PREHISTORY AND HUMAN ECOLOGY OF THE VALLEY OF OAXACA

Kent V. Flannery and Joyce Marcus
General Editors

Volume 1   *The Use of Land and Water Resources in the Past and Present Valley of Oaxaca, Mexico*, by Anne V.T. Kirkby. Memoirs of the Museum of Anthropology, University of Michigan, No. 5. 1973.

Volume 2   *Sociopolitical Aspects of Canal Irrigation in the Valley of Oaxaca*, by Susan H. Lees. Memoirs of the Museum of Anthropology, University of Michigan, No. 6. 1973.

Volume 3   *Formative Mesoamerican Exchange Networks with Special Reference to the Valley of Oaxaca*, by Jane W. Pires-Ferreira. Memoirs of the Museum of Anthropology, University of Michigan, No. 7. 1975.

Volume 4   *Fábrica San José and Middle Formative Society in the Valley of Oaxaca*, by Robert D. Drennan. Memoirs of the Museum of Anthropology, University of Michigan, No. 8. 1976.

Volume 5   Part 1. *The Vegetational History of the Oaxaca Valley*, by C. Earle Smith, Jr. Part 2. *Zapotec Plant Knowledge: Classification, Uses and Communication*, by Ellen Messer. Memoirs of the Museum of Anthropology, University of Michigan, No. 10. 1978.

Volume 6   *Excavations at Santo Domingo Tomaltepec: Evolution of a Formative Community in the Valley of Oaxaca, Mexico*, by Michael E. Whalen. Memoirs of the Museum of Anthropology, University of Michigan, No. 12. 1981.

Volume 7   *Monte Albán's Hinterland, Part 1: The Prehispanic Settlement Patterns of the Central and Southern Parts of the Valley of Oaxaca, Mexico*, by Richard E. Blanton, Stephen Kowalewski, Gary Feinman, and Jill Appel. Memoirs of the Museum of Anthropology, University of Michigan, No. 15. 1982.

Volume 8   *Chipped Stone Tools in Formative Oaxaca, Mexico: Their Procurement, Production and Use*, by William J. Parry. Memoirs of the Museum of Anthropology, University of Michigan, No. 20. 1987.

Volume 9   *Agricultural Intensification and Prehistoric Health in the Valley of Oaxaca, Mexico*, by Denise C. Hodges. Memoirs of the Museum of Anthropology, University of Michigan, No. 22. 1989.

Volume 10 *Early Formative Pottery of the Valley of Oaxaca*, by Kent V. Flannery and Joyce Marcus, with ceramic analysis by William O. Payne. Memoirs of the Museum of Anthropology, University of Michigan, No. 27. 1994.

Volume 11 *Women's Ritual in Formative Oaxaca: Figurine-Making, Divination, Death and the Ancestors*, by Joyce Marcus. Memoirs of the Museum of Anthropology, University of Michigan, No. 33. 1998.

Volume 12 *The Sola Valley and the Monte Albán State: A Study of Zapotec Imperial Expansion*, by Andrew K. Balkansky. Memoirs of the Museum of Anthropology, University of Michigan, No. 36. 2002.

Volume 13 *Excavations at San José Mogote 1: The Household Archaeology*, by Kent V. Flannery and Joyce Marcus. Memoirs of the Museum of Anthropology, University of Michigan, No. 40. 2005.

Volume 14 *Excavations at Cerro Tilcajete: A Monte Albán II Administrative Center in the Valley of Oaxaca*, by Christina Elson. Memoirs of the Museum of Anthropology, University of Michigan, No. 42. 2007.

Volume 15 *Cerro Danush: Excavations at a Hilltop Community in the Eastern Valley of Oaxaca, Mexico*, by Ronald K. Faulseit. Memoirs of the Museum of Anthropology, University of Michigan, No. 54. 2013.

Related Volumes

Flannery, Kent V.
1986   *Guilá Naquitz: Archaic Foraging and Early Agriculture in Oaxaca, Mexico*. New York: Academic Press.

Flannery, Kent V., and Joyce Marcus
2003   *The Cloud People: Divergent Evolution of the Zapotec and Mixtec Civilizations*. Clinton Corners, New York: Percheron Press.

Marcus, Joyce, and Kent V. Flannery
1996   *Zapotec Civilization: How Urban Society Evolved in Mexico's Oaxaca Valley*. London: Thames and Hudson.

Museum of Anthropology, University of Michigan
Memoirs, Number 54

PREHISTORY AND HUMAN ECOLOGY
OF THE VALLEY OF OAXACA

Kent V. Flannery and Joyce Marcus
General Editors
Volume 15

Cerro Danush

Excavations at a Hilltop Community in the Eastern Valley of Oaxaca, Mexico

Ronald K. Faulseit

Ann Arbor, Michigan
2013

©2013 by the Regents of the University of Michigan
The Museum of Anthropology
All rights reserved

Printed in the United States of America
ISBN 978-0-915703-82-1

Cover design by Katherine Clahassey

The University of Michigan Museum of Anthropology currently publishes two monograph series: Anthropological Papers and Memoirs. For permissions, questions, or catalogs, contact Museum of Anthropology Publications: 1109 Geddes Avenue, Ann Arbor, MI 48109-1079; umma-pubs@umich.edu; www.lsa.umich.edu/umma/

Library of Congress Cataloging-in-Publication Data

Faulseit, Ronald K., 1970-
 Cerro Danush : excavations at a hilltop community in the eastern valley of Oaxaca, Mexico / Ronald K. Faulseit.
     pages cm. -- (Memoirs of the Museum of Anthropology, University of Michigan ; Number 54) (Prehistory and human ecology of the Valley of Oaxaca ; Volume 15)
 Includes bibliographical references and index.
 ISBN 978-0-915703-82-1 (alk. paper)
 1. Cerro Danush Site (Mexico) 2. Zapotec Indians--Antiquities. 3. Excavations (Archaeology)--Mexico--Oaxaca Valley. 4. Oaxaca Valley (Mexico)--Antiquities. 5. Oaxaca Valley (Mexico)--Social life and customs. I. Title. II. Series. III. Series: Prehistory and human ecology of the Valley of Oaxaca ; Volume 15
 GN2.M52no. 54
 [F1219.1.O11]
 972'.74--dc23
                            2013035696

The paper used in this publication meets the requirements of the ANSI Standard Z39.48-1984 (Permanence of Paper)

Front cover:
Map of Macuilxóchitl and its jurisdiction, from the *Relación Geográfica de Macuilxóchitl*, 1580.
© Real Academia de la Historia, Madrid, C-028-007 (9-4663/19).

Contents

List of Figures	*vii*
List of Tables	*xiii*
Foreword, *by Kent V. Flannery and Joyce Marcus*	*xv*
Acknowledgments	*xvii*

1 Introduction — *1*

    Epiclassic Mesoamerica — *1*
    The Transition from Classic to Postclassic in the Valley of Oaxaca — *3*
    Classic to Postclassic Growth, Decline, and Abandonment: A Reassessment — *4*
    Collapse, Resilience, and Reorganization in Complex Societies — *5*
    Summary of Research Design — *7*
    Abandonment Patterns — *8*
    Summary of Field Methods — *8*

2 The Dainzú-Macuilxóchitl Region — *9*

    Dainzú-Macuilxóchitl: The Archaeological Site — *11*
    The Rise and Decline of Monte Albán — *17*
    The Late Classic/Terminal Classic Transition — *18*
    The Terminal Classic in the Valley of Oaxaca — *19*
    Postclassic Reorganization in the Valley of Oaxaca — *20*

3 Household Archaeology in the Valley of Oaxaca — *21*

    Project Research Scheme — *21*
    The Evolution of the House Complex in the Valley of Oaxaca — *22*
    Household Production, Specialization, and Political Economy in the Valley of Oaxaca — *24*
    Household Ritual in the Valley of Oaxaca — *26*
    Late/Terminal Classic Patterns of Site Abandonment in the Valley of Oaxaca — *28*
    Summary and Concluding Remarks — *30*

4 Mapping and Surface Collection on Cerro Danush — *31*

    Mapping Cerro Danush — *31*
    Terraces and Terrace Groups on Cerro Danush — *33*
    Surface Collection Procedures — *47*
    Artifact Analysis and Laboratory Procedures — *48*
    Concluding Remarks — *48*

5	**Density Distribution Analyses of Surface Artifacts**	*49*
	General Description of the Data Set	*49*
	Quantitative Assessment of the Ceramic Data Set	*50*
	Quantitative Assessment of the Chipped Stone Data Set	*54*
	Surface Distribution Patterns	*56*
	Principal Components and Correspondence Analyses	*91*
	Conclusions	*98*
6	**The Excavation of Terraces S19 and S20**	*103*
	A Description of the Excavation Area	*103*
	Establishing the Excavation Grid	*105*
	General Excavation Procedures	*106*
	Stratigraphy and Depositional History of the Terraces	*107*
	Horizontal Excavation of Terrace S19	*113*
	Description of Structures from the Most Recent Occupational Surface	*114*
	Stratigraphic Excavations on Terrace S19	*124*
	Description of Archaeological Features Associated with the Most Recent Occupation	*125*
	Earlier Occupational Structures and Features	*132*
	Radiocarbon Analyses	*132*
	The Occupational History of Terrace S19	*138*
	Conclusions	*139*
7	**Spatial Distributions of Artifacts and Implied Behavioral Patterns in an Early Postclassic Residence**	*141*
	Laboratory Procedures	*141*
	Qualitative Assessment of the Artifact Assemblage	*142*
	Domestic Offerings from the West Patio Complex, Terrace S19	*143*
	Quantitative Assessment of the Artifact Assemblage	*157*
	Characterizing Domestic Life in the Residential Compound, Terrace S19	*174*
	Conclusion	*178*
8	**Breakdown and Reorganization at Dainzú-Macuilxóchitl**	*179*
	Terminal Classic Abandonment Patterns on Cerro Danush	*179*
	Late Classic to Early Postclassic Community Ritual at Dainzú-Macuilxóchitl	*180*
	Late Classic to Early Postclassic Domestic Ritual	*183*
	Late Classic to Early Postclassic Household Production	*184*
	Classic Decline and Postclassic Reorganization in the Dainzú-Macuilxóchitl Region	*184*
	Resistance to Authority	*185*
	Appendix A: Ceramic Chronology for the Valley of Oaxaca	*187*
	Appendix B: Artifact Categories	*189*
	References Cited	*233*
	Color Plates	*247*

Figures

1.1. Topographic map of Mesoamerica with Classic and Epiclassic sites, *2*

2.1. The State of Oaxaca and the Valley of Oaxaca with archaeological sites, *10*
2.2. Geographical regions of Oaxaca, *11*
2.3. Cerro Danush (viewed from Dainzú Archaeological Zone), *11*
2.4. Jaguar tomb façade, Dainzú Archaeological Zone, *13*
2.5. Carved stone ballplayer (Building A, Dainzú Archaeological Zone), *14*
2.6. Monte Albán IV I-shaped ball court (Dainzú Archaeological Zone), *14*
2.7. Map of archaeological features with areas of previous excavations, *15*
2.8. Modern shrine constructed on the summit of Cerro Danush, *16*

4.1. Project map of Cerro Danush, *32*
4.2. Stone retaining wall, Terrace S6, *34*
4.3. Stucco floor exposed by water erosion on the slope of Cerro Danush, *34*
4.4. Terrace groups and surface collection circles, Cerro Danush, *35*
4.5. Summit Terrace Group, *36*
4.6. TIN surface depicting topography of the Summit Terrace Group, *37*
4.7. Carved stone doorjamb with image of Cociyo impersonator, *37*
4.8. Northeast Terrace Group, *38*
4.9. The North-Central Terrace Group, *39*
4.10. The North Terrace Group, *39*
4.11a. Terraces E1–E10 of the East Terrace Group, *40*
4.11b. Terraces E11–E20 of the East Terrace Group, *40*
4.12. Rock painting above Terraces E11–E20, *41*
4.13. The West Terrace Group, *42*
4.14. The Southwest Terrace Group, *43*
4.15. The South Terrace Group, *44*
4.16. Location of rock paintings and Terraces NC3–NC9, *45*
4.17. Rock paintings on cliff face below Terrace S6, *46*
4.18. Surface collection diagrams, *47*

5.1. Scatter plot of sherd counts vs. sherd volume, *51*
5.2. Scatter plot of total diagnostic vs. total sherd counts, *51*
5.3. Total diagnostic sherd counts vs. total volume, *51*
5.4. Distribution of total ceramic sherd counts per collection circle, *52*
5.5. Distribution of total volume of ceramics per collection circle, *53*
5.6. Distribution of diagnostic ceramics (sherd counts per circle), *55*
5.7. Diagnostic chipped stone vs. total chipped stone, *56*
5.8. Total chipped stone counts vs. total ceramic counts, *56*
5.9. Density plot of chipped stone counts per collection circle, *57*
5.10. Density plot of simple olla fragments, *60*

5.11. Density plot of cántaro fragments, *61*
5.12. Locations of manos, metates, molcajetes, and tejolotes, *62*
5.13. Distribution of ollas barriles, *63*
5.14. Distribution of apaxtles, *64*
5.15. Distribution of ceramic kiln waster fragments, *66*
5.16. Distribution of ceramic spindle whorl fragments, *67*
5.17. Distribution of raspadores, *68*
5.18. Distribution of chert debitage, *69*
5.19. Distribution of spent chert cores, *70*
5.20. Distribution of chert flakes (expedient tools), *71*
5.21. Distribution of mold-made figurines, *73*
5.22. Distribution of mold fragments for urns or figurines, *74*
5.23. Distribution of urn fragments, *75*
5.24. Distribution of botellón fragments, *76*
5.25. Distribution of silbato fragments, *77*
5.26. Distribution of hollow-handled sahumador fragments, *79*
5.27. Distribution of solid-handled sahumador fragments, *80*
5.28. Distribution of G23 fragments, *81*
5.29. Distribution of orange paste conical bowl fragments, *82*
5.30. Spatial distribution of G35 fragments, *83*
5.31. Distribution of brown paste (K14) conical bowl fragments, *84*
5.32. Surface distribution of G3M fragments, *86*
5.33. Surface distribution of ollas with appliqué glyph motifs, *87*
5.34. Total distribution of orange paste sherds, *88*
5.35. Terraces with total orange paste averages greater than 2.33%, *89*
5.36. Total distribution of gray paste sherds, *90*
5.37. Total distribution of brown paste sherds, *92*
5.38. Terraces with 33% or more total brown paste sherds, *93*
5.39. Terraces with 25% or more total brown pastes sherds, *94*
5.40. Scree plot for principal components analysis of surface ceramics, *95*
5.41. Coefficient values from the four principal components, *95*
5.42. *X-y* scatter plot of score values for principal component 1 and principal component 2, *96*
5.43. *X-y* scatter plot of score values for principal component 3 and principal component 4, *96*
5.44. Scree plot from principal components analysis of chipped stone assemblage, *97*
5.45. Coefficient values from principal components analysis of chipped stone data set, *97*
5.46. Variable and case loadings for components 1 and 2, *99*
5.47. Variable and case loadings for components 3 and 4, *100*
5.48. Variable and case loadings for components 2 and 3, *101*

6.1. Terraces S18–S20, *104*
6.2. Topographic depiction of excavation area, Terraces S18–S20, *104*
6.3. Profile sketch for Terraces S18–S20, *105*
6.4. Plan view of excavation grids, *106*
6.5. Project datum BNS18A, Terrace S18, *106*
6.6. Terrace S20, *108*
6.7. Plan view of excavation grid on Terrace S20, *108*
6.8. Terrace S19 prior to excavation, *109*

6.9.   Plan view of excavation grid for Terrace S19, *109*
6.10. Profile of western edge of Terrace S19, *110*
6.11. Relative artifact densities, Layer 2, Terrace S19, *111*
6.12. Profile sketch of Terrace S19, *112*
6.13. Layer 3, east side of Terrace S19, *112*
6.14. Wall fall, Blocks B and C, Terrace S19, *113*
6.15. Plan view of features and structures excavated on Terrace S19, *115*
6.16. East Patio Complex, *116*
6.17. Eastern edge of Terrace S19, *117*
6.18. Northern foundation wall, Structure A, *117*
6.19. Structure B, East Patio Complex, *117*
6.20. Eastern foundation wall, Structure C, *118*
6.21. Southern foundation wall, Structure C, *119*
6.22. Western edge of Structure C, *120*
6.23. Plan view of West Patio Complex with features, *121*
6.24. West Patio Complex, *121*
6.25. East edge and indented portion of North Wall, *122*
6.26. North Wall, *123*
6.27. Northern foundation wall, Structure E, *123*
6.28. Vertical excavation units and structures, Terrace S19, *124*
6.29. Burial 1, eastern structure complex, Terrace S19, *125*
6.30. Burial 2, Structure B, East Patio Complex, Terrace S19, *127*
6.31. Burial 2 drawing, *127*
6.32. Burial 3, *128*
6.33. G35-type conical bowl, Burial 3, *128*
6.34. Modified incisors from Burial 3, *129*
6.35. Comal hearth, West Patio Complex, *129*
6.36. Modern comal hearth, San Mateo Macuilxóchitl, *129*
6.37. Fire Pit 1, Layer 3, test unit 8, *130*
6.38. Fire Pit 1, Layer 3, test unit 8, *130*
6.39. Fire Pit 2, Layer 3, below North Wall, *131*
6.40. Fire Pit 2, Layer 3, below North Wall, *131*
6.41. Diagram of features from the earlier occupational surface, *133*
6.42. Structure D and patio, west of Structure C, *133*
6.43. Stone-lined drain, *134*
6.44. Remnants of structures below Structure E, *134*
6.45. Radiocarbon results from Terrace S19, Cerro Danush, *136*
6.46. Radiocarbon sample locations, most recent occupational surface, *137*
6.47. Radiocarbon sample locations, earlier occupational surface, *137*

7.1.   Terrace S19 residence with offerings, *143*
7.2.   Cajete/patojo pairs, test unit 3, West Patio Complex, *145*
7.3.   Cajete/patojo pair, test unit 5, West Patio Complex, *145*
7.4.   Cajete/patojo pair number 1, *146*
7.5.   Small G35-type conical bowl, cajete/patojo pair number 1, *146*
7.6.   Brown paste patojo, cajete/patojo pair number 1, *147*
7.7.   Postclassic-type conical bowl, cajete/patojo pair number 2, *147*

7.8. Postclassic patojo, cajete/patojo pair number 2, *148*
7.9. Cajete/patojo pair number 3, *148*
7.10. Postclassic-style conical bowl, cajete/patojo pair number 3, *149*
7.11. Postclassic-style patojo, cajete patojo pair number 3, *149*
7.12. Patojo number 4, *150*
7.13. Patojo number 5, eastern edge of North Wall, *150*
7.14. Cajete/patojo pair number 6, *151*
7.15. Postclassic brown paste conical bowl, cajete/patojo pair number 6, *152*
7.16. Brown paste patojo, cajete/patojo pair number 6, *152*
7.17. Test unit 8, West Patio Complex, *153*
7.18. Patojo number 7, *153*
7.19. Large gray paste G35 conical bowl, test unit 3, *154*
7.20. Test unit 6, West Patio Complex, *154*
7.21. Small G35 conical bowl, test unit 6, West Patio Complex, *155*
7.22. G35 gray conical bowl, excavation unit N8E5, *155*
7.23. Gray ware conical bowl with corncob impression, *156*
7.24. Volume densities of artifacts, plow zone, Terrace S19, *157*
7.25. Volume densities of artifacts, Layer 2, Terrace S19, *158*
7.26. Proposed areas of refuse deposits and their colluvial erosion zones, *158*
7.27. Soil volumes from excavated squares, Layer 2, Terrace S19, *159*
7.28. Raw artifact frequency counts, Layer 2, Terrace S19, *159*
7.29. Distribution of diagnostic ceramic fragments, *160*
7.30. Distribution of chipped stone materials, *161*
7.31. Distribution of faunal remains, *161*
7.32. Distribution of chert debitage, *161*
7.33. Distribution of chert points, *162*
7.34. Distribution of expedient flake tools, *162*
7.35. Distribution of ceramic spindle whorls, *163*
7.36. Distribution of prismatic blades, *163*
7.37. Distribution of obsidian debitage, *164*
7.38. Distribution of cal block fragments, *164*
7.39. Distribution of apaxtle fragments, *164*
7.40. Distribution of manos and metates, *165*
7.41. Distribution of fragments from ollas barriles, *165*
7.42. Distribution of tlecuil fragments, *166*
7.43. Distribution of K14 conical bowl fragments, *166*
7.44. Distribution of Classic period hemispherical bowls, *167*
7.45. Distribution of hollow-handled censers, *167*
7.46. Distribution of fragments from Classic period simple ollas, *167*
7.47. Distribution of Early Classic G23 bowl fragments, *168*
7.48. Distribution of Early Classic Dainzú conical bowls, *168*
7.49. Distribution of Early Classic orange paste hemispherical bowls, *168*
7.50. Distribution of solid-handled sahumador fragments, *169*
7.51. Distribution of miniature cups with appliqué claws, *169*
7.52. Distribution of Postclassic-style conical bowls, *169*
7.53. Distribution of globular jars with appliqué glyph motifs, *170*
7.54. Distribution of G3M bowl fragments, *170*

7.55. Case loadings for the fifty-six excavation units, *172*
7.56. Variable loadings for the artifact categories, *172*
7.57. Distribution of bajareque fragments, *173*
7.58. Distribution of botellón fragments (volume density index), *174*
7.59. Distribution of botellón fragments (raw frequency count), *174*
7.60. Distribution of plate fragments, *175*
7.61. Distribution of patojo fragments, *175*
7.62. Residential complex with proposed kitchen structure added, *177*
7.63. Artist's rendition of the Early Postclassic residence on Terrace S19, *178*

8.1. Map of Macuilxóchitl from the *Relación Geográfica de Macuilxóchitl*, *181*
8.2. Drawing of carved stone doorjamb with Cociyo image, *182*

B1. Small G35 conical bowl fragments, *191*
B2. Large G35 conical bowls, *192*
B3. Hemispherical bowl with concave curved walls, *193*
B4. Hemispherical bowl with composite silhouette walls, *193*
B5. Fragments of Postclassic G3M hemispherical bowls, *194*
B6. Fragments of cylindrical bowls, *195*
B7. Fragments of simple cups, *195*
B8. Fragments of G23-type bowls, *196*
B9. Fragments of G12-type bowls, *197*
B10. Rim sherds from Balancán Fine Orange vessels, *197*
B11. Rim and neck fragments from simple ollas, *197*
B12. Basic profile of simple ollas, with size ranges, *197*
B13. Fragments of small globular ollas, *198*
B14. Fragments of simple ollas with handles, *198*
B15. Fragments from barrel-shaped jars, *200*
B16. Fragments of jars with appliqué glyph motifs, *200*
B17. Early Postclassic patojos, *200*
B18. Fragments of an Early Postclassic olla, *202*
B19. Neck and rim fragments from cántaros, *202*
B20. Fragments of hollow-handled sahumadores, *203*
B21. Profile drawing of hollow-handled sahumador, *203*
B22. Fragments of solid-handled sahumadores, *203*
B23. Drawing of solid-handled sahumador, *203*
B24. Fragments of mold-made figurines, 13 Serpent type, *204*
B25. Fragments of mold-made figurines, 13 Serpent type, *204*
B26. Fragments of ceramic molds for figurine making, *205*
B27. Drawing of 13 Serpent, variant 1, mold-made figurines, *205*
B28. Close-up of 13 Serpent, variant 1, fragments, *205*
B29. Drawing of 13 Serpent, variant 2, figurines, *206*
B30. Fragments of 13 Serpent figurines, variant 2, *207*
B31. Body fragments of 13 Serpent, variant 2, *207*
B32. Fragments of ceramic whistles, *209*
B33. Whistles with jaw-of-serpent headdresses, *209*
B34. Fragments of whistles with jaw-of-serpent headdresses, *210*

B35. Whistle variant 2, *210*
B36. Male figurines with whistle attachments, *211*
B37. Close-up of Mazapan-type figurines/whistles, *211*
B38. Fragments of solid zoomorphic figurines, *212*
B39. Fragments from effigy urns, *212*
B40. Fragments from bottle jars, *213*
B41. Interior and exterior fragments of comales, *214*
B42. Chilmolera fragments, *215*
B43. Apaxtle fragments, *215*
B44. Tlecuil recovered from Terrace S19, *216*
B45. Fragments of cylindrical and hemispherical braziers, *217*
B46. Miniature vessels, *218*
B47. Fragments of shallow bowls or plates, *219*
B48. Fragments of shallow bowl or plate, *220*
B49. Perforated disks/spindle whorls, *221*
B50. Ceramic waster fragments, *221*
B51. Two- and one-handed manos, *222*
B52. Metates, *222*
B53. Tejolotes, *223*
B54. Molcajete, *223*
B55. Axes and celts, *224*
B56. Rueda, *224*
B57. Chert debitage, *225*
B58. Expedient flake tools, *226*
B59. Spent cores, *226*
B60. Prismatic blade fragments, *227*
B61. Small point derived from prismatic blade, *227*
B62. Obsidian eccentrics, *227*
B63. Obsidian needles or awls derived from prismatic blades, *228*
B64. Chert raspadores, *228*
B65. Illustration of raspador, *228*
B66. Chert points, *229*
B67. Quartzite points, *229*
B68. Volcanic tuff points, *229*
B69. Fragments of dog mandibles and teeth, *230*
B70. Fragments of turkey vertebrae, *230*
B71. Bone needles or punches, *230*
B72. Charred and broken antler, *230*
B73. Cal fragments, *230*
B74. Fragments of bajareque, *231*

Tables

5.1. Volume measurements and frequency counts for selected collection circles, *50*
5.2. Distributions of ceramic materials collected per individual terrace, *58*

6.1. Sample data from the radiocarbon analysis, *135*

A1. Ceramic chronology for the Valley of Oaxaca, *188*

Foreword
An Introduction to Volume 15 of the Series

by Kent V. Flannery and Joyce Marcus

Some of the most interesting research questions in Oaxaca prehistory grow out of the political reorganization of the Zapotec heartland following the decline of Monte Albán. That mountaintop city probably controlled as much territory in A.D. 200 as it would ever control. Between A.D. 300 and 500, it withdrew support from its more distant provinces so that it could focus most of its attention on the more heavily populated Valley of Oaxaca.

Finally, sometime between A.D. 600 and 900—during the period that Caso, Bernal, and Acosta called Monte Albán IIIb–IV—the Zapotec capital lost its grip on many of the valley towns that had served as secondary centers in its administrative hierarchy. These towns now controlled enough manpower to establish themselves as the capitals of autonomous petty kingdoms. Despite their growing independence, however, their hieroglyphic monuments indicate that the rulers of these small kingdoms sought to legitimize themselves by emphasizing their genealogical descent from the rulers of Monte Albán.

Such genealogical ties, of course, concerned only the ruling elite. What about the lesser Zapotec nobles, wealthy artisans, common farmers, and landless serfs? How did the decline of Monte Albán and the rise of the local petty kingdoms affect their lives?

One way to attack these questions is by investigating a community whose occupation spanned the transition from Classic to Postclassic. In this volume, Ronald K. Faulseit turns his attention to the area of Dainzú-Macuilxóchitl in the eastern, or Tlacolula, arm of the Valley of Oaxaca. This is an area that went from being a Tier 2 center within the Classic Monte Albán state to a small Postclassic polity in its own right. Faulseit focused his work on the area's most visible landmark—the artificially terraced hilltop site of Cerro Danush, which commanded a view of the entire polity.

Now consider Faulseit's logistic problems. At the time he took on Cerro Danush, he was not the director of a large, well-funded archaeological team; he was just a lone investigator on a limited budget. How could he possibly hope to accomplish his goals?

The answer: through the use of a superb work ethic, great discipline, and rigorous quantification of data. Faulseit mapped and intensively surface-collected Cerro Danush. He then selected a series of residential terraces whose size made them appropriate for his budget. He excavated them extensively, using excavation units small enough so that one could detect a variety of activities. At every level of analysis, Faulseit gives his sample size and evaluates the reliability of any conclusions drawn from it. He peels back the layers of each terrace so meticulously that we can see the residential changes between the Late Classic and Early Postclassic—the crucial transition from Monte Albán's hegemony to Macuilxóchitl's autonomous rule. Faulseit isolated the site's activity areas so rigorously that we can deduce which crafts were tied to state-level economies, which fed into local exchange, and which were carried out purely for household consumption.

This volume will not be the last to deal with the sociopolitical consequences of Monte Albán's decline, nor was that the sole reason we chose to include it in our publication series. We also chose it because it shows what one lone investigator—with limited resources—can accomplish with hard work, statistical rigor, meticulous attention to detail, and unusual intellectual honesty about what we can and cannot infer from his results. If we controlled a research foundation, we would be giving Faulseit a much bigger grant right now.

Acknowledgments

This book is based on research I conducted during my graduate studies at Tulane University. Since then, I have been able to think more deeply about the data I collected and what they mean for sociopolitical organization in the Early Postclassic Valley of Oaxaca. In that time, I have had the good fortune of continued guidance from my dissertation committee members, E. Wyllys Andrews V, Kit Nelson, and especially Chris Rodning, who have encouraged me to expand in new theoretical directions. I have also been very fortunate that both Gary Feinman and Linda Nicholas have taken time to challenge me to further develop my ideas and become a better scholar. They are always available and eager to discuss their knowledge of archaeology in Oaxaca, and their mentorship has been invaluable to me. Dan M. Healan has been an outstanding research advisor and continues to be a good friend and mentor, and I thank him for his continued support, guidance, and encouragement.

I would like to thank the Foundation for the Advancement of Mesoamerican Studies (FAMSI), Inc., as well as the Middle American Research Institute (MARI) at Tulane for providing funds to support this research. Additionally, I would like to thank the members of the *consejo de arqueología* from Mexico's Instituto Nacional de Antropología e Historia (INAH), for reviewing and approving my project proposals. I want to particularly acknowledge the *consejo* presidents, Nelly Robles García and Roberto García Moll, for the guidance and recommendations made prior to conducting the fieldwork. A special thanks goes to Betty Cleeland for preparing the outstanding artwork and illustrations that are used in this volume. I would also like to thank Stephen Kowalewski for permission to reproduce his survey map for the Macuilxóchitl area.

In Oaxaca, I would like to thank several members of the regional INAH office, who assisted me in every aspect of my field research. I am indebted to Enrique Fernández (director), Jorge Ríos, Angel Iván Rivera Guzmán, Jorge Bautista, and Cuauhtémoc Camarenas, who provided substantial logistical assistance and proved instrumental in coordinating my collaboration with the local community. I am also grateful to Robert Markens, Cira Martínez López, and Marc Winter for their advice and support during the project. A heartfelt thanks to all the people of San Mateo Macuilxóchitl, who allowed me to work on their *Bienes Comunales* property, and in particular, to the town's authorities, Joel Pérez and Ramón Martínez. Without their help, I could not have completed the project.

In the year I spent as Visiting Scholar at Southern Illinois University, much of which I spent writing and revising this manuscript, Mark Wagner and Heather Lapham were a greatly appreciated source of friendship and professional guidance. I want to thank Andrew Balkansky as well for sharing his insights on Oaxaca archaeology—may the Elvis bobblehead live forever!

I am very grateful to both Jill Rheinheimer and Katherine Clahassey for their patience in copyediting and helping to improve the figures in this manuscript. I also appreciate Kent Flannery's comments and criticisms on an earlier version of this work, which helped me to reorganize the manuscript and more thoroughly consider many aspects of the research. Most of all, I owe a sincere debt of gratitude to Joyce Marcus, who has been supportive, encouraging, and patient with me since the first moment I contacted her about my plans to conduct research in Oaxaca. Her Dynamic Model is a source of theoretical inspiration for me, and she has always provided helpful insights and thoughtful critiques of my work.

Lastly, I would like to thank my wife, Kate Ingold, for her unconditional support and love through the last 14 years. Although this manuscript would not have been possible without the encouragement and support I received from all of these people, any mistakes or faulty logic in the text are purely of my own making. Thank you.

1 | Introduction

From A.D. 1 to 600, the most powerful city in the southern Mexican highlands was Monte Albán. At its peak, between A.D. 200 and 300, it may have controlled 20,000 km² of what is now the State of Oaxaca. Even after its outer provinces began to break away, Monte Albán remained the capital of the Valley of Oaxaca, presiding over a political hierarchy of secondary, tertiary, and quaternary centers.

During the period from A.D. 650 to 950, the Zapotec state centered at Monte Albán began to weaken. As Monte Albán's control over its secondary centers and more distant provinces declined, the Valley of Oaxaca became reorganized as a series of petty kingdoms. One of the areas undergoing reorganization was the Dainzú-Macuilxóchitl region of the eastern (or Tlacolula) arm of the Valley of Oaxaca.

It is this Dainzú-Macuilxóchitl region that provides the setting for my research, which focuses on Cerro Danush, a prominent hilltop community near present-day Macuilxóchitl; the time span includes both the Late Classic (A.D. 600–900) and Early Postclassic (A.D. 900–1300) periods. I spent two field seasons investigating patterns of use and abandonment of residential terraces at Cerro Danush. At A.D. 600, the occupants of these terraces most certainly would have been subjects of the state centered at Monte Albán; by A.D. 900, they would have belonged to an autonomous local polity.

Working within the theoretical frameworks of political cycling (Anderson 1994; Marcus 1998a) and resilience theory (Holling and Gunderson 2002; Holling, Gunderson, and Peterson 2002), I am able to characterize both pre-Monte Albán and post-Monte Albán change as well as continuity in household activities, community ritual, and site settlement to identify patterns of behavior associated with resilient social institutions in the post-collapse environment. The overall goal is to understand how the important secondary center of Cerro Danush responded to the collapse of Monte Albán and reorganized itself during the dynamic sociopolitical environment of the Early Postclassic.

Epiclassic Mesoamerica

Between A.D. 650 and A.D. 950, societies across the Mesoamerican landscape—from northern Mexico to Honduras—experienced significant transformations in sociopolitical organization. By A.D. 1000, many, if not most, of the once prominent Classic (A.D. 200–900) and Epiclassic (A.D. 700–900) period centers (including all the sites in Fig. 1.1) were abandoned, in decline, or experiencing crises (Coe and Koontz 2002; Culbert 1973; Demarest, Rice, and Rice 2004; Inomata and Webb 2003; Sharer 2006). While it is beyond the scope of this book to attempt a

1

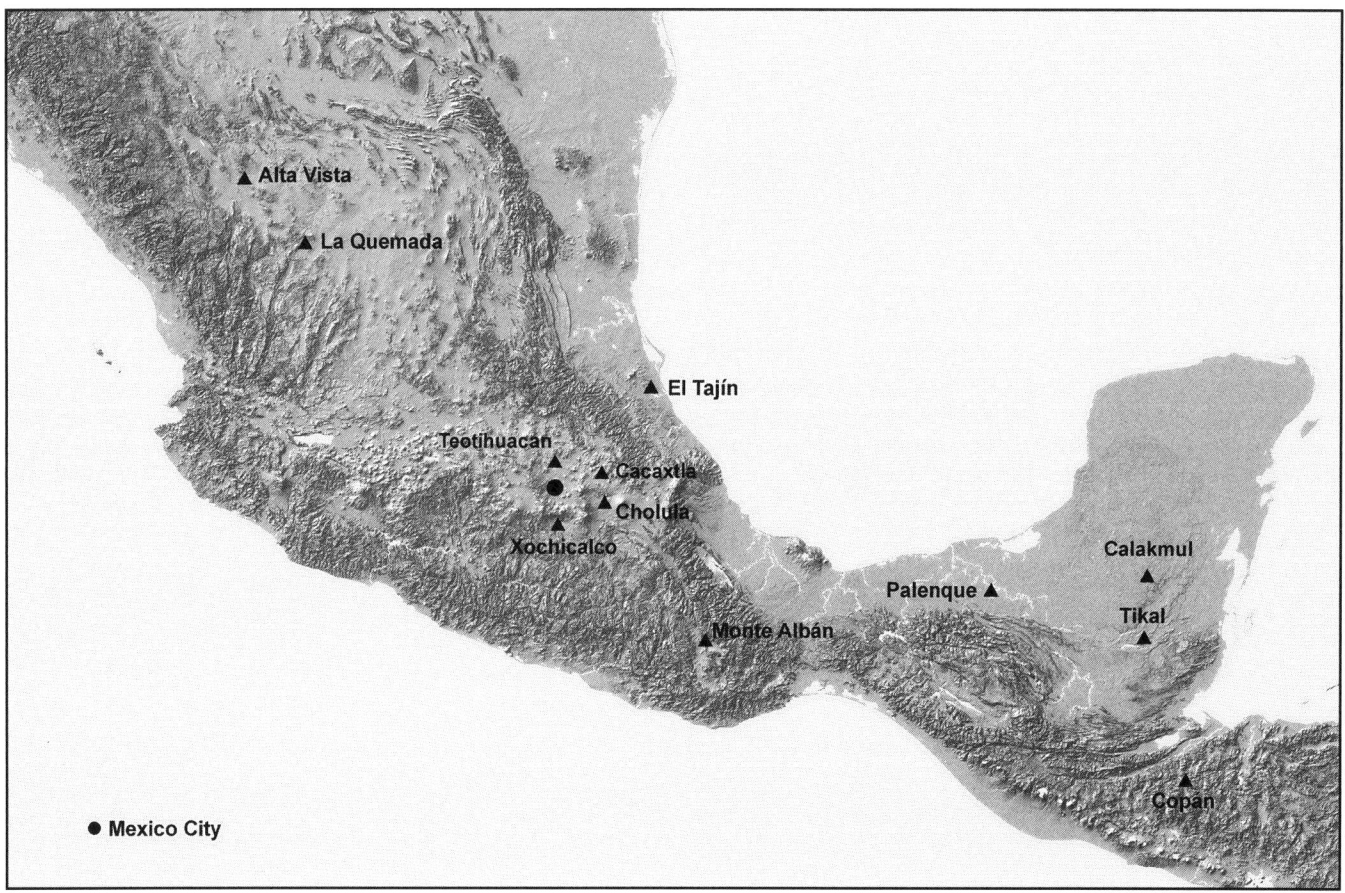

Figure 1.1. Topographic map of Mesoamerica with Classic and Epiclassic sites (shaded relief source SRTM NASA).

comprehensive explanation of this macro-regional phenomenon, it is important to place the events that occurred in the Valley of Oaxaca within this larger frame of reference.

The Epiclassic was most likely initiated by significant events that took place in the central Mexican basin in the sixth and seventh centuries A.D. Already experiencing population decline, "major structures" in the civic-ceremonial core of the largest and most populous Mesoamerican city of Teotihuacan, the seat of an influential and expansive state, "were desecrated and burned" around A.D. 600–650 (Cowgill 2012:306). Although there has been some disagreement over the dating of this event, which may have occurred even earlier (Manzanilla 2003), it most likely signifies the collapse of the ruling political structure at Teotihuacan and the end of its once vast influence, which had reached into many areas of Mesoamerica (Braswell 2003; Coe and Koontz 2002; Cowgill 1997; Flannery and Marcus 1983; Millon 1973, 1988). The subsequent decline and abandonment of the city marks the beginning of the Epiclassic (Diehl and Berlo 1989).

After Teotihuacan's decline, settlement in the central Mexican basin remained dispersed until the Early Postclassic (A.D. 900–1200) expansion of the Toltec state from its capital, Tula, in the state of Hidalgo (Diehl 1983; Mastache de Escobar, Cobean, and Healan 2002; Sanders, Parsons, and Santley 1979). Outside the basin, on the periphery of the Teotihuacan state, the void left by the loss of the centralized authority was filled by the development of several local kingdoms, often constructed in defensible and fortified locations (Marcus 1989) (Fig. 1.1). Many of these polities were ephemeral, however, and did not survive into the Early Postclassic, suggesting an unstable political environment in the region throughout the Epiclassic.

Much of the archaeological and iconographic evidence uncovered from Epiclassic sites in central Mexico is dominated by military or violent themes. The famous painted murals of Cacaxtla, a hilltop site in the state of Tlaxcala, depict a one-sided "battle," where feline warriors slaughter their bird warrior counterparts (Baird 1989). At Xochicalco, another hilltop site in the state of Morelos, ramparts, walls, ditches, and other defensive structures were built on the slope of the mountain so as to protect the city (Hirth 1989, 2000a, 2000b). These extraordinary measures were not enough, however, to prevent the destruction of its civic-ceremonial core and rapid abandonment of the site circa A.D. 900 (Webb and Hirth 2003). Yet another hilltop site, La

Quemada, located in Zacatecas on Mesoamerica's northern frontier, is known for the abundance of disarticulated human remains in its archaeological assemblage, which researchers interpret as evidence for both warfare and sacrifice (Nelson, Darling, and Kice 1992). As with the other centers, La Quemada was abandoned by the end of the Epiclassic, circa A.D. 900 (Nelson 2003).

Some Classic period central Mexican sites that existed on the periphery of the Teotihuacan state (such as Alta Vista, Teotenango, Cantona, El Tajín, and Cholula) appear to have flourished in the Epiclassic as well, taking prominent roles in the system of small or medium-sized polities (Coe and Koontz 2002). However, like the newly formed Epiclassic centers mentioned above, these sites went into decline by the Early Postclassic (Coe and Koontz 2002; Mastache and Cobean 1989). Farther afield, in regions like west Mexico (Michelet 1995) and the Gulf Coast (Ochoa Salas 1979, 1995), settlement patterns exhibit similar Epiclassic trajectories, but these areas have been less thoroughly studied.

The Terminal Classic (A.D. 750–1000) was also a time of dramatic change in the southern Maya Lowlands, where prominent cities such as Tikal, Calakmul, Copán, and Palenque were declining (Culbert 1973, 1988; Demarest 2004; Gill 2000; Sharer 2006). Both epigraphic and archaeological evidence show that warfare between major centers had become increasingly prevalent in the Late Classic (A.D. 600–750), reaching peak levels in the Terminal Classic (Demarest, Rice, and Rice, eds. 2004; Inomata 2003; Webster 2002). Like the central Mexican sites, by A.D. 900 many of the Lowland Maya centers were abandoned or dramatically reduced, but warfare was not the only factor contributing to their downfall—other stresses, such as environmental degradation, overpopulation, and a shift in the balance of trade mechanisms, have all been incorporated into multi-causal hypotheses for the Lowland Maya collapse (Culbert 1973; Demarest 2004; Demarest, Rice, and Rice 2004; Marcus 1995; Rathje 1973; Sharer 2006).

As in central Mexico, the void left by the demise of the great Lowland Maya centers may have led to the rise or expansion of peripheral entities (Marcus 1993), especially to the north in the modern Mexican states of Campeche (Carmean, Dunning, and Kowalski 2004) and Yucatan (Suhler et al. 2004). Like the Epiclassic centers of La Quemada, Cacaxtla, and Xochicalco, sites in these regions demonstrate defensive architectural features and bellicose iconography, suggesting warfare and instability at that time (Demarest, Rice, and Rice, eds. 2004; Marcus 2001). The florescence of the Terminal Classic sites in the Puuc region (Campeche) was also short-lived, with most sites either in decline or abandoned prior to the Early Postclassic (Carmean, Dunning, and Kowalski 2004). A similar pattern is evident in northern Yucatan, but the decline occurred later, ending with the abandonment of Chichén Itzá circa A.D. 1050 (Andrews, Andrews V, and Robles Castellanos 2003; Demarest 2004; Demarest, Rice, and Rice, eds. 2004; Sharer 2006).

The southern highlands of Mexico, where the Valley of Oaxaca is located, stand between the Maya Lowlands and central Mexico, and certainly were not immune to the macro-regional events that characterize the Epiclassic. Initially, perhaps in response to the decline of Teotihuacan, the Monte Albán state—which had dominated the Valley of Oaxaca since at least the Terminal Formative (200 B.C.–A.D. 100)—experienced Epiclassic growth in the construction of monumental architecture, size of settlement, and population, reaching its apogee sometime between A.D. 600 and 800. Like the central Mexican centers of Xochicalco, La Quemada, El Tajín, and Cacaxtla, this florescence was relatively short-lived, and by A.D. 900, Monte Albán and many other prominent sites in the valley, as well as other regions in the state of Oaxaca, were in decline or abandoned altogether (Blanton 1978; Joyce 2010; Joyce, Bustamante, and Levine 2001; Winter 2003). This monograph focuses on the Valley of Oaxaca and theories concerning this area, which are discussed in more detail below.

Although much has been written about the Epiclassic, the subsequent Early Postclassic remains one of the least understood periods within the Mesoamerican archaeological timeline. This is perhaps because (with the exception of the Maya Lowlands) until recently, most of the major archaeological research projects conducted were focused on the Formative (1500 B.C.–A.D. 200) rise of sociopolitical complexity (Blanton et al. 1999; Clark 1991; Coe and Diehl 1980; Cowgill 1997; MacNeish, Nelken-Terner, and Johnson 1967; Marcus and Flannery 1996; Sanders and Price 1968; Sanders, Parsons, and Santley 1979; Redmond 1983; Spencer 1982, 2006; Spencer and Redmond 1997). Additionally, far more data are needed from individual site excavations to complement the regional survey data already collected and allow for the type of comprehensive macro-regional study necessary to understand the broader context of the Classic to Postclassic transition in Mesoamerica (Balkansky 2006).

The research I present in this book is part of a growing corpus of investigations focused on Late Classic, Epiclassic, and Early Postclassic sites, and is intended to contribute to the discussion by assessing Epiclassic sociopolitical change at Dainzú-Macuilxóchitl, which was not only an important secondary center within the Monte Albán state, but was also never fully abandoned after the state declined. Instead, it was able to reorganize itself into a prominent local kingdom during the Postclassic.

The Transition from Classic to Postclassic in the Valley of Oaxaca

Caso and Bernal (1965) were the first researchers to discuss the Classic to Postclassic transition in the Valley of Oaxaca. Their conclusions were drawn mostly from excavations conducted at Monte Albán, Mitla, and Yagul, as well as survey and less extensive excavation at some other sites in the Valley of Oaxaca and Mixtec highlands (Acosta and Romero 1992; Caso 2003a, 2003b, 2003c). Because the artifact assemblage, architecture, and layout of the Postclassic sites of Mitla and Yagul differed so greatly from those of Classic period Monte Albán, they proposed that the Mixtec had expanded into the Valley of Oaxaca and replaced the Zapotec population in some parts of the valley

(Bernal 1965, 1966; Caso and Bernal 1965). Initially, other scholars picked up this theme (Paddock 1966), but soon rejected it in favor of a more complex relationship between Mixtec and Zapotec people in the Postclassic (Feinman and Nicholas 2011; Flannery and Marcus 1983).

In the 1960s, Paddock, Mogor, and Lind (1968) conducted extensive excavations at the site of Lambityeco, in the Tlacolula arm of the valley, which were designed to investigate differences between Classic and Postclassic sociopolitical organization in the Valley of Oaxaca. Because the ceramic assemblage at Lambityeco was different from Caso, Bernal, and Acosta's (1967) pre-decline Monte Albán IIIb phase, and appeared to closely resemble their post-decline Monte Albán IV phase, Paddock (1983a, 1983b) asserted that Lambityeco's florescence coincided with Monte Albán's decline, suggesting it "by then was independent in significant degree" (Paddock 1983a:187) from the capital.

Lambityeco was considered to exemplify Early Postclassic settlement in the Valley of Oaxaca (Paddock 1983b; Paddock, Mogor, and Lind 1968), and its diagnostic ceramics identified for the most recent (Monte Albán IV phase) occupation at the site were used by the Valley of Oaxaca Settlement Pattern Project (Kowalewski et al. 1989; Blanton 1978; Finsten 1983, 1995) as post-collapse Early Postclassic markers. Similarly, pre-collapse Late Classic markers were identified from the ceramic assemblage at Monte Albán (Blanton et al. 1999; Kowalewski et al. 1989). The resulting settlement patterns for these periods led to a model of collapse and reorganization in the Valley of Oaxaca that involved a slow transition from centralized valley-wide authority to regional balkanized authority (Blanton et al. 1993; Flannery and Marcus 1983).

In this model, regional centers became increasingly more autonomous during the Late Classic and began to challenge the centralized authority of Monte Albán (Balkansky 1998; Finsten 1983; Kowalewski et al. 1989). As control of economic resources and specialization shifted to these centers, the power of Monte Albán's ruling class waned and eventually collapsed, leaving the civic-ceremonial core of the site nearly abandoned (Blanton 1978, 1983). In the Early Postclassic, the regional centers developed into an organizational system of competitive balkanized states that held sway over the valley through the Late Postclassic (Blanton et al. 1982; Marcus and Flannery 1983).

From the evidence stated above, Blanton (1978, 1983) formulated a hypothesis concerning the causes for the collapse of the Monte Albán state. He saw both internal and external factors playing significant roles in the decline of the urban capital's dominance. The internal factors involved rapid population growth in the valley during the Late Classic, and perhaps an inability of the administrative system to settle increasing disputes over dwindling access to arable land. The external factors are related to the demise of Teotihuacan, as it had been postulated that Monte Albán's centralized power was at least partially in response to the outside threat from the central Mexican state (Blanton et al. 1999). With that threat removed, "local elites—especially those at emerging centers like Zaachila or Lambityeco—may have increasingly resisted pressure to support the capital, further diminishing its income at a time when there may have been pressing local problems and increased administrative costs" (Blanton 1983:186).

Work on the Classic–Postclassic transition has been impeded by two factors: (1) the difficulty of determining clear Late Classic and Early Postclassic ceramic markers owing to the dearth of decorative wares for these time periods (Feinman and Nicholas 2011; Kowalewski et al. 1989; Martínez López et al. 2000), and (2) a lack of radiocarbon dates for Late Classic and Early Postclassic contexts (Drennan 1983; Markens, Winter, and Martínez López 2010). These problems led to differing interpretations of the ceramic chronology, the development of competing phase assignments for the periods in question (Appendix A), and a considerable amount of debate (Kowalewski et al. 1989:251–54; Lind 1991–1992; Marcus 1990; see Marcus and Flannery 1990; Martínez López et al. 2000). Recently, an extensive seriation of well-dated Late Classic and Early Postclassic grave lots (Markens 2004, 2008) has made progress toward alleviating some of these difficulties, but data are still needed from other contexts, such as well-defined stratigraphically intact middens, to further define the diachronic percentage distributions of the ceramic types for these periods.

New research is providing a growing body of evidence from several Classic sites in central Oaxaca (Blomster 2008; Fargher 2004), such as Lambityeco (Lind and Urcid 2010), Ejutla (Feinman 1999), Jalieza (Casparis 2006; Elson 2011), El Palmillo (Feinman and Nicholas 2009; Feinman et al. 2002, 2006, 2008; Haines, Feinman, and Nicholas 2004), the Mitla Fortress (Feinman and Nicholas 2011), and Dainzú-Macuilxóchitl (Faulseit 2012a, 2012b; Markens, Winter, and Martínez López 2008; Winter et al. 2007). These data have allowed for the in-depth reassessment of settlement patterns derived from the Valley of Oaxaca Settlement Pattern Project (Feinman and Nicholas 2011) and have greatly increased our understanding of Late Classic sociopolitical organization in the Valley of Oaxaca.

Classic to Postclassic Growth, Decline, and Abandonment: A Reassessment

Results from the Valley of Oaxaca Settlement Pattern Project (Blanton and Kowalewski 1981; Blanton et al. 1982; Finsten 1983; Kowalewski et al. 1989) reveal population growth and increased centralization in the Valley of Oaxaca in the Late Classic, during the Monte Albán IIIb phase (A.D. 500–750). This growth seems to be centered mostly in the Etla arm of the valley and at Monte Albán, while the Tlacolula and Zimatlán Valleys were less densely populated. Then, in the Early Postclassic Monte Albán IV phase (A.D. 750–1000), population density shifted dramatically as the Late Classic centers in the Etla Valley, as well as Monte Albán, were abandoned, while settlement increased in the Tlacolula and Zimatlán Valleys (Kowalewski et al. 1989:251–306).

Subsequent excavations at many sites in these two valleys—including Lambityeco (Lind and Urcid 2010), Dainzú-Macuilxóchtil (Markens, Winter, and Martínez López 2008), El Palmillo (Feinman and Nicholas 2011), Ejutla (Balkansky, Feinman, and Nicholas 1997; Feinman and Nicholas 2000), and Jalieza (Casparis 2006; Elson 2011)—have produced radiocarbon data that suggest these communities were densely populated and nucleated settlements throughout the Late Classic, following nearly the same pattern of growth and decline as Monte Albán and the sites in the Etla arm of the valley. Based on these data, some researchers have refuted the model derived from the regional settlement pattern project, and suggest that the settlement diagrams for the Monte Albán IIIb and IV phases be combined to form one Late Classic settlement pattern (A.D. 600–800) (Lind and Urcid 2010; Markens 2011; Martínez López et al. 2000). In contrast to the settlement pattern project conclusions, this model envisions major growth in population density and settlement in the Late Classic, followed by extensive and rapid depopulation in the Early Postclassic throughout the Valley of Oaxaca (Winter 1989a, 2003).

Based on their experience on the regional survey project and subsequent extensive excavations in the valley, Feinman and Nicholas (2011) have updated, redrawn, and adjusted the chronologies of the Late Classic and Early Postclassic settlement pattern diagrams to accommodate the new data. They present a more complex settlement pattern than either previous model. For the Late Classic (A.D. 500–750), they combine the Monte Albán IIIb and IV phase settlement patterns, developed by Kowalewski et al. (1989:266, 291), into one phase they call Early Monte Albán IIIb–IV, which maintains the high population densities at Monte Albán and in the Etla Valley, but which also reflects the dense populations in the Tlacolula and Zimatlán Valleys implied by the new research.

Feinman and Nicholas (2011) then add a second Late Classic (A.D. 750–900) Late Monte Albán IIIb–IV phase, which can be viewed as the period of decline for the centralized polities. In this proposed settlement phase, population decreases significantly in the central portion of the valley around Monte Albán, and slightly increases in the southeastern part of the Tlacolula Valley, around Mitla. The Late Monte Albán IIIb–IV phase ceramic assemblage is designed to account for the different patterns of abandonment at sites throughout the valley. For example, the Late Classic at Monte Albán and Jalieza ends earlier (ca. A.D. 750–800) than it does at El Palmillo (ca. A.D. 850–900). This period should probably be renamed "Terminal Classic" to reflect the overall pattern of decline, but I will continue to use Late Classic here in order to maintain consistency with the other research projects.

Feinman and Nicholas (2011) also add a post-collapse Early Monte Albán V phase to the scheme. Population shows a continued decrease during the Early Postclassic around Monte Albán and in the Etla and Zimatlán Valleys; in contrast, population remains relatively steady in the Tlacolula Valley, although settlement becomes more dispersed. This contrasts with the settlement pattern project's Early Postclassic (Monte Albán IV phase) diagram because it suggests steady population densities between the end of the Late Classic and the Early Postclassic in the Tlacolula region, rather than rapid growth from a population shift. The newer model also changes the chronology for the Early Postclassic to A.D. 900–1300, as compared to Blanton et al.'s (1982) A.D. 700–1000, or Markens' (2008) A.D. 800–1200. It also disagrees with Winter's (1989a) proposed hiatus in the cultural sequence and decline in population throughout the Valley of Oaxaca.

While this settlement pattern reassessment provides an excellent base for interpreting excavation data from individual sites (e.g., Dainzú-Macuilxóchitl), comparative evidence from Early Postclassic contexts is still scarce and sociopolitical organization in the valley during this period of reorganization is not well understood. One purpose of my study is to present the results of intensive surface collections and excavations on Cerro Danush—where radiocarbon analysis clearly dates the most recent occupation to the Early Postclassic—in order to complement Feinman and Nicholas' (2011) reassessment and to begin to understand sociopolitical reorganization in the immediate aftermath of Monte Albán's decline.

There are currently two separate ceramic chronologies used in the Valley of Oaxaca. To maintain consistency with the previous volumes in the University of Michigan Museum of Anthropology series, through the remainder of this monograph I use the system developed by Caso, Bernal, and Acosta (1967). Because these competing systems differ in both phase terminology and chronology, I feel it is important to explain the differences between the systems, and describe how I reconcile these differences in my own research. To help the reader who is unfamiliar with the Valley of Oaxaca sequences, I have included a detailed discussion of my understanding of the Classic to Postclassic ceramic sequences in Appendix A.

Collapse, Resilience, and Reorganization in Complex Societies

When discussing the collapse of complex societies, archaeologists generally refer to a rapid (over a few generations) decline in sociopolitical complexity or the demise of a particular political system, and not the mysterious disappearance of a civilization (Railey and Reycraft 2008; Tainter 1988; Yoffee 1988a). Moreover, in both historic and ancient examples, such as ancient Mesopotamia (Yoffee 1988b, 2010) and the Soviet Union (Strayer 1998), civilizations that experience a decline or fragmentation in political complexity often demonstrate "resilience" in social aspects, such as worldview, kinship, and language (McAnany and Gallareta Negrón 2010; McAnany and Yoffee 2010). These leftover institutions form the "building blocks" for the regeneration of complexity (Schwartz 2006).

One of the most comprehensive definitions of collapse is provided by Renfrew (1984:367–69), who states that a sudden decline in sociopolitical complexity is marked by four general features: "1) The collapse of central administrative organization of the state, 2) the disappearance of the traditional elite class, 3) the collapse of centralized economy, and 4) settlement shift and population decline." Within these four general features, he lists items that are archeologically detectable, such as the "abandonment of palaces," "abandonment of public building works," "cessation of rich traditional burials," "abandonment of elite residences," "abandonment of settlements," and a "shift to a dispersed pattern of smaller settlements" (Renfrew 1984:367–69). These general characteristics are applicable for the study of the transformations that took place in the Valley of Oaxaca from the Late Classic to the Early Postclassic.

For this study, the term "collapse" or "decline" refers to the dissolution of the political apparatus that administered the Monte Albán state throughout the Classic period (Blanton 1983; Paddock 1983a). Although several studies suggest oscillating periods of high and low centralization during the thousand-year prominence of the Monte Albán polity in the Valley of Oaxaca (Blanton and Kowalewski 1981; Kowalewski et al. 1989; Marcus 1998a), this study focuses on the events that occurred directly before and after the decline of the urban center around A.D. 750. While far more dramatic in scope than earlier periods of decentralization, the Late Classic to Early Postclassic transformation does not necessarily involve the "devolution" of sociopolitical organization in the Valley of Oaxaca either, which implies the return to an evolutionary stage that had existed prior to the appearance of Monte Albán. In fact, researchers have acknowledged several pre-collapse/post-collapse continuities in material culture at several sites in the Valley of Oaxaca (Faulseit 2012a; Winter et al. 2007). Therefore, Zapotec civilization did not necessarily decline after the collapse of the Monte Albán state, but polities in the valley reorganized themselves into a different and perhaps even more stratified sociopolitical system (Marcus 1989), and this best defines the concept of post-collapse reorganization, which is the focus of the present study.

Railey and Reycraft (2008) point out that studies of collapse mostly follow two pathways. The first consists of regionally centered works focused on identifying the specific external factors that led to the decline of a particular complex society. This approach is best exemplified by the vast corpus of works concerning the collapse of the Classic Lowland Maya polities (Culbert 1973, 1988; Demarest, Rice, and Rice 2004; Gill 2000; Webster 2002). Such studies often incorporate the scientific examination of human-environment interactions, where collapse is hypothesized to be triggered by external climatic conditions such as drought (Gill et al. 2007; Haug et al. 2003; Hodell, Curtis, and Brenner 1995; Stuart 2000) or the result of internal organizational problems leading to environmental degradation (Diamond 2005; Webster 2002). The second pathway focuses on the process of collapse from a system perspective, attempting to identify the qualities shared by pre-collapse complex societies that led to their eventual fragmentation or disarticulation (Cowgill 1988; Flannery 1972; Renfrew 1978, 1984; Simon 1965; Tainter 1988). Although these models vary in details, they generally conclude that societies evolve through increasing sociopolitical complexity as a strategy for problem solving. Initially this strategy is effective, but it comes at increasing costs and ultimately reaches a peak in effectiveness, after which further increase in complexity creates instability and leads to collapse.

Scholarly interest in post-collapse reorganization has followed a similar trajectory to studies of collapse, with edited volumes producing either regionally diverse case studies aimed at identifying common resilient structures (McAnany and Yoffee 2010; Schwartz and Nichols 2006) or collective works intensively focused on the post-collapse reorganization that occurred in a particular region of study (e.g., Blomster 2008; Diehl and Berlo 1989; Hegmon, Nelson, and Ruth 1998). These works have yielded a fair amount of data, allowing for new challenges to previously held notions about "collapse," but they are lacking in the development of more general theoretical models for post-collapse reorganization (Schwartz 2006).

Eisenstadt (1988, 1993) suggested that collapse in complex societies involves the extreme case of "how social boundaries are constructed and reconstructed, with particular reference to the boundaries of political systems" (1988:236). This interplay of social and political boundaries is integral to the premises behind theoretical models that combine both collapse and reorganization into a cyclical understanding of the evolution of complex societies (Allen 2008; Adams 1978, 1988; Demarest 1992; Fish and Kowalewski 1990; Flannery 1999; Stark 2006). For example, Anderson's (1994) model of political cycling for the Savannah River chiefdoms of the Late Prehistoric southeastern United States envisions resilient small-scale sociopolitical institutions that remain intact during periods of decentralization and serve to hasten political reintegration in periods of reorganization. For Anderson (1994), "simple chiefdoms" in the Savannah River valley were integrated through slowly developing social institutions that evolved over long periods of time, while "complex chiefdoms" formed rapidly and were constituted mainly through the political integration of socially diverse simple chiefdoms. Because the more complex societies lacked the long-term development of unifying social institutions, they were relatively unstable and susceptible to fragmentation through a variety of external or internal stresses.

One of the most convincing and wide-reaching treatments of political cycling on a larger scale (i.e., archaic states) is Marcus' (1998a) dynamic model, which outlines cycles of "peaks" and "valleys" in political centralization that correspond to the rise, fall, and reorganization of societies over a variety of geographic regions and temporal scales. Marcus (1998a) views archaic states as expansionist entities, whose leaders extend their political boundaries well beyond their core social boundaries through conquest. At some point the state reaches a maximum territory of control, after which peripheral entities, which probably do not share social boundaries with the core, begin to assert their autonomy and disarticulate from the political integration of the state. In her most detailed treatment of this model, Marcus (1992a, 1993, 2012) incorporated ethnohistoric, archaeological, and epigraphic data to map the cyclical patterns of organization and transfer of power among Lowland Maya polities in the Late and Terminal Classic. Like Anderson (1994), Marcus identified resilient social units (i.e., Maya provinces) that remained intact, while regional political systems oscillated between high and low levels of integration.

The most recent cyclical treatments of sociopolitical complexity incorporate the tenets of resilience theory, which has been adopted from environmental scientists Holling and Gunderson (2002) and has been employed most extensively to model prehistoric decline, resilience, and reorganization in the regions of the U.S. Southwest (Nelson et al. 2006; Redman 2005; Redman and Kinzig 2003; Redman, Nelson, and Kinzig 2009) and Southeast (Thompson and Turck 2009; Delcourt and Delcourt 2004). While these studies have focused mostly on the interactions between humans and their ecosystems, resilience theory appears to also provide a promising explanatory tool for archaeologists to model sociopolitical evolution in complex societies beyond just the rise and fall of states.

Resilience theory is centered on the concept of the "adaptive cycle" (Holling and Gunderson 2002), which envisions ecosystems continuously cycling through four phases: exploitation (r), conservation (K), release or collapse (Ω), and reorganization (α). Rather than a sinusoidal undulation between peaks and valleys, however, the adaptive cycle is represented by a figure eight-shaped recurring loop, which is modulated by the overall potential in the system and the connectedness or vulnerability of its parts. The system is resilient while potential is high and connectedness is low, but becomes unstable and susceptible to collapse as key elements become more interconnected and interdependent. The Ω-phase rapid release or "collapse," however, is not triggered by the unstable conditions of the conservation phase, but by outside factors that induce the transition.

In this way, resilience theory does not replace or refute current models of sociopolitical collapse and reorganization, but complements and enhances subtle descriptions of these complex phenomena. For example, in the conservation K-phase, just prior to collapse, an ecological system becomes "overconnected and increasingly rigid in its control," which eventually leads to a sudden release that is triggered by "agents of disturbance such as wind, fire, disease, insect outbreak, and drought or a combination of these" (Holling and Gunderson 2002:35). Conceptually, this recalls the pre-collapse conditions of "hypercoherence," "declining marginal returns," and "cusp catastrophe" as outlined by Flannery (1972), Tainter (1988), and Renfrew (1984) respectively for sociopolitical systems. Similarly, the trigger agents are reminiscent of the causal factors, such as drought (Gill 2000) or warfare (Drews 1993), that are hypothesized to have induced the collapse of specific archaic states.

Additionally, the conditions that exist in the K-phase of the adaptive cycle do not always lead to release or collapse, because each local ecosystem's adaptive cycle is contained within a larger regional structure, known as a panarchy (Holling, Gunderson, and Peterson 2002), which consists of nested adaptive cycles that interact in a hierarchical manner. Thus, large and slow adaptive cycles influence small and fast cycles and vice versa (Delcourt and Delcourt 2004; Holling, Gunderson, and Peterson 2002; Redman and Kinzig 2003). Long-term slowly evolving adaptive cycles provide the impetus for short-term rapidly evolving cycles to skip from the K-phase of one cycle to the r-phase of another through a process described as "remember" (Holling, Gunderson, and Peterson 2002:76). Likewise, the smaller cycles can trigger release and reorganization in larger cycles through a process described as "revolt" (Holling, Gunderson, and Peterson 2002:74–75). Therefore, resilience theory provides a useful explanatory tool for modeling a variety of conditions and circumstances surrounding the collapse, resilience, and reorganization of archaic states.

In combining the concepts of political cycling with those of resilience theory, I suggest that the Valley of Oaxaca can be viewed as a regional panarchy that incorporates nested adaptive cycles of social, political, and ecological institutions. Thus, through the tenets of Anderson's (1994) and Marcus' (1998a) models, social boundaries are contained within long-term slowly evolving adaptive cycles associated with common ritual and ceremonial practices, while political boundaries belong to short-term rapidly evolving adaptive cycles associated with the charisma and capabilities of leaders. For the purposes of this study, I am mostly interested in explaining the α-phase to r-phase reorganization of polities in the Valley of Oaxaca after the collapse of the Monte Albán state.

According to Holling and Gunderson (2002:38–39), in the reorganization or α-phase, leftover institutions from the release or Ω-phase begin to "sequester and organize resources in a process that leads to the r species establishing founding rights over the remaining capital." Returning to the dynamic model (Marcus 1998a), the r species can be equated to the lower-level political leaders or intermediate elites that persist in the aftermath of collapse, such as those that belong to the head towns or loosely integrated provinces Marcus (1993) describes in the Maya Lowlands, and the available resources can be equated with the resilient structures that maintain social integration between communities after the disintegration of political ties. Therefore, opportunistic leaders can take advantage of the social connections through the "remember" process, leading to a rapid reorganization of sociopolitical complexity.

I suggest this is what occurred in the Valley of Oaxaca during the Late Classic to Early Postclassic transition. Working within this theoretical framework, my research at Dainzú-Macuilxóchitl incorporates both ethnohistoric and archaeological data to identify the "resources" or resilient social institutions that were exploited by the "r species," or local leaders, to regenerate sociopolitical complexity in the Valley of Oaxaca.

Summary of Research Design

In a special edition of *American Behavioral Scientist* "dedicated to the proposition that archaeology of the individual household is an essential building block in the reconstruction of past societies" (Willey 1982:613), Wilk and Rathje (1982:617) proposed that household archaeology could bridge the gap between mid-level and high-level theory. Since that time, household archaeology has become a prominent fixture in the general archaeological literature (Allison 1999; Blanton 1994; Netting, Wilk, and Arnould 1984), especially in Mesoamerica (Flannery and Marcus 2005; Flannery and Winter 1976; Healan 1989; Hendon 2010; Hirth 2009a; Santley and Hirth 1993; Wilk and Ashmore 1988). Projects involving survey, intensive surface collection, and excavation have been effectively employed to study household organization and craft specialization/production at sites in central and southern Mexico including Otumba (Charlton, Charlton, and Nichols 1993), Xochicalco (Hirth 2000a, 2000b), Teotihuacan (Millon 1973, 1988), Tula (Healan 1972, 1989; Mastache de Escobar, Cobean, and Healan 2002), Huexotla (Brumfiel 1980), and many others.

In the Valley of Oaxaca, the extensive record of household archaeology has provided a greater understanding of the developments in sociopolitical organization that took place from the Early Formative through the Early Classic (Blanton 1978; Elson 2007; Feinman 1999; Flannery 1976b; Flannery and Marcus 2005; González Licón 2003, 2009; Spencer 1982; Winter 1974). In my research, I build on these works by employing the tenets of household archaeology to study change and continuity in pre-collapse and post-collapse behavior at the site of Dainzú-Macuilxóchitl. In particular, I look at four aspects of behavior: abandonment, domestic ritual, community ritual, and political economy. It is my intention that through the reconstruction of household and community behaviors, I can identify resilient social institutions that may have served to keep dispersed communities loosely integrated in the Early Postclassic period of political fragmentation.

Abandonment Patterns

To understand the release phase conditions at the local level, it is important to understand patterns of abandonment at both the household and community level (LaMotta and Schiffer 1999). For example, a very rapid abandonment pattern was identified archaeologically by the presence of many large whole ceramic vessels left in their original contexts within residences at the site of Xochicalco (Webb and Hirth 2003). These data, coupled with the evidence for burning in the civic-ceremonial core, suggest that the site was hastily abandoned, perhaps because of an external threat. Sites in the Valley of Oaxaca, such as Monte Albán (Winter 2003), Lambityeco (Lind and Urcid 2010), and El Palmillo (Feinman and Nicholas 2011), show more gradual abandonment patterns with little evidence of violence (Chapter 3). I would therefore not have been surprised to find a similar abandonment pattern at Dainzú-Macuilxóchitl, pending the results of my excavations. Because colonial documents reveal that Dainzú-Macuilxóchitl was still an important center in the Late Postclassic (Whitecotton 1977, 2003), it seems reasonable to expect that the site was never completely abandoned. I wondered, however, if I might find a reduction in use of the terraces after the Late Classic, resulting in a less nucleated settlement in the Early Postclassic.

Given what we know of other sites in the area, I expected the residential pattern to reflect gradual abandonment as well. If commoner households were making the decision to move away from the nuclear settlement, they most likely would have had time to collect their belongings, and I expected to find little defacto refuse (LaMotta and Schiffer 1999). In addition, I did not expect to find evidence for violence, such as burning or destruction.

Summary of Field Methods

My research project targeted changes in settlement patterns and household organization from the Late Classic to Early Postclassic at Dainzú-Macuilxóchitl. I selected Cerro Danush as the focus of this study because previous research had suggested that it contained domestic terraces, and was the locus of Late Classic and Early Postclassic settlement at the site (Kowalewski et al. 1989; Markens, Winter, and Martínez López 2008). Because no extensive research had been previously conducted on the hill, my project was divided into two phases: an exploratory season of intensive survey, mapping, and surface collection, followed by the comprehensive excavation of two domestic terraces.

To study the settlement pattern of the terraces on Cerro Danush, I surveyed the entire hill, creating a detailed topographic map of all features and paying special attention to the man-made terraces. After that, I conducted a systematic surface collection on more than 70% of the terraces. Diagnostic ceramic markers were identified and counted so that I could study their density distributions across the terraces. The distributions of temporal ceramic markers were used to reconstruct the occupational history of Cerro Danush. Artifact distributions were also subjected to spatial and multivariate statistical analyses to model domestic and community behavioral patterns on the hill between the Late Classic and Early Postclassic periods.

To study Late Classic and Early Classic household organization, I selected for excavation two domestic terraces at the base of Cerro Danush. Both contained ceramic markers from the relevant periods on their surfaces. One of the terraces was then excavated extensively to uncover the most recent residential surface, which radiocarbon analysis revealed to be the Early Postclassic. Test units were then excavated to uncover the earlier, Early-to-Late Classic occupational surfaces. I then compared and contrasted the layout, design, and construction of the Early Postclassic housing complex uncovered during this project with Classic and Late Postclassic complexes excavated elsewhere in the Valley of Oaxaca. I also used the density distribution of artifacts and excavated features to compare and contrast household craft production and ritual activities between the Classic and Postclassic.

2 | The Dainzú-Macuilxóchitl Region

The archaeological sites of the Dainzú-Macuilxóchitl region are located in the eastern, or Tlacolula, arm of the Valley of Oaxaca. The geomorphology and botany of this region have been described by Kirkby (1973) and C. E. Smith (1978).

The Dainzú-Macuilxóchitl region lies about 25 km southeast of Oaxaca City, at a latitude of 17°01' and longitude of 97°33' (Figs. 2.1, 2.2). It is situated on the alluvial and piedmont soils between the Río Salado to the south and Sierra Norte to the north at an elevation of between 1640 and 1700 m. From the high mountains just north of the site, several tributaries drain southward to the Río Salado. One of the larger tributaries, known as the Río Grande, runs directly through the center of the archaeological remains, and must have played an important role in the site's history. Although these tributaries are seasonal, they flood periodically, depositing sediment in the area and replenishing the soil.

While the Tlacolula Valley is generally drier than the other two arms of the Valley of Oaxaca, its northwestern half, including Dainzú-Macuilxóchitl, receives more annual rainfall than do the areas to the south and east. Today, the inhabitants of the modern towns in this region practice milpa farming. This mostly consists of producing corn, beans, and squash for local consumption without the use of tractors or modern equipment. Since the site of Dainzú-Macuilxóchitl is located on community land within the boundaries of the modern towns of San Jerónimo Tlacochahuaya and San Mateo Macuilxóchitl, most of the alluvial lands surrounding the archaeological ruins are periodically plowed. Additionally, flocks of sheep and goats are pastured in the piedmont areas within the archaeological site.

Several prominent hills and small mountains dot the landscape around Dainzú-Macuilxóchitl and effectively serve as limits to the archaeological site. To the south we find the trio of Cerros Dainzú, Danyanwool, and Danypol; to the east lies Cerro Danez; and to the northwest lie Cerro Danush and Cerro Danso. These low-lying hills are rocky and sparsely vegetated with members of the genus *Agave*, mala mujer (*Jatropha* sp.), mesquite, and huizache (*Acacia* sp.). Because of their rocky nature and susceptibility to erosion during heavy rains, these hills are not very suitable for agriculture; however, they do provide a good source of firewood and small game (mostly rabbit). Archaeological remains—including petroglyphs, rock paintings, ceramics, chipped stone, and the remnants of structures—are found on three of these hills: Cerro Danush, Cerro Danez, and Cerro Dainzú, which mark the southern, northern, and eastern limits of the site, respectively.

The solitary peak of Cerro Danush (Fig. 2.3) rises 250 m over the alluvial floor of the valley. It is made up of volcanic tuff that appears to be rich in minerals. In several areas where the bedrock

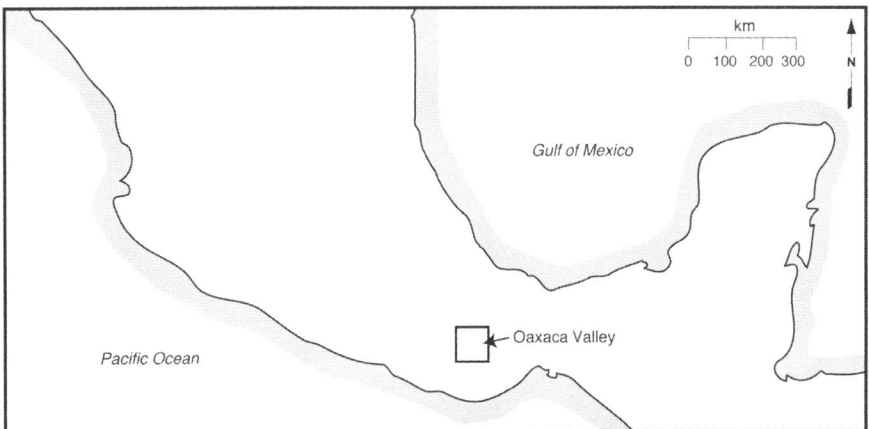

Figure 2.1.
The State of Oaxaca (image courtesy of ESRI ArcView software) (*above left*), and the Valley of Oaxaca with archaeological sites (shaded relief source SRTM NASA) (*left*).
A, Cerro Atzompa; *B*, Monte Albán; *C*, Dainzú-Macuilxóchitl; *D*, Lambityeco; *E*, Yagul; *F*, Mitla; *G*, El Palmillo; *H*, Jalieza; *I*, Ejutla; *1*, Etla arm of Oaxaca Valley; *2*, Tlacolula arm of Oaxaca Valley; *3*, Zimatlán Valley.

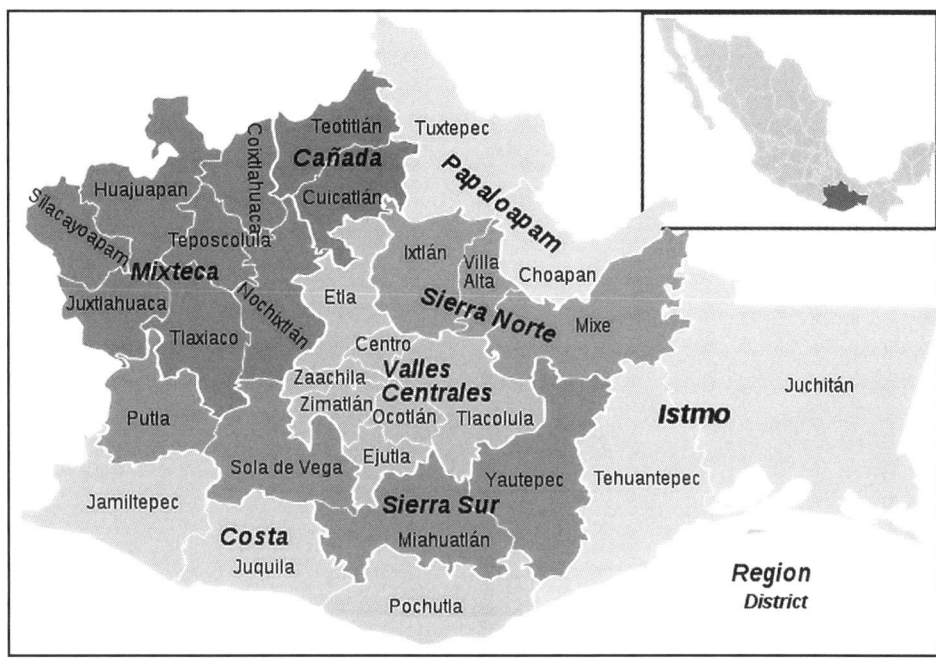

Figure 2.2. Geographical regions of Oaxaca (image courtesy of Wikimedia).

Figure 2.3. Cerro Danush (viewed from Dainzú Archaeological Zone).

is exposed, it shows signs of crumbling from erosion. The unexposed bedrock is white in color, but darkens relatively quickly after exposure, making it easy to spot recent areas of rock fall. The hill does not contain good sources of raw material for stone tool production, such as chert, but cobblestones of quartzite or silicified tuff from the nearby Río Grande may have provided raw material for many of the stone tools found at the site. Sources of limestone for burning (to produce lime for plaster) are found to the west of Dainzú-Macuilxóchitl.

Dainzú-Macuilxóchitl: The Archaeological Site

The site of Dainzú-Macuilxóchitl consists of over 150 artificial mounds spread over an area of roughly 4 km², located mostly on the communal lands (*bienes comunales*) of the modern towns of San Jerónimo Tlacochahuaya in the southwest and San Mateo Macuilxóchitl in the northeast. The highest concentration of archaeological materials (structures and surface artifacts) is found in the area between Cerro Dainzú and Cerro Danush.

Members of the Valley of Oaxaca Settlement Pattern Project (Blanton et al. 1993; Kowalewski et al. 1989; Balkansky 1998), who surveyed the region in the 1970s, group Dainzú-Macuilxóchitl within a larger system of loosely integrated archaeological sites that are found in the area surrounding the modern towns of Tlacochahuaya, Guadalupe, and Teotitlán del Valle; this they refer to as the Dainzú-Macuilxóchitl-Tlacochahuaya-Guadalupe (or DMTG) settlement cluster. Temporal ceramic markers recovered from the surface at Dainzú-Macuilxóchitl suggest that it was occupied from the Rosario phase (700–500 B.C.) through Spanish contact in the sixteenth century (Oliveros 1997).

Arturo Oliveros (1997:25) pointed out that the name *Macuilxóchitl*, which translates as "5 Flower" in the Nahuatl language, is also the name of the central Mexican deity associated with games, particularly the Mesoamerican ball game. This is an apt designation, considering the fact that archaeological research conducted at Dainzú-Macuilxóchitl has revealed a large corpus of iconography that some scholars have associated with an early form of ball game. The name "5 Flower"—*Guiebelagayo* in colonial Zapotec (Acuña 1984 [1580])—has deep roots in Zapotec cultural tradition. Several ceramic figurines found at Monte Albán and other sites in the Valley of Oaxaca, dating to the Classic period (A.D. 200–900), contain the glyphic representation of this name in their headdresses. Additionally, a small nearby Late Classic settlement, located between Dainzú-Macuilxóchitl and Lambityeco, bears the modern Zapotec translation *Gaii Guie'* (Fargher 2004). According to Whitecotton (1977:157), the *Relación Geográfica de Macuilxóchitl* of 1580 states that the people of the town worshipped "Coquehuilia, lord of the center of the earth, whose calendrical representation may have been 5-Flower." However, since this name includes the word *coqui*, or "hereditary ruler" in Zapotec, it could refer to a ruler whose calendric name was 5 Flower.

The first archaeologist to conduct excavations at Dainzú-Macuilxóchitl was Ignacio Bernal (1967), who initiated a salvage project for the Instituto Nacional de Antropología e Historia (INAH) in 1967 to recover some carved stones that had been exposed near an oxcart path along the western base of Cerro Dainzú. In the months and years that followed, he and Arturo Oliveros (Bernal and Oliveros 1988) directed extensive excavation and reconstruction projects on three large man-made terraces in the area that is now protected and open to the public, known as the Zona Arqueológica Dainzú. In the course of their work, Bernal and Oliveros (1988) uncovered monumental public architecture, elite residences, and a tomb (Tomb 7, Fig. 2.4) with the image of a jaguar carved on its lintel and doorjambs (Oliveros 1997). These buildings were found to have had several construction episodes, beginning in the Late Formative and extending into the Early Classic (Bernal and Oliveros 1988).

On the uppermost terrace, Bernal and Oliveros (1988) excavated Building A, a large rectangular stone platform with a central staircase that they suggest supported a building with ceremonial or religious functions. Like Building L at Monte Albán, Building A's lower wall was covered with stones carved in low relief, but unlike the prisoner carvings of Building L, the Dainzú carvings depict individuals wearing protective equipment (including helmets) and holding small rubber or stone balls in their hands (Fig. 2.5). Several of the figures also appear to be wearing jaguar outfits, or have been modified to include feline qualities such as spots (Bernal 1968, 1973).

These low-relief carvings have been interpreted as early evidence of ballplayers and the ball game (Bernal and Seuffert 1979; Orr 1997). Unlike the well-documented version of the Mesoamerican ball game that was played in I-shaped courts, where the participants did not use their hands but rather used their hips to bounce a soccer-sized rubber ball through a large stone hoop (Scarborough and Wilcox 1991), the Dainzú figures hold small balls in their hands (Fig. 2.5) and appear to be hurling them at one another (Orr 1997, 2003). Although Bernal and Oliveros uncovered an I-shaped ball court on the lowest terrace at Dainzú (Fig. 2.6), they found that it was constructed in the Late Classic (Bernal and Oliveros 1988:23). For earlier periods, they propose that the large open patios that formed the initial construction phase (Late Monte Albán I) of Building B, located on the terrace just below Building A, may have functioned as courts for playing a kind of ball game (Bernal and Oliveros 1988:10). Urcid (n.d.) suggests that the structure found on the summit of Cerro Dainzú may also have served as a ball court in the Terminal Formative period (Monte Albán II), whereas Marcus (n.d.) suggests that the summit structure was where victims were dispatched in a sacrificial ceremony.

The stone carvings at Dainzú have been the subject of several iconographic studies, most notably by Bernal and Seuffert (1968, 1979), Marcus (1983c, n.d.), and Orr (1997, 2001). Most recently, Baudez (2011), Berger (2011), and Taube and Zender (2009) argue against the notion that they are ballplayers, suggesting instead that they are combatants. While the interpretations of the iconography differ, this research establishes Dainzú-Macuilxóchitl as an important Late Formative site in the Valley of Oaxaca. Dainzú may have become an important second-tier center within the Monte Albán state (Balkansky 1998; Kowalewski et al. 1989).

In the 1970s, the settlement pattern project carried out full-coverage surveys of the Valley of Oaxaca (Blanton et al. 1982; Kowalewski et al. 1989). The survey team visited Dainzú-Macuilxóchitl and, through aerial photos and surface collections, created a map of more than 150 unexcavated mounds at the site (Fig. 2.7). They identified possible craft production areas, as well as developed a settlement history for the site based on surface ceramics (Kowalewski et al. 1989). Their data suggest that Dainzú-Macuilxóchitl underwent considerable expansion during the Early Classic (A.D. 200–500); the increased area of scatter for distinctive ceramic markers of this period shows the settlement growing to the north and west of Cerro Dainzú. Subsequent excavations in the area (Fernández Dávila and Gómez Serafín 1993; Markens 2004; Markens, Winter, and Martínez López 2008) confirmed this finding.

Figure 2.4. Jaguar tomb façade, Dainzú Archaeological Zone.

Figure 2.5. Carved stone ballplayer (Building A, Dainzú Archaeological Zone).

Figure 2.6. Monte Albán IV I-shaped ball court (Dainzú Archaeological Zone).

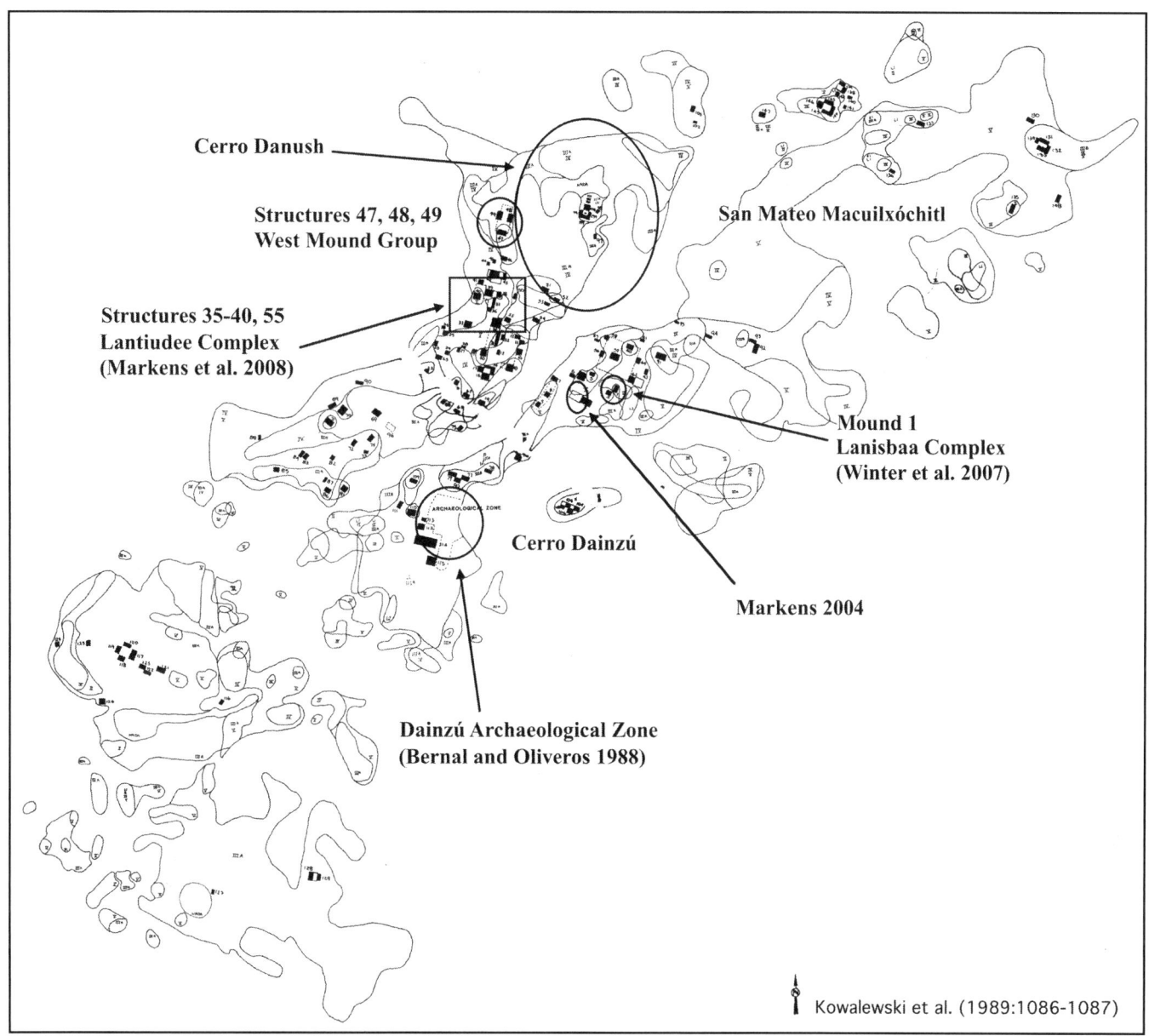

Figure 2.7. Map of archaeological features with areas of previous excavations (image redrawn and modified from Kowalewski et al. 1989:1086–87).

Toward the end of the Early Classic or the beginning of the Late Classic (A.D. 500–900), Dainzú-Macuilxóchitl experienced a rapid increase in the construction of monumental architecture, in overall size, and in population density. According to Kowalewski et al. (1989), the site grew to be second only to Monte Albán both in volume of monumental architecture (122,193 m³) and in population density (12,000); it was also comparable in both categories to Jalieza (33,500 m³/16,000), a large second-tier center in the Zimatlán Valley (Fig. 2.1). Settlement at the site of Dainzú-Macuilxóchitl also shifted at that time, with the near abandonment of the area surrounding Cerro Dainzú in favor of new settlements toward the northern end of the site, including the newly established civic-ceremonial precincts at the base and on the summit of Cerro Danush (Faulseit 2012a, 2012b; Markens, Winter, and Martínez López 2008). The only Late Classic construction in the Dainzú area involved the addition of an I-shaped ball court (Fig. 2.6), similar in design and orientation to those found at Monte Albán.

These changes at Dainzú-Macuilxóchitl were concurrent with and related to those at other major sites in the Valley of Oaxaca, such as Lambityeco (Lind and Urcid 2010) and Jalieza (Elson 2011), not to mention developments on hilltops at Santa Ana del Valle and San Miguel del Valle (Kowalewski et al. 1989). They also appear to be concurrent with increased construction and concentration of population on Cerro Atzompa near Monte Albán (Robles García and Andrade Cuautle 2011).

Dainzú-Macuilxóchitl, like many sites in the valley, appears to have experienced a period of decline at the end of the Late Classic (Markens, Winter, and Martínez López 2008), but was never fully abandoned. Instead, while many other sites were permanently abandoned, Dainzú-Macuilxóchitl was reorganized and emerged in the Late Postclassic (A.D. 1300–1521) as an important local kingdom whose nucleated center lay in the area where the modern town of San Mateo Macuilxóchitl is found today (Oudijk 2000, 2002, 2008; Whitecotton 1977, 1983, 1990, 2003).

While Dainzú-Macuilxóchitl was included in the regional survey (Kowalewski et al. 1989), and a few localized excavation projects have been conducted in the area since then (Markens 2004; Markens, Winter, and Martínez López 2008; Winter et al. 2007), no quantitative or spatially expansive study of the overall Late Classic abandonment pattern has been conducted at the site. Furthermore, prior to my work, no intensive archaeological investigations had been carried out on Cerro Danush, which had been identified as a major part of the site's Late Classic settlement (Markens, Winter, and Martínez López 2008). The data obtained during a recent salvage project (Markens, Winter, and Martínez López 2008; Winter et al. 2007), as well as Markens' (2004) additional excavations, have produced important information concerning the Classic to Postclassic transition in the area adjacent to Cerro Danush. This work included excavation of a Late Classic palace-temple complex (Markens, Winter, and Martínez López 2008), a portion of a Late Classic residence (Markens 2004), and an entire Late Postclassic residence (Winter et al. 2007). Markens and his colleagues (Markens 2004; Markens, Winter, and Martínez López 2008) concluded that the Late Classic structures and residences were abandoned around A.D. 800. They uncovered very sparse evidence for Early Postclassic occupation, essentially limited to intrusive burials, offerings of miniature vessels, and some modification and reuse of abandoned structures. No Early Postclassic residences were excavated, however, leaving settlement patterns during that period unclear.

Cerro Danush appears to have been first occupied toward the end of the Early Classic or the beginning of the Late Classic, when its slopes were terraced to support domestic structures and its summit dramatically reshaped to form a temple platform (Faulseit 2008, 2012b). At the end of the Late Classic, most of the settlement on the mountain appears to have been abandoned (Markens, Winter, and Martínez López 2008), but a small structure found on the summit appears to have served as a shrine (Kowalewski et al. 1989), perhaps for ritual pilgrimages (Orr 2001). A map provided by the town for the *Relación Geográfica de Macuilxóchitl* of 1580 (Acuña 1984 [1580]) shows the mountain in oversized proportions with a large cross at the top (Plate 7), indicating its continued importance into the Colonial period. Today, a modern shrine has been constructed on top of the ancient platform at the summit (Fig. 2.8), and the townspeople make a yearly (May 3) pilgrimage there to celebrate the Festival of the Cross (Markens, Winter, and Martínez López 2008).

Figure 2.8. Modern shrine constructed on the summit of Cerro Danush by local townspeople.

The Rise and Decline of Monte Albán

The Zapotec state—like a number of first-generation states worldwide—arose in the context of competition among rival chiefly societies (Flannery 1999). During the Rosario phase (700–500 B.C.), the Valley of Oaxaca was divided among at least three rank societies whose chiefly centers were San José Mogote in the north, San Martín Tilcajete in the south, and Yegüih in the east (Marcus and Flannery 1996: Fig. 128). At the end of the Rosario phase, at least 2000 people from San José Mogote and its satellite villages left the valley floor and moved to the summit of Monte Albán, a previously unoccupied mountain in the buffer zone between the three rival chiefly societies. There they began building an extensive defensive wall and launching attacks designed to acquire new territory. These attacks were aimed not only at rival societies such as Tilcajete (Spencer and Redmond 2004, 2005, 2006; Spencer 1982, 2007; Spencer and Redmond 1997), but at areas outside the valley, such as the Cuicatlán Cañada.

To place this development into the resilience/panarchy theory that I favor, the Monte Albán founding event represents a K-phase skip from one adaptive cycle, most likely that of the San José Mogote chiefdom, to the r-phase of a new adaptive cycle representing the early Monte Albán state. Holling, Gunderson, and Peterson (2002:75–76) suggest that this occurred through a process they define as "remember," where a slowly evolving adaptive cycle (in this case, representing the long-term social institutions developed over the entirety of the Formative in the Etla arm of the valley) provided the impetus for the quickly evolving political apparatus to exploit the available resources (manpower and land), allowing for quick reorganization in the face of a crisis. In this way, the social connections that developed between the Formative villages of the northern, or Etla, arm of the valley provided a means for the leaders of San José Mogote to relocate a large populace to the hilltop center of Monte Albán and establish Oaxaca's new capital. The subsequent Late Formative (500–100 B.C.) and Terminal Formative (100 B.C.–A.D. 200) represent the slow r-phase increase in both potential and connectedness of the early state adaptive cycle.

It is now clear that military force was required to create the Zapotec state, and that some 300 years were required to complete the process. Spencer and Redmond (2001, 2004, 2005) have documented Tilcajete's resistance to Monte Albán. When Monte Albán burned Tilcajete's ceremonial plaza in 330 B.C., Tilcajete refused to capitulate. Rather, it increased its size from 52.8 ha to 71.5 ha and moved its plaza uphill to a more defensible location. During Late Monte Albán I, Tilcajete erected several buildings characteristic of an archaic Zapotec kingdom, including a twelve-room palace and a number of two-room temples. Around 30–20 B.C., the palace (Structure 7) and one prominent temple (Structure 16) were burned. Tilcajete did not survive this second attack—it was abandoned, allowing Monte Albán to build a second-tier administrative center on a nearby mountain (Elson 2007).

For their part, the rulers of Monte Albán built monuments to their military conquests. On the main plaza of Monte Albán itself, they erected Building L, whose east wall once featured carvings of more than 300 slain (and occasionally mutilated) captives (Marcus 1974, 1983a 1992b). After defeating the village of La Coyotera in the Cuicatlán Cañada, the victorious Zapotec army erected a skull rack with the crania of some 61 victims (Spencer and Redmond 2001).

The Terminal Formative period (200 B.C.–A.D. 100) involved the consolidation and expansion of the Monte Albán state through conquest of several regions beyond its borders (Marcus and Flannery 1996; Redmond 1983; Redmond and Spencer 2006; Spencer 1982; Spencer and Redmond 1997). Caso (1947) was the first to interpret the approximately 40 carved stones set into Building J as "conquest slabs," places defeated by Monte Albán. At least half a dozen of those subjugated places have been identified with known places (Marcus and Flannery 1996:198). Among the subjugated places is Cuicatlán (Marcus 1976), whose conquest by Monte Albán has been confirmed (see Redmond 1983; Spencer 1982; Spencer and Redmond 1997, 2006). Not all outlying areas had to be conquered, however; Balkansky (2002) has shown that Sola de Vega was merely colonized by Monte Albán, and Ejutla seems to have been annexed peacefully during Monte Albán II (Feinman and Nicholas 1990, 1992, 1993).

Stone monuments of the Early Classic (A.D. 200–500) at Monte Albán suggest diplomatic ties—and perhaps even treaties—with Teotihuacan in the Basin of Mexico (Marcus and Flannery 1996:220–34). During this time, what has been variously called the Oaxaca *barrio* (Rattray 1993) or Zapotec enclave (Winter 1989b) was established at Teotihuacan, perhaps to facilitate trade between the two cities. Analysis of Monte Albán's Lápida de Bazán has led Marcus (1980, 1983g) to suggest that relations between Monte Albán and Teotihuacan were "without a hint of military activity" (1983g:180). During the Early Classic, many provinces previously conquered by Monte Albán during the Terminal Formative broke away, while many of those annexed peacefully remained closely tied to the Valley of Oaxaca.

Important sociopolitical changes were seen during the late Early Classic or early Late Classic in the valley. Opinions differ on what these changes mean. Blanton and his colleagues (Blanton et al. 1993; Kowalewski et al. 1989) proposed that during this period, political authority in the Valley of Oaxaca came to take the form of a triple alliance between Monte Albán, Jalieza in the southern valley, and the DMTG site cluster in the eastern valley. Jalieza (with an estimated population of 13,000) and DMTG (with an estimated population of 12,000) were similar in size to one another and second only to Monte Albán in estimated population density and mound volume at that time (Kowalewski et al. 1989). Such reorganization, they suggest, might have been initiated by the ruling elite at Monte Albán to more effectively facilitate activities within the Zimatlán and Tlacolula areas.

At the same time, just a few kilometers to the north of the main plaza at Monte Albán, a large and densely populated settlement was developing around an impressive civic-ceremonial core on the summit of Cerro Atzompa (Blanton 1978; Robles and Cuautle 2011). If it is the case that Dainzú-Macuilxóchitl and Jalieza reorganized to administer their respective arms of the valley, it is possible that Atzompa developed contemporaneously to administer the Etla arm.

Balkansky (1998) and Casparis (2006) suggest that this reorganization served to diffuse the political authority of the Monte Albán state, putting in place political institutions that would later compete with Monte Albán, setting the stage for the Late Classic decline of the urban capital and fragmentation of political authority throughout the valley. While this is reasonable, I suggest that the growth and reorganization at Jalieza, Atzompa, and Dainzú-Macuilxóchitl were initially permitted, or even encouraged, by the rulers at Monte Albán. Thus, these developments might represent an additional tier within the hierarchy of the overall political authority in the valley and a significant increase in the complexity of the Monte Albán state.

Based on the extensive resettlement that is documented for these three important sites, the Early to Late Classic transition may have involved an extensive reorganization of the political apparatus governing the Monte Albán state, perhaps representing another K-phase to r-phase skip from the early state adaptive cycle to the later state adaptive cycle. Unfortunately, aside from the excavations at Monte Albán and Jalieza, there are few comparative data to help explain this transitional episode. In any case, the period immediately following this reorganization—that is, the initial part of the Late Classic (A.D. 600–750)—saw valley-wide expansion of settlement, increases in the construction of monumental architecture, and a rapid increase in population density.

The Late Classic/Terminal Classic Transition

From the r- to K-phase of the adaptive cycle, competing species in an ecosystem become increasingly connected and interdependent as they exploit a greater and greater percentage of available resources. At some point in the Late Classic, the Monte Albán state experienced a transition to the K-phase, becoming unstable and susceptible to decline. Several archaeological projects have provided data on the nature of this transition in the Valley of Oaxaca, which is typified by the exploitation of marginal land for agriculture and the increasing efforts by elites to legitimize their authority by connecting themselves ideologically to long-term social institutions. These findings are summarized below.

Late Classic Population Growth and Intensification of Agriculture/Craft Specialization

According to Blanton and Kowalewski (1981:111–12), the Monte Albán state experienced a "cycle of growth" in the Late Classic, "characterized by population expansion, administered piedmont agricultural development, more centralized regional government, and increased levels of government 'meddling' in production and distribution." They argue that population expansion into the piedmont was initially beneficial to the integrated system, but continued growth, coupled with the eventual deterioration of the marginal piedmont soils, would have led to increasing disputes over land and water resources, requiring more administrative demands and costs.

Finsten (1983) argued that the Monte Albán state differentially administered the arms of the Valley of Oaxaca based on available economic resources. Because the Etla and Zimatlán Valleys contained greater potential for agriculture, the state encouraged intensified food production in these regions, even to the point where "it promoted development in the previously unoccupied and agriculturally productive southern Valle Grande to ensure adequate food supplies" (Finsten 1983:354). In the Late Classic, increased administrative control of the agricultural institutions produced a "hyper-interactive" system where individual polities were "over-integrated," so that "when the state fell, the entire area went down" (Finsten 1983:355–56). Like Blanton and Kowalewski's argument (1981), this model implies that the pressure of population growth prompted the state to expand settlement into previously uninhabited terrain, once again showing that the system was responding to problems with increased complexity.

To Finsten (1983:356), the Tlacolula Valley, with its lower potential for agricultural yield, was weakly integrated into the political system during the Late Classic and "began to participate in the state economy but in a very different way—as the producer of craft items whose production was not administratively regulated." This conclusion was based on data from the regional survey that showed low population in the Tlacolula Valley during the Late Classic. Recent research, however, has demonstrated that many sites in the Tlacolula Valley were, in fact, also densely populated.

Fargher (2004) has argued that increased craft production and specialization in the Tlacolula Valley were closely administered by regional authorities. Lind (2008) and Lind and Urcid (2010) assert that the rulers of Monte Albán took direct control of salt production activities at Lambityeco in the Late Classic, displacing the ruling line of nobles at the site, installing a new ruler, and replacing household production facilities with formal salt-producing workshops. While these scenarios remain to be proven, they mirror Blanton and Kowalewski's (1981) scheme, as well as Finsten's (1983), in that they imply that the state was responding to pressures by meddling in local production activities to increase yield, and therefore increasing administrative complexity.

Feinman and Nicholas (2000, 2007a, 2007b, 2007c, 2010) contend, however, that "specialized craft manufacture was not centralized at a few large Valley of Oaxaca settlements during the Classic; in fact, such economic activities have been noted through archaeological survey and excavation at many sites" (2010:91). The patterns of household production they found at Ejutla and El Palmillo were less indicative of state-controlled redistribution and more indicative of dependence on market-like transactions. They suggest that as population increased at El Palmillo, one of the driest localities in the Valley of Oaxaca, there was an increased dependence on the production of stone tools and textiles for exchange so that households could procure food by such transactions. (It should be noted that despite various authors' references to market-like *transactions*, no Classic [or earlier] site in the valley has produced convincing archaeological evidence for a market *place*, like those that existed in the sixteenth century.)

Late/Terminal Classic Efforts to Legitimize Authority by Elites

Archaeological research suggests that as complex societies encounter increasing costs or diminishing revenue, the ruling elites need to invest significant capital toward legitimizing their authority (Anderson 1994; Cowgill 1988; Renfrew 1984; Tainter 1988). Marcus (1998b:2) proposed that with the founding of the Monte Albán state, "full-time priests began to appropriate more and more of the ritual formerly conducted by ordinary families." Undoubtedly, many Early Classic state-level rituals and ceremonies at Monte Albán were performed in the large open plaza at the center of the site, where monumental carved stones were often put on display to show the power of the state apparatus (Marcus 1983b). Such displays most certainly served to solidify and institutionalize the authority of the ruling class.

In contrast to the Early Classic, carved stone monuments of the Late Classic tended to be smaller and were often located in private or restricted-access contexts, such as tombs, rather than being put on public display (Marcus 1983b). The messages contained on one type of Late Classic monument, referred to as a genealogical register, changed from depictions of militaristic state conquest and the subjugation of subordinate communities to the establishment or enhancement of a particular elite family's ancestral connection to supernatural or legendary forces (Marcus 1983b). According to Joyce (2004:209), Late Classic changes in the layout and design of civic-ceremonial architecture and carved stone monuments at Monte Albán indicate "a shift away from large-scale public ceremonies and toward restricted, private ones." For example, several elite residences were constructed in and around the main plaza of the site, effectively converting an area once used for "large-scale public ceremonies" to one with a "focus of elite domestic activities" (Joyce 2004:209).

Joyce (2004) suggests that this pattern is also reflected in the marked increase of civic-ceremonial complexes known as temple-patio-altar (TPA) systems constructed at Monte Albán during the Late Classic. The temple-patio-altar complex has been described by Winter (1989b:45–46) as a "formalized ritual ceremonial precinct . . . [that] consists of a large enclosed patio with a small raised platform or altar in the center and a temple situated atop a platform on one side of the patio." These structures contained high walls that enclosed the central patios, effectively restricting access to the rites or ceremonies that took place within them. They are often adjacent or connected to elite residences, and Winter (2002:79) suggests that these structures represent places where "the elite directly controlled community ritual and religion, as well as economic and political matters."

Two temple-patio-altar complexes excavated at Lambityeco have allowed for further characterization of these structures (Lind and Urcid 1983). The first, Structure 195, was considered to be the house of Lambityeco's ruling lineage (Lind and Urcid 1983). It consisted of a ritual or ceremonial space (TPA), with its patio and central altar surrounded by high platforms, connected to an elite residence, with central patio and surrounding house complex. The second temple-patio-altar complex, Structure 190-4, had a similar two-patio arrangement, but the temple in the center appears to have been devoted to the Zapotec deity *Cociyo* (Lightning). Lind and Urcid (1983) characterized this compound as the residence of the noble priest responsible for rites and ceremonies devoted to this important deity. Sellen (2002) suggested that Zapotec elites might assume the guise of Cociyo in ceremonies devoted to rain and agriculture, just as they are shown on Zapotec urns (Marcus 1983d). The closed and private nature of the temple-patio-altar complex suggests that Late Classic elites assumed responsibility and ownership of these rites to assert their legitimacy within the community.

Both of the temple-patio-altar compounds at Lambityeco contained elaborate tombs, and plaster friezes depict the ancestral lineage of the residents (Lind and Urcid 1983). This fact corroborates Marcus' (1983b) description of these monuments as genealogical registers that served to establish the legitimacy of the elites who maintained them. In the Late Postclassic, some *lienzos* in Oaxaca served as genealogical registers that established a connection between rulers and their deified ancestors. The latter were often believed to be responsible for the foundation of a sociopolitical entity or community (Boone 2000; Whitecotton 1990, 2003).

The Terminal Classic in the Valley of Oaxaca

We have conflicting scenarios for the decline of Monte Albán and the rise of competing smaller polities at the end of the Classic. The analyses of bones from graves excavated at Monte Albán suggest to González Licón (2009:15) that for low-status individuals in the Late Classic, "living conditions declined, with an increase in health problems, evidently because their diet consisted mainly of maize, with almost no meat," which was presumably limited to elite households. The abandonment patterns discussed earlier suggest that groups of individuals began to reject the elite's authority by moving away from the nucleated centers, probably to more dispersed settlements. These conditions could have then been exploited by intermediate elites from subordinate communities to challenge the political authority and found new centers.

Several authors suggest that growing competition and conflict between elite lineages or corporate groups played a significant role in the collapse of the Monte Albán state (Kowalewski et al. 1989:251). Although there is little direct evidence for violent conflict or warfare in the Valley of Oaxaca during the Late Classic, such as the destruction and burning of sites, there was an increase in the number of defensible hilltop settlements (Elam 1989). This suggests that the threat of hostilities was significant enough to be factored into the settlement plans of community leaders.

According to a number of authors (Balkansky 1998; Casparis 2006; Kowalewski et al. 1989), conflict within the political system arose as secondary centers began to break away from the control of Monte Albán. They suggest that competition developed among growing polities, such as Dainzú-Macuilxóchitl and Jalieza, as well as between those centers and the capital itself, with the former becoming increasingly independent and draining resources from Monte Albán. This inter-site conflict/competition also relates to the control of mechanisms for trade and exchange within and outside the valley, as localized settlement patterns "included more autonomous, specialized producers, and means of exchange that circumvented the primate center" (Kowalewski et al. 1989:251).

The most direct argument for conflict between Monte Albán and a subordinate center comes from Lind and Urcid (2010:322–24), who assert that toward the end of the Late Classic, the Monte Albán elite actually deposed the ruling lineage at Lambityeco, dismantling their residence and building a new one on top of the ruins. Underneath the new residence, Lind and Urcid found the remains of a "desecrated" altar and friezes associated with the previous residents. The architecture of the new Lambityeco civic-ceremonial complex was "built to Monte Albán standards," matching the design and layout of compounds at the capital city.

> In controlling their hegemonic state, the Monte Albán ruling elite must have deployed at various times different strategies toward their subject city-states, including marriage alliances, competitive generosity, patron-client relationships, and direct control backed up by military force. [Lind and Urcid 2010:330]

These data suggest that conflict and competition were part of the dynamics of the Late Classic in the Valley of Oaxaca, and that the Monte Albán state had to develop strategies to deal with the increasing instability. Strategies such as marriage alliances and royal generosity were probably initially effective, but as resources became scarce, these solutions would have been more costly, and less satisfying to the subordinate elites. The threat of or use of military force would have been even more costly, and may have been chosen as a last resort. Despite the renovations at Lambityeco, it was abandoned not long after.

The causal factors involved in the Late Classic collapse of the Monte Albán state are probably multiple, and remain poorly known to this day. Among the stresses that contributed to the Ω-phase release, intra- and inter-community competition and conflict probably played a significant role. Local centers of power may have attempted to maintain control of their regions with varying degrees of success, but eventually people rejected authority by simply voting with their feet (Feinman and Nicholas 2011:250).

Postclassic Reorganization in the Valley of Oaxaca

Most of what we know about the Postclassic reorganization of the Valley of Oaxaca is inferred from documents of the Early Colonial period (Flannery and Marcus 1983; Oudijk 2000; Whitecotton 1977), a period characterized by what have been described as small, "balkanized" kingdoms or polities (Flannery and Marcus 1983:217; Marcus 1989; Oudijk 2002; Winter 1989b). Documentary evidence, such as the early colonial *Relaciones Geográficas* (Acuña 1984 [1580]), indicates that these small kingdoms, including Dainzú-Macuilxóchitl, participated in conquest, marriage alliances, and tribute collection (Whitecotton 2003). Pressure and influence from Aztec and Mixtec states also become apparent in the archaeological record (Bernal 1966). Several Late Postclassic population centers in the valley, such as Yagul and Mitla (Flannery and Marcus 1983; Winter 1989b), maintained hilltop fortresses to which their populations could retreat. At one point, the Zapotec king moved his court and supporters to Tehuantepec to resist Aztec aggression (Marcus 1983e:302–8; Paddock 1983c:313).

This situation brings to mind the r species described by Gunderson and Holling (2002), which compete for available resources in the reorganization phase of the adaptive cycle. The purpose of the present monograph is to help explore all the factors that contributed to the α-phase to r-phase transition, a transition falling in the period between Monte Albán IIIb–IV and V.

3 | Household Archaeology in the Valley of Oaxaca

More than five decades ago, K. C. Chang (1958) proposed that social units—such as households and communities—should be the primary objects of study for archaeologists. The household forms one of the most basic social and economic units, presenting possibilities for interregional and diachronic comparisons. Archaeologists can readily identify physical remains, such as houses and domestic activity areas, related to households. Therefore, I employ household archaeology to characterize change and continuity in sociopolitical organization between the Late Classic and Postclassic at Dainzú-Macuilxóchitl, and in this chapter, discuss the scheme of this research project and present some of the relevant previous research on settlement patterns and household archaeology in the Valley of Oaxaca.

Project Research Scheme

From very early on, studies of household activities have played an important role in the archaeology of the Valley of Oaxaca. Investigations initiated by Flannery in the 1960s focused on "the units of society" (Flannery 1976:5–6), which included domestic activity areas, houses, neighborhoods, villages, and regions. The goal—through the excavation and survey of Formative sites—was to build a model for sociopolitical organization and the development of complexity in the Valley of Oaxaca. Excavations took place at the sites of Tierras Largas (Flannery and Winter 1976), Fábrica San José (Drennan 1976a, 1988), Santo Domingo Tomaltepec (Whalen 1981, 1988), San José Mogote (Flannery and Marcus 2005), and several other Formative villages in the Valley of Oaxaca. During this same period, Blanton (1978) directed a full-coverage survey of Monte Albán, and joined with Kowalewski, Feinman, Nicholas, and Finsten to survey the entire Valley of Oaxaca (Blanton et al. 1982; Kowalewski et al. 1989). Through these projects, we have some understanding of life in the Valley of Oaxaca at every level from household to region.

Subsequent research projects have focused on excavation and intensive surface collection in residential areas at a variety of central Oaxacan sites. Included are Monte Albán itself (Blanton 1978; González Licón 2003, 2009; Winter 1974) as well as sites such as Jalieza (Casparis 2006; Elson 2011; Finsten 1995), Lambityeco (Lind 2008, 2009; Lind and Urcid 2010), Ejutla (Feinman 1999; Balkansky, Feinman, and Nicholas 1997), San Martín Tilcajete (Redmond and Spencer 2006, 2008; Spencer and Redmond 2004, 2005), Dainzú-Macuilxóchitl (Fernández Dávila and Gómez Serafín 1993; Markens, Winter, and Martínez López 2008; Winter et al. 2007), El Palmillo (Feinman and Nicholas 2004a, 2007a, 2009, 2011), and a few smaller communities in the Tlacolula region (Fargher 2004). These projects have produced a large data set characterizing household organization, production, and ritual from the Terminal Formative through the Late Monte Albán IIIb–IV.

Prior to my project, however, little information was available concerning Early Postclassic household organization in the Valley of Oaxaca. One residence excavated at Monte Albán has been dated to this period, based on the presence of G3M-type bowls (Winter 2003). A few Postclassic graves intrusive into Late Classic deposits have been found (Elson 2011; Lind 2008), including some at Dainzú-Macuilxóchitl (Markens, Winter, and Martínez López 2008), but these discoveries did not include Postclassic households.

I chose to focus on the man-made residential terraces at Cerro Danush, which yield surface artifacts diagnostic of the Early Classic, Late Classic, and Early Postclassic (Kowalewski et al. 1989; Markens, Winter, and Martínez López 2008). Like the projects mentioned above, I employed both intensive surface collection and excavation in order to characterize household and community organization at Dainzú-Macuilxóchitl in the Late Classic and Early Postclassic, as well as to compare patterns of domestic behavior at the site both prior to and after Monte Albán's decline.

My fieldwork was divided into two phases. The first season consisted of survey, mapping, and systematic surface collection, which were designed to identify the extent of occupation and to document diachronic patterns of terrace use. The second field season was devoted to the comprehensive excavation of two domestic terraces, hoping to expose Early Postclassic residences. The specific goals of my fieldwork were to:

(1) Develop a detailed topographic map of Cerro Danush, marking the boundaries of the residential terraces, structural mounds, and other important features, in order to characterize the spatial relationships between them. This effort could potentially serve to identify sociopolitical units such as residential wards or "barrios,"[1] assuming they were present.

(2) Systematically surface collect as many of the terraces as possible in small standardized units, so that artifact density distributions could be spatially and statistically analyzed to model broad domestic behavioral patterns at the site.

(3) Characterize the patterns of use and abandonment for the domestic terraces found.

(4) Characterize the layout, design, and features associated with Early Postclassic residences.

(5) Systematically collect, identify, and count all the artifacts from standardized excavation units on the domestic terraces in order to analyze the spatial distributions of the materials.

(6) Collect radiocarbon samples and effectively date the history of use and occupation of residential terraces.

These analyses provide the basis for constructing a model to explain the process of Terminal Classic breakdown and Early Postclassic reorganization at the site. More specifically, I intend to reconstruct Terminal Classic abandonment patterns on the domestic terraces of Cerro Danush, and to compare and contrast the evidence for community ritual, domestic ritual, and household craft production before and after reorganization. These behavioral aspects are archaeologically detectable to a great extent, and several studies over the last decade have provided a plethora of data from Late Classic sites in the Valley of Oaxaca.

I begin by presenting some of the findings from these previous research projects, and I discuss how they informed my thinking with respect to the research hypothesis.

The Evolution of the House Complex in the Valley of Oaxaca

From the advent of settled villages in the Early Formative through today, the design and layout of residential architecture in the Valley of Oaxaca have conformed to some basic principles (Kowalewski, Murphy, and Cabrera 1984). The earliest Formative houses were surrounded by dooryards, but had no actual formal patios. By the Middle Formative, at least some households consisted of multiple one-room buildings, sharing a common patio. For these later households, Winter (1974) proposed three basic configurations: (1) open, with a single rectangular dwelling and corresponding open patio space; (2) semi-closed, with two to three dwellings arranged around a single patio in an L- or U-shape pattern; or (3) closed, with four dwellings fully enclosing the patio in a square configuration.

In the Tierras Largas and San José phases, all but the most high status families were restricted to one house, with no formal patio. Those houses excavated at the sites of San José Mogote (Flannery and Marcus 2005), Tierras Largas (Flannery, ed. 1976), Fábrica San José (Drennan 1976a), and Santo Domingo Tomaltepec (Whalen 1981, 1988) consisted of one-room rectangular wattle-and-daub buildings with compact earth floors (Flannery and Marcus 2005). Flannery and Marcus suggest that status differentiation is detectable between households at San José Mogote as early as the San José phase, where preferential access to materials such as magnetite, jade, and pearl oyster is evident in higher-status household artifact assemblages (Flannery and Marcus 2005).

In the Middle Formative Rosario phase, residential construction began to reflect more formalized differences in status between households at sites like San José Mogote (Marcus and Flannery 1996:131) and Santo Domingo Tomaltepec (Whalen 1988). At these sites, a few house complexes are distinguishable because they are larger in overall area, their houses are built on stone foundations rather than on compact earth platforms, and their structural walls are made of adobe blocks rather than wattle and daub. These higher-status house complexes have a more formal patio rather than a simple dooryard.

---

1. Smith and Novic (2012) have recently called into question the use of the term "barrio" for neighborhoods or residential wards in archaeological contexts, in order to prevent confusing the multiple modern uses of the term with an ancient construct. In this monograph, I use "residential ward," and include the term "barrio" in parenthesis when referring to previous works that used this term.

Status differentiation became even greater during the Late Formative (Monte Albán I phase). In the El Palenque sector of San Martín Tilcajete in the southern (or Zimatlán) arm of the valley, Spencer and Redmond (2004) excavated a large multiple-roomed masonry palace, which closely resembles later palaces excavated at Monte Albán. At other sites, the houses of less highly ranked Monte Albán I families were smaller, and some were even of wattle and daub.

For the Classic period at Monte Albán, a three-tier hierarchy has been proposed for the house complexes so far excavated (González Licón 2003; Winter 1974). Winter (1974:985) suggests that by the Late Classic, all house complexes at Monte Albán conformed to the closed configuration, and he distinguishes three size groups based on the calculated area of open patio space (12–14 m^2, 17–37 m^2, and 92–150 m^2). Mortuary practices were more standardized at that time, and many residents interred their dead within the house complex, in simple graves located beneath house and patio floors, or in centrally located tombs with patio entrances (Urcid 2008; Winter 2002). The following passages provide Winter's (1974, 2002) typology for house complexes and their burial patterns:

Type 1:
This is the small size [patio area = 12–14 m^2] and has a simple patio formed by a single line of faced stones. Room walls may have been made of wood or cane because stone foundations for adobe walls are not always present. [Winter 1974:984]

The smallest most common residence is usually found with slab-lined grave interments, but a subvariety with a small tomb exists. [Winter 2002:79]

Type 2:
This is the medium size with a small inner patio surrounded by a bench, which forms a larger outer patio [area = 17–37 m^2]. Building exteriors are delimited by stone wall foundations which once supported adobe walls. [Winter 1974:984]

Medium-size houses vary architecturally, and usually have slab-lined graves as well as a medium sized tomb. [Winter 2002:79]

Type 3:
This is a large walled compound or palace [patio area = 92–150 m^2]. [Winter 1974:984]

Large tombs usually occur beneath one of the rooms and are entered by a stairway which descends from the patio. [Winter 2002:79]

González Licón (2003:240–41) directed extensive excavations on several residential terraces at Monte Albán, uncovering all or part of twelve house complexes in three separate areas of the site. According to the floor plans published for these house complexes, each complex contained a central patio that was surrounded by rectangular rooms. González Licón (2003:84) argued that Winter's house complex size distinctions were not good indicators of household status, instead suggesting three status levels of his own based on associated artifacts and burial offerings:

a) The ruling elite in the upper social scale, living in palaces and large residences close to the Central Plaza, buried in well made tombs with decorated façades and mural painted walls, with abundant offerings including local and imported items;

b) Our sample distributed in three areas of the city, living in middle–small sized stone wall houses, built on terraces over the hill, buried in tombs or burials with some offerings;

c) The peasants and other low-income artisans or workers, living in small wattle-and-daub houses over earth platforms in the lower piedmont and the valley floor. [González Licón 2009:7–8]

Floor plans for Late Classic house complexes are available from a number of sites in the Valley of Oaxaca (Elson 2011; Feinman, Nicholas, and Haines 2002; Lind and Urcid 1983; Robles García and Andrade Cuautle 2011). These authors have also proposed three-part typologies among households at the respective sites. Most of the Late Classic house complexes excavated at these sites conform to the closed configuration identified at Monte Albán. They have single, closed-in stucco patios with rectangular rooms surrounding them in a square plan; this is especially true of the lower-status house complexes.

Toward the end of the Late Classic, it appears that some elite families began to reorganize the use of space within their residences by adding patios. Late Classic house complexes with two or three patios were identified at Jalieza (Elson 2011), Lambityeco (Lind and Urcid 1983), and El Palmillo (Feinman and Nicholas 2011). This phenomenon, however, seems to have been restricted to elite residences at those sites.

By the Late Postclassic, many elite house complexes in the Valley of Oaxaca contained multiple patios. This is evident both from the large palaces with three or more patios identified at Mitla (Robles García 1994) and Yagul (Bernal and Gamio 1974), and the more modest two-patio Lanisbaa household complex excavated at Mound 1 at Dainzú-Macuilxóchitl (Markens, Winter, and Martínez López 2008:205, Fig. 6.9). The Lanisbaa Complex was identified as a commoner residence, based on the burials and artifact assemblage the excavators recovered (Markens, Winter, and Martínez López 2008; Winter et al. 2007).

Multiple patios alter the shape of the house complex from square to rectangular, and may have served to separate household activities. Winter et al. (2007) assert that the division between the patios within the complex on Mound 1 of Dainzú-Macuilxóchitl may have served to delineate public from private space:

the north patio, with more restricted access, appears to have served as the residents' private retreat, whereas the south patio, open on the south side to the community beyond, provided a space for conducting public business as well as serving domestic needs. [Markens, Winter, and Martínez López 2008:204]

Household Production, Specialization, and Political Economy in the Valley of Oaxaca

Historically, archaeologists have adopted either "formalist" or "substantivist" approaches to the study of ancient economies (Fargher 2004; Garraty 2010), focusing debate on the dichotomy between ancient redistributive and modern market-based economies (Polanyi, Arensberg, and Pearson 1957). Recently, some scholars have attempted to go beyond this formalist-substantivist divide in favor of more holistic understandings of ancient political economies (Feinman and Nicholas 2007c), viewing these economies as complex combinations of various production and exchange mechanisms, such as tribute collection, market-like interactions, and administered distribution (Berdan 1983; Costin 1991; Hirth 1998, 2009a; Minc 2006; Smith 2003; Stark and Garraty 2010). In a similar vein, scholars now recognize that even within the palace-centered economies of the Bronze Age Minoan and Mycenaean societies, once considered dominated by the state-controlled redistribution of goods (Finley 1973), "a commercial network also operated" (Manning and Hulin 2005:273). Earlier treatments of the ancient Mesoamerican political economy favored the state-controlled redistributive model (Carrasco 1978; Sanders and Price 1968), but subsequent research suggests that, throughout the prehispanic era, craft production activities were often concentrated in residential contexts (Balkansky and Crossier 2009; Hirth 2009a; Feinman and Nicholas 2010; Flannery and Marcus 2005). "The ability of rulers to intervene or regulate such production seems nearly impossible" (Carpenter, Feinman, and Nicholas 2012).

Feinman and Nicholas (2007a, 2007b, 2007c, 2010) contend that specialized craft production, regardless of intensity, occurred in household contexts rather than in elite-controlled workshops (Feinman 1999; Balkansky, Feinman, and Nicholas 1997); instead of being centralized in administrative centers, craft specialization activities were organized within social units, such as residential wards. Blanton et al. (1982, 1984, 1993)—despite the fact that no marketplace has ever been discovered in the ancient Valley of Oaxaca—believe that they can detect market-like exchanges that were independent of any Zapotec state economy. Even as late as the Late Classic, at the height of the Monte Albán state, there is evidence for household strategies of "intermittent" and "multi-craft" (Hirth 2009a) production from excavations at Ejutla and El Palmillo (Fig. 2.1). Thus, Feinman and Nicholas (2007a, 2007b, 2007c) suggest that the political authority did not directly administer key components—such as local production and exchange mechanisms—of the economic system.

Evidence for craft production and specialization among individual households and communities has been identified at many sites throughout the Valley of Oaxaca (Blanton et al. 1982; Kowalewski et al. 1989; Finsten 1995; Flannery and Marcus 2005; Feinman and Nicholas 2000, 2007a, 2007b, 2007c; Whalen 1981). Flannery and Winter (1976) have proposed four categories of household specialization within Early Formative villages in the Valley of Oaxaca: (1) universal activities that all households take part in; (2) household specialization, where individual households within a community produce goods such as chert bifaces for extra-household exchange; (3) regional specialization, where several neighboring villages are involved in the production of a specific good (such as salt), and (4) unique specialization, where many households at a specific site are involved in the production of a particular good, such as iron ore mirrors. Subsequent excavations have demonstrated that these categories persisted into the Late Classic at some sites in the Valley of Oaxaca, although production and specialization were taking place on a higher scale at that time (Feinman and Nicholas 2000).

Universal household activities included food preparation and storage, and also the production and repair of chert tools (Parry 1987). Artifacts associated with food preparation and storage included grinding stones (*manos* and *metates*), ceramic cooking jars (*ollas*), and storage vessels for water (*cántaros*); features included hearths, earth ovens, and storage pits (Flannery and Marcus 2005; Martínez López et al. 2000). Haines, Feinman, and Nicholas (2004) found that all the Classic period house complexes they excavated at El Palmillo exhibited some degree of chipped stone working, which they suggest ranged from tool maintenance to the manufacture of stone tools for extra-household exchange.

Classic period regional and unique specialization is apparent in several areas of the Valley of Oaxaca (Finsten 1983). For example, several studies show that large-scale specialized salt production was taking place at Lambityeco in the Late Classic (Fargher 2004; Lind 2008; Paddock 1983b; Peterson 1976). Outside the valley, Feinman and his colleagues (Balkansky, Feinman, and Nicholas 1997; Feinman 1999; Feinman and Nicholas 2000) uncovered large amounts of shell fragments in the midden of a house complex at Ejutla that they suggest was involved in the specialized production of shell ornaments. The region surrounding the modern town of Mitla has long been known as a center for the production of stone tools (Hester and Heizer 1972; Kowalewski et al. 1989:359–60; Parry 1987). Feinman and Nicholas (2004, 2005) suggest that the residents of El Palmillo were involved in the specialized processing of xerophytic plants, particularly the production of textiles from maguey fiber.

Although possible production loci have been identified from surface materials at Dainzú-Macuilxóchitl (Kowalewski et al. 1989), particularly for ceramic and stone tool manufacture, excavations have not yet been extensive enough to show that this site was involved in unique or regional specialized production like that of the other sites mentioned above. The *Relación Geográfica de Macuilxóchitl* from 1580 indicates that prior to the Spanish Conquest, the town was subordinate to the Zapotec king (then resident at Tehuantepec), and supplied warriors for military campaigns as tribute, rather than goods (Acuña 1984 [1580]). Based on this document, I did not expect to find large-scale production of craft goods for tribute on the terraces of Cerro Danush, but instead, evidence that individual households (or groups of households) were involved in producing goods for local exchange.

Household Craft Production and Specialization

At the time of the valley-wide survey, large amounts of Classic period surface scatter associated with production (such as ceramic wasters and chert cores) were interpreted as evidence for the presence of formal workshops (Feinman et al. 1989; Finsten 1983, 1995; Kowalewski et al. 1989). Subsequent excavations in the Valley of Oaxaca (and elsewhere in Mesoamerica) suggest that such concentrations were actually associated with refuse dumps in and around residences. No formal workshops have come to light during subsequent excavation in the Valley of Oaxaca (Balkansky and Crossier 2009; Feinman 1999; Markens 2004).

Based on the data from Dainzú-Macuilxóchitl produced by the settlement pattern survey, plus artifact assemblages from other terraced hilltop sites such as Monte Albán, Jalieza, and El Palmillo, I expected to find evidence for household specialization and multicrafting, possibly involving ceramic production, textile production, and stone tool manufacturing. In the following sections, I discuss the artifacts found throughout the Valley of Oaxaca that are generally considered to be indicative of these activities.

Ceramic Production

Ceramic production has been identified in surface collections by the presence of wasters and kiln furniture (Fargher 2004; Finsten 1995) and through the kilns excavated within residences at Monte Albán (González Licón 2003; Winter and Payne 1976), Tomaltepec (Whalen 1981), Lambityeco (Payne 1970), and Dainzú-Macuilxóchitl (Markens, Winter, and Martínez López 2008). At Ejutla, Feinman and his colleagues (Balkansky, Feinman, and Nicholas 1997) excavated six oblong pits that "were associated with burned rock, charcoal, lenses of ash . . . as well as wasters, sherds that were overfired or fired more than once, slaglike material, and heavy densities of clay concentrations" (Feinman 1999:88). All of these features, identified as "pit kilns," were found within a Classic period house complex (Balkansky, Feinman, and Nicholas 1997). A similar feature was found within the house complex on Mound 1 at Dainzú-Macuilxóchitl (Markens, Winter, and Martínez López 2008).

Feinman and Nicholas (2000) also found large amounts of broken and distorted ceramic figurines within the midden of the house complex at Ejutla. Additionally, they recovered fragments of molds associated with the specialized production of mold-made figurines. This one household at Ejutla seems to have been producing pottery, figurines, and shell ornaments.

During the regional survey, Kowalewski et al. (1989:298) identified three possible loci of Late Classic ceramic production at Dainzú-Macuilxóchitl. None of these, however, were identified on the terraces of Cerro Danush, but rather to the southwest of the mountain.

Another Late Classic locus of ceramic production was identified by Fargher (2004) at the site of Gaii Guii, which is a small community, perhaps a residential ward, located between the site of Dainzú-Macuilxóchitl and Lambityeco. During his survey of the site, Fargher (2004:234) identified ceramic production by the presence of ceramic wasters (e.g., over-fired, over-oxidized, and bubbled sherds), clay balls that were used as kiln furniture, and "alluvial deposits that are easily mined for alluvial clay." He also documented a very large amount of pottery at the site (estimated 1.89 million sherds), which he believed to be refuse deposits associated with ceramic production.

Textile Production

Artifacts attributed to textile production include bone needles, awls, and spindle whorls, which consist of small perforated disks made out of fired clay and sometimes bone (Feinman and Nicholas 2004; Kowalewski et al. 1989:361). Perforated disks have been recovered at many sites in the Valley of Oaxaca, spanning the Early Formative to Late Classic (Caso, Bernal, and Acosta 1967; Feinman and Nicholas 2007a; Flannery and Marcus 2005; Redmond and Spencer 2008), and it is not clear that they all had the same function. Some have been found in place, serving as lids for cooking vessels (Flannery and Marcus 2005), while others are amazingly uniform in size (Appendix B), which suggests to me that they were used as weights for the spinning of a specific type of fiber. Carpenter, Feinman, and Nicholas (2012) have identified spindle whorls of this type at El Palmillo and suggest they were used to spin cotton.

Like Charlton, Charlton, and Nichols (1993), Carpenter, Feinman, and Nicholas (2012) also identified a larger type of spindle whorl at El Palmillo that they suggest was used for the spinning of maguey fiber. Other artifacts they recovered include bone needles and awls, as well as stone tools that they believe to be associated with textile production. In addition, Haines, Feinman, and Nicholas (2004) identified specialized chert scrapers, known as *raspadores*, which they conclude were used specifically to process maguey fiber. It should be noted that fiber production, the spinning of thread or yarn, and the sewing of garments are all tasks separate from the actual weaving of cloth.

Stone Tool Production

The most in-depth studies of stone tool production in the Late Classic come from excavations at the site of El Palmillo (Feinman, Nicholas, and Haines 2006; Haines, Feinman, and Nicholas 2004) and surface collections at Jalieza (Finsten 1995). The stone tool assemblages from these sites consist mostly of chert debitage and debris from knapping, but also include spent cores and production blanks, as well as formal and informal tools, including bifaces, scrapers, points, and expedient flake tools (Feinman, Nicholas, and Haines 2006:163–64, Fig. 8*a, b*).

Finsten (1995:62) found that the "production of chipped stone tools from local raw materials was extremely widespread at Jalieza." She recovered production debris and debitage from all the terrace groups she collected, suggesting generalized production within households at the site. The most abundant finished tools found at Jalieza, as well as at El Palmillo (Haines, Feinman, and Nicholas 2004), were expedient flake tools, which consist of percussion flakes that show signs of further working or use. Expedient tools of this type usually vary in size and thickness, and do not conform to any design, but generally contain a sharp edge that could be applied in a variety of tasks. In their excavations at El Palmillo, Haines, Feinman, and Nicholas (2004:259–60) found that stone tool production in the higher-status residences at the summit of the mountain involved "retouching or sharpening existing pieces, or 'nodule smashing' to create expedient tools," while lower-status households at the base of the mountain were "more intensely involved in the manufacture of formal tools (and possibly preforms and cores) that were intended for house-to-house exchange."

Summary and Expectations

The archaeological evidence presented above suggests that some households were participating in specialized production as early as the Formative. During the Classic, and especially the Late Classic, households were producing items on a relatively large scale and there is evidence for both site and regional specialization. Throughout this time, individual households were producing a variety of goods (multicrafting) within their residences, possibly for local house-to-house or village-to-village exchange. There is no evidence for state-controlled workshop production or distribution at any time in the prehispanic era in Oaxaca, although the highly integrated sociopolitical system that existed during the Late Classic may have enhanced the intraregional exchange of goods, and provided a stable atmosphere for local exchange.

Based on these data, it was reasonable to expect to find household craft production at Dainzú-Macuilxóchitl, and perhaps to find that the scale of production within individual households decreased from the Late Classic to the Early Postclassic, as the system responsible for integrating the individual polities collapsed and political organization in the Valley of Oaxaca became more fragmented.

Household Ritual in the Valley of Oaxaca

Previous research has demonstrated that rituals made up an important part of the activities that took place within prehispanic Mesoamerican households (Gonlin and Lohse 2007; Hendon 2010; Plunket 2002). Feinman, Nicholas, and Maher (2008:180) assert that "domestic ritual in Pre-Hispanic Mesoamerica encompasses a range of activities, including enactments using figurines, auto-sacrifice, divination, mortuary interment, and rites of dedication and termination." Several of these practices have been identified archaeologically through the recovery of material offerings buried within prehispanic residences in the Valley of Oaxaca (Lind and Urcid 2010; Marcus 1998b; Winter 2002; Winter et al. 2007).

In this section, I discuss some artifacts, recovered from domestic contexts, that have been associated with domestic ritual in the Valley of Oaxaca. This discussion is limited to mortuary patterns, ritual artifacts (particularly figurines), and material offerings because they have been widely discussed and are most evident in the archaeological record.

Burial Practices and Offerings

By the Late Classic, non-royal burial practices appear to have been formalized within Zapotec social structure, resulting in similar patterns at most of the sites excavated in the Valley of Oaxaca (Urcid 2008). Feinman, Nicholas, and Maher (2008:186) noted that for El Palmillo, "the population of the settlement shared similar ideas and attitudes regarding the interment of bodies, burying most of their dead under room and patio floors, whether in tombs, cists, or simple pits." At Monte Albán, Winter (2002) found the same pattern: non-royal burials were confined within and around the house complex, usually beneath the patio and room floors, and included simple interments, stone-lined graves, and tombs.

Simple burials were generally located beneath house and patio floors, but could also be found in areas directly outside the house complex, such as within household refuse dumps (Fernández Dávila and Gómez Serafín 1993). They were sometimes accompanied by offerings of ceramic vessels, such as conical bowls and censers (*sahumadores*), and/or sacrificed domesticated dogs (Feinman, Nicholas, and Maher 2008; Winter 2002). These types of burials have been found in residences of all status levels, but in some low-status residences, they are the only types of burials recovered (Winter 2002).

Feinman, Nicholas, and Maher (2008:187) found that intermediate residences at El Palmillo contained "sub floor tombs," which were "much less elaborate than the masonry tomb" they excavated in the high-status palace at the summit of the mountain. Winter (2002) found that intermediate-status or Type 2 residences at Monte Albán usually included a small tomb, but also contained simple burials, and he suggests that the differential treatment of individuals represents status differences among members of the household. González Licón (2003, 2009:15) identified a similar pattern, and he suggests that "adult males had greater prestige, with some holding leadership positions; at their death, they received the privilege of being buried in the family tomb with abundant offerings." At Monte Albán, medium-sized tombs were found with ceramic vessels such as frying-pan-like censers (sahumadores), bottle-shaped jars (*botellones*), and miniatures (Winter 2002:79–80).

Elaborate masonry tombs with carved stone doorjambs and lintels have been found in Late Classic palaces at Lambityeco (Lind 2008; Lind and Urcid 2010), El Palmillo (Feinman, Nicholas, and Maher 2008), Monte Albán (González Licón 2009; Winter 2002), Cerro de las Campanas (Franco Brizuela 1993), and other sites in the Valley of Oaxaca (Urcid 2008). Winter (2002:79–80) suggests that these types of tombs contained additional ceramic offerings not found in smaller tombs, such as "ceramic statues, ceramic boxes with removable effigy tops, and especially urns including representations of a wide range of deities as well as their *acompañantes*." Some of these large tombs were surrounded by simple burials, which may have consisted of the servants of the rulers interred within the tombs (Urcid 2008).

In their excavation of the Lanisbaa residence in Mound 1 at Dainzú-Macuilxóchitl, Winter et al. (2007) found evidence for continuity between Late Classic and Late Postclassic burial patterns. They found three simple interments within the house complex, each located beneath the floor in a corner of the house platform. In the fourth corner, there was another individual buried within a small tomb. "The individuals were laid to rest on their backs with legs extended and arms at their sides or, in one case, with hands resting on the pelvis" (Winter et al. 2007:201). They also found a similar burial beneath the patio floor, and the remains of a child, buried in the seated or flexed position. They propose that "the burial of family members in tombs and graves beneath household floors or within the confines of the residence during the . . . [Late Postclassic] continues the Zapotec tradition of funerary practices that crystallized during the Middle Formative period" (Winter et al. 2007:200–201).

Markens (2004, 2008) found changes in the ceramic offerings contained within tombs between the Late Classic and Early Postclassic. For example, tombs no longer included effigy jars, urns, or sahumadores, which suggests some change in mortuary patterns between these periods.

Figurines and Whistles

There are great differences in figurine use in Oaxaca. Early and Middle Formative figurines were handmade and, when found in situ, occurred in women's household work areas (Marcus 1998b) or were buried as dedications in house walls (Flannery and Marcus 2005: Fig. 9.14). While they are sometimes found in deliberately arranged scenes in women's work areas (Flannery and Marcus 2005:337–38), they were never found in situ in men's houses. This suggests that they were a component of women's ritual (Marcus 1998b).

These early figurines disappeared as the Zapotec state formed. Their place was taken by mold-made figurines and effigy urns (Marcus 1998b), which depict human figures or deities. In the Classic period, such mold-made figurines have been described as "monotonously mass-produced images" (Marcus 1998b:306). Marcus (1998b:306) suggests that this change represents the fact that under the Zapotec state, royal ancestors—rather than the ordinary ancestors depicted in every household during the Formative—were emphasized.

Although urns and effigy jars were usually confined to elite tombs, Late Classic mold-made figurines and whistles formed a consistent part of most household assemblages (Feinman, Nicholas, and Maher 2008). According to Caso and Bernal (1952:280–300), the standardized mold-made figurines they found at Monte Albán represent two separate images of an individual identified as 13 Serpent (Appendix B, Figs. B27, B29). According to Marcus (1980, 1983d), individuals with such calendar names are more likely to be mythologized rulers, culture heroes, or dynastic founders than deities. Another example of possible mythologized dynastic founders would be the "primordial couple," Lord 1 Jaguar and Lady 2 J, often depicted on Monte Albán IIIa beakers (Marcus and Flannery 1996:224; Marcus 2012).

Mold-made images of standardized male figures can appear on urns, effigy jars, and whistles (*silbatos*). The silbatos have standardized headdresses and bulbous bodies with small circular holes in the back. Caso and Bernal (1952:301–15) found three separate examples of these (Appendix B, Figs. B33–B35), each with its own particular headdress. Martínez López and Winter (1994:68–89) also identified whistles of this type; their sample had more variation in headdresses.

Another type of figurine/whistle that has been found in Late Classic (or perhaps Early Postclassic) contexts in the Valley of Oaxaca contains figures of warriors brandishing what appear to be spears and shields (Feinman and Nicholas 2011:255–56; Markens 2004:257–58). Figurines of this type are very similar to an Early Postclassic type identified in the Mexican basin, and known as Mazapan (Scott 1993). Examples of Mazapan style figurines (Appendix B, Figs. B36, B37) have been recovered from Lambityeco (Scott 1993), Dainzú-Macuilxóchitl (Markens 2004), and the Mitla Fortress (Feinman and Nicholas 2011). Feinman and Nicholas (2011:255–56) suggest that these Mazapan-style figurines came into use during the Late Classic and continued in use into the Early Postclassic.

Material Offerings

Feinman, Nicholas, and Maher (2008:180) recovered domestic offerings at El Palmillo within layers of fill "between occupational surfaces, beneath either the patio or a room floor." In the lower-status residences they excavated at the base of the hill, the majority of offerings consisted of ceramic vessels; less frequent were images of small animals like dogs or rabbits. Individual ceramic vessels were found buried within the construction fill between house floors; Feinman, Nicholas, and Maher (2008) suggest that these were part of dedicatory or termination rites that took place between construction episodes. Other offerings were found "placed in an adobe wall, under the floor of patios and rooms, or in an exterior area adjacent to the house" (Feinman, Nicholas, and Maher 2008:185).

The most abundant type of offering they found consisted of paired ceramic vessels, where a bowl was turned upside down and placed over a second bowl or jar as a lid. Similar paired-vessel offerings have been found at Lambityeco (Lind and Urcid 2010), Yagul (Bernal and Gamio 1974), and Dainzú-Macuilxóchitl (Winter et al. 2007). Winter et al. (2007:204), citing the ethnographic work of Parsons (1936:76), have suggested that they may have been used to hold the placentas of recently born children, a practice Parsons observed during her fieldwork in various Zapotec towns at the eastern end of the Tlacolula arm of the valley. Lind and Urcid (2010:277) documented the continuation of this practice in Zapotec communities into the 1980s and obtained modern ceramic bowls and jars that were being used for this purpose at the time.

At Monte Albán, González Licón (2009) found offerings of human skulls beneath the patios of a few residences. Feinman, Nicholas, and Maher (2008) also found offerings of this type at El Palmillo, as well as offerings of individual human hands and feet. Their excavations suggest that this type of offering was mostly limited to households of relatively high status. Animal offerings were also more abundant in these residences, along with items such as shell tinklers, stone pendants, obsidian tools, and high-quality chert (Feinman, Nicholas, and Maher 2008:185).

Feinman, Nicholas, and Maher (2008:189) also identified differences in domestic offerings between the five lower-status residences they excavated. For example, three of the residences contained mostly two-pot offerings, while another contained mostly individual ceramic vessels. They suggest that this type of differentiation may reflect separate practices conducted by members of distinct barrios or wards.

Summary and Expectations

Marcus (1998b:2) proposed that in Formative villages in the Valley of Oaxaca, "ritual at the household and community level was a major catalyst for social integration." As complexity in the valley grew, community rituals became more formalized and controlled by the state apparatus so that by the Late Classic, they were conducted by full-time priests in restricted-access temples. At the same time, private rituals conducted within residences of all status levels reveal highly standardized behavior, which is visible in domestic offerings and burials, as well as in the development of mass-produced and highly standardized ritual objects, such as figurines, urns, and effigy jars.

Winter et al. (2007) suggest that many of these practices were discontinued at the end of the Late Classic. For example, the standardized figurines, urns, effigy jars, and other ritual objects commonly found in Late Classic elite tombs were not found in any of the Postclassic burials or tombs they excavated. Markens (2011) proposed that this was part of a greater pattern related to the decline of the Monte Albán state, where items containing images of the deity Cociyo, which represent the Classic period Zapotec great tradition, fell out of use as the political system collapsed.

Based on the data presented above, it appears that ritual practices conducted within individual residences were very similar across Late Classic sites as distant from Monte Albán as Lambityeco and El Palmillo. This suggests that these communities were well integrated and that the practices of individuals within their homes were relatively standardized. I maintain that this situation persisted into the Early Postclassic, after the decline of Monte Albán, and I expected to find household offerings similar to those recovered from the Late Classic residences described above. I also expected, however, to find fewer signs of social inequality among households.

Late/Terminal Classic Patterns of Site Abandonment in the Valley of Oaxaca

Along with several other sites in the Valley of Oaxaca, Monte Albán experienced population growth and increased construction of monumental architecture during the Late Classic (Blanton 1978). Significantly, there was a dramatic increase in the number of residential terraces and the amount of monumental architecture on Cerro Atzompa (Robles García and Andrade Cuautle 2011), a hill approximately 4 km to the northwest of Monte Albán's civic-ceremonial core (Chapter 2, Fig. 2.1).

In the Terminal Classic, however, settlement at Monte Albán began to dwindle. Caso, Bernal, and Acosta (1967) found ceramics they identified as Early Postclassic offerings deposited within abandoned Late Classic structures. This suggests a slow process of decline in the Terminal Classic, where some buildings were still maintained, while others fell out of use. Winter (2003) points out that in the Late Classic, elite residences tended to be separate from the civic-ceremonial center, but in the Terminal Classic, two elite residences were installed adjacent to or on top of temples that had fallen into disuse. He sees this as a last-ditch effort on the part of the elites to maintain control. In Monte Albán IIIb–IV,

> the most important residences in the central part of Monte Albán were on the plaza and the North Platform, near . . . the principal temples, and the ball court, facilitating elite control of the city, perhaps as a desperate last attempt to keep it functioning. [Winter 2003:111]

Based on the data from more than fifty house complexes excavated on the domestic terraces outside the civic-ceremonial core of Monte Albán, Winter (2003:11) suggests a 98% population decline at the site from the Terminal Classic to the Early Postclassic. He did not, however, find any evidence to suggest violence, such as burning or destruction, and suggests that the site was gradually abandoned, with a few households remaining into the Monte Albán V phase. Although the Main Plaza was largely abandoned by the Early Postclassic, Winter et al. (2007) found Monte Albán V offerings there, just as Caso and Bernal had.

Abandonment Patterns at Lambityeco

Lambityeco is located in the central part of the Tlacolula arm of the valley, 2 km to the west of the modern town of Tlacolula (Chapter 2, Fig. 2.1). Evidence for prehispanic salt production there has been identified through both excavation (Lind 2008) and survey (Peterson 1976), and might explain why the site is located in a relatively indefensible position on the valley floor, near a salt marsh (Lind 2008:179–81).

Paddock (1983b) originally defined Lambityeco as the Early Postclassic (Monte Albán IV) component of the larger site of Yegüih, which shows evidence for occupation from the Middle Formative Rosario phase through the Postclassic Late Monte Albán V phase. Lind (2008) suggests that Lambityeco witnessed a dramatic increase in population and monumental architecture during the Late Classic (Monte Albán IIIb–IV), evidenced by an increase in its occupied mounds (from 29 to 159), and accompanied by a tenfold increase in site area (from 6.75 to 63.75 ha) (Lind 2008). This was followed by a dramatic decline during the Early Postclassic, marked by the disappearance of monumental architecture and a reduction of the site to just over 35 ha (Lind 2008).

Lind and Urcid (Lind 2008; Lind and Urcid 2010) document Terminal Classic changes at Lambityeco that resemble those proposed by Winter (2003) for Monte Albán. They propose that in the Late Classic, the rulers of Lambityeco were somewhat politically autonomous and salt production was a household activity (Lind 2008). In the Terminal Classic, however, they believe that Monte Albán instituted direct control over Lambityeco, disrupting the established ruling lineage and installing a new one (Lind and Urcid 2010). They suggest that this was done to increase salt production at the site, which Lind (2008:181) believes came to be carried out in workshops rather than in residences.

According to Lind and Urcid (2010), this takeover by Monte Albán was reflected in the presence of a new palace and temple built over the older houses of the former ruling lineage; these new structures were built to Monte Albán standards. Not long afterward, however, the site was hastily abandoned, leaving unfinished some construction projects that had been under way in one of the palaces. Lind (2008:189) suggests that the residents of Lambityeco may have rejected the authority of their new rulers by abandoning the area.

Abandonment Patterns at Jalieza

The area surrounding San Martín Tilcajete in the southern arm of the valley has played a major role in the prehistory of the region (Spencer and Redmond 2004, 2005). Diachronic settlement shifts have been identified in the region, including a move from the valley floor to a high hill during Monte Albán II (Elson 2007). Not far to the east of Tilcajete lies a second hilltop community, Jalieza (Fig. 2.1). This is a large, multiperiod site, consisting of thousands of residential terraces that surround a civic-ceremonial core at the summit of the hill (Casparis 2006; Elson 2011; Finsten 1983).

The Valley of Oaxaca Settlement Pattern Project originally characterized Jalieza as a Monte Albán IV phase settlement (Finsten 1983; Kowalewski et al. 1989). Recent excavations at Jalieza, however, have produced radiocarbon dates suggesting that the site existed in the Early Classic, expanded during the Late Classic, and was virtually abandoned by A.D. 800 (Elson 2011).

Unfortunately, we do not have much information on the process of abandonment of Jalieza. The presence of an Early Postclassic intrusive tomb in one of the Late Classic residences (Elson 2011) suggests a decline similar to that of Monte Albán or El Palmillo.

Abandonment Patterns at El Palmillo

El Palmillo is a large hilltop site consisting of residential terraces surrounding a civic-ceremonial core on the hill's summit (Feinman and Nicholas 2004). This site is located in the far end of the eastern, or Tlacolula, arm of the valley, near the modern town of Matatlán (Fig. 2.1). The excavation of eight residential terraces at the site, including elite houses on the summit, have led Feinman and Nicholas (2009, 2011) to propose a gradual pattern of abandonment during the Terminal Classic.

According to Feinman and Nicholas (2011), the elite houses on the summit of El Palmillo were abandoned over a considerable period of time. While parts of these residences were being sealed off, other rooms remained in use. Eventually these houses were abandoned, probably between A.D. 850 and 900. While this slow abandonment contrasts with the more rapid abandonment at Lambityeco, we should remember that only a small percentage of each site has been excavated.

Radiocarbon dates from the terraces at El Palmillo suggest that lower-level commoner residences were abandoned earlier than intermediate mid-level residences, which in turn were abandoned earlier than elite upper-level residences (Feinman and Nicholas 2011). This pattern led Feinman and Nicholas (2011:250) to suggest that rather than responding to some kind of overall catastrophe, El Palmillo's commoners began the abandonment process by voting with their feet.

Abandonment Patterns at Dainzú-Macuilxóchitl

Markens (2004) excavated the remains of two superimposed stucco floors and adobe block walls just to the east of a large pyramidal platform at Dainzú-Macuilxóchitl (Fig. 2.7). Based on ceramics found in the fill between the floors, he characterized the latter as belonging to two Late Classic structures, one built on top of the other. He also discovered intrusive trash pits, probably from a Late Postclassic residence located in a field nearby (2004:263). In addition, he recovered surface ceramics from the Early Postclassic, which led him to conclude that Dainzú-Macuilxóchitl contained Late Classic components as well as Early and Late Postclassic components. Due to the small scale of his project, however, Markens (2004) was unable to identify the extent of these components.

In 2002, INAH undertook excavations in the area just south of Cerro Danush, along the Pan American Highway corridor (Markens, Winter, and Martínez López 2008). During this project at Dainzú-Macuilxóchitl, several large mounds were excavated in an area christened the Lantiudee Complex (Markens, Winter, and Martínez López 2008; Winter et al. 2007). This complex consisted of seven pyramidal mounds (Fig. 2.7: nos. 35–40, 55) and an elite residence. Markens, Winter, and Martínez López (2008:203) interpreted the Lantiudee Complex as "the focus of a high-status family, that is a residence with associated temples. This kind of *señorio*, or royal house, . . . was the basic political unit" during the Monte Albán IIIb–IV phase.

Markens, Winter, and Martínez López (2008) suggest that the Lantiudee Complex was largely abandoned at the end of the Late Classic, except for two of the mounds (nos. 35 and 36) that were reused in the Early Postclassic. During this reuse, the original stairway to Mound 35 was blocked off and a new one constructed. The excavators found a "relatively simple tomb" there, suggesting to them that a house had been built over the earlier structure. They subsequently found a second Early Postclassic burial atop Mound 36. Based on these findings, they assert that "as we have noted for Monte Albán, . . . [Early Monte Albán V] is strikingly different from . . . [Monte Albán IIIb–IV]: the population declined, writing disappeared, and no urns or other representations of . . . [Monte Albán IIIb–IV] gods occur" (Markens 2008:207).

Markens, Winter, and Martínez López also excavated a two-patio house complex at Dainzú-Macuilxóchitl, dating it to the Late Postclassic based on the ceramics found within the complex (Winter et al. 2007: Fig. 7.9). This residence was also constructed on top of an earlier house complex that had been used in the Late Classic. Based on their findings, Markens, Winter, and Martínez López (2008:210) propose that "the Early Postclassic appears to be a time of political crisis in the Valley of Oaxaca, marked by a simplification of the social rank hierarchy and perhaps the dispersion of the valley population into smaller communities." Winter et al. (2007) identified several Early Postclassic vessels left as offerings within the Lantiudee Complex, including miniature cups and solid-handled sahumadores. Similar discoveries were made at the summit of Cerro Danush, continuing the widespread pattern of Postclassic offerings found in Late Classic buildings.

Summary and Expectations

The abandonment patterns discussed above suggest that during the Late/Terminal Classic, a major reorganization was taking place, and the political structure at many sites was breaking down. Based on these findings, I expected to see a significant reduction in the number of occupied terraces at Cerro Danush between the Late Classic and Early Postclassic, as well as a decrease in civic-ceremonial architecture and elite residences. Our data for Early Postclassic settlement are by no means abundant, but because both Late Classic and Late Postclassic houses were known to be present at Dainzú-Macuilxóchitl, I expected to find evidence for community ritual such as that reported for Monte Albán and Dainzú-Macuilxóchitl during the same transitional period.

Summary and Concluding Remarks

The data presented in this chapter show that during the Late Classic, household and community organization was highly structured and standardized throughout the Valley of Oaxaca. This suggests a highly integrated and hierarchically ordered system. Many of the excavated residences show a pattern of rectangular dwellings opening onto central patios. Upon death, household members were buried beneath house or patio floors, or in a family tomb, depending on their status within the household. Status differentiation is evident on three levels, defined by the size and construction techniques employed in individual house complexes and their associated tombs, as well as by the materials found in burials and domestic offerings. Community rituals appear to have been conducted by the elite in secluded temple precincts, but domestic rituals were evident in all households.

At hilltop sites such as Monte Albán, Jalieza, and El Palmillo, elite residences were found in the highest places, near civic-ceremonial architecture. They consisted of large masonry structures with elaborate tombs and a range of offerings. Ceramics associated with these residences included large vessels used in ceremonies or for feasting activities. Economic activities within these elite households appear to have been limited to the production of prestigious items.

Intermediate residences were found downslope from the elite residences, and comprised more modest adobe structures with small tombs. Low-status residences were located even farther downslope, and consisted of small houses with wattle-and-daub walls; they might, or might not, include small slab-lined tombs. Ritual offerings in these houses were limited to ceramics and small animals. Residents of low-status or intermediate-level households appear to have participated in modest production of items for outside exchange.

Because Cerro Danush is a terraced hill, it seemed to offer an opportunity for comparison with the other Oaxacan sites mentioned in this chapter. The results of my excavation help to evaluate the spatial patterns derived from the examination of surface artifacts on Cerro Danush, and contribute to our understanding of the sociopolitical organization at Dainzú-Macuilxóchitl during the Late Classic–Postclassic transition. I hope that by comparing Late Classic and Postclassic households at Cerro Danush, I can confirm or modify some of the patterns detected at sites such as Monte Albán, Jalieza, and El Palmillo.

4 | Mapping and Surface Collection on Cerro Danush

Prior to my research, no intensive archaeological investigations had taken place on Cerro Danush. My project was divided into two phases: (1) detailed mapping and intensive surface collection, and (2) follow-up excavations. The goals for my first field season were to (a) develop an accurate and informative topographic map of Cerro Danush, clearly depicting all man-made features; (b) conduct a controlled, intensive surface collection so that the distribution patterns of surface materials could be probed through spatial and statistical analyses; and (c) identify a specific area for follow-up excavations (which would be phase two). In this chapter, I discuss in detail the field and laboratory methods used during the first phase of the project, as well as some of the important characteristics of the site that were identified through this research.

Mapping Cerro Danush

The mapping project began in early September of 2007 and was completed on October 31 of the same year. During that time, I used a Nikon DTM-420 total station and TDS 48GX data recorder in combination with a reflecting prism and graduated rod to measure the horizontal coordinates and vertical elevations of more than three thousand points on Cerro Danush. The Universal Trans Mercator (UTM) coordinates of all station points were also measured using a Garmin G-V GPS device. My goal was to develop a topographic map of the hill, paying special attention to the boundaries and retaining walls of man-made terraces, stone wall supported paths, structural mounds, cliff paintings, and other man-made features. In addition, I mapped significant natural features such as springs and caves, as well as many general topographic points between these features. The resulting map (Fig. 4.1) not only provides an accurate depiction of the archaeological features on the hill, but it gives a more detailed presentation of the hill's topography than does the 1:50,000 scale Instituto Nacional de Estadística y Geografía (INEGI) map.

With the help of a five-member field crew, I began the process by establishing the main station point or benchmark for the project with a wooden 5 cm × 5 cm stake driven into the ground on the hill's summit. A nail was hammered into the center of the stake for precise placement of the total station. Once the total station was set up and leveled over the project benchmark, it was calibrated and oriented to magnetic north using a compass. To reduce problems caused by human error in daily compass measurements and fluctuations in the magnetic to grid declination angle, this is the only station where the zero angle was set with a compass. All subsequent station points, identified with large nails and orange flagging tape, were established using back azimuth

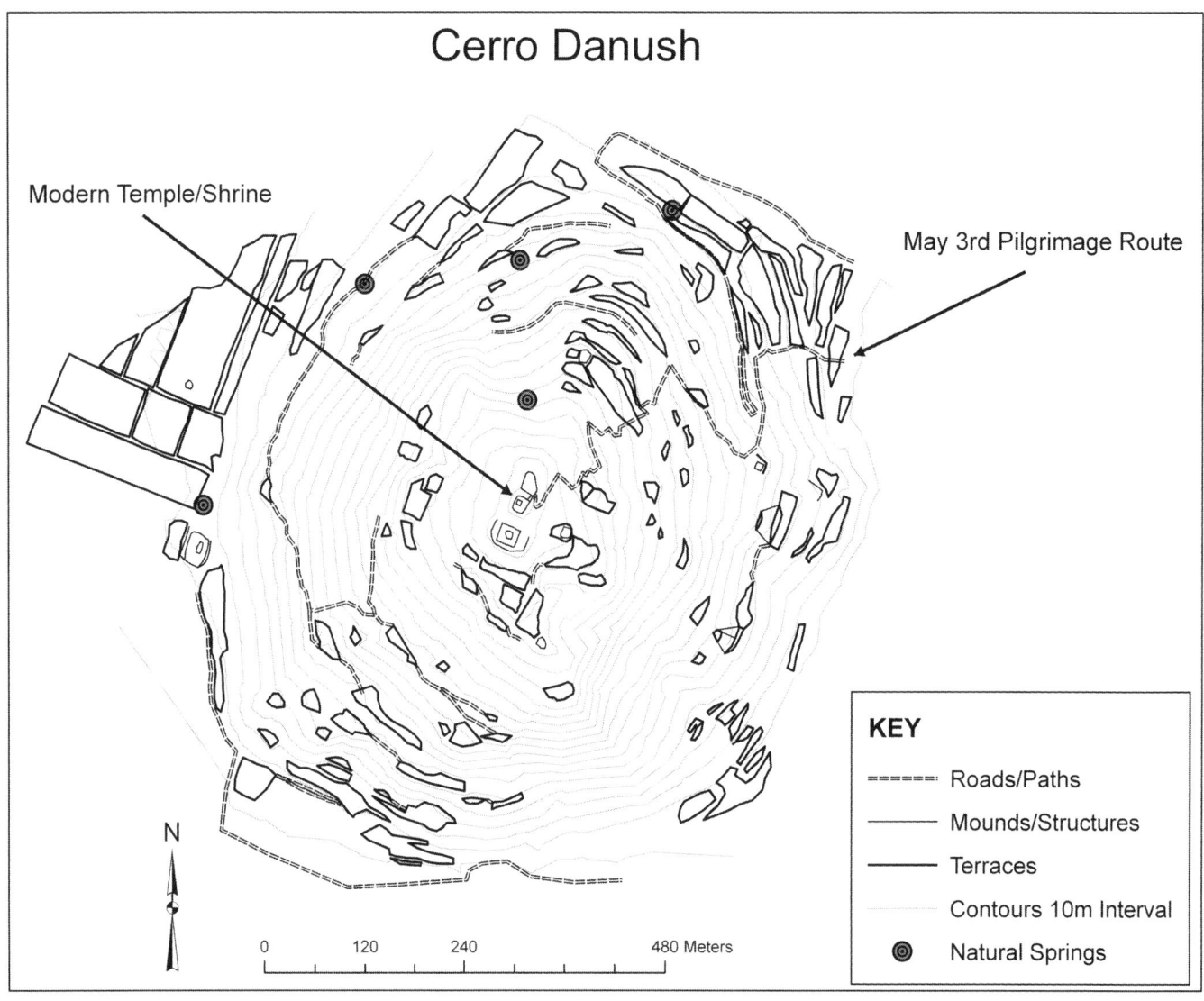

Figure 4.1. Project map of Cerro Danush.

measurements to the preceding station points. To reduce error, each time the total station was moved to a new station point, the coordinates of a third station point were also measured to ensure they closely matched their original measured values.

With the total station set over the project benchmark, we began mapping the terraces and features immediately surrounding the summit. This proved difficult because the crew had to traverse steep terrain with all the equipment in tow, and the total station had to be moved frequently in order to obtain good vantage points. Once the summit was completed, however, we followed successive station points down the slope of the hill to the base, and from there were able to work our way around the hill using station points established on the valley floor. This enabled us to cut down on both measurement error and time by increasing the number of points that could be recorded using a single station point.

Two mapping notebooks were kept during the project: one maintained by the archaeologist with the prism team and the other with the total station. The prism notebook was used to develop sketches and to record notes about the placement of each point measured, while the total station notebook was used to record the coordinates, angles, and distances of each measurement. Although the data recorder saved all of this information, we ensured that the data would not be susceptible to loss via electronic or digital issues by maintaining a hard copy. The information from the data recorder and the GPS was downloaded and compared every night. The notebooks were invaluable for tracking our activities, as well as for detecting human errors and correcting them.

In the field, the project benchmark was assigned the arbitrary location of 5000 N, 5000 E, and 2000 m elevation. All the measured points were referenced from that location and stored in the data recorder in the same coordinate system. After we downloaded the data from the recorder, the mapping points were transformed and rotated into the UTM coordinate system using the program ForeSight DXM by Tripod Data Systems (TDS). First, I changed the project benchmark location from the arbitrary coordinates to the UTM coordinates recorded by the GPS unit, and then I mathematically translated all the remaining points by the same distances north and east. This changed the reference system of the north and east distances to the reference points for the UTM 14N zone.

Because I oriented all the total station measurements to magnetic north, I also had to rotate all the points to the UTM grid using the magnetic to grid declination angle. Unfortunately, the declination angle reported on the INEGI map was not accurate enough for this procedure, which may be due to annual or long-term fluctuations in this value. Instead, the exact angle of rotation was determined through a process of tweaking, whereby secondary station point measurements recorded by the total station were compared with those recorded by the GPS unit on successive iterations of test rotation angle values. The optimal angle of rotation (2.01°) placed the maximum number of total station measurements the shortest distances from the GPS points. The final transformed station points were all within 2 m of their GPS counterparts, and the majority fell within 1 m. As a further check, all the measured points (total station and GPS) were then overlaid digitally onto the INEGI topographic map, which was used to verify horizontal accuracy by examining points plotted near obvious locations such as bridges and road intersections.[1]

Elevation measurements recorded by GPS devices are not accurate because they are based on the assumption that the surface of the earth closely approximates a smooth ellipsoid, whereas in reality the earth's surface is irregularly shaped. For this project, the elevation values of the measured points were approximated using the contour lines from the INEGI map. To do this, I first overlaid the project data onto the INEGI map and examined several areas where measured points intersected contour lines. Then, the elevation values for all points were translated based on a single point, which was selected because it demonstrated the shortest horizontal distance to the center of a contour line. To ensure the efficacy of this translation, I examined many of the new values for points located on or between contour intervals to ensure that their adjusted measurements made sense. For example, all the elevation values for points located between two contour intervals on the map should fall between the specified elevations, and they should increase or decrease in value as they near a specific contour. While this method is preferable to relying on the GPS data, it is not an extremely effective means for determining true elevation. This was made evident by comparing the estimated elevations of points measured on Terraces S19 and S20 from both field seasons, which suggest an error of 1–3 m.

Once the accuracy of the points was established within acceptable limits, terrace boundaries, walls, paths, and other man-made features were drawn in using TurboCAD v3 Computer Assisted Drawing (CAD) software. The point and line data were then downloaded into the ArcView v9.2 Desktop Geographic Information System (GIS) software and geographically referenced with the WGS 84 datum and UTM 14N projected coordinate system. The elevation measurements from the mapping point file were converted to a Triangulated Irregular Network (TIN) raster surface using the 3D Analyst extension in ArcMap, and contour lines were made at varying intervals from this surface to depict the topography of the hill. The resulting project map (Fig. 4.1) is oriented to UTM grid north (not astronomical true north or magnetic north).

Terraces and Terrace Groups on Cerro Danush

During the first phase of the project, I mapped the boundaries of 130 man-made terraces (Fig. 4.1). The builders had constructed these terraces (which varied in size [surface area] from fewer than 100 m^2 to over 3000 m^2) by erecting stone retaining walls (Fig. 4.2), often on top of bedrock platforms, and filling in the area upslope of the walls with stone and sediment so as to provide a level surface to support both residential and civic-ceremonial architecture. The retaining walls were generally two or three stones thick (roughly 50 cm) and constructed without mortar, which I believe was intentionally done to allow water to drain freely through the stones, rather than to build up pressure behind a sealed wall. Regardless of the reason, the fact that so many terraces are still in very good condition today—centuries after their initial construction—is testament to their structural integrity.

I mapped each terrace by first measuring points along the centerline of the retaining wall on the downslope edge; this was usually the most well defined border. The remaining edges were mapped by following the edge of the terrace, typically indicated by sharp changes in the incline of the surface. Because of water erosion, most of the terrace surfaces were slightly inclined, making it difficult at times to accurately map the upslope border. In some places, I found evidence for residential terraces (such as exposed stucco house floors [Fig. 4.3]), but was unable to find

---

1. The error in relative horizontal and vertical accuracy recorded by the total station between points measured during the first field season was evaluated by recording multiple readings of a single station point from total station positions at varying distances and comparing the results. The resulting error is estimated to be no more than 50 cm at its greatest fluctuation for the long distances covered in the first field season. For the shorter distances covered during the second field season, relative accuracy was measured on a daily basis and specific measurements varied by no more than 1 cm.

Figure 4.2. Stone retaining wall, Terrace S6.

Figure 4.3. Stucco floor exposed by water erosion on the slope of Cerro Danush.

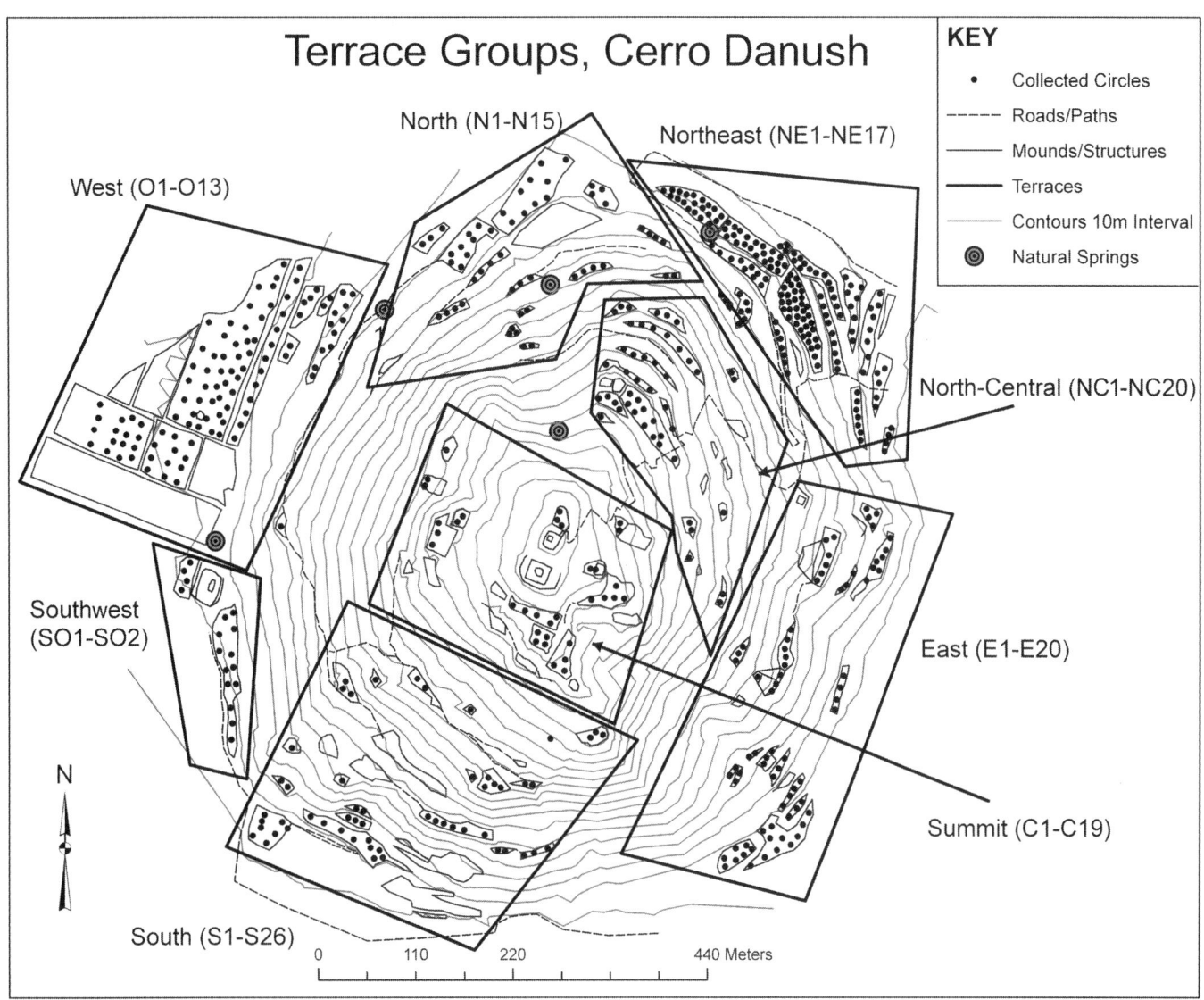

Figure 4.4. Terrace groups and surface collection circles, Cerro Danush.

any associated retaining walls or other indicators of a terrace, which suggests that the project map of Cerro Danush is incomplete. There were most likely several more terraces that cannot be seen today owing to erosion and destruction, and, for the same reasons, it is likely that many of the terraces mapped during this project were larger and more clearly delineated during their period of use.

For the purposes of identification and reference, the terraces were divided into eight groups based on their horizontal location on the hill (Fig. 4.4): Summit (C, *cumbre*), Northeast (NE, *noroeste*), North-Central (NC, *norte-central*), North (N, *norte*), East (E, *este*), West (O, *oeste*), Southwest (SO, *suroeste*), and South (S, *sur*). Within these groups, terraces were assigned numbers so that each particular terrace could be further identified. For example, terraces in the Summit Terrace Group were named C1–C19 (Fig. 4.5). The abbreviated terrace designations correspond to their Spanish titles, so that summit terrace number one is written Terrace C1 (Cumbre 1). I chose to do this rather than assign each terrace a unique number because the relative location of any given terrace could be quickly established by its group/number designation, without having to constantly reference the map.

Residential wards, neighborhoods, or "barrios" have been identified archaeologically at a number of Mesoamerican sites (Healan 1993; Millon 1973; Smith and Novic 2012), including the hilltop centers of Monte Albán (Blanton 1978), Xochicalco (Hirth 2000b), and Calixtlahuaca (Smith and Novic 2012). It is possible that similar social units existed at Dainzú-Macuilxóchitl,

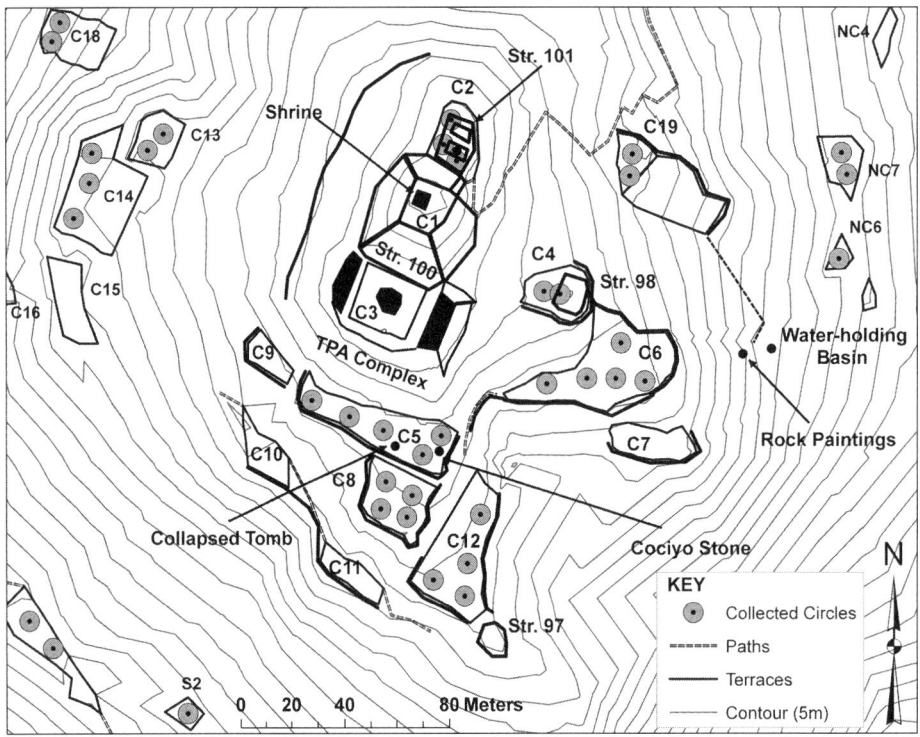

Figure 4.5. Summit Terrace Group.

but the terrace groups defined for Cerro Danush represent units that were arbitrarily designated for reference purposes and hold no other significance. To be sure, terraces within groups appear to be spatially connected in many cases and perhaps related to one another, sometimes separated from other terraces or terrace groups by imposing terrain. It is possible, therefore, that Cerro Danush had social units larger than the household, knowledge of which would increase our information on sociopolitical organization at the site.

The Summit Terrace Group (Figs. 4.5, 4.6)

The Summit Terrace Group is distinct from the others and appears to be an important civic-ceremonial precinct for the community of Dainzú-Macuilxóchitl. This group is made up of residential terraces surrounding a monumental stone structure built on the peak of the hill. The TIN surface (Fig. 4.6) clearly depicts the design and layout of the architecture, which Kowalewski et al. (1989:1086–87) identified as their Structures 99–101. My Terrace C1 is the flattened top of the central pyramidal platform (Kowalewski et al.'s Structure 100), which was constructed through a combination of modifying the original bedrock and adding cut stone blocks. The builders also constructed a stone retaining wall on the slope of the hill below the structure to create a flat surface in support of the structure's west wall.

This structure appears to have served as the base for a temple, and today it supports a small shrine that is used for ceremonies associated with the Festival of the Cross. Terrace C3 lies just below the temple platform, to the south, and consists of a patio with a central altar. The patio is closed on three sides by high stone walls (Kowalewski et al.'s Structures 99, 199, and 299); these stand 2–4 m above the patio surface and adjoin the temple platform on the north side. Working from the patio, I found the remnants of stone steps that led up the south wall of the pyramidal platform. The architectural design and layout of this system are similar to structures found at Monte Albán and other Classic period sites in the Valley of Oaxaca, known as temple-patio-altar systems or TPAs (Winter 1986).

Many Classic period TPAs in the Valley of Oaxaca are associated with elite residences (Joyce 2000, 2004, 2010; Lind and Urcid 1983, 2010; Winter 2001), and it is likely that the domestic terraces C5–C12, found just below the temple-patio-altar complex, contained the residences of an elite household. Stucco floors and stone foundations exposed by looting pits were visible on the surface of Terrace C5, along with a large carved stone, extracted by looters but left behind presumably because

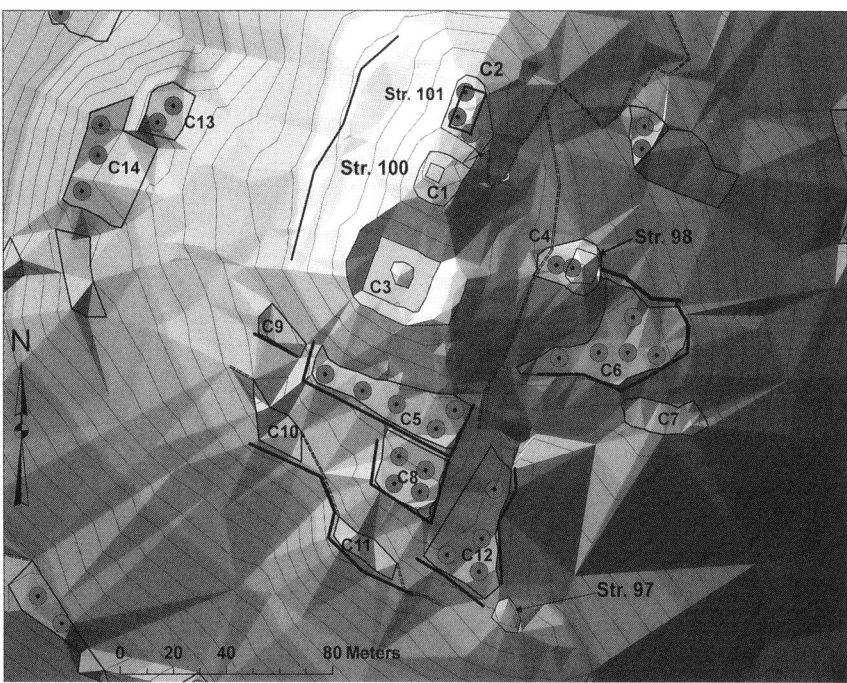

Figure 4.6.
Triangulated Irregular Network (TIN) surface depicting the topography of the Summit Terrace Group.

Figure 4.7.
Carved stone doorjamb with image of Cociyo impersonator.

of its weight. This carved stone appears to be the doorjamb for a tomb, and it contains the image of an individual wearing a Cociyo mask (Fig. 4.7). Only a person of high status would be buried in such an elaborate tomb, and the individual depicted on the stone seems to be "impersonating" (Sellen 2002) Cociyo or Lightning. The Zapotec ruling stratum is known to have claimed close ties to Lightning (Marcus 1983d, 1983f).

Access to the Summit Terrace Group appears to have been very limited. The summit is isolated on three sides (west, south, and north) by very steep terrain, augmented by high retention walls. On the fourth side (east), it is set off by a stone mound on Terrace C4 and a reinforcing wall that runs along the northern edge of Terrace C6. Access to the residential terraces of the area is limited to a small footpath that runs between the temple-patio-altar and the mound on Terrace C4. The difficult terrain in this area required more effort for the construction of terraces than was the case with other groups, and the retaining walls are generally taller and thicker in this group than anywhere else on the hill. These factors clearly demonstrate the elevated status of the inhabitants of the Summit Terrace Group. In fact, no other structural complex or terrace group within the site of Dainzú-Macuilxóchitl is as restricted as this civic-ceremonial precinct.

The Northeast Group (Fig. 4.8)

This terrace group consists of seventeen terraces that lie in close proximity to one another along the northeast base of the hill. The group is separated from the North-Central and East Groups by steep terrain, and the North Group lies a considerable distance away. The terraces of this group are stacked one above the next in such a way that when viewed from the base of the hill, they have the appearance of large steps.

Several terraces in this group exhibit clear signs of destruction caused by the recent development of a dirt road, used by trucks to carry supplies up the hill during the construction of a cistern. A small footpath that leads to the summit also cuts through several terraces, and has exacerbated erosion in the area. The close physical relationship between these terraces suggests they represent a sociopolitical unit of organization above the level of household, perhaps a residential ward.

The North-Central Group (Fig. 4.9)

The terraces of the North-Central Group are built on top of a rocky outcrop, elevated above the North and Northeast Groups by a short but steep slope. As with many of the other groups, it consists of terraces of varying sizes stacked one above another. In between Terraces NC11, NC12, and NC13, I mapped a stone mound (Mound 300); its upper surface was flush with Terrace NC12 but rose above NC13, NC11, and NC19. Although it is difficult to ascertain the function of this mound, it probably served as a platform for a structure.

Like the terraces of the Northeast Group, the close proximity and connections between Terraces NC10 through NC18 suggest they may form part of a supra-household unit of organization. Several small terraces, NC4–NC9, are separated from the bulk of this group, and may not be directly related.

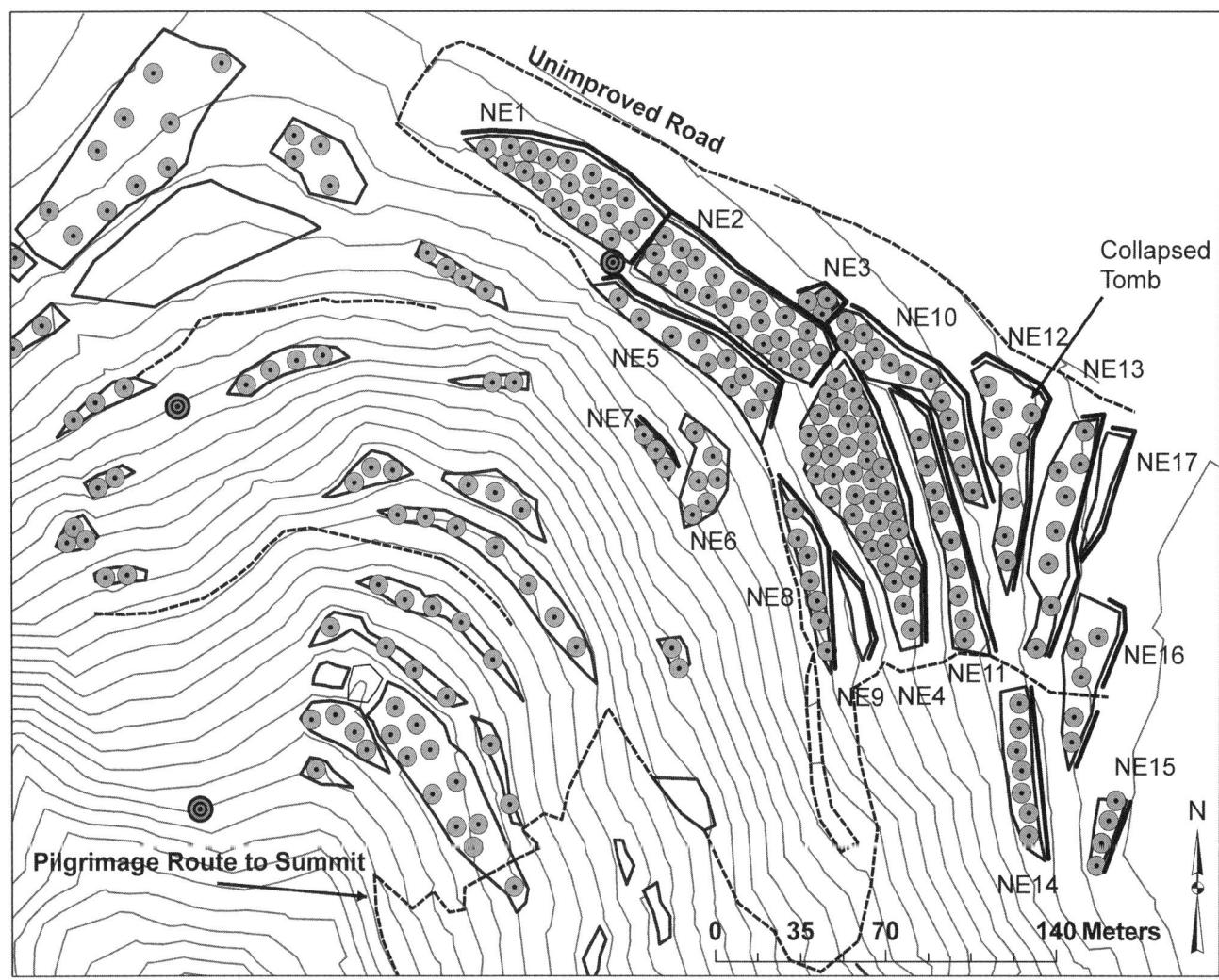

Figure 4.8. Northeast Terrace Group (see key, Fig. 4.5).

The North Terrace Group (Fig. 4.10)

The terraces in this group are more dispersed than is the case with the Northeast or North-Central Groups. The larger terraces at the base of the hill (N10–N15) are constructed on top of gently sloping bedrock, which is exposed in many places. The smaller terraces (N1–N9) are constructed in steep terrain to the west of the North-Central Group, and a stone-lined path connects the two groups. Within the North Group, there are two natural springs that provide water for most of the year; two paths provide access to these springs. One of these paths, supported by a stone wall, starts on the western edge of Terrace N13 and extends all the way around the west side of the hill, connecting with the terraces of the South Group. While the lower terraces are physically connected to one another, their relation to the upper terraces is unclear.

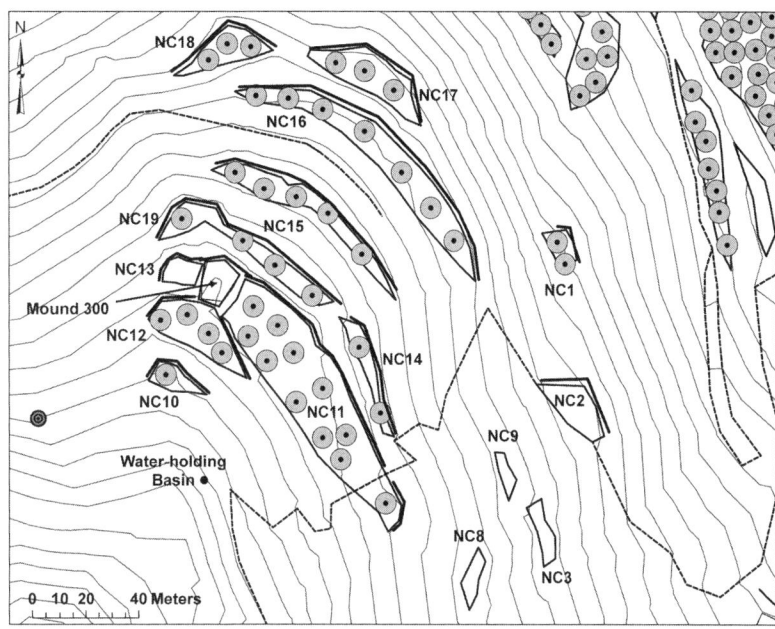

Figure 4.9. The North-Central Terrace Group (see key, Fig. 4.5).

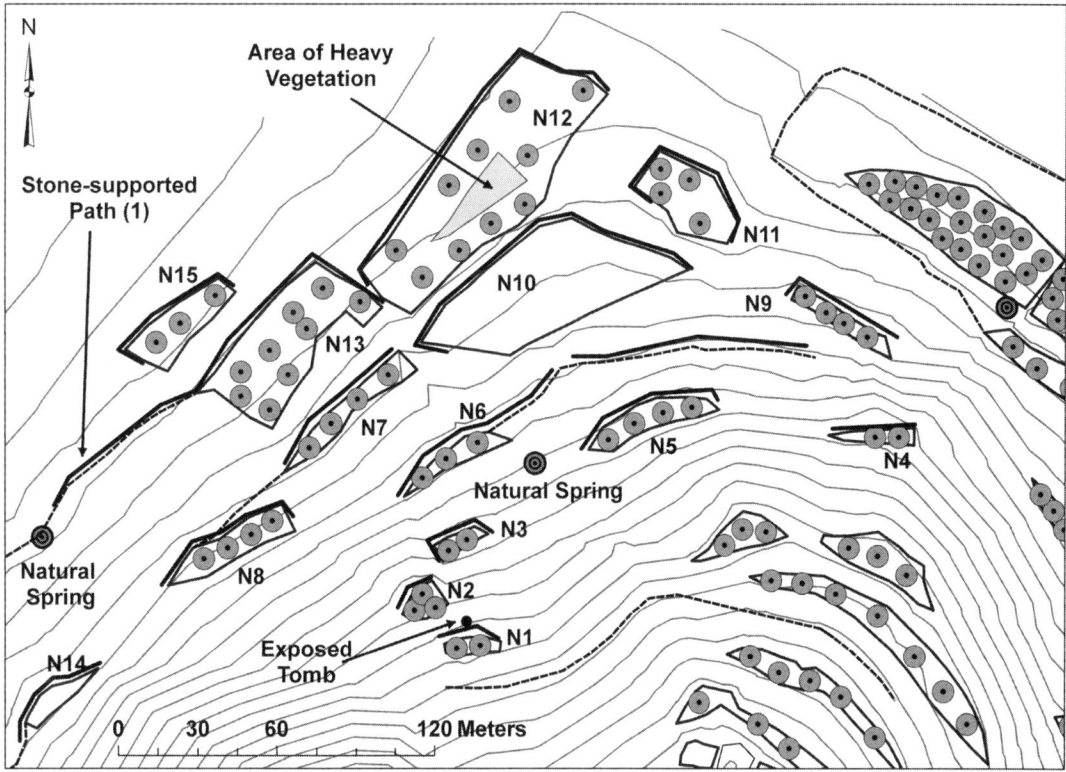

Figure 4.10. The North Terrace Group (see key, Fig. 4.5).

The East Terrace Group (Fig. 4.11)

The eastern slope of Cerro Danush is steep and rocky. It includes a vertical cliff face along the higher part of the hill, just below the Summit Terrace Group (Fig. 4.1). The terraces that make up the East Group are located on the less steep, but still sharply inclined, lower slope of the hill.

I present the East Group in two maps (Fig. 4.11a, b) because its terraces appear to form two distinguishable residential wards or precincts. Terraces E1–E10 are arranged around two structures (301 and 302), located on either side of an arroyo. These structures are highly eroded but similar, in the sense that solid stone rectangular platforms support pyramidal structures built into the slope of the hill in each case. I collected many solid-handled

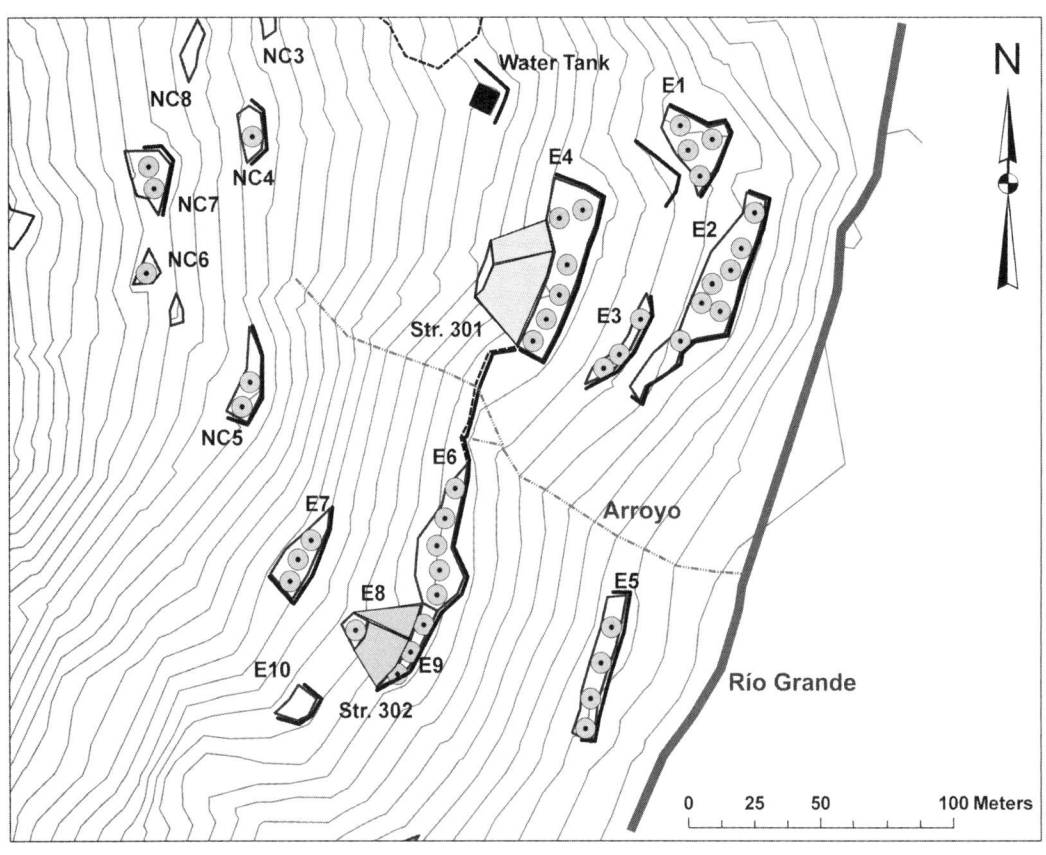

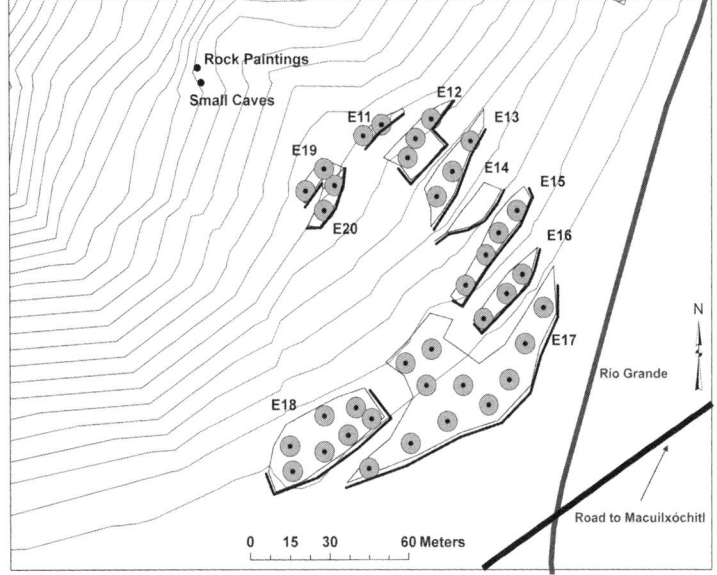

(*above left*) Figure 4.11a.
Terraces E1–E10 of the East Terrace Group (see key, Fig. 4.5).

(*left*) Figure 4.11b.
Terraces E11–E20 of the East Terrace Group (see key, Fig. 4.5).

frying-pan-shaped censers (sahumadores; Appendix B) at the base of Structure 302, suggesting ceremonial activity (see Chapter 8).

Terraces E11–E20 are located on the southeast corner of the hill, and consist of another closely connected group of stacked terraces. The lower terraces, E17 and E18, are larger, and have recently been used as agricultural fields. The upper terraces are quite small, with an average size of 4 m by 15 m, perhaps big enough to support individual houses but not entire house complexes. This may reflect an attempt by the inhabitants to adapt their residences to steep, rocky terrain.

Several of the terraces in this group were severely eroded. In fact, on the slope below Terrace E20, I found the remains of a few stucco floors resting directly on the bedrock, with no evidence for terracing in the vicinity. Immediately upslope from the terraces, near the base of the cliff, there is an area with small circular caves and rock paintings (Fig. 4.12). Because of their close proximity to the terraces, I believe this area may have served as a ritual venue for the occupants of this group, but no artifacts were visible on the surface.

Figure 4.12. Rock painting above Terraces E11–E20.

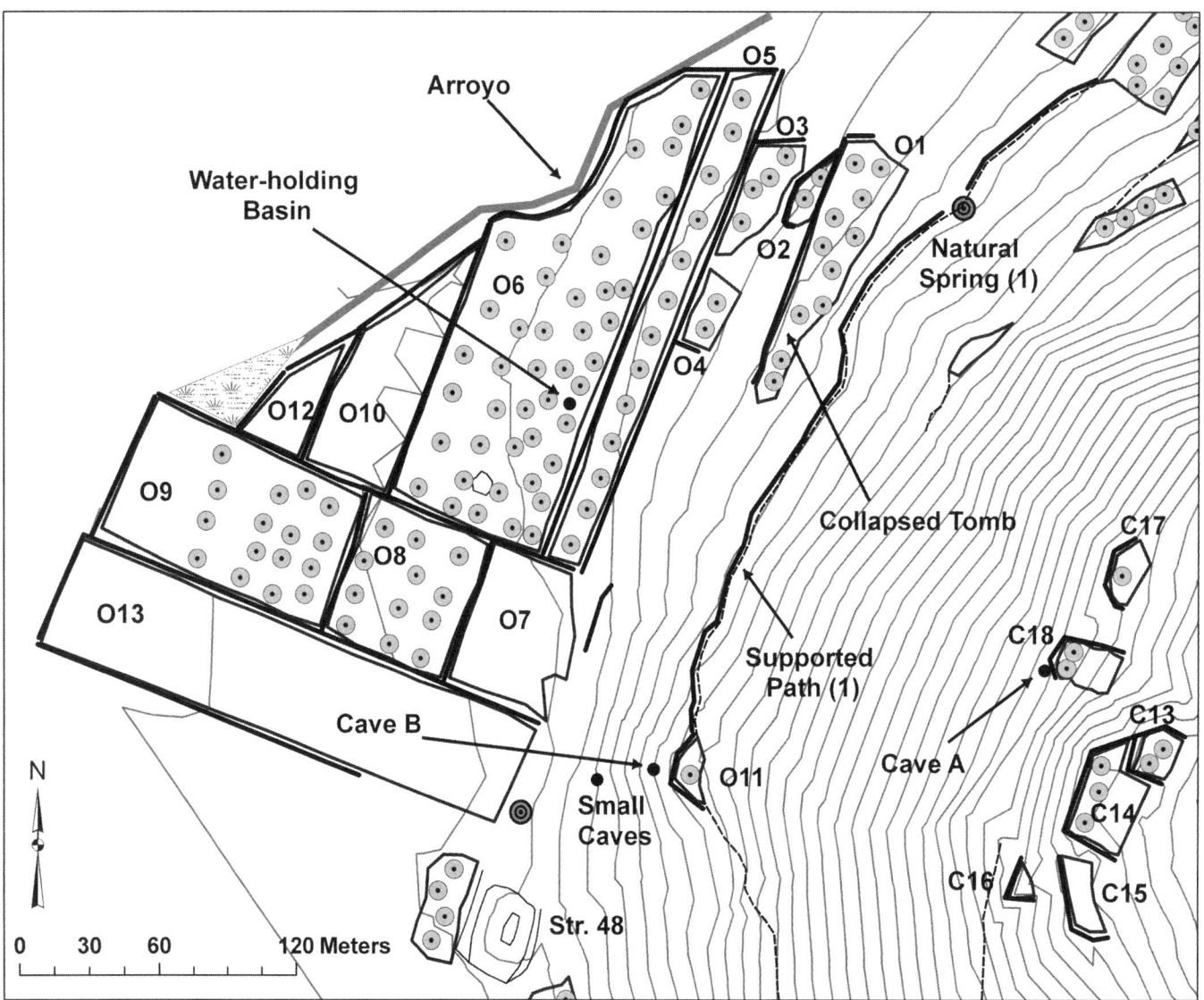

Figure 4.13. The West Terrace Group (see key, Fig. 4.5).

The West Terrace Group (Fig. 4.13)

The terraces of the West Group are located at the base of the hill. They step down a gentle slope that extends from the steep, rocky incline below the Summit Terrace Group toward an arroyo. Like many other groups, the West Group consists of terraces that are stacked one above another and are potentially related.

Two variables that separate these terraces from the others are their great size and their straight edges. The retaining walls and surfaces of these terraces do not show signs of severe erosion, perhaps because the soils in this area are so infertile that they have not been used for agricultural purposes in a very long time. The lack of recent plowing, in fact, may account for the low density of artifacts recovered from the surfaces of Terraces O1–O6 (Chapter 5).

Two natural springs flank the West Terrace Group. The first (Fig. 4.13, Spring 1) supplies water well into the dry season, and is located along the main path up the hill, while the other functions only during the rainy season. There are also some caves located on a small, steep bluff below Terrace O11. The largest of these (Fig. 4.13, Cave B) is the only one found on Cerro Danush that was big enough for humans to enter. Once inside the opening of Cave B, one finds an oval-shaped chamber with a high ceiling that could accommodate five or six individuals comfortably.

Ethnographic studies have shown that caves and springs retain ritual significance among the various indigenous groups

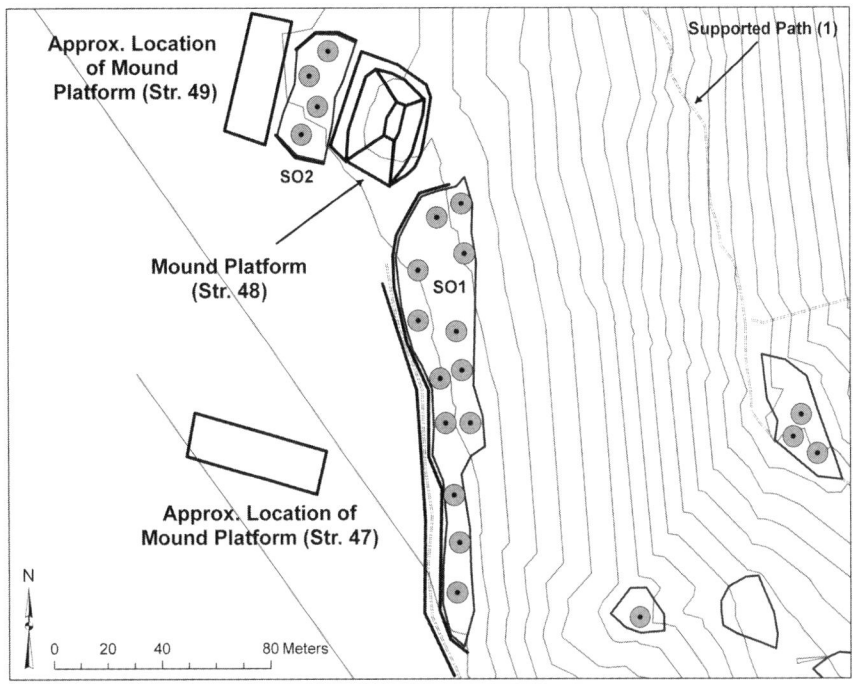

Figure 4.14. The Southwest Terrace Group (see key, Fig. 4.5).

of Oaxaca (Barabas 2003), and are generally considered to be venues for communication with ancestors and other spirits that dwell within the mountains. Perhaps for this reason, located directly below the caves one sees a large Classic period civic-ceremonial center, consisting of three monumental structures (47, 48, and 49) arranged around an elevated patio/platform (Kowalewski et al. 1989:1086–87).

On Kowalewski et al.'s (1989:1086–87) map for Dainzú-Macuilxóchitl, we see several similar three-mound groups at various points on the site. These might reflect civic-ceremonial precincts associated with specific residential wards. My mapping did not extend to the three-mound complex near the West Group because most of it lay outside the bounds of my project. However, I did map the mound called Structure 48 (Figs. 4.13, 4.14) by Kowalewski et al. (1989:1086–87). This was a high pyramidal platform, similar in design to Structure 100 of the Summit Terrace Group. I also mapped the patio between Structures 48 and 49 (Fig. 4.14, Terrace SO2). I believe that this ceremonial complex may have united the terraces of the West and Southwest Groups into one large sociopolitical unit.

The West Group is perhaps the only unit on Cerro Danush that resembles the residential wards ("barrios") identified by Blanton (1978) at the site of Monte Albán. Unlike the situation with the Summit Terrace Group, however, I found no evidence for elite residences in the vicinity of the civic-ceremonial complex. It should be noted, however, that the area downslope from the three-mound group had been severely damaged from recent agricultural activity, and Mounds 47 and 49 were almost completely eroded. It is, therefore, possible that any elite residence in this area is now too eroded to detect on the surface.

The Southwest Terrace Group (Fig. 4.14)

This group consists of only two terraces. One (SO2) is the patio of the civic-ceremonial complex mentioned above, and the other (SO1) is a long, heavily eroded terrace running along the southwest base of the hill, directly below a steep rocky slope. The remnants of several short stone walls were visible on the surface of Terrace SO1; it was difficult to tell whether these were house foundations, or simply the remains of retaining walls that would once have divided Terrace SO1 into smaller, stacked terraces. Whatever the case, this area seemed clearly related to Structures 47, 48, and 49, and, therefore, the West Terrace Group. The area is also located just north of the largest concentration of prehispanic artificial mounds mapped at the site of Dainzú-Macuilxóchitl by Kowalewski et al. (1989:1086–87). These include the Late Classic Lantiudee Complex excavated by Markens, Winter, and Martínez López (2008).

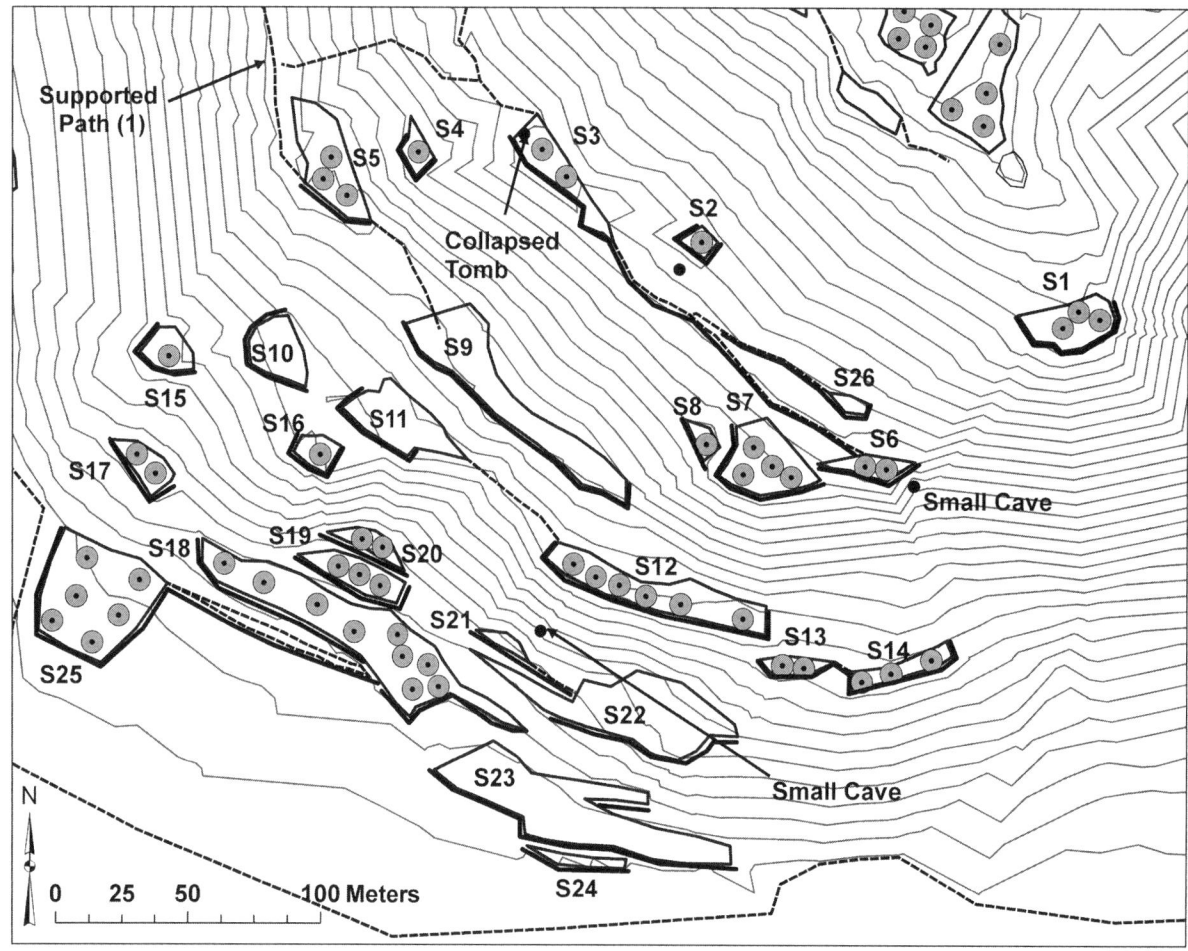

Figure 4.15. The South Terrace Group (see key, Fig. 4.5).

The South Terrace Group (Fig. 4.15)

The terraces of the South Group are located on a steep rocky slope that contains thick vegetation, especially thorn forest species such as mesquite, *huizache*, and *mala mujer*, on the inclines between the terraces. The tough terrain made it difficult to map this part of the hill, and thick grass on some of the terraces made surface collection difficult. Nevertheless, in this area I was able to identify and map twenty-six distinct terraces and surface collect eighteen of them.

When viewed from the west, the southern slope of the hill has the appearance of a gigantic stepped pyramid. There are three very steep natural slopes at varying heights on the hill that give this appearance, but this phenomenon has been enhanced by the construction of the terraces on this side of the hill. The first steep incline, which separates the Summit Terrace Group from a thin line of small terraces and masonry-supported paths below, was heightened by the construction of high retaining walls to support the terraces above. Further down, at the bottom of the second steep incline, we see another strip of terraces and paths that make up the level surface of the next step, which also rests atop a vertical rock face. Below that, one finds the remaining terraces at the base of the hill.

Unlike the terraces of the other groups, which are relatively isolated from the remainder of Dainzú-Macuilxóchitl, the terraces of the South Group directly face Cerro Dainzú. This group of terraces would therefore be visible from the valley floor structures that make up the bulk of the site of Dainzú-Macuilxóchitl. In fact, the basal terraces of the South Group (S18–S25) lie close enough to the so-called Lantiudee Complex (Markens, Winter, and Martínez López 2008; Winter et al. 2007) to be considered an outlying residential ward.

The remaining terraces of the South Group are elevated and difficult to reach, yet all are interconnected through paths; the largest of these paths (Fig. 4.15, Path 1) extends all the way around the hill to the springs of the North Group. This group

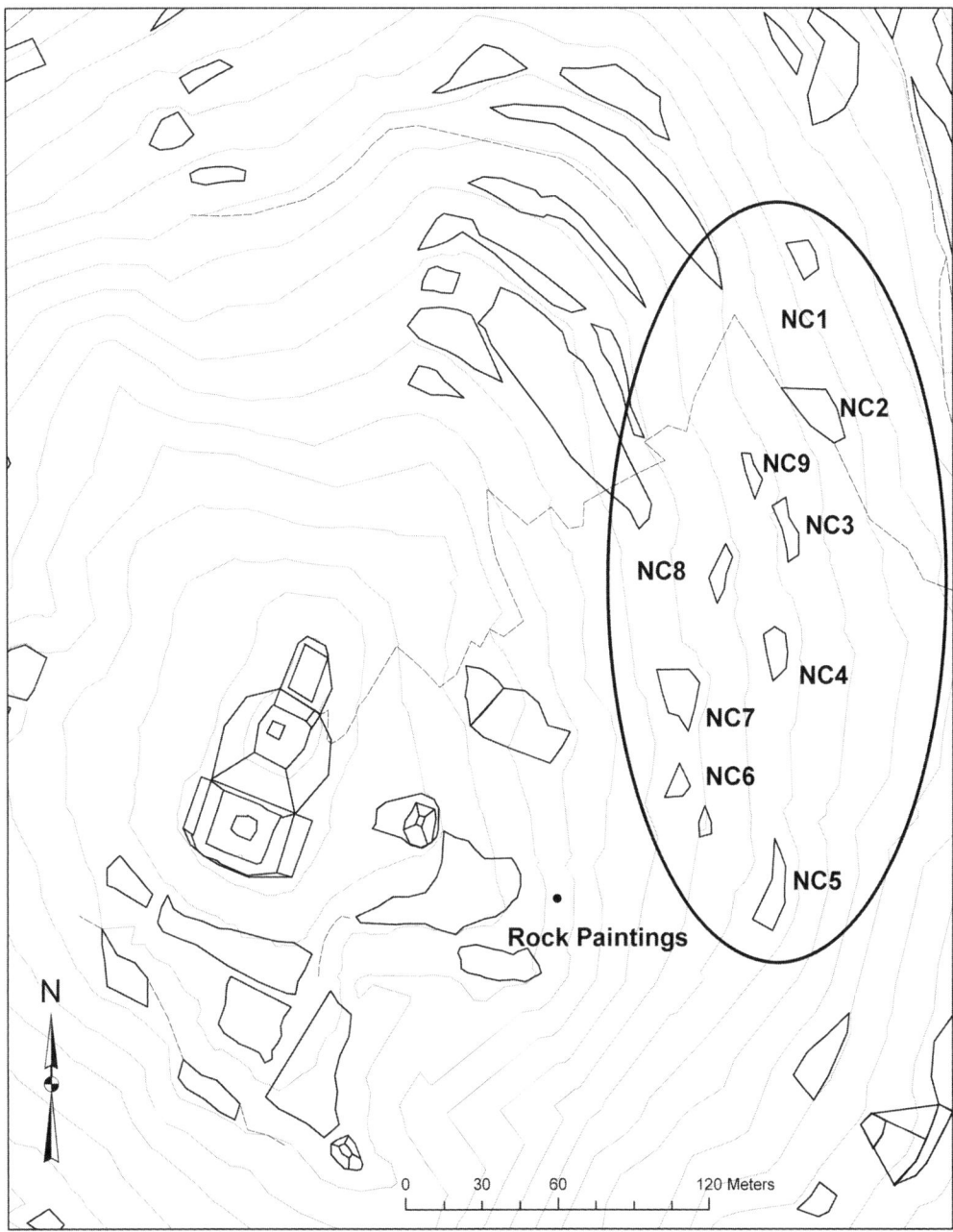

Figure 4.16. Location of rock paintings and Terraces NC3–NC9.

of closely related terraces (S3–S16) might represent a suprahousehold organizational unit, similar to that proposed for Terraces E11–E20 but spatially adapted to the different physical conditions presented by the hill. Terrace S2 appears to be the top of a heavily eroded pyramidal mound similar to those found in the East Terrace Group, and may have had a ritual function. Terrace S1, on the other hand, is an isolated terrace atop a high cliff below the Summit Terrace Group. It has no clear connection to any other terrace, and no distinguishing features.

Terraces NC3–NC9 (Fig. 4.16)

Several small terraces (NC3–NC9) were found on the northeast side of the hill, below the Summit Terrace Group (Figs. 4.16, 4.11a). Although they had no physical connection with any of the other terraces, they were arbitrarily assigned to the North-Central Group because they were located in roughly the same area and at the same elevation. These terraces had loose soils and lay on a medium incline above the East and Northeast

Figure 4.17. Rock paintings on cliff face below Terrace S6.

Groups. Their retaining walls were difficult to follow, and none of the terraces appear to be sizable enough to have contained residential structures. Because all the other areas with similarly graded slopes contained residential terraces, it is possible that NC3–NC9 are all that remain of a larger terrace complex that had been degraded through major erosion.

Just to the south of these terraces, along the base of a cliff below Terrace C6 of the Summit Terrace Group, my field crew identified another area with rock paintings (Fig. 4.17). Like the paintings above Terraces E11–E20, the images are rendered in monochrome red. The drawings are simple in design, almost like stick figures, and appear to show mythical creatures with both human and animal qualities. For example, one of the figures stands like a human, holding a spear-like instrument in its hands, but also has a turtle shell on its back and a bird head. The creatures appear to be either hunting or taking part in combat. These paintings have not been dated, and at this time I have no interpretation of their content.

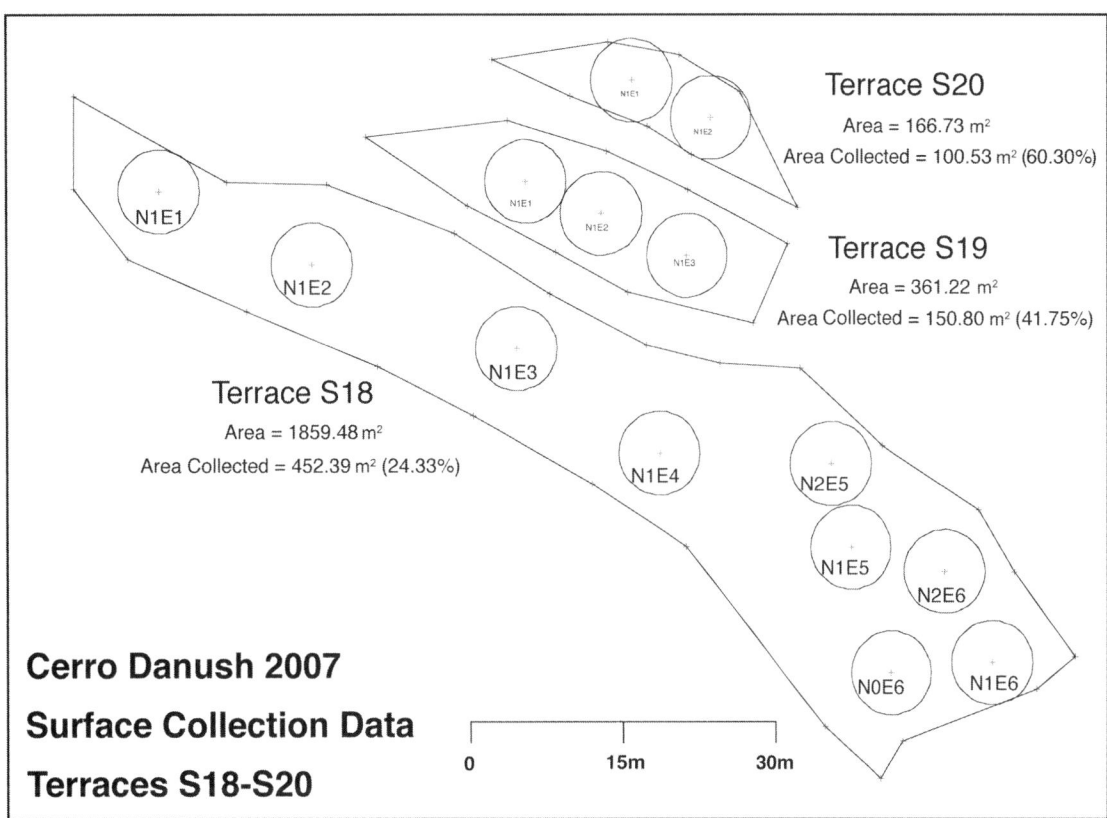

Figure 4.18. Surface collection diagrams. (Polygons represent the mapped boundaries of terraces of various sizes. Circles within a given terrace are to scale.)

Surface Collection Procedures

Intensive surface collection of the residential terraces on Cerro Danush began on November 5, 2007, and concluded on December 21. My goal was to recover enough data to explore the density distribution patterns of surface artifacts on all the residential terraces. To accomplish this, the collection units had to be of comparable size and also represent a significant portion of the surface space on each terrace. The high number of terraces, abundant surface materials, and large area, however, eliminated the possibility of establishing collection grid systems on every terrace within the project time and budgetary constraints. Therefore, a collection scheme had to be developed that allowed for the relatively quick and intensive collection of as many terraces as possible.

The solution was simple but effective. Artifacts were collected using circles of equivalent surface area, which were arbitrarily placed on each terrace so that most of the horizontal space was represented in the sample. (I use the term "space" here to keep separate the notions of horizontal position and surface area.) I was not necessarily interested in collecting a similar amount of surface area for each terrace, but rather in distributing the collection circles so that I could identify discrete activity areas within a terrace, assuming they existed. The resulting terrace diagrams (Fig. 4.18) reveal that the percentage of surface area collected differs between terraces, but most of the space on a given terrace was covered.

The circles were made using two chaining pins tethered with twine at a distance of 4 m apart, yielding a surface area of 50.27 m^2. One chaining pin, which served as the circle's center, was placed firmly in the ground and its coordinates were recorded with the GPS device. Then crew members used the second chaining pin to mark the outer boundary of the circle. All cultural materials within the circle were collected and placed in marked Ziploc bags. Circles were then distinguished by recording the terrace designation, the relative position north and east on the terrace (beginning from the southwest corner), and the UTM coordinates recorded for its center point. For example, the circles on Terrace S18 were named starting in the southwest corner with N1E1, and numbers increased as one moved east and north (Fig. 4.18).

A total of 540 circles were collected, involving 98 (75%) of the 130 terraces that were mapped; the individual collection circles are depicted in the terrace group maps (Figs. 4.5, 4.8–4.11, 4.13–4.15). Some terraces were not collected, usually because they contained so much undergrowth vegetation (mostly in the form of tall thick grass) that surface visibility was reduced to a point where collection would yield misleading results. Thick grass was especially problematic on the southern part of the hill, which contained thicker vegetation than other areas in general. Undergrowth also prevented the collection of certain circles within terraces that were otherwise suitable for collection, such as C5 and O9. In those cases, I collected as many circles as possible. Another reason that individual terraces might not be collected is that corn and beans were planted on them (Terraces S23, S24, and N10). Although we were allowed to map the boundaries of these terraces, the owners asked us not to disturb their crops.

Surface collection began in the Northeast Terrace Group, and as the maps show (Figs. 4.4, 4.8), collection circles in that area are more closely spaced than elsewhere on the hill. This is because I initially wanted to cover as much of the surface area as possible from each terrace, but time constraints—coupled with the enormous amount of artifacts collected—eventually necessitated a change in collection strategy. The maps also depict some overlap between adjacent circles, but this is due to the error inherent in GPS measurements, and does not reflect actual overlap on the ground.

Adjacent circles were collected simultaneously and the field crew always fully extended their lines toward one another to ensure no overlap before collecting. If overlap was detected, then one of the circle's center points was relocated before collection began.

Artifact Analysis and Laboratory Procedures

The analysis of artifacts collected during surface survey took place between January 2 and February 15, 2008. The purpose of this analysis was to sort the collected materials into meaningful diagnostic categories and to record the counts of all items within each collection circle. I did not intend to establish or even refine artifact types, but to use those already defined through extensive previous research (Caso, Bernal, and Acosta 1967; Kowalewski et al. 1989; Markens 2008; Martínez López et al. 2000). Materials were visually inspected and sorted into categories, and their counts were recorded on standardized forms prepared for each collection circle. These counts were then manually input into a geo-referenced spreadsheet so that the density of their distributions across the terrace groups could be spatially and statistically probed for patterns, revealing important information about activities that took place on the terraces (Chapter 5).

For the classification of categories within the project ceramic assemblage, I used a combination of forms and types developed from previous research projects throughout the Valley of Oaxaca. These include categories defined by: Caso et al. (1952, 1965, 1967) during their extensive excavations at Monte Albán; Kowalewski et al. (Blanton et al. 1982:375–82; Kowalewski et al. 1989:829–37; Kowalewski, Spencer, and Redmond 1978) from the valley-wide survey and surface collection project; Bernal et al. (1974, 1988) from their excavations at Dainzú and Yagul; Paddock, Mogor, and Lind (1968) from their excavations at Lambityeco; and Markens et al. (Markens 2004, 2008; Markens et al. 2008; Martínez López et al. 2000) from their excavations at Dainzú-Macuilxóchitl.

Ceramic categories associated with form and function included cooking jars (ollas), conical bowls (*cajetes cónicos*), hemispherical bowls (*cajetes semiesféricos*), cylindrical bowls (*cajetes cilíndricos*), cups (*vasos sencillos*), figurines (*figurillas*), ceremonial whistles (silbatos), hollow-handled frying-pan-shaped censers (sahumadores), effigy urns (*urnas*), tortilla griddles (*comales*), salsa bowls (*chilmoleras*), water jugs (cántaros), and kiln wasters (*desechos*). These categories were further organized by rim diameter, basal decoration and supports, paste color, incised patterns, and rim shape.

Since the majority of ceramics collected fit within the established categories for the Late Classic, it appears that the major occupation of the terraces on Cerro Danush took place during that time. Ceramic artifacts belonging to other time periods included solid-handled censers (sahumadores) (Blanton et al. 1982, cat. 2220) and G3M bowls (Kowalewski et al. 1978, cat. 1102 and 1105) from the Early Postclassic; small numbers of incised G23 bowls (Blanton et al. 1982, cat. 1312) from Monte Albán IIIa; and G12 conical and hemispherical bowls, which began in Late Monte Albán I and lasted until Monte Albán II (Spencer, Redmond, and Elson 2008).

Chipped stone artifacts were sorted into categories such as expedient flake tools, debitage, points, prismatic blades, scrapers, spent cores, and bifaces. They were further separated by color and source material (chert, volcanic tuff, and obsidian). These materials are generally not useful in relative dating, but were very similar to materials found at contemporary sites in the Valley of Oaxaca (Haines, Feinman, and Nicholas 2004).

Ground stone artifacts were sorted into categories such as: manos, metates, mortars (*molcajetes*), pestles (*tejolotes*), *ruedas* (large stone wheels with a perforation in the center), and *hachas* (axes or celts). Once again, these materials are not useful in relative dating, but do match artifacts found at Monte Albán, Yagul, El Palmillo, Mitla, and other sites in the Valley of Oaxaca. Since many of these tools are still in use, they are excellent indicators of domestic activities.

A detailed description of the artifact categories used during both phases of this project, including photographs and drawings, is included in Appendix B.

Concluding Remarks

The procedures and qualitative descriptions presented in this chapter reveal how I was able to achieve the goals laid out in the introductory paragraph. In-depth analyses of the topographic map developed during the project provide a base for understanding the organization and layout of terraces, structures, and other features that were surveyed on Cerro Danush. The description of the surface collection procedures and the depiction of the collection circles on the project maps allow the reader to better understand the units of analysis studied in detail in the following chapter. Lastly, the field season's exploratory research of survey, mapping, and surface collection provided me with an intimate knowledge of Cerro Danush, and allowed me to target specific areas for excavation, not only in the Phase 2 field season (Chapters 7 and 8) but during future projects as well.

5 | Density Distribution Analyses of Surface Artifacts

The goal of my first field season was to acquire a sample of diagnostic artifacts from many small units (collection circles) over a broad area (the terraces of Cerro Danush), sufficient to allow me to calculate broad patterns of artifact densities across the site. In this chapter I discuss the nature of the data set, its preparation for analyses, and the ancient behavior patterns deduced from it. Included are discussions of the inherent limitations in the data and analyses.

General Description of the Data Set

In the laboratory, I recorded the frequency counts of all materials from each collection circle on a form. This form was organized like a spreadsheet, with types or categories (e.g., point/olla) as the column headings and artifact material (e.g., chert/brown paste) as the row headings. The use of this form standardized the frequency count process so that circles would have comparable data. It also allowed for relatively quick processing of a large amount of material.

The most important limitation of this technique is that minor variations between individual artifacts of the same type are not generally recorded, making it impossible to conduct spatial and statistical analyses of such variations. For most of the artifact categories, however, this limitation was negligible. In the ceramic assemblage, for example, artifacts for the time periods were highly standardized and lacked decorative treatments, thus reducing the possible variations. In the lithic assemblage most of the material consisted of debitage or expedient tools, which also lacked stylistic variation.

The data from the analysis forms were next input into an Excel spreadsheet, with the diagnostic categories serving as variables (columns) and the individual collection circles (540 in total) serving as cases (rows). The resulting file became the project master database; once it was created and the data verified, it was not modified again. To maintain the integrity of the master file, and to retain it as a means to verify subsets, all spatial and statistical analyses were conducted on sub-databases created from the master file.

The raw data for ground stone, chipped stone, and ceramic materials were downloaded into separate spreadsheets for analysis. This was done because the mean surface density for chipped stone materials (measured in pieces per square meter) was significantly lower (by a factor of 100) than the mean surface density of ceramic materials (measured in sherds per square meter). This meant that any type of quantitative analysis of the ceramics and chipped stone taken together would overweight the ceramic data; as a result, important spatial relationships could be lost. Ground stone was found in only 47 of the 540 collection circles, limiting the analysis of these items to qualitative means.

Quantitative Assessment of the Ceramic Data Set

A total of 119,649 potsherds were recovered during the surface collection of 540 circles. Sherds with gray paste were by far the most abundant, amounting to 95,374 or 79.71% of the assemblage. Brown paste sherds were second, totaling 22,344 or 18.67% of the assemblage. Orange paste sherds were the least abundant, with a total of 1931 or 1.61% of the assemblage. Of the sherds collected, 24,398 (22.4%) were considered diagnostic, meaning that their forms were sufficiently clear to identify them as belonging to one of the specific categories defined in Appendix B.

During my analysis, I adhered to a strict method of classifying the sherds into diagnostic categories. Only unambiguous examples were counted, with questionable sherds left out of the counts. While this scheme resulted in a smaller count of overall diagnostics, it did not appear to skew the results for or against any particular category. The most abundant sherds in the diagnostic assemblage were rim fragments from G35 conical bowls, and the majority of questionable sherds were body fragments that could have come from this type.

Before conducting spatial analysis of the diagnostic ceramic materials, it is important to understand the general relationship between raw sherd counts, relative sherd size, and the distribution of diagnostic materials across the data set. In general, areas with relatively high surface sherd counts tend to yield more diagnostic materials and skew the analyses. Similarly, areas with notably higher sherd size tend to yield more diagnostic materials, simply because larger pieces are easier to characterize. With this in mind, several control aspects were recorded for individual collection circles in the spreadsheet. These included the total number of sherds per circle, the number of diagnostic sherds per circle, the percentage of diagnostic sherds per circle, and the total volume of ceramics per circle. The following discussion is an assessment of these characteristics across the data set.

Because it proved impractical to measure every sherd to determine its size, relative fragment size was approximated through the use of volume density measurements. The volume density was calculated by dividing the total number of ceramic fragments per circle by the total volume of sherds per circle. Volume density relates to estimated sherd size in an inverse manner: the lower the volume density, the greater the relative size of the sherds. An alternative means of estimating relative sherd size would be to measure the overall weight of the materials per circle, where sherd size is estimated by dividing the total number of ceramic fragments by the overall weight. I chose volume density over weight density because I believe it to more accurately portray sherd size. This method was also far less time consuming.

Both methods carry limitations, the most obvious being that thicker sherds will, in general, be heavier and result in more volume than thinner sherds with similar surface areas. Weight density measurements also skew the results in favor of ceramics that are more densely constructed, whereas volume density measurements do not. For example, sherds made of more porous material will generally weigh less than sherds of similar size made of compact material.

The relative volumes of the ceramics in each circle were measured using standardized storage bags (1-gallon Ziploc bags). Converting to the metric system, a full bag of this size would then contain 3.875 liters. After the analysis and count of the ceramics were complete, the bags were carefully filled and counted. Bags were recorded as 1/4, 1/3, 1/2, 2/3, 3/4, or completely full. This set of six rough-and-ready categories provided a rapid way of estimating volume densities, and assessing the relative size of fragments among circles.

Table 5.1 shows the measured volumes in liters, the total sherd counts, volume densities, percentage of diagnostic sherds, and diagnostic sherd counts for a few selected collection circles, as well as the ranges and mean values of these measurements for all the collection circles. The first three circles displayed in the table had different volumes and sherd counts but were similar in volume density, suggesting that they contained sherds of roughly equal sizes. The last two circles listed in the table had nearly equal sherd counts, but their density numbers reveal a distinct difference in the size of the sherds.

When we turn to the last two columns in the table—the percentage of diagnostic sherds and the number of diagnostic sherds—we can observe a relationship between them; large differences in volume density generally reflect similar differences in the percentage and absolute number of diagnostic sherds. We also see that small differences in volume density have little or no effect on the number or percent of diagnostic sherds. This trend can be observed throughout the data set, where scatter plots of volume density yield negative Pearson's r correlation coefficients of -0.29 vs. number of diagnostics and -0.5 vs. percent of diagnostics.

Table 5.1. Volume measurements and frequency counts for selected collection circles.

Circle ID	# Bags	Volume	Count	Vol. Density	% Diagn.	# Diagn.
NE4N10E3	3	11.36	345	30.38	44.35%	153.00
NE6N3E2	3.25	12.30	335	27.23	39.40%	132.00
NE6N2E2	2	7.57	218	28.80	38.07%	83.00
NE10N12E2	0.75	2.84	249	87.71	16.87%	42.00
NE7N1E1	3	11.36	250	22.02	29.60%	74.00
minimum	0.25	0.94625	7	7.40	4.11%	1
maximum	7.5	28.39	920	188.11	71.43%	279
mean	1.28	4.86	221.16	52.19	22.50%	49.66

To further understand the effects of relative sherd size within my data set, it helps to understand the relationship between sherd volume and sherd count. Figure 5.1 demonstrates a strong positive correlation ($r = 0.85$) between total sherd count and volume of sherds per circle. Thus, I did not expect relative sherd size to be a limiting factor in my study of the spatial distribution of diagnostics.

When we plot the frequency counts of diagnostic sherds per circle against the frequency counts of total sherds per circle (Fig. 5.2) we see a relatively high positive correlation ($r = 0.80$), which further supports the notion that sherd size is not a major limiting factor in the density distribution of diagnostic materials in this data set. Instead, the raw frequency count of ceramics appears to be a stronger indicator than relative sherd size for the number of diagnostics collected in any given circle. As noted above, there is little correlation between volume density and diagnostic sherd count. When we plot total sherd volume against the number of diagnostic sherds (Fig. 5.3), we get an even greater positive correlation ($r = 0.90$). This suggests that sherd volume incorporates both the small effect of relative sherd size and the larger effect of overall sherd count.

The analysis above seems to verify our intuition: the number of diagnostic sherds found in a given circle increases with the total number or volume of materials collected. Therefore, before drawing conclusions about the distribution of any specific diagnostic, it is important to look at the spatial distributions of both total sherd count and volume measurements for the circles.

For both quantitative and qualitative spatial analysis of the Cerro Danush surface collection, I employed surface density plots. These plots show the surface density in sherd count or sherd volume per square meter for each of the collection circles. Since the surface area of each circle was standardized (50.26 m^2), surface densities are directly proportional to the sherd count frequencies. The mean surface density of sherds per circle was 4.41 sherds per square meter, with a range between 0.14 sherds/m^2 and 18.40 sherds/m^2. On the surface density plots presented here, this variation in surface density is depicted using the relative darkness of the circles, with specific numbers provided in the keys.

Figures 5.4 and 5.5 present surface density plots based on total sherd counts and total volume, respectively, for the circles on Cerro Danush. The plots reveal similar patterns, with localized areas of high and low surface densities. Although the plots reveal striking variation among individual circles (including circles located on the same terrace), fewer

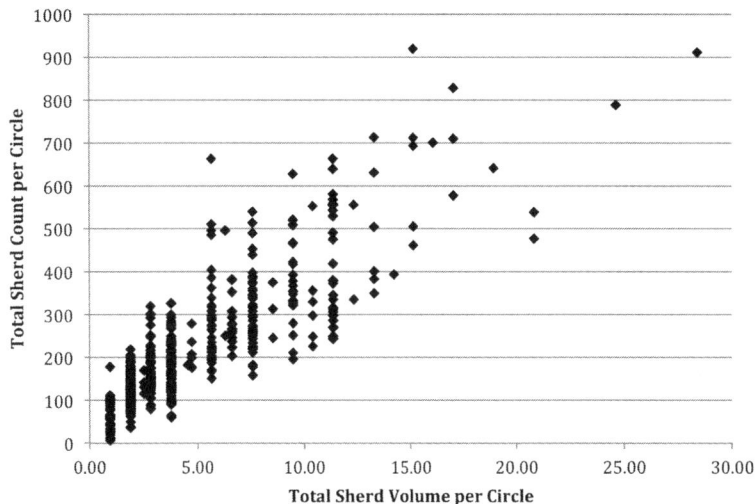
Figure 5.1. Scatter plot of sherd counts vs. sherd volume ($r = 0.85$).

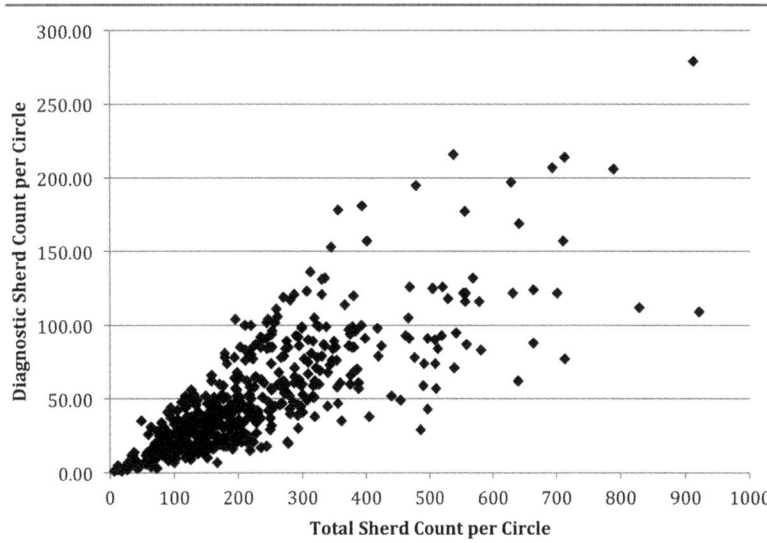
Figure 5.2. Scatter plot of total diagnostic sherd counts vs. total sherd counts ($r = 0.80$).

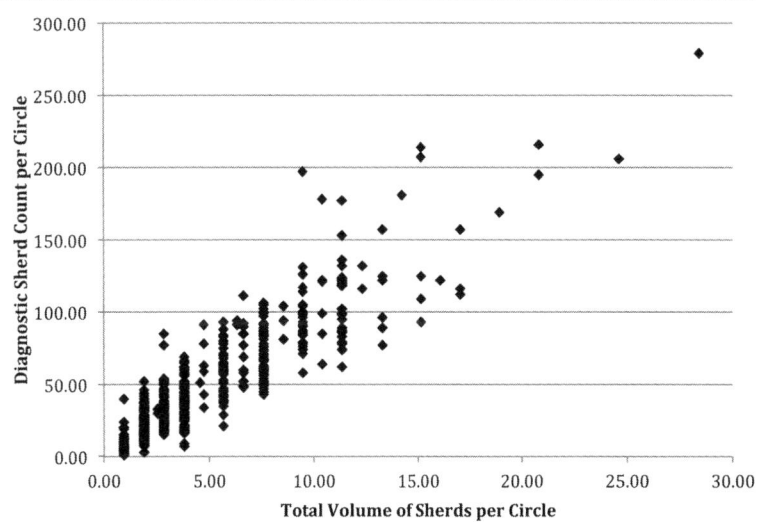
Figure 5.3. Total diagnostic sherd counts vs. total volume ($r = 0.90$).

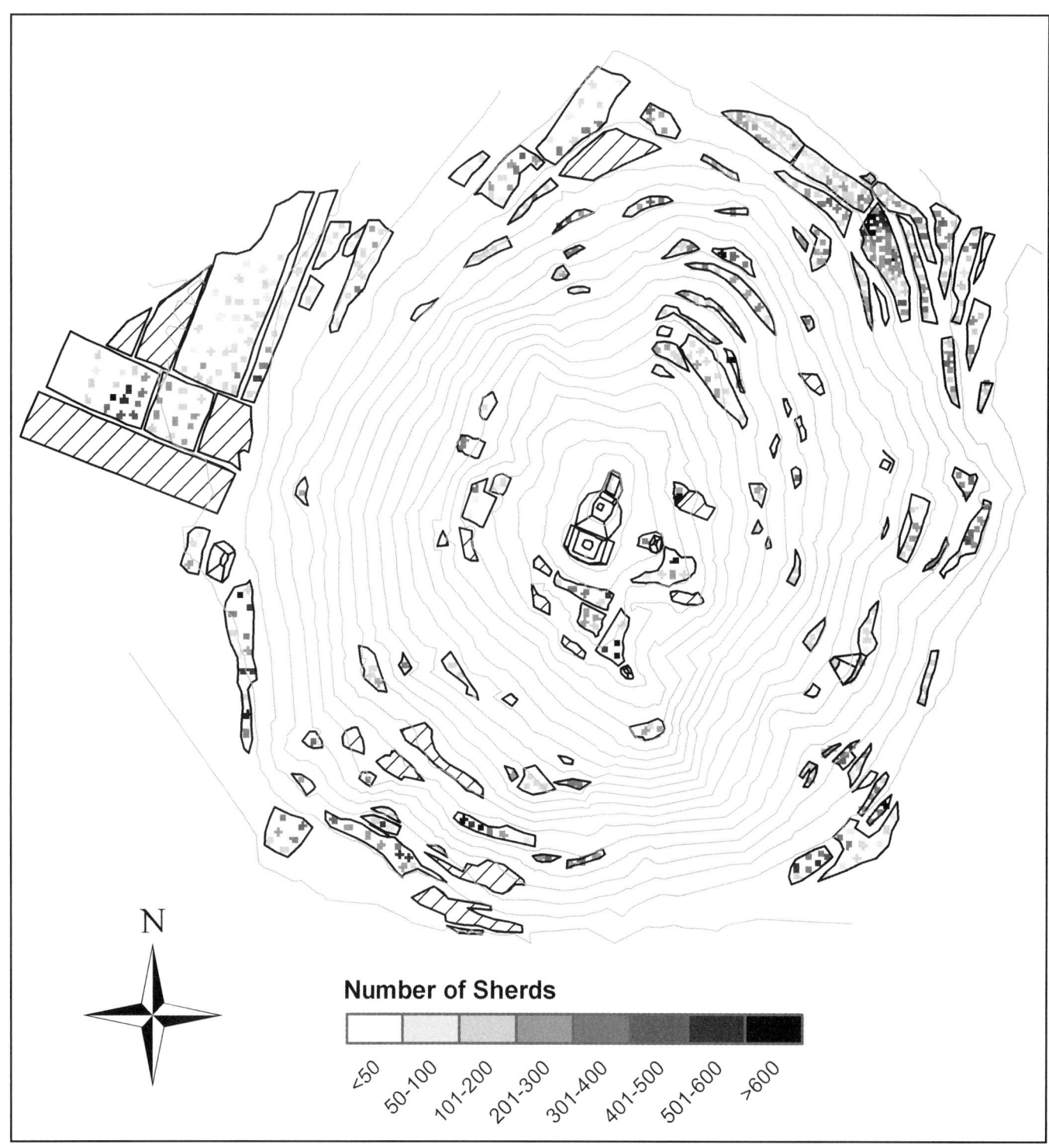

Figure 5.4. Distribution of total ceramic sherd counts per collection circle.

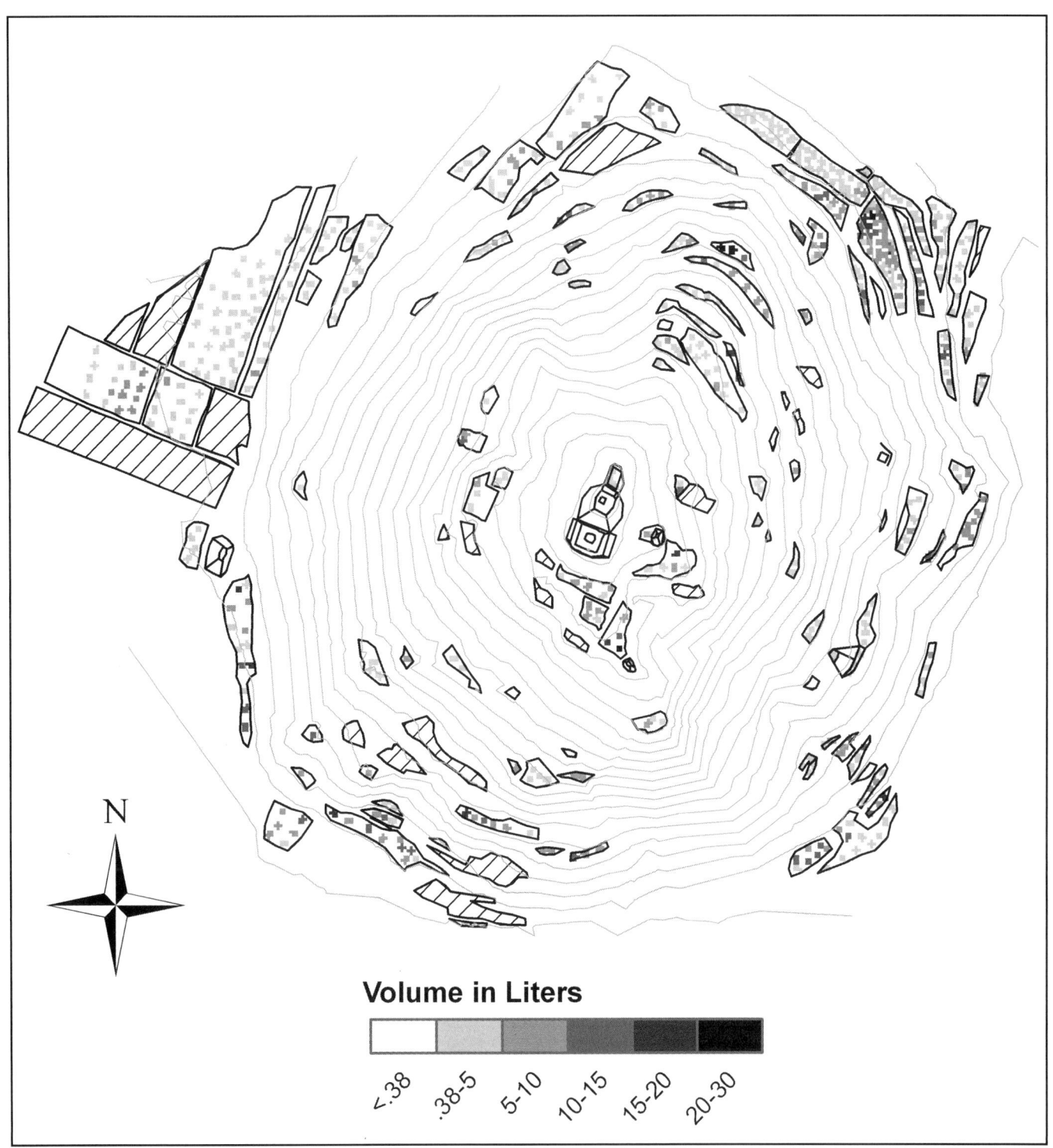

Figure 5.5. Distribution of total volume of ceramics per collection circle.

differences appear when terraces from different areas of the hill are compared. It is therefore possible that the terrace provides a better unit of analysis than does the collection circle.

As Figure 5.1 suggests, surface density plots for sherd count and sherd volume are generally in good agreement. Several of the circles in the West Group, however, show high surface density with respect to sherd count and low surface density with respect to sherd volume. This is especially true of Terrace O9. The surface distribution of diagnostic materials in the West Group (Fig. 5.6) appears to follow more closely the distribution of sherd volume. This pattern recalls the strong correlation between sherd volume and diagnostics found in Figures 5.2 and 5.3. It appears, therefore, that the West Group is the only area of Cerro Danush where sherd size was sufficiently small to affect the number of diagnostics.

Having discussed the relationships among sherd volume, sherd size, sherd count, and number of diagnostics, let us now look at those terraces that may yield misleading results owing to their extremely low densities of surface ceramics. The most obvious candidates are Terraces C13 and C14 of the Summit Terrace Group and Terraces S1–S7 of the Southern Group, which yielded extremely small amounts of diagnostic materials (Fig. 5.6). Significantly, these terraces all occur in similar physical environments. All are located at intermediate elevations on some of the steepest slopes of Cerro Danush, making access to them difficult. Also, all contained significantly more vegetation than did the other terraces I collected. These terraces were collected, in spite of the difficulty, so that some data could be recorded from them. The low amount of surface material found on them, however, demonstrates that these terraces are more useful for qualitative, rather than quantitative, analyses.

Other terraces exhibiting lower than average surface concentrations are O5 and O6 in the Western Group, NC11 in the North-Central Group, and E4 in the Eastern Group. The surfaces of these terraces had diagnostic sherd densities of fewer than 2 sherds per square meter (100 sherds per circle). For Terraces O5, O6, and NC11, I have two reasons to believe that their spatial analysis will nevertheless yield meaningful results: (1) they have sufficiently large surface areas so that despite their low surface concentrations, the overall count of diagnostic materials is comparable to other terraces; and (2) they lie in close proximity to potentially related terraces with high concentrations of diagnostic materials. These conditions do not apply in the case of Terrace E4, however, limiting its usefulness in our analysis.

Fortunately, every terrace group includes terraces with at least moderately high amounts of diagnostic surface materials. Once outlier terraces are removed from the analysis, both the individual terraces and the larger terrace groups serve as good units for my quantitative spatial analysis. While the individual collection circles are probably less useful than entire terraces, both appear to be useful in determining relationships among diagnostic materials. Principal components analysis (PCA) is the statistic I chose to identify relationships among individual diagnostics across the data set.

Quantitative Assessment of the Chipped Stone Data Set

A total of 1301 chipped stone items were recovered from 374 of the collection circles on the terraces of Cerro Danush. The majority of these items (947 pieces, or 72.79%) were of chert; 183 (14.07%) were of silicified volcanic tuff; and 171 (13.14%) were obsidian. The mean surface density of chipped stone materials was 0.069 pieces/m^2, with a range between 0.020 pieces/m^2 and 0.358 pieces/m^2.

A total of 234 (17.99%) chipped stone items were considered diagnostic and separated from the debitage. The relationship between diagnostic and non-diagnostic materials in the chipped stone assemblage, however, is different from that of the ceramic assemblage. All of the sherds found in my sample are fragments of larger vessels. It follows, therefore, that the more sherds one finds, the more diagnostic sherds will be present. The same is not true for chipped stone since the debitage consists not of fragments of larger items, but of tool production byproducts. The relationship between diagnostic and non-diagnostic materials is thus less predictable than that for sherds, a notion supported by the low Pearson's r relationship (0.43) found between the total chipped stone and the diagnostics (Fig. 5.7).

Furthermore, materials within the chipped stone assemblage are less susceptible to damage than is the case with sherds. I therefore determined that an analysis of size distribution would not be necessary, since relative size in the sample did not limit analysis in the same way that it did for sherds. As an example, consider the fact that a large, spent core made from volcanic tuff is no more diagnostic than a small prismatic obsidian blade fragment, despite the great differences in weight and volume between such items.

One possible means of assessing the chipped stone data set is through comparison to the sherd data set. The scatter plot of the total distribution of chipped stone materials vs. the total distribution of sherds (Fig. 5.8) shows little correlation between the two ($r = 0.53$). One reason is that no chipped stone at all was found in 166 of the 540 collection circles. Removing these circles from the analysis did not, however, improve the correlation between the two, which remained at $r = 0.50$. Comparing the density distribution of total ceramics (Fig. 5.4) and total chipped stone (Fig. 5.9) underscores this poor correlation.

The most obvious differences between the two surface density plots occur within the Summit and North-Central Terrace Groups, where areas with high concentrations of sherds do not have comparable densities of chipped stone. A similar pattern was found on the terraces of El Palmillo (Feinman et al. 2006; Haines, Feinman, and Nicholas 2004), where the majority of artifacts associated with chipped stone production were found on the lower terraces of the hill. It is possible, therefore, that a genuine ancient behavioral pattern was involved. It also appears that the chipped stone data set, like the sherd data set, works best when terraces or terrace groups—rather than the individual collection circles—are used as the units of analysis.

Density Distribution Analyses of Surface Artifacts

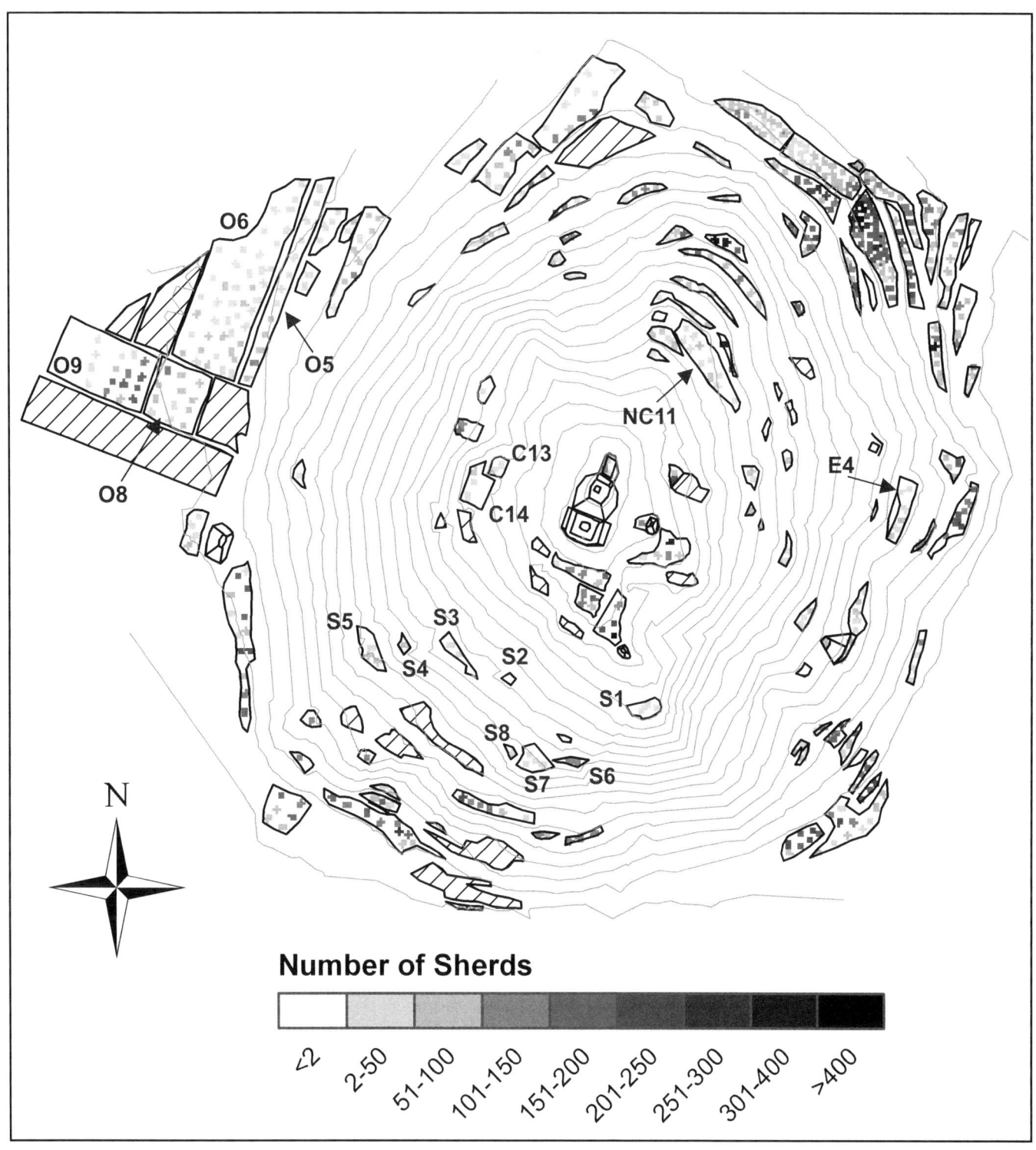

Figure 5.6. Distribution of diagnostic ceramics (sherd counts per circle).

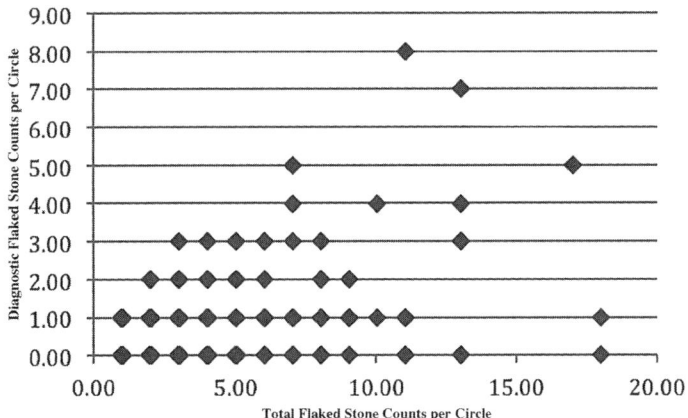

Figure 5.7. Diagnostic chipped stone vs. total chipped stone ($r = 0.43$).

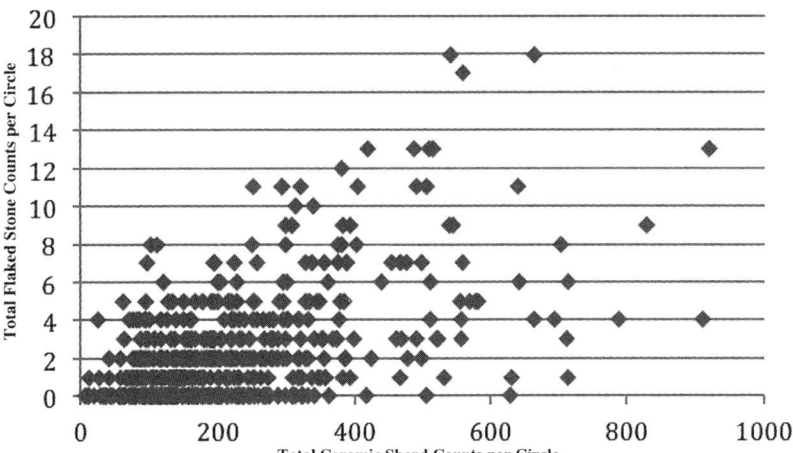

Figure 5.8. Total chipped stone counts vs. total ceramic counts ($r = 0.53$).

Surface Distribution Patterns

In this section I use density plots to identify temporal and spatial patterns within the surface distribution of diagnostic materials. To take into account the uneven distributions of the total diagnostics collected (Figs. 5.6, 5.9), most data are row or case standardized; that is, the surface densities of individual diagnostic items are presented on the plots as percentages of the total diagnostic materials per collection circle. In the case of certain diagnostic materials, found in very low quantities, I use raw counts and rely on qualitative assessments. Table 5.2 contains numeric data for the percentage distributions of the more important ceramic indicators discussed in this section.

Typologically, the artifact assemblage from the surface of Cerro Danush closely resembles the materials found on the surface of other Classic period terraced hilltop sites in the Valley of Oaxaca, such as Monte Albán (Blanton 1978), Jalieza (Finsten 1995), and El Palmillo (Feinman and Nicholas 2004a, 2004b). Subsequent excavations at all sites uncovered residential complexes on the terraces (Feinman, Nicholas, and Haines 2002; González Licón 2003; Winter 1974). I therefore had reason to expect that the majority of the terraces on Cerro Danush supported residential units, and bore this in mind during the initial stage of surface remains analysis.

Throughout the prehistory of the Valley of Oaxaca, food preparation and storage were common activities within households. That was true of Late Classic residences such as those excavated at Monte Albán by González Licón (2003). I was confident, therefore, that the common indicators of food preparation and storage could be used to identify domestic terraces on Cerro Danush.

Because of their relative abundance within the ceramic assemblage, I chose simple ollas and cántaros as residential indicators. Their surface density plots (Figs. 5.10, 5.11) show that fragments of these vessels were found in significant amounts on nearly all terraces. In addition, nearly 80% of the ground stone collected—which includes manos, metates, tejolotes, and molcajetes—could be considered diagnostic of food preparation. While our sample of ground stone is too small to allow further analysis based on frequency counts or percentages, the general distribution of the four categories mentioned above (Fig. 5.12) indicates widespread use in all areas of Cerro Danush. These data support the likelihood that the majority of terraces were used for domestic purposes.

One area where simple olla and cántaro fragments were found in relatively low percentages is the Summit Terrace Group. The terraces of this group likely supported high-status residences and may have been the focus of civic and ceremonial activities. It may be significant that large storage and food preparation vessels such as *ollas barriles* (Fig. 5.13; Table 5.2) and *apaxtles* (Fig. 5.14; Table 5.2) make up a greater portion of the assemblage from the Summit Group (particularly on Terrace C12) than was the case with most of the other terrace groups. The presence of these larger vessels suggests that the meals prepared included food for the kind of extra-familial individuals typically associated with high-status settings, including participants in community rituals, high-status visitors, and even a staff of servants.

Feinman, Nicholas, and Maher (2008) also found higher percentages of large serving bowls in their high-status residences at El Palmillo, which they attribute to feasting and drinking rituals. It is also possible, of course, that the higher percentages of apaxtles on Terraces C14, NC11, and C12

Density Distribution Analyses of Surface Artifacts 57

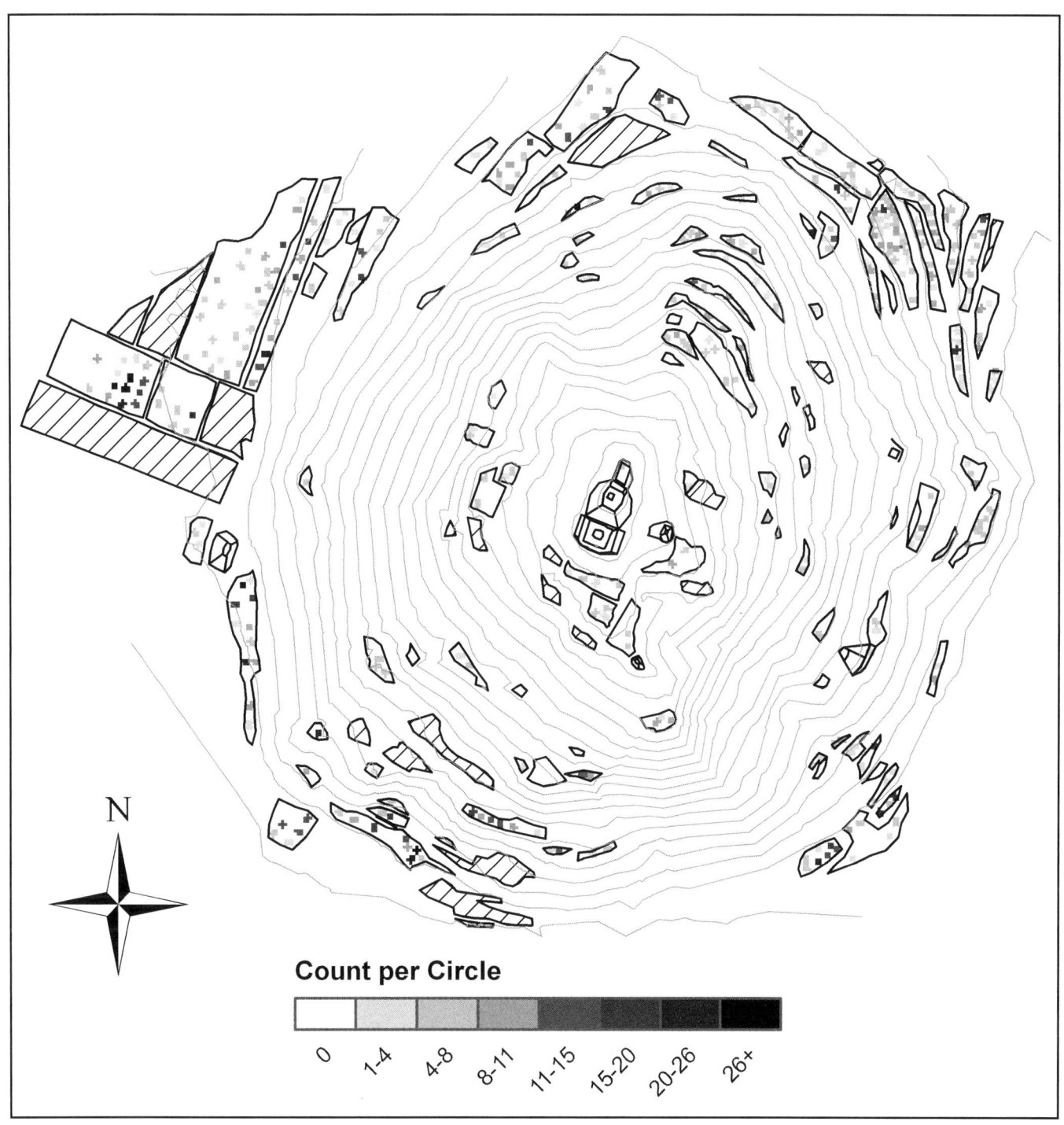

Figure 5.9. Density plot of chipped stone counts per collection circle.

Table 5.2. Distributions of ceramic materials collected per individual terrace.

Terrace	Temporal										Other		
	Paste			G35[b]	K14[b]	Dainzu[b]	G3M[b]	Sahumador[b]		G23[c]	Figurines[b]	Ollas Barriles[b]	Apaxtles[b]
	gray[a]	brown[a]	orange[a]					hollow	solid				
C2	42.08	56.83	1.09	17.59	13.89	0.93	4.63	2.78	42.59	0.00	1.85	0.00	0.93
C4	80.05	19.71	0.24	66.67	17.39	0.00	1.45	0.00	0.00	0.00	0.00	0.00	0.00
C5	77.19	20.03	2.79	54.10	13.11	2.30	2.30	0.66	0.66	1.00	0.00	0.98	0.66
C6	75.13	23.09	1.79	54.03	19.13	2.01	2.68	0.67	0.00	0.00	0.34	0.00	0.34
C8	72.61	22.50	4.89	48.54	17.57	4.60	2.51	0.84	0.42	0.00	1.26	0.00	0.84
C12	86.12	10.58	3.29	65.05	6.41	0.97	0.39	0.19	0.19	0.00	0.19	0.97	2.91
C13	84.29	15.18	0.52	60.00	4.00	0.00	0.00	0.00	0.00	0.00	0.00	4.00	4.00
C14	78.32	16.77	4.91	65.28	11.11	1.39	0.00	0.00	0.00	0.00	0.00	2.78	4.17
C18	72.55	24.86	2.58	52.83	14.47	1.89	0.63	0.00	0.63	0.00	0.63	0.00	2.52
NE1	83.89	15.98	0.13	58.96	7.00	0.42	5.60	0.42	0.42	0.00	0.70	0.14	0.00
NE2	83.26	16.44	0.29	60.32	11.94	0.12	1.62	0.75	0.25	0.00	1.24	0.00	0.12
NE3	81.96	17.53	0.52	57.14	14.29	0.95	0.95	1.90	0.95	0.00	0.95	0.00	0.00
NE4	85.32	14.24	0.45	58.65	9.25	0.34	1.26	0.71	0.29	1.00	1.34	0.26	0.37
NE5	82.75	16.84	0.41	56.73	11.42	0.12	0.72	0.72	0.24	0.00	1.32	0.24	0.12
NE6	84.49	15.14	0.38	54.46	9.90	0.40	1.19	1.19	0.00	0.00	1.58	0.59	0.79
NE7	85.23	14.43	0.34	56.07	11.21	0.47	0.00	1.40	0.00	0.00	0.00	0.47	1.87
NE8	89.13	10.48	0.40	55.66	5.54	0.23	0.46	2.08	0.00	0.00	0.69	0.23	0.23
NE10	81.76	17.75	0.48	66.61	10.75	0.00	0.48	0.00	0.96	0.00	1.28	0.00	0.32
NE11	88.38	11.24	0.38	62.98	6.43	0.13	1.93	0.51	0.26	0.00	0.13	0.39	0.51
NE12	79.23	20.45	0.32	54.68	8.99	0.19	8.99	1.15	0.76	0.00	1.34	0.19	0.00
NE13	82.08	16.87	1.05	65.52	7.21	0.94	0.63	0.63	0.31	0.00	2.51	0.00	0.94
NE14	80.13	19.13	0.73	59.28	7.69	0.68	0.90	0.23	0.45	0.00	1.36	0.00	0.23
NE16	79.73	19.98	0.29	47.41	12.75	0.00	5.98	0.40	1.20	0.00	2.39	0.80	0.40
NC11	75.32	19.50	5.18	47.48	6.30	5.46	0.00	1.68	0.00	2.00	2.52	0.00	2.94
NC12	79.61	15.46	4.93	50.74	7.35	5.15	1.47	2.21	0.00	0.00	2.94	0.00	0.74
NC14	82.24	16.61	1.15	60.85	8.53	1.55	2.71	0.39	0.00	0.00	0.78	0.00	0.78
NC15	78.05	18.56	3.39	47.74	10.32	3.87	3.87	1.94	0.00	0.00	0.65	0.00	0.00
NC16	86.73	11.53	1.74	56.98	6.27	1.42	0.00	1.71	0.28	2.00	2.28	0.00	0.57
NC17	89.84	9.71	0.45	62.28	5.44	0.53	1.23	1.23	0.00	1.00	0.70	0.18	0.70
NC18	83.46	14.80	1.73	53.33	8.67	2.67	1.33	0.67	0.00	0.00	1.33	0.00	1.33
NC19	81.26	15.86	2.88	51.89	8.49	4.72	0.94	0.94	0.00	0.00	0.00	0.00	0.00
N1	79.52	17.14	3.33	42.86	7.14	7.14	3.57	3.57	0.00	0.00	0.00	0.00	7.14
N2	71.86	23.19	4.94	42.11	17.11	7.89	3.95	0.00	0.00	0.00	1.32	0.00	0.00
N3	76.28	20.97	2.76	44.93	7.97	4.35	2.17	2.17	0.00	0.00	2.17	0.72	1.45
N4	87.38	12.30	0.32	49.02	9.80	1.96	0.00	1.96	0.00	0.00	3.92	3.92	0.00
N5	80.39	18.39	1.23	48.91	13.04	4.35	2.72	1.63	0.54	0.00	4.35	0.00	0.54
N6	77.43	21.83	0.74	45.99	8.56	2.14	5.88	2.14	0.53	0.00	1.07	0.00	0.00
N7	81.08	18.12	0.79	50.77	6.92	2.31	1.54	1.54	0.00	0.00	0.77	0.00	3.08
N8	78.02	19.46	2.52	51.55	18.56	3.09	0.00	0.00	0.00	0.00	3.09	0.00	0.00
N11	72.26	26.94	0.80	42.07	11.72	3.45	1.38	2.07	0.00	0.00	3.45	0.00	0.69
N12	70.08	29.44	0.47	39.94	10.06	0.30	10.06	2.74	1.83	0.00	3.96	0.91	1.22
N13	75.34	23.77	0.89	47.16	11.94	1.49	0.00	0.60	0.90	1.00	2.09	0.30	0.90
N15	78.16	20.69	1.15	44.44	0.00	0.00	13.89	0.00	0.00	0.00	0.00	2.78	0.00

Table 5.2 continued.

Terrace	Temporal										Other		
	Paste			G35[b]	K14[b]	Dainzu[b]	G3M[b]	Sahumador[b]		G23[c]	Figurines[b]	Ollas Barriles[b]	Apaxtles[b]
	gray[a]	brown[a]	orange[a]					hollow	solid				
E1	77.92	21.61	0.47	55.37	8.68	0.41	1.24	0.00	0.00	0.00	2.07	0.00	0.00
E2	78.41	21.22	0.37	54.15	15.92	0.35	1.38	0.52	0.52	0.00	0.69	0.17	0.69
E3	80.35	19.50	0.15	57.95	10.80	0.00	1.14	1.70	0.00	0.00	2.27	0.00	1.70
E4	75.74	23.24	1.02	60.96	9.59	1.37	1.37	0.00	0.00	0.00	2.05	0.00	0.68
E5	72.65	26.38	0.97	47.20	12.00	2.40	4.00	0.00	0.00	0.00	0.80	1.60	0.00
E6	68.56	30.57	0.87	42.37	9.32	0.00	0.85	0.00	4.24	0.00	0.85	0.85	0.85
E7	68.84	27.76	3.40	51.52	19.70	3.03	0.00	0.00	0.00	0.00	4.55	0.00	0.00
E8	66.41	31.30	2.29	45.45	15.15	0.00	6.06	0.00	6.06	0.00	6.06	0.00	0.00
E9	64.48	34.36	1.16	29.21	15.73	0.00	4.49	0.00	21.35	0.00	0.00	0.00	0.00
E11	75.94	23.26	0.80	61.18	8.24	0.00	4.71	1.18	0.00	0.00	2.35	0.00	0.00
E12	74.01	25.53	0.46	55.18	11.89	0.61	3.05	0.61	0.91	1.00	0.61	0.00	0.00
E13	79.06	20.35	0.59	51.90	8.86	1.27	5.06	0.63	0.63	0.00	2.53	0.00	1.27
E15	76.70	22.47	0.84	51.63	10.70	1.40	0.93	0.47	1.86	0.00	0.93	0.00	0.47
E16	79.34	19.20	1.46	49.66	8.22	2.40	0.00	0.34	1.03	0.00	2.74	0.00	0.68
E17	83.22	15.37	1.41	48.82	6.21	1.28	3.85	0.64	1.28	0.00	1.28	0.00	1.50
E18	83.81	15.19	1.00	51.99	6.20	0.89	1.62	0.44	0.44	4.00	1.92	0.00	1.18
E19	81.04	16.62	2.34	39.34	9.84	3.28	1.64	0.00	0.00	0.00	8.20	0.00	0.00
E20	78.40	19.51	2.09	47.27	9.09	0.00	1.82	0.00	0.00	0.00	5.45	0.00	3.64
O1	77.42	19.73	2.85	51.49	8.63	2.38	0.00	0.00	0.30	2.00	3.87	0.00	0.89
O2	77.07	18.05	4.89	45.76	3.39	1.69	0.00	0.00	0.00	0.00	3.39	0.00	3.39
O4	87.18	9.62	3.21	61.54	7.69	0.00	0.00	0.00	0.00	0.00	0.00	0.00	0.00
O5	87.01	10.67	2.32	61.30	6.51	1.37	0.34	0.68	0.00	0.00	1.03	0.00	0.00
O6	86.13	12.06	1.81	60.81	5.85	1.08	1.55	0.36	0.00	0.00	1.79	0.00	1.08
O8	82.24	17.11	0.65	53.50	8.88	0.47	0.23	0.00	0.00	0.00	2.10	0.00	0.23
O9	83.46	16.31	0.23	50.77	6.17	0.59	3.91	0.24	0.36	0.00	4.03	0.00	0.71
SO1	77.99	16.38	5.63	39.88	9.07	4.42	3.49	1.98	0.12	8.00	3.14	0.00	1.40
SO2	79.38	17.70	2.92	43.48	7.25	2.90	1.45	0.00	1.45	0.00	5.80	0.00	0.00
S5	56.69	33.52	9.79	25.97	20.78	19.48	0.00	0.00	0.00	0.00	4.00	1.00	0.00
S12	68.99	28.23	2.78	37.31	13.99	3.37	0.52	2.07	1.55	0.00	0.78	0.52	1.81
S13	68.70	29.70	1.61	48.86	12.50	1.14	0.00	1.14	1.14	0.00	2.27	0.00	3.41
S14	70.70	27.02	2.28	51.66	10.43	0.47	0.00	1.42	0.47	0.00	0.95	0.47	2.37
S15	73.06	24.90	2.04	43.24	14.86	5.41	0.00	0.00	2.70	0.00	0.00	0.00	1.35
S16	83.77	15.58	0.65	68.66	2.99	1.49	0.00	0.00	0.00	0.00	0.00	0.00	2.99
S17	82.94	15.72	1.34	53.33	11.67	1.67	0.00	0.00	0.00	0.00	5.00	0.00	1.67
S18	72.75	25.37	1.88	50.74	12.17	1.78	0.89	1.34	1.04	0.00	1.48	0.59	0.89
S19	64.24	33.42	2.34	49.08	12.88	3.07	3.07	0.61	0.61	0.00	0.61	0.00	0.61
S20	72.61	26.11	1.27	41.38	3.45	6.90	0.00	3.45	0.00	0.00	0.00	0.00	0.00
S25	80.32	18.96	0.72	47.00	10.70	0.78	0.00	1.31	0.78	1.00	1.57	0.26	2.35

[a]Percentage of paste color fragments in total assemblage
[b]Percentage of individual ceramic category in the diagnostic assemblage
[c]Raw frequency count

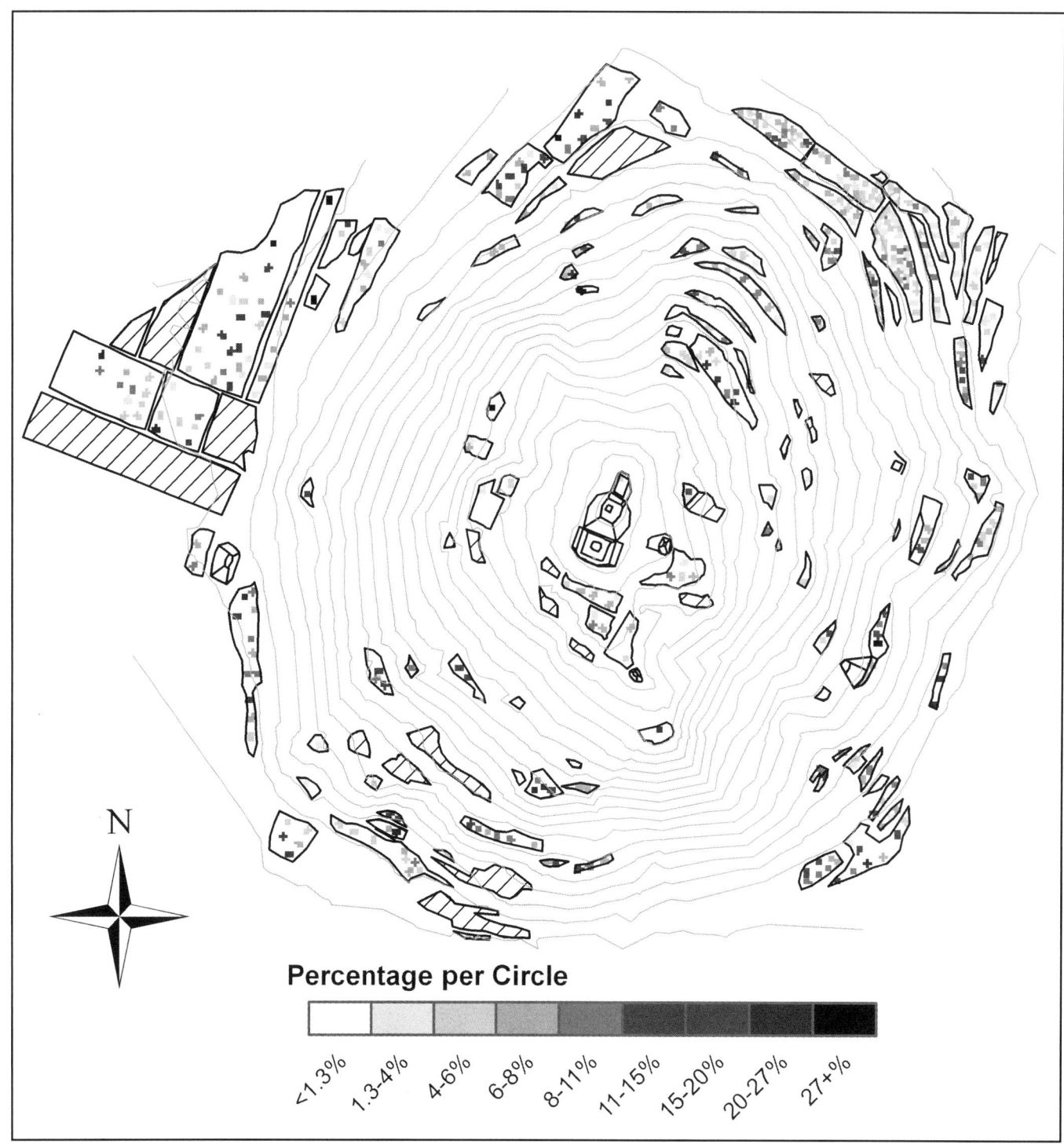

Figure 5.10. Density plot of simple olla fragments.

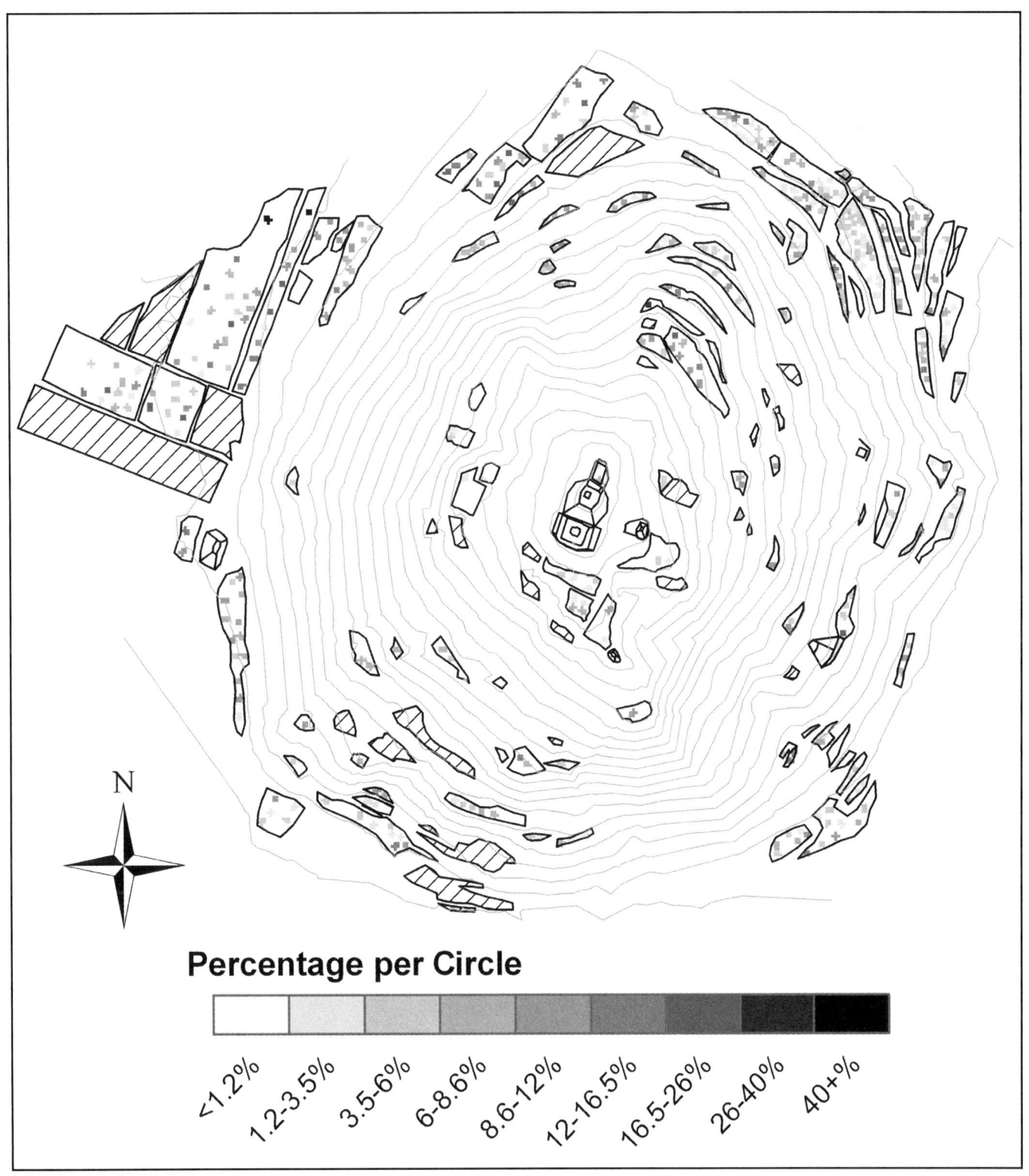

Figure 5.11. Density plot of cántaro fragments.

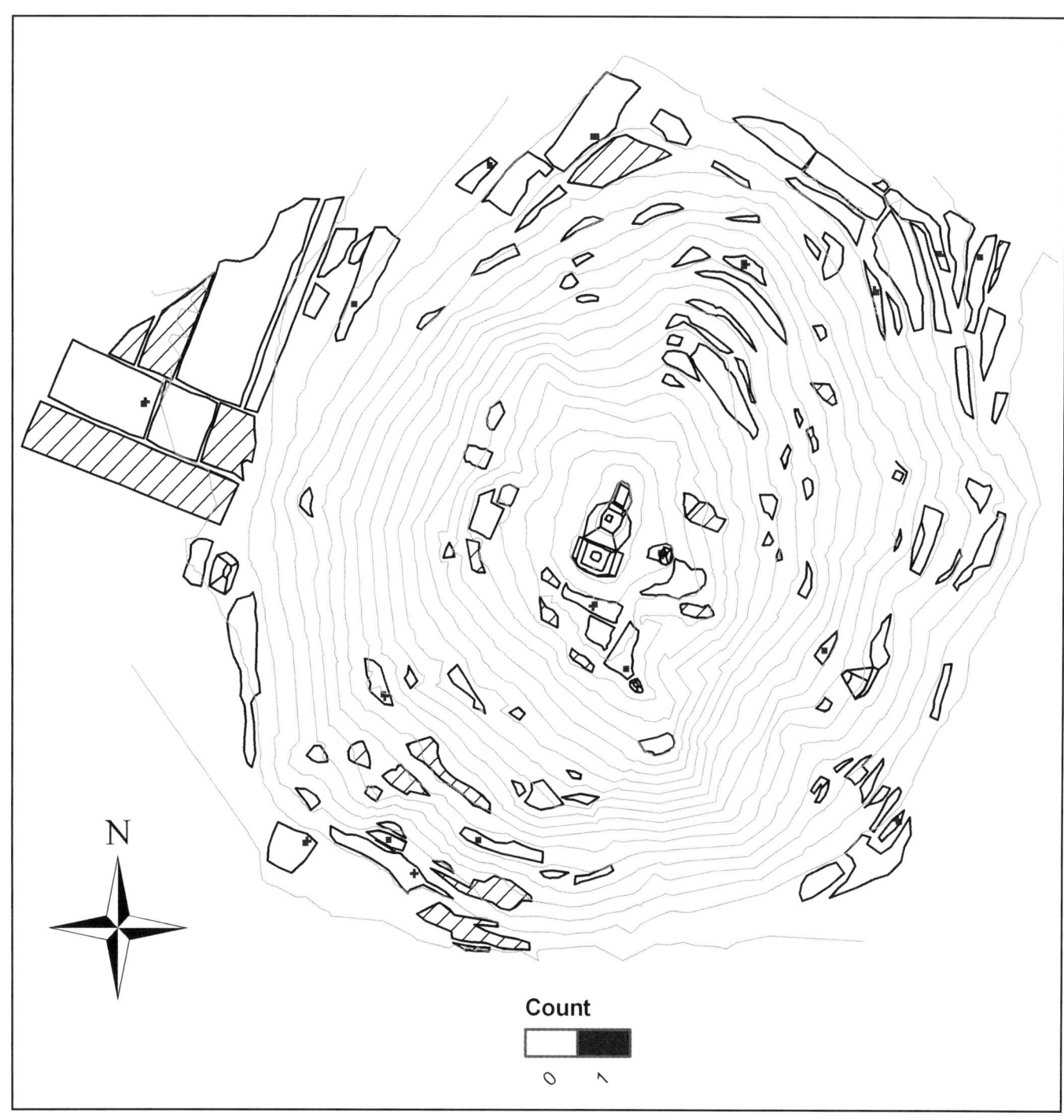

Figure 5.12. Locations of manos, metates, molcajetes, and tejolotes.

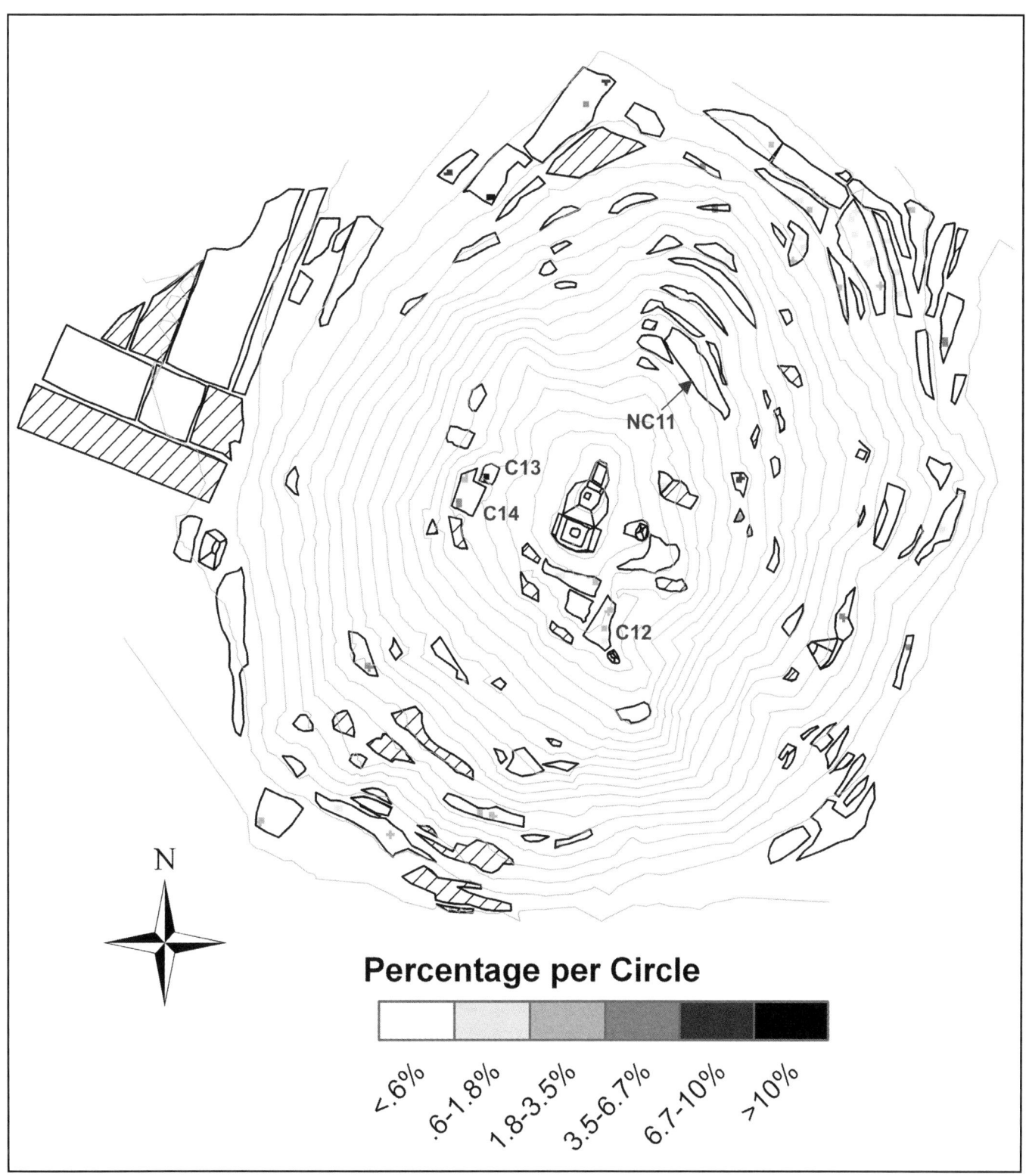

Figure 5.13. Distribution of ollas barriles.

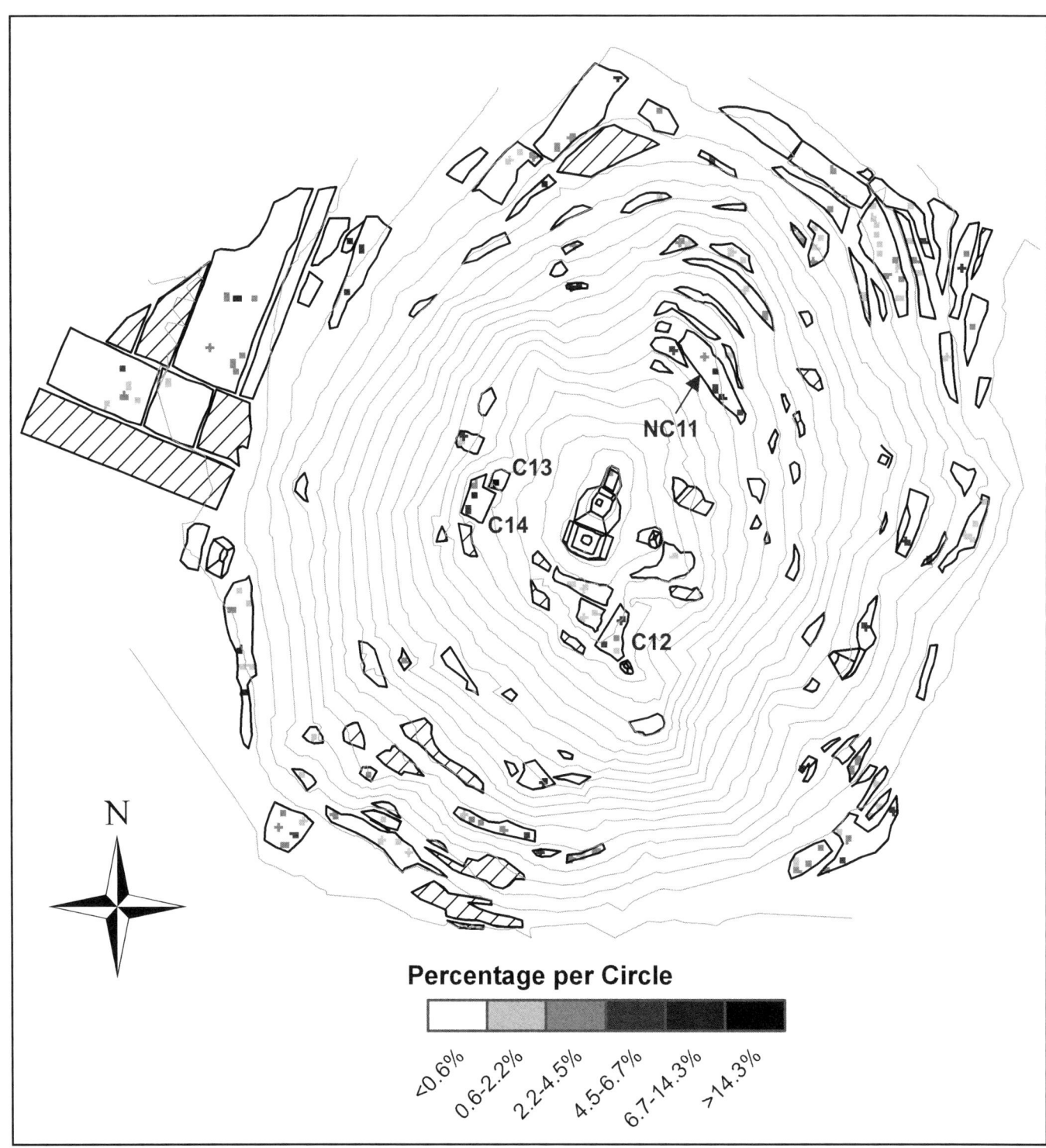

Figure 5.14. Distribution of apaxtles.

at Cerro Danush reflect increased storage needs, based on their distances above the valley floor.

Two terraces exhibiting relatively high concentrations of both apaxtles and ollas barriles are C13 and C14, situated on top of a high cliff just below and to the west of the temple-patio-altar complex on the summit of Cerro Danush. These vessels were the most abundant diagnostic materials recovered from these terraces (other than the ubiquitous Classic period conical bowls). One collection circle in this area, C13N1E1, in fact, yielded only 2 diagnostic sherds—one an apaxtle fragment and the other an olla barril fragment. The presence of these items, combined with the lack of other diagnostic materials, may mean that Terraces C13 and C14 (and although not collected, C15) served as a storage area for the Summit Terrace Group, although the extremely low quantities of ceramics recovered from these terraces make it difficult to be certain.

The location of these three terraces makes them very difficult to reach from any place other than the summit. Their restricted access could have been used strategically, to limit access to the materials stored on the terraces to high-status individuals and/or the ceremonial buildings of the summit.

Domestic Production and Craft Specialization

Previous studies in Oaxaca, and Mesoamerica in general, have established the household as an important unit of economic production and craft specialization (Charlton, Charlton, and Nichols 1993; Feinman 1999; Feinman and Nicholas 2000; Hirth 2009a; Santley and Hirth 1993). Several items in the assemblage from Cerro Danush are considered to be indicative of production; included are spindle whorls, ceramic molds and kiln wasters, and chipped stone cores and debitage. The excavation of several domestic terraces at El Palmillo revealed a pattern of use of similar items that researchers have linked to differential social organization among households of varying statuses (Carpenter, Feinman, and Nicholas 2012; Feinman et al. 2002, 2006; Haines, Feinman, and Nicholas 2004). In this section, I consider the surface distribution of items associated with production at Cerro Danush and compare them to the data from El Palmillo and other terraced hilltop sites in the valley (Blanton 1978; Finsten 1995).

If one excludes kiln wasters, the production diagnostics at Cerro Danush, taken as a group, follow a general pattern with respect to their surface distributions. They are more abundant (and relatively evenly spread) among the low-lying terraces, and hardly present at all on the terraces of the Summit Terrace Group. This pattern suggests that small-scale production of textiles and chipped stone tools occurred largely in lower-status households, and was not limited to one specific area of terraces.

Kiln wasters were found in small percentages in every terrace group (Fig. 5.15), superficially suggesting that some ceramic production took place within households at all levels. Many of the "wasters" recovered during the project, however, were simply fragments of G35 bowls with cracks or bubbles; some imperfect versions of these vessels may have been used despite their flaws (Appendix B). In other words, the low level of craftsmanship of some G35s makes it hard to decide whether one is dealing with a true waster (and hence a locus of ceramic production).

A total of 21 objects were identified as spindle whorls. This number is probably too small to allow for any strong conclusions based on the presence or absence of whorls on individual terraces. Spindle whorls, for example, were the only diagnostics recovered during the excavation of Terrace S19 that had not been found when the terrace was surface-collected. That being said, the overall surface distribution of whorls (Fig. 5.16) follows the general pattern for other artifacts: they were found on the surface of every terrace group except for the Summit. While this fact does not rule out the possibility that some textile production took place in residences of the Summit Terrace Group, it does suggest that lower-status households participated in this activity to a greater degree than did higher-status households.

Finsten (1995:64) found little evidence for textile production at Jalieza, but spindle whorls formed a significant part of the assemblage at El Palmillo (Carpenter, Feinman, and Nicholas 2012). Haines, Feinman, and Nicholas (2004:260) report that the larger whorls used for processing maguey fiber were more abundant at El Palmillo (especially on the lower terraces), while the smaller whorls used for spinning cotton were found in greater quantities in high-status residences. El Palmillo also produced significant quantities of chert raspadores, which studies suggest were for extracting fiber from maguey leaves (Hester and Heizer 1972). Raspadores also form a significant portion of the assemblage from other sites located in the eastern Tlacolula Valley (Haines, Feinman, and Nicholas 2004), where conditions are drier and maguey is more commonly grown.

In contrast, the majority of spindle whorls identified during both surface collection and excavation on Cerro Danush appear to fit within the size ranges used for finer threads. Larger whorls and raspadores (Fig. 5.17) were indeed recovered at Cerro Danush, but the small quantities involved (6 raspadores total) suggest that maguey fiber processing was less common than at sites in the eastern Tlacolula Valley.

As was the case at El Palmillo (Haines, Feinman, and Nicholas 2004:257) and Jalieza (Finsten 1995:62), chert debitage was by far the most abundant chipped stone collected on Cerro Danush (66% of the total assemblage). The surface distribution of this material (Fig. 5.18) reflects that of El Palmillo (Haines, Feinman, and Nicholas 2004:259) and conforms to the general pattern for other items: there were high concentrations on nearly all the lower terraces, but very little found on the Summit Terrace Group (although 1 spent chert core was recovered from that group [Fig. 5.19]). This distribution presumably reflects a higher degree of production activity on lower-status terraces.

The chert flakes from Cerro Danush are considered to be expedient tools, similar to those found at Jalieza (Finsten 1995:64) and El Palmillo (Haines, Feinman, and Nicholas 2004:257). Interestingly, these were the only chipped stone items found in higher concentrations in the Summit Terrace Group than anywhere else (Fig. 5.20). The distribution of chert flakes, as well as chert debitage and cores,

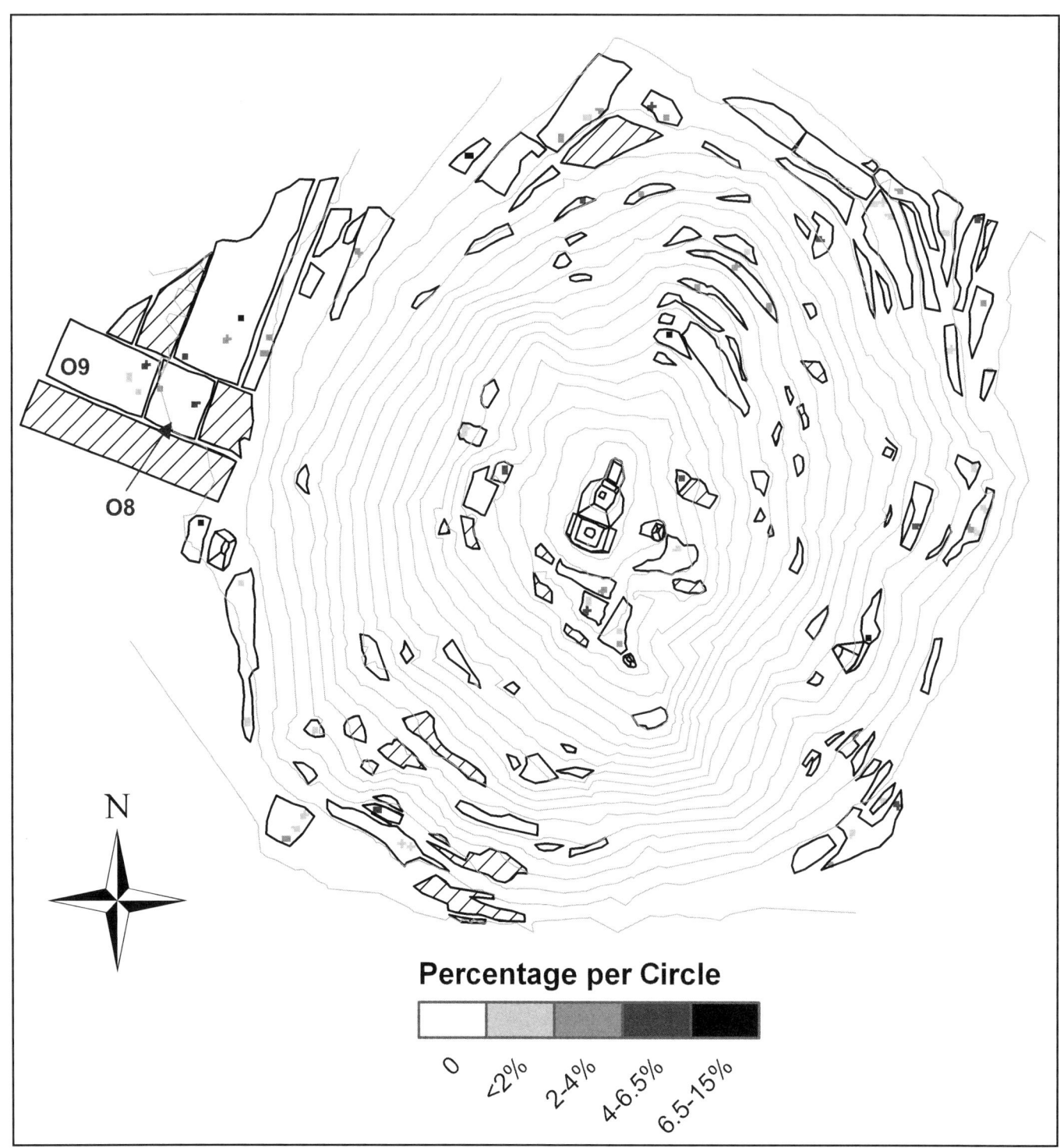

Figure 5.15. Distribution of ceramic kiln waster fragments.

Density Distribution Analyses of Surface Artifacts

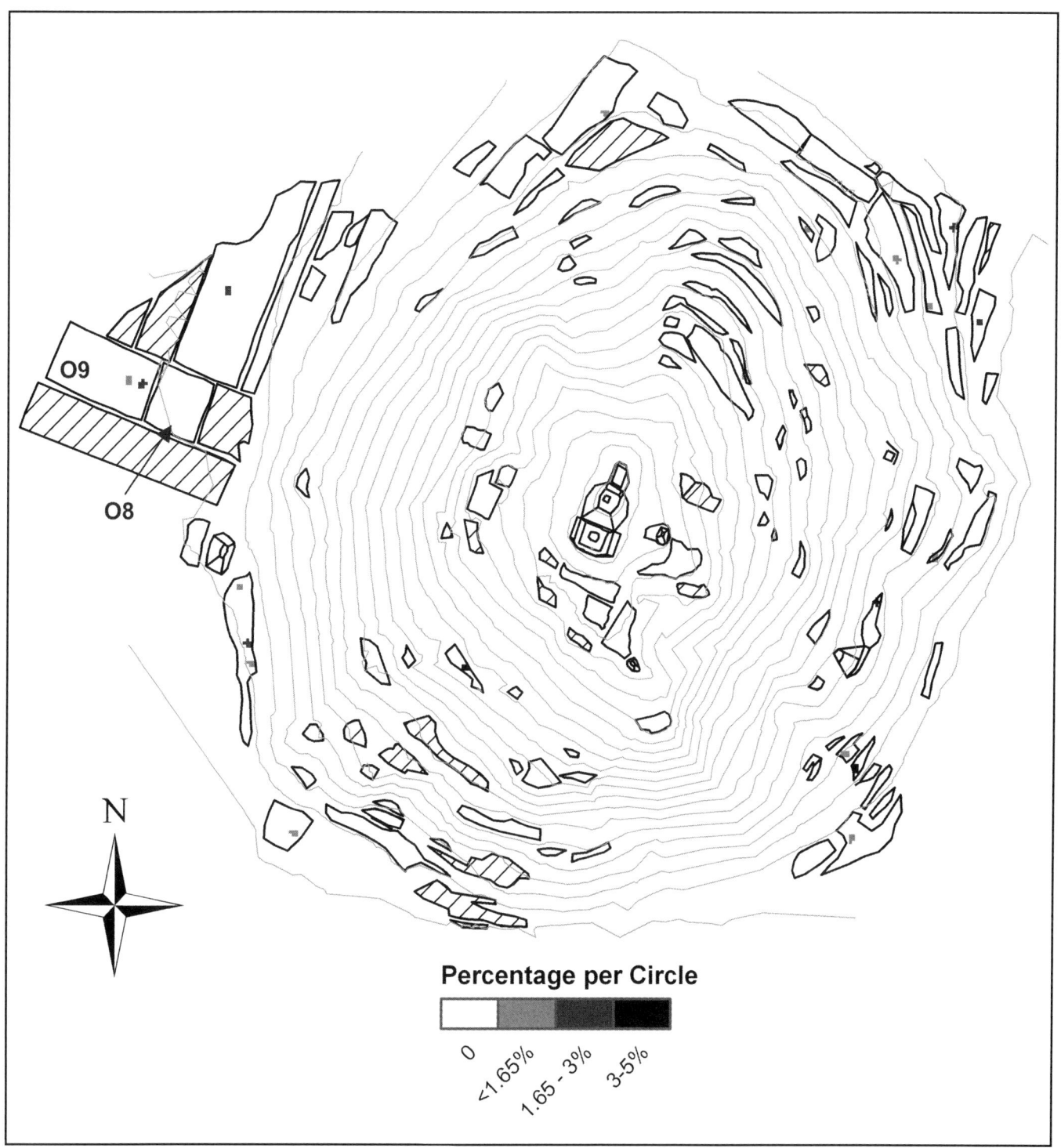

Figure 5.16. Distribution of ceramic spindle whorl fragments.

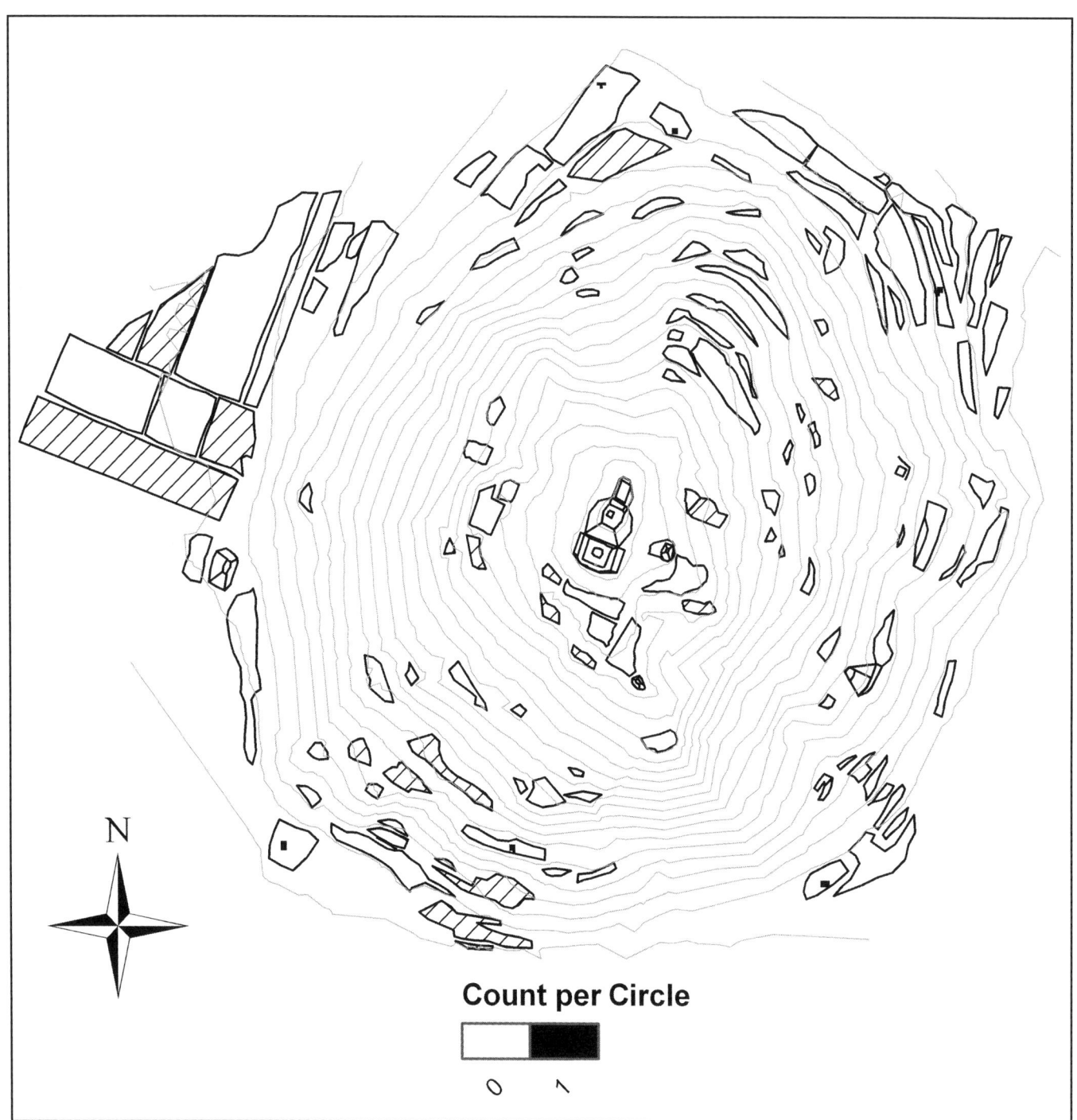

Figure 5.17. Distribution of raspadores.

Figure 5.18. Distribution of chert debitage.

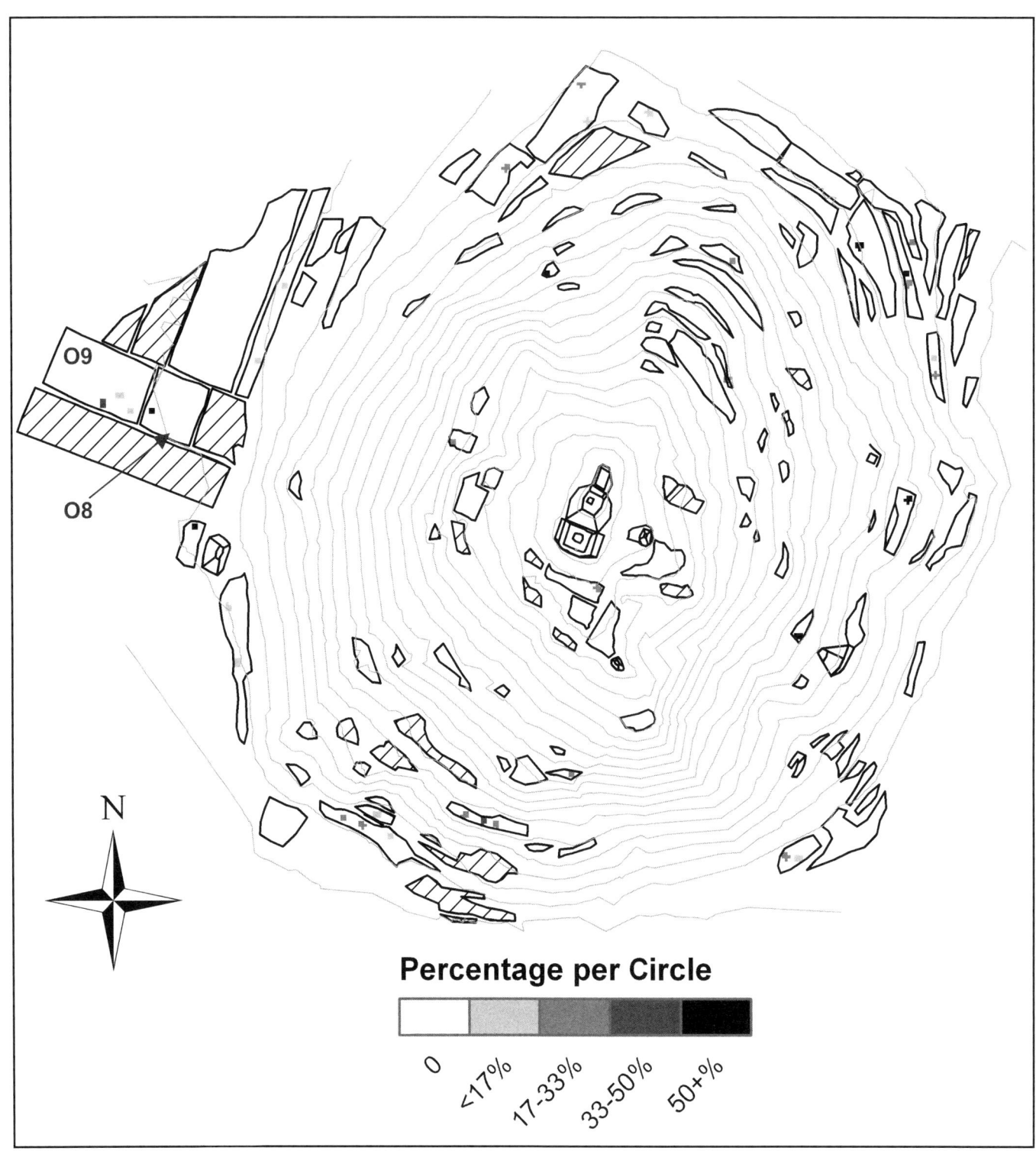

Figure 5.19. Distribution of spent chert cores.

Density Distribution Analyses of Surface Artifacts 71

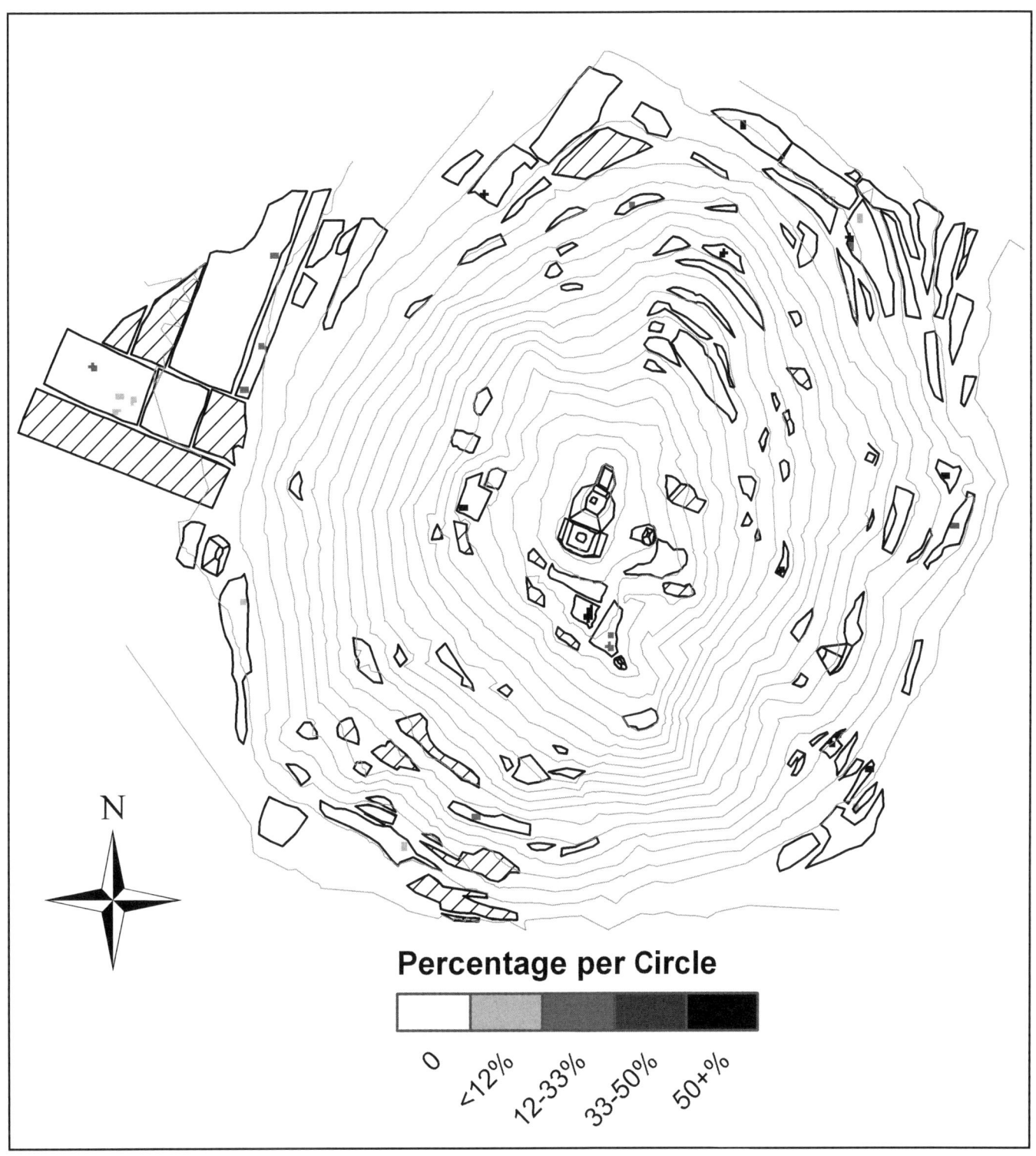

Figure 5.20. Distribution of chert flakes (expedient tools).

is similar to that found at El Palmillo. There, Haines, Feinman, and Nicholas (2004:259–60) concluded that chipped stone production within the higher-status households consisted mostly of retouching and creating their own expedient tools, while "the residents of the lower terraces appear to have been more intensely involved in the manufacture of formal tools (and possibly preforms and cores) that were intended for house-to-house exchange."

Follow-up excavation holds out the possibility of adding strength to the above conclusion. For example, if the chert debitage found on the lower-status terraces was the byproduct of formal tool production, one might expect to find partially completed tools that were broken and discarded during the process. Such was the case during the excavation of Terrace S19 at Cerro Danush, where a relatively high number of chert points were recovered. Many of these points were poorly formed or broken, suggesting that formal tool production was indeed one of the activities taking place there (Appendix B).

With the possible exceptions of Terraces O8 and O9 (see below), the surface distribution of production materials on the terraces of Cerro Danush did not indicate any specific areas where large-scale production might have taken place. This is consistent with what has been found at Monte Albán (Blanton 1978) and Jalieza (Finsten 1995).

Kowalewski et al. (1989:294) did identify several possible Late Classic–Early Postclassic ceramic, chert, ground stone, and obsidian production contexts within the greater site of Dainzú-Macuilxóchitl during their settlement pattern survey. These possible areas of production were found on the valley floor to the south of Cerro Danush, near two plaza-and-mound groups on either side of the Río Grande tributary (Fig. 2.7). In general, Kowalewski et al. (1989:296) noted "the tendency for work areas for several commodities, and public buildings, to coincide" at the site. The surface collection data appear to support this conclusion.

The large terraces at the base of Cerro Danush's West and Southwest Terrace Groups flank one of the aforementioned plaza-and-mound groups (Fig. 2.7, Structures 47–49). In fact, Terrace SO2 of Cerro Danush could be considered an elevated plaza between Structures 48 and 49 of that mound group (Fig. 4.14). Significantly, many of the production materials listed above (kiln wasters, chert cores, spindle whorls, and chert debitage) were found in relatively high concentrations in this area of Cerro Danush, particularly on Terraces O8 and O9 (Figs. 5.15, 5.16, 5.18, 5.19). This fact supports Kowalewski et al.'s claim, and I can add that the distribution of two other materials may indicate that these terraces were also the center of a particular kind of craft specialization, involving mold-made figurines.

On Cerro Danush, mold-made anthropomorphic ceramic figurines were collected from the surface of nearly every terrace (Fig. 5.21), but they were found in higher concentrations in the North and West Terrace Groups. In the area where Terraces O9 and O8 meet, mold-made figurines made up significant percentages of the materials from every collection circle. In addition to this, 3 of the 5 figurine molds that were recovered during the project were also found in this area (Fig. 5.22), while the other 2 were found on the Southeast Terrace Group. These data suggest that in addition to the textile and stone tool production common to all the terrace groups, the households of the West Terrace Group carried out specialized production of mold-made figurines.

To be sure, some mold-made figurine production could have been for inter-household exchange. Figurines are not typical utilitarian items, however, and at least some of the figurines produced in this area may have served another purpose. Relatively high percentages of figurines were collected from the plaza between Structures 48 and 49 (Terrace SO2), and many more were visible on the surface within the plaza/mound group beyond the limits of my collection area. These data suggest that figurines may have played an important part in rituals associated with this plaza/mound group.

Domestic Ritual and Status Differentiation

In addition to the mold-made figurines discussed above, other items associated with ritual were recovered from the terraces of Cerro Danush. Several of these items are commonly found in Classic period tombs; included are ceramic urns, botellones, anthropomorphic whistles, and hollow-handled sahumadores (Caso and Bernal 1952; Caso, Bernal, and Acosta 1967).

Winter (2002) has proposed three house types at Monte Albán based on their relative size and corresponding tomb size during the Classic period. In Type 1 houses, with simple burials and small tombs, burial offerings were limited to G35 bowls and occasional hollow-handled sahumadores. In Type 2 houses, which had medium-sized tombs, there were higher numbers of ceramic offerings, including sahumadores and botellones. In the highest status houses, Type 3, the large tombs also included urns and whistles. Winter also pointed out that throughout the Valley of Oaxaca, the highest status Classic tombs tend to have carved stone lintels and doorjambs, like the tomb recovered within the Summit Complex on Cerro Danush.

Armed with this knowledge, I looked at the distribution of these items to see if the status levels of houses on different terraces could be inferred from their surface remains. For example, I would not have been surprised to find urns concentrated in the Summit Terrace Group, and hollow-handled sahumadores more evenly distributed. Figures 5.23–5.26 show the distribution patterns for urns, botellones, silbatos, and hollow-handled sahumadores respectively, and unfortunately, these items all appear to be pretty evenly distributed across the terraces. In fact, the terrace group with the lowest concentration of fragments from these diagnostics was the Summit Group, which I knew to contain a high-status residence with a large tomb.

Unfortunately, therefore, little can be said about the status differentiation of households on Cerro Danush from these data alone. The spatial distributions do, however, demonstrate an important aspect of my data set: Late Classic diagnostics can be found in significant quantities throughout the terrace groups on Cerro Danush. In contrast, Early Classic and Early Postclassic indicators were less evenly distributed. This point is clearly

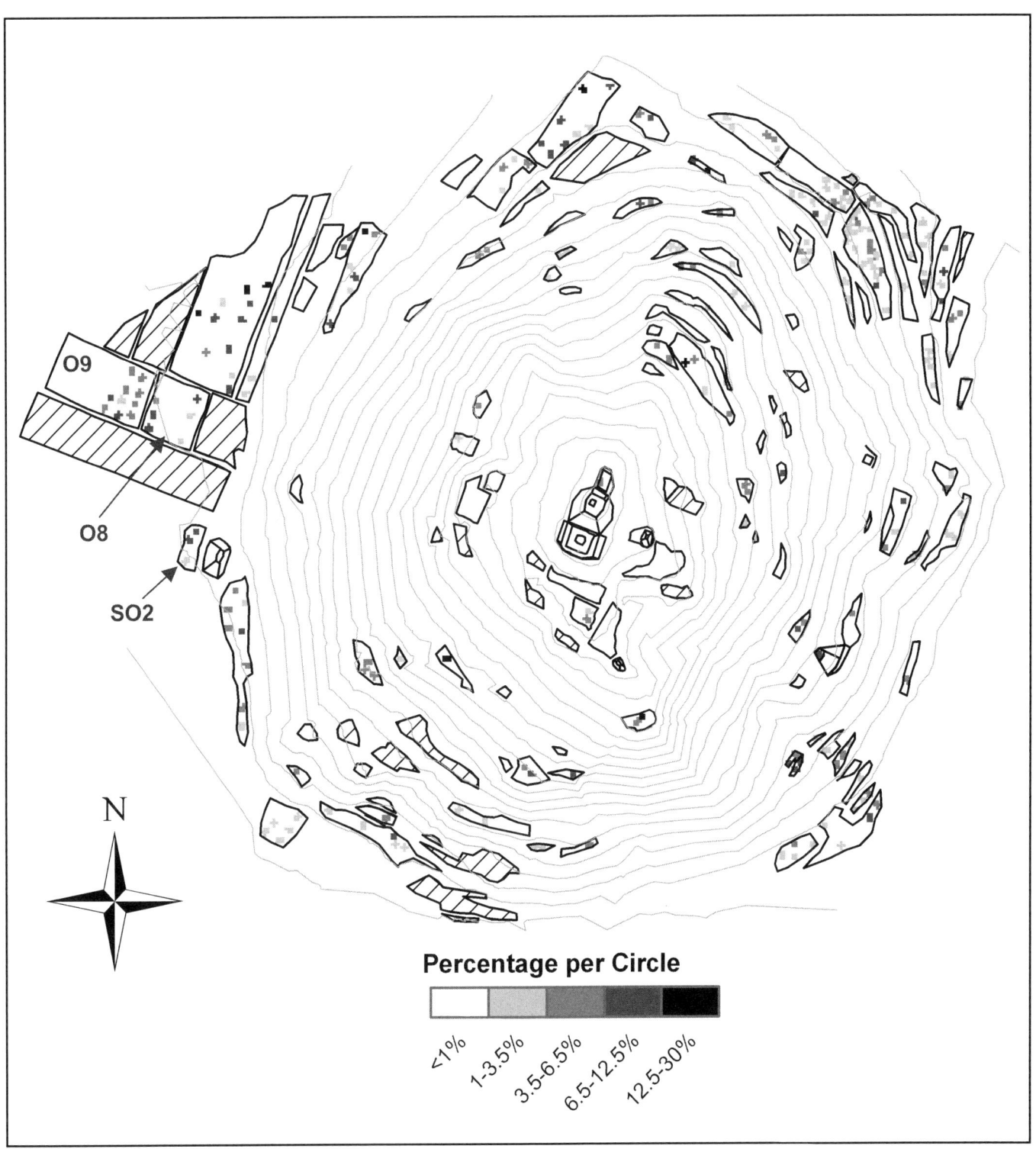

Figure 5.21. Distribution of mold-made figurines.

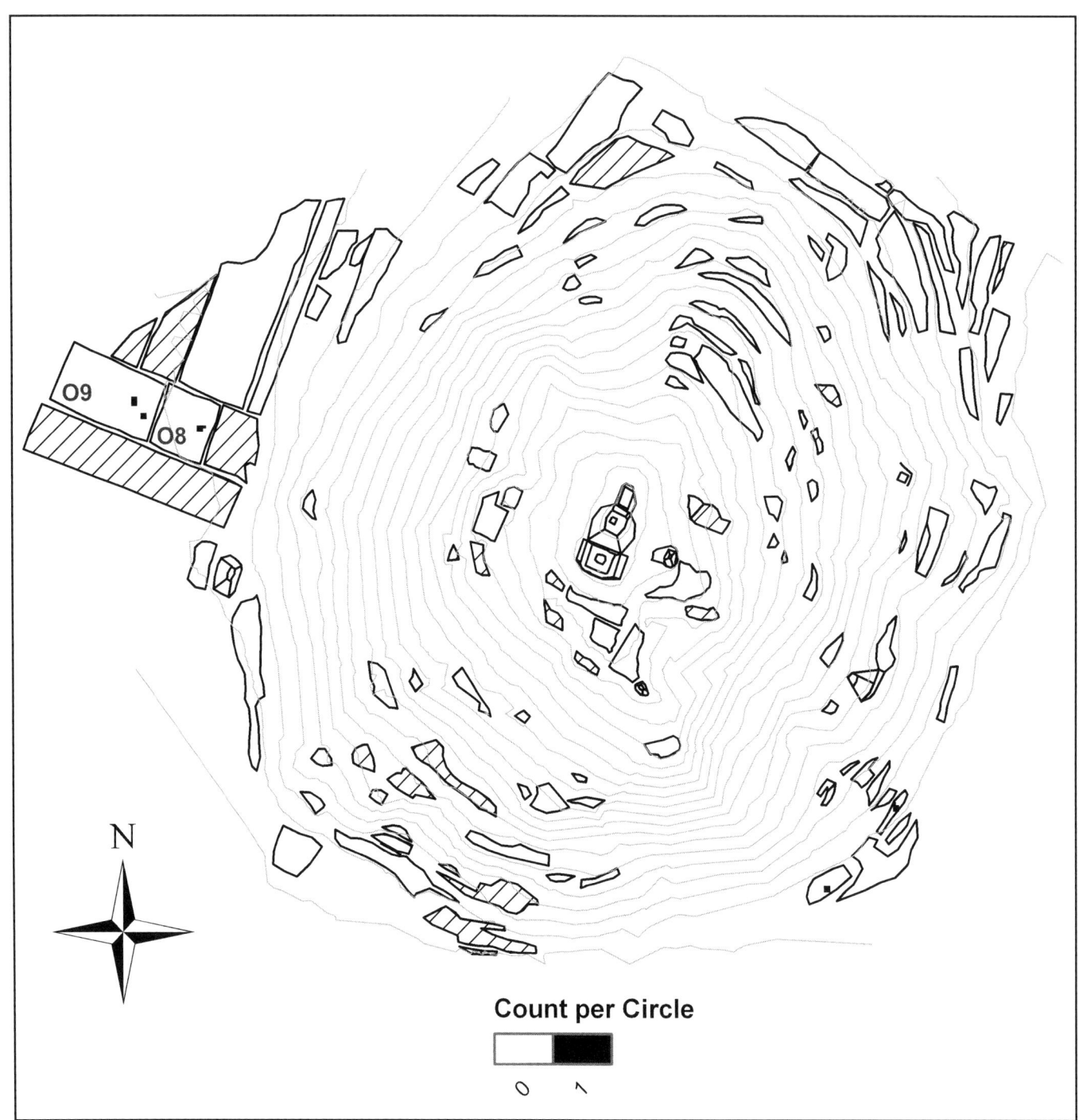

Figure 5.22. Distribution of mold fragments for urns or figurines.

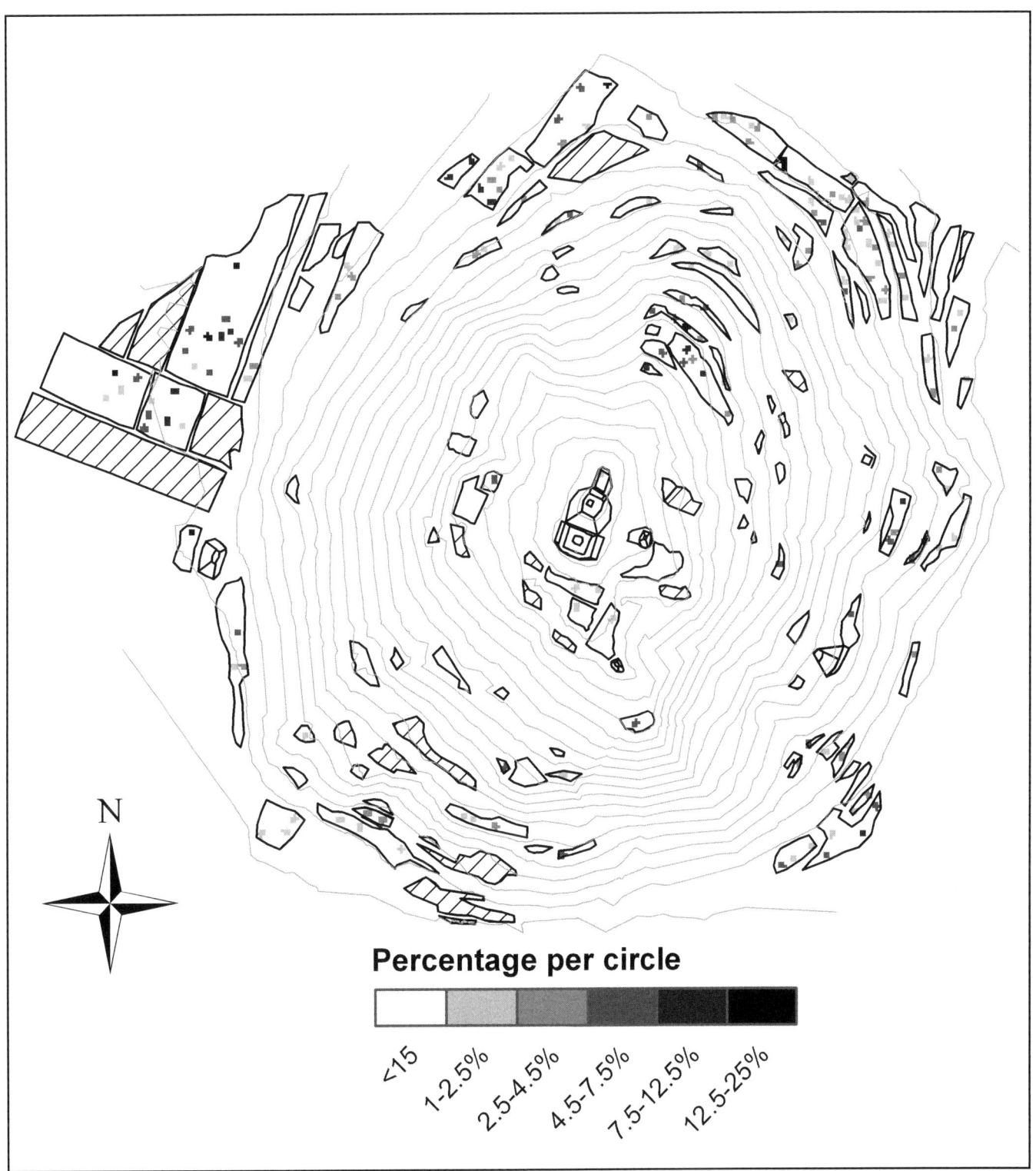

Figure 5.23. Distribution of urn fragments.

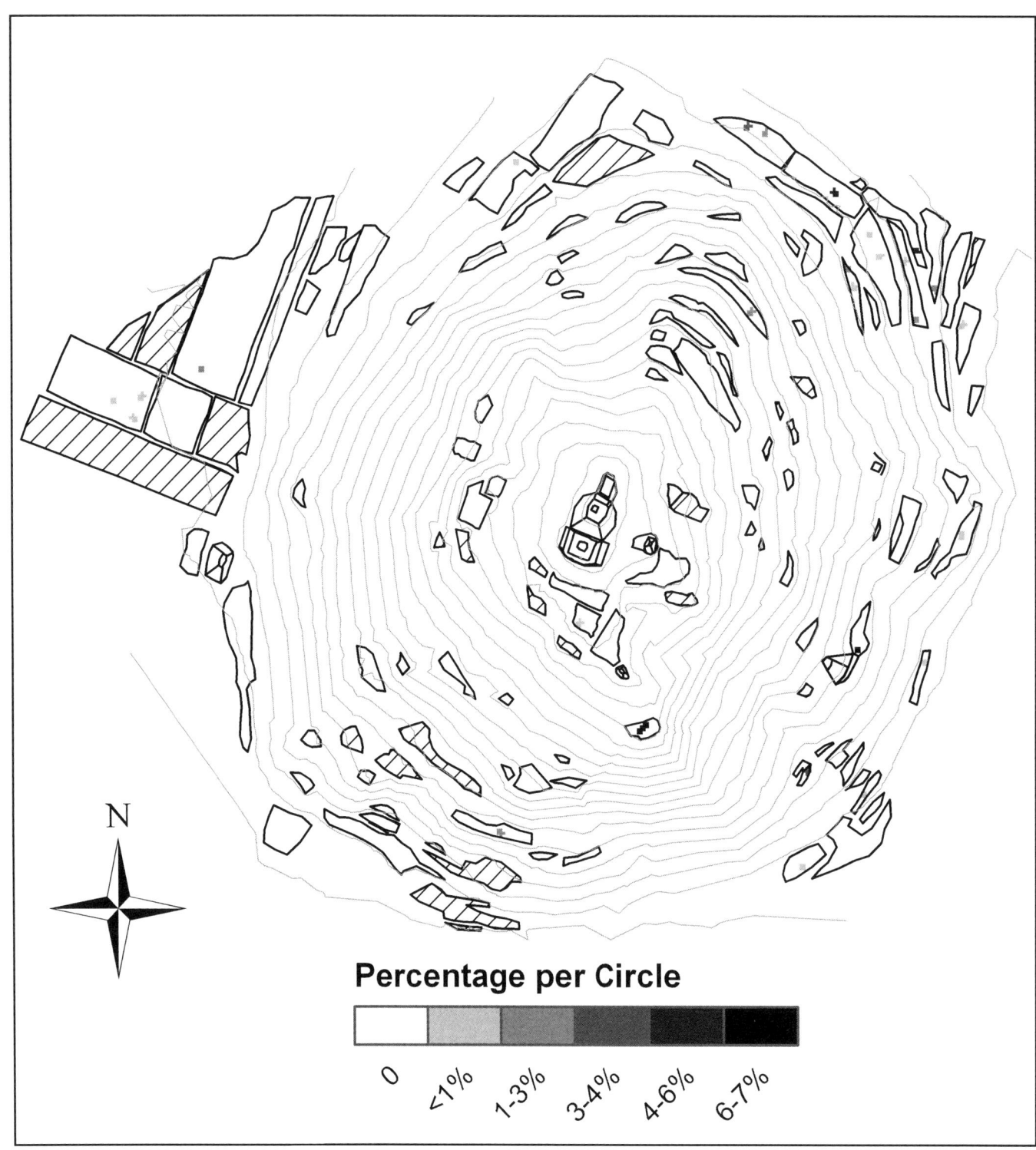

Figure 5.24. Distribution of botellón fragments.

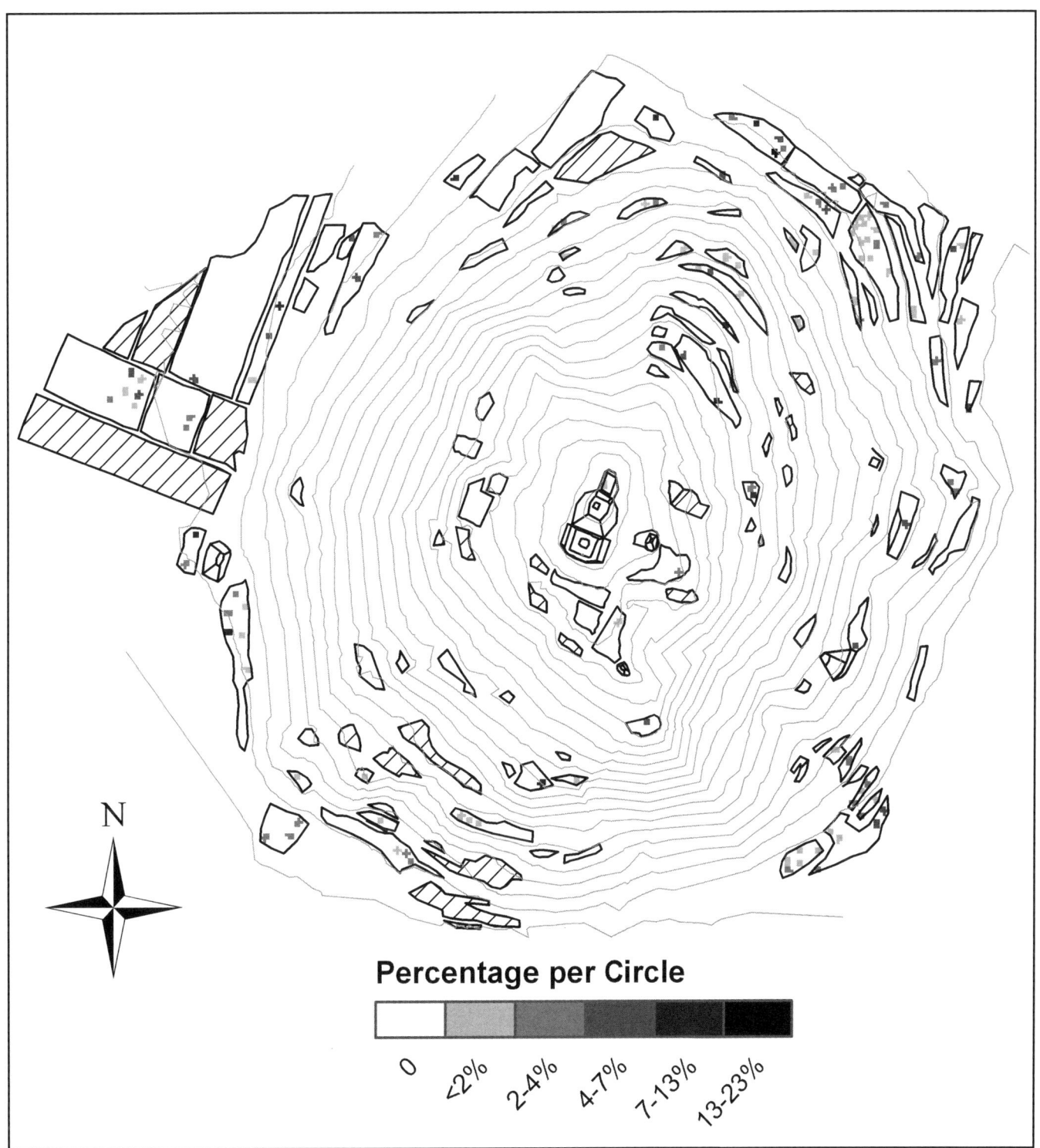

Figure 5.25. Distribution of silbato fragments.

demonstrated when we compare the spatial distributions of Late Classic hollow-handled sahumadores (Fig. 5.26) and Early Postclassic solid-handled sahumadores (Fig. 5.27; Table 5.2). The former artifacts follow the same basic pattern as urns, silbatos, and botellones, making up between 2 and 25% of the diagnostics recovered from many collection circles in all areas of the hill.

In contrast, Early Postclassic solid-handled sahumadores were found in low concentrations on some terraces of the North, Northeast, Eastern, and South Terrace Groups, and were far less frequent on terraces of the North-Central, West, and Summit Terrace Groups. In addition, clusters of solid-handled sahumador fragments were identified in two small areas around Terraces C2 and E9. Seventy-three fragments (40% of the total) were recovered from just four collection circles—C2N2E1, C2N1E1, E9N1E1, and E6N1E2—located at the bases of the two small pyramidal structures described in Chapter 4.

The spatial distribution of Early Postclassic sahumadores at Cerro Danush is therefore similar to the general pattern found by Kowalewski et al. (1989:342) in their regional survey:

> But it seems safe to conclude that sahumadores were discarded in low frequency in ordinary domestic contexts. They occur in the greatest numbers in special contexts: formal mound groups occupied as palaces in Period V, earlier mounds now treated as sacred places, hilltop prominences, and ballcourts . . . but the places where we find the highest numbers of sahumadores are neither domestic nor palace buildings, but hilltop shrines.

Kowalewski et al. suggest that this pattern reflects a shift in ritual activities that took place during the Early Postclassic. My surface collection data, as well as the available ethnographic and ethnohistoric evidence, seem to support their conclusions and may help further define the ritual activities represented by the sahumador clusters (discussed further in Chapter 8). In general, the differences in spatial distribution between hollow-handled and solid-handled sahumador fragments reflect changes in the use and occupation of Cerro Danush that occurred between the Late Classic and Early Postclassic.

Reconstructing the Occupational History of Cerro Danush

Analysis of ceramic types and their relative quantities within the surface collection provides an understanding of the archaeological timeline for the occupation of terraces on Cerro Danush. Because significant amounts of diagnostics for three consecutive ceramic phases (covering the period from the Early Classic to the Early Postclassic) were recovered, it is reasonable to assume that domestic use of the hill spanned that period. Furthermore, the extremely high frequencies of Late Classic ceramic markers, when compared to the low frequencies of Early Classic and Early Postclassic markers, suggest that the Late Classic was the apogee for use of the terraces. In the section that follows, I look more closely at the spatial distribution of both individual ceramic phase markers and paste colors to better characterize the pattern of occupation and abandonment of Cerro Danush.

For the Early Classic (Monte Albán IIIa), I examined the spatial distribution of sherds of G23 bowl fragments (Fig. 5.28), as well as rim sherds from the orange paste conical vessels, characterized by Kowalewski et al. (1989:201) as "Dainzú Bowls" (Fig. 5.29). These two vessel types have been found in both high- and low-status domestic contexts, and were recognized as good period markers both in excavations (Bernal and Oliveros 1988; Caso, Bernal, and Acosta 1967) and in valley-wide survey (Blanton et al. 1982; Kowalewski et al. 1989). Although not many G23 sherds were recovered, those that were found appear to match the high concentration areas for "Dainzú Bowls," with the highest concentrations in the Southwest, West, North-Central, and Summit Terrace Groups, as well as on Terrace E18 at the southeastern base of the hill. This relationship was also identified during multivariate analyses of the data set (see below).

There were many ceramic markers for the Late Classic (Monte Albán IIIb–IV) identified in the Cerro Danush assemblage, including the urns, silbatos, botellones, and hollow-handled sahumadores already discussed. The most widely accepted indicator of Monte Albán IIIb–IV is the G35 conical bowl, which was also the most ubiquitous material found on the terraces. Although this type occurs in low quantities in both Early Classic and Early Postclassic contexts, it is considered far more abundant in the Late Classic. The high concentrations of G35s shown in Figure 5.30 make it appear that almost all the terraces on Cerro Danush were occupied or used at some point during the Late Classic.

Brown paste correlates of the G35 bowl, referred to as K14 (Caso, Bernal, and Acosta 1967), were also common in the Late Classic, and their spatial distribution (Fig. 5.31) generally mirrors that of the G35, with only minor differences. This similar distribution of brown paste and gray paste conical bowls, however, contrasts sharply with the orange paste "Dainzú Bowls"; the latter seem to reach lower concentrations where G35 bowls are lower. A comparison of the relative frequencies of these materials may, therefore, help identify which terraces were occupied exclusively in either the Early Classic or the Late Classic, and which were occupied in other periods.

Occupation exclusively in the Early Classic is most strongly suggested for Terrace SO1, a long narrow terrace located at the base of the hill on the southwest side, just south of the Mound Plaza Group. This terrace shows relatively high frequencies of both "Dainzú Bowls" and G23 bowls, but has relatively low frequencies of G35s and K14s. To be sure, it is possible that Terrace SO1 was first occupied toward the end of the Early Classic or the beginning of the Late Classic, when the shift in settlement at Dainzú-Macuilxóchitl began. The other terrace groups (North-Central, Summit, and West) that show Early Classic temporal markers may be among the first terraces occupied on the hill, but occupation of these terraces expanded during the Late Classic; several terraces in these groups show very high concentrations of G35s and low concentrations of "Dainzú Bowls."

Judging by the distribution of G35 and K14 bowls, several terraces of the Northeast Terrace Group appear to have been oc-

Density Distribution Analyses of Surface Artifacts

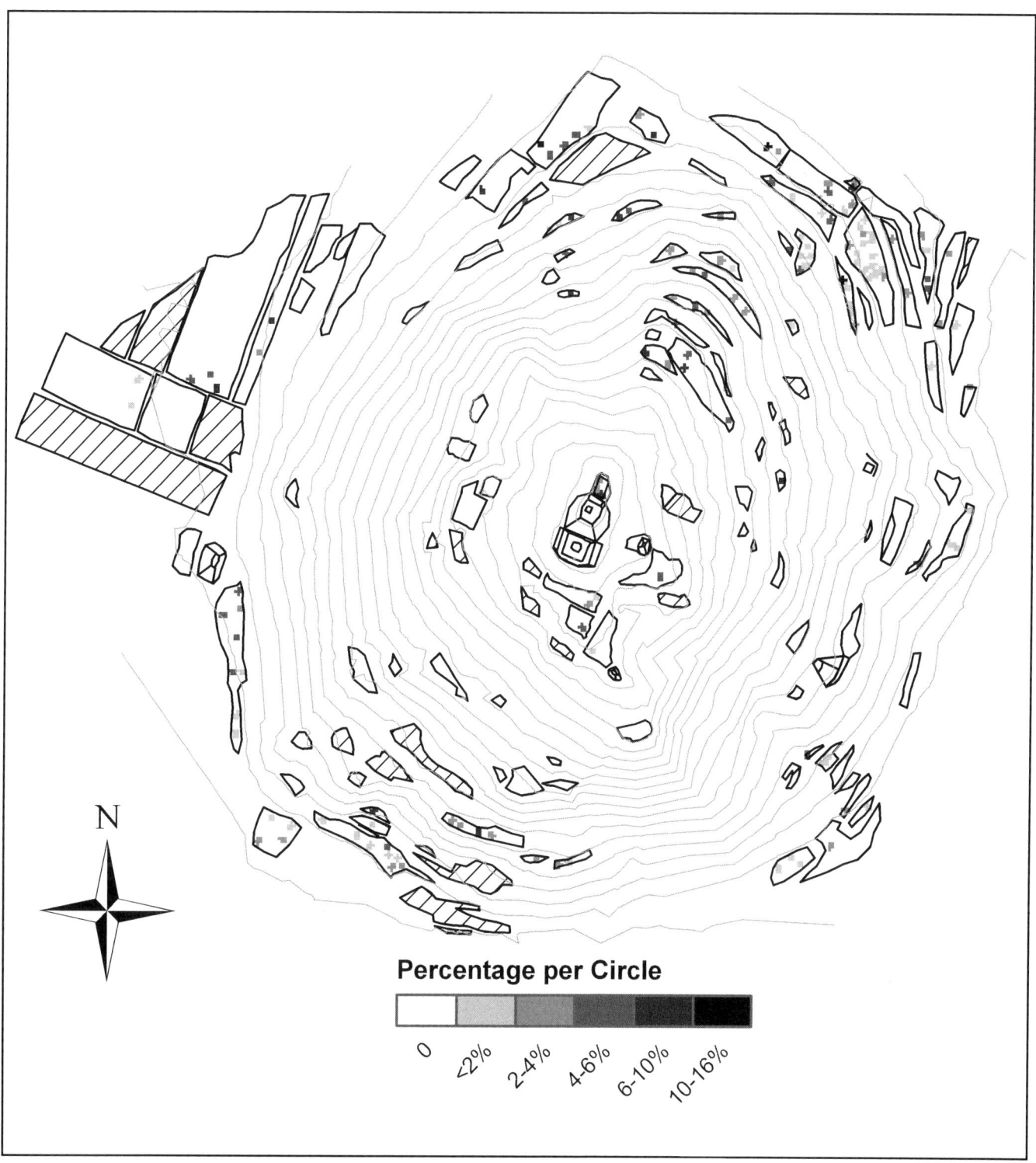

Figure 5.26. Distribution of hollow-handled sahumador fragments.

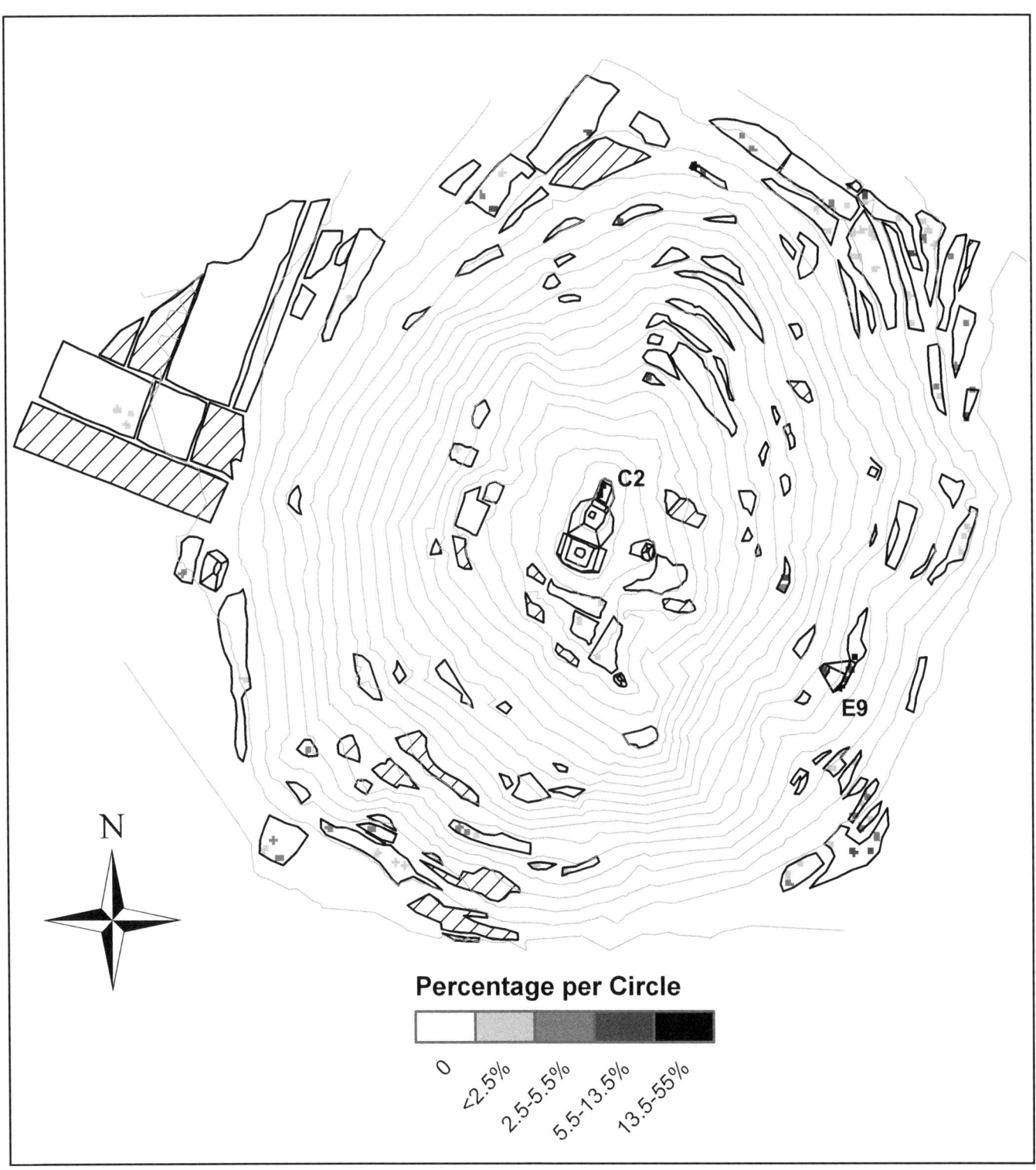

Figure 5.27. Distribution of solid-handled sahumador fragments.

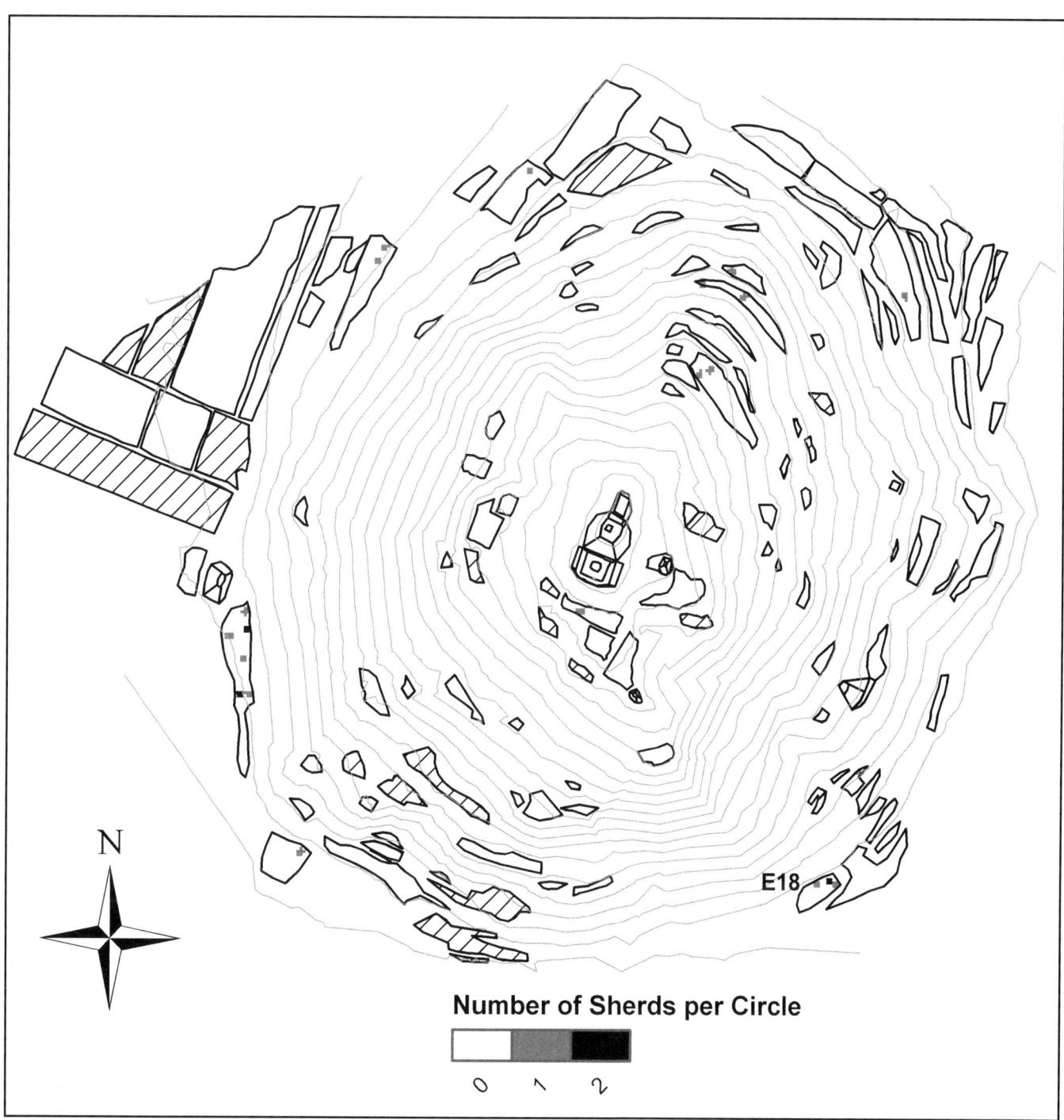

Figure 5.28. Distribution of G23 fragments.

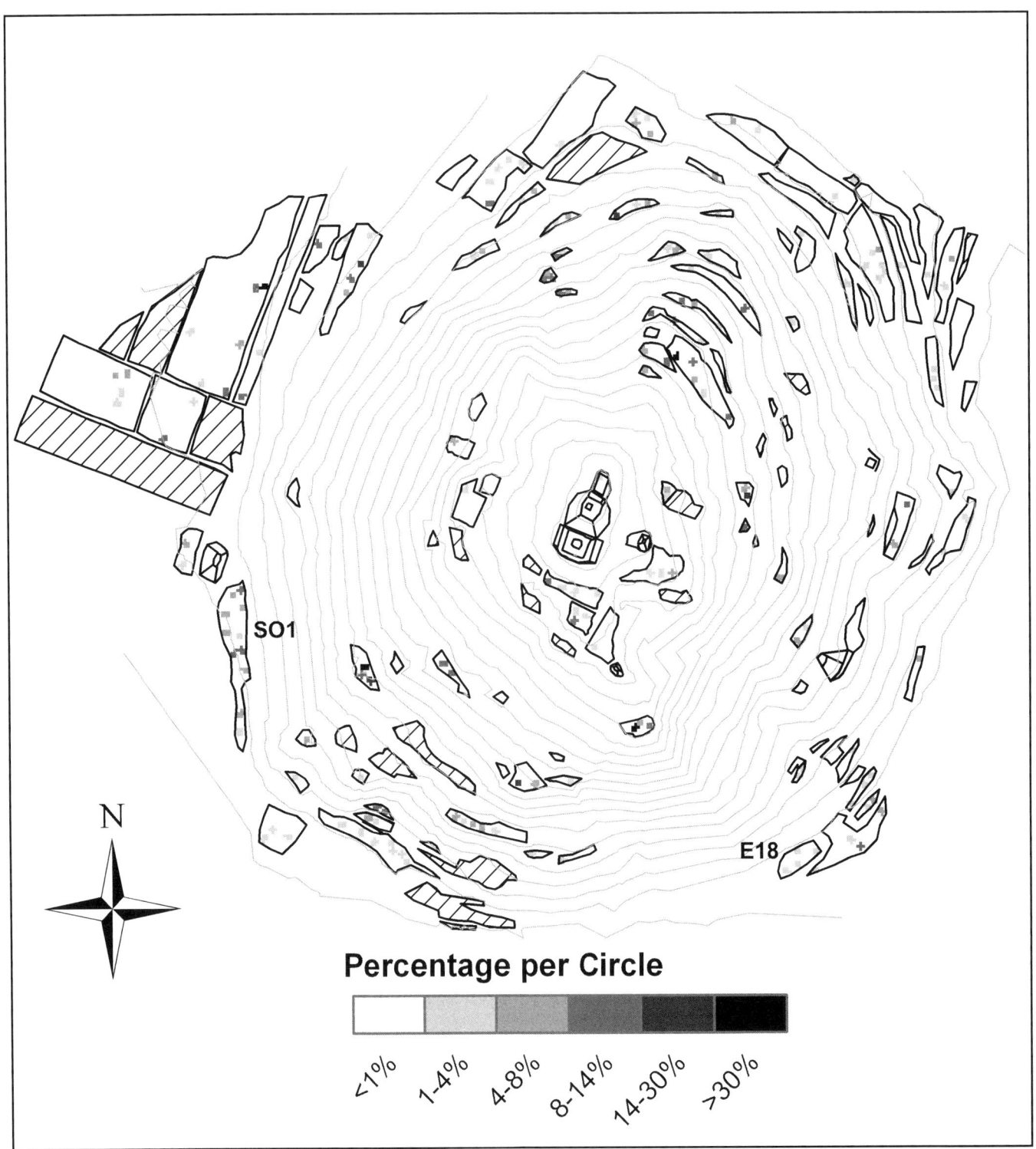

Figure 5.29. Distribution of orange paste conical bowl fragments.

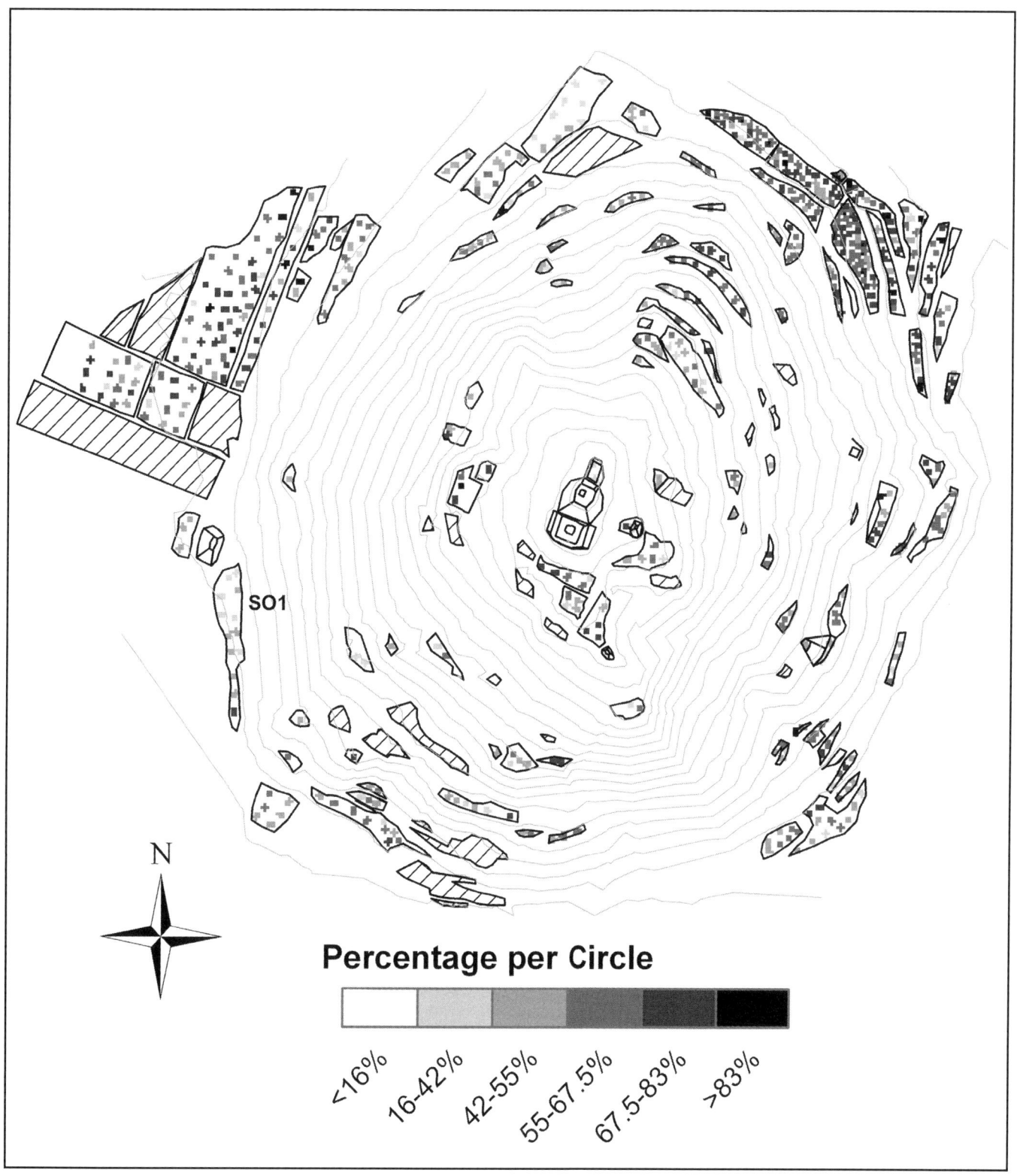

Figure 5.30. Spatial distribution of G35 fragments.

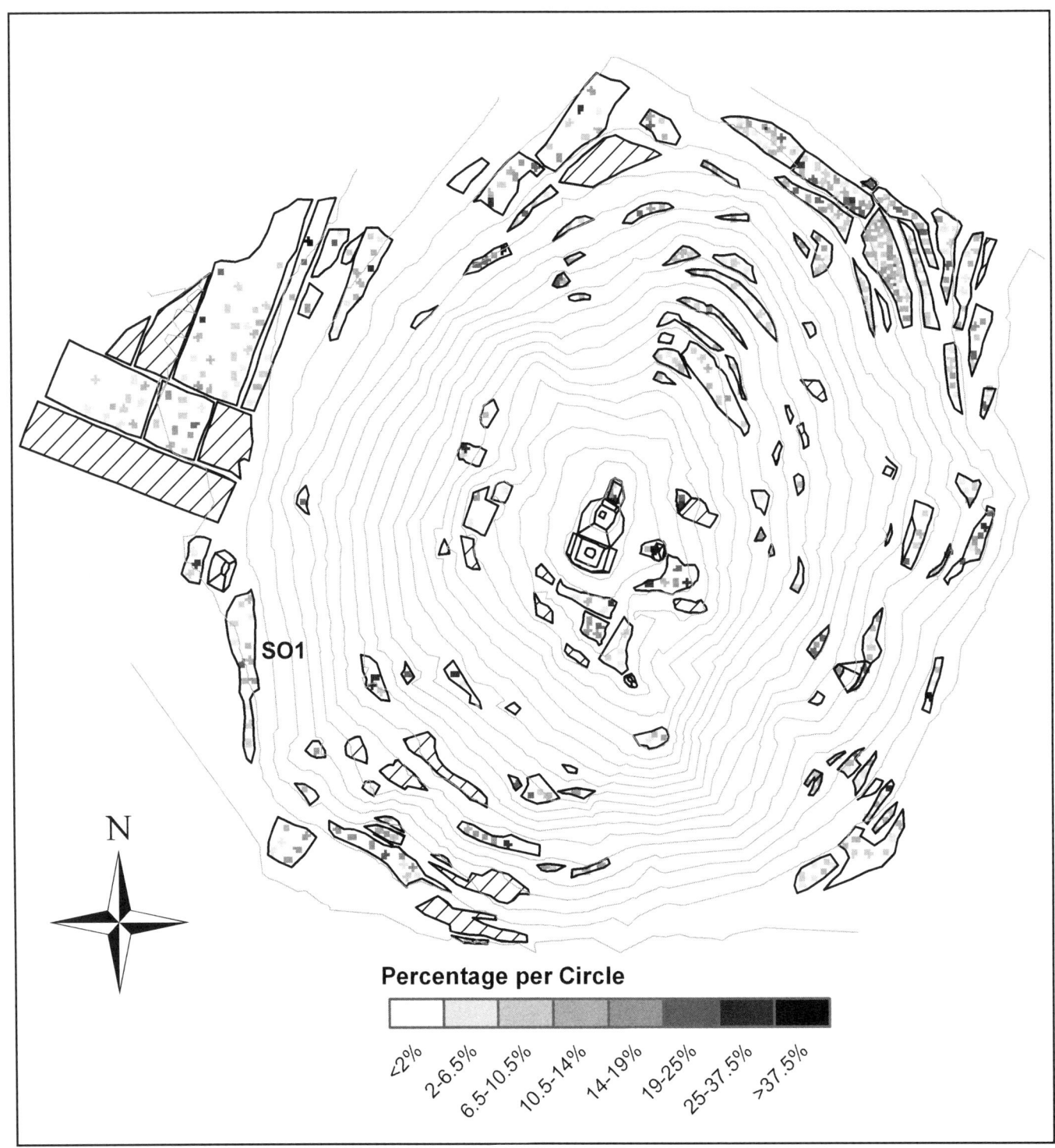

Figure 5.31. Distribution of brown paste (K14) conical bowl fragments.

cupied exclusively during the Late Classic. This group, however, along with the South, East, and North Terrace Groups, has a more complicated history, since many of these terraces may have also been occupied during the Early Postclassic.

To identify Early Postclassic (Monte Albán V) period use and occupation, I relied on solid-handled sahumadores and G3M bowls. While the former seem to be restricted to this period (Markens 2004, 2008), the case with G3M bowls is more complicated. Caso, Bernal, and Acosta (1967) suggest that G3M might begin in low frequency late in Monte Albán IIIb–IV, as does Flannery (pers. comm.), based on his work at Abasolo. I believe that I can detect intermediate types between the Late Classic gray paste hemispherical bowls and the Postclassic G3M hemispherical bowls.

Unlike the solid-handled sahumadores, which occur in the Postclassic, I therefore expected to find G3M bowls more evenly distributed on the terraces. Since they do become more abundant in Early Postclassic contexts, however, I focus less on their presence or absence and more on their relative densities. In other words, I treated the G3M distribution (for Early Postclassic purposes) in a manner analogous to the G35 distribution (for Late Classic purposes).

If we turn now to the two best Monte Albán V diagnostics, the distribution of solid-handled sahumadores seems to be greatest along the basal terraces of Cerro Danush. The G3M distribution (Fig. 5.32) appears to be consistent with this: low percentages occurred on the higher terraces of the Summit and North-Central Groups, while higher percentages occurred at the base of the hill. There are, however, some unique concentrations of G3M bowls. In a number of individual circles, G3M fragments amount to 15 to 40% of the materials collected; this is especially true in the North and Northeast Terrace Groups. Excavation will be necessary to determine the nature of these concentrations.

The spatial distribution of ollas with appliqué glyph motifs (Fig. 5.33) appears to be similar to that for both G3M and solid-handled sahumadores: low densities in the North-Central and Summit Terrace Groups, and high densities in the Northeast and North Terrace Groups, as well as on Terrace S19. Paddock (1983b) and Kowalewski et al. (1989) have argued that this type of olla is a temporal indicator for the Early Postclassic. Martínez López et al. (2000), however, assert that it is part of the Late Classic assemblage, arguing that whole vessels of this type have been recovered only from Late Classic contexts.

If the latter were the case, I would expect to see such ollas more evenly distributed on Cerro Danush, like the rest of the Late Classic indicators. Instead, they occur in relatively high amounts in the Northeast Terrace Group, where we found so many Postclassic solid-handled sahumadores, as well as the highest concentrations of G35 bowls. Here is another case where further excavation will be necessary to determine whether ollas with appliqué glyphs are useful chronological markers, or whether they began in the Late Classic and continued into the Early Postclassic.

Based on the surface density plots of the diagnostics mentioned above, I tentatively conclude that the first terraces occupied at Cerro Danush were those on the southwest, summit, and north-central part of the hill. Their occupation may have begun during the initial part of the Early Classic to Late Classic settlement shift. During the Late Classic, settlement grew until nearly all the terraces were occupied. By the Early Postclassic, many of the terraces had been abandoned, leaving only a few at the base of the hill (on the east, south, and northeast) occupied. However, post-abandonment rituals were conducted on several terraces during the Early Postclassic.

While the presence or absence of diagnostics on the surface of a site does not always mirror what is under the surface, the above analysis provides a model for a site's settlement history that can then be tested with excavation.

The Distribution of Ceramic Pastes

In addition to the progression of pottery types mentioned above, the relative percentages of gray, brown, and orange ceramic pastes reflect diachronic differences for this region of the Valley of Oaxaca (Kowalewski et al. 1989). Since paste color could be identified in all the ceramic sherds collected at Cerro Danush, whether or not the sherd could be identified to type, the density distribution of paste colors provides a separate line of evidence to evaluate terrace occupation over time.

The overall ceramic assemblage from the surface collection consisted of 79.70% gray paste, 18.68% brown paste, and 1.62% orange paste. The relative percentages from the surface of Terrace S19 were 64.24% gray paste, 33.42% brown paste, and 2.34% orange paste. Significantly, these paste color percentages very closely matched those recovered from the excavation of the same terrace (65.89% gray paste, 31.55% brown paste, and 2.55% orange paste). My excavation revealed that Terrace S19 had been occupied continuously from the Early Classic to the Postclassic. Based on my results, I came to consider any terrace with an orange paste percentage of 2.3% or higher among its surface sherds to present a possibility for Early Classic occupation.

Orange paste sherds ranged between 0.13% and 9.79% of the surface collection on any terrace (Fig. 5.34). While the surface distribution of such sherds matches the distributions of both G23 and "Dainzú Bowl" fragments (Figs. 5.28, 5.29), the areas with percentages of 2.3% or higher suggest additional areas of Early Classic occupation along the base of the hill in the south and southeast. This picture becomes clear when we consider the distribution of ceramics on individual terraces rather than the sum of the collection circles. Figure 5.35 depicts all terraces that yielded a percentage of orange paste sherds greater than or equal to that found on Terrace S19. I suspect that these terraces approximate the Early Classic occupation of Cerro Danush.

Gray paste sherds ranged between 42.08% and 89.84% of the assemblage found on any given terrace (Fig. 5.36), with only two terraces exhibiting gray paste percentages below 64%. Since gray ware is known to have dominated the Classic period ceramic assemblage (Caso, Bernal, and Acosta 1967; Martínez López et al. 2000), the high frequency found on all terraces is consistent

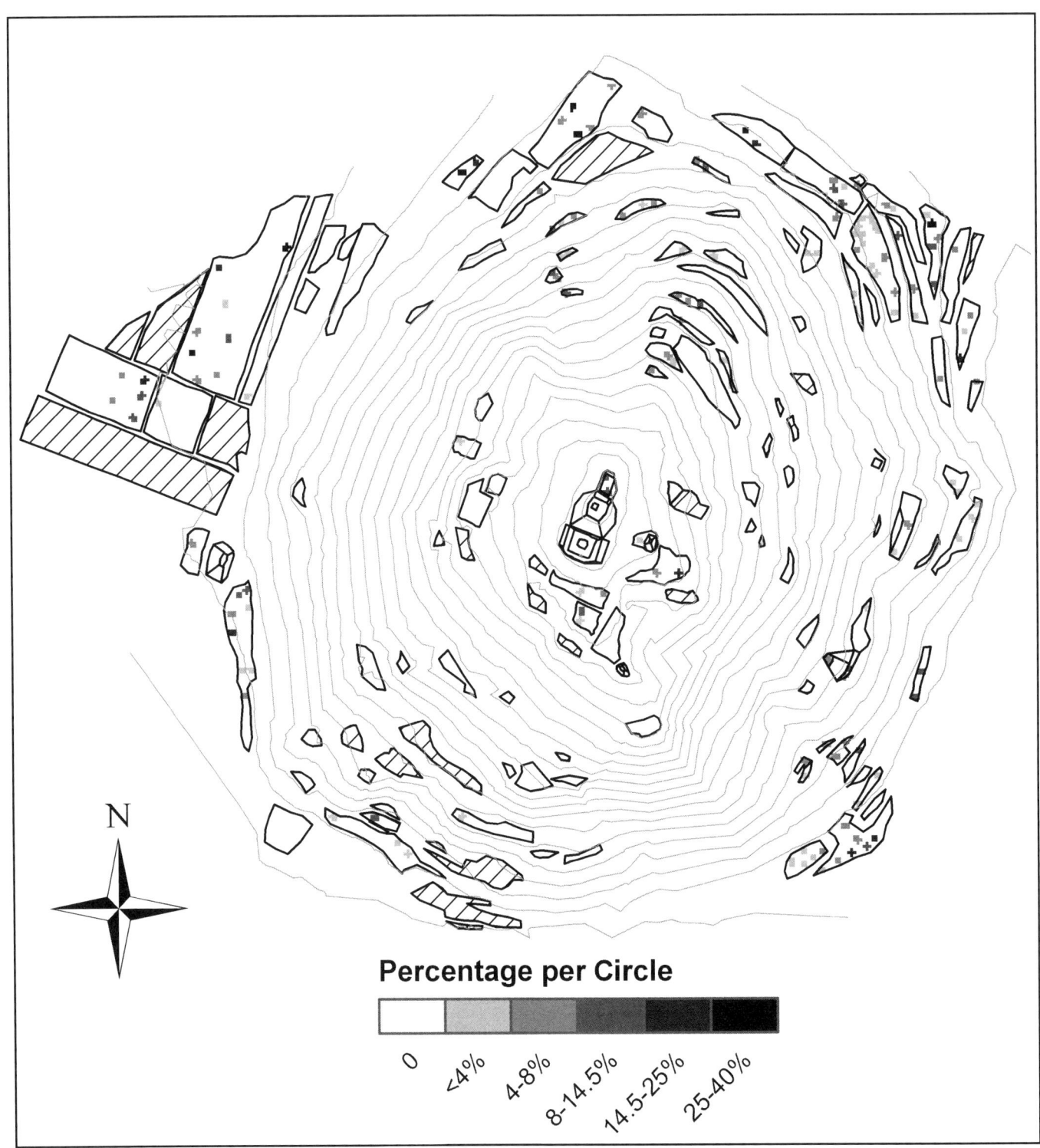

Figure 5.32. Surface distribution of G3M fragments.

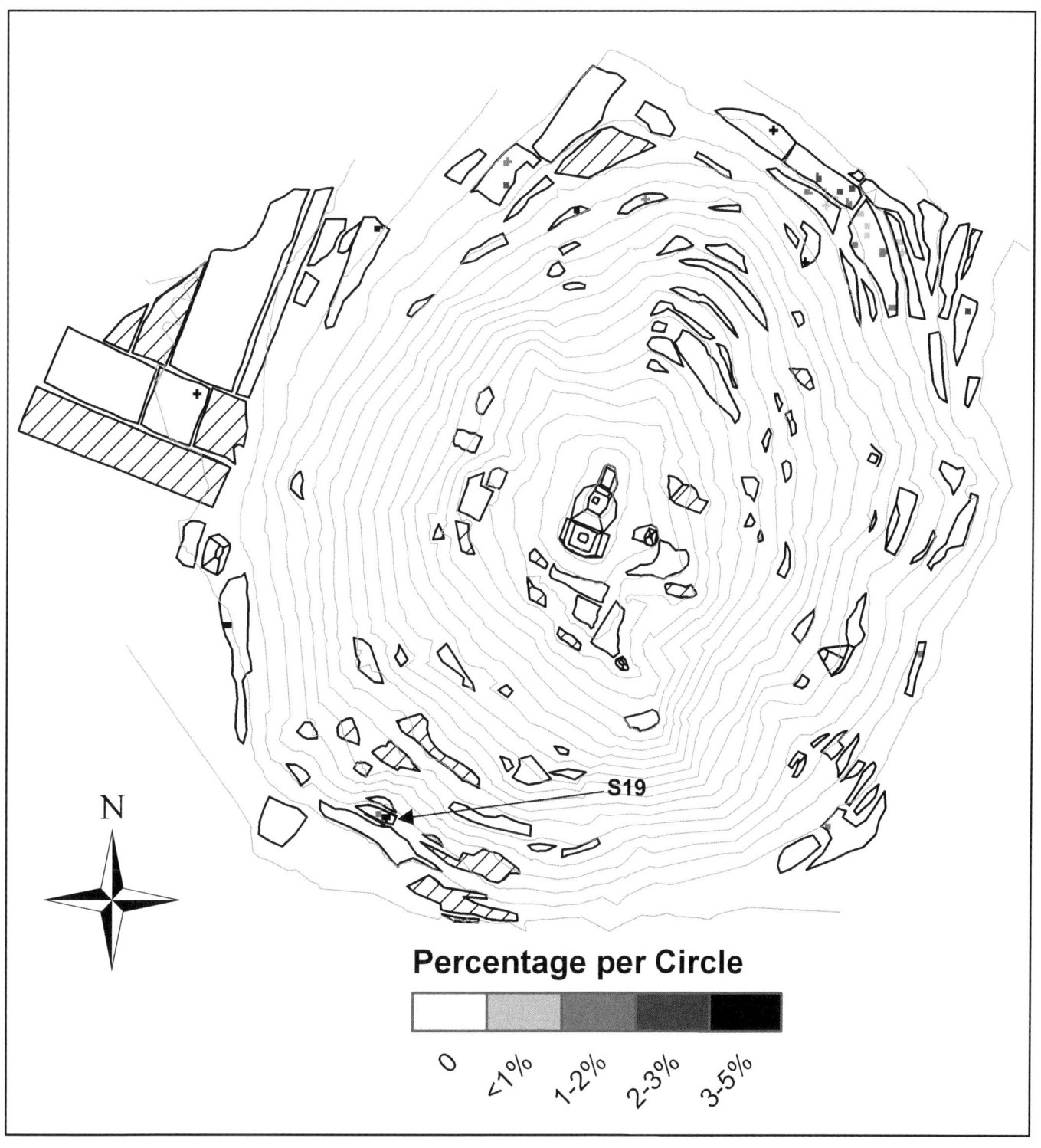

Figure 5.33. Surface distribution of ollas with appliqué glyph motifs.

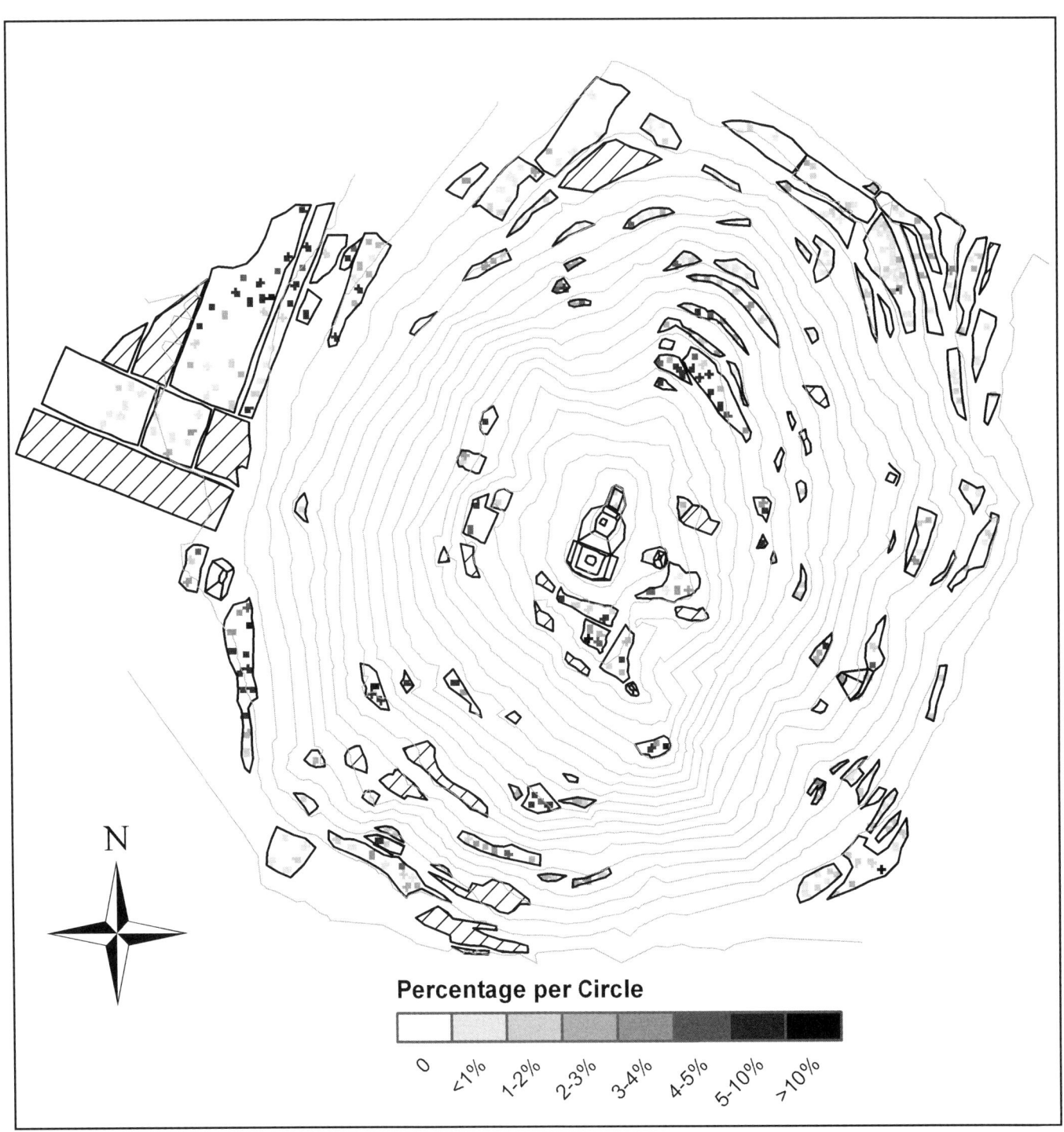

Figure 5.34. Total distribution of orange paste sherds.

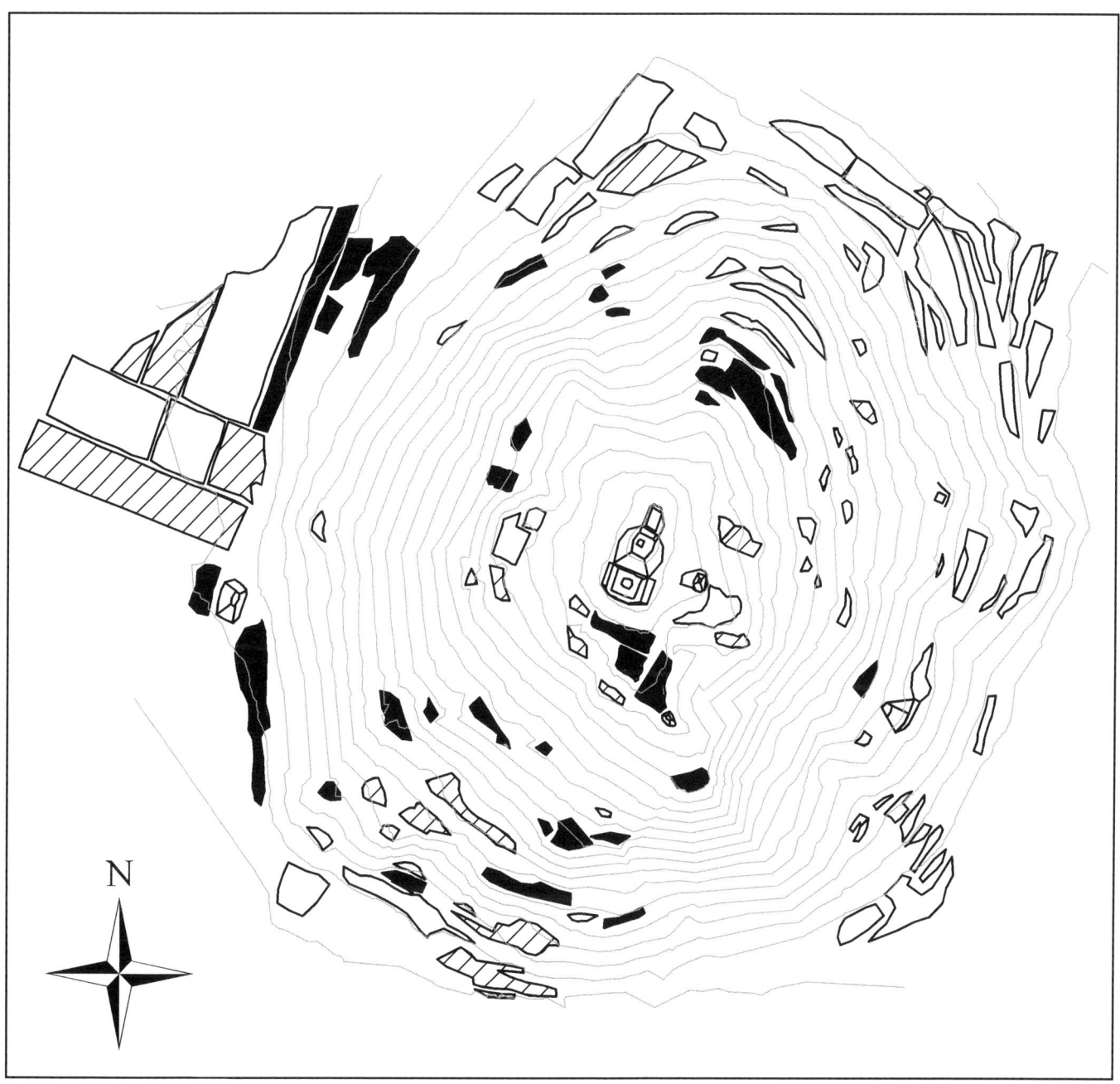

Figure 5.35. Terraces with total orange paste sherd averages greater than 2.33% (shown in black).

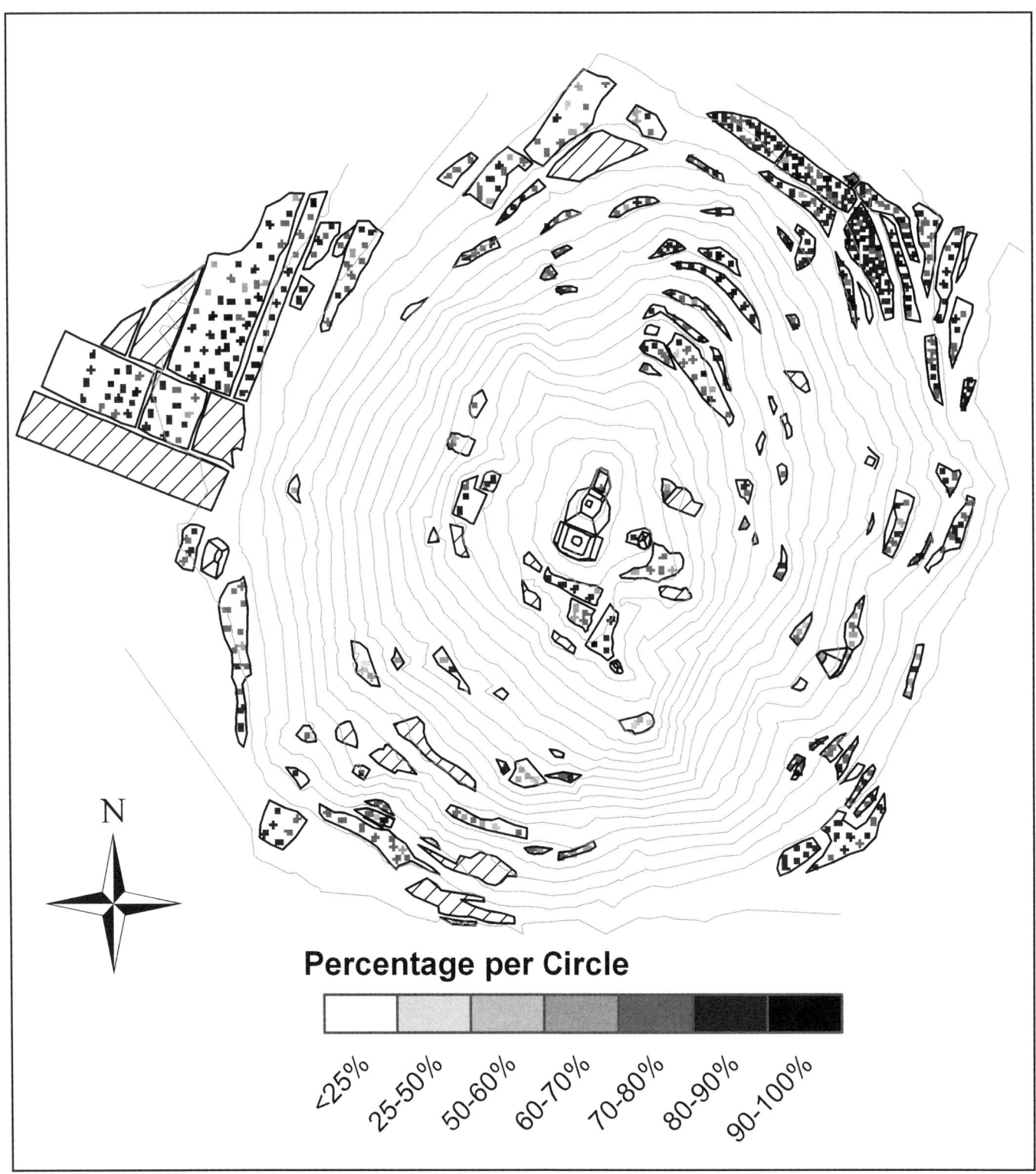

Figure 5.36. Total distribution of gray paste sherds.

with Late Classic occupation, and supports the conclusions drawn from the analysis of the surface density plot for G35 fragments. In addition, the percentage of gray paste sherds was higher than 80% on many terraces; on most of the latter I found no Early Classic or Early Postclassic diagnostics on the surface, suggesting that these terraces were used only during the Late Classic.

Brown paste sherds ranged between 9.62% and 56.83% of the assemblage found on any given terrace. While brown paste sherds do make up a small percentage of the Classic period assemblage for the Valley of Oaxaca (Caso, Bernal, and Acosta 1967; Martínez López et al. 2000), recent research (Markens 2008) has demonstrated that the Postclassic assemblage consists of a much higher percentage of brown paste sherds, with gray paste sherds declining in frequency. Terraces with high percentages of brown paste sherds, therefore, are likely to have been occupied in the Postclassic. Figure 5.37 depicts the distribution of brown paste fragments, and Figure 5.38 shows the terraces that exhibited brown paste sherd frequencies of 33% or greater on their surfaces. What these figures suggest is a striking reduction in the number of occupied terraces during the Early Postclassic. Even if the standard is lowered to 25% brown paste sherds (Fig. 5.39), the number of terraces is still less than 15% of the number occupied in the Late Classic, and they remain distributed mostly along the base of the hill. With a few possible exceptions (most notably, the terraces at the base of the hill in the Northeast and Southeast Terrace Groups), the terraces with the highest frequencies of brown paste sherds correspond well with the highest densities of Postclassic sahumadores. Combining the two distributions thus gives us a good picture of the terraces occupied during the Early Postclassic.

Although brown paste sherds do appear to be present in higher concentrations throughout the Valley of Oaxaca in the Early Postclassic (Feinman and Nicholas 2011; Markens 2008), their percentages do vary considerably among sites and regions within the valley. Thus, while I believe my approach to be effective for Cerro Danush, in other parts of the valley one has to consider the composition of a particular assemblage and adjust the percentage thresholds accordingly.

Principal Components and Correspondence Analyses

To quantitatively compare the data between collection circles, I employed principal components analysis (PCA) and correspondence analysis (CA). These analyses serve as an independent means to verify patterns identified visually with the surface density plots. Initially, I also intended to use these analyses to probe the data set for associations that might correspond to specific activities. For example, it would be interesting to see if food storage items and food preparation items were negatively associated, making it possible to identify specific areas where these activities took place. Unfortunately, neither analysis tool was sensitive enough to identify patterns beyond the most obvious ones presented in the surface density analysis. This is probably a limitation of the data set itself. It is difficult to identify anything but broad patterns in such a surface collection. In addition, site abandonment brings about its own set of destructive processes, making it difficult to identify specific activity areas even in the case of excavated terraces such as Terrace S19 (Chapters 7 and 8). Nevertheless, the multivariate analyses were useful in quantifying the patterns described above and merit some further discussion. All analyses were conducted with Minitab v15 software.

Principal Components Analysis

In principal components analysis, a matrix of Pearson's r-values is created based on the correlation between cases (collection circles). In this distance matrix, high r-values are shared between cases that exhibit similar patterns with respect to the variables (artifact categories). For example, two circles that show high frequencies of the same diagnostic materials share relatively high positive r-values. Cases that exhibit high frequencies of a specific diagnostic material will, in turn, share relatively high negative r-values with cases that exhibit low frequencies of the same material. The overall variation among cases throughout the data set is then mathematically characterized so that the variables that are responsible for the high and low r-values between cases are identified and grouped into principal components. Each principal component is then assigned a weight (Eigen value) that corresponds to the amount of variation that that particular component is responsible for in the data set. Once the principal components are identified, the variables and their corresponding cases can be examined for spatial patterns.

In general, principal components analysis is susceptible to problems associated with size within the data set. In this specific data set, "size" refers to frequency count. For example, G35 conical bowls were found in very large numbers in most of the circles, while other materials were found in low numbers. If these data are not treated in some way before analysis, this size difference will account for most of the variation, and very little spatial information will be recovered.

To reduce this problem, my data were row standardized before analysis. This confined the data set to a range, where all the individual datum points were converted to percentages of the total count per row, with a minimum value of 0% and maximum value of 100%. Even with this standardization, I expected the large percentages of G35 conical bowls to cause at least one principal component to be dominated by the variation of this one item. Further, because of the large size differences between ceramics and chipped stone, they were separated into two data sets for analysis.

Principal Components Analysis of the Ceramic Data Set

For analysis of the ceramics, I used 537 of the 540 collection circles (cases), with a total of 45 categories (variables). Three of the circles were removed from the analysis because they

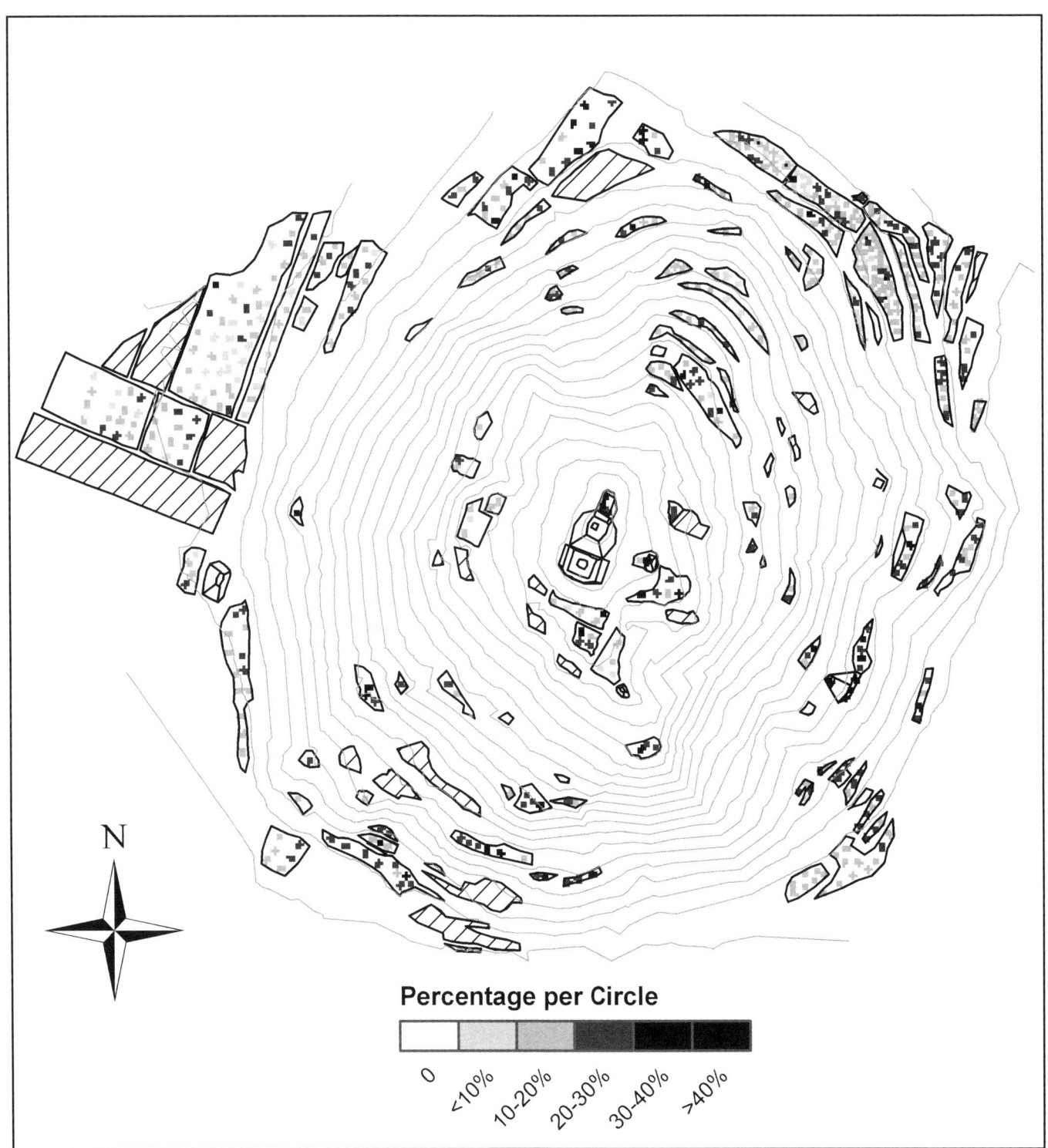

Figure 5.37. Total distribution of brown paste sherds.

Density Distribution Analyses of Surface Artifacts

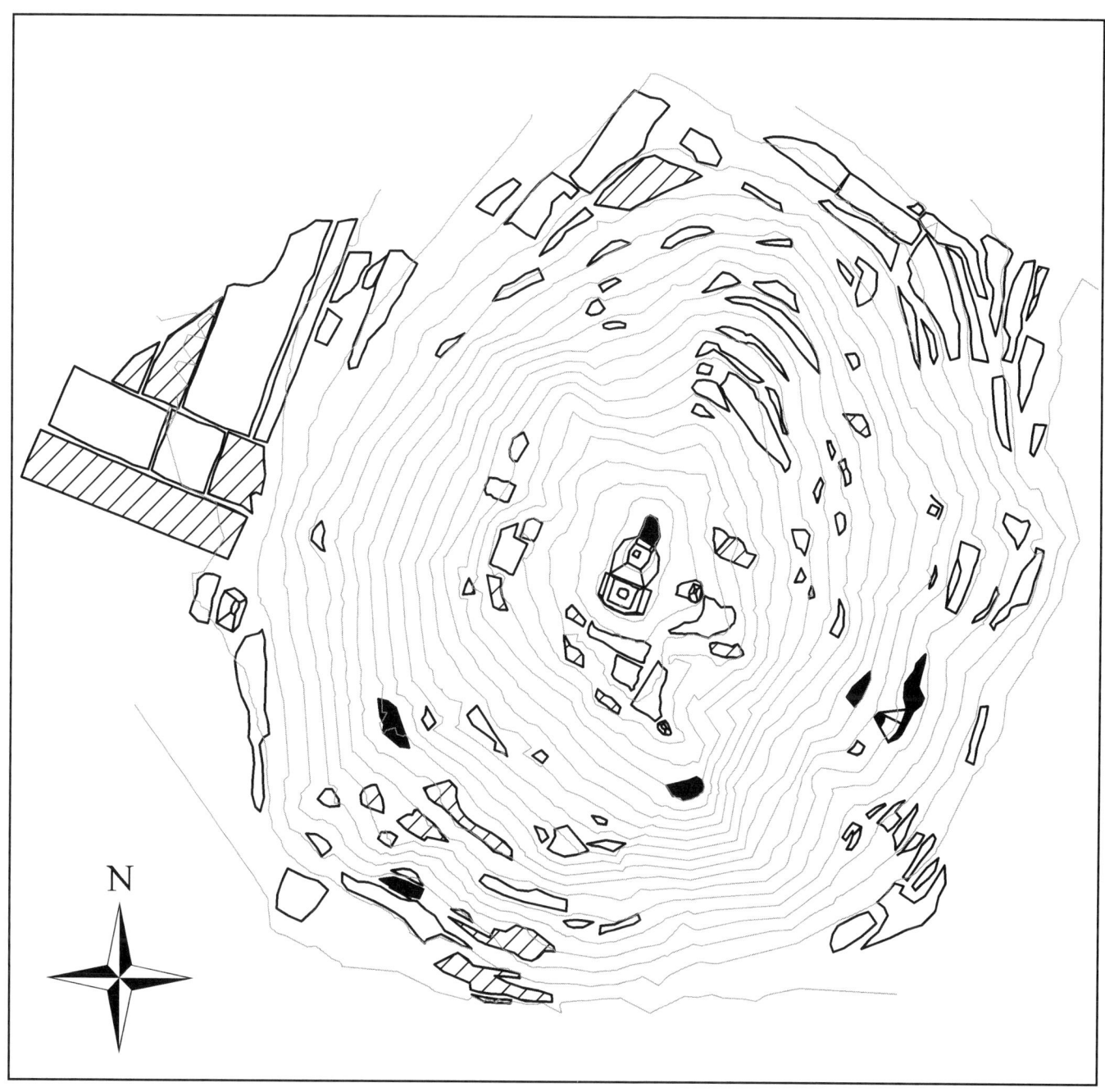

Figure 5.38. Terraces with 33% or more total brown paste sherds (shown in black).

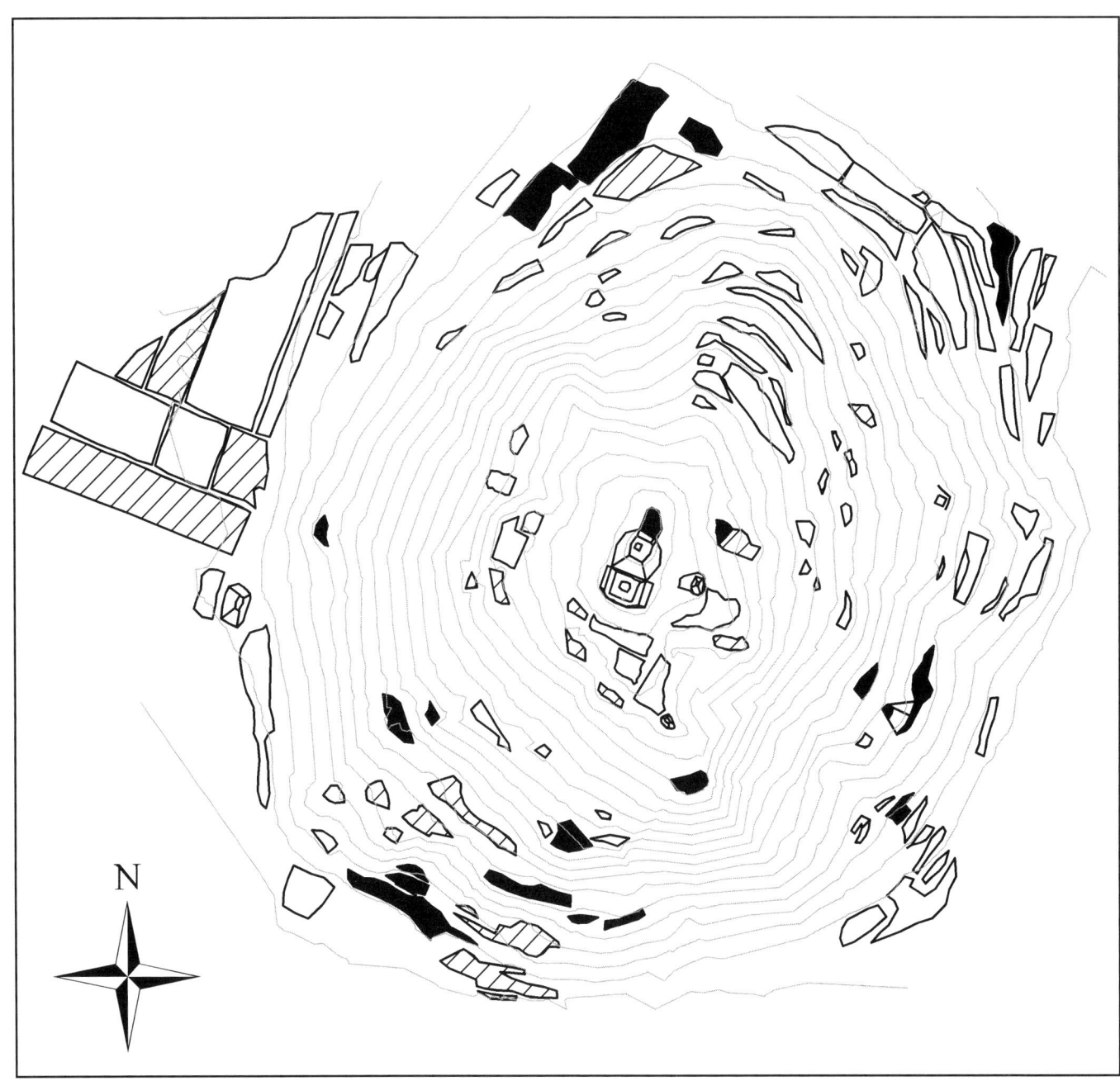

Figure 5.39. Terraces with 25% or more total brown paste sherds (shown in black).

contained no G35 conical bowls, and only a minimal amount of other materials. For example, circle C13N1E1 produced only 2 diagnostics (1 apaxtle and 1 olla barril), giving each fragment a value of 50%. Obviously, this places far too much emphasis on just 2 ceramic fragments. Two other circles, SO2N2E1 and NC11N2E5, were removed for similar reasons.

Variables were likewise pared from the sample based on too few recovered materials. For example, there was only 1 orange paste apaxtle within the entire data set, and a total of 3 G12 bowls, so these were removed. Some of the items were reduced to type rather than being separated into the 3 color categories. For example, solid-handled sahumadores were so often of brown paste that gray paste and orange paste examples were too rare to separate out.

Once principal components analysis is conducted, the program produces a scree plot (Fig. 5.40), which shows the overall Eigen value (total variation) vs. the principal components. This graph provides a visual indication for how much variation each principal component is responsible for. In the case of ceramics, the first three to four components were responsible for most of the variation in the data set. I thus limit my analysis to the first four components.

Once the number of principal components is decided upon, the program produces coefficients for each of the variables (ceramic categories) per principal component. In the ceramic distribution data set, each of the 45 categories is assigned a value for each principal component. The coefficients are an ordinal data set, ranging between +1.0 and -1.0. The higher the coefficient value, the greater the effect—positive or negative—any ceramic category has within the principal component. One can therefore identify specific variables responsible for the variation in the data set by examining the coefficient values. Variables with coefficients between -0.15 and 0.15 are generally considered to be unimportant with respect to the variation. Rather than providing the entire table of coefficients, I decided to plot the coefficient values for the four principal components with dot plots (Fig. 5.41), and identify the most important variables.

As expected, most of the negative value in the first principal component was assigned to the G35 conical bowl. This results from the size effect discussed above, and most of the variation for this principal component is explained by the large amounts of G35 conical bowls collected.

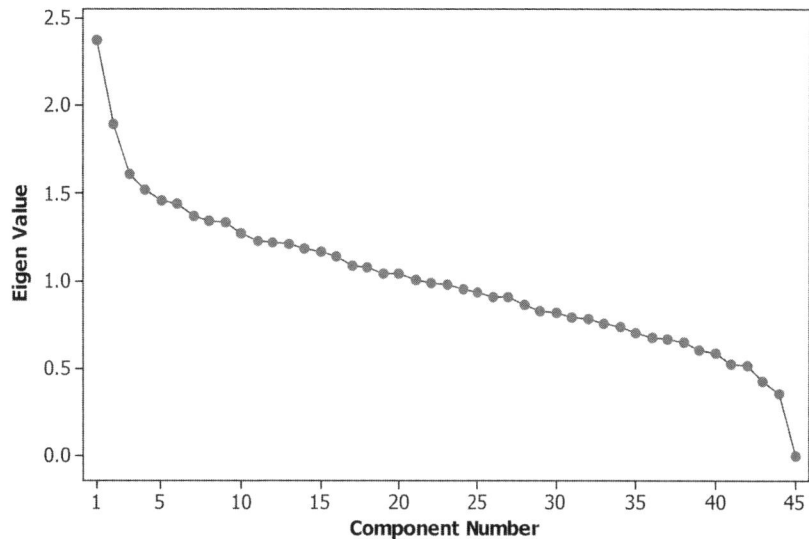

Figure 5.40. Scree plot for principal components analysis of surface ceramics.

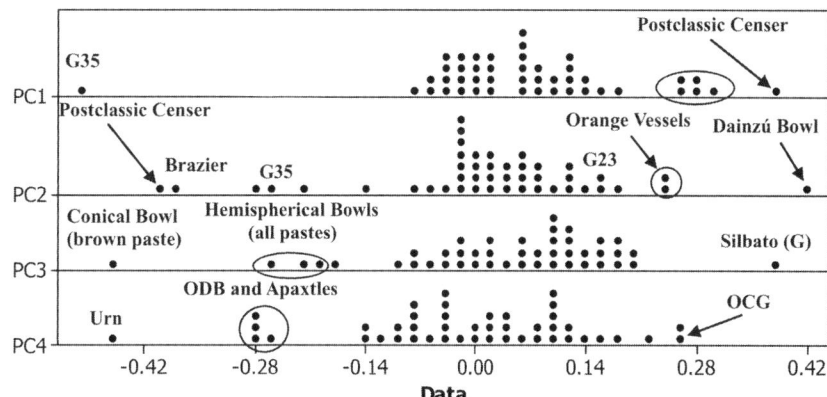

Figure 5.41. Coefficient values from the four principal components.

There is, however, some important information generated on the positive side of the coefficient plot. The ceramic categories of solid-handled sahumadores, café braziers, and gray solid figurines contribute the greatest number of positive values. This is a mathematical reflection of the clustering of these items on Terraces C2 and E9, already seen in the surface density plots.

The dot plot for the second principal component displays the two most prevalent orange paste vessels—conical and hemispherical bowls—on the right side, while G35s and gray paste cylindrical bowls are plotted on the left. The majority of the gray paste vessels have negative values, while most of the orange paste vessels have positive values.

Significantly, G23 bowls have a coefficient value of 0.151 with orange paste vessels. While not a particularly high correlation, this nevertheless confirms that both are Early Classic diagnostics. Here is a case where principal components analysis appears to verify our conclusions based on the surface density analysis. Solid-handled sahumadores and café braziers also contribute a lot of the value in this principal component, showing just how important their clustering is to the overall variation in the sample.

The effect that each of these principal components (and therefore the relevant ceramic categories) has on a given collection circle is mathematically weighted and given a numeric score. Due to the size of the table of score values (4 columns vs. 537 rows), it is more effective to plot these values than to look for patterns in the numerical data. Since principal components 1 and 2 show similar tendencies, an *x-y* scatter plot (Fig. 5.42) should reveal (for example) which collection circles are most defined by the solid-handled sahumador and brazier, and which are most defined by high percentages of orange paste sherds.

The plot for the first two principal components reveals that Terraces C2 and E9 are different from the majority of circles because of their high concentrations of solid-handled sahumadores and café braziers (Fig. 5.42). The large cluster of points in the center reflects the majority of the circles, which have high surface concentrations of G35 bowl fragments. On the right-hand side of the plot (along the PC 2 axis), one finds many of the circles from terraces with relatively high concentrations of orange paste ceramics, such as those from the North-Central, West, and South Groups. Significantly, the same circles identified during surface density analysis as having relatively high concentrations of orange paste sherds and G23 bowls have positive scores along the axis of principal component 2. Principal components analysis thus confirms the pattern detected during our earlier spatial analysis.

The third and fourth principal components do not account for as much variation as the first two, and interpretation of the dot plots is more difficult. Brown paste urn fragments apparently play an important negative role in principal component

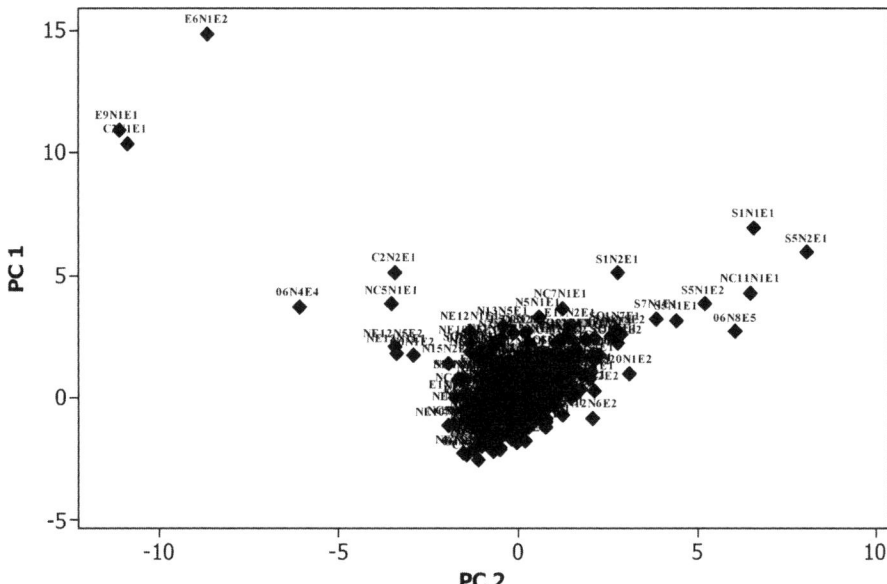

Figure 5.42. *X-y* scatter plot of score values for principal component 1 and principal component 2.

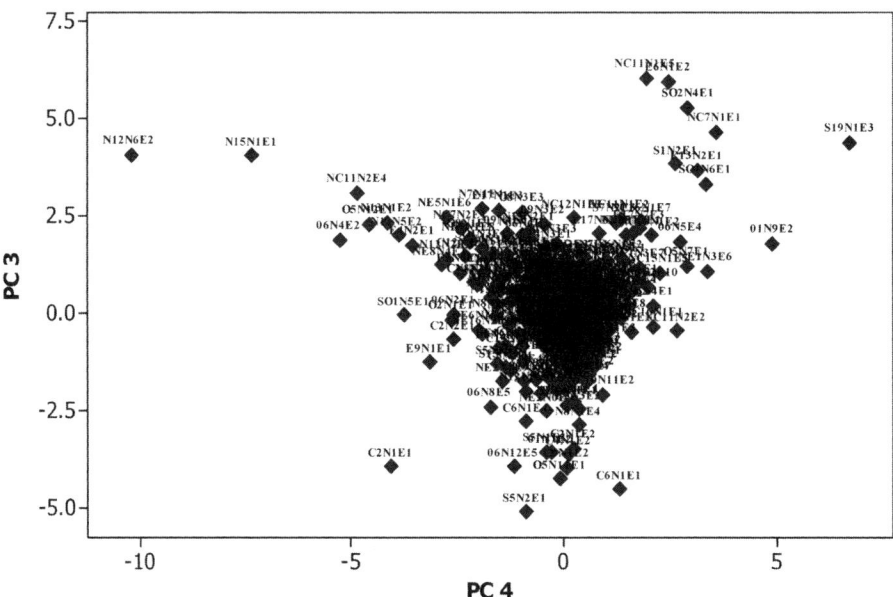

Figure 5.43. *X-y* scatter plot of score values for principal component 3 and principal component 4.

4, which the scatter plot attributes mainly to two circles in the Northern Group (Fig. 5.43). On the positive end of the same dot plot, café ollas with appliqué glyphs contribute significantly to the variation; here collection circle S19N1E3 is implicated, since it is the only unit where café ollas of this type were found. Neither of these spatial patterns is particularly informative, since both gray and café pastes were used for these vessels in the Late Classic.

The diagnostic categories accounting for most of the remaining variation in principal components 3 and 4 are gray paste whistles (silbatos) and large storage vessels (apaxtles and ollas barriles). It is apparent from the graph that gray paste whistles have higher-than-average concentrations in a few circles of the North-Central and Southwestern Terrace Groups. It is difficult to provide a satisfactory explanation for this pattern, given the fact that whistles with both gray and café pastes were relatively evenly distributed among the terraces in our surface density analysis. The pattern displayed by the large storage vessels appears similar to that identified during surface density analysis; collection circles on Terraces C12, C13, C14 and NC11 all exhibit negative score values in principal component 4.

Principal Components Analysis of the Chipped Stone Assemblage

During principal components analysis of the chipped stone data set, I eliminated all the collection circles that did not contain any materials; this left a total of 374 cases. The diagnostic categories were then organized into 10 variables: chert debitage, volcanic tuff debitage, obsidian debitage, chert flakes, volcanic tuff flakes, raspadores, chert bifaces, spent chert cores, spent volcanic tuff cores, and fragments of obsidian prismatic blades. Once again, the data were row standardized before analysis.

The scree plot (Fig. 5.44) immediately reveals the difficulty this data set presents for principal components analysis: nearly all the variation is accounted for by the first principal component. This is likely because the assemblage is heavily dominated by chert debitage. The dot plot for the first principal component (Fig. 5.45) underscores this problem; it shows chert debitage with a value of -0.752 on one side of the graph, directly opposite the next two most abundant materials—prismatic obsidian blades and volcanic tuff debitage (circled in the figure). The remaining principal components accounted for extremely small amounts of the variation, and none of the patterns detected during surface density analysis were duplicated during principal components analysis.

Correspondence Analysis

Correspondence analysis works in a manner very similar to principal components analysis, but is considered to be more effective with frequency count data (Shennan 1997:308–9). For one thing, CA reduces the steps in data preparation. In PCA, the data must first be standardized, after which a distance matrix (*r*-values) is developed to define the relationship between variables. Next, the cases are scored with respect to their relationship to the variables. In CA, on the other hand, the data

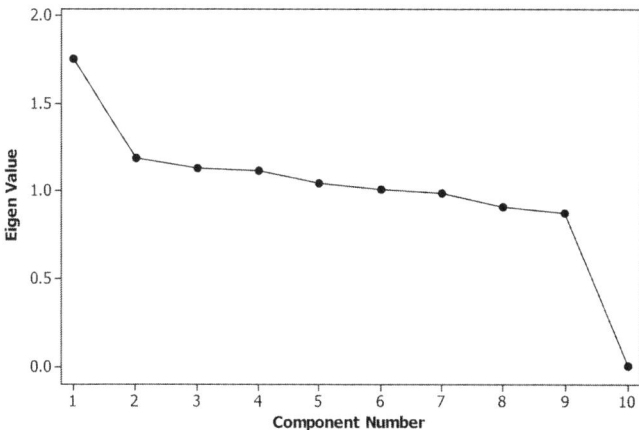

Figure 5.44. Scree plot from principal components analysis of the chipped stone assemblage.

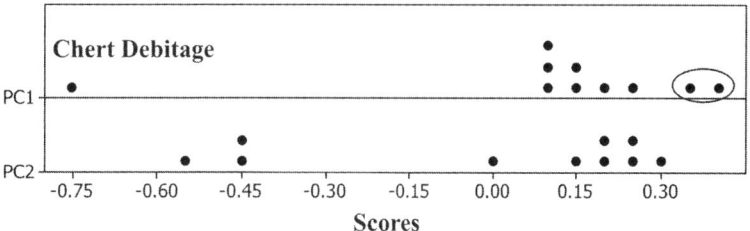

Figure 5.45. Coefficient values from principal components analysis of the chipped stone data set.

are converted into a table of partial chi-squared values (referred to as chi-squared distances), which serves to both standardize the data set and define the relationships between both variables and cases. The variation in the sample is then defined by the distance the individual chi-squared values display in a given case or variable when compared with an overall expected chi-squared value, often called total inertia. This value is analogous to the Eigen value in PCA and is used to measure the amount of variation each component (sometimes referred to as axis) in the analysis contributes.

Another advantage of correspondence analysis over principal components analysis is that the score values (referred to as loadings) are calculated in the same coordinate system for both variables and cases. In PCA, the coefficients for the variables are different measurements than those for the case scores, requiring separate analysis for the two. In CA, the loading values for variables and cases can be overlain on the same plot or placed side by side in similar plots, making it easy to see the relationships between diagnostic categories and collection circles. When dealing with large amounts of data, such as I am here, visual analysis is often faster and more effective for pattern recognition.

Correspondence Analysis of the Ceramic Data Set

The same 45 variables and 537 cases used in my principal components analysis were used for the correspondence analysis. The results were a bit more productive, however, since the size problem caused by the large numbers of G35 bowls appears to have been eliminated, and several additional patterns appear to be visible. For example, when we plot the variable (Fig. 5.46 *top*) and case (Fig. 5.46 *bottom*) loadings from component 1 and component 2, we see the same cluster pattern that we found during PCA with respect to solid-handled sahumadores and café braziers on Terraces C2 and E9. Therefore, CA provides further quantitative means to independently verify the patterns seen during surface density analysis.

Let us now look at a second pattern, not initially detected through either surface density analysis or PCA. On the left-hand side of the variable loading scatter plot, G3M bowl fragments are separated from the rest of the variables. This appears to be because G3M bowls were found in very high densities in a few circles of the North, West, and Northeast Terrace Groups. The specific collection circles where these bowls were clustered are identified in the case loading plot in the bottom of Figure 5.46. This is an important discovery because it reveals significant depositional patterns for a pottery type considered diagnostic of the Early Postclassic, and it separates that type from the materials diagnostic of earlier periods. This suggests that the patterns of occupation and use of Cerro Danush during the Early Postclassic were different from those seen in the Late Classic.

Our second CA graph (Fig. 5.47), which plots component 3 against component 4, also confirms one of the patterns identified during surface density analysis. In the variable loading scatter plot (Fig. 5.47 *top*), diagnostic materials below the zero line of the *y* axis are mostly Early Classic indicators (orange paste sherds and G23 bowls), while the highest variable above the zero line is the G3M bowl, an Early Postclassic indicator. Most of the Late Classic indicators are clustered in the center of the plot. Therefore, the *y* axis can be used as a way of tracking terrace occupations from the Early Classic to the Early Postclassic.

The collection circles found below the zero line of the case loading scatter plot (Fig. 5.47 *bottom*) are from the West, Southwest, South, and North-Central Terrace Groups, all of which were identified in the surface density analysis as having been occupied in the Early Classic. Interestingly, among the variables found above the zero line of the *y* axis are brown paste sherds and ollas with appliqué glyph motifs. Correspondence analysis of the ceramic data set, therefore, rather nicely supports the findings from surface density analysis.

Correspondence Analysis of the Chipped Stone Assemblage

As with the ceramic assemblage, the same data set that was used for principal components analysis was used for correspondence analysis of the chipped stone. Unlike the case with PCA, however, the resulting components from the CA were not dominated by size factors such as the abundance of chert debitage. In fact, all the patterns visible in the surface density analysis of chipped stone are remarkably well represented in the scatter plots of the variable and case loadings for components 2 and 3 (Fig. 5.48).

When we focus on the scatter plot for variables (Fig. 5.48 *top*), four separate clusters are readily apparent. The first is found in the center left portion of the graph, and is made up of three items: chert flakes, prismatic blades, and volcanic tuff debitage. All of these materials were found in significant amounts in all terrace groups on Cerro Danush, including the Summit Terrace Group. A second cluster of variables is found in the center right of the variable loading scatter plot, and is made up of chert cores, chert debitage, raspadores, and obsidian debitage. These materials were found in high percentages in every group except the Summit Terrace Group. The third cluster consists of volcanic tuff flakes and cores, and is found in the lower portion of the variable loading scatter plot. These materials were found in significant quantities only on terraces in the South and West Groups. Finally, 5 of the 6 chert bifaces recovered during survey were isolated finds; there were no other chipped stone items found in the same circles. Appropriately, chert bifaces appear separated from other variables on the graph.

Conclusions

In this chapter I have analyzed the spatial distributions of the artifacts from the Cerro Danush surface collection both qualitatively and quantitatively, using surface density plots, principal components analysis, and correspondence analysis. The patterns identified have been compared with data from other Valley of Oaxaca sites, such as Monte Albán, Jalieza, and El Palmillo. In the following paragraphs I summarize the most important findings from this analysis.

Cerro Danush was most likely first occupied at the threshold between the end of the Early Classic and the start of the Late Classic, a time when northward expansion of the site of Dainzú-Macuilxóchitl led residents to construct terraces along the base of the hill on the south and southwest sides. At this same time, the Summit Terrace Group and the North-Central Terrace Group were constructed.

The Late Classic saw a considerable increase in the population living on Cerro Danush, a trend reflected by significant increases in domestic terrace construction. This period represented the apogee in both population size and number of occupied terraces at Cerro Danush. Activities identified for lower-status households during this period included textile production and chert tool production, as well as the production and likely ritual use of mold-made figurines. Activities of the high-status residents at the summit of Cerro Danush may have included large-scale public rituals.

During the Early Postclassic, many of the domestic terraces on Cerro Danush appear to have been abandoned, including those of the Summit Terrace Group. The greater significance of

Density Distribution Analyses of Surface Artifacts

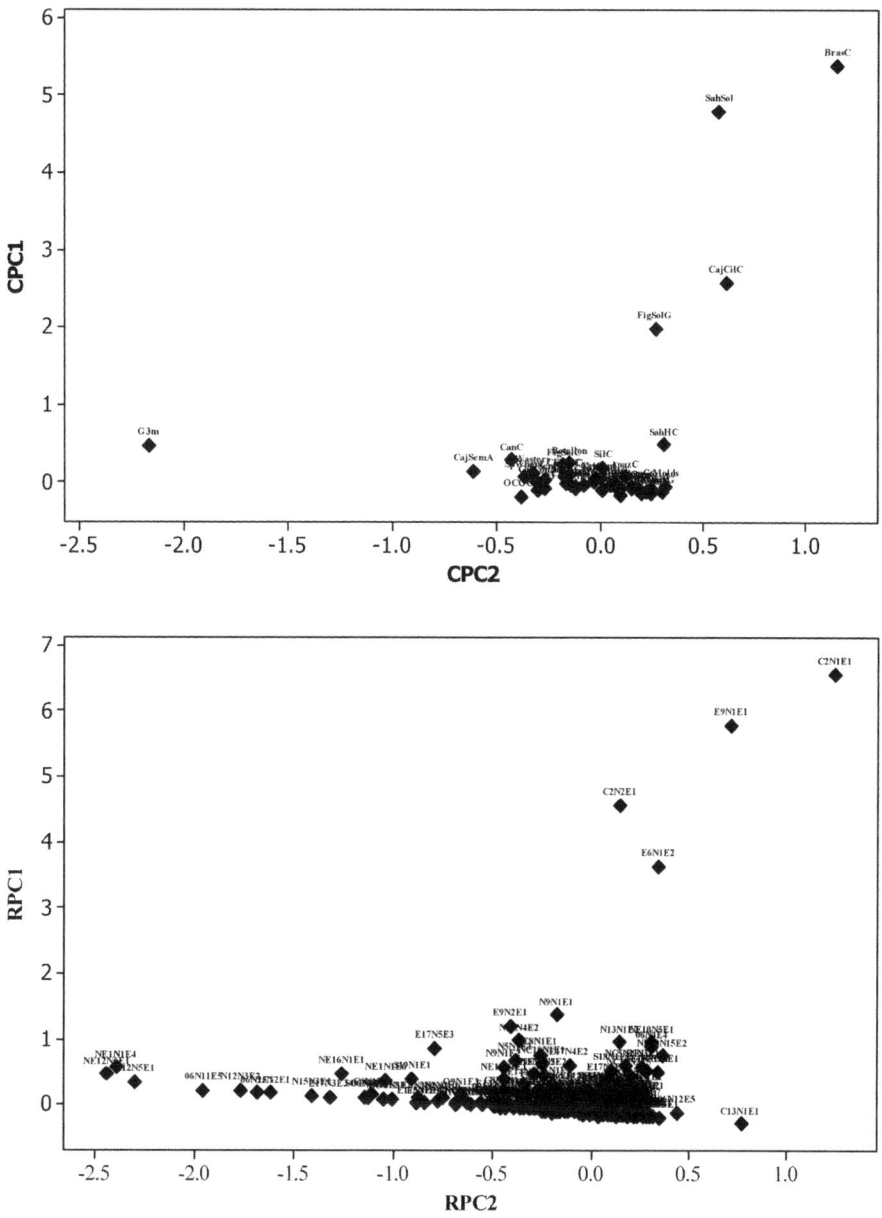

Figure 5.46. Variable (*top*) and case (*bottom*) loadings for components 1 and 2.

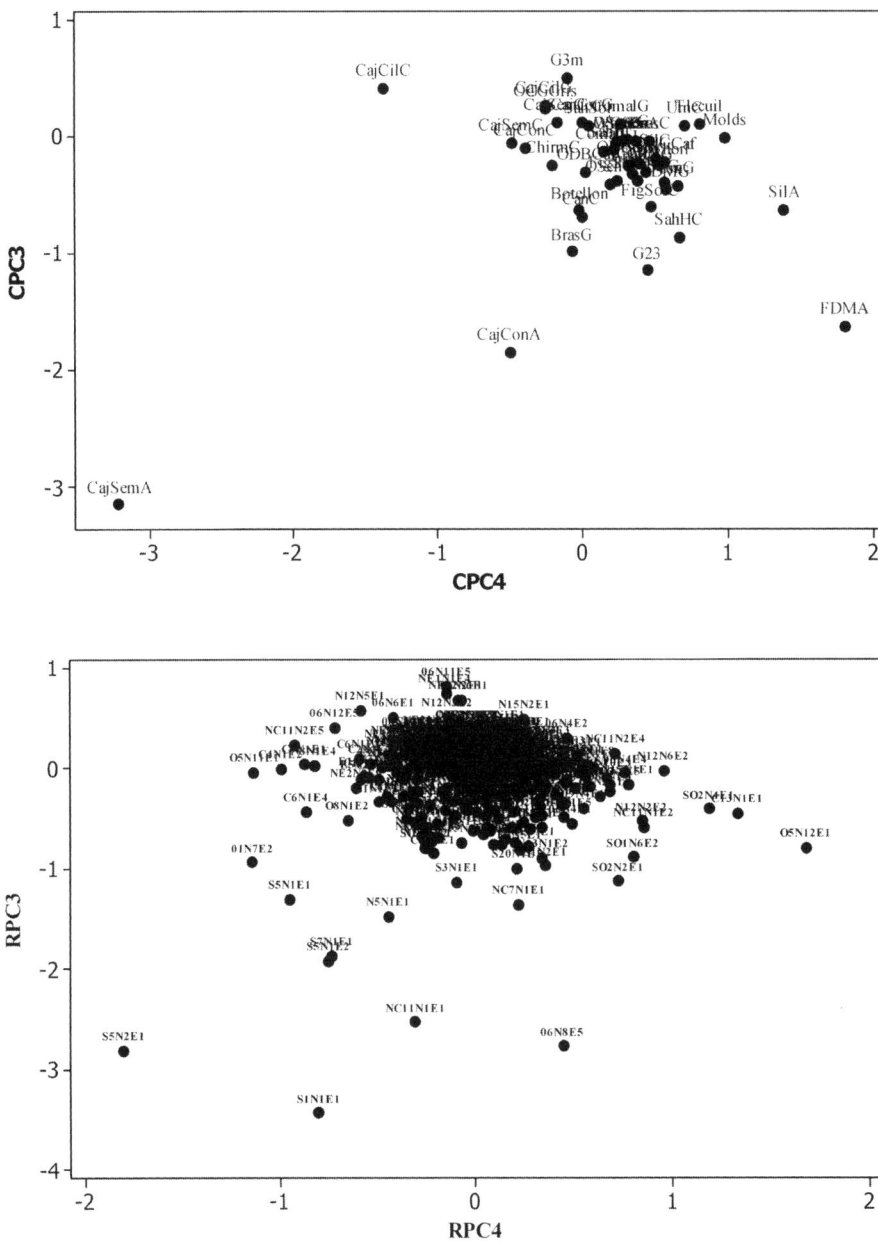

Figure 5.47. Variable (*top*) and case (*bottom*) loadings for components 3 and 4.

Density Distribution Analyses of Surface Artifacts 101

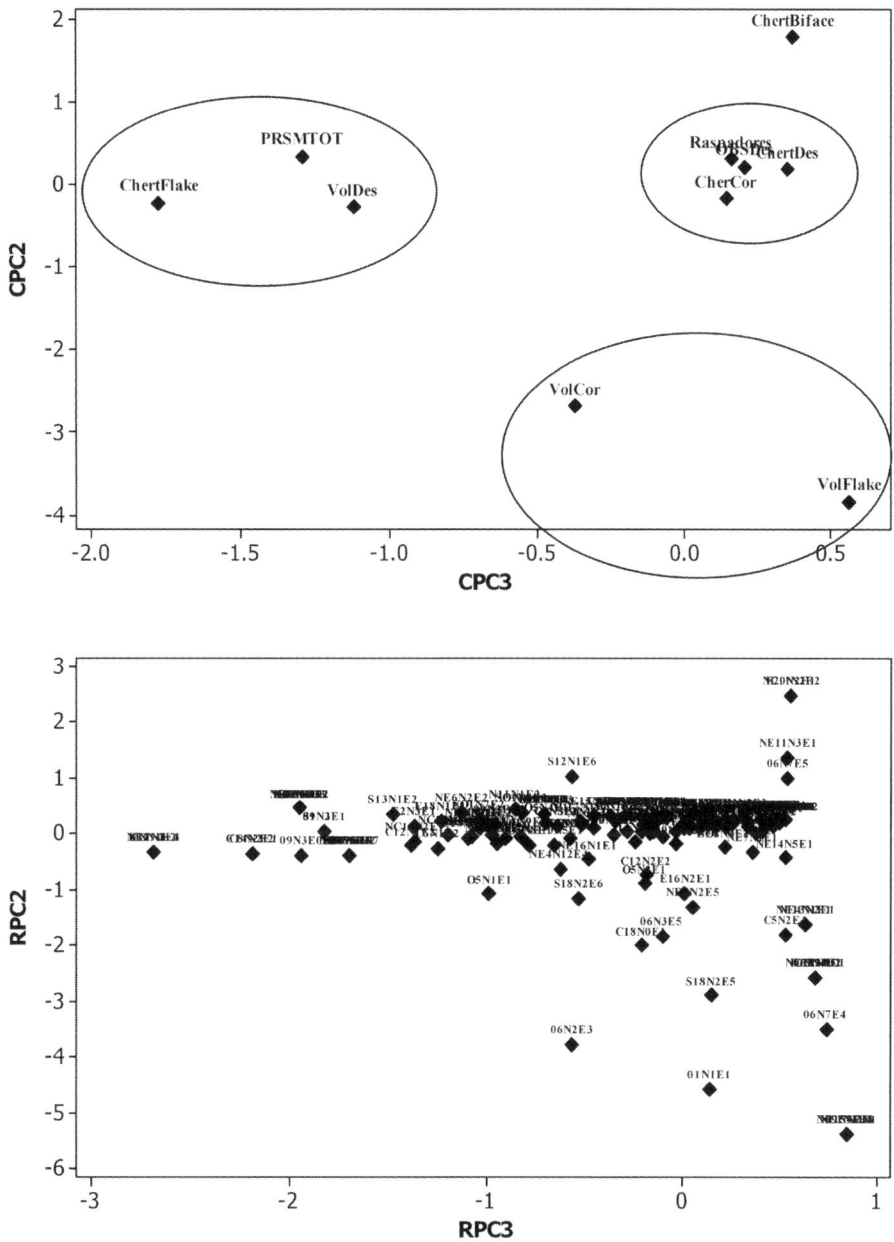

Figure 5.48. Variable (*top*) and case (*bottom*) loadings for components 2 and 3.

this abandonment for social organization will be presented in the concluding chapter.

In addition to the analyses described in this chapter, my survey and surface collection served another purpose: to identify appropriate areas for excavation during my second field season. Initially I planned excavation blocks for several terraces in the Northeast, West, and South Terrace Groups. After considering the logistical constraints of my project and the recommendations of the Consejo de Arqueología, however, I decided to conduct comprehensive excavations on just two terraces, S19 and S20.

I chose these terraces for several reasons: (1) their surface areas were small enough to allow me to excavate them in their entirety, yet large enough to contain complete Classic house complexes; (2) they were relatively well preserved, without much visible erosion damage to their retaining walls; (3) diagnostic ceramic markers for the Early Classic, Late Classic, and Early Postclassic periods were present on their surfaces; (4) they had a relatively high density of surface remains indicative of stone tool production; and (5) they displayed a recurring pattern seen throughout Cerro Danush, one in which contiguous terraces were stacked one above another and decreased in size with elevation.

I hoped that excavation of these terraces would allow for the investigation of factors such as (1) the relationship between adjacent terraces; (2) differences in terrace function based on size; (3) the relationship between surface materials and excavated materials; and most importantly, (4) diachronic differences in the layout and organization of house complexes from the Late Classic to the Early Postclassic. I also hoped that excavation data would help me evaluate the reliability of my surface data analyses. The following chapters describe my field methods and present the results from the second field season of my project.

6 | The Excavation of Terraces S19 and S20

The second phase of my project consisted of the complete excavation of two man-made terraces in the South Terrace Group. My goal was to excavate completely each terrace's most recent occupational surface, then probe vertically with test pits to identify/characterize earlier occupational surfaces. I hoped to (1) uncover house structures and other features indicative of domestic activities, (2) collect radiocarbon samples from different contexts in order to reconstruct the occupational history of each terrace, and (3) analyze the distribution of artifacts on each terrace. A secondary goal of my excavation was to obtain data that would allow me to evaluate my surface collection analyses. In this chapter I discuss the field operations and qualitative results of this second phase of my project.

A Description of the Excavation Area

Terraces S18, S19, and S20 are found in the South Terrace Group (Fig. 4.15) at the base of Cerro Danush, directly below a low-lying vertical rock face (Figs. 6.1, 6.2). They form a system of three stacked terraces, constructed directly on top of bedrock (Fig. 6.3). The lowest terrace—S18—is the largest, with a surface area of about 1860 m². It was the first of the three terraces constructed, and the retaining wall for Terrace S19 (with its surface area of about 400 m²) was built on top of Terrace S18's northeast corner. The smallest terrace, S20 (with a surface area of about 200 m²), was built directly atop bedrock on the northern edge of Terrace S19, most likely at or around the same time as the construction of S19.

These three terraces are directly connected to Terrace S25 (Fig. 4.15) by a reinforced path, and appear to relate to several artificial mounds in the vicinity. Just 200 m to the south, Markens, Winter, and Martínez López (2008) excavated the Lantiudee Complex, a cluster of seven mounds that include a civic-ceremonial complex and an elite residence. Roughly the same distance to the west lies the West Terrace Group (Figs. 4.4, 4.13).

Terraces S18–S20 have been periodically plowed in preparation for the planting of corn and beans, with the most recent episode occurring 3–5 years prior to the start of my project. When the terraces are not in use for agricultural purposes, goats and sheep are allowed to graze on the grass that grows on their surfaces. Other human activities in the area include small game hunting and firewood collecting.

Another source of post-abandonment human disturbance includes the placement of three concrete posts for high-tension wires in the southeast corner of Terrace S18. Although this activity caused damage, it appears to have been confined to a relatively small area, and is sufficiently distant from Terraces S19 and S20 to have not affected them directly. Because of project time and budget constraints, Terrace S18 was not excavated.

Figure 6.1. Terraces S18–S20.

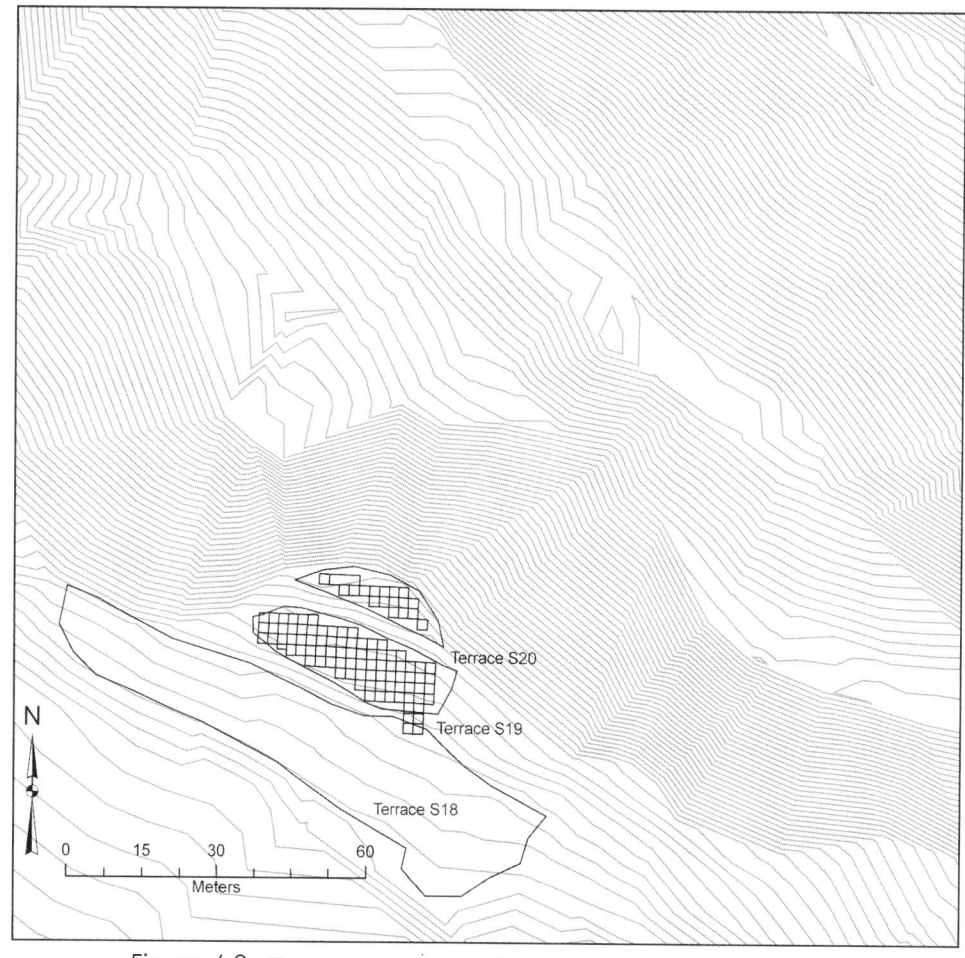

Figure 6.2. Topographic depiction of excavation area, Terraces S18–S20.

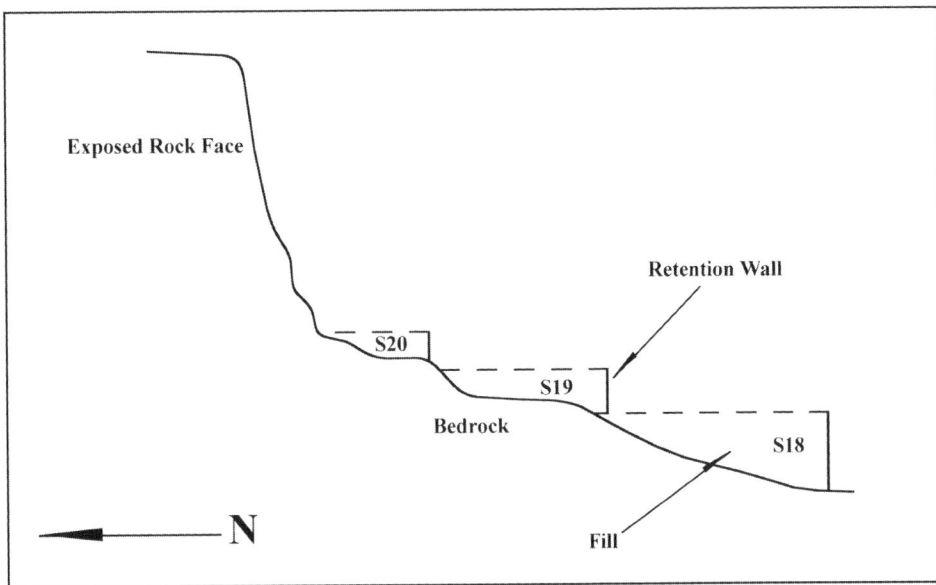

Figure 6.3. Profile sketch for Terraces S18–S20 (not to scale).

Establishing the Excavation Grid

The first week of my second field season (August 3–7, 2009) was spent setting up the excavation grid. Five site station points were established for horizontal and vertical reference (Fig. 6.4): the main site datum (BNS18A) and station point (BNS18B) on Terrace S18, two station points on Terrace S19 (BNS19A and BNS19B), and one on Terrace S20 (BNS20). These reference points were marked with 5 cm × 5 cm wooden stakes. The main datum point (BNS18A) was referenced to a reasonably permanent landmark, having been established exactly 5 m due north (magnetic azimuth) from the northwest corner of the most northerly of the three high-tension wire posts on Terrace S18 (Fig. 6.5). All of the points measured during this project were collected with a Nikon DTM-420 total station from these reference positions. The relative horizontal and vertical total station accuracy was established on a daily basis to within 1 cm by backsighting designated control points.

The UTM coordinates were also measured for each of the station points on a daily basis with a Garmin G-V handheld GPS device. Only readings with a reported accuracy of 3 m or better were saved. At the end of the project, the daily measurements were averaged to provide the horizontal UTM coordinates for the station points. The same procedures were used to translate and rotate the total station measurements into the UTM projected plane as in the first field season (Chapter 4). Based on comparison of the independent GPS and total station measurements for the reference points—BNS18B, BNS19A, BNS19B, and BNS20—the reported horizontal UTM coordinates are well within 1-m accuracy. The site datum BNS18A was used as the reference point for the translation and rotation of total station measurements.

The excavation grid for the site was established using a Silva Ranger compass to determine the reference azimuth, making the horizontal zero angle for the total station measurements magnetic north (2.01° east of UTM grid north). As in the first season, after the initial establishment of the zero angle, the total station was calibrated daily by using a backsight point rather than a compass. Using the Stake Out function of the total station software, I marked the locations for the excavation block corners with a prism rod and tape measure.

Once the total station confirmed the desired locations, they were marked with 30-cm nails. After that, strings were tied between the corner points, forming a box, and the rest of the grid was set up making measurements along the string lines. During the process, each individual nail location was verified using Pythagorean theorem measurements with adjacent nails. When the process was complete, the coordinates of each nail were recorded with the total station. Once the grid of 2 m × 2 m units was in place, string was tied between all the nails to guide the excavation.

Individual excavation units were assigned numbers based on the terrace, the excavation block, and the location of the nails in their southwest corners. These designations were based on distances north and east of the baselines for the overall grid on a given terrace. For example, the nail in the southwest corner of unit N6E0 in excavation Block A on Terrace S19 was located on the most westerly grid line of excavations on that terrace, some six units (12 m) north of the most southerly grid line. These designations provide relative provenience of the materials collected from those units, while the UTM coordinates of the nails provide actual proveniences.

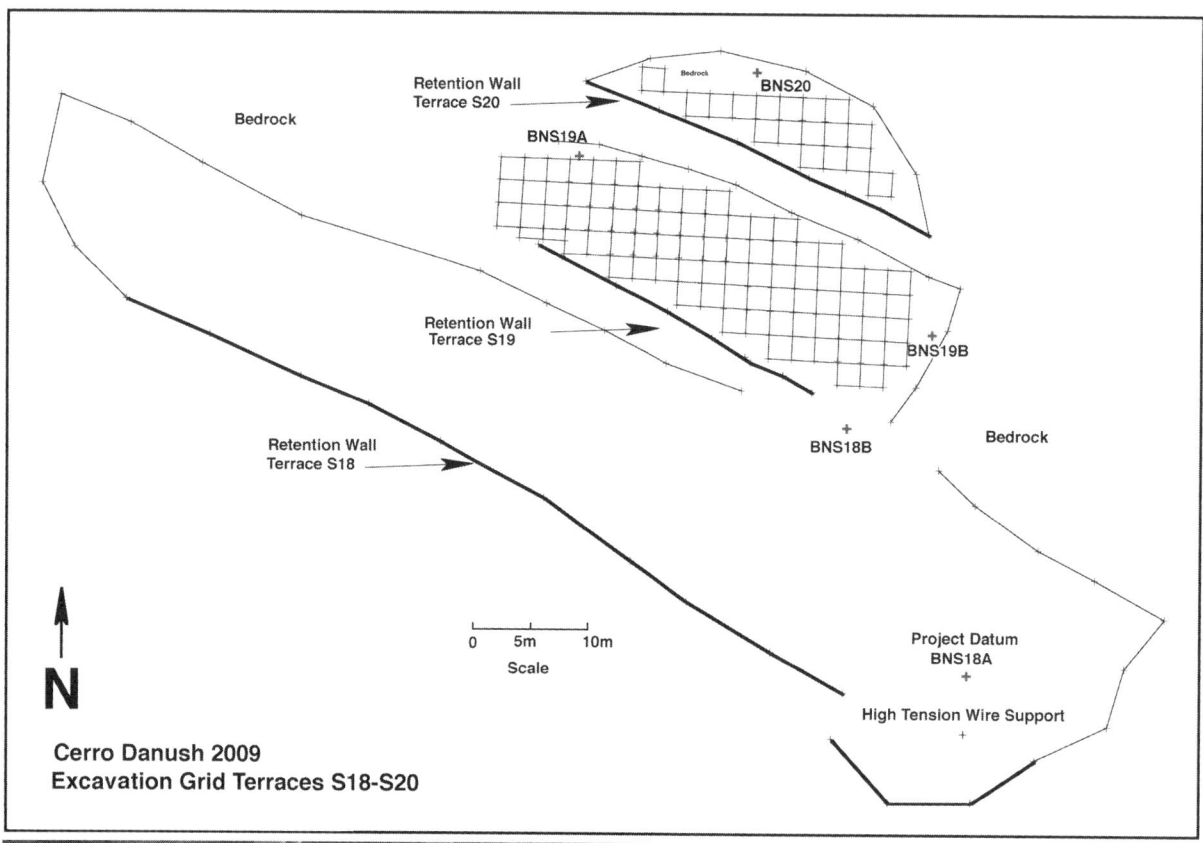

(*above*) Figure 6.4. Plan view of excavation grids.

(*left*) Figure 6.5. Project datum BNS18A, Terrace S18.

General Excavation Procedures

Excavations began on August 10 and were concluded on November 27, 2009, with backfill operations completed the following week. For field operations, the eight project workers were divided into two excavation teams, with two people screening and two people excavating in each team. Using handpicks, shovels, and trowels, the project workers excavated 2 m × 2 m squares in natural layers, meaning that they stopped digging vertically either when soil color or texture changed, or when they came upon a feature such as a patio floor. Identified structures and features were then carefully excavated with paintbrushes, ice picks, and trowels. All excavated soil was collected, using shovels, dustpans, and buckets, and was screened using 6-gauge mesh ($\approx$ 5-mm squares).

Standardized excavation forms were used to record information (such as soil color, volume, and depth) from the excavation of each layer for every square. All objects of interest, such as complete or nearly complete ceramic vessels, were drawn onto the map of the corresponding excavation form, and their locations were recorded with the total station. Excavation forms, bags for material collection, and storage boxes were prepared before excavation of individual units began. Excavation teams did not begin new units until the corresponding excavation forms, material bags, and boxes from current excavation units had been completed and approved by the project archaeologist, including measurements, drawings, and photographs. All excavation forms are now bound in a notebook, a copy of which is stored with the registered artifacts in the town of Macuilxóchitl.

A total of 173, 410 liters of soil were screened, with the majority coming from Terrace S19 (163,550 liters, 94.3%). All the soil removed from the excavation units was screened, and all stone, ceramic, and bone artifacts were collected and saved in marked 1-gallon (3.785 liters) Ziploc bags. The soil volume was measured through the use of calibrated 20-liter buckets. The excavators filled each bucket to a 20-liter mark before it was screened, and the screeners kept track of the number of buckets by placing a mark on the corresponding excavation form for every new bucket screened. In the case of incomplete final buckets, they were recorded as being 1/4, 1/2, or 3/4 full, and the measurements for each layer were rounded to the nearest liter, making the error in reporting individual layers approximately 1–2 liters. After screening, the soil was sorted into heavy materials (the portion that did not go through the screen) and light materials (the portion that did go through the screen). Both portions were stored at the edges of the terrace, to be used later as backfill.

Stratigraphy and Depositional History of the Terraces

Like all the terraces on Cerro Danush, Terraces S19 and S20 were constructed by first building a retaining wall of loose stones and then filling in the area upslope. Their modern surfaces, however, are the product of several natural and cultural formation processes that have occurred since their abandonment. In this section, I describe the stratigraphic layers encountered on both terraces and try to reconstruct the depositional history as it relates to the systemic and archaeological contexts (LaMotta and Schiffer 1999, 2001; Schiffer 1975, 2000). This will inform the following discussions concerning the archaeological features and structures excavated at the site.

Terrace S20

Terrace S20 (Fig. 6.6) is located directly underneath the low cliff face. Prior to excavation, fallen stones littered its surface, which was gently inclined from south to north. Although an excavation block (Block H, Fig. 6.7) was set up on this terrace, a large area of bedrock was visible on the surface, and excavation of six 2 m × 2 m units (N1E11, N4E9, N2E8, N3E6, N4E3, N5E1) quickly exposed bedrock just below the surface as well. On the upslope part of the terrace, excavation units N5E1 and N4E9 yielded low artifact densities (just 0.03 artifacts per liter of soil removed), and bedrock was reached within 10–14 cm of the surface.

The lower part of the terrace (just north of the retention wall), between excavation units N4E3 and N1E11, contained deeper soils than did the upper part, but we reached bedrock relatively quickly in those units as well, with N1E11 being the deepest unit at 24 cm. In the plow zone (approximately 15–20 cm), soil was loose, sandy, and light brown in color, but the lower soils found just above the bedrock were much lighter and denser. This change in color is probably due to the terrace's depositional history. The plow zone layer is darkened from the addition of organic materials, while the lower soil, which has a more compact, clay-like texture, is whitened by calcium carbonate, and may actually be soil formed by the decomposition of the bedrock below it.

Artifact densities from the excavated units on Terrace S20 were much lower than those on Terrace S19, averaging about 0.55 artifacts per liter of soil screened. This figure would be still lower if unit N1E11 (which contained a density of 0.93 artifacts per liter) was excluded. N1E11 was the most southern and lowest excavation unit on Terrace S20; it was also the closest to Terrace S19. The soil in this unit (particularly in the second layer) was much darker than the rest of the terrace, and many of the artifacts collected from it were found immediately on top of the bedrock. This pattern was similar to that seen in excavated areas of bedrock on Terrace S19, just downslope. The density of artifacts and dark soil suggest the possibility that domestic refuse may have been dumped in this area from the residents of Terrace S19.

No archaeological features were found on Terrace S20. Indeed, had such features existed, they most surely would have been destroyed when the terrace was plowed. The low density of artifacts recovered, its location below the cliff, its relatively small size, and its stratigraphy all suggest that Terrace S20 was never used to support domestic structures, but served to support Terrace S19. While Terrace S19 was in use, Terrace S20's retention wall served as a barrier to falling rocks; the area upslope filled in over time through a combination of rock fall and soil erosion from above, as well as the deposition of refuse from below.

A total of 9860 liters of soil was screened from Terrace S20. Plans for further excavation were abandoned after the exposure of the six excavation units revealed its nature. The excavation of Terrace S20 shows that while most terraces on Cerro Danush may have served domestic purposes, not all supported residences.

Terrace S19

The modern surface of Terrace S19 is slightly inclined from south to north (Fig. 6.8), albeit to a lesser degree than that of Terrace S20. An excavation grid consisting of eighty-seven 2 m × 2 m units was established on its surface (Fig. 6.9). Because of the large grid size, it was divided into seven excavation blocks. This provided further spatial references for the excavation areas.

Figure 6.6. Terrace S20 (viewed from the east).

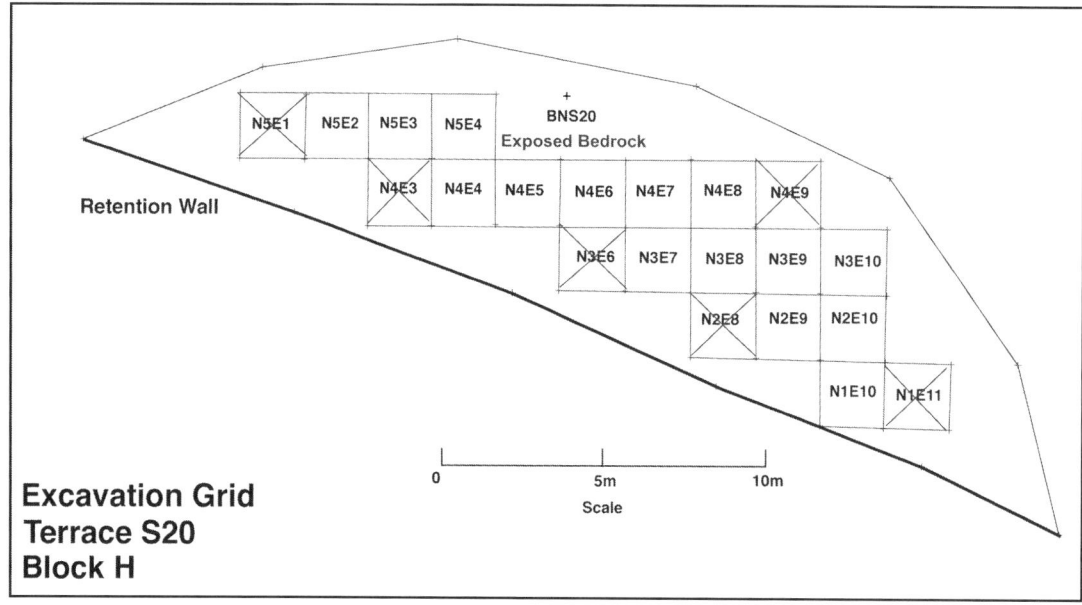

Figure 6.7. Plan view of excavation grid on Terrace S20 (Xs mark excavated units).

Figure 6.8. Terrace S19 prior to excavation (viewed from the eastern edge).

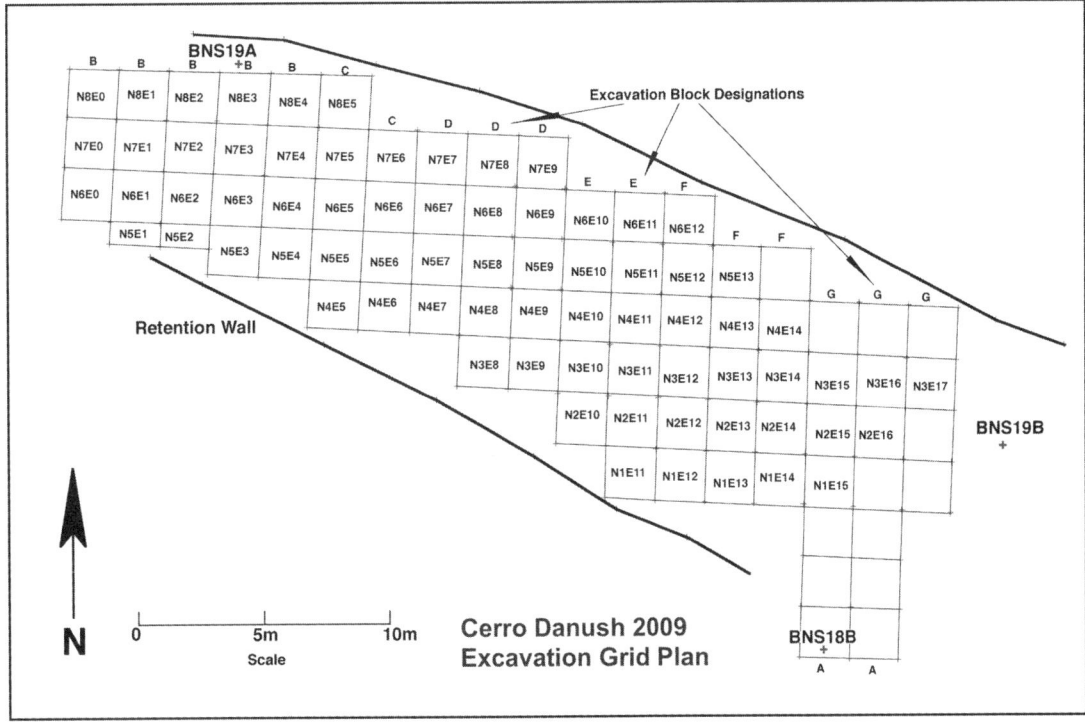

Figure 6.9. Plan view of excavation grid for Terrace S19.

Block B was located on the west side of the terrace; the remaining blocks were lettered sequentially from west to east, ending with Block G. Block A was established on the southeastern edge of Terrace S19 and extended into Terrace S18 in order to investigate physical connections between the terraces. Owing to the extensive erosion found in Blocks F and G, I decided that it would not be productive to excavate this area.

Like Terrace S20, S19 had been plowed recently. Because of this, the terrace did not contain any large woody vegetation, only grass, and as a result little root disturbance was encountered during the project. On the eastern edge of the terrace there is a bedrock platform that slopes gently out from the steeper exposed rock face above, and protrudes from the surface just below Terrace S20's retention wall. We uncovered this platform all along the eastern edge of the terrace, and its dark weathered appearance suggested that it lay exposed during occupation, marking the terrace's eastern boundary. On the opposite end of the terrace, part of the retaining wall had collapsed, and subsequent water erosion washed a small portion of the terrace downhill onto Terrace S18, causing a steep mound of eroded sediment on the lower terrace's west side (Fig. 6.1). Excavations along this edge of the terrace confirmed that it previously extended farther to the west, though probably only by 5–10 m. Beyond that point, bedrock once again rose to form an exposed vertical rock face (Figs. 6.1, 6.2).

Four stratigraphic layers were identified on Terrace S19. From upper to lower, they were: (1) modern plow zone; (2) a mixed natural/cultural layer of fill from erosion and refuse deposition; (3) a cultural layer resulting from human activities in the Early Postclassic; and (4) a second natural/cultural layer, resulting from human activities prior to the Postclassic. Seventy-four of the units established (Fig. 6.9, numbered squares) were excavated to at least the first level, and fifty-six were excavated to the base of the second.

When units were not excavated beyond the first level, it was either because I came down on bedrock in the first layer (units N3E17 and N6E12) or because they were located where the erosion layer was not as deep, and an important patio floor was found just below the plow zone (see discussion below). The latter was the case for most of the southern units, in excavation Blocks E, F, and G. A total of fourteen test units (either 1 m × 2 m or 2 m × 2 m in size) were excavated into the third stratigraphic layer, and four of those were further excavated to the base of the fourth layer.

The stratigraphic profile drawn at the western edge of Terrace S19 (Fig. 6.10) shows the superimposed layers found there. The upper two layers have resulted from natural erosion, so their surfaces slope more from north to south; the surfaces of the third and fourth layers were man-made and are relatively flat. Because of the sloping nature of the two upper layers, the distance from the modern terrace surface and the ancient one decreases greatly as one moves southward across the terrace. In some areas we found no second layer, since the ancient surface was found just below, or even within, the plow zone. Massive erosion has damaged some of the structures we found, and perhaps destroyed others that once existed on the southern end of the terrace.

The plow zone of Terrace S19 was brown in color and roughly 20–25 cm deep. No archaeological features were found within this layer. A total of 77,710 liters of soil were screened from the plow zone, with an average artifact density of 1.25 artifacts per liter (a/L). The depth of the second stratigraphic layer varied, ranging from 25 cm to 60 cm; this layer was generally darker in color and more compact than the plow zone. A total of 71,810 liters of soil was screened from the second layer, and the average artifact density was higher than for the first layer (1.62 a/L). This was especially true along the northern and eastern edges of the terrace, where artifact density was between 2.5 and 4.0 a/L.

The second stratigraphic layer was a complex mixture of erosion products, wall collapse, and refuse deposition, and its depositional history differed slightly on the east and west sides of the terrace. On the west side, the upper portion of a protective wall (North Wall, see below) collapsed onto the terrace after abandonment, making the second layer a combination of

Figure 6.10. Profile of western edge of Terrace S19.

wall fall and sediment deposited through water erosion onto an ancient occupational surface. The depositional pattern for the second layer was similar on the east side of the terrace, with the exception that bedrock played the same protective role that the man-made wall did on the western side, and the second layer was made up entirely of sediment there. In both cases, the second layer was deepest just below the wall on the west and the bedrock platform to the east, preserving many of the archaeological features uncovered during the project.

The artifact densities in the second layer were greatest (2.5 to 4.0 a/L) in three areas to the north, upslope of the protective wall and northeast of the bedrock platform. Density decreased toward the south, or downslope of these areas (Fig. 6.11). The densest artifact distributions may reflect areas used for dumping refuse during the occupation of the terrace. Outside these dump areas, the density distribution pattern was consistent with erosion. Soil color suggested that the lighter soils migrated downslope more easily than the heavier artifacts. We can propose, therefore, that the northern/upslope portion of the second layer was the result of both cultural processes (dumping of refuse) and natural processes (erosion), while the southern/downslope portion was largely the result of erosion.

On the west side of the terrace, the third layer consisted of 15–20 cm of fill, the result of human efforts to bury an earlier occupational surface and create a new one. This new surface may have been covered with stucco during use, as we found small patches of that material on the surface during excavation. Most of the stucco had eroded away, however, probably because of post-abandonment exposure to the elements. The color of the soil in this layer was generally dark brown—lighter than the layer above it—and its texture was that of compact sandy loam.

At the base of the third layer, we found the intact stucco house floors and foundation walls of the fourth layer, whose more deeply buried condition had most likely protected them from the effects of erosion. We mapped these early features, but did not remove them by continuing on to bedrock.

I excavated a total of eleven 2 m × 2 m and three 1 m × 2 m test units to the base of the third stratigraphic layer, with 12,385 liters of soil screened. As one moved across the terrace from west to east, the stratigraphy of the third and fourth layers became more difficult to interpret. This happened because the most recent occupational surface on the west side (the top of the third layer) was elevated above its eastern counterpart by a stone-lined step in the center of the terrace. The stratigraphy was further complicated by the fact that the surface of the third layer on the east side was level with the surface of the fourth layer on the west (Fig. 6.12).

On the east side of the terrace, the third layer consisted of a thin cap (≈ 15–20 cm) of burned earth, charcoal, soot, and ash (Fig. 6.13, Plate 1). Below that (fourth layer), we found no evidence of an earlier occupational surface, just a thick layer of compact fill above bedrock (Fig. 6.12, Layer 4). It appears that the east side of the terrace was filled in in advance of its use for residential purposes, allowing brush to accumulate on its surface. Before constructing an occupational surface there, the residents first burned off the vegetation and compacted the remains into the thin cap that makes up the third layer.

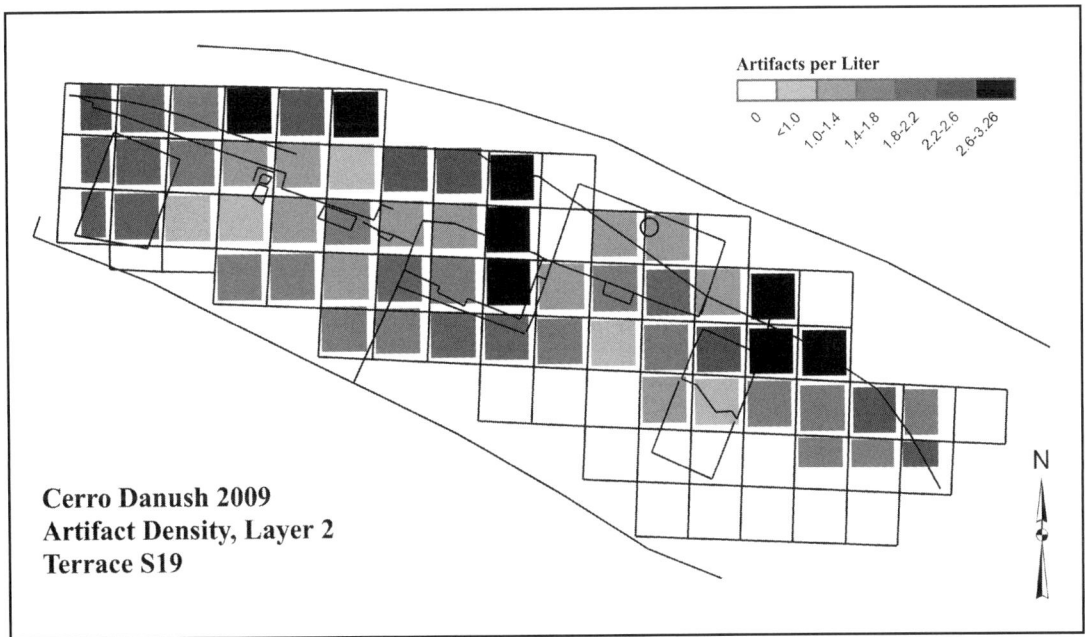

Figure 6.11. Relative artifact densities, Layer 2, Terrace S19. (Blank units were not excavated beyond Layer 1.)

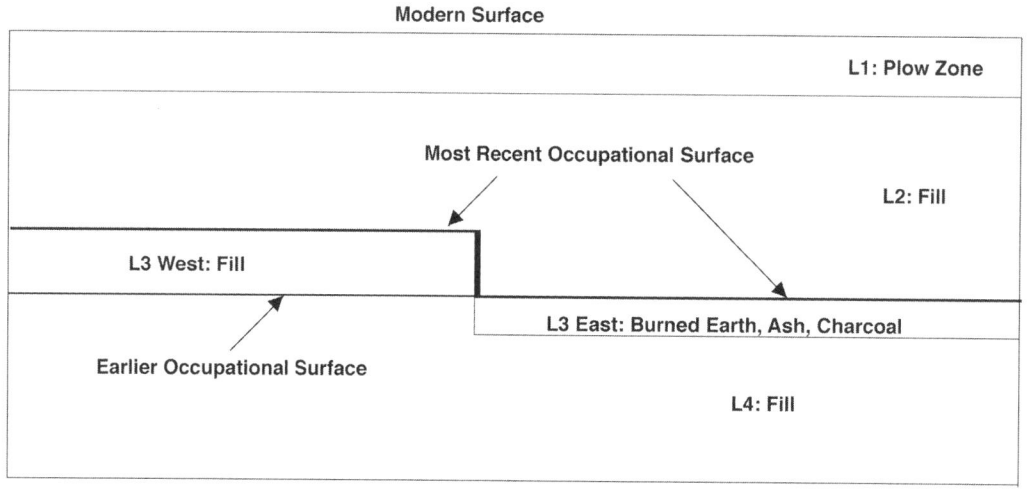

Figure 6.12. Profile sketch of Terrace S19 (not to scale).

Figure 6.13. Layer 3, east side of Terrace S19 (also see Plate 1).

Horizontal Excavation of Terrace S19

I initiated excavations in Block B, on the west side of the terrace, digging alternate squares so that the stratigraphy in the profiles of the first units could be used to guide our excavation of later units. In the initial excavation squares, we found a high density of stones, just beneath the plow zone, that appeared to come from the collapse of a wall. The excavation of adjacent units revealed these stones in nearly the entire area of Blocks B and C (Fig. 6.14). Although a faint line of stones was distinguishable on the northern edge of the wall fall, it was difficult to discern any obvious structural features. Rather than digging down into the stones and possibly missing or damaging features, I decided to move to the east and backtrack, with the hope that things would become clearer if I came in from a different angle.

I then opened up Block F, particularly unit N6E12, because its location made it possible to follow exposed bedrock downslope until we reached an ancient living surface. Once this surface had been identified, it would be easy to follow it westward toward Block B. This strategy worked well, as there was no confusing wall fall in the area, and we quickly uncovered the remains of a stone house foundation, designated Structure A. Horizontal expansion of excavations in the area uncovered two more house foundations, Structures B and C, with a central patio between them. These features were collectively designated the East Patio Complex, and are discussed in detail below.

I followed the patio surface to the east until bedrock rose up again, marking the eastern limit of the terrace. On the west we followed the patio surface to the central portion of the terrace, where heavy erosion made it more difficult to interpret structures. An intact stucco floor was uncovered, along with some stone lines that did not seem to relate well to the structures found to the east. The initial ambiguity in this central region of the terrace was cleared up after we had exposed a large east-west-running

Figure 6.14. Wall fall, Blocks B and C, Terrace S19.

wall, designated the North Wall, which was clearly elevated above the other features in the vicinity. Because the base of this wall was also elevated some 20 cm above the surface we were following, I concluded that a nearby line of cut stones, extending north to south, were actually facing stones for a partially eroded step that elevated the occupational surface. Once this fact was clear, we went ahead and excavated all subsequent units to the west until they were level with the base of the wall and the top of the step (Fig. 6.12).

Because the most recent occupational surface was now clearly defined, it became relatively easy to remove the wall fall mentioned above, carefully exposing the face of the North Wall and following it to the western edge of the terrace. In Block B, we exposed another stone house foundation, designated Structure E, and grouped it with the North Wall as part of the West Patio Complex. Due to time constraints and the heavily eroded nature of the western edge of the terrace, we concluded our horizontal excavations after the end of the North Wall was exposed. At this point the terrace sloped steeply downward toward Terrace S18, and further excavation in this direction might have placed Structure E at risk of collapse.

Description of Structures from the Most Recent Occupational Surface

The top of the third stratigraphic layer (Fig. 6.12) constituted the most recent occupational surface found on Terrace S19. Once horizontal exposure of this surface had been completed, all the structures were cleaned with brushes, carefully mapped, and photographed. The resulting plan (Fig. 6.15) is referred to continuously in this section. The solid lines on the drawing represent walls or alignments of stone that were mapped with the total station in the field, while the dashed lines represent the proposed locations of walls that have been destroyed by erosion.

Due to the uneven nature of the terrace surface, the structures found to either side of the central step are divided into two separate complexes, the East Patio Complex and the West Patio Complex. On first inspection of the radiocarbon results, the construction of the former appeared to predate the latter by a significant period of time (Faulseit 2011). Analysis of the buried ceramic vessel offerings found in Layer 3 of the West Patio Complex (Chapter 7), however, suggests that the two patio complexes form a single residential unit. That unit was constructed at the end of the Late Classic or the beginning of the Early Postclassic, and remained in use for as long as 200–300 years. It appears that some reconstruction took place after the major reconfiguration of the terrace, in particular the addition of a low buttress to the original protective wall. What follows is a detailed description of the design, orientation, and layout of the structures that make up this residential unit.

The East Patio Complex

The East Patio Complex consists of three rectangular house foundations arranged around a central patio (Structures A, B, and C, Fig. 6.16). The structures appear to be contemporary with one another, as they share the same orientation and construction technique and are situated atop the same surface. The layout of the house foundations and patio follows a typical pattern found in the Valley of Oaxaca, one that became common during the Classic period (Winter 1974; Feinman and Nicholas 2009; González Licón 2003) and continued into the Postclassic (Winter 2002, 2003). Its general properties are similar to those of the Late Postclassic Lanisbaa house complex excavated in Mound 1 at Dainzú-Macuilxóchitl during the highway salvage project of Winter et al. (2007). Although there is variation among the three structures involved (discussed in detail below), they all measure between 2–3 m wide and 4.5–6 m long, and consist of stone wall façades filled in to form solid rectangular platforms.

The central patio is roughly square. It measures 6.22 m in length (the distance between Structures C and A, Fig. 6.16), and covers approximately 40 m². The downslope portion of the complex was highly eroded, with the southern foundation walls of both Structures A and C completely destroyed, and large portions of their east and west foundation walls missing as well. It is possible that a fourth structure once existed at the southern end of the patio, fully enclosing it, but this is now impossible to verify. Excavations elsewhere in the Valley of Oaxaca have shown that complexes of this type can have as many as four, or as few as one, house platforms (Winter 1974).

Structure A

Structure A consists of what was once a rectangular house foundation. Because its southern end is so thoroughly eroded away, its exact measurements are unknown, but it probably approximated 2.5 m × 5 m. It is located on the east side of the East Patio Complex, roughly 8–10 m from the eastern edge of the terrace (Fig. 6.17). I found no evidence to suggest which way the entrance to the structure faced, but it most likely opened onto the patio that it shared with Structures B and C to the west. Both of these structures had stairs that led into the same patio (see below).

Structure A's northern foundation wall (Fig. 6.18) was orientated 113° east of north (grid angle, not magnetic), and was the only wall that remained completely intact. It measured 2.38 m long and between 30 cm and 32 cm high. The construction style is *bloque y laja*, where small rectangular cut stones were used to fill in the spaces between larger blocks. The wall was finished with a layer of thin flat stones, placed along the top to provide a smooth flat surface. Part of the wall's base made contact with bedrock, and the rest was leveled with soil, ash, and charcoal.

Several rim sherds were embedded between the stones of the foundation wall (Fig. 6.18). These were intentionally placed in the mud mortar as spacers during its construction, and were identified as fragments of G35 bowls (Appendix B, Figs. B1, B2).

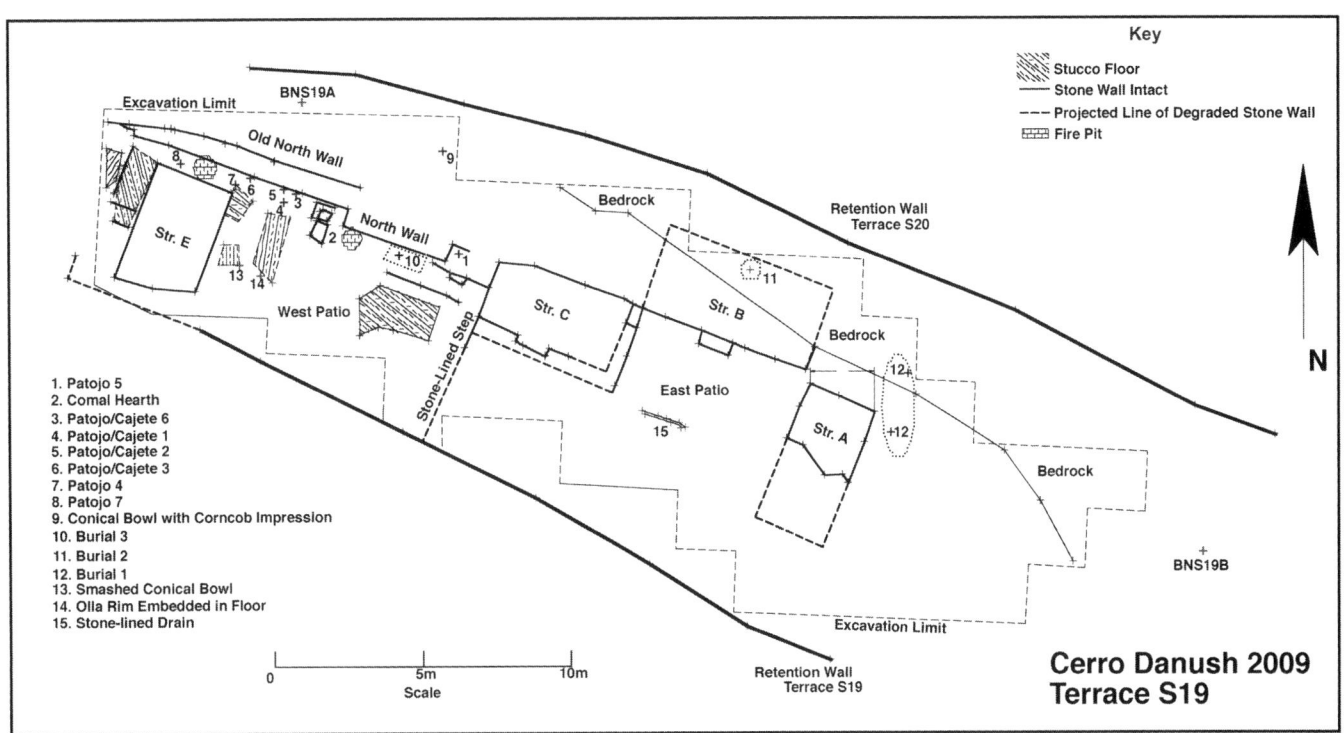

Figure 6.15. Plan view of features and structures excavated on Terrace S19.

This ceramic type was most heavily used during the Late Classic, and the "chinking" of sherds within the mortar was common at other sites (such as Lambityeco) during that time. Because it was possible to identify these sherds as G35s in situ, we left them in place rather than risk damaging the wall by removing them.

The east and west walls were heavily damaged and traceable only for a short distance (about 2.5 m) to the south. They were oriented perpendicular to the northern wall (23° east of north). The center of the platform was filled in with stones and earth and contained very few sherds. The top of the platform may have been covered in stucco, but no remains of this material had survived. A circular area of burned earth was exposed in the northwest corner of the structure (Figs. 6.16, 6.17).

Along the eastern edge of the structure, at the base of the second layer, we recovered several pieces of burned daub (*bajareque*, Appendix B). This discovery suggested that the walls above the foundation were made of wattle and daub, a construction technique typical of commoner houses in prehispanic Oaxaca. In this same area we also found fragments of prepared chalk blocks (*cal*, Appendix B), which may have been destined for either the production of stucco or the preparation of corn flour (Chapter 7).

Northeast of Structure A, in an area where bedrock projects above the patio's surface, the soil became darker and the density of artifacts increased considerably (Fig. 6.11); this area may have been used as a refuse dump by the occupants of the complex. In this same region, parts of an adult burial (Burial 1, see below) were found dispersed among several excavation units. No other features were found in or around Structure A.

Further east, along the edge of the bedrock platform (Fig. 6.17), the surface was darkened with soot and ash, and I uncovered a large stone that appeared to have a smooth, flattened surface. This stone was resting on the same level as the base of the structures in the East Patio Complex and may have served as a metate (Fig. 6.17). Its size and weight evidently allowed it to remain in place despite the plowing of the terrace, and we decided to leave it in place after the excavation had been completed.

Structure B

Structure B (Fig. 6.19) was another rectangular house platform, located just north and west of Structure A. It appears to have been oriented perpendicular to the latter, with its long end running east-west rather than north-south. The base of the structure's southern foundation wall rests atop the patio, but the rest of the structure was built directly on top of the bedrock platform on the northern edge of the terrace. Its elevated position placed most of Structure B within the plow zone, and it had been damaged as a result. Fragments of its southern and eastern

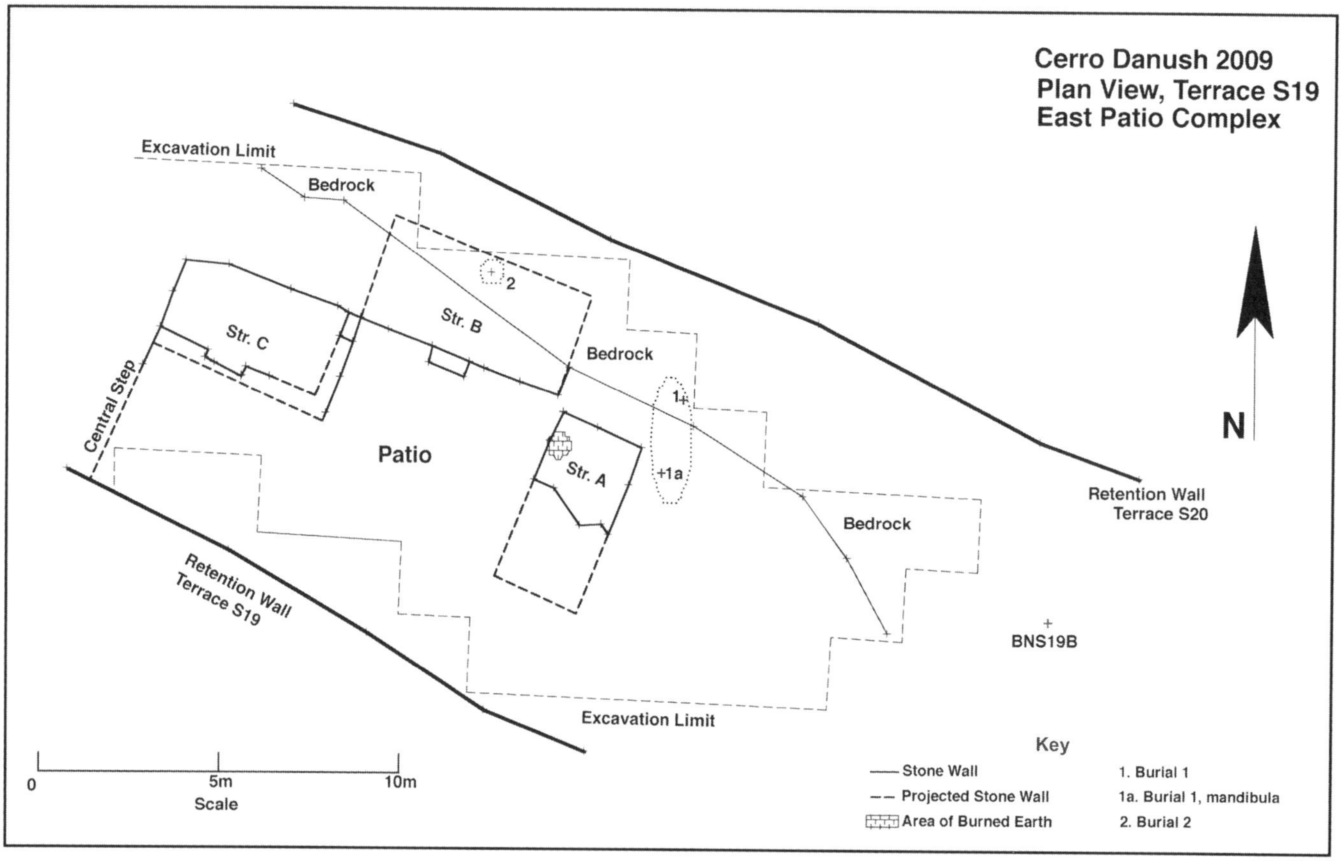

Figure 6.16. East Patio Complex: *top*, plan drawing; *bottom*, photograph (viewed from the east).

Figure 6.17.
Eastern edge of Terrace S19.

Figure 6.18.
Northern foundation wall, Structure A.

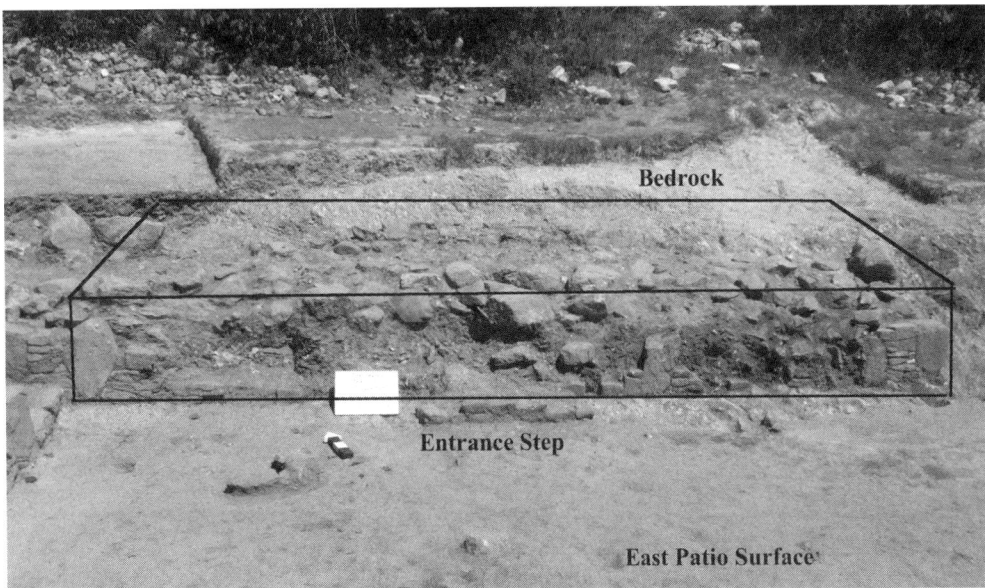

Figure 6.19.
Structure B, East Patio Complex (lines indicate proposed platform).

foundation walls were all that remained, and they were in poor condition. Nevertheless, enough of the structure remained to ascertain its basic form.

Structure B's southern foundation wall, constructed in the bloque y laja style, was oriented 113° east of north (magnetic) and measured 5.9 m long from the southeast corner to its intersection with Structure C, making the structure's estimated size a little larger than that of Structure A (3 m × 6 m). Owing to erosion I was unable to measure the original height of this wall above the patio, but it must have been considerably higher than the remaining stones suggest. This conclusion is based on the assumption that the house platform surface was level and not sloping, meaning that the wall would need to extend higher to match the sloping bedrock and maintain a level floor.

A small line of cut stones protrudes into the patio from the center of the wall. These are most likely the remains of what was once a step that led into the structure from the patio. The line measured 1.15 m long by 0.43 m wide, but I was unable to ascertain how high it might have been originally, or if there was more than one step.

Although I was unable to identify any trace of a western or northern foundation wall, much of the compact sediment and stone fill that made up the platform was still visible (Fig. 6.19). It is in a portion of this fill that I found the remains of an infant burial (Burial 2, see below), nearly cut in half by the plow. To the north and east of the burial the bedrock rises sharply, and artifact densities in the thin layer of soil excavated there were very low (Fig. 6.11). This rise in bedrock may have been exposed during the occupation of the house complex; indeed, it is probable that bedrock itself was used as a foundation for the northern wattle-and-daub structure wall.

Structure C

Like Structures A and B, Structure C consisted of a rectangular house foundation with a stone façade; it is located on the west side of the East Patio Complex (Fig. 6.16). Excavation of Structure C revealed a more complex construction history than we saw in the other two structures, with at least two periods of occupation/use separated by reconstruction and reorientation. The most recent version of the structure had an estimated size similar to that of Structure A—approximately 2.5 m × 5 m—but it is oriented like Structure B, with its longer side running east-west.

The eastern foundation wall of Structure C (Fig. 6.20), constructed in the bloque y laja style, was heavily eroded on its southern end, making it nearly impossible to ascertain its original length. Its southern corner no longer exists, and no evidence for the corresponding southern foundation wall was found. In the northeast corner, the eastern wall abutted the southern wall of Structure B, and there was a two-step staircase leading into the

Figure 6.20. Eastern foundation wall, Structure C.

structure from the patio. In the area immediately surrounding the eastern wall, both inside and outside the structure, I found a large amount of ash and carbon. This is probably part of the fill that was used during the expansion of the structure in the Early Postclassic.

Along the southern edge of the structure, I identified a line of stone blocks that ran perpendicular to the eastern wall and probably served as one of the structure's southern foundation walls. It was inset nearly a meter from the southern extension of the eastern foundation wall, however, making it unlikely that the two once shared a corner. In the central portion of this wall, we found the base for another step, which faced southward (Fig. 6.21). The different construction style and inset position suggest that this wall was part of an earlier construction/use period for the structure. Along the base of the wall, I found well-preserved portions of a stucco patio floor, probably protected from erosion when it was buried during the remodeling of the house platform (Fig. 6.21).

It appears that Structure C was older than the other structures of the East Patio Complex, and was expanded (and reoriented to face eastward) when the residence was reconfigured and the East Patio Complex constructed. To test this conclusion, I excavated a test pit (Fig. 6.20) in the center of the structure to see whether I could find carbon samples or features that might date the earlier construction. Although no feature came to light, I did recover a carbon sample yielding a Classic period date (see below). Thus my conclusion would seem to be confirmed.

I did not find a northern foundation wall for Structure C, but rather a line of cut facing stones (Fig. 6.21) that rested on the interior house floor. These stones may have provided a support for a wattle-and-daub wall. To the north of this line of stones I found a thick layer of stone and earth fill on top of bedrock. The density of ceramics in this region was very high (Fig. 6.11), suggesting it may have been a site for refuse disposal during occupation of the terrace.

The western wall of Structure C was the most difficult to interpret. The northern half of the wall, about 2 m long, shares a corner with the interior southern wall and has the same single block construction style. This is most likely the original western limit of the structure. Sometime later, a line of thinly cut rectangular facing stones was added to the southwest corner, extending it southward at least another 1.3 m (Fig. 6.22). At first, I interpreted this extension as part of the Postclassic remodeling of Structure C, and indeed, part of it may have served as an extension of the western wall at that time. The top of this line of cut stones, however, is roughly even with the base of the North Wall of the West Patio Complex. As noted above, the entire surface of the terrace to the west of this point was elevated above the level of the patio on the eastern side of the terrace, and there was no evidence for such an elevated surface to the east of the facing stones. This eventually led me to conclude that this construction was part of a stone-lined step that originally extended the entire width of the terrace.

Figure 6.21. Southern foundation wall, Structure C.

Figure 6.22. Western edge of Structure C.

The West Patio Complex

The West Patio Complex (Figs. 6.23, 6.24) consisted of two structures: (1) a large stone wall that extended east to west, designated the North Wall, and (2) a rectangular house foundation with stone façade, designated Structure E. These structures were part of the most recent episode of reconstruction on the terrace, which took place at the end of the Late Classic or the beginning of the Early Postclassic (probably around the same time as the expansion of the terrace and the construction of the East Patio Complex). Both of these structures rest on top of the same fill layer (Fig. 6.12) and exhibit the same bloque y laja construction technique, which supports the conclusion that they were constructed at or around the same time.

During the course of excavation we found seven pairs of ceramic vessels intentionally buried in the layer of fill between these structures (Chapter 7). In fact, there was no space along the edge of the North Wall where I did not encounter an offering or some other kind of feature. In addition to the paired vessels, I found a human burial, a comal hearth, and two small fire pits.

The North Wall

The North Wall began just to the west of Structure C (Fig. 6.25) and stretched 12.5 m to the western edge of the terrace. Its base was elevated between 10 and 20 cm above the level of the patio of the East Patio Complex and oriented 113–115° east of north. The wall was constructed mostly in the bloque y laja style, but did not exhibit uniform technique throughout its length. The eastern end of the wall was marked by a large corner block and some smaller cut stones, but it then turned abruptly at a right angle and ran 60 cm to the south, where its construction changed from bloque y laja to a base layer of fine cut stones. It then continued for 3.6 m at a 113° angle until it turned another corner; there the wall returned to the bloque y laja style.

The section of fine cut stones reminded us of the northern foundation wall of Structure C. On either side, it was connected to the North Wall at right angles, giving it a step-like appearance; upslope, however, I found only a dense concentration of fallen stones and no further evidence of a structure. Based on the ethnographic descriptions of traditional house lots, I suspect that this area may have supported something like a cook shack or kitchen. I discuss this structure in further detail in Chapter 7.

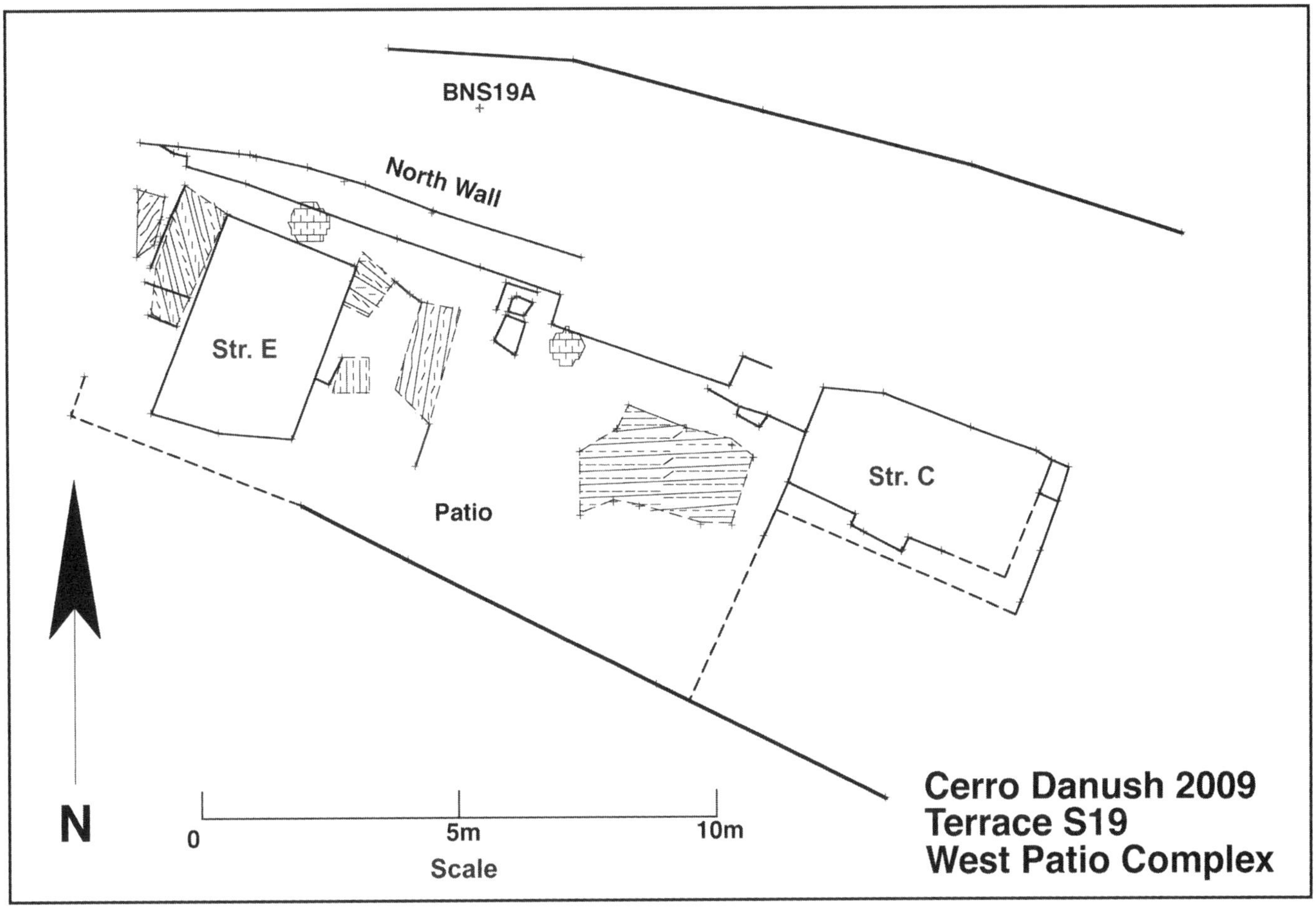

The Excavation of Terraces S19 and S20

Figure 6.23. Plan view of West Patio Complex with features.

Figure 6.24. West Patio Complex (viewed from east).

Dense areas of artifact deposition, perhaps indicating refuse dumps, were found just upslope of this area and to the east (Fig. 6.11). The gap between the North Wall and Structure C probably served to provide access to the upper part of the terrace.

To the west of its fine cut stone section, the North Wall was actually made up of two separate but adjoined stone walls (Fig. 6.26): (1) an older wall consisting of large stacked stones and (2) a newer buttress wall consisting of bloques y lajas that was built right up against the former. Because the lower wall clearly abuts the higher wall, it is possible to conclude that it was constructed at a later time; unfortunately, we recovered no radiocarbon samples that could provide an absolute date for the construction of the original wall. This made it difficult to ascertain to which period of terrace occupation it pertained.

The North Wall may have been built to protect the structures below from falling stones, as the cliff above is close to the terrace. Whatever the case, it had functioned this way, since the area upslope was filled with fallen stones. It is likely that the original wall was constructed during the earlier occupational period, while the second wall was built to buttress the original.

The original wall was higher than the buttress, giving the overall structure a bench-like appearance. Because of erosion and destruction from plowing, it was impossible to determine the original height of the older wall, but at the time of my excavations it stood between 1 and 1.5 m above the base of the lower wall. For its part, the lower wall rose only between 45 and 55 cm above its base. Taken together, the two walls measure between 0.75 and 0.90 m thick; the lower wall alone measures between 35 and 50 cm. At the western edge of the terrace the newer wall merges into the original, which extends another 1–2 m to the base of the cliff (Fig. 6.26).

Structure E

Structure E (Fig. 6.24), located on the western edge of the terrace (9 m to the west of Structure C), was a stone-lined rectangular house foundation similar in both design and orientation to Structure A. It measured 2.7 m wide and between 5 and 6 m long. Although Structure E was the best preserved of the structures on Terrace S19, its southern foundation wall had been thoroughly destroyed. Its northern foundation wall was completely intact, however, and the majority of the east and west walls remained intact as well. All the surviving foundation walls exhibited the bloque y laja construction technique.

Structure E's northern foundation wall was oriented 115° east of north and measured 2.67 m long and 30–32 cm high. The eastern foundation wall measured about 3.5 m long and 33 cm high, and the western wall measured approximately 4.05 m long and 35 cm high. As was the case with Structure A and the North Wall, sherds were found embedded in the mortar of the northern foundation wall (Fig. 6.27). We carefully extracted a few of these sherds and identified them as rim fragments of G35-type bowls.

Figure 6.25. East edge and indented portion of North Wall.

The Excavation of Terraces S19 and S20

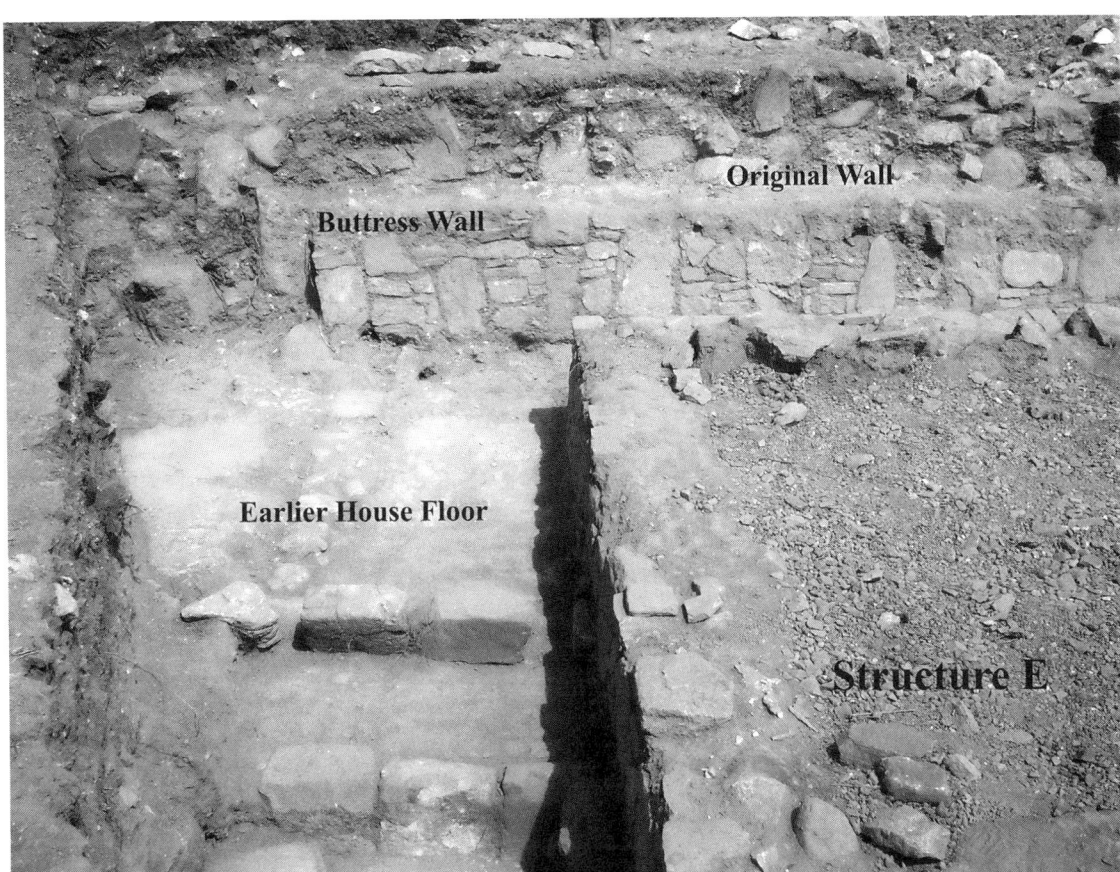

Figure 6.26. North Wall (viewed from the south).

Figure 6.27. Northern foundation wall, Structure E.

It appeared, therefore, that all the ceramic fragments used for wall chinking on the terrace were of this type.

We excavated a 2 m × 2 m test unit into the center of Structure E in an attempt to find any objects that may have been buried within the house. Unfortunately, nothing was found. However, this test unit did provide us with information as to the construction method. The exterior walls were not very thick, only the width of one block, or between 20 and 25 cm. These walls were constructed first, and then the structure was filled in with soil and compacted. After that, the floor surface was likely plastered with stucco, with the supports for the wattle-and-daub walls built right into the stucco surface.

While the foundation walls of Structures A and E had very similar dimensions, orientation, and construction technique, it is interesting to consider the differences between the two. First, the platform fill for Structure E was compacted earth, while the Structure A platform was filled in mostly with stones. Second, all the walls in Structure E were vertical and straight, while the northern foundation wall of Structure A appeared to lean in from bottom to top, like a talud. We are not sure whether these differences have implications for the structures' uses or simply reflect variations in construction.

Stratigraphic Excavations on Terrace S19

Once the most recent occupational surface had been completely exposed, I set up test units to probe further into stratigraphic Layers 3 and 4 (Fig. 6.28). Test units were strategically placed on the surface of Layer 3 with the intention of characterizing and dating earlier occupational surfaces, as well as finding any buried features associated with the most recent occupation surface. Lateral expansion of these test units was limited in order to avoid causing any damage to structures already exposed on the most recent surface. While too limited to provide a comprehensive picture for any earlier occupational periods, these vertical excavations did provide data useful for reconstructing the occupational history of the terrace.

Figure 6.28 depicts the structures found at the base of Layer 2, as well as the vertical test units, numbered 1 to 14, that were excavated into Layers 3 and 4. Most of these units were not set up along the north-south axis of the original grid, but were aligned to the structures. The test units were either 1 m × 2 m units (as is the case with units 2, 9, 12 and 13) or 2 m × 2 m units (as is the case with units 1, 3, 4, 5, 6, 7, and 11). The remaining three units (8, 10, and 14) were not given uniform shapes because they were designed to fit between structures or features found on the surface of either Layer 3 or 4.

Aside from their orientation, the test units were set up in a similar manner to that of the other units, using nails to mark their corners. The nails were then mapped using the total station, and unit excavation forms were used to collect all the excavation data. In addition to the numbered test units, some of the original excavation units were excavated to the base of Layer 3 along the face of the Northern Wall. Included were units N6E4, N6E5, and N8E0.

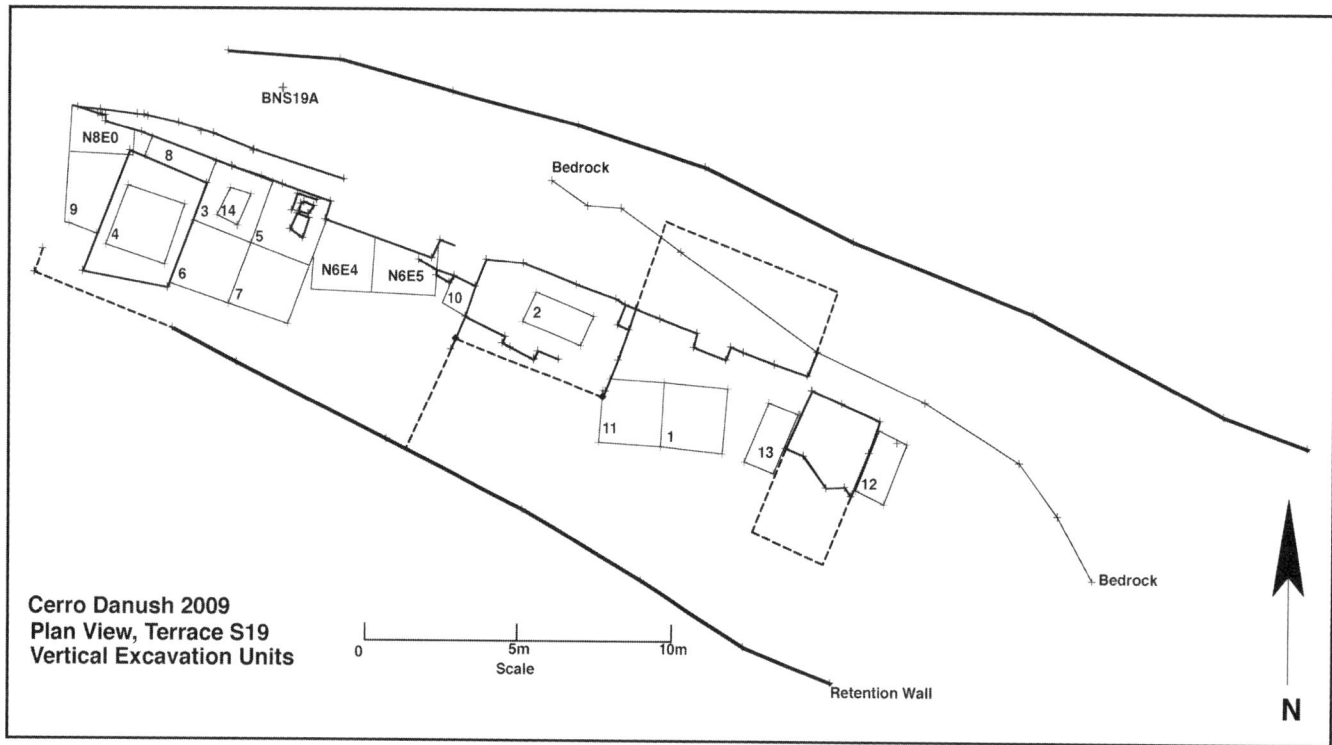

Figure 6.28. Vertical excavation units and structures, Terrace S19.

Description of Archaeological Features Associated with the Most Recent Occupation

I excavated several burials, significant artifacts, and features associated with the most recent occupational surface. Most of these were recovered in the layer of fill (Layer 3) below the West Patio Complex. These discoveries are shown in Figure 6.15, and in the following discussion their descriptions are accompanied by the corresponding numbers so that they can be easily located on the drawing.

Burials

Three human burials were excavated on Terrace S19 (Fig. 6.15). Since it is common to find tomb entrances in the patios of Classic period house complexes in the Valley of Oaxaca, I fully expected to find one within the patio of the East Patio Complex. It was partially for this reason that I excavated test units 1, 11, 12, and 13 to bedrock. In those units, however, I did not find anything that could have been interpreted as a tomb. In fact, we encountered bedrock within 20–30 cm of the patio's surface. Either the residences on Terrace S19 were too low-status to have tombs, or else the relatively late date of the East Patio Complex precluded its display of the Classic tomb pattern. Markens (2011) has argued that by the Late Postclassic, tombs appear to have shifted away from domestic to more public contexts.

Burial 1 (Fig. 6.15, Feature 12)

Burial 1 was found east of Structure A, on the eastern side of the terrace just outside the eastern household complex (Fig. 6.29). While all the bones collected appear to be from the same individual, they were found scattered in the second layer of excavation squares N5E13, N4E13, N4E14, and N3E13, above the patio surface. The principal cluster of bones lay directly on top of bedrock between excavation units N4E13 and N5E13 (Fig. 6.29). In this area I found several fragments of long bones, ribs, and vertebrae. It seemed likely that from this position, several of the remaining bones had washed downhill. Several pieces of the cranium and maxilla were found scattered in excavation unit N4E13. In addition, half of the mandible was found in the southern part of N4E13 and the remaining half in N3E13.

No artifacts were found in association with this burial, but the individual may have been accompanied by a dog. I found the remains of a canine mandible at the same level in the northwest corner of excavation unit N4E14, immediately to the east of the human remains.

All the bones from Burial 1 were very fragile. Many fragments were so small and splintered that it was impossible to identify them. Based on the teeth, the individual can be identified as an adult, probably between 22 and 40 years of age. Owing to the poor condition of the bones, it was not possible to ascribe the sex of, or estimate the stature of, the individual. In addition, because of the post-burial erosion, we were unable to determine the original

Figure 6.29. Burial 1, eastern structure complex, Terrace S19.

position or orientation of the individual. If we assume that the long bones and ribs were lying in their original positions, then it is possible that the burial was oriented south-to-north (with the feet to the south and head to the north) and in the extended position.

Burial 2 (Fig. 6.15, Feature 11)

Burial 2 was found just above the bedrock within the fill of Structure B of the East Patio Complex (Fig. 6.19). The location of this burial suggests that it was interred beneath the floor of Structure B, a practice common in prehistoric Oaxaca (Flannery and Marcus 2005; Urcid 2008). The body was flexed, without any offerings accompanying it (Figs. 6.30, 6.31). It was oriented from southeast to northwest, and appeared to be facing southwest. Unfortunately, the burial was located near the modern surface of the terrace, making it susceptible to damage from plowing. In fact, the skeleton appeared to have been very nearly cut in half, with the upper part completely missing; the bones that remained were very weak and fragile.

The size (roughly 32 cm long in the flexed position) as well as analysis of the skeleton (particularly the teeth) suggest that it was of a very young child. All the teeth that were found were primary. The lower molar had erupted, but the second, while already formed, had not. In addition, the proximal end of one femur showed that the epiphysis had not yet ossified (the other femur was too damaged to make an assessment). These data suggest a very young age, and most tooth eruption charts would place the child between 12 and 18 months old.

Burial 3 (Fig. 6.15, Feature 10)

Burial 3 was heavily eroded, but not to the same extent as Burials 1 and 2 (Fig. 6.32). It was found in association with the North Wall of the West Patio Complex, in Layer 3 of excavation unit N6E5. The burial was located right at the point where the construction style of the North Wall changed (see discussion above), and was placed directly on the surface of an earlier patio. While it was buried too deeply below the modern surface to have been disturbed by the plow, this burial had been subjected to periodic wetting and drying over many years, causing many of the bones to disintegrate. We found the spinal column, fragments of ribs, parts of the sacrum and pelvis, parts of the right radius and ulna, several phalanges and metacarpals of the left hand, large parts of both femora and fibulae, parts of the left tibia, and several metatarsals, phalanges, and tarsals of the left foot. Some of the bones appear to have migrated after burial; we found parts of the right foot, hand, and arm in excavation unit N5E5, and parts of the cranium in unit N6E4. This migration may have been caused by water moving beneath the surface, or perhaps happened during reconstruction of the North Wall.

The burial lay in the extended/supine position with the feet to the east and head to the west, along the same orientation as the North Wall (113° east of north). The right arm had been apparently placed across the stomach of the individual, and the radius and ulna were found in this position. A large gray conical G35 bowl (Fig. 6.33, Plate 1) with red paint in its interior had been inverted and placed over the thighs of the individual; no other artifacts were found in association.

Analysis of the skeleton revealed the individual to be an adult between the ages of 18 and 40. The third molar was present. Insufficient diagnostic materials were recovered to verify the sex of the individual, but the sharp angle of the greater sciatic notch on the right pelvic bone suggests that it was the skeleton of a young male. Significantly, this was the only burial with a ceramic vessel offering found on the terrace, and two of the incisors had been deliberately modified (Fig. 6.34)—one incisor was filed down on the left side, and the second had a circular indentation for some type of inlaid material.

The individual was probably buried not too long after the circa A.D. 1000 reconfiguration of the terrace residence because the burial was found in the layer of fill (Layer 3) used to cap the earlier structures and to prepare the new patio surface. This placement—above the earlier patio surface and associated with the most recent version of the residence—is supported by both the radiocarbon data and the remaining ceramic offerings found in the same stratigraphic layer (Chapter 7). The presence of the Late Classic G35 offering further suggests that this burial most likely occurred shortly after the building renovation, or perhaps even as part of the dedicatory rites associated with this event. The remaining ceramic offerings found in Layer 3 include both Late Classic G35 bowls and later Postclassic types. Thus, there may have been continuous occupation of the residence during the transition from Classic to Postclassic.

Comal Hearth (Fig. 6.15, Feature 8)

In test unit 5, just to the west of the change in construction style of the North Wall, I found the remains of a circular hearth. This hearth was made up of an interior circle of stones that exhibited exposure to heat and fire, supported by an exterior line of stones that abutted the face of the North Wall. To the south of the hearth, several more stones were placed at its base to create a flat surface (Fig. 6.35). The interior of the inner circle measured between 30 and 40 cm, the length of the oven measured about 1.2 m, and its width was about 80 cm at its widest point. It had a perpendicular orientation with respect to the North Wall, making its main axis around 23° east of north.

This design very closely matches the modern comal hearths commonly used in Oaxaca today (Fig. 6.36), and it may have served the same purpose during the occupation of the terrace since many comal fragments were found during excavation. I suspect that the comal, which would presumably have been level with the patio floor, was plastered in place with stucco on top of the circular oven. Fuel for the fire was presumably added via the opening below, which faced the flat surface of stones. Contemporary comal ovens are very useful in that tortillas and other materials can be cooked on the comal surface while beans can be cooked in *patojos* (shoe pots) inserted into the opening.

The Excavation of Terraces S19 and S20 127

Figure 6.30. Burial 2, Structure B, East Patio Complex, Terrace S19.

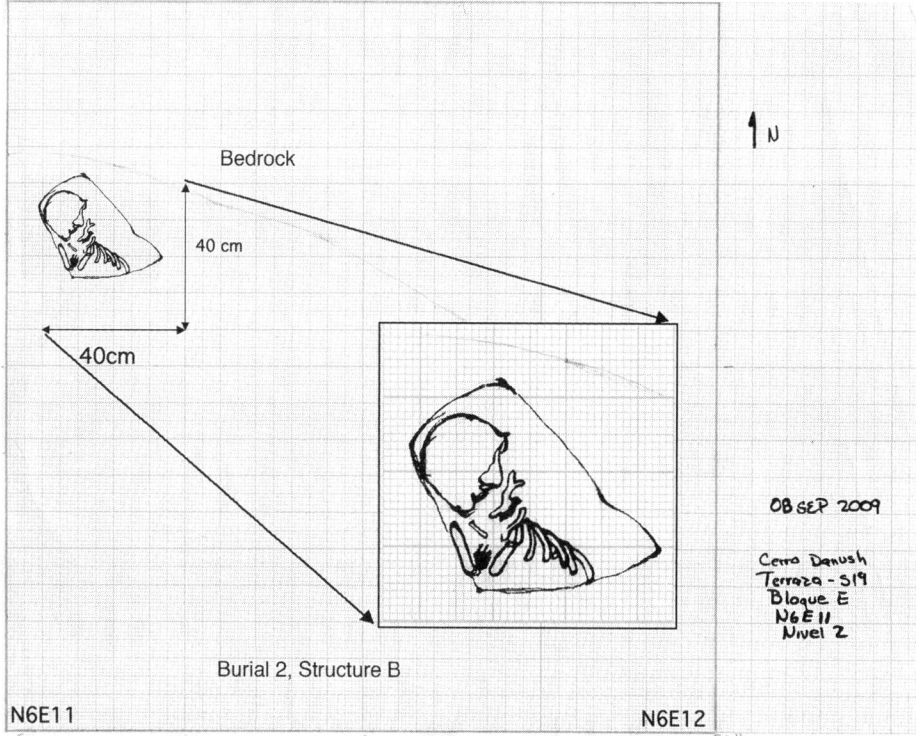

Figure 6.31. Burial 2 drawing (to scale).

Figure 6.32. Burial 3 (viewed from north).

Figure 6.33. G35-type conical bowl, Burial 3 (also see Plate 1).

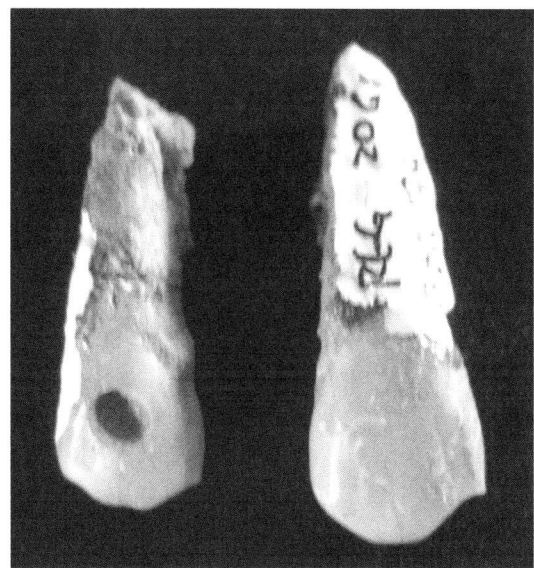

(*above*) Figure 6.34. Modified incisors from Burial 3.

(*right*) Figure 6.35. Comal hearth, West Patio Complex.

(*below right*) Figure 6.36. Modern comal hearth, San Mateo Macuilxóchitl.

Figure 6.37.
Fire Pit 1, Layer 3, test unit 8 (prior to excavation) (also see Plate 1).

Figure 6.38.
Fire Pit 1, Layer 3, test unit 8 (after excavation) (also see Plate 1).

Parsons (1936:33) published a drawing of a hearth of this type (which she refers to as a "griddle") along with many early twentieth-century versions of ceramic vessels akin to those I found during my excavation. Parsons' assemblage includes ollas, patojos, cántaros, manos, metates, and apaxtles, which she identified as the kitchen implements used by one of her informants from Mitla in the Tlacolula Valley.

Fire Pits

Two small, irregularly shaped areas of burned earth, ash, and carbon were found along the North Wall (Fig. 6.15, Fire Pits).

The first fire pit was found in the third layer on the west side of the terrace, in test unit 8, between patojos (Fig. 6.15, numbers 7 and 4). It consisted of a layer of fine gray ash with charcoal inclusions on top of a reddened layer of burned earth (Figs. 6.37, 6.38, Plate 1). The second fire pit was found beneath the fine cut stone section of the North Wall, in the third layer of Square N6E4 (Fig. 6.28), just to the west of Burial 3. It was also made up of a layer of fine gray ash on top of burned earth (Figs. 6.39, 6.40).

The fire-reddened earth found at the base of both features implies that they were burned in situ, but no artifacts were recovered from either one. In both cases the carbon, ash, and burned earth extended beneath the base of the North Wall, implying that the

Figure 6.39. Fire Pit 2, Layer 3, below North Wall (prior to excavation).

Figure 6.40. Fire Pit 2, Layer 3, below North Wall (after excavation).

burning event took place before its construction. These events might be related to an offering associated with the modification of the North Wall, the time when the buttress wall was added or reconstructed. At both ends of the buttressed portion of the wall, I recovered patojos (Fig. 6.15, numbers 1 and 8), oriented so that the "toe" portion of the vessel faced outward, or away from the wall (Figs. 6.37, 7.16, Plates 1, 5). These vessels may also have been placed there as part of a dedicatory rite.

Earlier Occupational Structures and Features

The features we found on the earlier occupational surface at the base of Layer 3 were difficult to interpret because of the modification of the terrace during remodeling. We found patches of stucco floors and stone lines that belonged to earlier structures, but they were difficult to map completely. What is clear from the evidence is that there had been an earlier house complex—perhaps similar in design to the eastern household complex—and that it was first constructed in the middle of the Classic (A.D. 400–500), more than 500 years before the newer complex was built. Figure 6.41 depicts the features that we identified, and probably suggests what the terrace looked like before the remodeling took place.

On the western edge of Structure C, a perpendicular stone wall extended out about 2 m until it intersected the North Wall of the West Patio Complex (Fig. 6.42). The base of this wall was level with the west wall of Structure C, and it was constructed in the same manner (large singular blocks), suggesting that it was built around the same time as the original version of Structure C. It may represent the remains of another related house foundation (Structure D, Fig. 6.41) from the initial occupation, but it appears that most of it was eliminated with the construction of the North Wall. The wall probably represents what remains of an earlier structure that was incorporated into the new terrace design to support the construction of the North Wall.

Directly to the south of Structure D's remaining foundation wall, we found a large patch of intact stucco floor (Fig. 6.42). This patch was level with the eastern patio floor, and is probably what remains of an earlier patio surface. Between the patio and Structure D, some stones had been arranged to form a flat surface. It is not clear whether this was a walkway or *banqueta*, or whether the stones were placed during the interment of Burial 3.

To the east of Structures C and D, below the patio of the East Patio Complex (Fig. 6.28, test units 1 and 11), I found the remains of a stone-lined drain (Fig. 6.43). The drain had been placed directly on top of bedrock and followed its natural slope downward, away from the structures at an angle 113° east of north. Finally, after a few meters, the drain turned sharply to the south and descended from the terrace.

The floor of the drain consisted of flat stones, leveled with a thin layer of carbon, ash, and soil atop bedrock. The sides were formed of cut stones, as was the roof. Because two roof stones remained in place at the time of excavation, we were able to measure the drain, which was between 20 and 30 cm wide and 8 to 15 cm high. The position, construction style, and dimensions of the drain are consistent with those of Classic period house complexes at Monte Albán (Winter 1974; González Licón 2003). This fact, coupled with the available radiocarbon dates (below), suggests that this drain was contemporaneous with the original Structure C, and most likely drained water away from its patio. It does not appear to have been reused as a drainage system for the East Patio Complex, as several of its roof stones had been removed and the drain filled in during the expansion of the terrace.

To the west of Structures C and D, we found evidence for a second patio beneath the remains of Structure E. As can be seen from the photos (Figs. 6.26, 6.44), I found there the outline of a stone foundation for what probably was a rectangular house. At the southern end of this house outline we uncovered a line of large cut facing stones (Fig. 6.44). Since we found remains of stucco floor both above and below these facing stones, they would seem to have been the southern wall of the house structure, facing south onto a patio (Fig. 6.41). Although the full layout of the structure cannot be determined owing to its poor condition, its pattern is consistent with domestic architecture. So, too, was the associated artifact assemblage.

Several of the stucco floors on the stratigraphic surface of Layer 4 were fairly well preserved, perhaps because they were buried when the terrace was reconstructed. In many cases, it was possible to see the method of construction. Apparently the builders incorporated small, smooth flat stones into the plaster for the purpose of strengthening the floors. This same construction pattern was visible in the stucco floor we found to the south of Structure D, in the central part of the terrace.

To prevent further erosion of these early floors, I decided not to excavate below them. I did, however, excavate one test unit (Fig. 6.28, unit 14) to bedrock without finding any evidence for an earlier occupational level.

Both the radiocarbon dates (see below) and the ceramic assemblage from our excavation (Appendix B) suggest that the initial occupation of the terrace took place in the middle Classic, between A.D. 400 and 600. That means that the terrace may have been occupied for as many as 600 years before its area was expanded to the east during the Postclassic. Certainly, its structures did not remain static throughout that time; there must have been many episodes of reconstruction and reorganization of structures on the terrace. The surviving architectural traces enabled me to identify only the three most recent episodes of reconstruction/reorganization.

Radiocarbon Analyses

During the excavation of Terrace S19 we collected a number of charcoal samples, wrapped them in aluminum foil, and sealed them in Ziploc bags. All samples were collected using metal trowels, and care was taken so that the samples did not come

The Excavation of Terraces S19 and S20

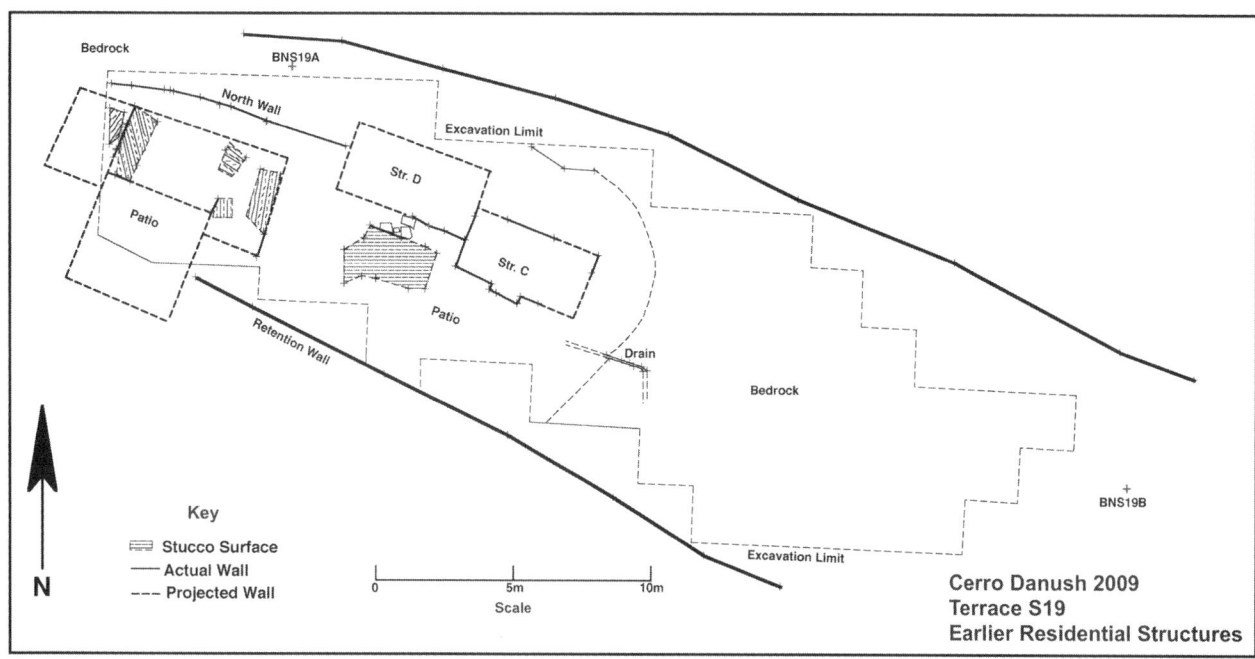

Figure 6.41. Diagram of features from the earlier occupational surface.

Figure 6.42. Structure D and patio, west of Structure C.

Figure 6.43. Stone-lined drain.

Figure 6.44. Remnants of structures below Structure E.

into contact with possible contaminants such as human skin or plastic. Ten charcoal samples from significant contexts (Table 6.1) were submitted to Beta Analytic.

Table 6.1 gives the results of these ten samples. I charted the dates' 2-sigma (95% confidence) ranges (Fig. 6.45), and prepared maps indicating the locations on the terrace where the samples were extracted (Figs. 6.46, 6.47). Below, I discuss the radiocarbon dates from the East Patio Complex, the West Patio Complex, and the earliest occupation of the terrace.

Radiocarbon Dates for the East Patio Complex

Four samples were submitted to date the construction and occupational period of the three houses (Structures A, B, and C) and central patio that made up the East Patio Complex (Fig. 6.46). The orientation and arrangement of these structures suggest that they made up a single household unit. Ceramics collected in and around the complex dated it to sometime between the Late Classic and Early Postclassic periods (A.D. 600 to 1300).

The calibrated intercept dates for these four samples (Beta 277780, 277782, 277783, and 277784) are A.D. 990, A.D. 1030, A.D. 1000, and A.D. 1010 respectively, with a collective 2-sigma (95%) range between A.D. 890 and A.D. 1160. These dates fall within a relatively short period of time and all their ranges overlap in the Early Postclassic (Fig. 6.45). No ceramic diagnostics of the Late Postclassic were found in the area during our excavations. In general, the dates suggest that the house complex was constructed sometime after A.D. 900 and abandoned sometime before A.D. 1300.

Structure A, N4E12ESTA (Beta 277780)

This sample consisted of a single piece of charcoal, extracted from a thin layer of soil below the platform of Structure A (specifically, between the base of its northern foundation wall and bedrock; Fig. 6.18). This layer of soil represents Layer 3, likely the result of the burning of vegetation and surface leveling that took place prior to the construction of the house complex. The resulting date, therefore, can be viewed as terminus post quem for Structure A. The calibrated intercept date was A.D. 990, with a 2-sigma (95%) range of A.D. 890–1030.

Table 6.1. Sample data from the radiocarbon analysis.

Lab ID	Material	Uncal. Years BP	13C/12C	Provenience	Cal. Range (2-sigma)
Earliest Occupation					
Beta 277781	wood charcoal	1630 +/- 40	-23.4	Structure C (int. wall)	A.D. 340–540
Beta 277785	wood charcoal	1540 +/- 40	-24.9	stone-lined drain	A.D. 420–610
East Patio Complex					
Beta 277780	wood charcoal	1060 +/- 40	-10.3	Structure A	A.D. 890–1030
Beta 277783	wood charcoal	1050 +/- 40	-24.4	central patio	A.D. 900–1030
Beta 277784	wood charcoal	1040 +/- 40	-25.2	Structure C (ext. wall)	A.D. 900–920 A.D. 950–1040
Beta 277782	wood charcoal	980 +/- 40	-23.8	central patio	A.D. 990–1160
West Patio Complex					
Beta 277789	wood charcoal	860 +/- 40	-26.4	fire pit (west)	A.D. 1040–1100 A.D. 1120–1260
Beta 277787	wood charcoal	850 +/- 40	-23.3	fire pit (east)	A.D. 1050–1090 A.D. 1130–1140 A.D. 1140–1260
Beta 277786	wood charcoal	830 +/- 40	-23.7	fire pit (east)	A.D. 1160–1270
Beta 277788	wood charcoal	830 +/- 40	-25.5	fire pit (west)	A.D. 1160–1270

House Complex Patio, POZO1N1A (Beta 277782) and POZO1N1B (Beta 277783)

These two samples consist of pieces of charcoal extracted from the layer of soot, ash, charcoal, and burned earth found beneath the level of the patio floor of the East Patio Complex (Fig. 6.12). These samples were collected within Layer 3 of test unit 1, a 2 m × 2 m excavation unit in the center of the patio between Structures A, B, and C (Fig. 6.46). In the northern section of this unit, there were roughly 15–20 cm between the patio floor level and bedrock (Fig. 6.13, Plate 1). Several pieces of charcoal were extracted from this area, and due to the evidence for in situ burning, two separate pieces were chosen with the intention of ascertaining whether or not this layer represented a single burning episode, or repeated episodes over a period of time. The calibrated intercept dates were A.D. 1030 (2-sigma range of 990–1160) and A.D. 1000 (2-sigma range of 900–1030) respectively. While these data support the notion of a single burning event that took place prior to patio floor construction, one cannot rule out the possibility of multiple burning events during a short period of time. In either case, burning was concluded before construction of the stucco patio floor, making these dates terminus post quem for the construction of the patio. Both of these dates are also in good agreement with those taken from Structures A and C, supporting the idea that the entire house complex was built and used around the same time.

Structure C, N5E9N2ESTC (Beta 277784)

This sample consisted of a piece of carbon extracted from Layer 3 beneath the eastern foundation wall of Structure C (Fig. 6.46) (specifically between the base of its foundation and bedrock). It is also a terminus post quem date, preceding the construction (or at least the reconstruction) of Structure C. Like Structure A, part of Structure C's foundation was located immediately on top of the bedrock, making it possible to assert that this thin layer of soil was placed immediately prior to construction of the house foundation as a means of leveling the area. The resulting date is therefore likely a close approximation for the construction/reconstruction of Structure C. The calibrated intercept date was A.D. 1010, with a 2-sigma (95%) range of A.D. 950–1040.

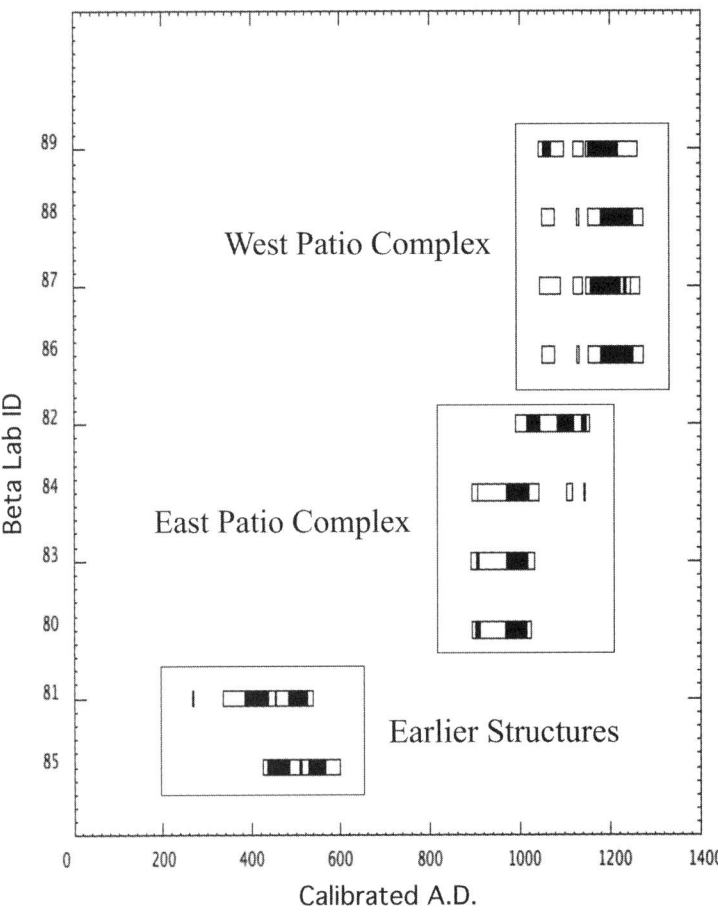

Figure 6.45. Radiocarbon results from Terrace S19, Cerro Danush.

Radiocarbon Dates for the West Patio Complex

Four charcoal samples were submitted to date the construction and occupation of the North Wall and Structure E, which make up the West Patio Complex. Because these two structures were built on the same surface, and share an orientation and construction style (bloque y laja), I consider them to be contemporaneous. The ceramics from excavations in and around the complex (Chapter 7) indicate a date in the Early Postclassic (A.D. 900–1300).

The calibrated intercept dates for these four samples (Beta 277786, 277787, 277788, and 277789) are A.D. 1220, A.D. 1210, A.D. 1220, and A.D. 1200 respectively, with a collective range between A.D. 1040 and A.D. 1270. These dates fall within a relatively short period of time, and all of their 2-sigma (95%) ranges overlap, leaving a nearly two hundred-year gap between these dates and those of the East Patio Complex (Fig. 6.45). The mix of Late Classic and Early Postclassic ceramic offerings described in Chapter 7, however, suggests that the West Patio Complex and the East Patio Complex were probably built around the same time.

The fire pits (whose dates are given below), therefore, may represent some type of burned offering made prior to the addition of the buttress wall, circa A.D. 1200. The fact that a few of the paired ceramic offerings as well as the two fire pits were underneath the buttress wall supports this interpretation. Furthermore, two of the ceramic offerings were found on either end of the buttress wall, suggesting that they were made just prior to or immediately after its construction. As with the East Patio Complex, no ceramics diagnostic of the Late Postclassic were found in the area during our excavations. From these data, we can suggest that the West Patio Complex was constructed sometime after A.D. 1000 and fell out of use sometime before A.D. 1300.

Fire Pit 1, POZO8N1A (Beta 277788) and POZO8N1B (Beta 277789)

These two samples consist of pieces of charcoal from an area of soot, ash, charcoal, and burned earth found in Layer 3 of test unit 8 (Fig. 6.28), specifically between the North Wall and

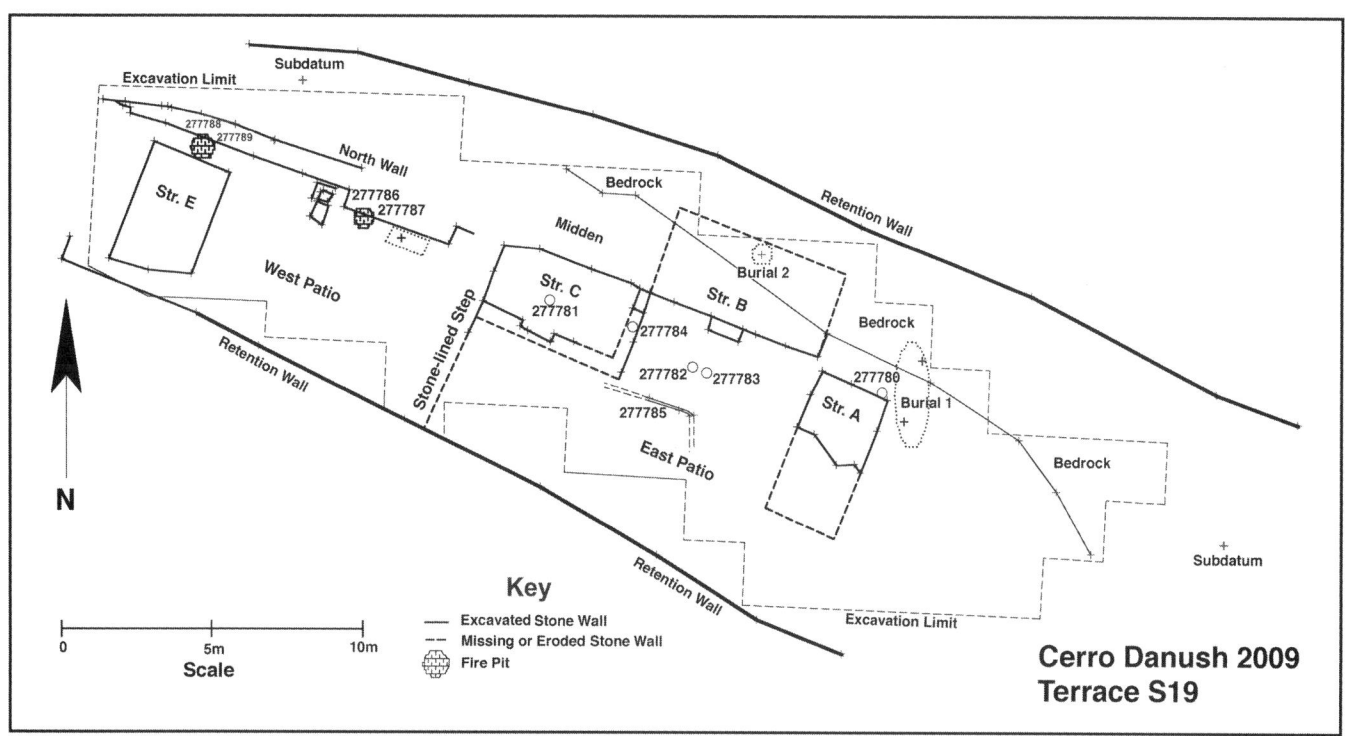

Figure 6.46. Radiocarbon sample locations, most recent occupational surface.

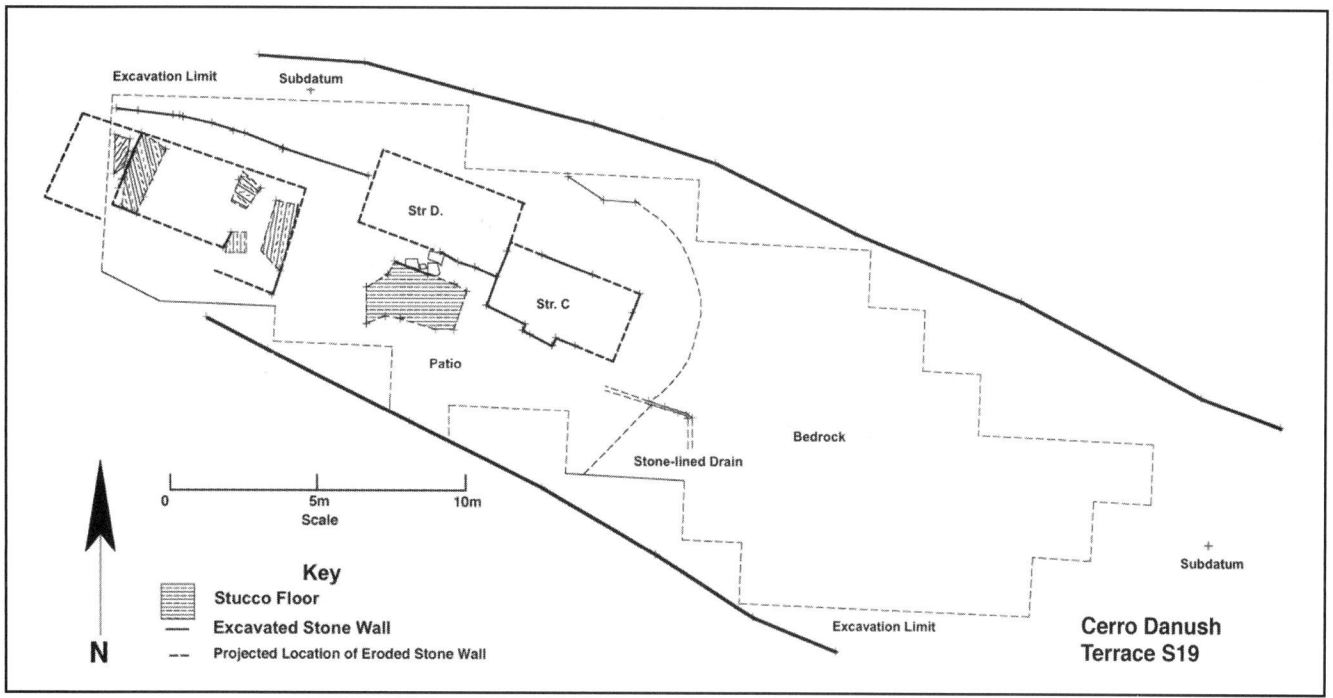

Figure 6.47. Radiocarbon sample locations, earlier occupational surface.

Structure E (Figs. 6.37, 6.38, Plate 1). These samples were taken from the same stratigraphic layer as the two from unit N6E4 in Level 3 (see below). Two pieces were chosen for analysis, in hopes of establishing whether this feature was the result of a single burning event or was used over a long period of time. The calibrated intercept dates were A.D. 1220 (2-sigma range of 1160–1270) and A.D. 1200 (2-sigma range of 1120–1260). These dates suggest a single burning event, one that took place prior to the construction of the buttress wall. Since this feature also extended below the buttress wall, the date serves as a terminus post quem for that wall.

Fire Pit 2, N6E4N3 (Beta 277786) and N6E4N3 (Beta 277787)

These two samples consist of pieces of charcoal extracted from an area of soot, ash, charcoal, and burned earth in Level 3 of excavation unit N6E4, specifically beneath the southern edge of the North Wall (Figs. 6.39, 6.40). Several pieces of charcoal were extracted from this area, and due to the evidence for in situ burning, two pieces were chosen in hopes of ascertaining whether or not this feature represented a single burning episode, or repeated episodes over a long period of time. The calibrated intercept dates were A.D. 1220 (2-sigma range of 1160–1270) and A.D. 1210 (2-sigma range of 1140–1260) respectively. These dates are close enough to suggest a single episode. Because this feature extends beneath the buttressed addition to the North Wall, these dates provide a terminus post quem for the remodeling of the North Wall and the construction of the buttress wall.

Radiocarbon Dates for the Earliest Occupation of Terrace S19

Two charcoal samples were submitted to date the initial use of the terrace. Stone-lined stucco floors found below the level of Structure E and the North Wall had revealed an earlier occupation of the terrace, and the associated ceramics dated this initial occupation to the Classic period (A.D. 200–800). The details of the stucco floors matched those of Classic period house complexes at other sites. The charcoal we submitted did not come from the stucco floors, but from features in the central part of Terrace S19 that appeared to be contemporaneous with the floors.

The calibrated intercept dates for the two samples (Beta 277781 and 277785) are A.D. 420 and A.D. 540 respectively, with a range between A.D. 340 and A.D. 610 (Fig. 6.45). These dates fall within the latter part of the Early Classic or the early part of the Late Classic. Such a date is supported by the presence of Early Classic G23 vessels and orange Dainzú conical bowls, as well as Late Classic G35 conical bowls and hollow-handled sahumadores.

Structure C, POZO2ESTC (Beta 277781)

This sample consisted of a single piece of carbon recovered from test unit 2 (Fig. 6.28), a 1 m × 2 m unit excavated into the house platform beneath the floor of Structure C (Fig. 6.20). Unlike some of our other samples, this charcoal cannot be related to an in situ burning event. It was included in the fill of the house platform, and therefore represents only a loose terminus post quem for the construction of the house platform. The excavation of this platform suggested that it may have been constructed during the initial occupation of the terrace, and later remodeled and reused as part of the East Patio Complex. The calibrated intercept date, A.D. 420 with a 2-sigma (95%) range of A.D. 340–540, supports that temporal placement.

Stone-Lined Drain, POZO11N2 (Beta 277785)

This sample consisted of a piece of carbon taken from the thin layer of soil between the bottom of the stone-lined drain and bedrock (Fig. 6.43). Stratigraphy suggested that this drain was partially destroyed during the Postclassic terrace reorganization.

There was no evidence for in situ burning, but the position of the soil layer beneath the drain makes this date a loose terminus post quem date for construction of the drain. The calibrated intercept date was A.D. 540, with a 2-sigma (95%) range of A.D. 420–610. This date, along with the sample from Structure C (Fig. 6.45), provides further support for the presence of a Classic period house early in the history of Terrace S19.

The Occupational History of Terrace S19

In the introduction, I stated that the goals of our second field season were (1) to uncover house structures and other features indicative of domestic activities, and (2) to collect radiocarbon samples from different contexts in order to reconstruct the occupational history of the terraces. The complete horizontal excavation of Terrace S19 led to the discovery of many domestic features, including house foundations, stuccoed patios, burials, an oven, and ritual offerings. These materials make up the living space of a household unit and support many of our conclusions based on surface collections (Chapters 4 and 5). The horizontal and vertical excavation of Terrace S19 led to an understanding of the formation processes for individual stratigraphic layers, as well as the sequence of construction episodes that took place. These data provide us with a means for reconstructing the terrace's occupational history.

The ceramic assemblage we recovered contained temporal diagnostics from the Early Classic through the Early Postclassic (Appendix B). The least abundant diagnostics were those from the Early Classic, accounting for only 1–3% of the diagnostic materials. Late Classic diagnostics were by far the most abundant, making up as much as 50–60% of the collection. Early Postclassic markers comprised about 3–5% of the diagnostics; the remaining sherds were not good temporal markers.

The overall assemblage consisted of 65.90% gray paste sherds, 31.55% brown paste sherds, and 2.55% orange paste sherds. These percentages weight the collection heavily to the span from Early Classic to Early Postclassic, and our dates support a similar placement. Architectural traces allowed us to identify three periods of construction and remodeling that occurred on Terrace S19 during the period A.D. 420–1220.

Initial construction and occupation of the terrace probably occurred toward the end of the Early Classic, A.D. 400–600. Construction at this time included a rectangular house foundation and a stone-lined drain that were probably part of a residential complex constructed in what is now the center of the terrace.

The second building episode we detected dated to the Late Classic. The evidence included the stone foundations and stucco floors found at the base of Layer 3 on the west side of the terrace. Their layout and construction design (single large cut facing blocks) are similar to those of other Late Classic commoner house complexes excavated in the Valley of Oaxaca (see Chapter 3). As far as can be determined after all the erosion and disturbance, construction consisted of a patio flanked by house platforms (Fig. 6.47).

In the Early Postclassic, the vegetation on the east side of the terrace was burned and the surface was leveled to support the construction of an additional patio and residential structures. Structure C was remodeled and reoriented, and Structures A and B were constructed to form the East Patio Complex. Similar types of terrace expansion to accommodate residential remodeling or new construction have been documented in several Late Classic residences at El Palmillo (Feinman and Nicholas 2009).

Our evidence suggests that the terrace was not abandoned between the Late Classic and Early Postclassic. Rather, occupation continued on Terrace S19, and our third construction episode represents the expansion of a living surface that was already in use. This interpretation is supported by the fact that the patio on the west side of the terrace is flush with the newly constructed patio on the east side, and none of the Late Classic structures on the west side show evidence of remodeling. In fact, the stucco floors of both the house platforms and patios on the west side of the terrace were found in good condition, suggesting they were buried during the reconstruction.

Probably not long after the eastern expansion of the terrace, the west side of the terrace was buried within a layer of fill to create a new surface that was elevated above the East Patio Complex patio by a stone-lined step. One new house foundation, Structure E, was built on this surface, and the North Wall may have been constructed or modified at that time. Several ceramic offerings were left on the earlier patio surface before it was filled in (see Chapter 7), including two Late Classic G35 conical bowls. These activities provide further evidence for continuous use of the terrace from the Late Classic into the Early Postclassic. Finally, around A.D. 1200, the North Wall was modified with the addition of the buttress wall.

After that final reconstruction episode, however, the residence on Terrace S19 may have been used only for a few more generations. It appears that by A.D. 1300, the terrace was no longer occupied. This conclusion is supported by a complete lack of Late Postclassic ceramic diagnostics, such as polychrome pottery, three-legged composite silhouette bowls, and cántaros with burnished star patterns (Markens 2004, 2008). In contrast, all the latter diagnostics were recovered from a similar residential compound—the Lanisbaa Complex—excavated in Mound 1 at Dainzú-Macuilxóchitl and radiocarbon dated to the Late Postclassic (Winter et al. 2007).

Conclusions

Previous research in the Valley of Oaxaca has demonstrated that Classic period commoner house complexes consisted of single patios with up to four surrounding rectangular house platforms (Chapter 4). With the exception of actual palaces, classic residential complexes excavated at Monte Albán, while exhibiting differences in construction technique (adobe vs. wattle and daub) and overall size, maintained this same general layout (González Licón 2003; Winter 1974). This is most likely the form that the house complex on Terrace S19 took in its initial construction episode. The remains of this residence were found on the central part of the terrace.

Toward the end of the Late Classic, several residential complexes at El Palmillo and Jalieza were remodeled to incorporate multiple, rather than single, patios (Elson 2011; Feinman and Nicholas 2009). This change in residential design is mirrored on Terrace S19, as the terrace was expanded to convert a single-patio house complex into a two-patio residence.

By the Late Postclassic, most residential structures in the Valley of Oaxaca contained multiple patios, and Winter et al. (2007) suggest that the number of patios may relate to the status of the residents. For example, they propose that the Late Postclassic two-patio house complex excavated in Mound 1 at Dainzú-Macuilxóchitl was a low-status residence, while the six-patio residence found at Yagul has been described as a palace (Bernal and Gamio 1974). All indications from my research suggest that the residential complex on Terrace S19 was of commoner status. It is similar in both design and layout to the Lanisbaa residence (although it is oriented at right angles to that structure).

In addition to the aforementioned changes in the design and layout of house complexes, construction style appears to have changed as well. While many Postclassic house platforms retained the Classic rectangular shape and size, the building technique incorporated in the foundation walls changed from single block to bloque y laja. This style was first documented in the Mixtec region of Oaxaca during the Late Classic, but did not become common in the Valley of Oaxaca until the Postclassic. The intact foundation walls of Structures A and E (Figs. 6.18, 6.27) match closely the design described and illustrated by Winter (2007:86–89) for Late Classic phase structures at Cerro de las Minas, Oaxaca, a site located in the Mixteca Baja or Ñuiñe region (see Chapter 2).

Other possible Mixtec influences become evident in the Valley of Oaxaca during the Postclassic, such as the introduction of red-on-cream and polychrome pottery. The introduction of these materials into the Zapotec region may reflect a growing number of royal marriages between Mixtec *cacicazgos* and petty Zapotec states at that time. The continuity of occupation and domestic activities identified within the residence on Terrace S19, however, indicate that these "foreign" stylistic influences were adopted into Zapotec households, and do not represent either a population replacement or a conquest by Mixtec people.

7 | Spatial Distributions of Artifacts and Implied Behavioral Patterns in an Early Postclassic Residence

The previous chapter focused on the structures and features of Terrace S19. In this chapter I present the results from qualitative and quantitative analyses of the artifact assemblage recovered by excavating the terrace. My goal is to better understand the use of space within the residential complex and to identify the range of domestic activities that took place there. I also discuss the limitations inherent in the particular analyses employed.

Laboratory Procedures

Laboratory analysis of the materials collected during my excavations occurred over the duration of the project—on days during field operations when the weather prohibited excavation, and then on a full-time basis after field operations were complete. The collected materials were stored in 1-gallon (3.785 liters) Ziploc bags labeled with terrace number, unit ID, excavation layer, date, and excavation block. Tags with the identical information were placed inside each bag for redundancy.

All the ceramic and lithic materials were washed and placed in large six-gauge mesh screens to dry. Careful attention was paid toward ensuring that the corresponding provenience tags accompanied the artifacts in the screens, and throughout the process, maintaining provenience integrity of the washed items.

Once dry, all the materials were sorted into the same categories used during the first season (Appendix B), and their counts were recorded on forms prepared for the individual excavation units. After the counts were verified, diagnostic materials were separated out for the project sample or *muestrario*, while non-diagnostic materials were returned to their appropriate marked bags. The diagnostic materials were marked with terrace number, unit ID, and excavation layer, as well as specific identification numbers designated for the project by INAH. They were then placed in labeled archival boxes and stored in Macuilxóchitl's community museum.

Bone fragments from the project were first separated into animal vs. human categories; the majority could not be sorted further than that because they were too splintered to characterize. The fragments that could be identified were sorted into more specific categories, such as "canine mandible" or "bone needle" (Appendix B). The human remains from the three excavated burials (Chapter 6) were placed directly into prepared aluminum foil packets during extraction, and then into labeled Ziploc bags. Like the other diagnostic materials collected, the bone materials were marked, counted, and stored with the project muestrario.

The lab analysis consisted of physical inspection and characterization based on the known artifact categories described in Appendix B. As in the first season, standardized forms were used to record the frequency count data. The data set for the second season was prepared in the same manner as for the first field season (Chapters 4 and 5), with the data being stored in an Excel master file. From there, individual data sets were created for each excavation layer. The spreadsheets were converted into georeferenced feature classes using ArcGIS v9.2 desktop software, and the frequency counts were converted into raster shape files, so that density distributions could be plotted on the project map.

The spreadsheets were also imported into Minitab v15 software for multivariate statistical analysis of the frequency count data. Based on my experience with the surface collection data set, however, I decided not to conduct principal components analysis with the excavation data, but to rely on correspondence analysis alone. All the remaining laboratory and statistical treatment of the materials and data were identical to the procedures outlined for the first field season (Chapters 4 and 5).

Qualitative Assessment of the Artifact Assemblage

Overall, the excavation artifact assemblage was similar to that of the intensive surface collection, and reflected the domestic activities that took place within and around the residential complex. Bone fragments (which had not been preserved on the surface) were an addition to the assemblage from the excavation phase, providing further insight into the domestic activities on the terrace. The following section contains a brief assessment of the assemblage to facilitate the discussion of analyses below. A more detailed description of artifact categories is provided in Appendix B.

Ceramics

Some 249,477 sherds were recovered during the second field season, and 37,717 of these were considered diagnostic. On Terrace S19, gray, brown, and orange paste sherds represented 65.90%, 31.55%, and 2.55% of the assemblage, respectively. These percentages matched the surface collection results (64.24%, 33.42%, and 2.34%, respectively) quite closely. The diagnostic sherds from the excavation assemblage were very similar to the surface collection, with the same categories represented (Chapter 5).

In general, the assemblage contained materials used in food preparation and storage (such as ollas, comales, and cántaros), as well as in domestic ritual (such as figurines and sahumadores). These items are commonly recovered in prehispanic residences in the Valley of Oaxaca (Feinman, Nicholas, and Maher 2008; Winter 2002) and many of them have been described in traditional ethnographic contexts (Parsons 1936:30–38).

As mentioned previously, the temporally diagnostic sherds complement our radiocarbon dates. Early temporal indicators such as G23 bowls, as well as orange paste Dainzú Bowls, were present in small numbers. These forms suggest that the terraces were first occupied in the very beginning of the Late Classic, and our radiocarbon analyses support this. Our earliest dates fall between A.D. 400 and 600, at the transition between the Early and Late Classic. In addition, we found sizable amounts of brown paste sherds from items such as sahumadores, ollas, patojos, and conical bowls indicative of the Early Postclassic (Markens 2008), which our radiocarbon data suggest was the final phase of occupation for the residence on Terrace S19.

While we obtained no Late Classic (A.D. 500–900) dates, the majority of the diagnostic sherds recovered during excavation consist of utilitarian gray paste forms common in the Late Classic, such as G35 conical bowls (36.33% of the diagnostics collected), hemispherical bowls (16.43%), ollas (4.41%) and cántaros (1.25%). Such high frequencies of Late Classic diagnostics indicate that Terrace S19 had continuous occupation from the Late Classic into the Early Postclassic (see below).

Only 2 sherds found during excavation could be considered diagnostic of the Late Postclassic, and given this low frequency, we feel confident that Terrace S19 was no longer occupied at that time.

Stone Tools

Some 1610 flaked stone and 36 ground stone materials were collected during the excavation. Once again, the results were consistent with our surface collection assemblage. The most abundant ground stone items reflected food preparation activities; examples include whole or broken one-handed and two-handed manos (21 total), metates (2), tejolotes (4), and molcajetes (2). The remainder of the stone tools consisted of fragmented axe heads (2) and a few miscellaneous items such as small polished cubes and stone beads (Appendix B).

The most abundant chipped stone raw material was local chert (846 pieces, 52.77% of the total assemblage), represented mostly by debitage (552 pieces), but with a significant number of expedient flake tools (241) and points (32), as well as a few raspadores (4) and spent cores (17). The number of chert points recovered during excavation, along with the quantities of cores and debitage, suggests production of this tool on a scale greater than the household itself required. Recall that the surface collection analysis (Chapter 5) also revealed large amounts of chert debitage and cores in the area of Terraces S25, S18, and S19. Thus, this area may have been a production locus for consumption outside the household.

Volcanic tuff was the least abundant raw material (152 items), with debitage (58), expedient flake tools (80), spent cores (9), raspadores (3), and even points (2) represented in the assemblage. These items are very similar to those of the chert assemblage, but represent production on a smaller scale.

Obsidian was the second most abundant lithic raw material (612 items), consisting of 531 fragments of, or whole, prismatic blades; 74 pieces of debitage; 4 sharp pointed punches/needles derived from prismatic blades; and 3 eccentrics, which are C- or E-shaped items also derived from prismatic blades (Appendix B). The obsidian sample is quite different from the chert and volcanic tuff sample, and most likely represents the use of finished products incorporating either whole blades or sections of them. The tiny obsidian debitage fragments found during the project appear to represent small parts of broken prismatic blades, which probably fractured during use. The presence of the eccentrics does suggest some limited reworking of prismatic blades, but probably only for the use of house complex inhabitants.

Faunal Remains

Some 373 animal bone fragments were collected during excavation. The majority of these bones could not be assigned to species, but some fragments of ribs and long bones appeared to belong to canids or deer. One of these fragments was positively identified as the distal end of a deer metapodial, while several teeth and mandible fragments likely belonged to domestic dogs (Fig. B69). In addition, a few vertebrae of turkeys were recovered during excavation (Fig. B70).

Evidently the inhabitants of Terrace S19 had access to several meat sources. It is likely that they maintained both domesticated turkey and dog, and supplemented this with an occasional deer. Although no bones of cottontails or jackrabbits were identified from my excavations, rabbits are regularly hunted in the area today. Late Classic households in El Palmillo and Lambityeco ate rabbits and turkeys, and turkey eggs have been found in Early Postclassic households at the Mitla Fortress (Lapham, Feinman, and Nicholas 2013).

Five bone items were identified as possible tools. Four were polished to a point and were probably used as either punches or needles for sewing or textile production (Fig. B71). Three of these were found on the west side of the terrace, in the same area where the majority of spindle whorls were recovered (see below). The fifth item appears to be the burned and broken end of a deer antler that could have been used for flintknapping (Fig. B72).

Domestic Offerings from the West Patio Complex, Terrace S19

During the excavation of the West Patio Complex, I recovered 15 complete or nearly complete ceramic vessels buried in the layer of fill between two successive residential patio surfaces (Fig. 7.1). Feinman, Nicholas, and Maher (2008:180) describe domestic offerings as "the remains of non-mortuary rituals that occurred in or near a residential complex and may include dedicatory and termination rites." In their excavation of residential terraces at the Classic period hilltop center of El Palmillo, the majority of domestic offerings they found consisted of ceramic vessels either "placed in layers of relatively clean fill during construction episodes between occupational surfaces" or "just beneath room floors while structures were still occupied" (Feinman, Nicholas, and Maher 2008:180). Similar vessel offerings have been recovered within Classic and Postclassic residences

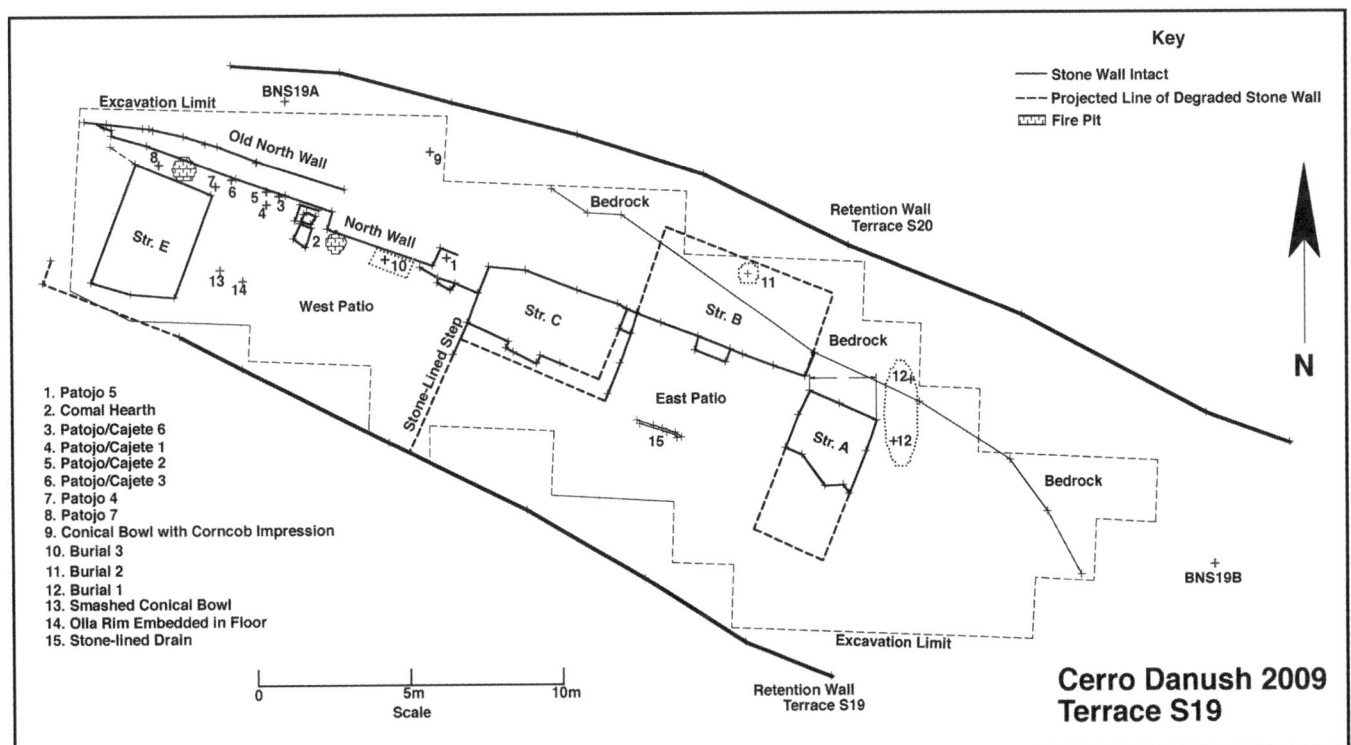

Figure 7.1. Terrace S19 residence with offerings.

throughout the Valley of Oaxaca (Casparis 2006; Feinman, Nicholas, and Maher 2008; Lind and Urcid 2010:277; Winter 2007).

Feinman, Nicholas, and Maher (2008) suggest that these types of vessel interments make up the only material offerings found within low-status residences, and also comprise part of the more expansive material offerings found within residences of high status, such as the Palace of the Six Patios at Yagul (Bernal and Gamio 1974). No other types of material offerings were found on Terrace S19, which is consistent with the other factors indicating the residence's commoner status (Chapter 6). The ceramic offerings recovered from the Terrace S19 house complex are very similar to those found within Classic period residences at Lambityeco (Lind and Urcid 2010:277), El Palmillo, and Ejutla (Feinman, Nicholas, and Maher 2008), and the Late Postclassic Lanisbaa residence excavated in Mound 1 at Dainzú-Macuilxóchitl (Markens, Winter, and Martínez López 2008; Winter et al. 2007). This suggests continuity in domestic ritual behavior between those periods, and is a strong indicator for continuous occupation at the site of Dainzú-Macuilxóchitl.

Thirteen of the ceramic vessels recovered from the west patio appear to represent either termination or dedicatory rites. Their horizontal proveniences are depicted on the terrace plan map (Fig. 7.1). One unique feature of these ceramic vessel offerings is that they contain a mixture of what are considered Late Classic and Early Postclassic markers. Included are 3 Late Classic G35 bowls, 3 Early Postclassic brown paste conical bowls, and 7 Early Postclassic patojos, all buried within a layer that was radiocarbon dated to circa A.D. 1200 (see Chapter 6). Burial 3, which was found beneath the same patio along the edge of the North Wall, also contained an offering of a G35 bowl. In addition, all the sherds found embedded within the foundation walls of Structure A, Structure E, and the North Wall were rim sherds of G35 bowls.

Previous research in the Valley of Oaxaca (Caso, Bernal, and Acosta 1967; Markens 2004, 2008) has shown that G35 bowls first appeared in the Early Classic, making up a small portion of the ceramic assemblage for that period, but later became the most abundant form used in the Late Classic, making up a significant portion of the ceramic assemblage for that period. After that, they appear to have fallen out of favor and are generally not considered to be part of the Postclassic Valley of Oaxaca assemblage; they were replaced by G3M hemispherical bowls and brown paste conical bowls (Caso, Bernal, and Acosta 1967; Markens 2008). Recently, however, G35 bowls have been found in Early Postclassic contexts at the Mitla Fortress (Feinman and Nicholas 2011), suggesting some continued use into that period. The buried ceramic offerings found on Terrace S19 support this conclusion.

Paired Ceramic Vessel Offerings (Fig. 7.1)

During the excavation of test units 3 (Fig. 7.2) and 5 (Fig. 7.3), along the North Wall of the West Patio Complex, several intentionally buried ceramic vessels were found. They were discovered at varying depths within Layer 3, below the base of the North Wall and above the earlier stucco floors. Four of these were paired vessels, consisting of conical bowls turned upside down and then placed over the mouths of shoe-shaped jars, known as patojos. In addition, there were 3 patojos that appeared to be left without accompanying conical bowls, although their poorly preserved context makes it difficult to be sure.

These types of offerings have been found in both Late Classic and Late Postclassic domestic contexts (Lind and Urcid 2010; Feinman, Nicholas, and Maher 2008; Winter et al. 2007). Like the pairs recovered during this project, they are almost always found empty and without any residue, which makes their purpose uncertain, although they may have been part of rites associated with the placenta of newborn infants (Chapter 3).

Because these offerings occur at varying depths below the patio surface, it seems that they were buried on separate occasions. A similar conclusion was drawn by Winter et al. (2007) for the paired-vessel offerings they found within the Lanisbaa residence.

Cajete/Patojo Pair 1 (Fig. 7.4, Plate 2)

During the excavation of test unit 3 (Fig. 7.2), I found the remains of a cajete or conical bowl (Fig. 7.5, Plate 2) that was turned upside down, 40 cm to the south of the base of the North Wall. The bowl was made with gray paste, and could easily be identified as a G35. Its dimensions (17.3 cm rim diameter, 7.4 cm base diameter, and 4.3 cm height) and design fit well within our project's sample of small Classic period cajetes (Appendix B).

Directly below the bowl, I excavated a patojo (Fig. 7.6, Plate 2) that was interred with its base oriented to the west (Fig. 7.2). This was the smallest of the patojos collected, and measured 15.5 cm long, 11.2 cm wide, and 12.5 cm tall, with an outside rim diameter of 9.3 cm and a thickness of 5 mm. Like all the patojos recovered during the project, it was made with brown paste that was differentially fired and had diorite temper, which is diagnostic of Early Monte Albán V (Markens 2008).

This is our only ceramic vessel pair with mixed (or transitional) period indicators, perhaps suggesting that it was one of the first to be buried. It certainly implies some continued use of G35 cajetes into the Early Postclassic.

Cajete/Patojo Pair 2

About 15 cm to the west of the first vessel pair, I found a second cajete/patojo pair buried directly beneath the North Wall (Fig. 7.2). Unlike the first pair, however, the conical bowl (Fig. 7.7, Plate 3) was made with brown paste, similar to the patojos. This bowl fits Markens' (2008) description of the Early Monte Albán V type. The conical bowl was found intact, with measurements of 16.4 cm rim diameter and 5 cm height. Beneath the bowl, I found patojo number 2, with its base also oriented toward the west (Fig. 7.8, Plate 3). Although this patojo was in poor condition (broken into more than 30 fragments), we were able to reconstruct it sufficiently to determine its measurements. Its rim had an inside diameter of 8 cm and an outside diameter of 11.5 cm; its length was 24.5 cm, width 19.5 cm, height 15 cm, and wall thickness 6 mm.

Spatial Distribution of Artifacts and Implied Behavioral Patterns 145

Figure 7.2. Cajete/patojo pairs, test unit 3, West Patio Complex.

Figure 7.3. Cajete/patojo pair (no. 6), test unit 5, West Patio Complex.

Figure 7.4. Cajete/patojo pair number 1 (also see Plate 2).

Figure 7.5. Small G35-type conical bowl, cajete/patojo pair number 1 (also see Plate 2).

Spatial Distribution of Artifacts and Implied Behavioral Patterns 147

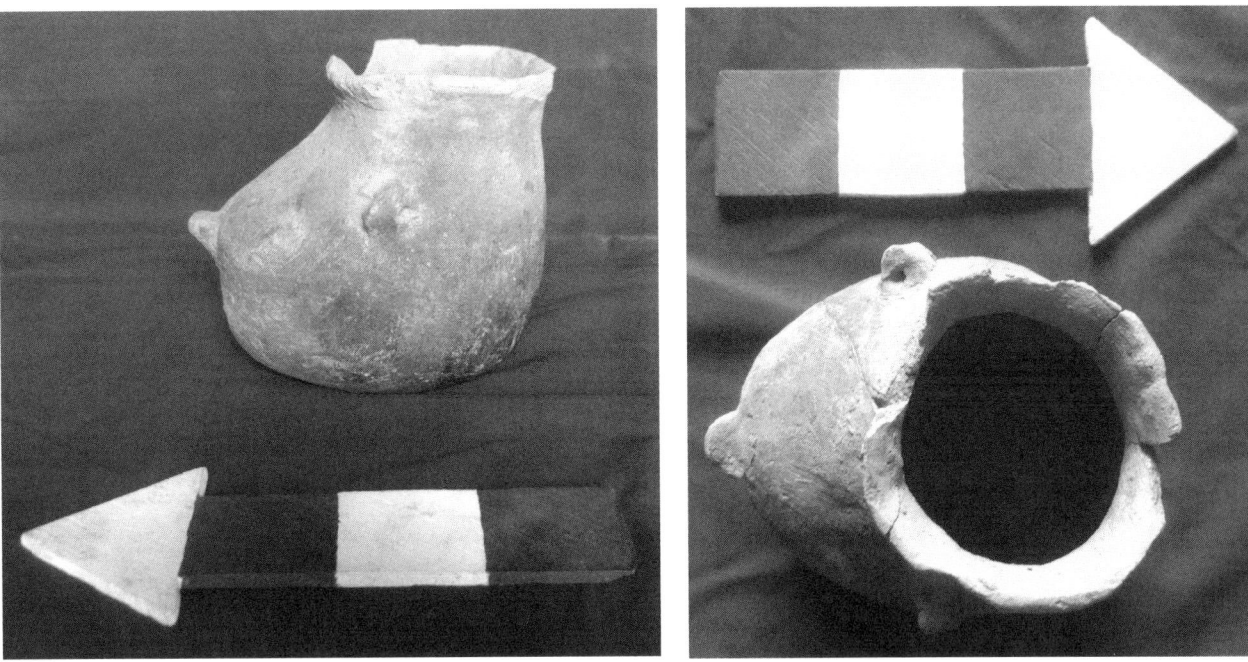

Figure 7.6. Brown paste patojo, cajete/patojo pair number 1 (also see Plate 2).

Figure 7.7. Postclassic-type conical bowl, cajete/patojo pair number 2 (scale has 5-cm sections) (also see Plate 3).

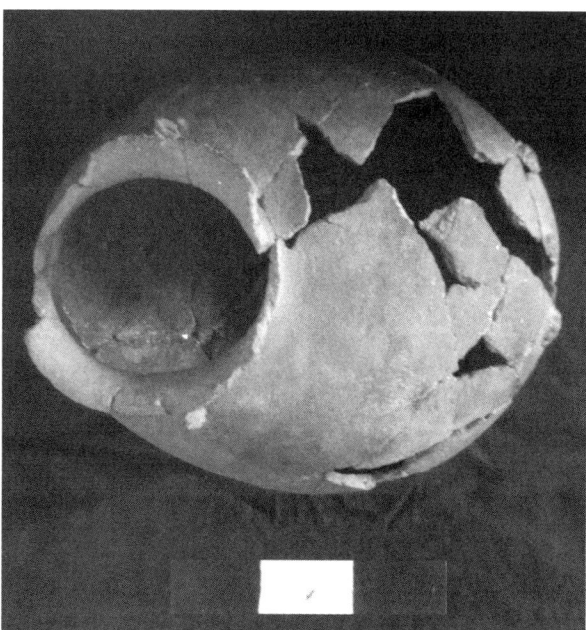

Figure 7.8. Postclassic patojo, cajete/patojo pair number 2 (also see Plate 3).

Figure 7.9. Cajete/patojo pair number 3 (also see Plate 3).

Cajete/Patojo Pair 3

Buried beneath the North Wall, 130 cm to the west of the second pair (Fig. 7.2), we found the third vessel pair (Fig. 7.9, Plate 3). As with the others, the cajete was placed upside down over the mouth of the patojo. The bowl (Fig. 7.10, Plate 3) was made with the same orange/brown paste as our second cajete. Although the cajete was broken into many pieces, the patojo was found in excellent condition (Fig. 7.11, Plate 4). Like the majority of the other patojos, its "toe" was facing west, and it was made with brown paste that was differentially fired.

Patojo 4

Large fragments of a patojo (Fig. 7.12)—which appeared to be all that remained of another cajete/patojo pair—were found in test unit 3, some 35 cm to the west of the third vessel pair and 45 cm south of the base of the North Wall (Fig.7.2). I found no evidence for a corresponding conical bowl, and the patojo was sufficiently destroyed that I was unable to determine its measurements. It did, however, appear to have had its toe to the west, like the others.

Patojo 5

This patojo was found nearly intact at the base of the North Wall, at its eastern edge in excavation unit N6E6 (Fig. 7.13). This was the largest of the patojos we found, with a length of 22 cm, width of 18.8 cm, height of 18 cm, inside rim diameter of 8.7 cm, outside rim diameter of 11.7 cm, and general wall thickness of about 5 mm. Unlike the other patojos, this one was found oriented to the east, and no cajete was found with it.

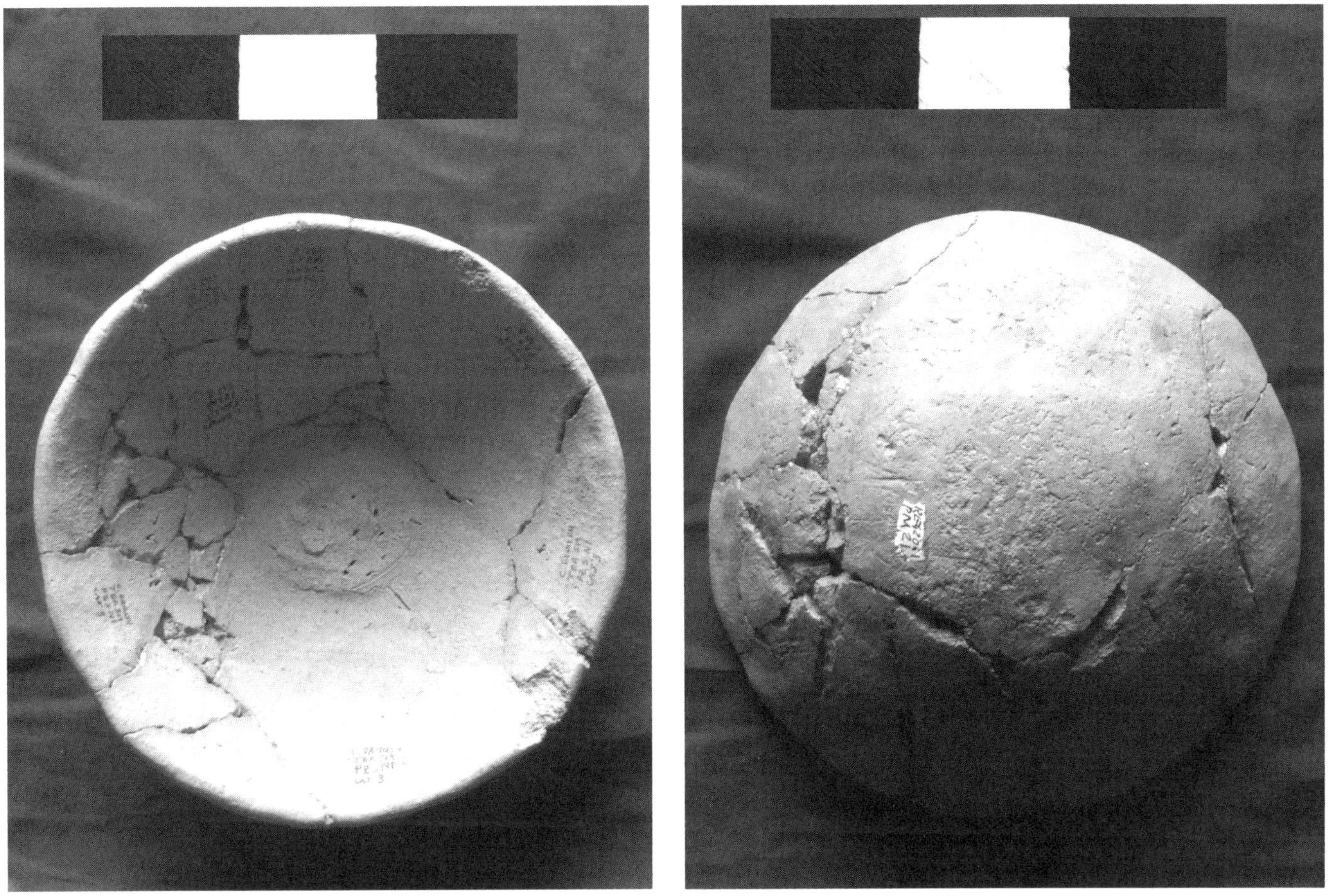

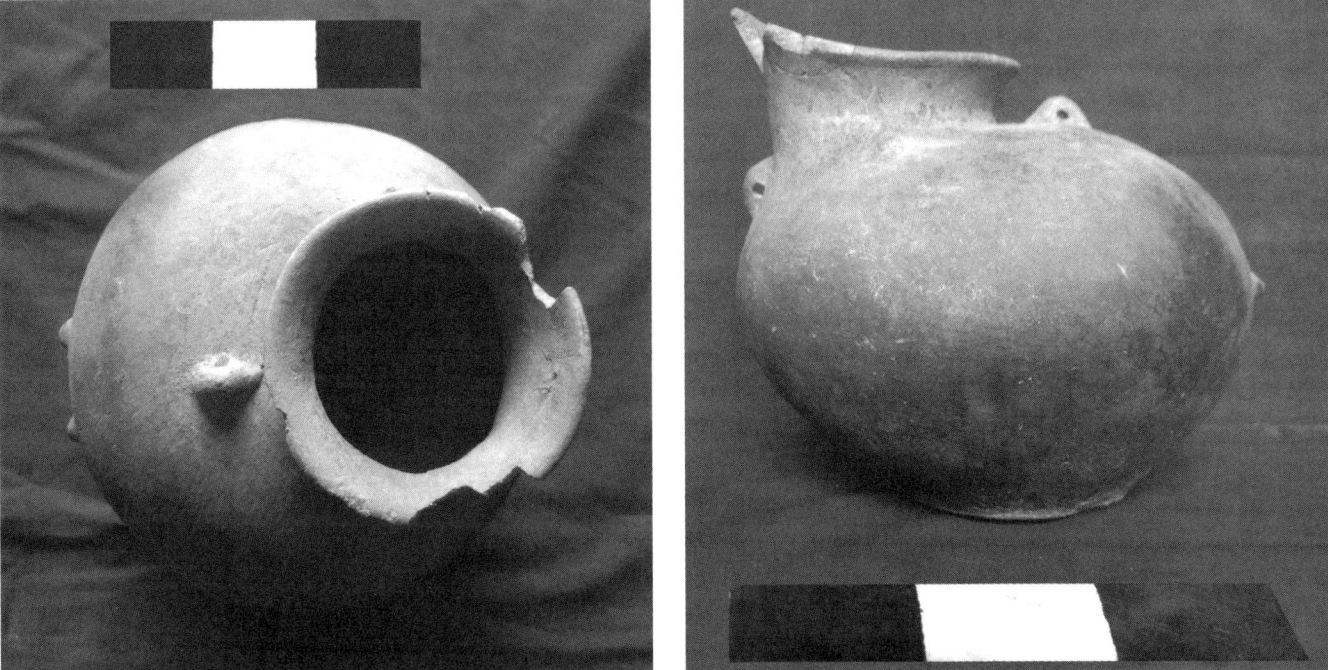

Figure 7.10. Postclassic-style conical bowl, cajete/patojo pair number 3 (also see Plate 3).

Figure 7.11. Postclassic-style patojo, cajete/patojo pair number 3 (also see Plate 4).

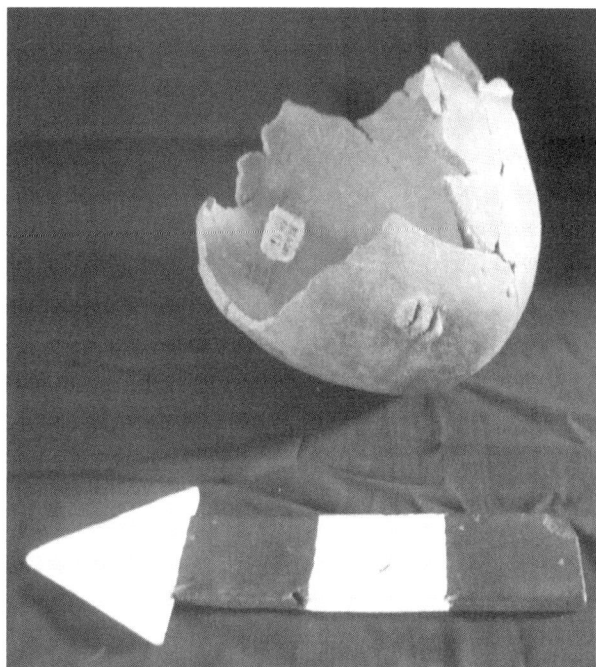

Figure 7.12. Patojo number 4 (arrow has 5-cm sections).

Figure 7.13. Patojo number 5, eastern edge of North Wall (north arrow has 10-cm sections).

Figure 7.14. Cajete/patojo pair number 6 (arrow has 5-cm sections) (also see Plate 4).

Cajete/Patojo Pair 6 (Fig. 7.14, Plate 4)

In test unit 5 (Fig. 7.3), 50 cm to the east of the second cajete/patojo pair, I found another paired-vessel offering buried beneath the North Wall. The cajete (Fig. 7.15, Plate 5) was found in relatively good condition. It was made of brown paste that was differentially fired, had a flat bottom and straight rim, and fits the Monte Albán V variety. Patojo 6 (Fig. 7.16, Plate 5) was found intact directly beneath the bowl. Like patojos 1–4 and 7, it was oriented to the west, and made of brown paste that was differentially fired. Its outside rim diameter was 10.3 cm, inside diameter 7.4 cm, length 18 cm, width 16.2 cm, height 14.5 cm, and general wall thickness 5 mm.

Patojo 7

The base of a seventh and final patojo was found oriented to the west in test unit 8 (Fig. 7.17), about 180 cm to the west of patojo 4 and nearly centered between the northern foundation wall of Structure E and the North Wall. It was heavily damaged, with most of the neck and rim missing (Fig. 7.18), and no evidence for an accompanying cajete. Consequently, I was able to determine only its length (20.2 cm), width (16.5 cm), and general wall thickness (5 mm).

Other Ceramic Vessel Offerings

On top of the stucco floor found at the base of test unit 3, I found a dense area of ceramic sherds that turned out to be the remains of a nearly complete gray ware G35 conical bowl with hollow supports (Fig. 7.19, Plate 6). This piece fits within the category of large conical bowls (Fig. B2) and has the following measurements: outside rim diameter 30 cm, inside rim diameter 25 cm, base diameter 14 cm, height 7.2 cm, and general wall thickness 5 mm. It may have been deliberately smashed on the earlier floor as part of a termination ceremony, immediately prior to the construction of the West Patio Complex.

In test unit 6 (Fig. 7.20), directly to the south of test unit 3, 2 other vessels were found below the surface of the patio floor (Fig. 7.1, nos. 13, 14). The first was a small G35-type bowl (Fig. 7.21), which was found upside down and broken into 23 pieces. Like the larger conical bowl discussed above, this item was found directly on top of the earlier patio surface, suggesting it may have been placed there as part of a termination offering.

About 90 cm to the east of the conical bowl, I found the rim and neck of an olla that appears to have been embedded in the earlier stucco surface. It was made with gray paste consistent with Classic period types, with an outside rim diameter of 19 cm, and an inside rim diameter of about 13 cm. The bottom of the neck was cut straight, suggesting that the severed rim was being used for a secondary purpose, perhaps as a stand for a round-bottomed cooking vessel. In support of this possibility, the stucco immediately surrounding the olla rim was reddened (Fig. 7.20) from heat. This piece may not represent an offering, but rather a floor feature left over from the previous construction phase.

Directly upslope of the North Wall, in the second layer of unit N8E5 (Fig. 7.1, no. 9), I found a small G35 conical bowl with its face down (Fig. 7.22). Unlike the other vessels, this bowl did not appear to be associated with any other feature, and probably should not be considered an offering. The inside of this bowl was filled with dried stucco, which had the impression of a shelled corncob embedded in it (Fig. 7.23, Plate 6). It may be that the

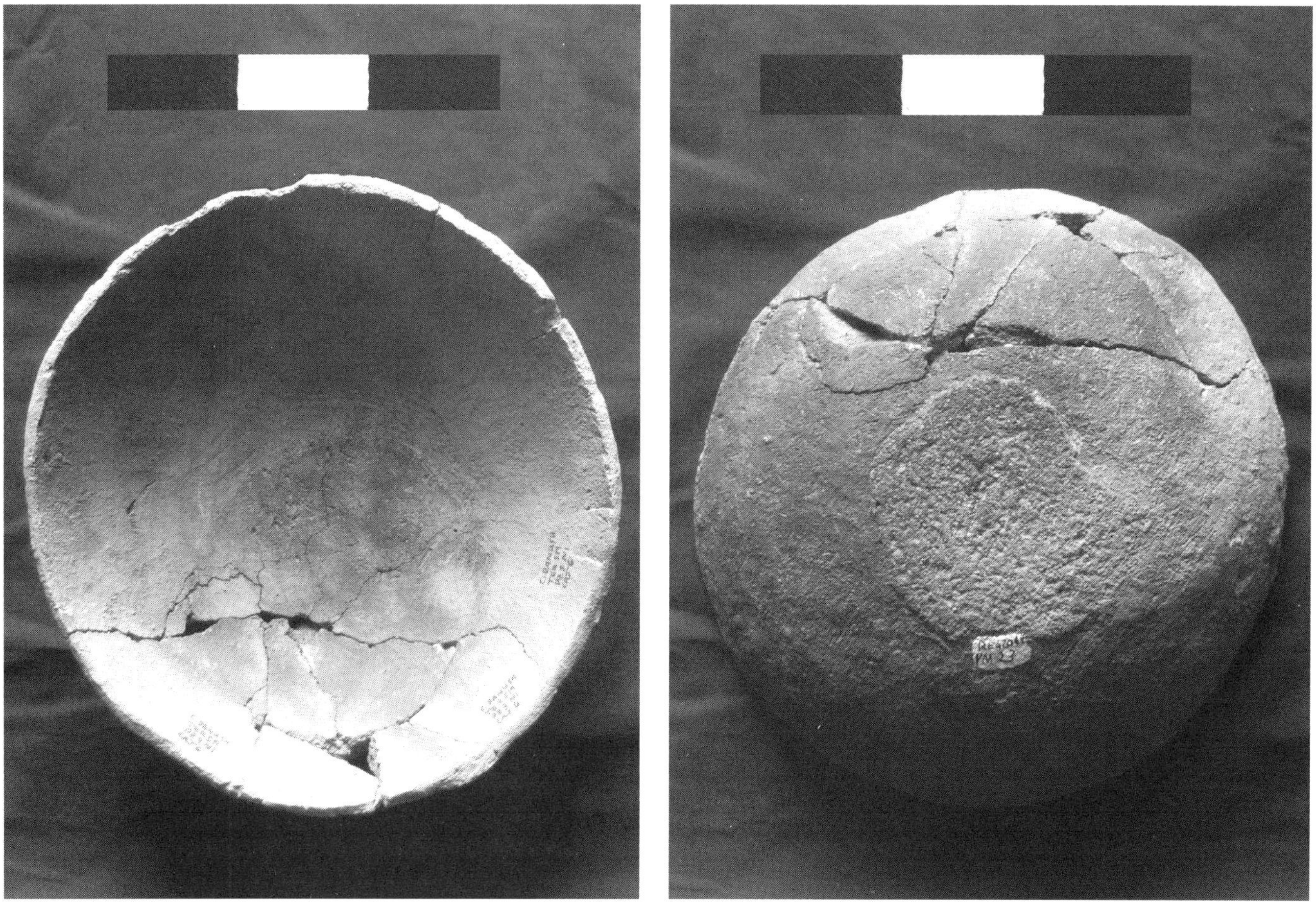

Figure 7.15. Postclassic brown paste conical bowl, cajete/patojo pair number 6 (scale has 5-cm sections) (also see Plate 5).

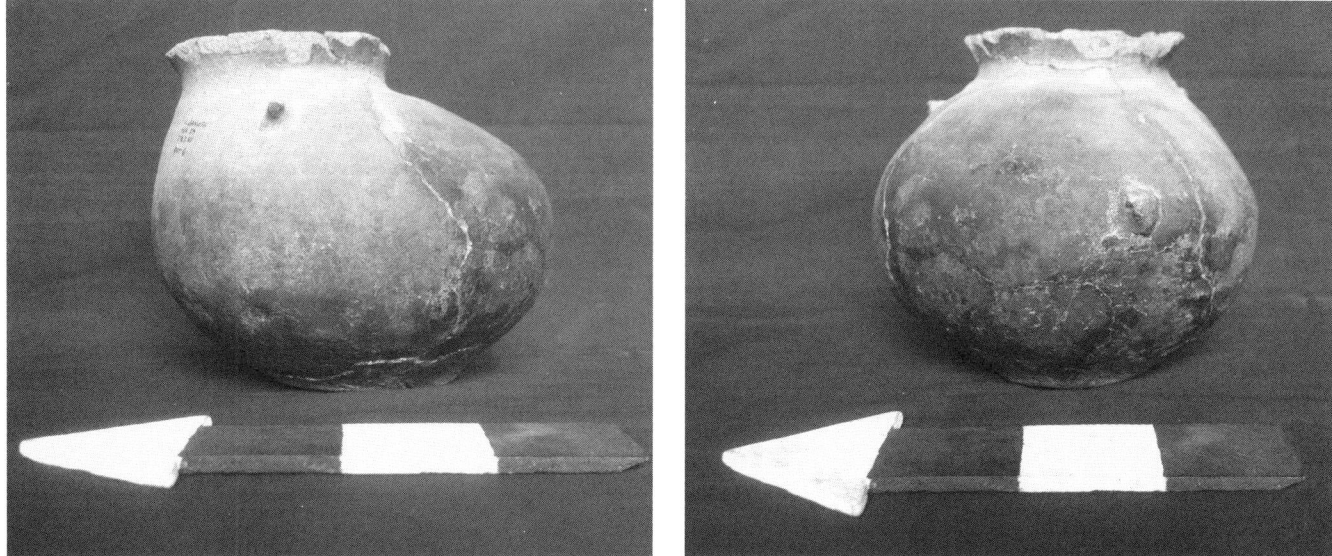

Figure 7.16. Brown paste patojo, cajete/patojo pair number 6 (arrow has 5-cm sections) (also see Plate 5).

Spatial Distribution of Artifacts and Implied Behavioral Patterns 153

Figure 7.17. Test unit 8, West Patio Complex (north arrow has 10-cm sections).

Figure 7.18. Patojo number 7 (arrow has 5-cm sections).

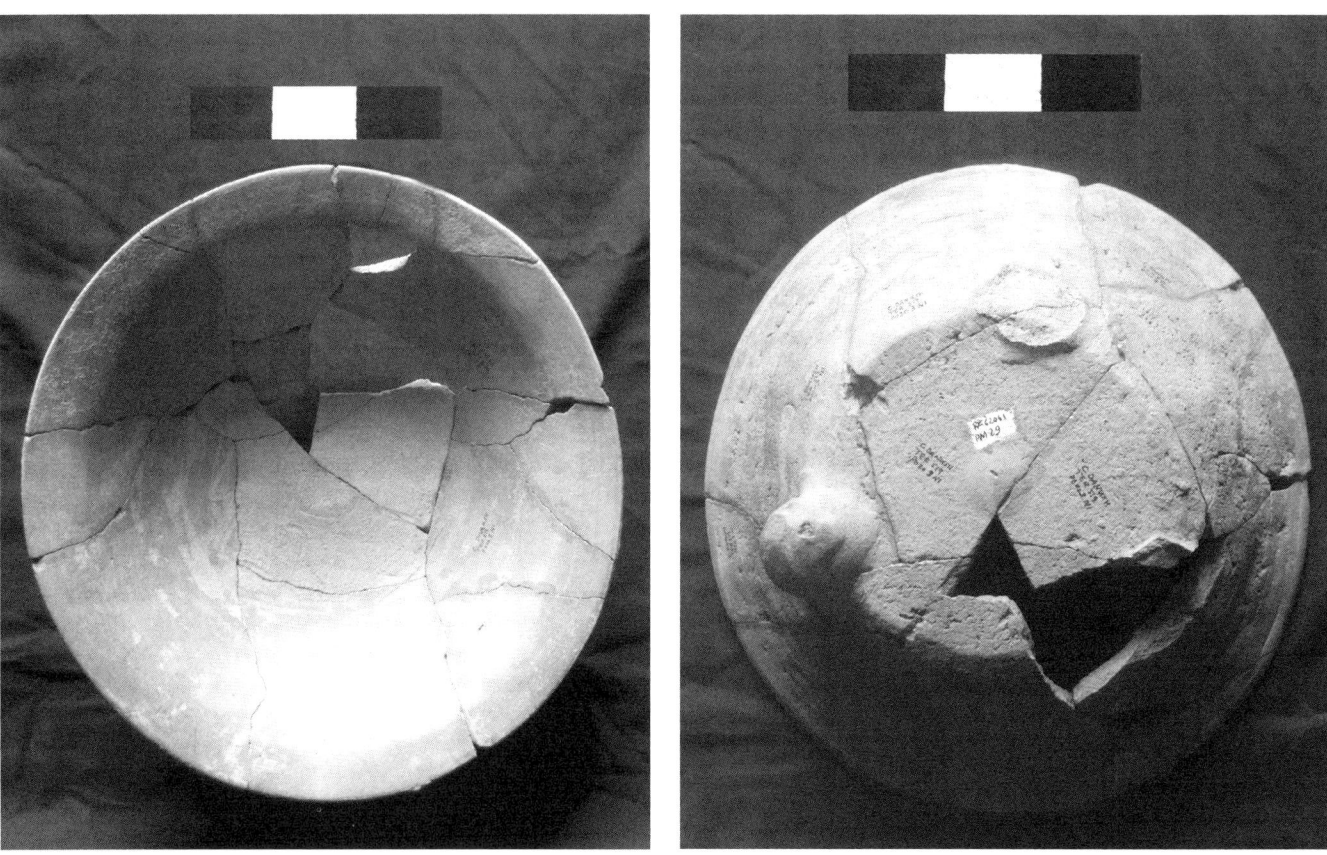

Figure 7.19. Large gray paste G35 conical bowl, test unit 3 (scale has 5-cm sections) (also see Plate 6).

Figure 7.20. Test unit 6, West Patio Complex (north arrow has 10-cm sections).

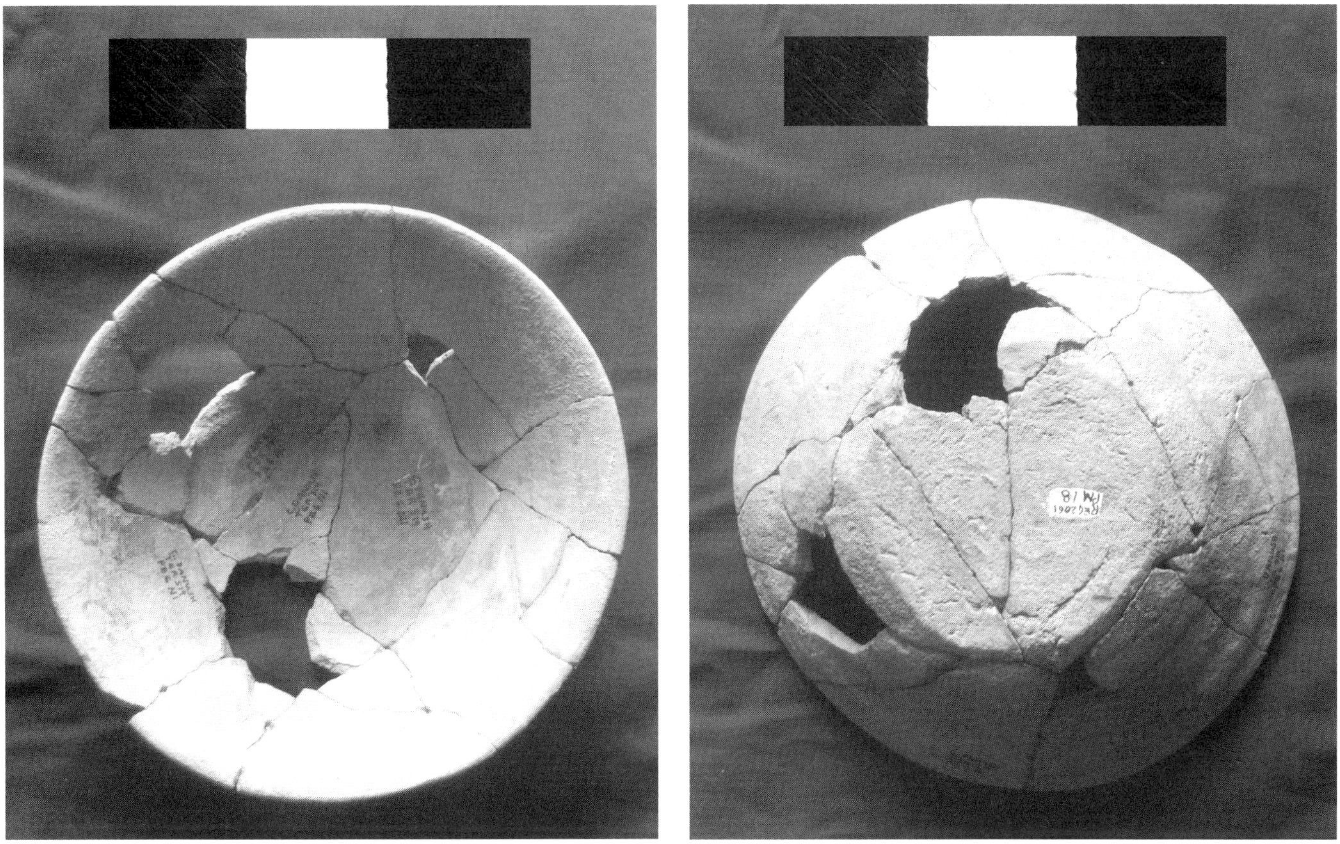

Figure 7.21. Small G35 conical bowl, test unit 6, West Patio Complex (scale has 5-cm sections).

Figure 7.22. G35 gray conical bowl, excavation unit N8E5 (north arrow has 10-cm sections).

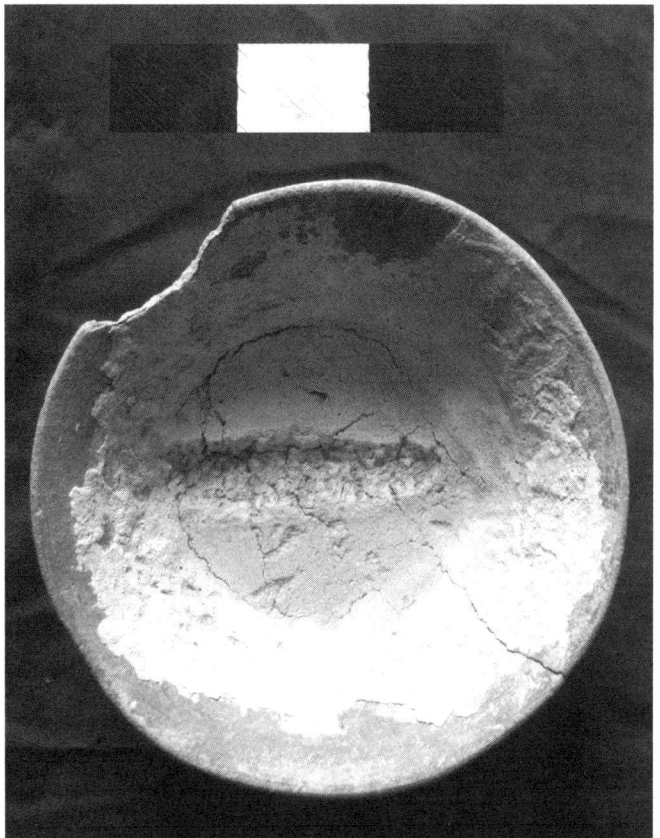 

Figure 7.23. Gray ware conical bowl with corncob impression (scale has 5-cm sections) (also see Plate 6).

stucco dried up while waiting to be used, and the bowl was then discarded in the refuse area upslope of the North Wall. While the bowl is mostly gray, there is a small patch of brown along the rim, revealing a differential firing process. The form and dimensions of this bowl fit well within the Classic period small G35 bowl category (Fig. B1), with an outside rim diameter of 19.3 cm, inside rim diameter of 18.7, base diameter of 10.8 cm, height of 6.2 cm, and general wall thickness of about 5 mm. The shelled corncob might have been used as an applicator for stucco.

The Overall Qualitative Pattern

The pairing of Late Classic G35s and Early Postclassic patojos on Terrace S19 suggests a transitional period. The two G35 bowls positioned immediately on top of the earlier patio surface may have been part of an offering left just before the reconstruction of the patio. The third G35 was found as part of a paired cajete/patojo offering made after the new patio was constructed.

Because the remaining cajete/patojo pairs contain only Postclassic-type yellow or brown paste cajetes, I propose that the mixed pair was the first to be buried, perhaps shortly after the patio reconstruction. The later paired offerings probably reflect a pattern of diminishing use for the Late Classic-type G35 cajetes during the Early Postclassic; eventually, they were completely replaced with brown paste cajetes and gray paste G3M vessels.

We should not be surprised to learn that gray paste G35 bowls did not simply vanish at the Classic/Postclassic boundary. These bowls made up such a large part of the ceramic assemblage during the Late Classic that it is only reasonable that local households continued to use them until they were no longer serviceable, even after potters were going over to yellow or brown paste. Virtually every Late Classic community would have been making and using G35s, and it is doubtful that all potters gave up making them simultaneously.

Another piece of evidence for the continued use of G35 conical bowls during the Early Postclassic occupation of Terrace S19 is the ceramic offering that accompanied Burial 3 (Chapter 6). This individual was interred beneath the patio floor of the West Patio Complex, above the earlier patio surface along the edge of the North Wall. The burial offering consisted of a large G35 cajete (Fig. 6.33, Plate 1) with red paint on its interior surface. This vessel had been placed upside down over the individual's thighs, a mortuary pattern typical of commoners in Classic and Postclassic residences (Winter 2002; Winter et al. 2007). The stratigraphic location of this burial (in the same layer of fill where the other offerings were found) suggests that it occurred sometime after the Early Postclassic residence was constructed, but while gray paste G35 cajetes were still being manufactured.

The ceramic offerings found beneath the patio floor of the Early Postclassic house complex therefore suggest a transitional pattern during which Late Classic and Early Postclassic types coexisted (perhaps A.D. 1000–1250). The types of offerings found—and their location beneath the patio floor—present great continuity in ritual behavior between the Early Postclassic inhabitants of Terrace S19 and their Late Classic ancestors. This ritual continuity persisted despite the adoption of Early Postclassic behaviors such as bloque y laja construction technique and G3M ceramics.

The facts summarized above allow me to propose that the residence on Terrace S19 was occupied continuously by a multigenerational household from the Late Classic through the Early Postclassic, perhaps for a period of more than 700 years. Further support for this hypothesis comes from the large number of sherds recovered on Terrace S19 (more than 230,000). For a residence with no evidence of kilns, such an accumulation of broken pottery suggests an extensive period of occupation.

To be sure, over such a long span of time, one would expect major episodes of architectural reconstruction, such as the one that occurred around A.D. 1000. Despite this renovation, many aspects of household behavior on Terrace S19 appear to have changed little. Evidently, the members of this particular household on Terrace S19 continued many of their regular routines despite the significant political changes going on in the Valley of Oaxaca.

Quantitative Assessment of the Artifact Assemblage

Analysis of our surface collections gave us a way to infer behavioral patterns at the level of the individual terrace. Only excavation, however, allowed us to infer the behavioral patterns within each terrace, and such inference had to be informed by an understanding of the cultural and natural processes involved in the formation of each stratigraphic layer, and how those processes had affected the distribution of artifacts.

The plow zone, or Layer 1, had been disturbed by post-abandonment processes such as plowing and erosion. The artifact density distribution (artifacts recovered per liter of soil excavated) within this layer closely resembled that of the circles surface-collected during the first field season. Artifact migration caused by plowing and erosion has rendered density distribution analysis in this layer unreliable beyond the level of the terrace; in other words, it is unlikely that artifact distribution patterns in this layer reflect the activities carried out on the ancient living surface. The volume density plot (Fig. 7.24) of artifacts from the plow zone illustrates this concept. Artifact distribution is more uniform, and densities low, in comparison to the second layer (Fig. 7.25). Therefore, I did not include the plow zone in my spatial or statistical analyses.

Both Layers 3 and 4 consisted of fill (Chapter 6), which means that the artifacts found in these layers have been removed from their original contexts. Spatial analysis of artifact density distributions in these layers, therefore, would not be useful with regard to characterizing household activities or the use of space. For these reasons, I chose not to subject the data sets for the third and fourth layers to detailed analysis.

Of all the layers, it was the second that had the greatest potential for spatial analysis. These materials were deposited on top

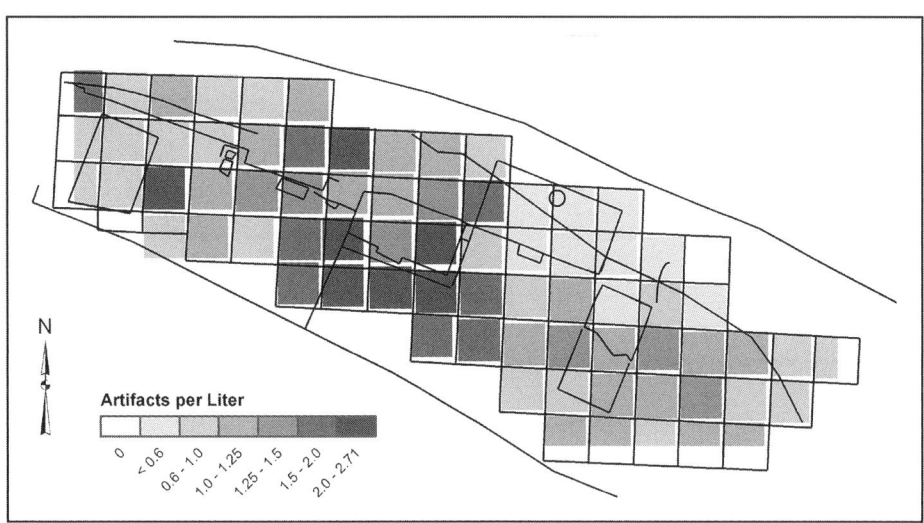

Figure 7.24. Volume densities of artifacts, plow zone, Terrace S19.

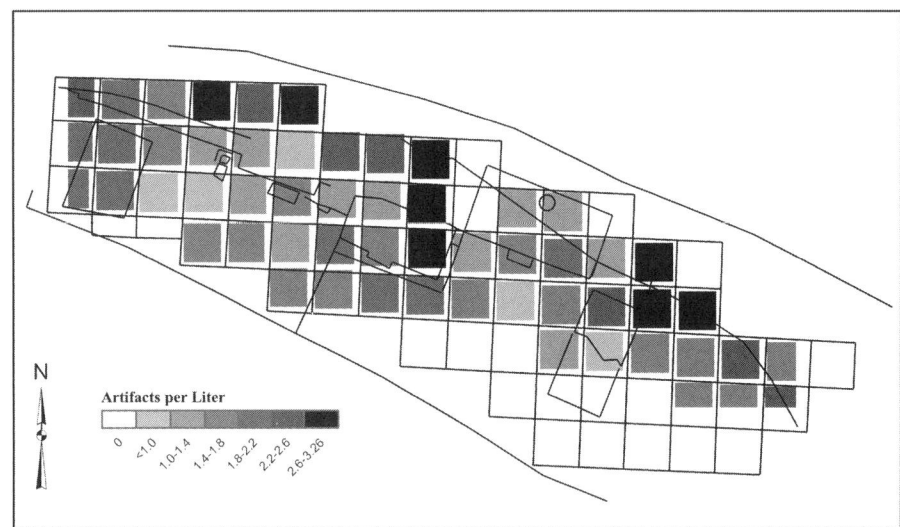

Figure 7.25. Volume densities of artifacts, Layer 2, Terrace S19.

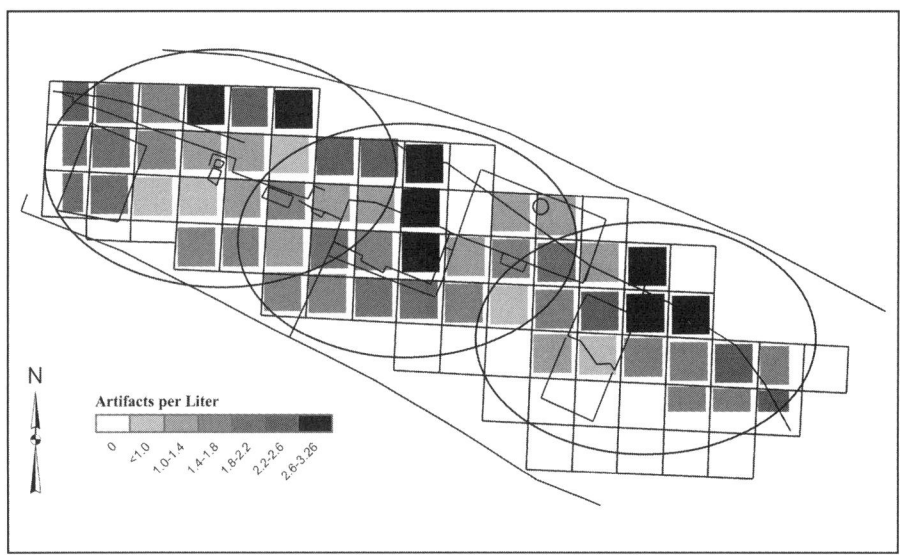

Figure 7.26. Proposed areas of refuse deposits and their colluvial erosion zones.

of the most recent occupational surface, which consisted of two separate patios and their adjacent structures. Patios have long served as the focal points for domestic activities (including food preparation and storage) within Oaxacan house complexes, and the patios on Terrace S19 are no exception. Without claiming that all Level 2 artifacts were in the exact locations where they had been left (see LaMotta and Schiffer 1999; Schiffer 1975), their density distributions ought to yield information concerning the division of activities between the two patios.

The highest artifact concentrations in Layer 2 were found lying on bedrock just outside these patio spaces (Fig. 7.26). Three areas were identified as probable refuse deposits and appear to relate to the patios in the following manner. The first area was upslope of the North Wall, just north of the West Patio Complex; the second was on bedrock to the north of Structure C, and may relate to both patios; the third area was found to the north and east of Structure A, just east of the East Patio Complex. If we assume that materials were discarded close to their use and that subsequent artifact migration was limited to a fan-shaped area just downslope of their original point of deposition, then it may be possible to use these "erosion fans" (Fig. 7.26, circled areas) to identify the activities that produced the debris. To be sure, there may be overlap in the case of some erosion fans.

Let us now proceed to an analysis of the second stratigraphic layer. Note that owing to the sloping surface of the terrace, the depths of individual excavation units in this layer

Spatial Distribution of Artifacts and Implied Behavioral Patterns 159

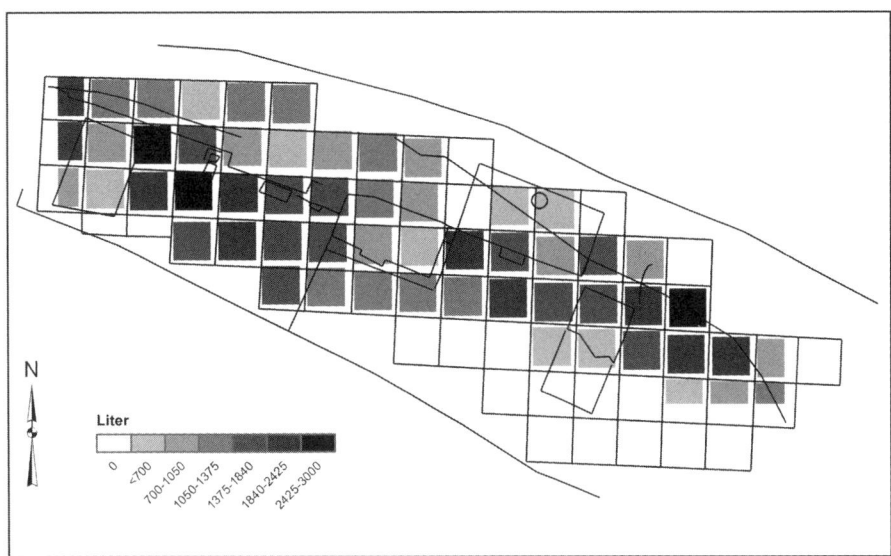

Figure 7.27. Soil volumes from excavated squares, Layer 2, Terrace S19.

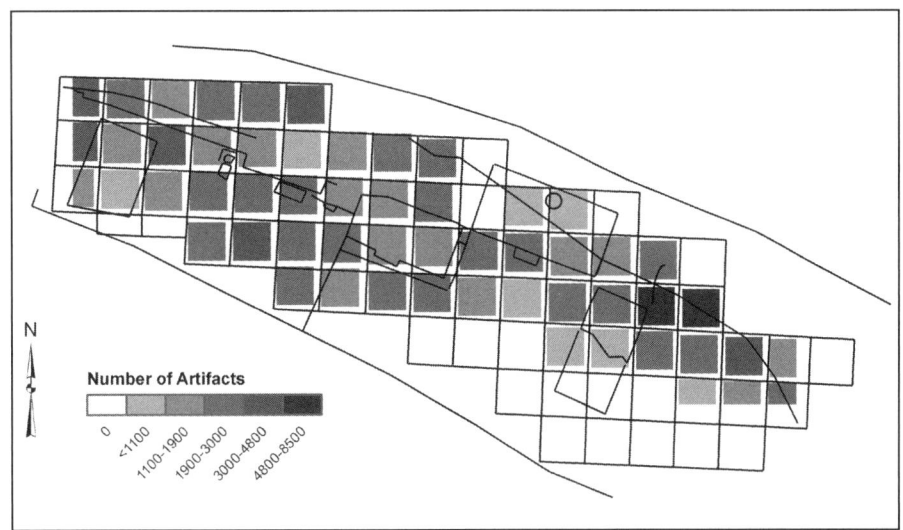

Figure 7.28. Raw artifact frequency counts, Layer 2, Terrace S19.

varied significantly, which resulted in a significant variation in the volume of soil removed per unit (Fig. 7.27). This raises the possibility that direct analysis of the spatial distributions based on artifact frequency counts could be misleading, since one would naturally expect to find more artifacts where more soil was removed. A comparison of the plots of unit volumes (Fig. 7.27) with the unit artifact densities based on simple frequency counts for the second layer (Fig. 7.28) demonstrates this point. To take this problem into account, I first standardized the data by dividing the frequency count of artifacts from a specific excavation unit by the corresponding volume of soil removed (in liters).

Spatial Analysis of the Artifact Density Distribution, Terrace S19

I subjected the artifact frequency counts from the second layer of Terrace S19 to multivariate statistical analysis. My goals were to provide an independent evaluation of the results from the spatial analysis and to identify patterns that might not be readily inferred from the density distribution plots. During my analysis of the surface collection data, principal components analysis had proven limited in its ability to distinguish anything more than the most obvious spatial patterns; correspondence analysis had proven more effective, serving as a quantitative complement to

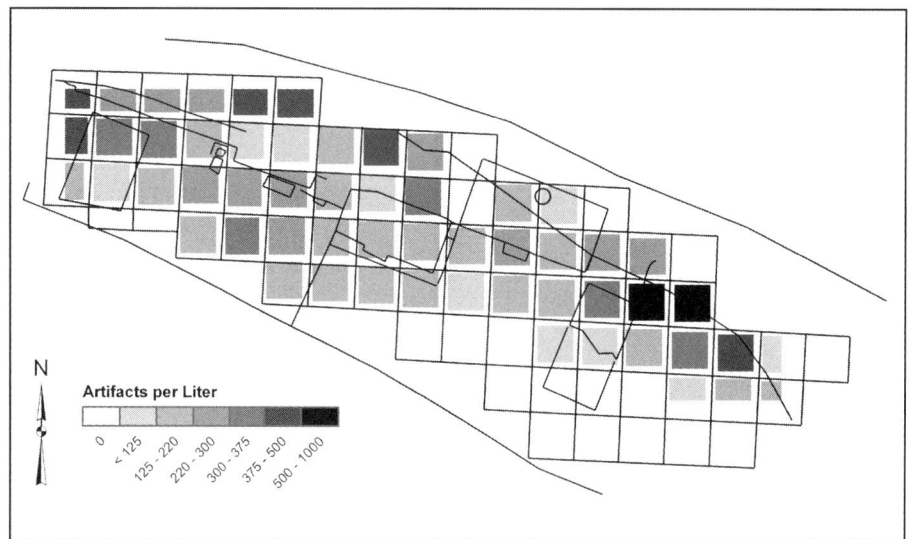

Figure 7.29. Distribution of diagnostic ceramic fragments.

the spatial analysis. For this reason, I limited my multivariate study to correspondence analysis.

The total of 53 artifact categories used in my correspondence analysis (Appendix B) included G35 and K14 conical bowls, Dainzú Bowls, hemispherical bowls (orange, gray, and brown), cylindrical bowls (orange, gray, and brown), G23 bowls, G3M hemispherical bowls, Postclassic conical bowls of yellow or brown paste, small bowls with exterior red paint, cups with appliqué claws attached, miniature ceramic vessels, simple ollas, large barrel-shaped ollas, small globular ollas with appliqué glyph motifs, silbatos, *tecomates*, botellones, *tlecuiles*, comales, cántaros, chilmoleras, patojos, apaxtles, ceramic wasters, plates, solid figurines, mold-made figurines, figurine molds, urns, spindle whorls, *cucharones* (ladles), braziers, solid-handled censers, hollow-handled censers, chert points, chert debitage, chert flake tools, chert cores, raspadores, volcanic tuff debitage, volcanic tuff flake tools, volcanic tuff cores, obsidian prismatic blades, obsidian debitage, animal bone fragments, burned daub, chalk, manos, and metates.

Because the soil volumes for individual excavation units were very high (often containing more than 100 liters), the volume densities for individual artifact categories were converted to a volume density index. In this index, individual artifact counts were first divided by the soil volume in liters for each excavation unit and then the result was multiplied by one hundred (volume index = $a/L \times 100$). I did this to avoid dealing with excessively small numbers, and because all the data were treated this way, the index did not bias the relative comparison of density distributions. All density plots contain a gray scale that reflects varying densities of the artifacts reported in the volume index format.

Let us look first at the overall distribution patterns of diagnostic ceramics, chipped stone, and faunal remains. Because sherds (diagnostic and non-diagnostic) made up the bulk of the artifacts recovered during excavation, they tend to dominate the overall artifact distribution represented by the plots in Figures 7.25 and 7.26. Diagnostic sherd (Fig. 7.29) densities follow the same basic pattern, with high concentrations in all three zones, but these sherds appear to be most concentrated in the eastern zone. The plot of chipped stone (Fig. 7.30) shows a slightly different pattern from that of ceramics, with high densities on both the central and western fans, but lower densities on the eastern fan. The density plot for faunal remains (Fig. 7.31) shows them to be more dispersed than the other two items, but they nevertheless show concentrations on all three fans.

Chert debitage makes up the greatest portion of the chipped stone assemblage from excavation. The density distribution for this category shows that debitage was most concentrated in the central portion of the terrace (Fig. 7.32), specifically in the units immediately surrounding the eastern patio, with the lowest concentrations in units on the western side of the terrace. The only spent chert core found in this layer was recovered from excavation unit N3E14, just east of Structure A.

The distribution of volcanic tuff cores and debitage displayed a pattern similar to that of chert, possibly because silicified tuff was simply used to supplement chert. The distribution suggests that stone tool production may have been an activity concentrated in the eastern patio.

Two products of the chert industry—points (Fig. 7.33) and expedient flake tools (Fig. 7.34)—show differing distribution patterns. Points appear to follow the debitage pattern, with concentrations around the east patio and many fewer found on the fans to the east and west sides of the terrace. One explanation for this pattern could be that points were being produced for consumption outside the household and that many of the points we recovered had been discarded because they either broke during production or were poorly formed (Figs. B66–B68).

Spatial Distribution of Artifacts and Implied Behavioral Patterns 161

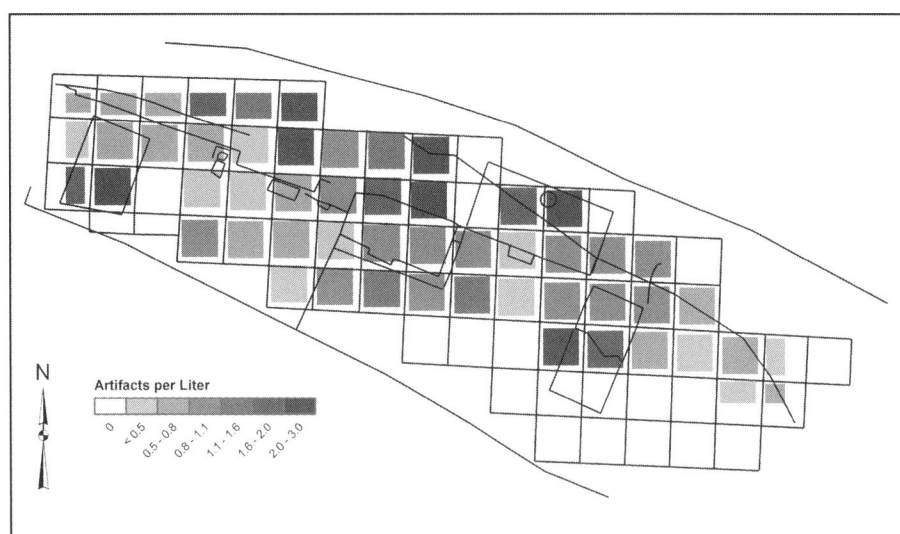

Figure 7.30. Distribution of chipped stone materials.

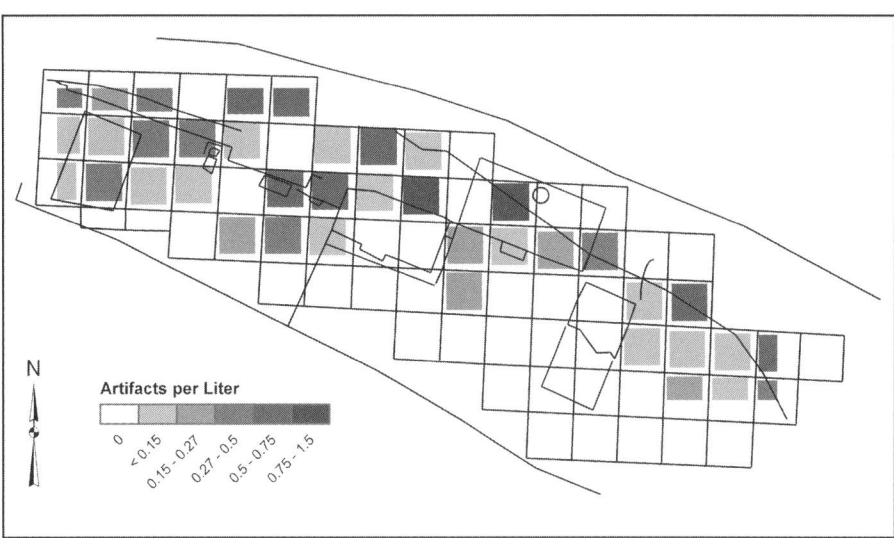

Figure 7.31. Distribution of faunal remains.

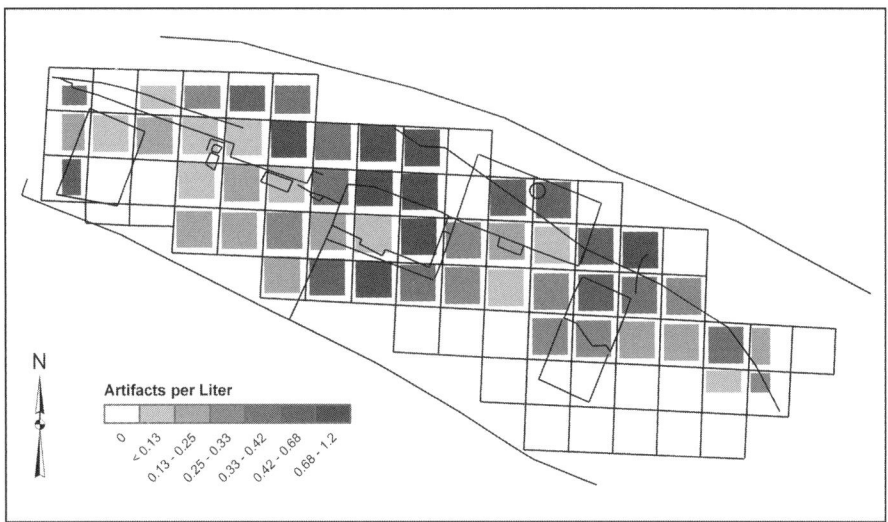

Figure 7.32. Distribution of chert debitage.

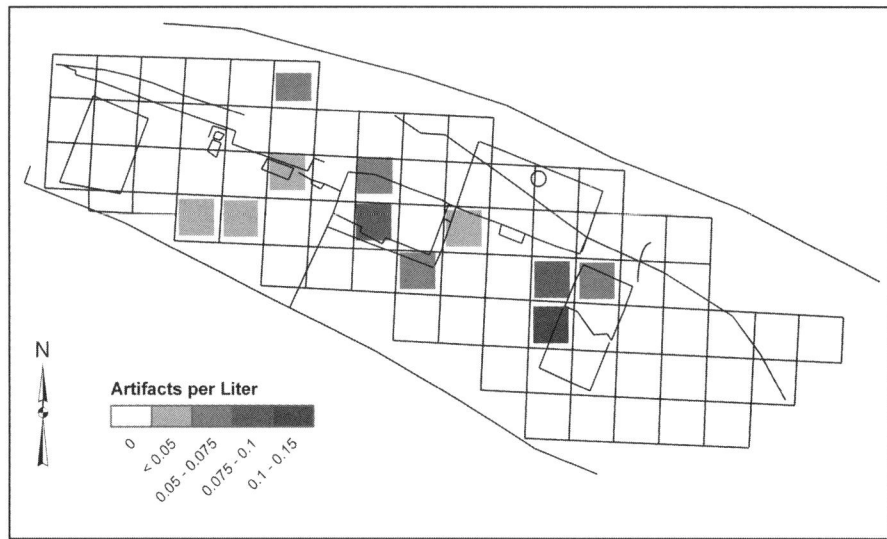

Figure 7.33. Distribution of chert points.

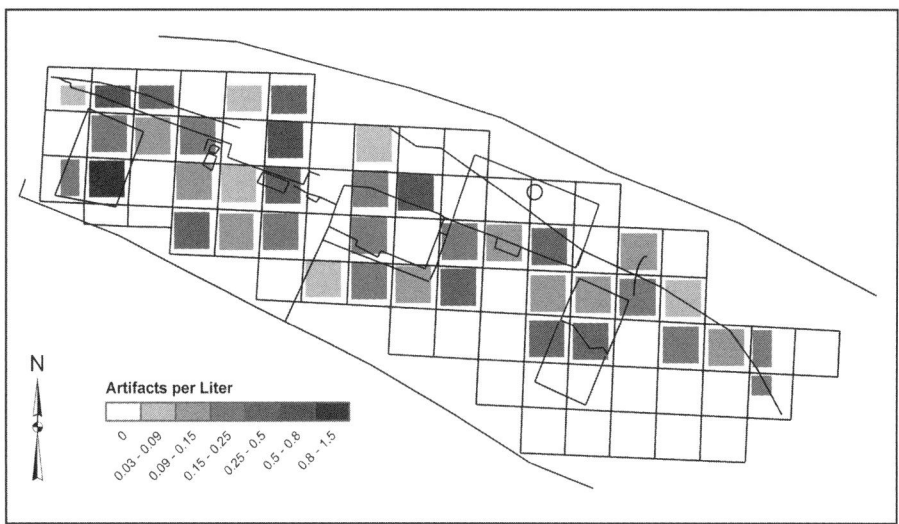

Figure 7.34. Distribution of expedient flake tools.

In contrast to points, I suspect that expedient chert flake tools were most likely produced not for external consumption, but for various tasks performed by household members. I would therefore expect these artifacts to be more spread out across the terrace, which appears to be the case (Fig. 7.34). The highest concentration of expedient chert flake tools occurred on the western side of the terrace, around Structure E. Our lone chert raspador (a tool likely used in maguey working; see Figs. B64, B65) was also recovered in this area. So, too, were 3 of the 4 bone awls/needles recovered by excavation. In addition, the density distribution of ceramic spindle whorls (Fig. 7.35) reveals that they were most concentrated on the terrace's western side. This evidence for fiber production, spinning, and sewing suggests that textile production within the residential complex may have been focused on the western patio.

The distribution of obsidian prismatic blade fragments (Fig. 7.36) is similar to that of expedient flake tools (Fig. 7.34), with high concentrations around both patios and a low distribution on the far eastern side of the terrace. Thus, the correspondence analysis reinforces our qualitative assessment of this artifact category. Since all the obsidian artifacts consisted of prismatic blades or were derivative of them, and no production materials such as spent obsidian cores were found, I suggest that prismatic blades produced elsewhere were used throughout the residential complex. This would explain their distribution.

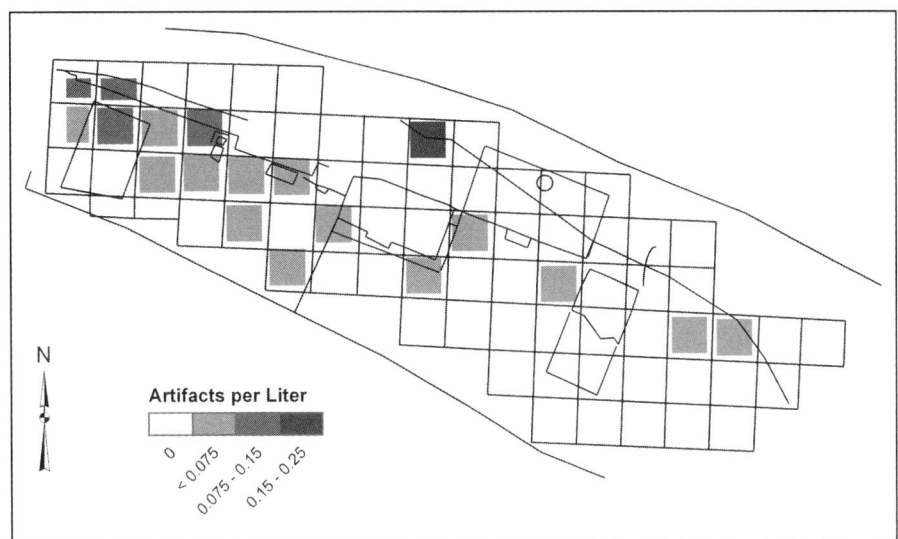

Figure 7.35. Distribution of ceramic spindle whorls.

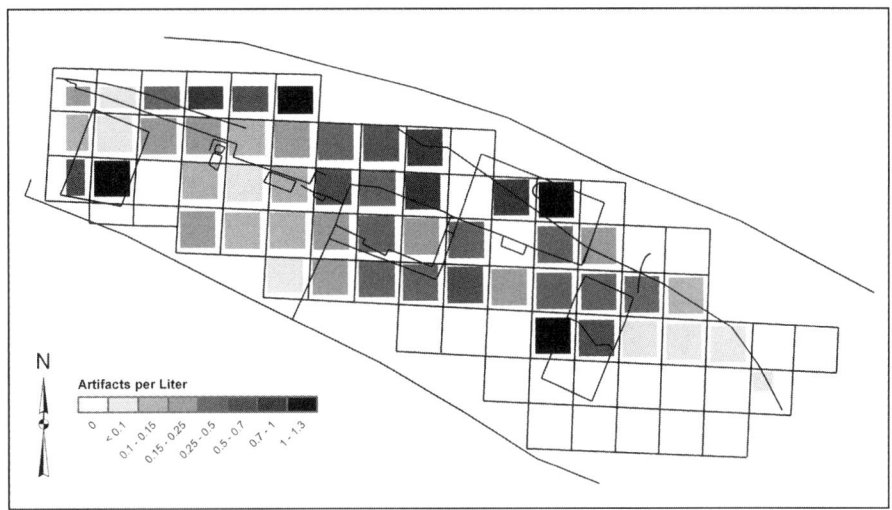

Figure 7.36. Distribution of prismatic blades.

Since obsidian is brittle, the bulk of the obsidian debitage probably represents fragments of blades broken during use. To be sure, some forms derived from obsidian blades—such as the eccentrics mentioned above and one small point (Fig. B61) collected during the surface pickup on Terrace S18—suggest occasional reworking. The most concentrated areas of obsidian debitage seem to be around the east patio (Fig. 7.37); this is an area where other chipped stone tools were worked.

One item found in great quantities to the east of Structure A—and nowhere else on the terrace—was cal (the local term for chalk blocks; Fig. 7.38). This material is produced by cooking limestone at high temperatures for prolonged periods of time, and is used both for the production of stucco and in the preparation of corn flour (*masa*) for tamales and tortillas. Interestingly enough, we found no lime kilns of the type used in cal production, which suggests that the Terrace S19 residence was acquiring this material from elsewhere.

The distribution of the large ceramic vessels known as apaxtles (Fig. 7.39), which were probably used for large-scale food preparation, shows them to be concentrated on the east side of the terrace. Here the soil is darkened by what appear to be soot and ash inclusions (Fig. 7.17), perhaps materials left over from cooking. In this same area we found a large flattened stone, lying atop the patio surface, that may have been used as a metate (Fig. 7.17). Broken one-handed and two-handed grinding stones (manos) were also more densely distributed around the east patio

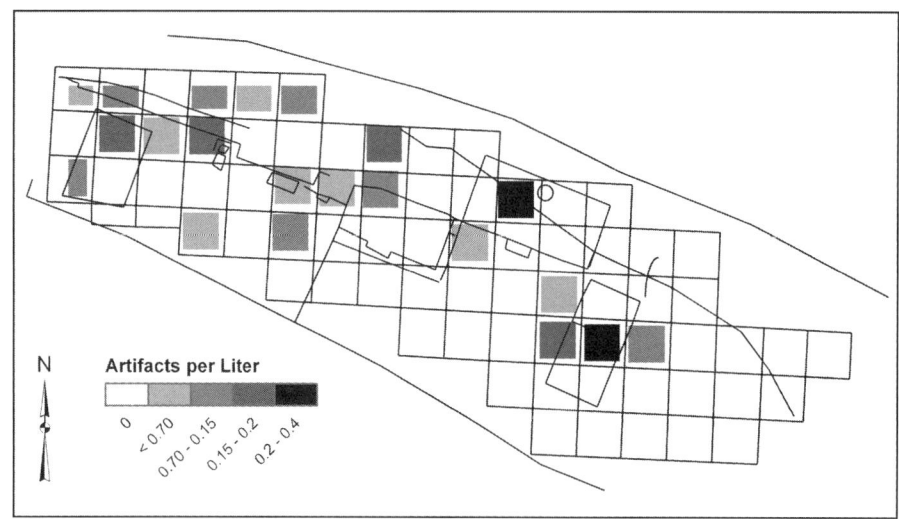

Figure 7.37. Distribution of obsidian debitage.

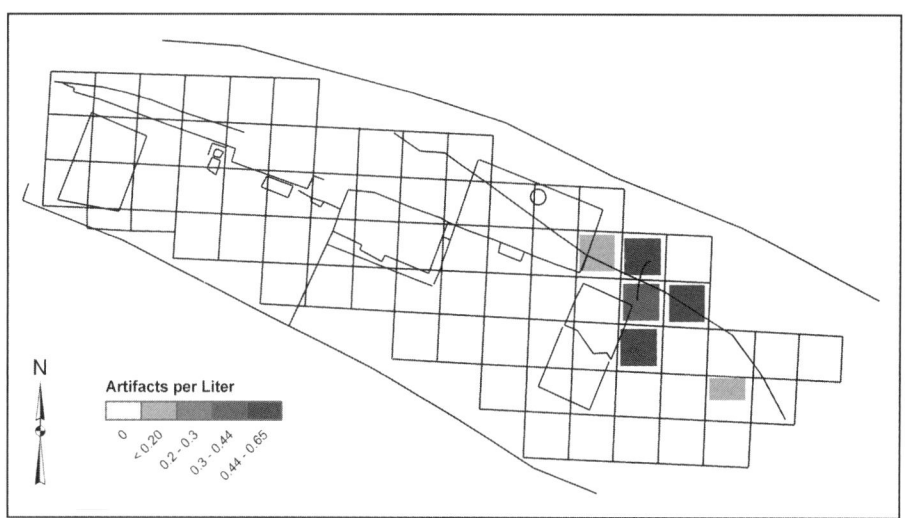

Figure 7.38. Distribution of cal block fragments.

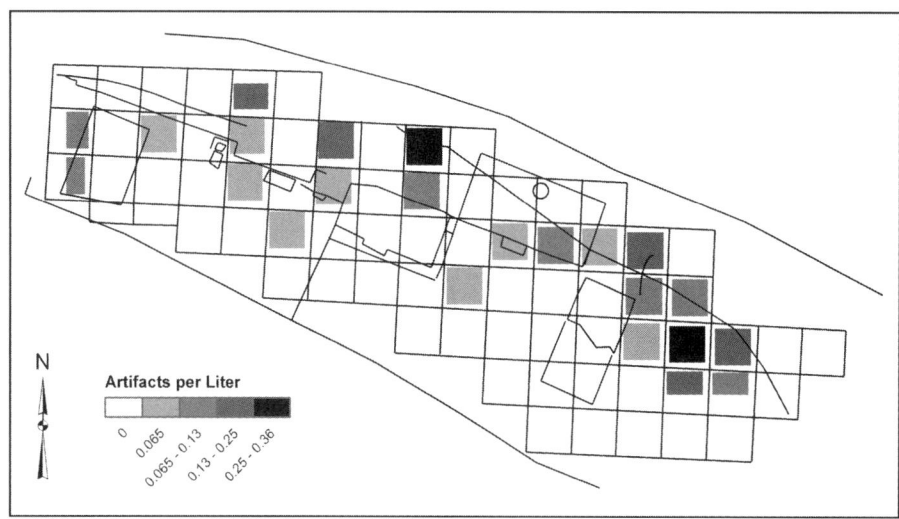

Figure 7.39. Distribution of apaxtle fragments.

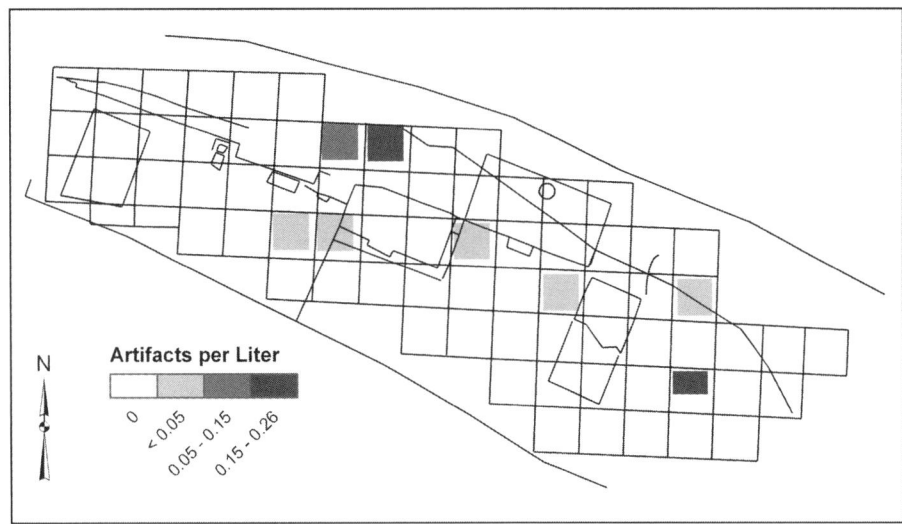

Figure 7.40. Distribution of manos and metates.

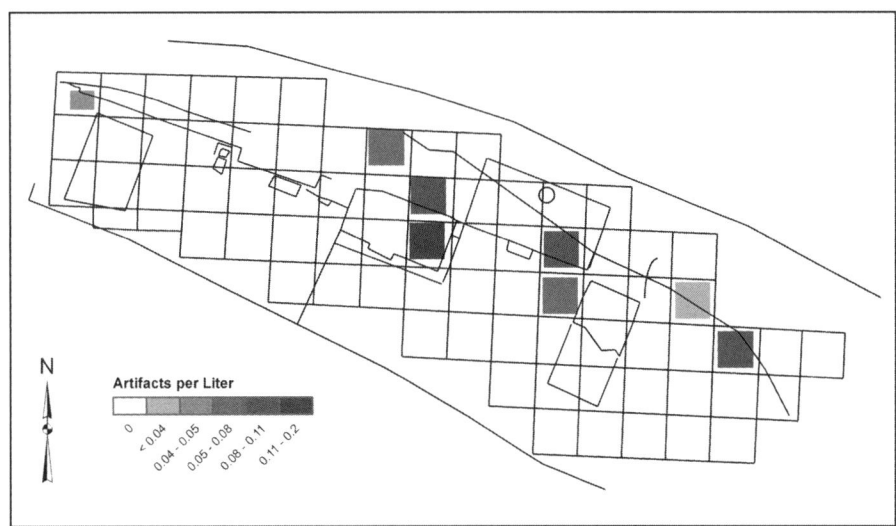

Figure 7.41. Distribution of fragments from ollas barriles.

(Fig. 7.40). Taken together, the presence of cal, apaxtles, manos, and a large metate suggests that corn flour preparation may have taken place on the east side of the terrace. The presence of a comal oven on the west patio suggests that tortillas were cooked there. This spatial separation of masa production and tortilla preparation is potentially interesting in terms of division of labor within one large residential unit.

Ollas barriles (Fig. 7.41), barrel-shaped jars with lids (Appendix B), were likely used to store materials such as dried corn kernels. These vessels generally appear to be concentrated around the east patio of the terrace as well, providing further support that this area may have been used for food storage and the early stages of preparation.

Tlecuiles were stone-lined hearths set into house or patio floors in such a way as to be flush with the surface of the floor. Also set flush with the floor surface were large, thick-walled, cylindrical ceramic vessels (Fig. B44) (see Martínez López et al. 2000:163). While the stone-lined hearths usually show evidence of burning, the large ceramic vessels usually do not, even though local people sometimes refer to them as tlecuiles.

Parsons (1936:32) noted that—unlike the practice in other areas of Mexico—Zapotec women in Oaxaca did not use outside granaries, but stored both ears of corn and shelled kernels in their houses. Perhaps these large ceramic vessels, set flush with the floor, were used to store such items at Cerro Danush. The 7 fragments of such vessels recovered from Layer 2 of Terrace S19

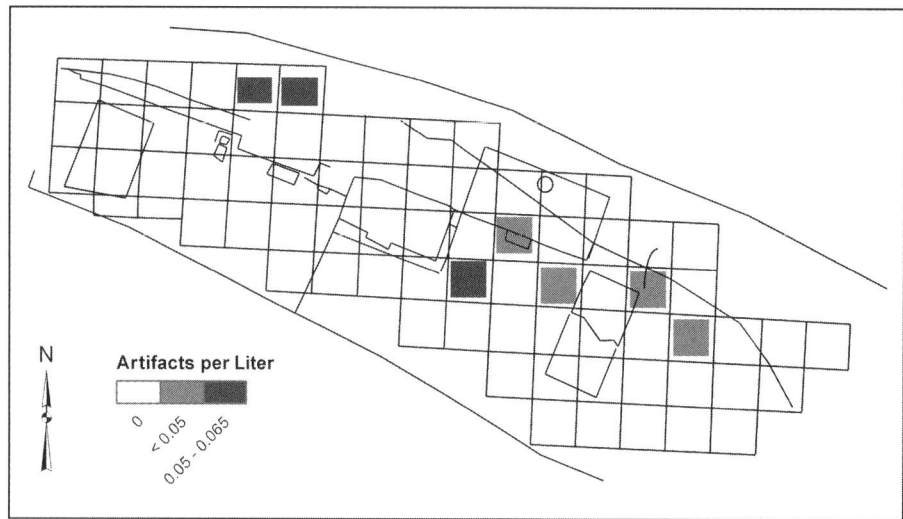

Figure 7.42. Distribution of tlecuil fragments.

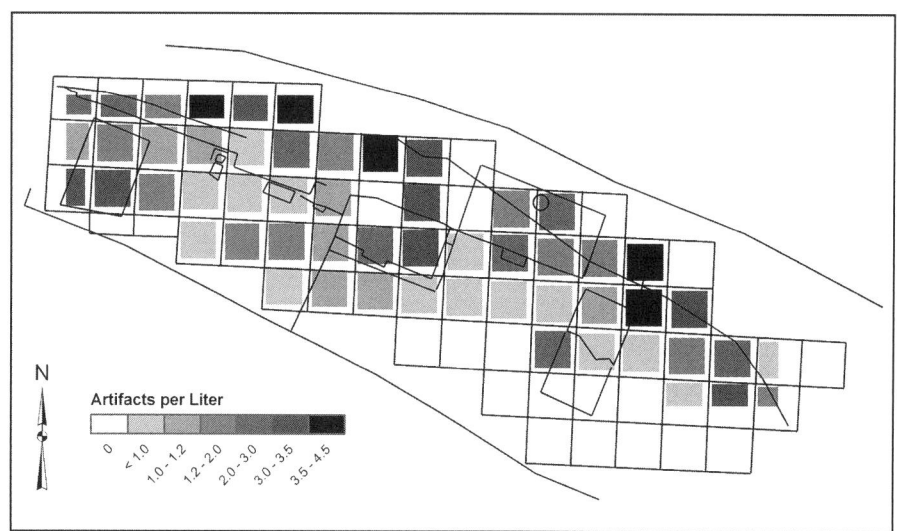

Figure 7.43. Distribution of K14 conical bowl fragments.

mostly appear to be distributed on the eastern side of the terrace, near the house platforms (Fig. 7.42). This may be an indication of storage activity.

The spatial patterns discussed above most likely reflect behavior during the Early Postclassic. Diagnostics of both the Early and Late Classic are so evenly distributed over the three fans in Layer 2 as to suggest that they were included in architectural fill. Certainly this is true of K14 conical bowls (Fig. 7.43), hemispherical bowls (Fig. 7.44), hollow-handled sahumadores (Fig. 7.45), and simple ollas (Fig. 7.46). In fact, nearly all the Classic period diagnostics display this pattern. During the Early Postclassic reconstruction process, considerable materials had to be moved around, first to expand the terrace eastward and then to build up the elevated patio on the west. Earlier refuse was undoubtedly incorporated into the fill, leaving Classic diagnostics thoroughly spread around (Figs. 7.47–7.49).

In contrast to the Classic diagnostics mentioned above, Early Postclassic materials display the same east/west dichotomy observed with chipped stone, spindle whorls, and needles. For example, solid-handled sahumadores (Fig. 7.50) and miniature cups with appliqué feet (Fig. 7.51) tend to be concentrated on the west side of the terrace, while brown paste conical bowls (Fig. 7.52) and globular ollas with appliqué glyph motifs (Fig. 7.53) tend to be concentrated on the central area and east side of the terrace. The sahumadores and miniature cups have often been associated with ritual activity; thus, it is no surprise to find them most concentrated

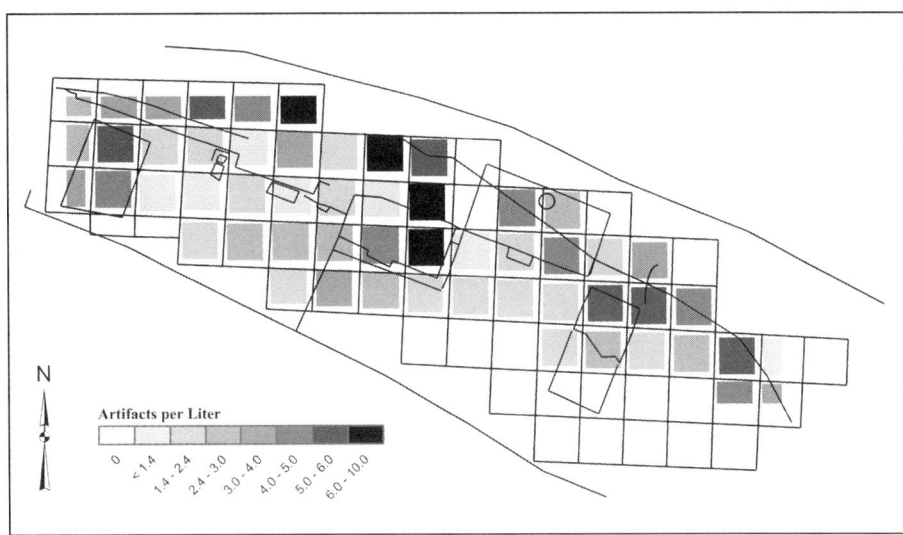

Figure 7.44. Distribution of Classic period hemispherical bowls.

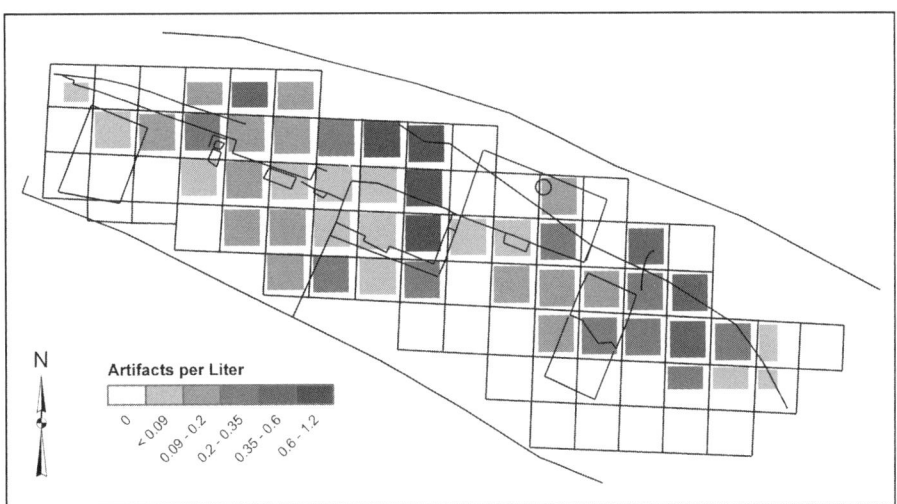

Figure 7.45. Distribution of hollow-handled censers (sahumadores).

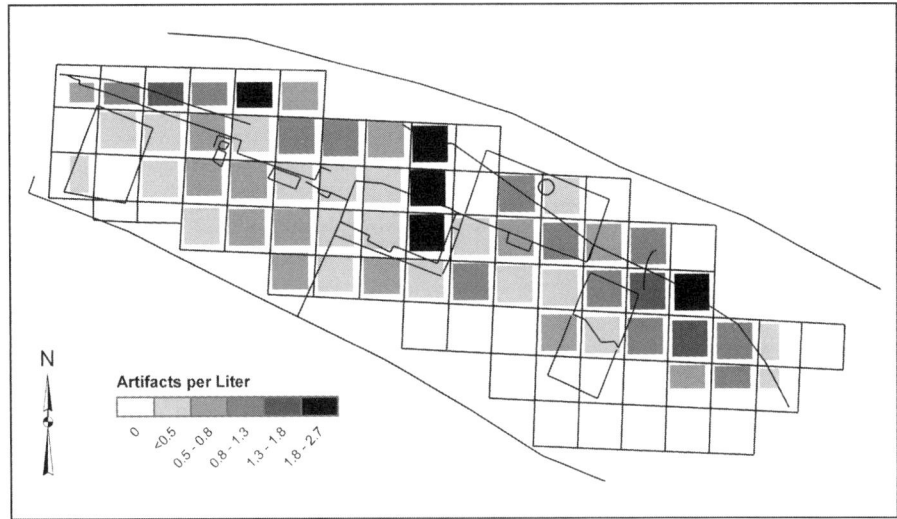

Figure 7.46. Distribution of fragments from Classic period simple ollas.

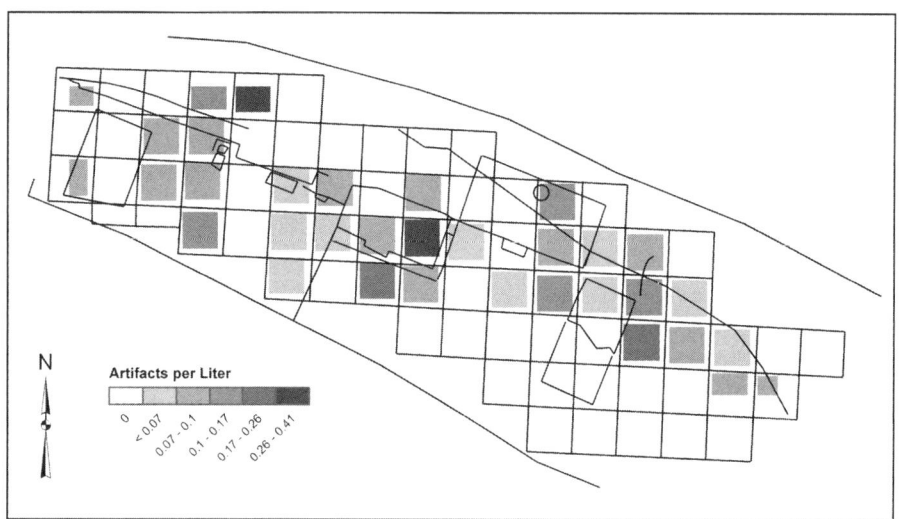

Figure 7.47. Distribution of Early Classic G23 bowl fragments.

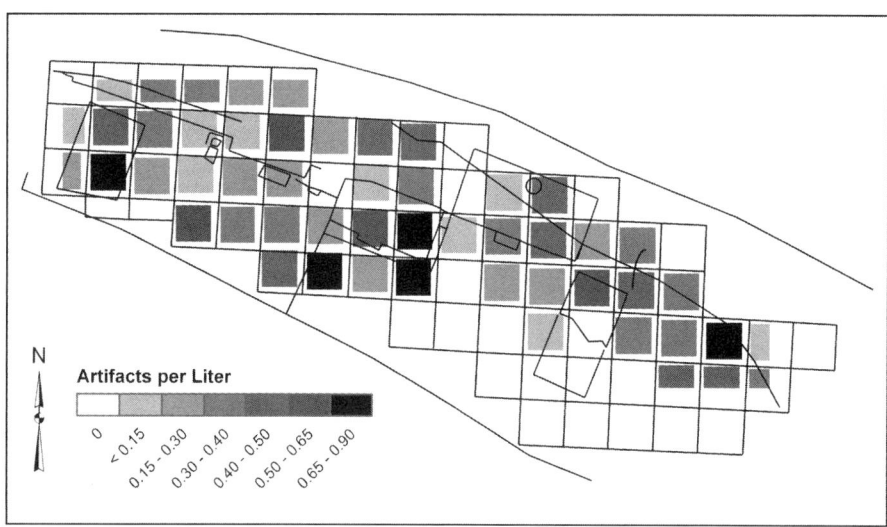

Figure 7.48. Distribution of Early Classic Dainzú conical bowls.

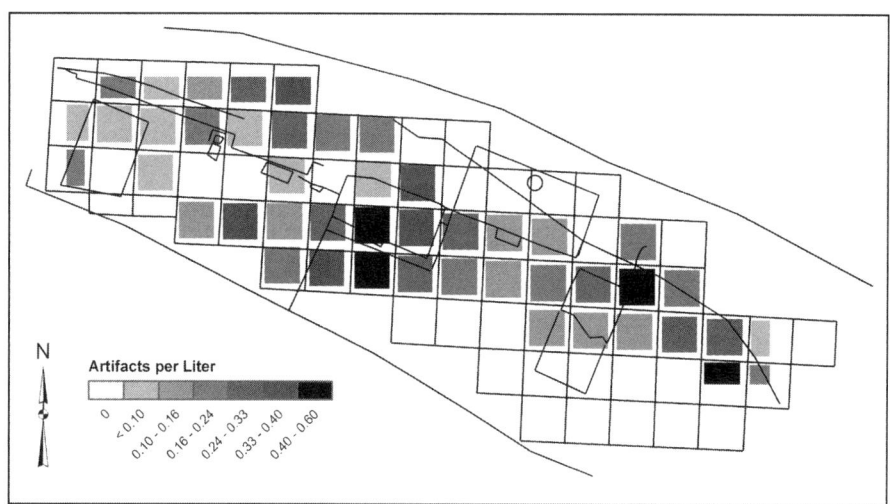

Figure 7.49. Distribution of Early Classic orange paste hemispherical bowls.

Spatial Distribution of Artifacts and Implied Behavioral Patterns 169

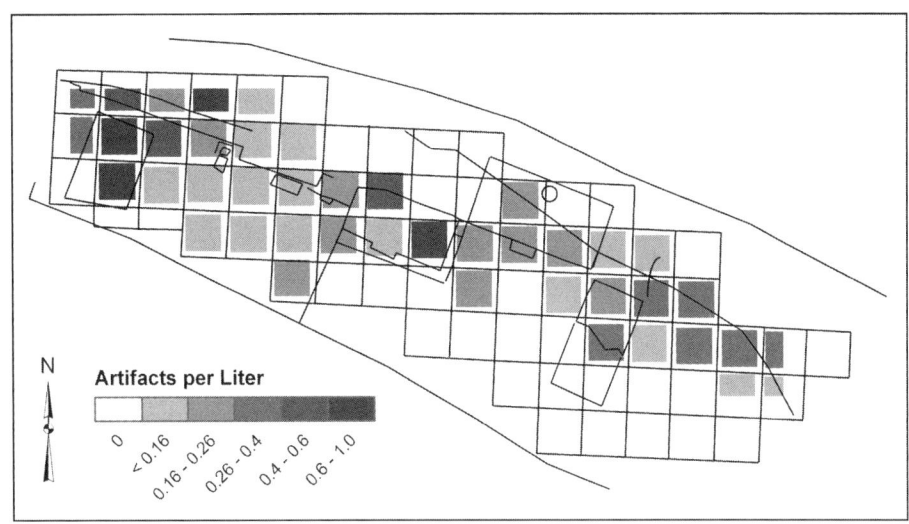

Figure 7.50. Distribution of solid-handled sahumador fragments.

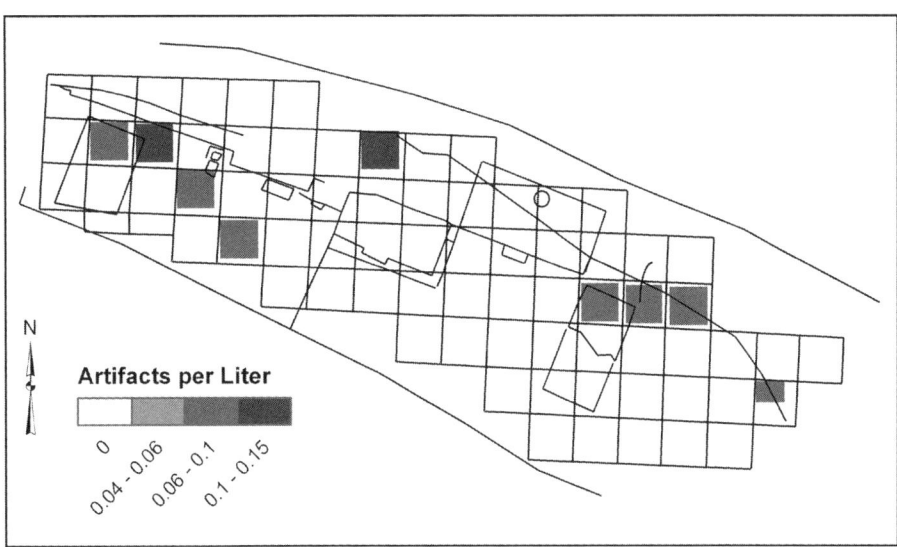

Figure 7.51. Distribution of miniature cups with appliqué claws.

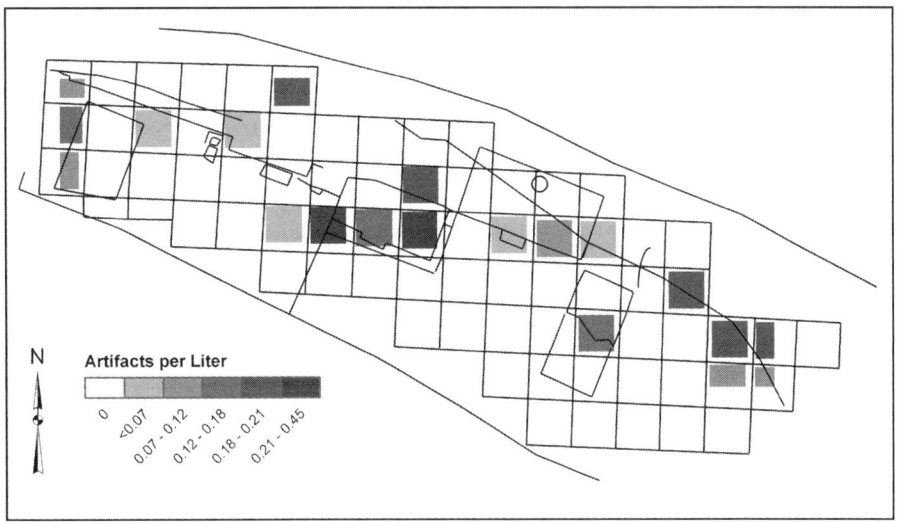

Figure 7.52. Distribution of Postclassic-style conical bowls.

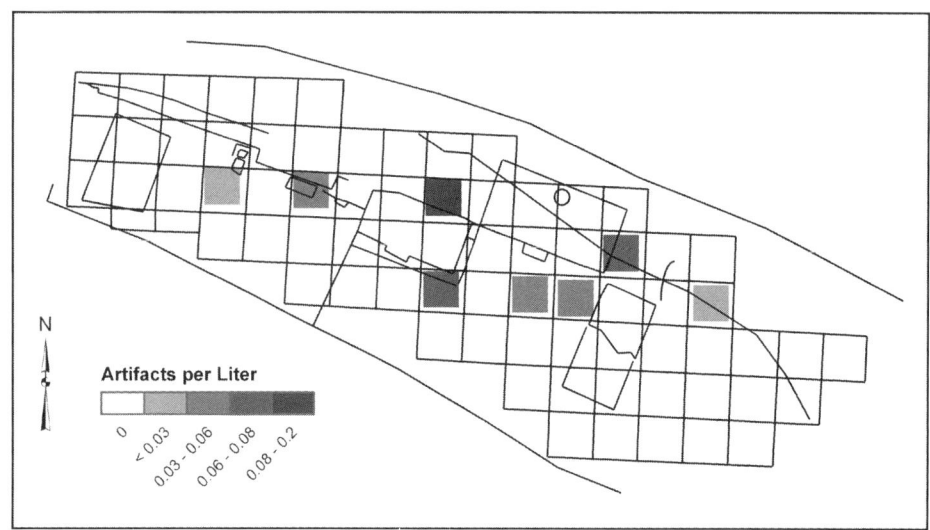

Figure 7.53. Distribution of globular jars with appliqué glyph motifs.

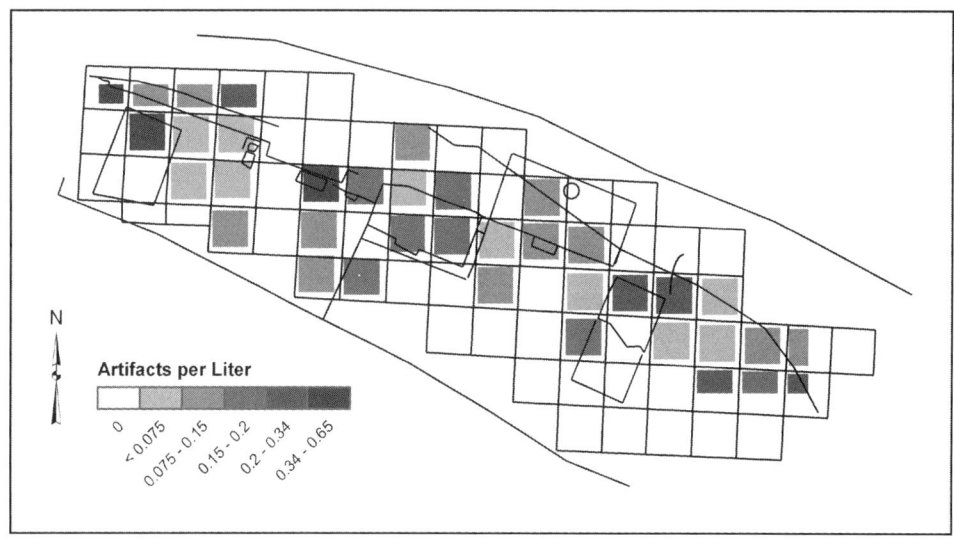

Figure 7.54. Distribution of G3M bowl fragments.

in the same patio where so many intact domestic offerings were found. For their part, the ollas and conical bowls were more likely associated with food preparation and consumption.

The final resting place for most of the Early Postclassic artifacts was just downslope of our proposed refuse dump areas, suggesting that these artifacts had migrated downhill. Since these materials would have been discarded during the most recent occupation of the terrace, they may have been in the topmost stratum of midden and hence susceptible to gravity and erosion. Early Postclassic G3M bowl fragments (Fig 7.54) also seem to have moved downslope somewhat, although their more uniform distribution on opposite sides of the terrace suggests that G3M bowls were used in a variety of household activities.

Correspondence Analysis of the Artifact Density Distribution, Terrace S19

The excavation data set consisted of 55 variables (artifact categories) and 56 cases (excavation units). Unlike the spatial analysis data set, however, the *frequency counts used in the correspondence analysis were not volume-standardized*. The reason for this is that correspondence analysis requires frequency data as its raw input in order to provide the chi-square distances used to measure the variation (see discussion in Chapter 5). As a result, the possibility exists for some bias, based on the large differences in volume between individual excavated units. Fortunately, my correspondence analysis was independent of the spatial analysis described earlier, and as a result, any biases can be detected by comparing the volume density distribution vs. the raw count density distribution.

While the excavation data set shows quantitative similarities to the surface collection data set, it differs qualitatively because it represents contiguous spatial units in a continuous layer, rather than discrete collection circles. The excavation data set is also much smaller than the surface collection data set, making the resulting scatter plots less cumbersome. For these reasons (and because the usual size effects caused by large differences in frequency count data were muted by the partial chi-squared standardization in correspondence analysis), I decided to group all the artifact categories (sherds, stone tools, and fauna) into one analysis rather than analyzing one raw material at a time. The artifact categories employed, of course, were the same ones used in the spatial analysis.

The bulk of meaningful patterning derived from the analysis was contained within the first two components or axes and declined steadily with the addition of more components. This suggested that most of the variation in the data set was accounted for by those components, and my discussion is limited to them. Once again, the results of the analysis are best presented in graphic form, especially by plotting the loading values for component 1 against the loading values for component 2.

The scatter plot of case loadings (excavation units) for the first two components is shown in Figure 7.55. It will be noted that many of the excavation units cluster around the origin point in the graph ($y = 0, x = 0$), while others extend out from that central point in three directions. When one adds a few arbitrary dividing lines to the plot, it becomes easy to see that units extending below and to the right of the origin point are mostly from the east side of the terrace (Blocks F and G, units E13–E15). Units to the left of the origin point, however, are from the west side (Blocks B and C, units E0–E6), and units that are above and to the right of the origin tend to be from the center of the terrace (Blocks C, D, and E, units E7–E12). This result provides independent statistical support for my three proposed refuse dumps and the three proposed debris fans downslope of them. The only obvious outliers in Figure 7.55 are two units I excavated on the far eastern edge of the terrace (E16). These units are grouped with the squares on the west side of the terrace.

The scatter plot for the variable loadings (artifact categories) of the first two components (Figs. 7.56) provides useful artifact distribution information. We note immediately that the scale for the variable loadings plot is much greater than that of the case loadings. This probably resulted from the fact that some artifact categories—for example, bajareque (daub), cal (chalk), metates, raspadores, and chert points—are concentrated in a few excavation units within one of the three proposed downslope fans, making their scores/loadings extend outside the scale for the excavation units. These results reinforce the findings from the spatial distribution analysis for both chalk and chert points; that is, chalk is concentrated on the far east side of the terrace while chert points are concentrated around the eastern patio.

The artifact categories of bajareque, metate, and raspador were included in the analysis for the purpose of testing the correspondence analysis. Each of the latter two categories is represented by a single artifact, found in the west patio to either side of Structure E. While it is difficult to interpret a distribution pattern based on a single artifact, correspondence analysis should at least identify these materials as concentrated on the west side of the terrace; that pattern is evident in the loadings plots (Figs. 7.56). In the case of bajareque, burned fragments of daub were found on the east side of Structure A (Fig. 7.57) and were probably part of the structure's wall at some point. These materials were preserved only because they were burned and their distribution pattern likely reflects a conflagration rather than a locus of activity. Despite the problems presented by small sample size, correspondence analysis successfully plotted all three materials within the terrace.

The remainder of the artifact categories fit within the scale for the case loadings scatter plot (Fig. 7.55). As for the Classic diagnostics distributed through architectural fill, almost all are located near the origin point, within the rectangle marked on the loading plot (Fig. 7.56). So, too, are G3M bowls.

One Classic diagnostic, the botellón (Fig. 7.56), was plotted outside the central origin region. This is probably an anomalous result caused by very low sample size and a disparity between the volume density and the frequency count plots. The volume density plot (Fig. 7.58) shows botellones to be relatively evenly distributed over the three debris fans, while the raw frequency count plot (Fig. 7.59) shows them to be concentrated on the terrace's east side. Fortunately, this is the only artifact category that appears to have been susceptible to this problem.

For the most part, the variable loadings scatter plot places the artifact categories on the parts of the terrace one would expect, based on the results from the earlier spatial analysis. Items found to be concentrated around the eastern patio—such as chert points, debitage, ceramic tlecuiles, and ollas with appliqué glyphs—are all located in the upper right quadrant of the scatter plot (Fig. 7.56). Apaxtles, chalk, and spent cores—all concentrated to the east of the East Patio Complex—can be found in the plot's lower right quadrant. Items concentrated on the west side of the terrace—such as solid-handled sahumadores, miniature claw cups, and spindle whorls—are located on the plot's left side, although not as obviously separated as the other categories mentioned above.

Three categories—ollas barriles (Fig. 7.56, ODB), manos (Fig. 7.56, located within the central rectangle), and fauna—do not appear where one might expect, given the spatial analysis. Because of their distribution patterns in Figures 7.40 and 7.41, I expected to find ollas barriles and manos plotted on the right side of the scatter plot, near ceramic tlecuiles and ollas with appliqué glyphs. The third item, fauna, remains near the origin point.

The fact that these items were not plotted within the areas expected cannot be explained by differences in their volume density and raw frequency count plots. If, however, we examine the scatter plot closely (Fig. 7.55), the reason for their unex-

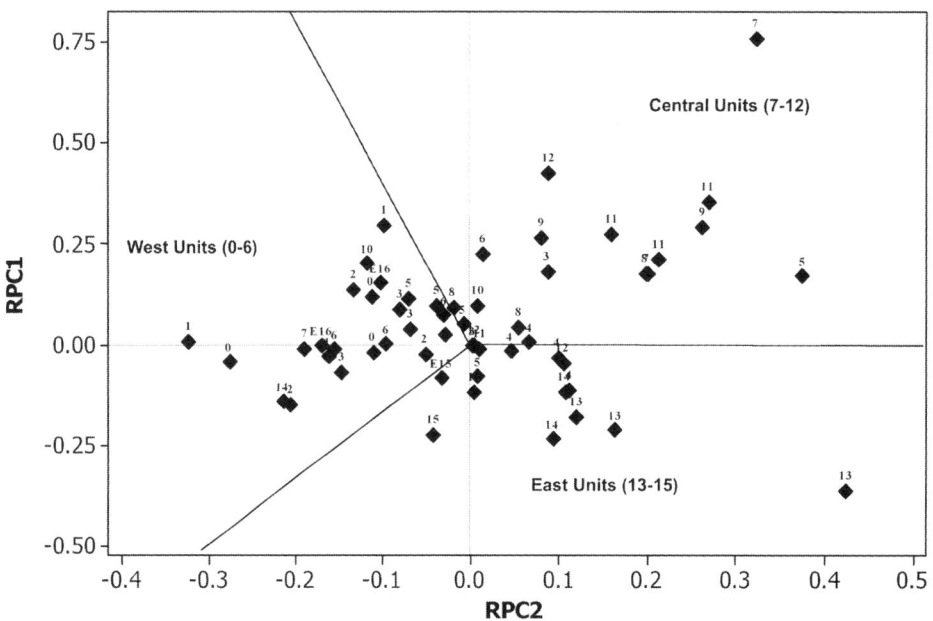

Figure 7.55. Case loadings for the fifty-six excavation units (numbers indicate location on terrace, 0 = west edge, 16 = east edge).

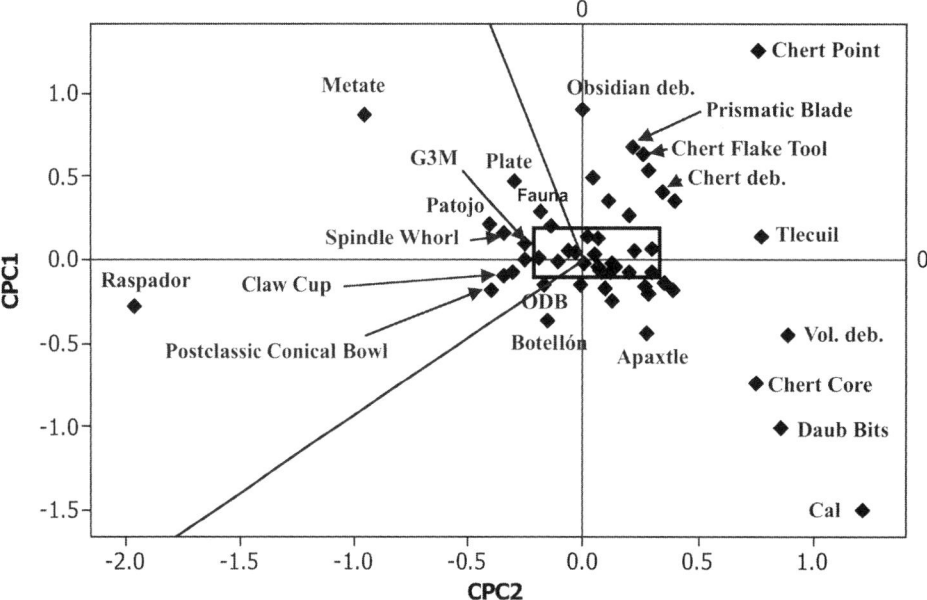

Figure 7.56. Variable loadings for the artifact categories

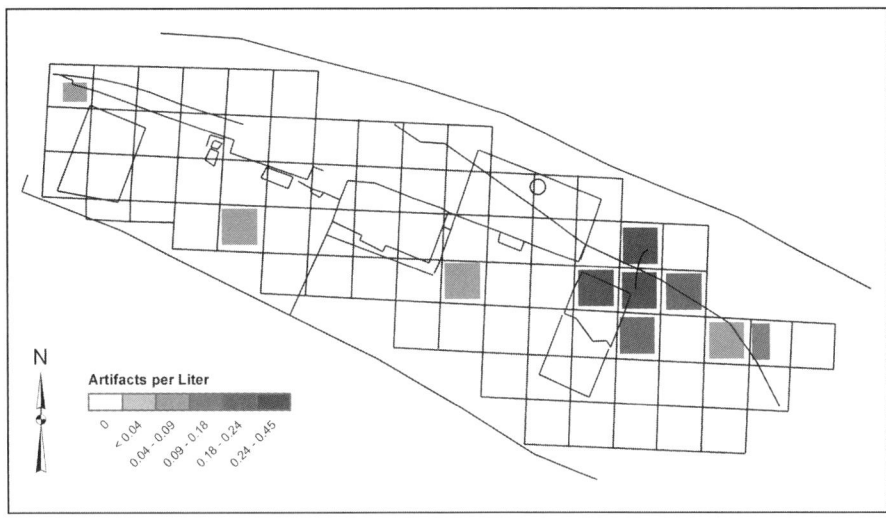

Figure 7.57. Distribution of bajareque fragments.

pected position becomes clear. For example, the loadings from two debris fans on the eastern and central parts of the terrace (units N3E16 and N6E10) are plotted in the upper left quadrant of the scatter plot, among units that are mostly from Block B on the west side of the terrace. This happened in part because the overall distribution of the 53 artifact categories found in these two excavation units is similar to that of units located on the terrace's west side. In addition, faunal remains were more concentrated in excavation units N3E16 and N6E10 than in the units flanking them. As a result, the variable loading for fauna was plotted in the same region as these two units, rather than near the origin point. Similar causes can be found to explain the unexpected plotting of manos and ollas barriles.

Finally, let us turn to plates and patojos (Fig. 7.56), two artifact categories appearing in the plot's upper left quadrant. Plates are clearly concentrated on the terrace's west side (Fig. 7.60), while patojos are somewhat more evenly distributed (Fig. 7.61). It is likely that patojos were plotted in the upper left quadrant because they were more common in contiguous units on the west side of the terrace (particularly around Structure E) than they were in either the center or the east. Recall that in Oaxaca today, patojos are used to cook beans in comal ovens. Assuming that they were used the same way at Cerro Danush, one would expect to find more patojo fragments near the comal oven we discovered in the west patio. That would explain their unexpected plotting.

Summary of Results

Our results indicate that there were separate loci for a variety of household activities, and that those loci tended to be concentrated either around one of the two residential patios, or in the open area on the terrace's east side.

Of the two patios, the western one is the larger and more open, reminiscent of the south patio of the Lanisbaa residence (Winter et al. 2007). The western patio appears to be the locus of many household activities, including food preparation, spinning and sewing, and domestic ritual.

The eastern patio was closed in on three sides by house structures, like the north patio of the Lanisbaa residence. The concentrations of chert debitage, broken or malformed points, and obsidian debitage in this area are indicative of stone tool production or reworking. The open area to the east of the residence appears to have been a locus for food storage and preparation.

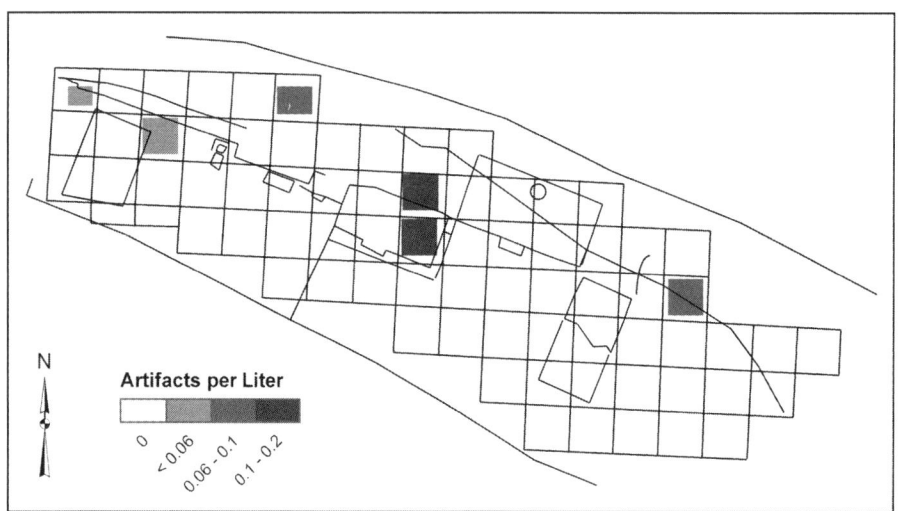

Figure 7.58. Distribution of botellón fragments (volume density index).

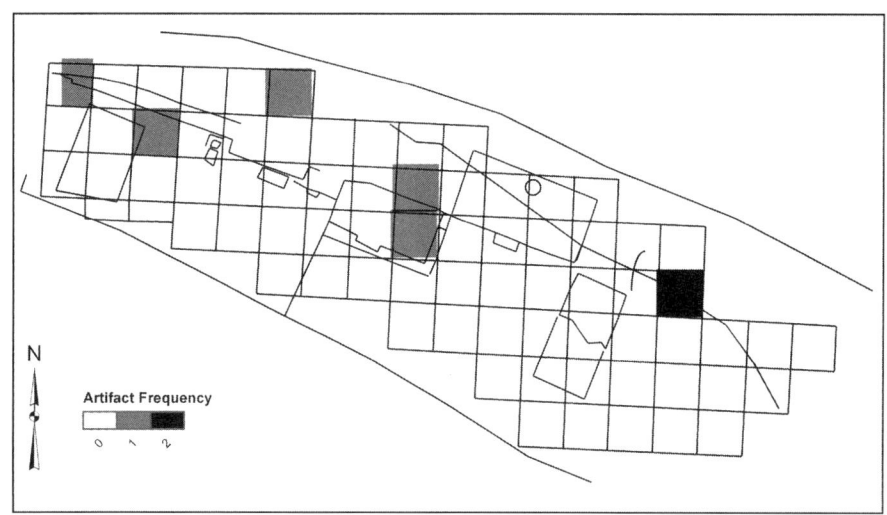

Figure 7.59. Distribution of botellón fragments (raw frequency count).

Characterizing Domestic Life in the Residential Compound, Terrace S19

Studies have shown that house lots within the traditional Zapotec communities of the Valley of Oaxaca today share many similarities with their prehispanic counterparts (Kowalewski, Murphy, and Cabrera 1984). Ethnographic descriptions of domestic activities and household artifacts are relevant to the material assemblage from my project, and traditional Zapotec house construction, layout, and design share elements with the residential complex on Terrace S19. In the discussion below, I use data from two ethnographic studies—Parsons' (1936) work in the eastern Tlacolula Valley, and Sutro and Downing's (1988) study of traditional Zapotec house construction—to relate domestic behavior to the spatial patterns identified on Terrace S19.

The plan view of Terrace S19 (Fig. 7.1) shows a rectangular residential compound, bounded above and below by terrace retention walls, and organized around two interior patios. The east patio is closed in on three sides by dwellings, while the west patio is more open, bounded only by Structure E on the far western edge of the terrace. Winter et al. (2007) describe the rectangular two-patio Lanisbaa residential complex they excavated in Mound 1 of Macuilxóchitl as being divided between public and private domains. They suggest that the patios served

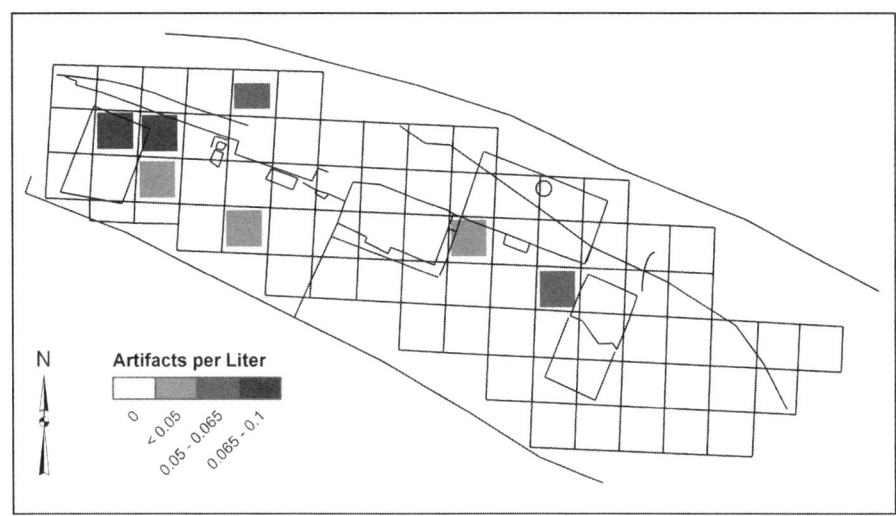

Figure 7.60. Distribution of plate fragments.

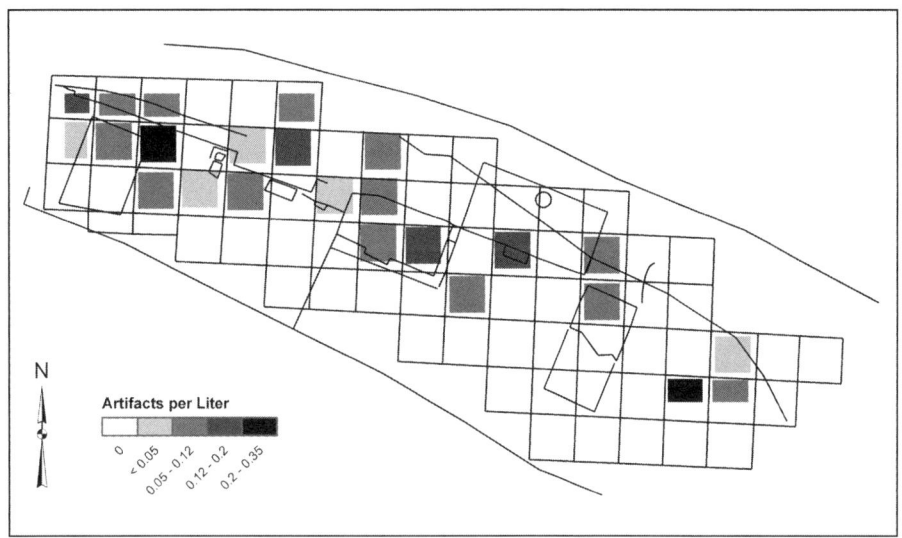

Figure 7.61. Distribution of patojo fragments.

separate functions: one as a workspace and area for interaction with neighbors, and the other as private living quarters. The results of my analyses suggest a similar pattern for the patios on Terrace S19.

Sutro and Downing (1988) assert that the traditional house lots (*solares*) of the Zapotec villages they studied in the Tlacolula Valley—being the residences of poorer community members—were the products of communal work effort since the owners could not afford the extra labor needed to complete them otherwise. Because this unpaid work force consists of community members who also live in solares, they have creative input with respect to the design of the house complex, which leads to standardization. Sutro and Downing (1988:36) define a Zapotec "grammar of space" where "house construction and space utilization are subject to shared and sometimes unconscious norms."

Sutro and Downing (1988:37–40) present a list of rules for the physical aspects of solares, including the layout and orientation of dwellings and other structures. The diagrams they present bear many resemblances to the residence on Terrace S19, suggesting that it may have been subject to a similar set of rules or norms. One of the house lots in particular—Solar 42-6 in the village of Díaz Ordaz (Sutro and Downing 1988:34, Fig. 2.3)—is strikingly similar, with two patios divided between living and work spaces, and containing features such as a comal hearth.

The first rule—"house lots tend to be rectangular" (Sutro and Downing 1988:37)—appears also to be true for the Late Classic and Postclassic multi-patio residences excavated at El Palmillo (Feinman and Nicholas 2009), Yagul (Bernal and Gamio 1974), Mitla (Caso 2003a), and Dainzú-Macuilxóchitl (Winter et al. 2007). Additional rules limit dwellings to one-room rectangular structures, with the kitchens and storage spaces being separate. The norms for these structures serve to create patios within the complex. Secondary dwellings are oriented parallel to or perpendicular to existing dwellings, creating L-shaped (two-dwelling), U-shaped (three-dwelling), or completely enclosed (four-dwelling) patios. The East Patio Complex on Terrace S19 (Fig. 7.1) fits the U-shaped pattern.

To be sure, today's Zapotec house complex most often incorporates facilities for introduced Old World domestic animals. Such facilities include exterior and interior compound walls and fences, as well as animal pens and food storage facilities. Despite these modifications to the prehispanic residential design, however, the traditional rectangular multi-patio model is maintained (Sutro and Downing 1988:39). Obviously, some traditional Zapotec rules are so strong that even the introduction of Old World animals could not invalidate them.

Parsons (1936) provides a plethora of information concerning domestic activities and residential life in early twentieth-century Zapotec communities. Although she does not provide detailed descriptions of the layout of residential structures or the use of space, her discussions of domestic features and activities provide useful information. She describes houses as rectangular, windowless one-room buildings of adobe or wattle and daub with stone foundations (Parsons 1936:22–26). This description fits Structures A, B, C, and E on Terrace S19.

Parsons (1936:24) states that, "in every yard or house lot, there is a cook shed." Many of the kitchen implements she describes and illustrates resemble items in the ceramic assemblage from Cerro Danush (Appendix B), including cántaros, simple ollas, manos, metates, patojos, chilmoleras, and even the comal hearth, which Parsons calls a griddle.

Sutro and Downing (1988) also describe separate rectangular kitchen structures in Zapotec households, but they say that when the house lot contains a comal hearth, it is usually outside (and adjacent to) the kitchen building. In both ethnographies, kitchens are generally smaller and not as well constructed as the house structures.

These ethnographic accounts of kitchen space may help explain why one section of the North Wall on Terrace S19 employed an unusual construction technique. Recall that this section of the wall (Fig. 6.25) consisted of a flat line of cut stones laid directly on top of the west patio surface, similar to Structure C's northern foundation wall (Fig. 6.21). To either side of this flat line of cut stones, the North Wall forms a corner that I suggest was part of a cook shed or kitchen. Figure 7.62 presents the proposed plan and location of this kitchen, which, like its modern counterparts, would have been smaller and more crudely constructed than the house itself. This would explain the lack of genuine foundation walls, as the kitchen probably consisted of wattle and daub without the usual supporting layer of stones. The fact that the comal hearth was found directly adjacent to the proposed kitchen provides further support for this interpretation.

While whole (or nearly complete) ollas and patojos can easily be separated, their small sherds cannot. I therefore grouped sherds of Early Postclassic patojos and ollas into a single category (Appendix B), which I used to represent kitchen activities of that period. The distribution of ollas and patojos, depicted in Figure 7.61, makes sense in terms of my proposed kitchen area, since they are concentrated to either side of it. The presence of a kitchen in this area also makes sense when considering the locations of our proposed refuse deposits (Fig. 7.62). If the gap between Structure C and the North Wall served to provide access to the upper part of the terrace, one would expect to find high concentrations of artifacts just upslope of the proposed kitchen and Structure C, which is the case. Figure 7.63 shows how the space may have been divided when the residence was occupied. In my reconstruction, the East Patio was living space, while the West Patio was work space.

Despite our evidence for a general separation of living and cooking areas, the distributions of apaxtles, ollas barriles, and cal suggest that the division of activities within the residence may have been a bit more complex than the dichotomy between the two patio spaces. Apaxtles, olla barriles, and cal were concentrated on the opposite side of the living space from the kitchen, suggesting that the storage and preparation area for masa may have been separate. Sutro and Downing (1988) depict houses in which corn storage areas are removed from the kitchen. For her part, Parsons (1936:30–33) describes the use of lime pots, manos, and metates in the production of the corn flour, but does not indicate whether corn storage and cooking take place in different areas.

Our spatial distribution data for spindle whorls (Fig. 7.35) suggest that the spinning of yarn was an activity that took place on the West Patio. Parsons (1936:41–46) describes the use of cotton and wool within traditional residences in the town of Mitla. The implements included small ceramic disks like the spindle whorls recovered at Cerro Danush, which served as flywheels for spinning yarn. According to Parsons (1936:43, 45), "spinning is by the familiar method of stick and disk or whorl, the butt of a small, plain spindle resting in a little bowl." The cloth produced on the looms of the families that Parsons studied was used in the home or sold in local markets. Parsons does not discuss the locus of the spinning or weaving activities within a house complex, but her photographs (Parsons 1936: Plates XIV, XV) show both activities taking place outside the residence. One problem with the use of Parsons' data is that Spanish-introduced looms and the wool of introduced sheep are involved. In addition, the *Relación de Mitla y Tlacolula* (Canseco 1905 [1580]) indicates that the cotton used in the Tlacolula region was imported, not locally grown.

The North Wall must have been a very important feature of the residential compound on Terrace S19; based on the amount

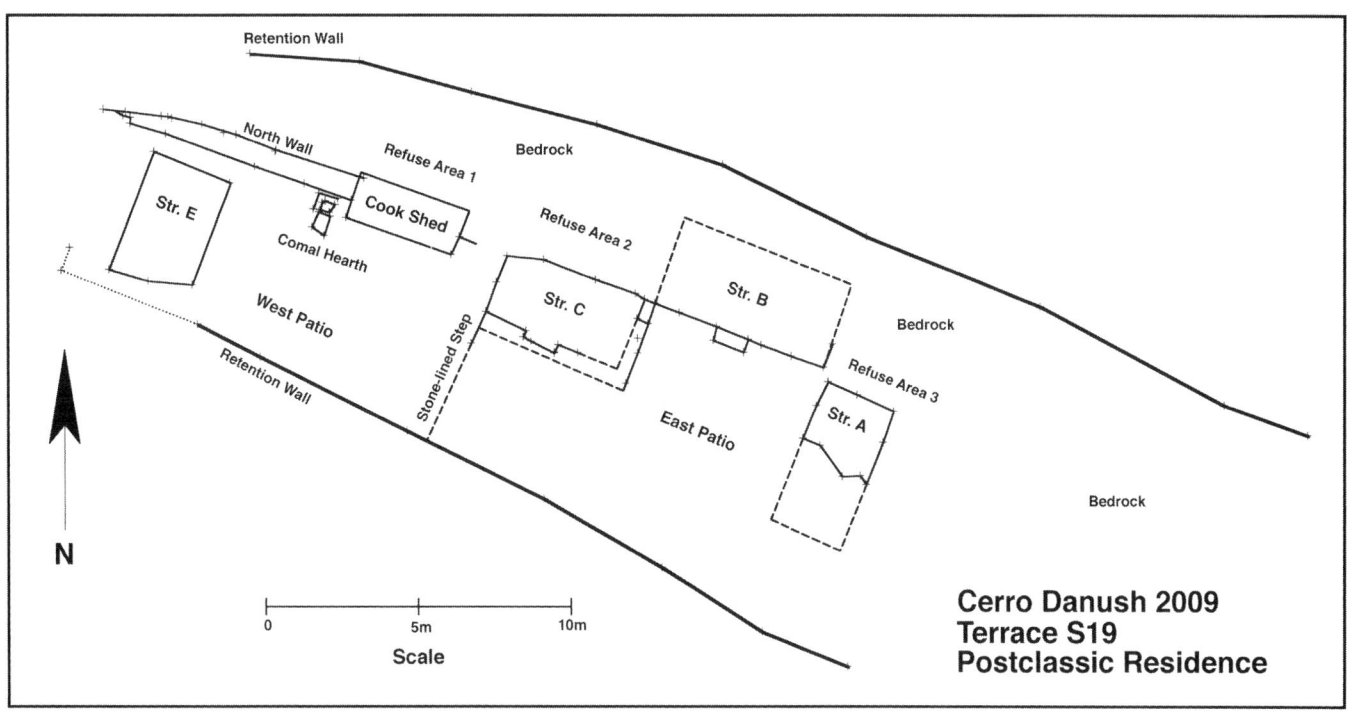

Figure 7.62. Residential complex with proposed kitchen structure added.

of wall fall found within Layer 2, it probably stood quite a bit taller when the terrace was occupied. This wall served to protect the residence from rocks falling from the cliff above, and also effectively separated the patio area below from the waste disposed above. We are unsure exactly why the North Wall was buttressed in the Early Postclassic; whatever the reason, the act of buttressing was accompanied by the burial of ritual offerings along the wall's entire length (Fig. 7.62). This area also saw the burial of an individual of higher than average status (Burial 3).

Finally, Parsons (1936:27–28) describes the most conspicuous item within a traditional Zapotec house as the altar. Today, such altars consist of wooden tables where offerings of perishable materials are left. Parsons discusses the use of plates to leave offerings of food on the altars and in other sacred places around the community. She also describes clay censers for burning incense at the altars.

To be sure, the rites that Parsons describes involve syncretism, a mixture of Catholic and indigenous religion. At the same time, we know that offerings were made and incense burned in prehispanic times. Markens, Winter, and Martínez López (2008) have identified both solid-handled sahumadores and miniature claw cups as items found in Early Postclassic offerings at both Monte Albán and Dainzú-Macuilxóchitl. Sahumadores (Fig. 7.50), plates (Fig. 7.60), and claw cups (Fig. 7.51) all appear in high densities on the west side of Terrace S19, between Structure E and the North Wall. In this area, the buttressed portion of the North Wall forms a shelf (Figs. 6.24, 6.26) that may have served a purpose similar to that of today's syncretic altars. We recovered nearly intact claw cups from the Terrace S19 residence (Appendix B). Their condition suggests that these offerings were left in place long after the terrace was abandoned, or that they continued to be placed there after abandonment.

Our data indicate that the West Patio was the scene of food production, spinning, and sewing, with perhaps some storage on the terrace's eastern edge. While the East Patio seems to have been a living area, the high density of chert debitage, discarded points, and cores found nearby (as well as on the surrounding terraces) suggests that point production beyond the needs of the household may have been carried out here. Clearly, such craft production was kept separate from food preparation. Unfortunately, chipped stone tool production is not a significant activity in today's Zapotec households, so there are no ethnographic analogies.

Figure 7.63. Artist's rendition of the Early Postclassic residence on Terrace S19 (illustration by Betty Cleeland).

Conclusion

The information from Chapters 6 and 7 provides a basis for reconstructing how the Terrace S19 residence appeared during its final period of occupation in the Early Postclassic. Figure 7.63, an artist's rendition of the house complex, shows the juxtaposition of the open West Patio and closed East Patio spaces. It also depicts the relationship between the work spaces (patios) and refuse deposition areas, whose locations I deduced from the artifact density distributions (Figs. 7.25, 7.26).

The material presented here documents the variety of activities that took place within the Terrace S19 residence. These activities and their locations within the residence show significant continuities in patterns between Postclassic commoner households and their twentieth-century counterparts, despite the major events that took place over that time.

In the next chapter, I go back farther in time and consider the changes and continuities identifiable between Late Classic and Early Postclassic households. These changes and continuities should tell us something about the decline of Monte Albán and the subsequent sociopolitical reorganization of the Valley of Oaxaca.

8 | Breakdown and Reorganization at Dainzú-Macuilxóchitl

In the preceding chapters I presented the results from two seasons of fieldwork on Cerro Danush. Here, I summarize and contextualize those results within the theoretical framework described in Chapter 1 and the previous research findings outlined in Chapter 3. The discussion is presented in terms of the project research design, and provides evidence for continuity or discontinuity in community ritual, household ritual, and production at the site, in light of widespread Terminal Classic abandonment in the Dainzú-Macuilxóchitl region.

Terminal Classic Abandonment Patterns on Cerro Danush

Analyses of the surface distributions of time-sensitive diagnostics and changes in ceramic paste preferences have served to show the growth, decline, and abandonment of the residential terraces on Cerro Danush. We have learned that a few terrace groups (Summit, South, West, and North-Central) were first occupied toward the end of the Early Classic or at the beginning of the Late Classic, and that during the Late Classic, nearly all of the 130 terraces that I mapped were occupied. During the Early Postclassic, however, fewer than 35 of those terraces continued to be used, a 75–80% reduction in settlement. By the beginning of the Late Postclassic (ca. A.D. 1250–1300), it appears that all the remaining residential terraces on Cerro Danush were abandoned.

There is some evidence to suggest that many terraces within a group were occupied and abandoned in unison (or, at least, in close succession). For example, terraces with Classic diagnostics and orange paste sherds were concentrated in the West and North-Central Groups. In other words, these groups of terraces might represent units of sociopolitical organization above the household level, such as residential wards. None of the terraces in these two groups show evidence for Early Postclassic occupation, suggesting that they were abandoned simultaneously (or in close succession) during the Terminal Classic. The Summit Terrace Group, which most likely represents a palace and temple complex, also seems to have been abandoned as a unit.

The Late/Terminal Classic period spans 300–400 years, and there must have been many sociopolitical changes in the Valley of Oaxaca (and Cerro Danush) during that time. Unfortunately, we still lack diagnostics that would enable us to distinguish the Late and Terminal Classic in surface collections. As a result, I am unable to determine whether adjacent or related terraces within the groups on Cerro Danush were abandoned simultaneously or sequentially. To confirm the possibility that entire residential wards arrived and left together, I would have to excavate a great many more terraces within each group.

Early Postclassic diagnostics and concentrations of brown paste sherds were found mostly on terraces in the North, South, Northeast, and East Terrace Groups, perhaps indicating that some residential wards on Cerro Danush lasted into that period. A number of adjacent terraces were occupied in the Early Postclassic, although population seems to have declined even within those groups.

Late Classic to Early Postclassic Community Ritual at Dainzú-Macuilxóchitl

It is likely that Cerro Danush was always an important part of the landscape for the people of Dainzú-Macuilxóchitl. In the Early Colonial period, the authors of the *Relación Geográfica* for the town of San Mateo Macuilxóchitl (Acuña 1984 [1580]:324–41) included a map of the area; Cerro Danush is depicted in oversized proportions, in the center of the map (Fig. 8.1, Plate 7). Residents of the town today have told me that Cerro Danush is sometimes called *buun zhab*, which literally translates to "devil," but can be loosely interpreted to mean that the mountain is possessed by a spirit. Every May 3, members of the community make a pilgrimage to the summit of Cerro Danush to perform overnight ceremonies and leave offerings of food as part of the Festival of the Cross (Markens, Winter, and Martínez López 2008; Orr 2001). This ritual is undertaken to petition for a healthy rainy season and bountiful maize harvest.

Broda (1991, 1993, 2001) has observed similar pilgrimage ceremonies associated with the Festival of the Cross in modern indigenous communities in the neighboring state of Guerrero, and suggests that they are the products of syncretism between the Catholic liturgical calendar and a pre-Columbian festival calendar. She specifically notes the similarities between this ceremony and the Aztec festival *Huey Tozoztli* (described by fray Diego Durán [1971]) that took place on April 29 and was devoted to the Aztec god of rain, Tlaloc. During this ceremony, Moctecuhzoma, along with many high-ranking officials, climbed Mt. Tlaloc in Puebla, where they sacrificed a child in front of an altar. In addition, offerings of food were made, and a carved stone image of the deity was adorned with flowers and clothing. The offerings made during Huey Tozoztli were intended to petition Tlaloc for plentiful rains and an abundant crop (Broda 2001:206).

In the case of Cerro Danush, it appears that toward the end of the Early Classic or the beginning of the Late Classic (ca. A.D. 400–600), the leaders of Dainzú-Macuilxóchitl directed a massive construction project on the hill's summit. The peak of Cerro Danush was transformed into a large pyramidal platform, roughly 15 m high, and a square walled-in patio with a central altar was constructed on the terrace below it (see Figs. 4.5, 4.6). The terraces below this temple complex evidently contained elite residences, and the high densities of fragments from large storage and cooking vessels found there suggest that this was a center of ceremonial activities (Figs. 5.13, 5.14). I have designated this area as the Summit Terrace Group.

A few weeks before I began mapping Cerro Danush, looters sacked a tomb on Terrace C5 and uncovered a carved stone doorjamb (Fig. 4.7), which is now housed in the community museum (Faulseit 2008, 2012b; Markens 2011). The image on the stone appears to be that of an individual wearing a mask to impersonate Cociyo, or Lightning, a Zapotec supernatural loosely analogous to the Aztec deity Tlaloc (Kowalewski 1970), who was believed to reside on the summit of a mountain and is associated with rain, lightning, and sky (Sellen 2002). Urcid (pers. comm.) has identified the glyph in the upper right corner as a representation of maize (Fig. 8.2). Just below is a cloud glyph with a raindrop within it. In the upper left corner of the stone is a possible corn plant. Although the right side of the doorjamb is eroded, the location of the maize glyph (just above the spot where the individual's hand should be) suggests that the figure may have been carrying a cornstalk. As pointed out by Joyce Marcus (pers. comm.), Monument 3 at Macuilxóchitl shows a woman performing a similar rite by holding a corncob (see also Bernal and Seuffert 1973).

Sellen (2002) and Caso and Bernal (1952) have identified the same maize cob and stalk iconography on Classic period ceramic effigy vessels that contain the image of Cociyo. In fact, the image on one of the vessels, ROM 1435, is nearly identical to the image on the carved jamb (Sellen 2002: Fig. 8b). According to Sellen (2002), the effigy vessels depict Zapotec elites who have assumed Cociyo's identity and are using cornstalks during dances or rituals associated with the agricultural cycle of corn.

> For the ancient Zapotec, adequate rainfall depended on Cocijo, the storm god invested with the power to control climatic conditions. Offerings to this deity of food and blood, including human sacrifices, may well have been accompanied by dances in which the community leaders or priests wore his guise. [Sellen 2002:12]

The fragmentary data we have from the Summit Terrace Group at Cerro Danush are only enough to suggest that a noble family resided there, near what was probably one of the site's most important temples. The iconography of the looted tomb is consistent with what we know of Late Classic Zapotec monuments elsewhere in the valley. Until the whole of the Summit Terrace Group can be carefully excavated, it would be unwise to speculate on what it may or may not contain.

It is safe to say, however, that the construction of the palace and temple atop Cerro Danush probably came at a very high cost in labor to the community. During my mapping of the site, the crew members and I climbed Cerro Danush for days to record the terraces of the Summit Terrace Group. With some admittedly heavy equipment in tow, we were able to reach the summit only after a grueling 20- to 25-minute climb, giving us an idea of the effort needed for community members in the Late/Terminal Classic to carry water and supplies to the palace and to maintain the temple precinct. This type of labor would probably be feasible as long as the rituals conducted on the summit were regarded as beneficial to the greater community—that is, agricultural yields remained high enough to feed everyone and support the ceremonies.

Our density distribution analysis of surface artifacts suggests that the temple complex at the summit and its corresponding

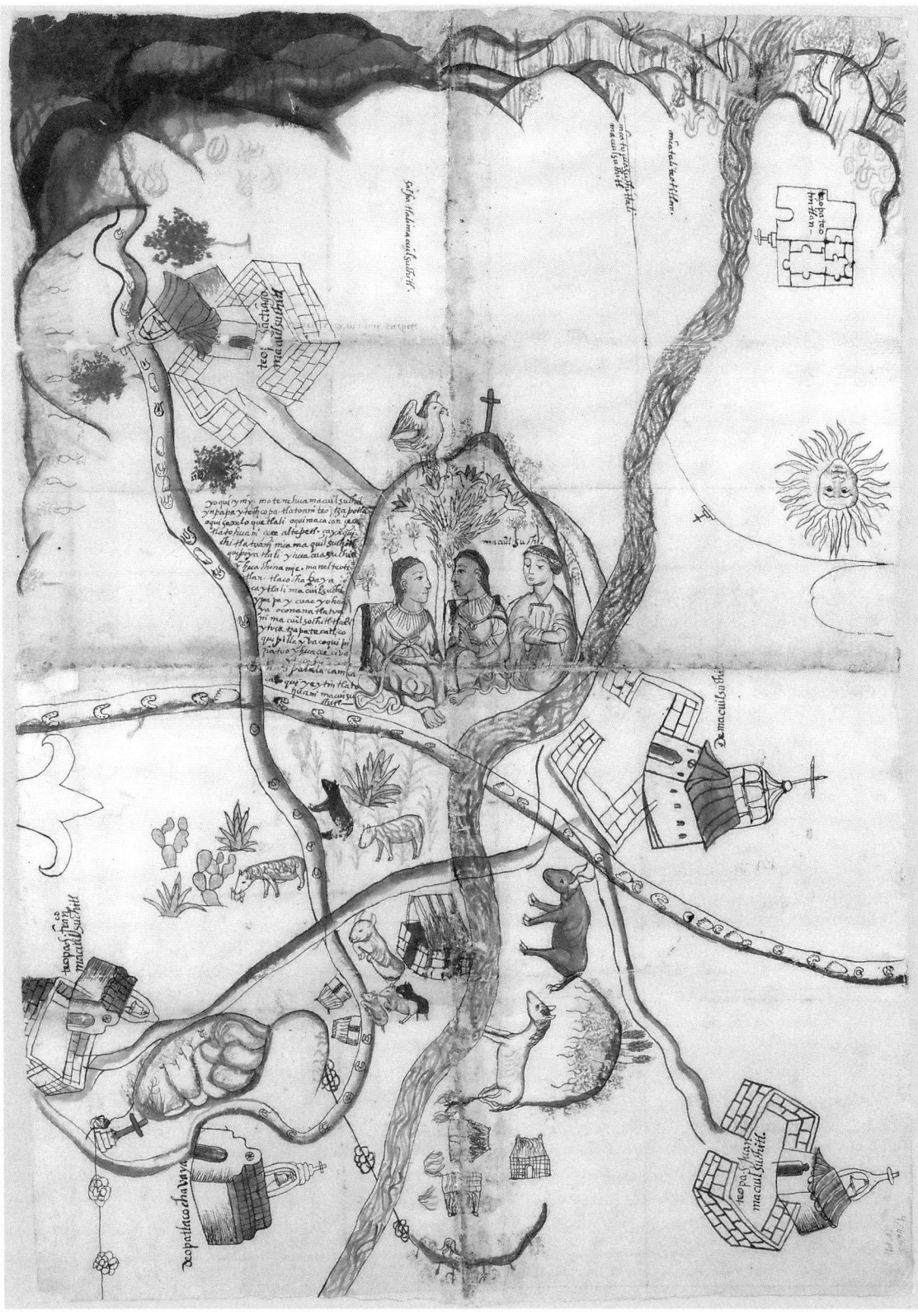

Figure 8.1. Map of Macuilxóchitl and its jurisdiction, from the *Relación Geográfica de Macuilxóchitl*, 1580. © Real Academia de la Historia, Madrid, C-028-007 (9-4663/19). (Also see Plate 7.)

Figure 8.2. Drawing of carved stone doorjamb with Cociyo image (illustration by Betty Cleeland).

elite residences were abandoned by the end of the Terminal Classic. Two other civic-ceremonial precincts—the Lantiudee complex at Macuilxóchitl (Markens, Winter, and Martínez López 2008), and the three-mound complex associated with Cerro Danush's West Terrace Group (Chapters 4 and 5)—also appear to have been abandoned around the same time. Because there is no evidence for Terminal Classic violence at Dainzú-Macuilxóchitl, I suspect that these monuments fell out of use because of political breakdown—for example, because a declining population could no longer support them.

The evidence for Early Postclassic rituals on Cerro Danush consists of three high-density clusters of solid-handled sahumadores, located at the bases of eroded artificial mounds (Figs. 5.27). The first two sahumador clusters were found at the base of a double-mound platform constructed at the summit of Cerro Danush on Terrace C2 (Fig. 4.5, Structure 101). Compared to the Late Classic temple complex on the summit, this shrine is much smaller and not nearly as well constructed. As a result, erosion has reduced it to two roughly conical stone mounds on a rectangular platform. Unlike the Summit Temple Complex, this Postclassic shrine is not enclosed within any walls; instead, it faces an open area where any ceremonies would be visible to many spectators. This type of arrangement suggests that access to the summit was not as restricted as it was during the Late Classic.

The third mound yielding a solid-handled sahumador cluster (Fig. 4.11a, Structure 302) is located in the East Terrace Group and consists of a pyramidal structure built into the slope of the hill and supported by a small rectangular terrace, Terrace E6. Like the double-mound shrine at the summit, this structure does not compare in size or construction to the Late Classic pyramidal mounds found at the summit or in the West Terrace Group. This shrine faces east and is quite visible from the base of the hill, suggesting that it, too, was designed for public ceremonies.

Kowalewski et al. (1989b:343–44) suggest that the "low, square-top stone mounds" they found on prominent hilltops throughout the valley, "with *sahumadores*, obsidian blades, and a few serving bowls," were typical of the Postclassic; they propose that these hilltop shrines witnessed pilgrimages and rituals "directed toward [the] supernaturals" associated with lightning, clouds, and rain. In other words, the changes described above for Dainzú-Macuilxóchitl were probably part of a valley-wide shift in community ritual that took place between the Late Classic and the Early Postclassic (Kowalewski et al. 1989:343–44; Markens 2011).

Although the transformation in community ritual described above suggests a major change in political organization at Dainzú-Macuilxóchitl (and perhaps the entire Valley of Oaxaca) between Late Classic and Early Postclassic times, there are also signs of continuity in social organization. Cerro Danush, with all of its links to supernatural forces such as lightning and rain, never lost its importance. Even after its

Classic temples had been abandoned, local people continued to perform ceremonies and leave offerings at newly constructed shrines on its summit. Even though settlement became more dispersed during the Early Postclassic, communities attempted to preserve as much of the ancient ritual as they could despite the loss of elite religious specialists.

Late Classic to Early Postclassic Domestic Ritual

During the excavation of Terrace S19, I uncovered evidence of both mortuary practices and domestic rituals. In general, the continuity in domestic ritual from the Late Classic to the Early Postclassic was notable.

Burials

The three burials (two adults and one child) excavated on Terrace S19 reflect local traditions that began in Early Formative Oaxaca and appear to have characterized commoner burials well into the Late Postclassic. All were simple graves; no tomb was found within the Terrace S19 residence, indicating its lack of elite occupants. The small size of the patios, the wattle-and-daub construction, and the simplicity of the burials all suggest that the Terrace S19 house complex fit within the commoner-status categories established by Winter (1974, 2002) and Gonzalez Licón (2003, 2009) at Monte Albán.

Burial 1 consisted of the disarticulated bones of a single adult, found in a refuse dump to the east of Structure A. There were no associated offerings, but I recovered the mandible of a dog that may have been originally included with the burial. This is similar to a burial excavated by Fernández and Gómez (1993:27) in a Terminal Formative house complex near the Dainzú Archaeological Zone, where "in the midden, two individuals were buried, along with a dog, among the refuse deposits from the houses" (my translation).

Burial 2 consisted of a very young child interred in the flexed position, without any offerings, beneath the floor of a house (Structure B). Winter (2002:70) suggests that "children, infants, and the aged received less careful treatment" in the commoner house complexes he excavated at Monte Albán. The Late Classic children there tended to be buried in simple graves or within ceramic vessels, which is the same pattern seen by Fernández and Gómez (1993).

Burial 3 was found beneath the patio floor along the North Wall, on the west side of the house complex. This individual lay buried fully extended with at least one arm folded over the pelvic region, a position similar to an interment Winter et al. (2007:201) excavated in the Late Postclassic Lanisbaa complex. A large G35 bowl was placed upside down over the thighs of the individual in Burial 3, which was a common pattern found in the Late Classic residences excavated at Monte Albán (Winter 2002). This individual had deliberately modified incisors, a somewhat surprising trait given the modest burial offering, which leads us to wonder whether deliberate tooth modification was less rigidly restricted to elite individuals in the Early Postclassic.

Domestic Offerings

The domestic offerings recovered from the house complex on Terrace S19 also show continuities with Late Classic and Late Postclassic commoner house complexes in the Valley of Oaxaca. Offerings were limited to ceramic vessels, which is essentially what Feinman, Nicholas, and Maher (2008) found in the Late/Terminal Classic low-status house complexes they excavated at El Palmillo.

The paired-vessel offerings I recovered in the West Patio of the Terrace S19 complex were very similar to ceramic offerings found in Late Classic residences at El Palmillo (Feinman, Nicholas, and Maher 2008) and Lambityeco (Lind and Urcid 2010). They also resembled offerings in the Late Postclassic Lanisbaa complex at Dainzú-Macuilxóchitl (Winter et al. 2007). Indeed, such ceramic vessel offerings represent a ritual practice that persisted into the twentieth century (Parsons 1936).

In addition to the G35 offering found with Burial 3, three more G35 bowls were left as offerings within the same stratigraphic layer. One of these was paired with an Early Postclassic patojo. The remainder of the vessels found in this layer were Early Postclassic types. This mixture of ceramic diagnostics buried beneath the West Patio of the Terrace S19 house complex suggests that the manufacture of G35 bowls (perhaps not surprisingly) continued for some time into the Early Postclassic. It is also one more line of evidence for continuous use of Terrace S19 from the Late Classic through the Early Postclassic.

Figurines and Whistles

Although many fragments of anthropomorphic figurines and whistles (Appendix B, Figs. B24–B37) were recovered during my project, no examples were found in primary contexts. Our sample consists mostly of flat Late Classic mold-made female figurines and bulbous male whistles, nearly identical to those found in Late Classic contexts at Monte Albán (Caso and Bernal 1952; Caso, Bernal, and Acosta 1967; Martínez López and Winter 1994). In addition, we found several fragments of anthropomorphic figurines and whistles resembling Early Postclassic Mazapan types described by Scott (1993); Feinman and Nicholas (2011) found examples of these at the Mitla Fortress. These figurines and whistles were made with a brown paste similar to that used for Early Postclassic sahumadores (Appendix B, Fig. B22, Plate 8). This paste probably reflects Early Postclassic clay sources rather than any change in ritual behavior.

Summary of Domestic Ritual Behavior

Despite valley-wide changes in settlement patterns, our evidence suggests continuity in commoner mortuary practices and household ritual between the Late Classic and the Early

Postclassic. Evidently, commoner families held onto a number of traditional behaviors, even as Monte Albán's power faded and a whole series of petty kingdoms arose. Figurines, whistles, and sahumadores might be of different pastes, but there was a great deal of continuity in the overall domestic ritual assemblage. Paired-vessel offerings from the Late Classic houses at El Palmillo (Feinman, Nicholas, and Maher 2008) and Lambityeco (Lind and Urcid 2010:276–77) contained gray paste G35 bowls turned upside down and placed over the mouths of simple ollas; Early Postclassic offerings of the same type on Terrace S19 contained brown paste G35 bowls placed over the mouths of patojos. There is no reason to believe that the modest changes in paste and jar shape reflected differences in the ritual implications of these offerings.

Late Classic to Early Postclassic Household Production

The surface distributions of items such as spindle whorls, ceramic wasters and molds, and chipped stone cores and debitage have allowed us to infer patterns of domestic production on the terraces of Cerro Danush. In general, the surface patterns at Cerro Danush appeared to correlate well with the findings of Feinman, Nicholas, and Haines (Feinman, Nicholas, and Haines 2002, 2006; Haines, Feinman, and Nicholas 2004) on the terraces they excavated at El Palmillo. The majority of households at Cerro Danush seem to have participated in "intermittent" (Hirth 2009a) or part-time craft production, and in some cases multicraft production (Shimada 2007) or "multicrafting" (Balkansky and Crossier 2009; Feinman and Nicholas 2000). The only terrace group at Cerro Danush that did not show much evidence for craft production was the high-status residence in the Summit Terrace Group, which is not surprising—it was likely the home of one of the site's most elite family.

Surface densities of ceramic figurine fragments and figurine molds appeared to be more concentrated in the West and Southwest Terrace Groups than in other parts of the site, perhaps representing production loci. These are the only groups that exhibited specialized production of this kind. I have already suggested that these groups, along with the central three-mound civic-ceremonial precinct, may represent a residential ward. It was not uncommon throughout Mexico for specialized production to be organized at the neighborhood level (Berdan 1982; Carrasco 1971; Feinman and Nicholas 2012; Smith and Novic 2012). The lack of Early Postclassic ceramic diagnostics suggests that this entire area was abandoned at the end of the Late Classic, perhaps in response to a widespread breakdown in the sociopolitical hierarchy.

Almost all of the lower-status terraces at or near the hill's base contained high densities of chert debitage, cores, and points, suggesting household production of formal chipped stone tools for exchange. In addition, ceramic spindle whorls were found in nearly every terrace group, implying that the spinning of yarn also took place within many households. This type of multicrafting appears to have continued into the Early Postclassic, as demonstrated by the bone needles, spindle whorls, raspadores, and chert points and debitage found in and around the house complex on Terrace S19. Although it would be difficult to determine the scale of textile production on Terrace S19 without finding actual loom parts, the number of broken and incomplete chert points recovered appears to suggest that these items were being produced for extra-household consumption.

An interesting passage in the *Relación Geográfica de Macuilxóchitl* of 1580 (Acuña 1984 [1580]:330–31) states that that community paid its tribute by supplying its overlords with warriors equipped with bows and arrows. While we do not know exactly when the bow and arrow reached the Valley of Oaxaca, the making of points for atlatl darts (or arrows) might have a long history in the Macuilxóchitl region.

Considering the apparent decline in both community nucleation and political organization that took place at Dainzú-Macuilxóchitl at the end of the Late Classic, I did not expect to see as much continuity in household economic behavior as we see at Cerro Danush. To be sure, we are still a long way from understanding the full economic history of the Valley of Oaxaca. Cerro Danush is simply not a good vantage point from which to view the tribute system and the demands of the Monte Albán state. What Cerro Danush does show us is that there was a very resilient system of craft production and exchange operating at the level of commoner households.

We should never forget that our view of Zapotec economics is sometimes colored by today's thriving system of local markets. We cannot simply project that system back into prehistory, because the empirical archaeological evidence is not there. One day we may find proof of a prehispanic marketplace, but none has been found so far. Not every prehispanic state had markets; the Inca, for example, did not even have a word for "market." To be sure, there was both local and long-distance exchange, but we cannot show that it even vaguely resembled today's Oaxaca markets.

Classic Decline and Postclassic Reorganization in the Dainzú-Macuilxóchitl Region

In this final section, I look at what previous authors have said about the Postclassic reorganization of the Valley of Oaxaca, and consider what the Cerro Danush data can add to that dialogue.

The fact that the terraces I excavated were occupied by commoners limits what I can say. Fray Juan de Córdova (1578) was a Spanish priest and lexicographer who lived for years at Tlacochahuaya, not far from Macuilxóchitl. He describes the Zapotec as having *tija coqui*, royal lineages; *tija joana*, lineages of nobles reminiscent of Spanish *caballeros*; and *tija joana huini*, lineages of lesser nobles reminiscent of Spanish *hidalgos*. While the Summit Group at Cerro Danush may have housed such nobles, Terrace S19 did not. What it presumably housed was one of Córdova's *tija peniqueche*, "lineages of townspeople."

Whitecotton (1977) has suggested that individuals within Zapotec *tija*, or lineages, may have been ranked like the individuals within the unit that Paul Kirchhoff called a "conical clan." If such ranking was present at Cerro Danush, it could explain why Burial 3 had artificially modified teeth, while our other burials did not. (It should be remembered, of course, that "conical clan" refers to a form of chiefly organization, whereas the Postclassic Zapotec were organized as a state.)

Let us consider where the hereditary elite of the area might have lived. During the Late Classic, Dainzú-Macuilxóchitl was part of a cluster of large sites, known for convenience as DMTG. In addition to the nucleated settlements of Dainzú, Macuilxóchitl, Tlacochahuaya, and Guadalupe, there were smaller outlying communities like Gaii Guii (Fargher 2004). Within the boundaries of Dainzú-Macuilxóchitl, Kowalewski et al. (1989) mapped several three- and four-mound groups that may represent the civic-ceremonial precincts for a series of residential wards. One of these mound groups, consisting of a patio flanked by Structures 47, 48, and 49 (Fig. 2.7), may have served as the civic-ceremonial precinct for the ward headed by a noble family living on the west side of Cerro Danush.

I suspect that the highest-ranked leaders of Dainzú-Macuilxóchitl resided in the Lantiudee complex and the Summit Terrace Group at Cerro Danush. Their power clearly waned in the Terminal Classic, a time when whole groups of terraces at Cerro Danush were abandoned. On the summit of Cerro Danush, major temples fell into disuse. Their importance was remembered, however, and a lesser shrine was erected there in the Early Postclassic.

In contrast, the "lineages of townspeople" seem to have been so resilient that during the Early Postclassic, they continued to build houses of the same general type, maintained a number of household rituals, and buried their dead in much the same way they had in the Late Classic. Indeed, many aspects of their ritual and economic life probably survived the Spanish Conquest, allowing us to use the available sixteenth-century documents to interpret our data.

Resistance to Authority

Ethnohistoric sources suggest that resistance to authority was one reason for the site abandonments and relocations of late prehistoric times. Even in the most well integrated state systems, the constant elite demands for tribute and labor could generate resentment. Whenever the power of the tija coqui or hereditary rulers began to wane, it is likely that leaders of lesser rank (the tija joana or tija joana huini), bolstered by the commoners loyal to them, expressed their resistance to the demands of the ruling family by abandoning their old neighborhoods and establishing new ones. This may be one explanation for the apparent abandonment of entire residential wards at Cerro Danush in the Terminal Classic.

Nor is Cerro Danush the only site showing such abandonment and relocation during the Classic–Postclassic transition. For example, Paddock (1966) and Lind and Urcid (2010) have suggested that many residents of Lambityeco abandoned that site to resettle in nearby Yagul, a mesa-top site that became a nucleated community in the Postclassic (Bernal and Gamio 1974). Likewise, the area surrounding San Martín Tilcajete reveals several diachronic settlement shifts, some dating back to the Late Formative (Casparis 2006; Elson 2007; Redmond and Spencer 2008). In the Tilcajete region, Jalieza, like Cerro Danush, was the focus of Late/Terminal Classic occupation. Evidence for a significantly reduced Early Postclassic occupation has been found at Jalieza, and that hilltop appears to have been completely abandoned by the Late Postclassic (Elson 2011), perhaps in favor of settlement on the valley floor where the modern town is located.

This strategy of resistance by abandonment continued even after the Spanish Conquest of Oaxaca. As Taylor (1972) tells us:

> Pressures within a community or excessive demands by the colonial authorities often forced Indians to choose between flight and active resistance, and many chose to abandon their homes. Residents of even the largest and most affluent towns demonstrated great mobility when faced with involuntary service in the mines or a tyrannical native leader. Large numbers of able-bodied men and their families left Macuilxóchitl, Tlacolula, and Ejutla in the first half of the seventeenth century, for example, to avoid serving in the repartimiento for the Chichicapa mines.... Rather than work for the Spaniards who held the encomienda for their town, a large group of Tlacochahuayans left in the 1630's and established a new town.... After a disputed election in San Juan Teitipac in 1701, the barrio of Luyuxe was completely abandoned. [Taylor 1972:28]

The colonial history of San Mateo Macuilxóchitl not only documents this process of resistance, but also shows how some of the population shifts were justified by relating them to the will of supernatural figures (in this case, saints). The 1580 map (Fig. 8.1, Plate 7) from the *Relación Geográfica de Macuilxóchitl* (Acuña 1984 [1580]:324–41) shows two small settlements. The settlement in the lower right-hand corner of the map is identified as Teopa San Juan Macuilxóchitl, indicating that it was a ward of the larger community and its patron saint was San Juan. In the upper left, one finds Teopa Santiago Macuilxóchitl, a ward under the patron saint of Santiago. During the Colonial period, these wards separated themselves from the authority of San Mateo Macuilxóchitl, and became autonomous *municipios*, known today as San Juan Guelavía and Santiago Ixtaltepec.

As for San Juan Guelavía, its founding is recounted in a folktale transcribed by the Summer Institute of Linguistics (Hernández 1984). According to the author, Sr. Pedro Hernández, the ward of San Juan was initially settled by a few families seeking to protect San Mateo Macuilxóchitl's border from incursions by the neighboring community of Magdalena Teitipac. As this community grew, its residents petitioned San Mateo Macuilxóchitl for their own patron saint and received San Juan; after a short time, however, the authorities of the parent community recanted and took the image of the saint back. Miraculously, however, the saint's image kept reappearing within the San Juan ward, which prompted the members to found their own township and seek independence from San Mateo Macuilxóchitl. The story also relates that the community members subsequently gained their autonomy and ownership of the surrounding lands through a combination of legal means and armed confrontation with the communities of Magdalena Teitipac and San Mateo Macuilxóchitl.

Founding narratives like these provide hints about the diachronic changes in settlement evident at the site of Dainzú-Macuilxóchitl. In the Late Postclassic, settlement once again became nucleated around a civic-ceremonial core, located in the area where the town of Macuilxóchitl is today. Colonial documents suggest that Macuilxóchitl was a petty kingdom in its own right when the Spaniards arrived (Oudijk 2001, 2002; Whitecotton 1977). It had, by that time, come a long way from its humble beginnings as a residential ward under the control of a Late Classic royal family. With the political breakdown of Terminal Classic times, it became sufficiently independent to develop its own noble line.

We learn a bit about this line from a colonial genealogy showing fourteen generations of ruling couples. Oudijk (2008) suggests that this noble line can be traced back to the Early Postclassic. The gloss in the genealogy does not connect the founder with elite ancestral lines, but states that he emerged from a primordial pool of blood (Oudijk 2008:107). The mythologized origin is typical of a new lineage that is attempting to validate itself in spite of its lack of genuine credentials. Whatever the details, this new lineage—established at the place where San Mateo Macuilxóchitl stands today—grew in power and prestige until the settlement became more concentrated around it. By the Late Postclassic, the remaining settlement on Cerro Danush had been abandoned in favor of the growing kingdom discovered by the Spaniards.

Since the Late Classic, the history of the Dainzú-Macuilxóchitl region is one of cyclic breakdowns in higher-level political authority, followed by population movements that—among other things—probably reflect resistance to authority and a desire for autonomy on the part of lower-level leaders. Having gained that autonomy, some leaders established new hereditary lineages and grew powerful enough to initiate a new cycle of nucleation and power. Through it all, the tija peniqueche or commoner lineages managed to show remarkable continuity in residential layout, burial practices, and household ritual. It is my hope that future research at Dainzú-Macuilxóchitl in general, and Cerro Danush in particular, will provide greater resolution of the theoretical issues touched on in this volume.

Appendix A
Ceramic Chronology for the Valley of Oaxaca

The original Valley of Oaxaca ceramic sequence was developed by Alfonso Caso and his collaborators (Caso and Bernal 1965; Caso, Bernal, and Acosta 1967) on the basis of eighteen field seasons at the site of Monte Albán. The sequence is based on stratigraphy and employs phase designations that combine the name of the ancient urban capital with Roman numerals (e.g., Monte Albán I, Monte Albán II). Because the site of Monte Albán was founded in the Middle Formative (ca. 500 B.C.), the earliest ceramic phase, Monte Albán I, was assigned to this period. Subsequent research in the valley has uncovered Early and Middle Formative sites that predate Monte Albán I, requiring five new phase names (Flannery and Marcus 1994).

While the Caso, Bernal, and Acosta chronology works for the entire Valley of Oaxaca, a paucity of diagnostics that can separate Monte Albán IIIb and IV has provided survey crews with problems to confront (Blanton et al. 1982; Kowalewski et al. 1978, 1989). Recently, Feinman and Nicholas (2011) have tweaked Caso's chronology slightly to accommodate radiocarbon data from their excavations at El Palmillo and the Mitla Fortress.

Stratigraphy in excavations in Monte Albán's North Platform allowed Bernal (1946) to divide Monte Albán I into subphases Ia, Ib, and Ic. Lind (1991–1992) expressed dissatisfaction with Caso's Roman numeral chronology, and proposed replacing those numerical designations with day names from the Zapotec calendar, such as Xoo and Liobaa (Table A1). While some of Lind's colleagues have adopted this system (Joyce 2010; Markens 2004, 2008; Martínez López et al. 2000; Urcid 2001), most Oaxacanists continue to use some version of the original Caso system (Feinman 2007; González Licón 2003). I present all current versions in Table A1.

As suggested above, the thorniest problem with the Caso chronology is distinguishing Monte Albán IIIb and IV (and to a lesser extent, IV and Early V). These problems have led to a considerable amount of debate (Finsten 1983:16–25; Marcus and Flannery 1990; Markens 2004, 2008; Martínez López et al. 2000; Kowalewski et al. 1989:251–54; Lind 1991–1992). The problems lie not in what one calls the phase, but in a lack of reliable ceramic diagnostics (Kowalewski et al. 1989:251–54). At some of the larger sites, there are Maya Fine Orange trade wares that help resolve issues, but we need local diagnostics. Adding to the problem is the fact that only a small number of radiocarbon dates have been run from Late Classic and Early Postclassic contexts (Drennan 1983; Markens, Winter, and Martínez López 2010).

Markens (2004, 2008) has recently completed an extensive phyletic seriation of Late Classic and Early Postclassic materials from well-dated grave lots, which has made progress toward alleviating the difficulties mentioned above. This research has produced clear distinctions between ceramic vessels from the

Table A1. Ceramic chronology for the Valley of Oaxaca.

Period	Dates	Feinman and Nicholas	Lind
Late Postclassic	A.D. 1300–1521	Late Monte Albán V	Chila
Early Postclassic	A.D. 900–1300	Early Monte Albán V	Liobaa
Late/Terminal Classic	A.D. 600–900	Late Monte Albán IIIb–IV	Xoo
Late Classic	A.D. 500–600	Early Monte Albán IIIb–IV	Peche
Early Classic	A.D. 200–500	Monte Albán IIIa	Pitao
Early Classic	A.D. 100–200	Transitional II–IIIa	Tani
Terminal Formative	200 B.C.–A.D. 100	Monte Albán II	Niza
Late Formative	300–200 B.C.	Late Monte Albán I	Pe
Late Formative	500–300 B.C.	Early Monte Albán I	Danibaan
Middle Formative	700–500 B.C.	Rosario	Rosario
Middle Formative	850–700 B.C.	Guadalupe	Guadalupe
Early Formative	1150–850 B.C.	San José	San José
Early Formative	1400–1150 B.C.	Tierras Largas	Tierras Largas
Early Formative	1900–1400 B.C.	Espiridión	Espiridión
Archaic	8000–1900 B.C.	n.a.	n.a.

Late Classic and the Early Postclassic, and Markens' descriptions provide part of the basis for classification of the ceramic materials recovered during my project (Appendix B). Seriation, however, cannot replace stratigraphy. Because burial offerings reflect one-time events, more data are needed from contexts such as stratified middens. Only the latter can truly define the diachronic distributions of ceramic types for these periods.

In my work, I take no position on any given chronology, but simply attempt to accommodate the contributions of all relevant researchers. When necessary, I combine more than one system based on similarities in the diagnostic materials rather than phase names (Table A1). My broad view of the Late Classic incorporates Markens' (2008) proposed Peche (A.D. 500–600) and Xoo (A.D. 600–800) phase diagnostics with Feinman and Nicholas' (2011) tweaking of Caso's chronology (Chapter 1), which results in Monte Albán IIIb–IV lasting from A.D. 500 to 900. For the Early Postclassic, I also use Markens' (2004, 2008) proposed Liobaa phase (A.D. 800–1200) diagnostics, but incorporate them into the chronology recently developed by Feinman and Nicholas (2011), in which Early Monte Albán V lasts from A.D. 900 to 1300.

Appendix B
Artifact Categories

Because of the large body of previous work in the Valley of Oaxaca, I did not need to concern myself with establishing or even refining artifact types; I was almost always able to use preexisting artifact categories. This appendix defines each of the artifact categories used in the Cerro Danush data set.

General Description of the Project Ceramic Assemblage

In general, the ceramic assemblage from Cerro Danush is indicative of domestic activities, and matches similar assemblages from other terraced hilltop sites in the Valley of Oaxaca, such as Monte Albán (Blanton 1978), Jalieza (Finsten 1995), and El Palmillo (Feinman and Nicholas 2004). Almost all the diagnostic ceramics fit within the categories described for Monte Albán IIIa (Early Classic), Monte Albán IIIb–IV (Late Classic), or Early Monte Albán V (Early Postclassic). No diagnostics clearly attributable to earlier periods were found, and only a few Late Monte Albán V (Late Postclassic) ceramic indicators were recovered during our two field seasons on Cerro Danush.

For the classification of categories within the project ceramic assemblage, I used a combination of forms and styles developed through previous research projects in the Valley of Oaxaca. These include categories defined by Caso, Bernal, and Acosta (1967) during their 18 seasons at Monte Albán; Kowalewski et al. (1989b:829–37; 1978; Blanton et al. 1982:375–82;) from their valley-wide survey; Bernal and Oliveros (1988) from excavations at Dainzú; Bernal and Gamio (1974) from excavations at Yagul; Paddock, Mogor, and Lind (1968) from excavations at Lambityeco; and Markens and his colleagues (Markens 2004, 2008; Markens, Winter, and Martínez López 2008; Martínez López et al. 2000) from excavations at Dainzú-Macuilxóchitl and several other sites in the Valley of Oaxaca.

The sherds collected at Cerro Danush were also separated by the color of their pastes. Three paste colors were identified (orange, brown, and gray), effectively expanding the number of categories recorded within the data set. Overall, gray wares (*gris*) were the most abundant, making up 65% of the excavation assemblage and 80% of the surface collection assemblage. Brown paste sherds (*café*) were the second most abundant, accounting for 32% of the excavation assemblage and 19% of the surface collection assemblage. Orange paste sherds (*amarillo*) were the least abundant, amounting to 2.55% of the excavation assemblage and 1.62% of the surface collection assemblage.

Minor color variations existed within the overall paste designations, especially in the case of the brown pastes, which ranged from light brown or tan to dark reddish brown. Further analysis revealed, however, that this color variation was likely due to differential exposure to heat while firing, as the full range of browns can usually be found among individual examples of the same type. Many of the orange and brown paste vessels appeared to be made of the same actual clay as the gray pastes, their color difference due mainly to their firing in an oxidizing environment rather than in the reducing environment used for gray ware.

The combination of vessel form and paste color yielded a total of 62 ceramic categories. These categories are described in greater detail below, with special attention paid to the activities they may reflect and their temporal significance. Not all categories were used in the quantitative analyses presented in earlier chapters, and some had to be eliminated because they were found in extremely small quantities.

Conical Bowls (Cajetes Cónicos)

The most abundant diagnostic fragments found during the project fit within the description of the G35 conical bowl (Figs. B1, B2), first defined by Caso, Bernal, and Acosta (1967:348). Although variations in rim shape, rim diameter, and presence/absence of hollow or solid supports have been documented by Kowalewski, Spencer, and Redmond (1978: categories 1137, 1138, 1140, 1263, 1274, 1122, 2086) and Martínez López et al. (2000), the basic vessel has a flat circular base with straight or convexly curved walls that lean outward. The G35 type is made with gray paste; however, identical vessels made with brown paste, known as type K14, may be often found in the same contexts with less frequency. Conical bowls were further divided into two rim diameter categories: the first (Fig. B1) consists of bowls with rim diameters of 20 cm or less, and the second consists of bowls with rim diameters between 20 and 40 cm. Conical bowls with rim diameters greater than 40 cm were generally much thicker, and have been grouped in the apaxtle category described below.

While there is an early form of G35 found in Monte Albán II, classic G35s become the dominant form in Monte Albán IIIb–IV, and are often considered diagnostic of the Late Classic. In the Tlacolula arm of the valley, orange paste conical bowls were also present in significant numbers along with the usual G35 and K14 types. Kowalewski et al. (1989b:201, category 3500) have identified this orange paste vessel as the "Dainzú Bowl," and suggest that they were more abundant in the Late Formative and Early Classic than in the Late Classic. Spatial analysis of orange paste Dainzú Bowls from the surface collection at Cerro Danush supports this conclusion.

Conical bowls have been found in many different contexts, with a number of implied functions. One need look no further than our sample of whole vessels recovered during the excavation of Terrace S19. Several G35 bowls were collected from ritual contexts; for example, one (with its interior surface painted red) was found with a human burial (Figs. 6.32, 6.33, Plate 1). Others, such as the one recovered from the midden on Terrace S19 (Figs. 7.22, 7.23, Plate 6), had a utilitarian purpose; that example contained dried white plaster with the impression of a corncob brush, indicating its use for the stuccoing of house or patio floors. Conical bowls were also likely used for serving food.

Given their variety of uses, the surface distribution of cajetes cónicos will not always be useful for identifying specific activity areas across the site. Their great abundance in nearly every terrace group, however, does suggest that Cerro Danush was most heavily occupied during the Late Classic. Our total collection includes 15,652 gray paste G35 sherds, 4155 brown paste K14 sherds, and 801 orange paste Dainzú Bowl sherds. Together, these types make up approximately 30% of the diagnostic materials we recovered.

Late Classic Hemispherical Bowls (Cajetes Semiesféricos)

Hemispherical bowls (Figs. B3, B4) were the second most abundant category (approximately 10% of the diagnostic sherds) recovered during my project. They are also a temporal diagnostic of Monte Albán IIIb–IV (Caso, Bernal, and Acosta 1967; Martínez López et al. 2000). Variation in the design and finish of these bowls has been noted, such as flat vs. rounded bottoms and presence/absence of hollow or solid supports, but the basic form consists of a curving (Fig. B3) or somewhat composite silhouette (Fig. B4) wall that gives the vessel its hemispherical shape. Most importantly, Late Classic hemispherical bowls are undecorated, which contrasts with the hemispherical bowls of earlier and later periods.

The Late Classic hemispherical bowl generally has the same paste and finish as the G35 conical bowl, but sherds were found with gray (5617), brown (1637), and orange (386) pastes. These bowls could also be divided into two size categories based on rim diameters: the first measuring 30 cm or less, and the second greater than 30 cm. The larger bowl class was generally thicker-walled, and the rims were reinforced on the interior. Like G35 bowls, it is likely that hemispherical bowls served a variety of uses, making it difficult to associate them with specific activities.

G3M Hemispherical Bowls

Six hundred and forty-seven fragments of small, well-fired gray paste hemispherical bowls, belonging to the G3M type (Caso, Bernal, and Acosta 1967), were collected during my project (Fig. B5). These thin, well-made ceramics are considered diagnostic of Monte Albán V (Kowalewski et al. 1989; Kowalewski, Spencer, and Redmond 1978; Markens 2004). In fact, G3M bowls replace G35 bowls as the most abundant type in the Postclassic, and probably also represent a great variety of uses. Therefore, their distribution is most useful as a temporal marker and not as an indicator of specific activities.

Most vessels belonging to the G3M ware category are very standardized, and the majority lack decoration. The G3M hemispherical bowl can easily be distinguished from Late Classic gray paste hemispherical bowls because it is thinner-walled, is more thoroughly double burnished, and has a less porous paste. G3M

Appendix B

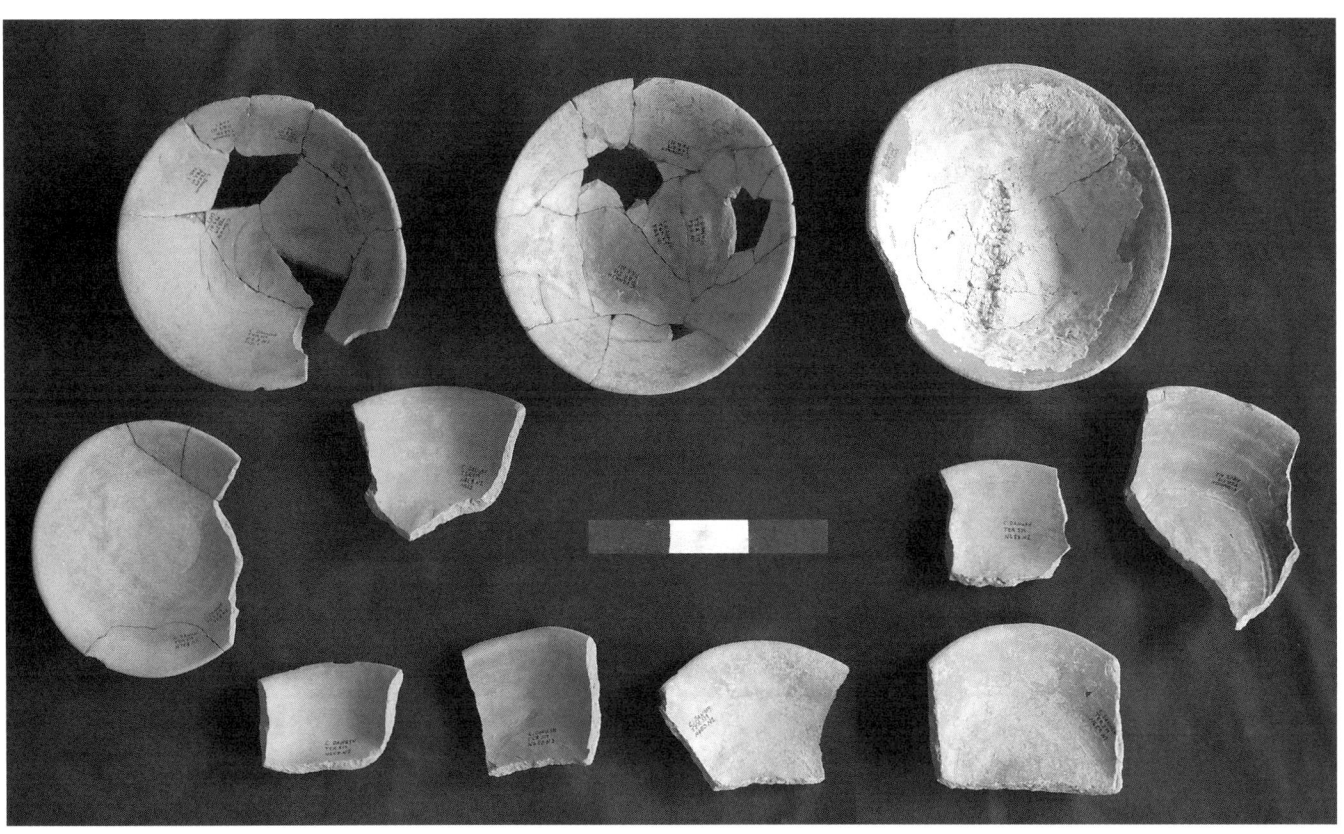

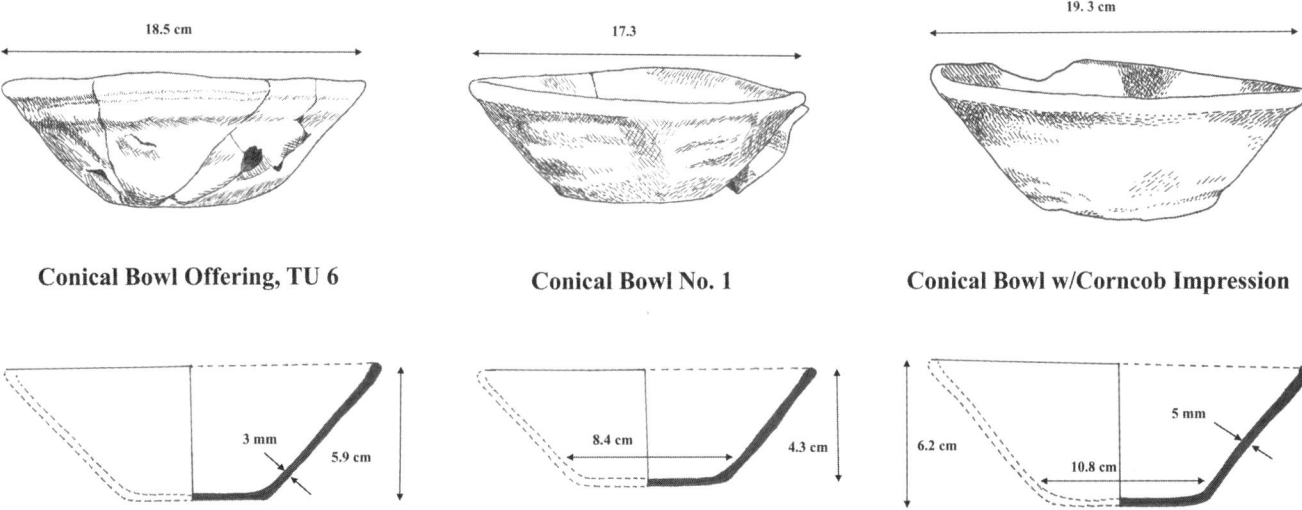

Figure B1. Small G35 conical bowl fragments (rim diameter of 20 cm or less).

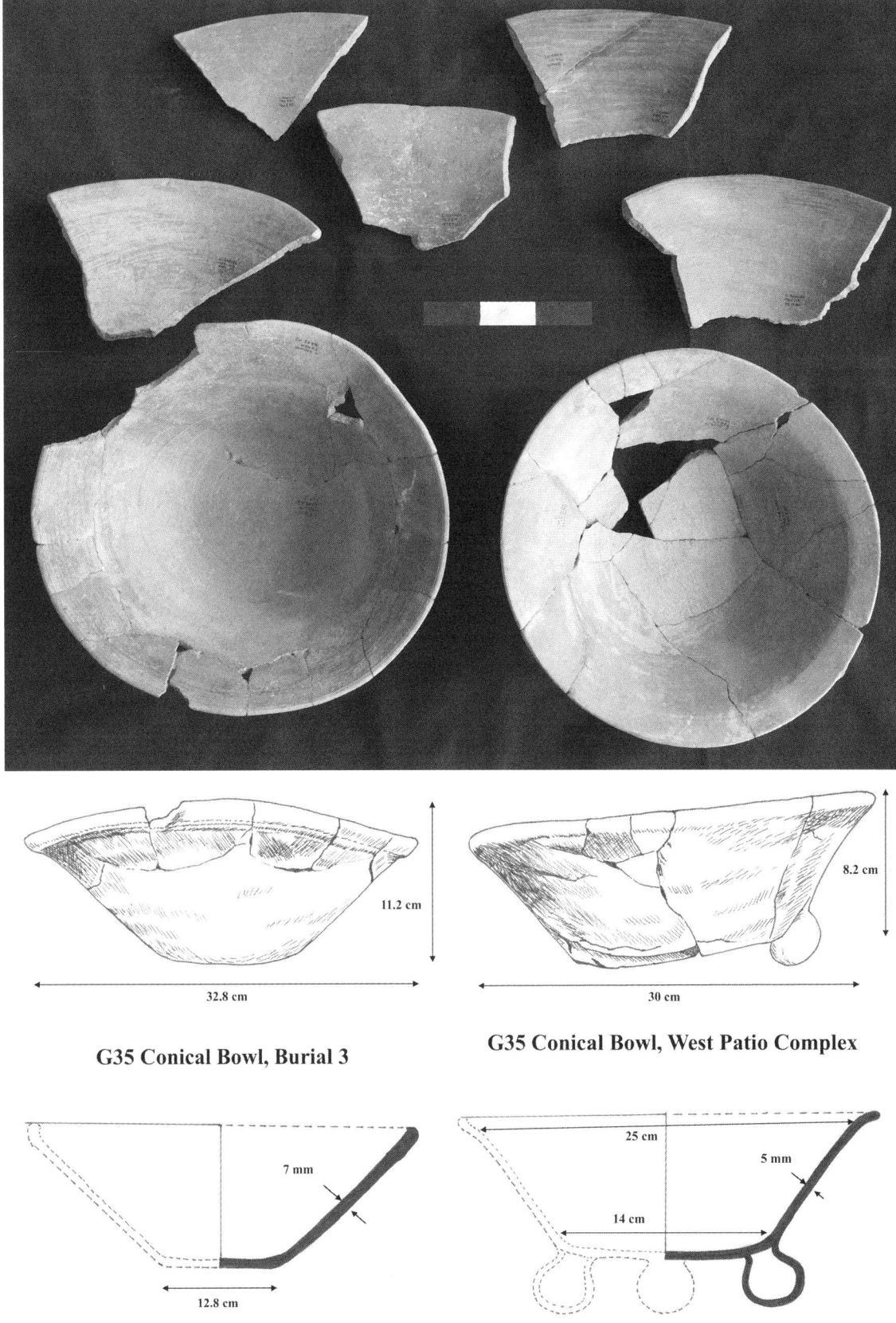

Figure B2. Large G35 conical bowls (rim diameter between 20 cm and 40 cm).

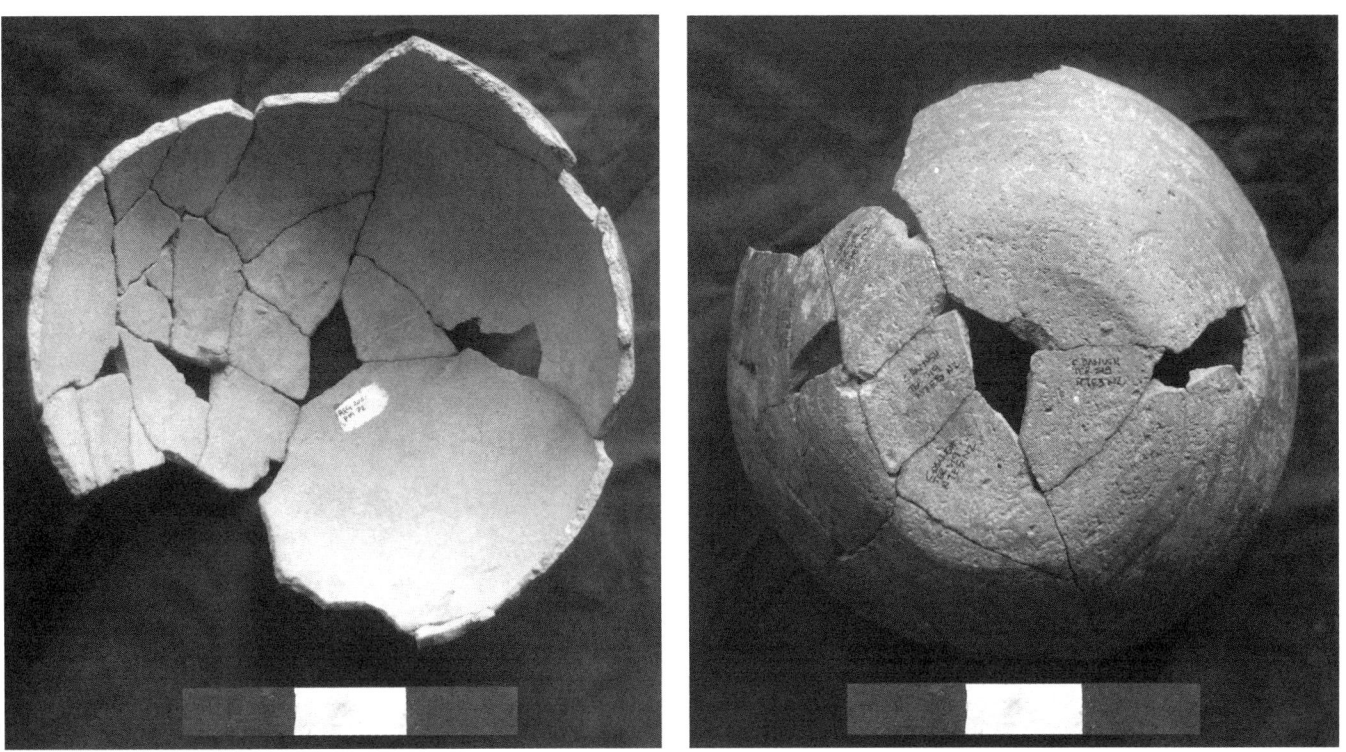

Figure B3. Hemispherical bowl with concave curved walls.

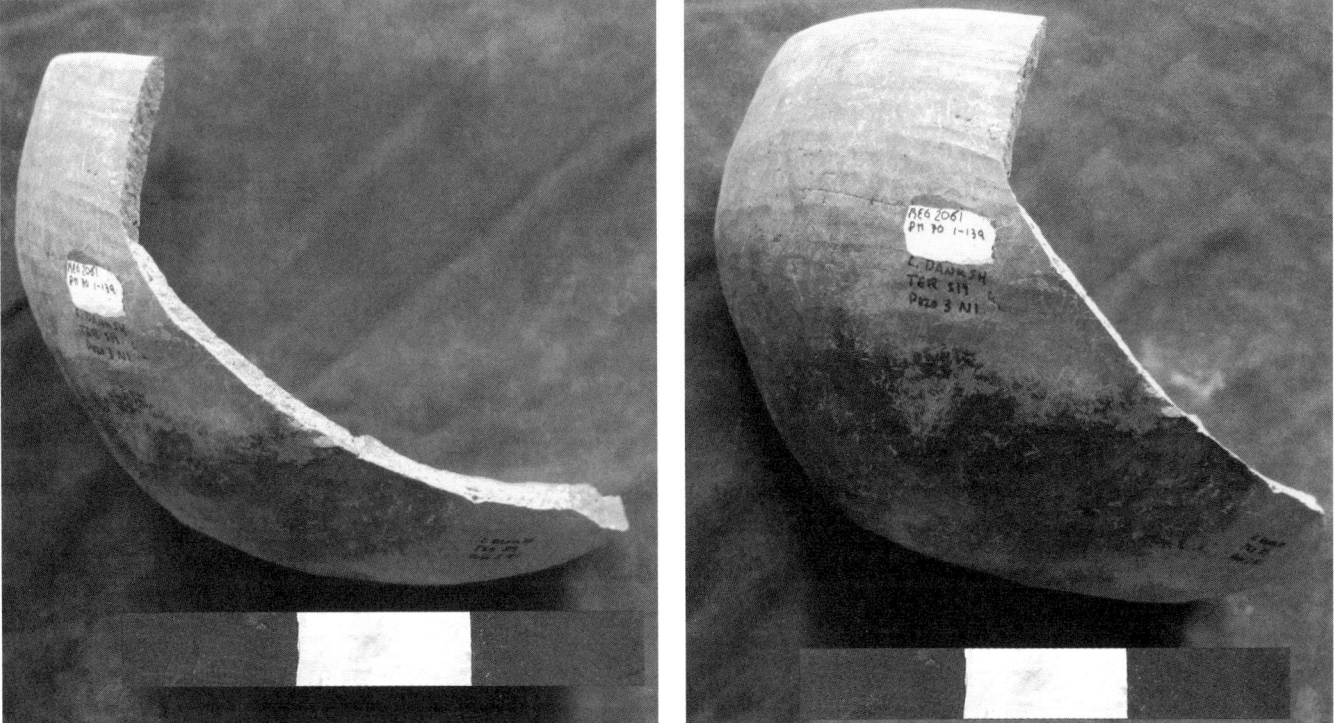

Figure B4. Hemispherical bowl with composite silhouette walls.

Figure B5. Fragments of Postclassic G3M hemispherical bowls.

is unslipped, but is often differentially fired so as to have black and gray zones. One theory is that the black zone is submerged in sand during firing; another theory is that the darker zones are smudged. G3M, in fact, would seem to be the forerunner of today's black ware from Coyotepec.

During the analysis of materials from the excavation of Terrace S19, I found several examples of hemispherical bowls that appeared to represent a transition from the Late Classic (G35) to the Postclassic (G3M) type. Included were bowls that were not as thoroughly fired or burnished as a typical G3M, but more so than the Late Classic bowls. Kent Flannery (pers. comm., 2013) tells me that he found similar transitional vessels while excavating at San Sebastián Abasolo in the 1960s. The stratigraphy at Abasolo—just south of Tlacochahuaya—indicates that Monte Albán V ceramics grew out of Monte Albán IV, rather than bringing an exotic intrusion into the Valley of Oaxaca. Obviously, however, more work needs to be done.

Cylindrical Bowls and Cups
(Cajetes Cilíndricos/Vasos Sencillos)

In addition to our conical and hemispherical bowls, fragments from straight-walled vessels, characterized by Martínez López et al. (2000) as cylindrical bowls (Fig. B6) and cups (Fig. B7), were also identified in the ceramic assemblage. When nearly complete vessels are recovered, one can generally distinguish cups from cylindrical bowls by the overall vessel size, as well as by the ratio between wall height and base diameter. When only sherds are present, it is more difficult to separate bowls and cups; I have therefore decided to group them into one category.

Cylindrical bowls and cups generally were found to have the same finish as the Late Classic conical and hemispherical bowls, and are also considered diagnostic of Monte Albán IIIb–IV (Martínez López et al. 2000). Fragments of these vessels were found both in gray paste (183 pieces) and brown paste (26), but not orange. These vessels are not considered indicative of any specific activity, and serve mainly as temporal diagnostics.

Figure B6. Fragments of cylindrical bowls.

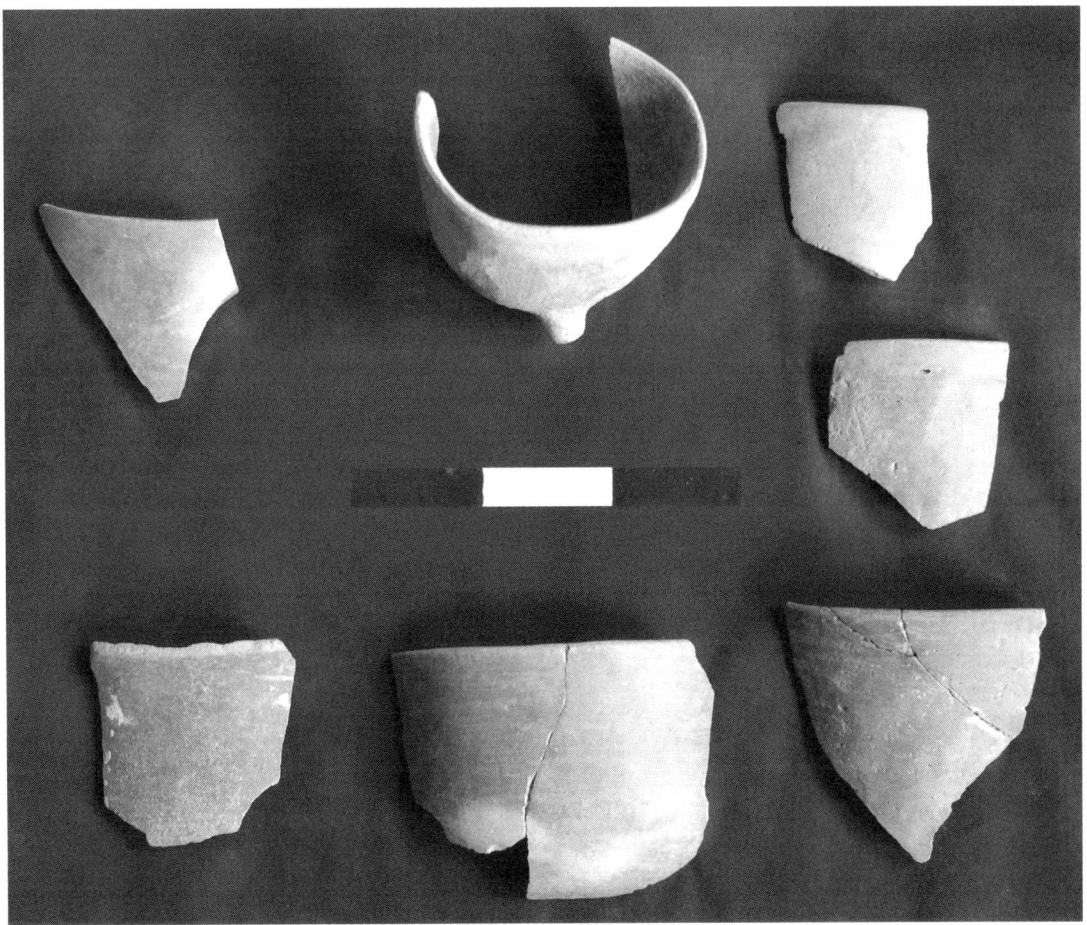

Figure B7. Fragments of simple cups.

Figure B8. Fragments of G23-type bowls.

G23-Type Bowls

A small but significant number of fragments (154) of bowls carefully incised on the exterior were recovered during the project (Fig. B8). They represent the remains of both cylindrical and hemispherical bowls, and were found in both gray and orange pastes. Caso, Bernal, and Acosta (1967) defined similar vessels from Monte Albán as G23 (gray paste) and A7 (orange paste) types, and assigned them to Monte Albán IIIa (Early Classic). They have subsequently been used as Early Classic diagnostics in excavations (González Licón 2003; Martínez López 1994; Redmond 1983; Spencer and Redmond 1997) and during surface survey (Balkansky 2002; Kowalewski, Spencer, and Redmond 1978; Kowalewski et al. 1989).

Because of their low frequency in the assemblage from Cerro Danush, I was forced to group all the G23 and A7 fragments into one single analytical category, using it as a temporal diagnostic only, and not as an indicator of a specific activity.

G12 Bowls

Five fragments of conical bowls with two incised parallel lines running along the interior rim were recovered, 3 from the surface collection and 2 from excavation (Fig. B9). Bowls of this type were identified as type G12 by Caso, Bernal, and Acosta (1967). More recently, Spencer, Redmond, and Elson (2008) have subdivided this type into varieties G12a, G12b, and G12c. While G12s are most abundant in Late Monte Albán I, the variety G12b spans Late I and Early II, and G12c occurs mainly in Monte Albán II. Owing to a lack of Monte Albán I and II diagnostics, I suspect my 5 G12 rims were from vessels that survived into the Early Classic. Unfortunately, the tiny sample size excludes the use of G12s for quantitative analyses.

Red-Painted Vessels

Several fragments of small red-painted cylindrical bowls or cups (rim diameters of less than 15 cm) made with thin gray or cream-colored paste were recovered during my project. These vessels resemble ceramic category 3035 as defined by Kowalewski, Spencer, and Redmond (1978:192). They assign 3035 to Monte Albán IIIb–IV. The significance of this type within the Valley of Oaxaca ceramic sequence has not been fully established, and our sample made up less than half a percent of the diagnostic sherds recovered. This category serves to do little more than provide further evidence of Late Classic occupation at Cerro Danush.

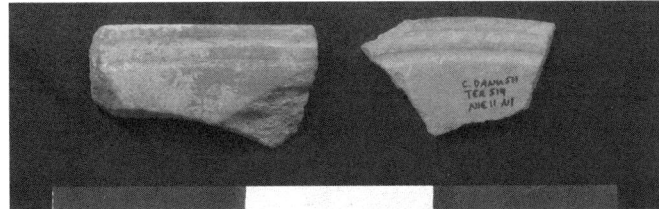

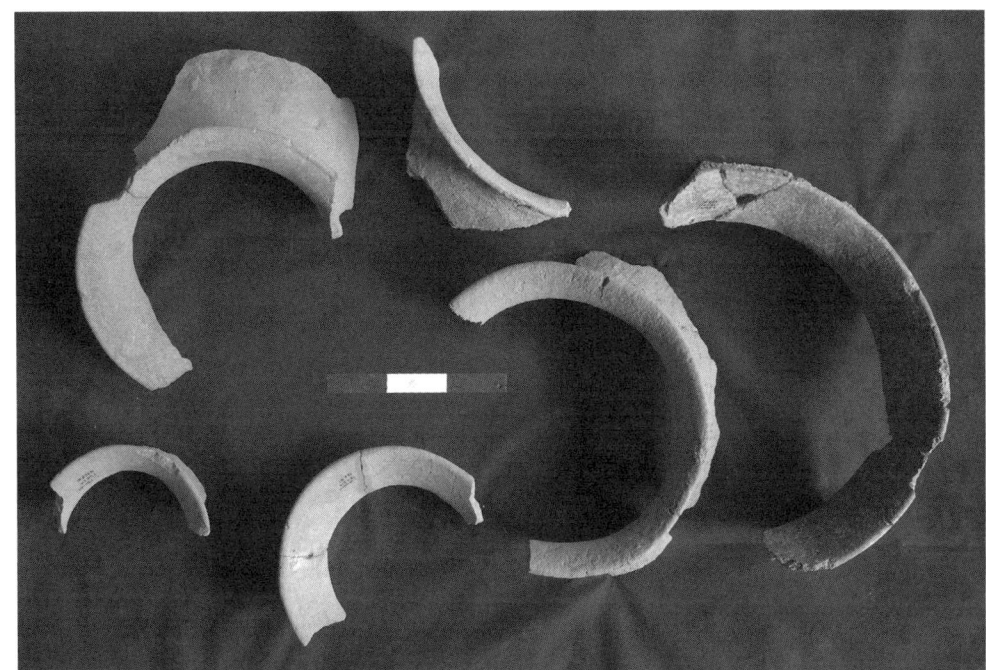

(*above left*) Figure B9. Fragments of G12-type bowls.

(*above right*) Figure B10. Rim sherds from Balancán Fine Orange vessels.

(*right*) Figure B11. Rim and neck fragments from simple ollas.

Balancán Fine Orange

Only 2 rim sherds, both recovered during the excavation of Terrace S19, were assigned to Balancán Fine Orange, a Maya import ware (Fig. B10). They are brick red in color and contain fine exterior incised designs similar to those described by Markens (2004) and Martínez López et al. (2000:218, Fig. 43). Fine Orange ceramics like these have been a central item in the debate over the Late Classic and Early Postclassic ceramic chronology (Marcus and Flannery 1990). They have been assigned to the Early Postclassic by Paddock, Mogor, and Lind (1968) and Kowalewski et al. (1989b), and to the Late Classic by Martínez López et al. (2000). Because Terrace S19 was occupied in both the Late Classic and the Early Postclassic, my sample of 2 sherds cannot help resolve this debate.

Simple Cooking Jars (Ollas Sencillas)

Rim and neck fragments from simple cooking jars (Fig. B11) made up the third most abundant sherd category I recovered (3236 total fragments). These vessels have globular bodies with restricted necks and flaring conical rims (Fig. B12). They vary greatly in size and thickness (Fig. B13), and are some-

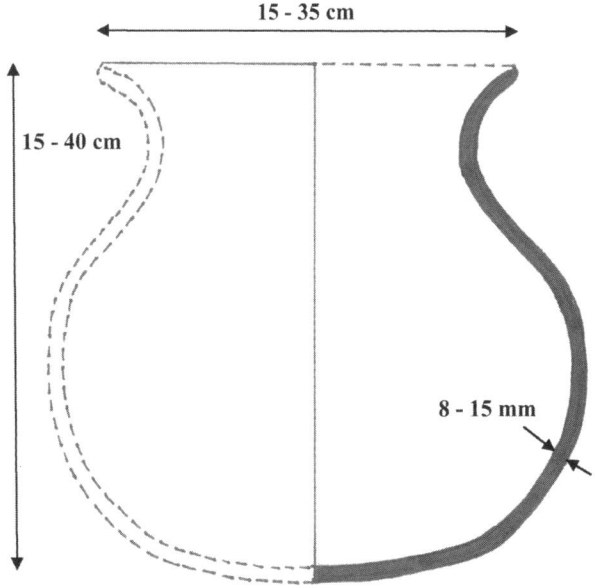

Figure B12. Basic profile of simple ollas, with size ranges.

Figure B13.
Fragments of small globular ollas.

Figure B14.
Fragments of simple ollas with handles.

times found with external handles, usually attached just above or below the neck (Fig. B14). While most of the examples I found appear to fit well with the descriptions of Martínez López et al. (2000) for Late Classic ollas, similar vessels have been found in Formative through Late Classic contexts in the Valley of Oaxaca (Caso, Bernal, and Acosta 1967). As a result, fragments of this type are not particularly useful as temporal markers; they are, however, useful indicators of food storage and preparation activities.

Barrel-shaped Storage/Cooking Vessels (Ollas Barriles)

Ollas barriles are easily distinguished from simple jars (ollas sencillas). They are thicker, have open rather than restricted mouths, and are barrel-shaped rather than globular. Diagnostic fragments consist mostly of large thick rims with a lip for a lid to rest on (Fig. B15). Markens (2008:80–81) and Martínez López et al. (2000:139) assign these vessels to the Late Classic. I collected fragments of these vessels in all three paste colors (52 gray, 31 brown, 2 orange), but at much lower frequencies than simple jars. Because these vessels were most likely used for food storage, they are a good indicator of this activity.

Jars with Appliqué Glyph Motif (Ollas con Glifo)

Fifty-five fragments of small globular or bottle-shaped jars with exterior appliqué motifs were recovered (Fig. B16). These jars are easily identified by the presence of a distinctive appliqué to the body or neck. Only one motif, which has been identified as the hieroglyphic representation of a hill, occurs (Paddock 1983b). While Martínez López et al. (2000:145) assign this vessel to the Late Classic, others maintain that it is an Early Postclassic diagnostic (Kowalewski et al. 1989; Marcus and Flannery 1990; Paddock, Mogor, and Lind 1968). Intact jars of this type have been found as tomb offerings, and Lind and Urcid (2010) suggest it may be related to ceremonies involving Cociyo (Lightning). Fragments were found only in gray and brown pastes.

"Shoe Pots" (Patojos)

During excavation, the remains of several intact or nearly intact brown paste "shoe pots" were found as part of paired-vessel offerings (Chapter 7). These vessels, called patojos in Spanish, derive their shoe-like shape from the fact that the mouth is offset to one side, allowing the contents to be stirred while the bulk of the vessel remains in the fire (Fig. B17). Patojos have been identified in Formative and Postclassic contexts in the Valley of Oaxaca (Caso, Bernal, and Acosta 1967), but are not known from the Late Classic. The shoe pots I recovered came from a stratigraphic layer radiocarbon dated to the Early Postclassic. Markens (2004, 2008) assigns brown paste patojos to the Early Postclassic.

All the patojos I found during my project had brown paste, with clouding or smudging visible on the outside and striations from brushing on the surface. Unfortunately, in the Early Postclassic some simple ollas (Fig. B18) were made from this same type of paste, and show similar smudging and striations on their surfaces (Markens 2004). As a result, small sherds from such ollas could not always be separated from sherds of patojos. Since both vessels were used in food preparation, occasional lumping should not affect our ability to identify areas devoted to that activity.

Water Storage Vessels (Cántaros)

Cántaros are large, globular, thin-walled narrow-mouthed jars that were likely used to carry and store water (Fig. B19). They were the fourth most abundant sherd found in my excavations. Most cántaros were not diagnostic of a particular period; in fact, similar vessels have been found in Late Classic, Early Postclassic, and Late Postclassic contexts (Markens 2008:83–85). At Cerro Danush, fragments of cántaros displayed mostly gray paste (1515), but a small number with brown (99) or orange (5) paste were recovered. Markens (2008:83–84) has assigned one type of cántaro—with a "starburst burnished pattern radiating downward from the neck"—to the Late Postclassic; only 1 fragment of this type was found at Cerro Danush.

Censers (Sahumadores)

Two types of frying-pan-shaped incense burners, known in Spanish as sahumadores, were found at Cerro Danush. These vessels came in two varieties, one diagnostic of the Late Classic and the other diagnostic of the Early Postclassic.

The oldest variety, which appeared in the Early Classic but became more common during the Late Classic, is the larger of the two, has a hollow handle, and features a hemispherical or conical receptacle for burning incense (Figs. B20, B21, Plate 8). I recovered fragments of this sahumador in gray (364), brown (155), and orange (10) paste, and there were even a few with cream paste and a red-painted exterior (7). The interior of the receptacle could either be smooth or contain incised designs or perforations (Caso, Bernal, and Acosta 1967:434; Markens 2008:84). These vessels were commonly found as offerings in small tombs and slab-lined graves during the Late Classic (Winter 2002).

The second variety of sahumador is smaller, has a shallower receptacle, and features a thin handle that is nearly solid, having just a small (2- to 4-mm diameter) tube running the length of its interior (Figs. B22, B23, Plate 8). The receptacle's interior often contains two incised lines that cross in the center, as well as four stamped circles, one in each corner of the cross (Fig. B23). The majority of the fragments (489) we recovered were made from the same type of brown paste found in our Early Postclassic patojos and ollas; only a few were made of gray (11) or orange paste (3). These vessels are typical of the Early Monte Albán V assemblage in the Valley of Oaxaca (Kowalewski, Spencer, and Redmond 1978: category 2220; Markens 2008:84).

Flat Figurines and Molds

During the course of my work, I recovered 1062 fragments of flat-backed figurines (Fig. B24). Several still show evidence of finger marks on their backs, made during the process of pressing the clay into the mold (Fig. B25). In addition to the figurine fragments, I recovered 9 fragments of the ceramic molds used to make figurines (Fig. B26). These items made up 1.67% of the excavation assemblage and 1.64% of the surface collection assemblage. A large majority (890) consisted of fragments that were either too small or eroded to be categorized more specifically, but the remaining samples were found to fit very well within the diagnostic categories defined by Caso and Bernal (1952), Scott (1993), and Martínez López and Winter (1994). I organized them into separate categories, based on these works.

13 Serpent Figurines, Variant 1

This figurine type (Figs. B24, B25, B27, B28) portrays a woman with an elaborate headdress, tasseled belt, and necklace. Caso and Bernal (1952:283–93) identified this woman on a number of ceramic urns and figurines, where she is accompanied by her name (13 Serpent) from the Zapotec 260-day calendar. Half

Figure B15. Fragments from barrel-shaped jars (ollas barriles).

Figure B16. Fragments of jars with appliqué glyph motifs.

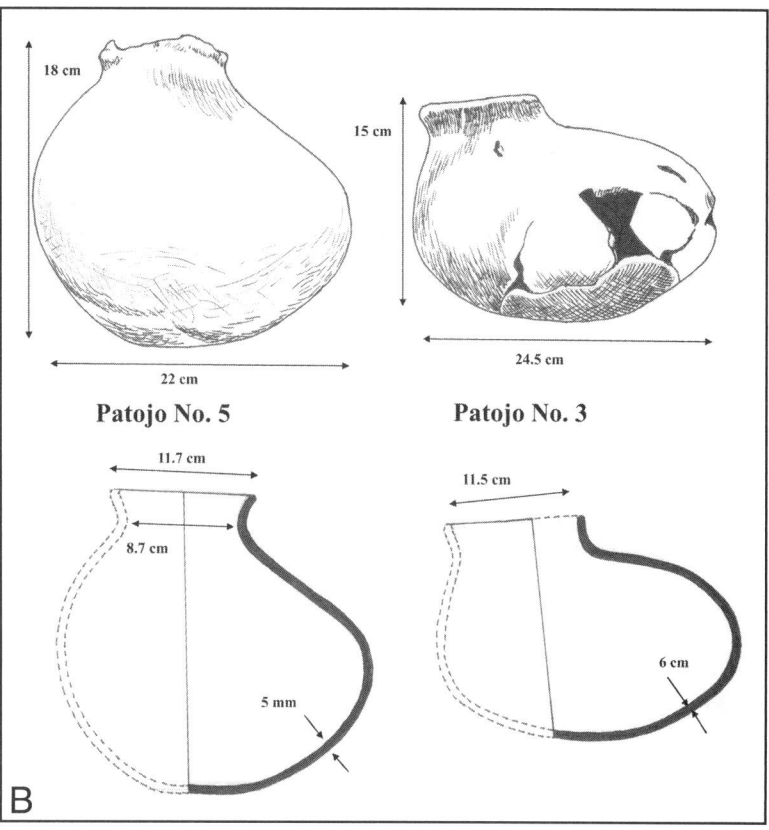

Figure B17. Early Postclassic patojos. *A*, Patojo number 5; *B*, drawings with profiles and measurements, patojos numbers 5 and 3 (drawing by Betty Cleeland); *C*, drawings and profiles with measurements, patojos numbers 3 and 6 (drawing by Betty Cleeland); *D*, patojo number 6.

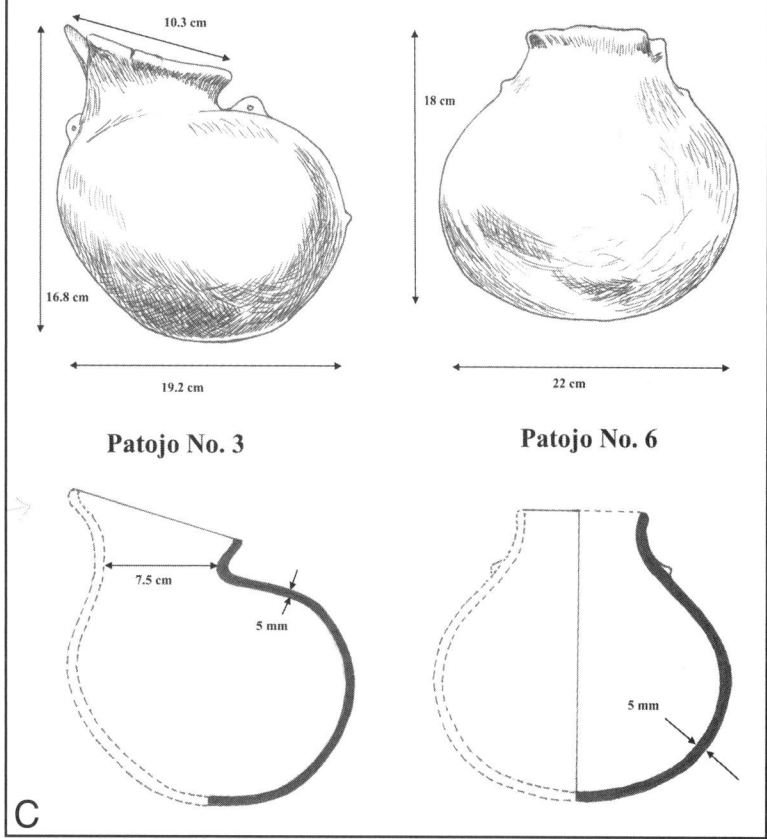

Figure B18. Fragments of an Early Postclassic olla.

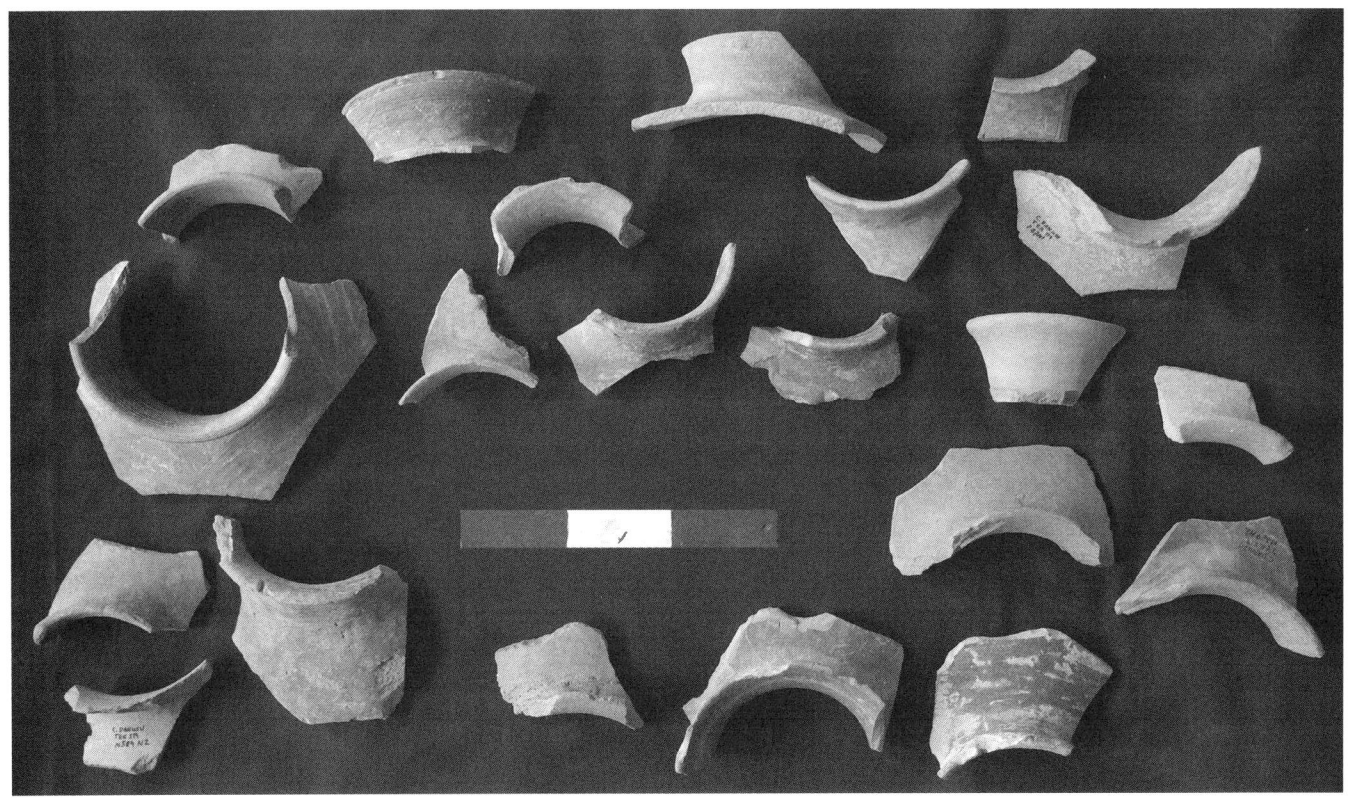

Figure B19. Neck and rim fragments from cántaros.

(*left*) Figure B20. Fragments of hollow-handled sahumadores (also see Plate 8).

(*below*) Figure B21. Profile drawing of hollow-handled sahumador (drawing by Betty Cleeland).

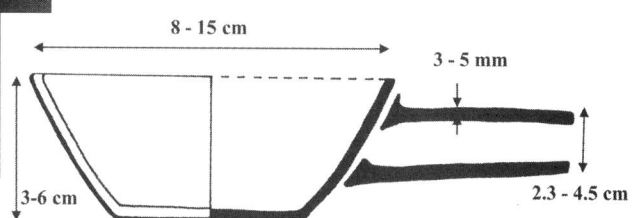

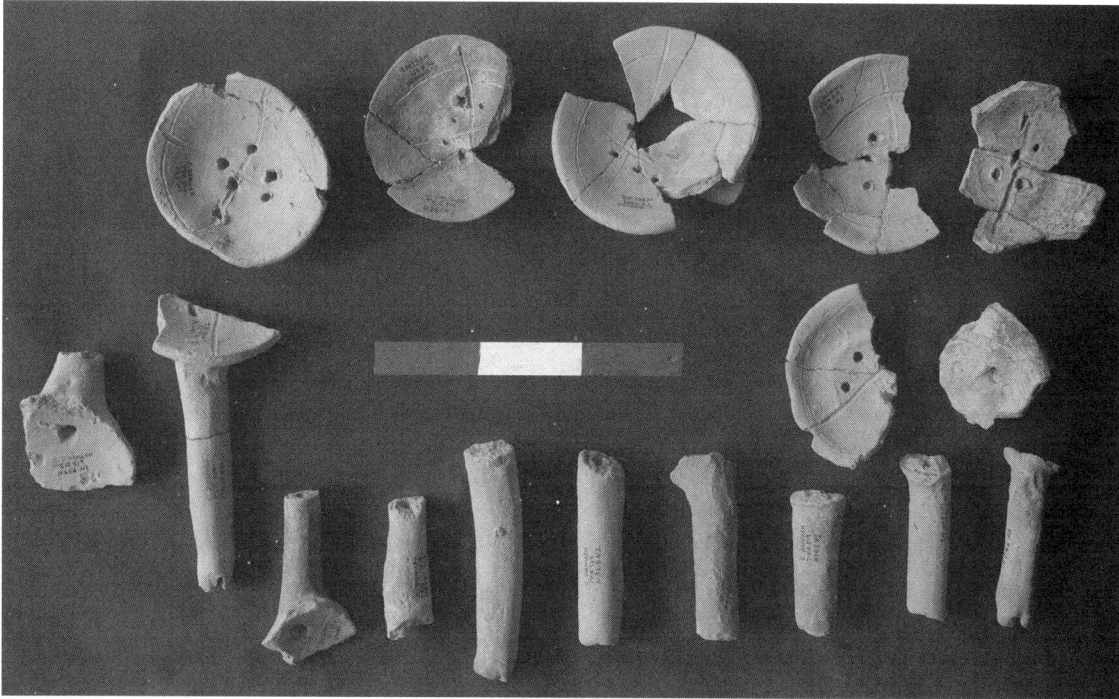

(*above right*) Figure B22. Fragments of solid-handled sahumadores (also see Plate 8).

(*right*) Figure B23. Drawing of solid-handled sahumador (drawing by Betty Cleeland).

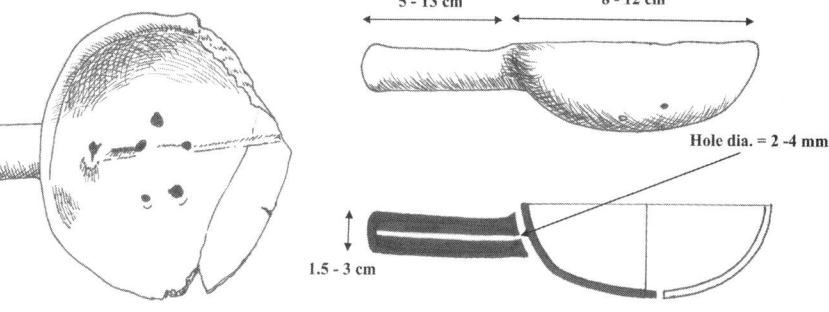

Figure B24. Fragments of mold-made figurines, 13 Serpent type (front).

Figure B25. Fragments of mold-made figurines, 13 Serpent type (back).

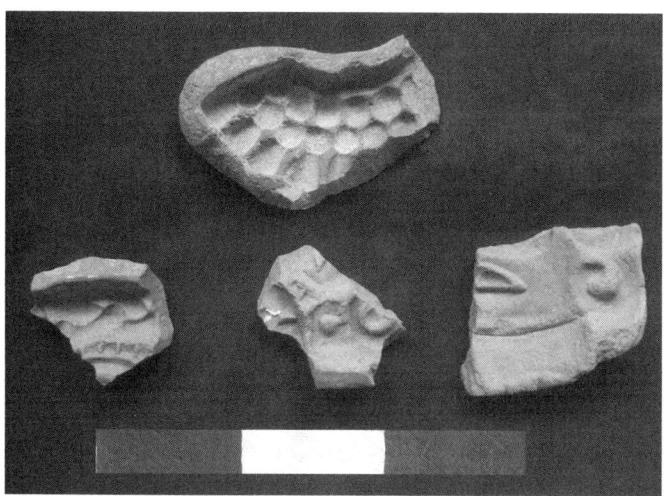

(*above*) Figure B26. Fragments of ceramic molds for figurine making.

(*above right*) Figure B27. Drawing of 13 Serpent, variant 1, mold-made figurines (after Caso and Bernal 1950:293).

Figure B28. Close-up of 13 Serpent, variant 1, fragments.

a century ago it would have been common to hear such figurines interpreted as deities, but as pointed out by Marcus (1983d), the calendric names identify them as ancestors, whether real or mythologized. Martínez López and Winter (1994:53) identified fragments of this variant in both Early and Late Classic contexts at Monte Albán. The headdress and body of the figure are so distinctive that they are easy to recognize from even the smallest of fragments. Perhaps for this reason, variant 1 wound up being the most abundant in my sample. A total of 121 fragments were collected (60 with gray paste, 47 with brown paste, and 15 with orange paste).

13 Serpent Figurines, Variant 2

These figurines are also a variant of Lady 13 Serpent, but with different attire (Figs. B29–B31). In this version, the woman has a braided headdress and the kind of overblouse referred to in Nahuatl as a *quechquemitl* (Fig. B29). Twenty-eight fragments of this type were recovered, 6 with gray paste, 6 with brown paste, and 16 with orange paste.

Martínez López and Winter (1994:58) found variant 2 in Late Classic contexts at Monte Albán, but suggest that some examples

Figure B29. Drawing of 13 Serpent, variant 2, figurines (after Caso and Bernal 1952:295)

Appendix B

Figure B30.
Fragments of 13 Serpent figurines, variant 2.

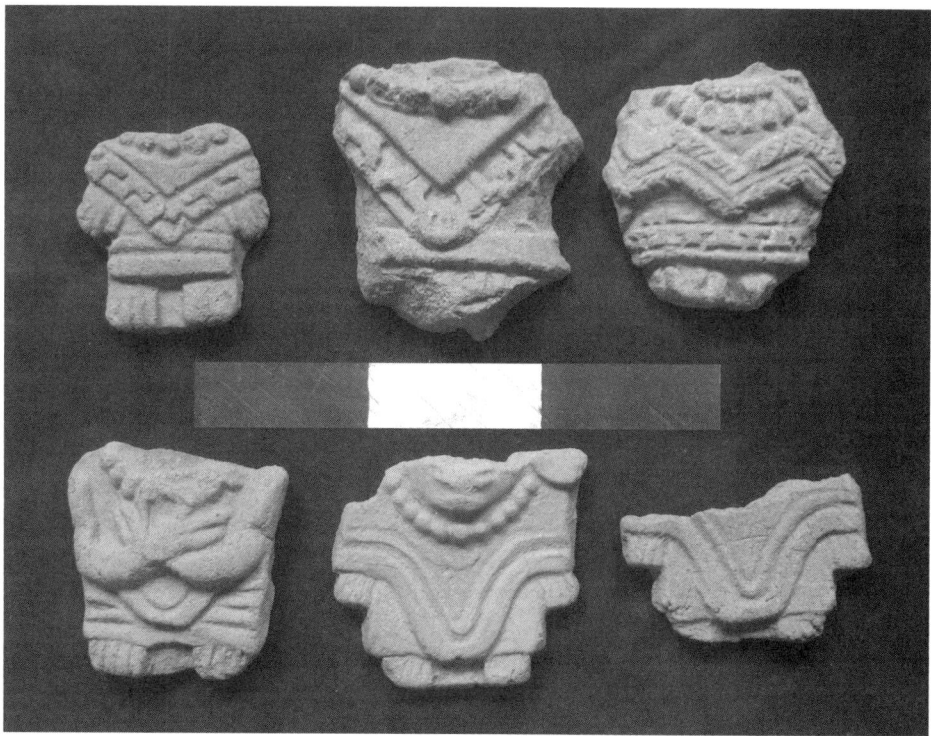

Figure B31.
Body fragments of 13 Serpent, variant 2.
top row, Late Classic; *bottom row*,
possible Early Postclassic examples.

may last into the Early Postclassic, based on specimens found at Yagul (Bernal and Gamio 1974). Fragments of variant 2 figurines from Terrace S19 at Cerro Danush resemble those depicted by Caso and Bernal (1952) and Martínez López and Winter (1994) as a Late Classic diagnostic (Fig. B31, *top row*). I also found fragments of figurines wearing a similar quechquemitl, but made with the same brown paste used for Early Postclassic sahumadores. These brown paste examples tended to be thinner and flatter, and their overblouses had a different design from most variant 2 examples (Fig. B31, *bottom row*). A larger sample might show the brown paste examples to be a later version of Lady 13 Serpent.

Late Classic Whistles (Silbatos)

I recovered 406 fragments of globular whistles, similar to the silbatos identified by Caso and Bernal (1952:167–69, 308–9) and Martínez López and Winter (1994:68–89). These date to both the Early and Late Classic. Silbatos are mold-made and typically consist of flat images of human heads with elaborate headdresses, attached at the neck to globular, birdlike bodies with wings and tails (Figs. B32–B35). Although the majority of the Cerro Danush specimens (322 fragments) consisted only of faces, necks, wings, and tail tips (Fig. B32), it was nevertheless possible to identify three variants.

The first variant depicts a young male with a headdress featuring the eyes and open jaw of a serpent (Figs. B33, B34). The second variant (Fig. B35) also depicts a young male, but with a different type of headdress. The third variant features the face of an older male (Fig. B32, *top left*); unfortunately, only 2 examples of this variant were found, and neither included a headdress. All three variants of whistle that I recovered (along with several that I did not) were found in Early and Late Classic deposits at Monte Albán (Caso and Bernal 1952; Martínez López and Winter 1994:68–93).

A recent acoustic analysis of complete whistles like these, found in tombs at Monte Albán, has shown that they emit sounds similar to the cry of an owl (Sánchez Santiago 2005). Because owls were considered to be messengers between the living and the dead in ancient Mesoamerica, Sánchez Santiago suggests that they may have been used in rituals involving the ancestors.

Mazapan-type Figurines/Whistles

During the excavation of Terrace S19, I found 23 mold-made figurines that appeared to have the same type of café paste as the Early Postclassic solid-handled sahumadores. Some depicted women wearing quechquemitls (Fig. B31, *bottom row*), while others depicted men carrying scepters in their right hands and (sometimes) wearing feathered capes (Figs. B36, B37). I recovered no items of this type during surface collection. Neither Caso and Bernal (1952) nor Martínez López and Winter (1994) recovered male figurines like these while excavating at Monte Albán. Bernal and Gamio (1974:78–81), however, do describe figurines like these in their collection from Yagul, a site to the east of Macuilxóchitl, which was occupied in both the Late Classic and Early Postclassic.

Scott (1993) has called attention to the similarity between figurines of this type from nearby Lambityeco, and Early Postclassic Mazapan-type figurines from Teotihuacan in the Basin of Mexico. Several examples in Scott's sample—as well as in Bernal and Gamio's (1974:78) sample from Yagul—feature small bulbous attachments on the back of the legs, with circular holes and a lip. Most male figurines of this type recovered from Terrace S19 at Cerro Danush also feature bulbous attachments, or the broken remnants of them (Figs. B36, B37). Significantly, none of the female figurines show any evidence for such attachments. Bernal and Gamio (1974:78) suggested that the bulbs on the male figurines served as whistles, and intact examples from Cerro Danush did produce loud, high-pitched whistle sounds when I tested them in the lab.

Feinman and Nicholas (2011) have found similar figurines in their excavations at El Palmillo and the Mitla Fortress. Like Martínez López and Winter (1974), they suggest that this type of figurine may have originated toward the end of the Late Classic, and continued in use into the Early Postclassic. Based on my observations and those of the other scholars mentioned above, I also conclude that these figurines may be Terminal Classic–Early Postclassic variants of the Late Classic figurines (and whistles) described above.

Solid Figurines

I recovered 301 fragments (212 with brown paste, 89 with gray paste) of zoomorphic, handmade solid figurines (Fig. B38). Most appear to represent roughly formed four-legged animals such as dogs or deer, although a few appear to be birds, lizards, or toads. Similar zoomorphic figurines have been found at Monte Albán (Martínez López and Winter 1994) and Yagul (Bernal and Gamio 1974). The four-legged ones are typical of (but not restricted to) Monte Albán IIIa, and my specimens from Cerro Danush were likely Late Classic survivals.

Funerary Urns (Urnas)

A total of 419 fragments of effigy urns were recovered at Cerro Danush, 235 from the surface and 184 from Terrace S19. Such urns typically consist of seated human figures attached to a cylindrical vessel. Present as early as Monte Albán II, they reached their peak in Monte Albán III–IV. The full range of these urns, which were often included in royal or noble tombs, can be glimpsed in *Urnas de Oaxaca* (Caso and Bernal 1952) or the catalogue by Frank Boos (1966). My evidence for urn use consisted mainly of small diagnostic fragments such as ear spools, feet, hair, and headdresses (Fig. B39).

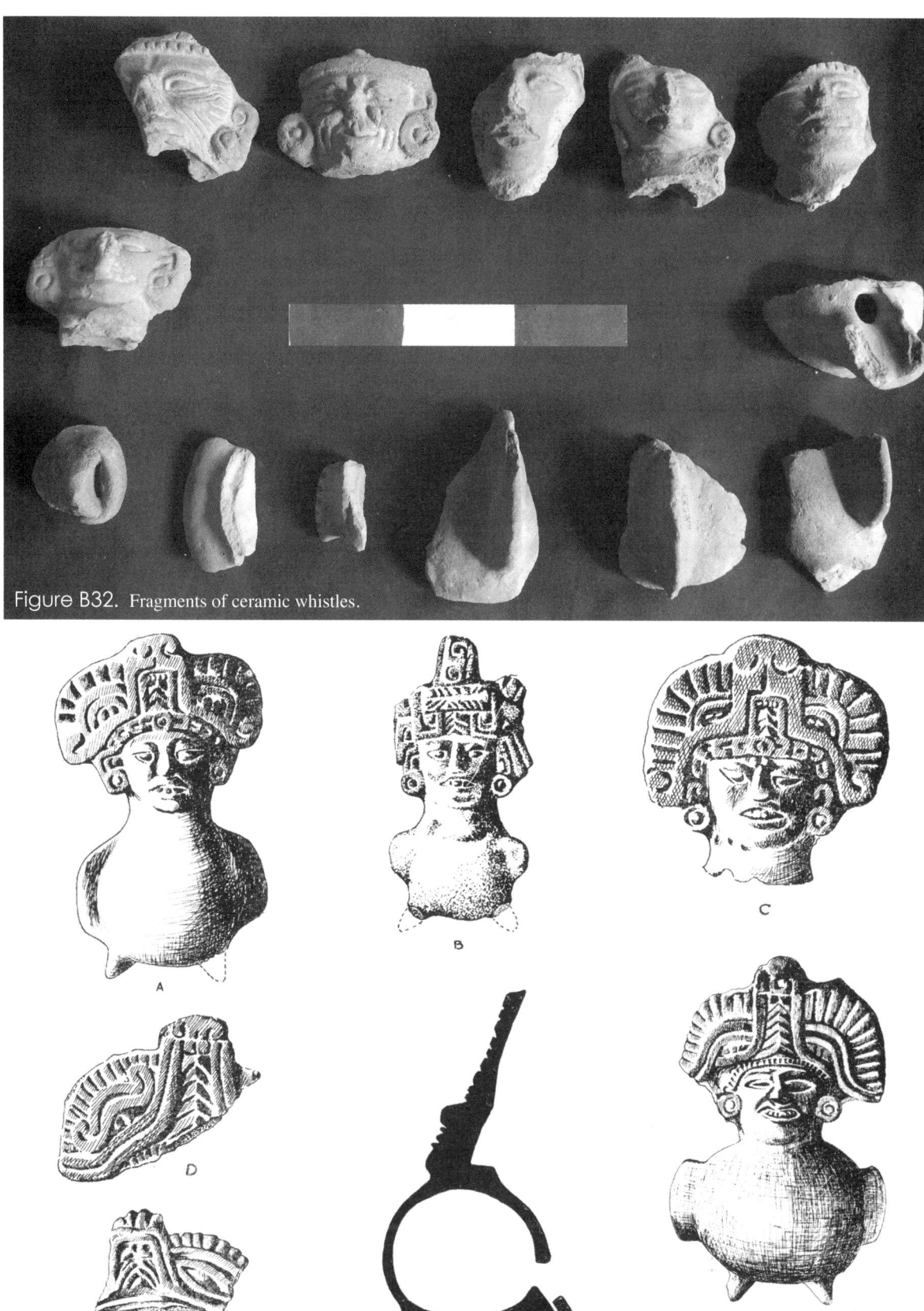

Figure B32. Fragments of ceramic whistles.

Figure B33. Whistles with jaw-of-serpent headdresses (after Caso and Bernal 1952:168).

Figure B34. Fragments of whistles with jaw-of-serpent headdresses.

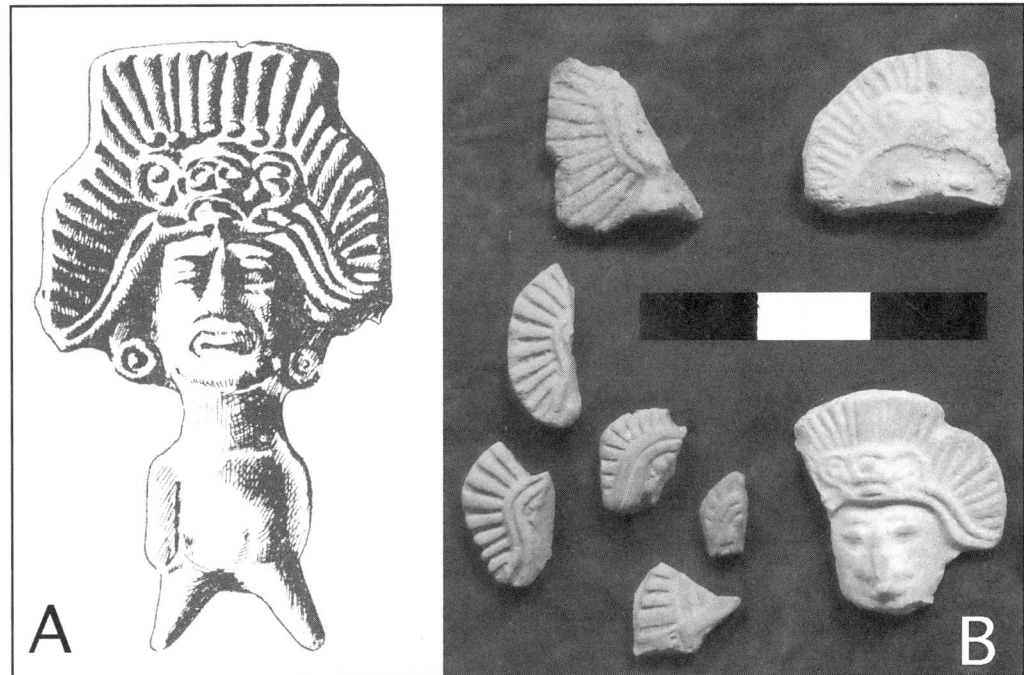

Figure B35. Whistle variant 2. *a*, drawing (after Caso and Bernal 1952:309); *b*, fragments from Terrace S19 ceramic assemblage.

Appendix B

Figure B36. Male figurines with whistle attachments.

Figure B37. Close-up of Mazapan-type figurines/whistles.

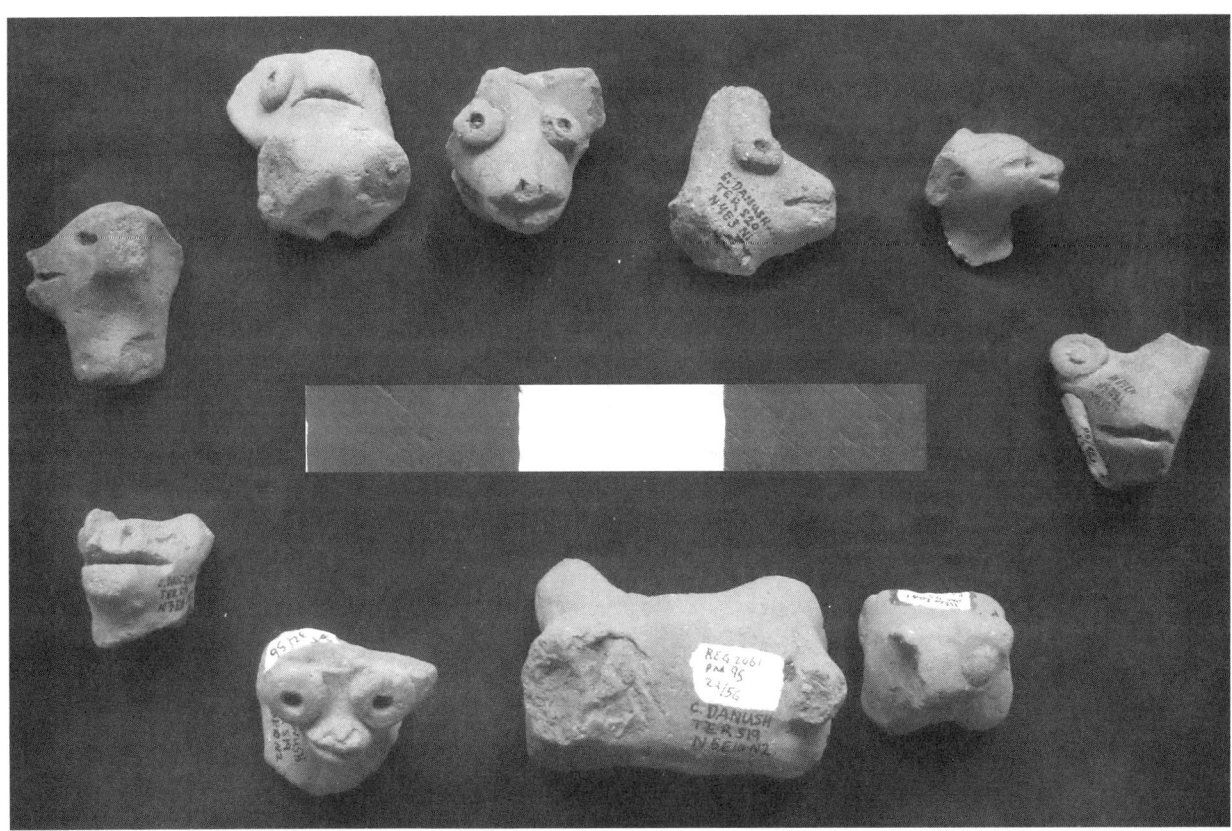

Figure B38. Fragments of solid zoomorphic figurines.

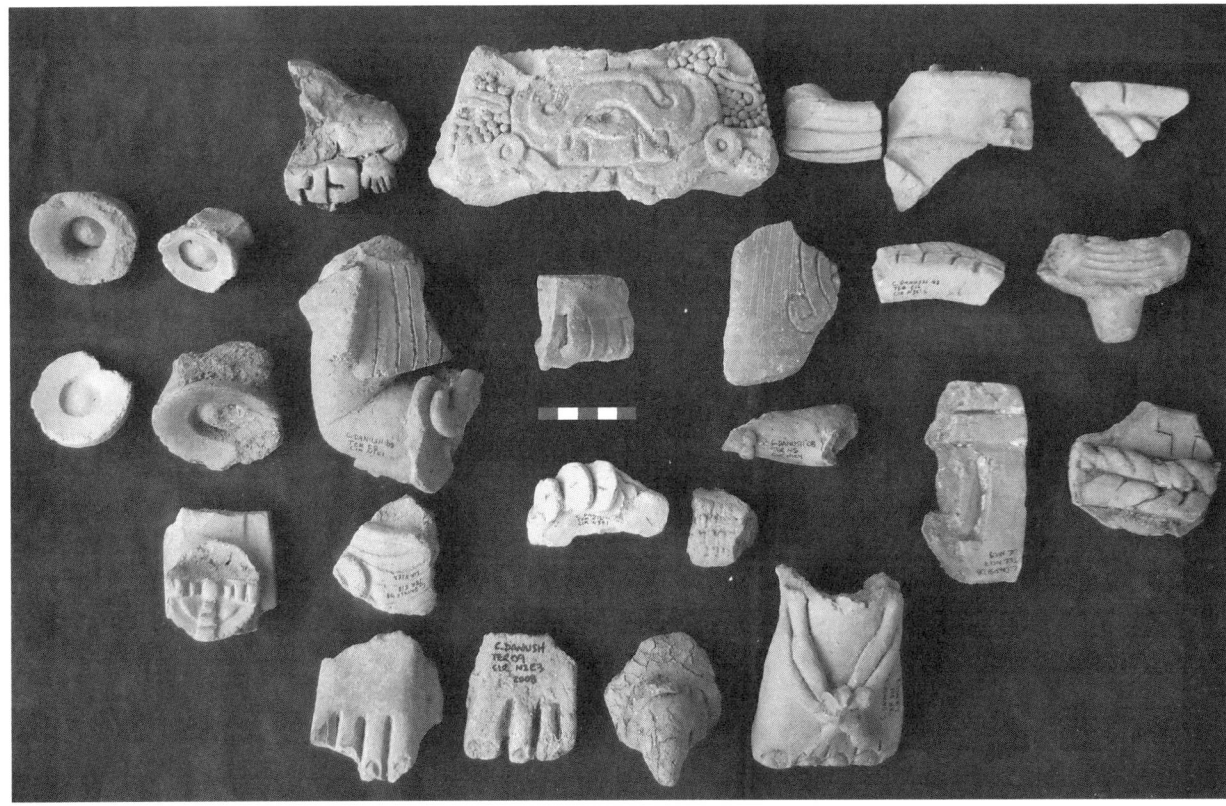

Figure B39. Fragments from effigy urns.

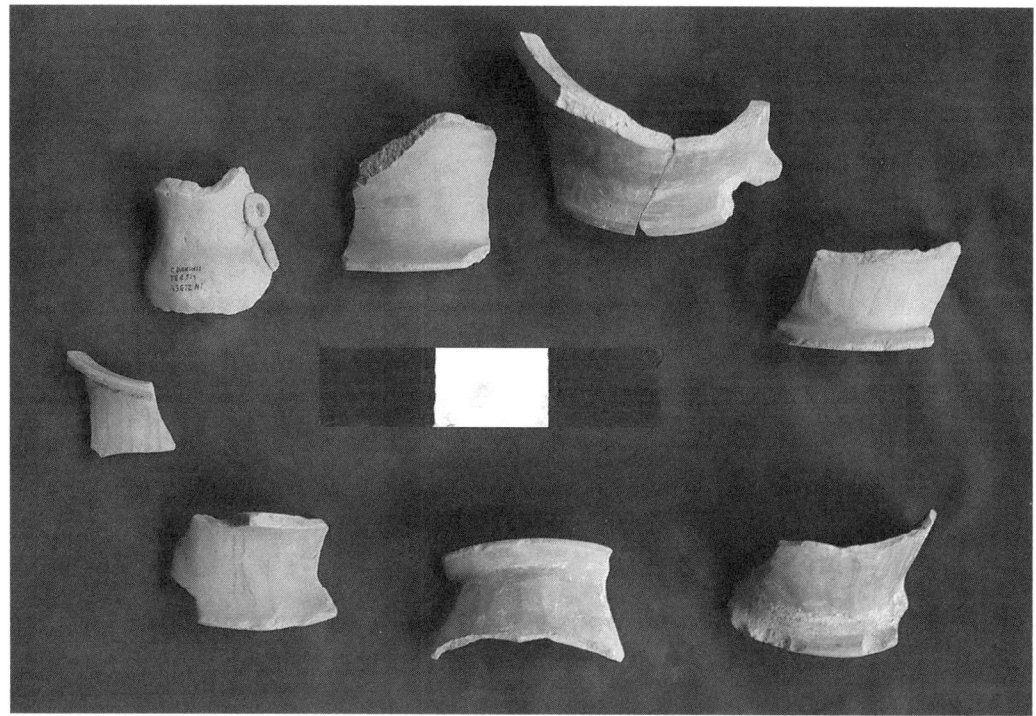

Figure B40. Fragments from botellones.

Bottles (Botellones or Floreros)

These vessels have long thin necks, flaring rims, and small globular bodies, making them look somewhat like flower vases. Only 59 fragments of these vessels were recovered, 35 from the surface collection and 24 from the excavation of Terrace S19. These vessels date to the Early and Late Classic, and are often found as offerings in high-status tombs. Diagnostic fragments from Cerro Danush consisted mainly of rim and neck fragments (Fig. B40). One example featured an attached appliqué motif of a hill glyph, like the jars depicted in Figure B16.

Comales

Comales are large flat ceramic griddles that first appeared in Monte Albán I and are still used today (see Chapter 6) for cooking tortillas. Fragments of these vessels are relatively easy to identify because comales are circular and flat, the rim is slightly upturned, and the bottom usually has a rough surface (Fig. B41). A total of 344 fragments were found (216 on Terrace S19 alone). The majority (258) were made of brown paste, which was also true of Martínez López et al.'s (2000:198) sample of comales from Late Classic levels at Monte Albán.

Grater Bowls (Chilmoleras)

I recovered 270 fragments of shallow bowls, deeply incised on the interior to facilitate grinding (Fig. B42). Grater bowls have a long history in highland Mexico, and their Spanish name—chilmolera—comes from the fact that they are often used to grind chiles (chile + moler) during the preparation of sauces. Their presence should be evidence for food preparation.

Large Conical Vessels (Apaxtles)

These vessels have a long history in Mexico. They are similar in form to conical bowls, but are much larger and thicker, usually having a rim diameter of over 40 cm (Fig. B43). Martínez López et al. (2000:167) have also identified these vessels in Late Classic deposits. I recovered a total of 198 fragments of this type of vessel during surface collection, and another 82 during the excavation of Terrace S19.

Tlecuiles

Tlecuiles are thick-walled (2–4 cm), shallow vessels (Fig. B44) that have been found embedded in the floors of Formative and Classic houses and temples (Martínez López et al. 2000:163).

Figure B41. Interior (*top*) and exterior (*bottom*) fragments of comales.

Appendix B

Figure B42. Chilmolera fragments.

Figure B43. Apaxtle fragments.

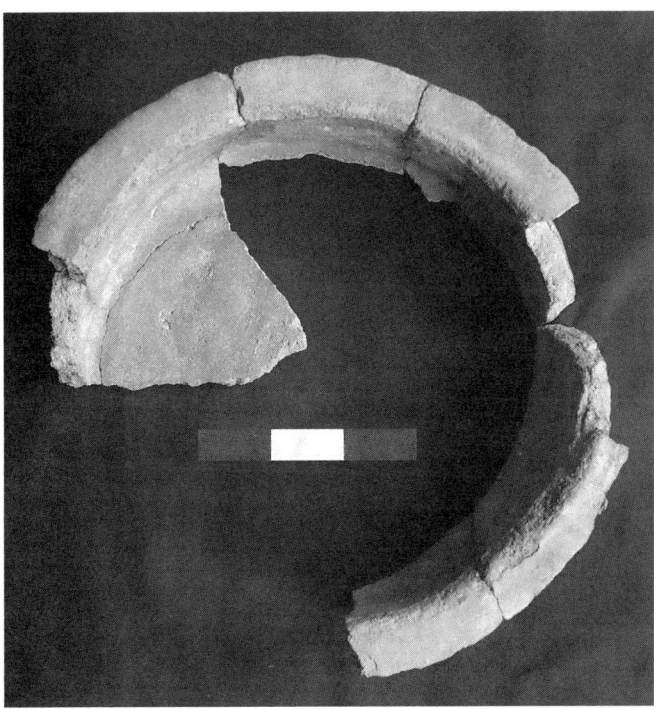

Figure B44. Tlecuil recovered from Terrace S19.

Their name is borrowed from Nahuatl, where it refers to a fire basin built into a stucco floor. Such a loan word implies that ceramic tlecuiles were used in the same manner as the fire basins with the same name.

I recovered a total of 25 fragments of these vessels. One example, from Layer 3 of Terrace S19, was large enough to allow the reconstruction of its size and shape (Fig. B44). Most of the fragments found during the project showed no signs of burning, such as soot stains or ash, in spite of the fact that their borrowed name implies burning. Interestingly enough, this is true even of the non-ceramic tlecuiles in Zapotec temples, some of which seem to have been built-in basins for water rather than fire.

Braziers (Braseros/Incensarios)

I found 79 fragments of cylindrical vessels with appliqué braid or cord decorations (Fig. B45, *top*) or hemispherical bowls with appliqué spines (Fig. B45, *bottom*). Some 34 were from excavation, and 45 were from the surface. Similar braziers were recovered by Martínez López et al. (2000) and Caso, Bernal, and Acosta (1967) from Late Classic deposits. It is generally believed that these vessels held incense and were used during rituals.

Miniature Vessels

Seventy-six fragments of brown paste miniature vessels were found during the excavation phase of the project, many of them intact or nearly intact (Fig. B46). Two types of miniatures were identified: (1) simple plates (Fig. B46, *top*) and (2) "claw vessels," that is, cups shaped like a bat's foot, complete with claws (Fig. B46, *bottom*). The Cerro Danush miniatures are similar to those that Markens and his colleagues (Markens, Winter, and Martínez López 2008; Winter et al. 2007) found in Early Postclassic offerings at Dainzú-Macuilxóchitl and Monte Albán. "Claw vessels" were widely used during Monte Albán IIIb–IV as well, and have been found in levels of that age even at caves like Guilá Naquitz (Kent Flannery, pers. comm., 2012).

Plates

I found 23 fragments of shallow bowls or plates during excavation (Figs. B47, B48). All were made from brown or gray pastes similar to those used for Late Classic G35 or K14 bowls. Unlike the latter vessels, however, the exterior bases of these plates were rounded. Caso, Bernal, and Acosta (1967:395) identified 4 vessels they characterized as plates, based on their shallow depth compared to their rim diameter. One of these (Caso, Bernal, and Acosta 1967:395, Fig. 323a) matched the plate depicted in Figure B48 exactly. The Caso et al. (1967) samples were recovered from tombs.

Ceramic Disks/Spindle Whorls

I recovered 79 ceramic disks with central perforations (21 from surface collection, 58 from excavation) (Fig. B49). Most were small, with an outside diameter between 3.5 and 5 cm, and a diameter for the perforation between 0.4 and 0.5 cm. I also recovered 3 fragments of larger disks, however, measuring between 6 and 8 cm in diameter with a perforation measuring 0.5 cm. Similar disks have been identified at many sites throughout the Valley of Oaxaca (Carpenter, Feinman, and Nicholas 2012; Feinman and Nicholas 2010; Kowalewski et al. 1989), as well as in other parts of Mesoamerica (Charlton, Charlton, and Nichols 1993); they have generally been characterized as spindle whorls, the flywheels placed on spindles while spinning yarn. Mary Parsons (1972) was the first to argue that the larger whorls were for spinning maguey fiber, while the smaller whorls were for cotton. Charlton, Charlton, and Nichols (1993) and Feinman and Nicholas (2004) concur.

Possible sherd disk spindle whorls were present in all periods in Oaxaca from Early Formative to Postclassic (Flannery and Marcus 2005; Kowalewski et al. 1989; Spencer and Redmond 2004). Flannery and Marcus (2005:77) have found sherd disks in situ serving as lids for small jars, however, so it would be premature to assign one function to all examples. The more symmetrical a perforated sherd disk is, the more likely it was used as a flywheel.

Appendix B

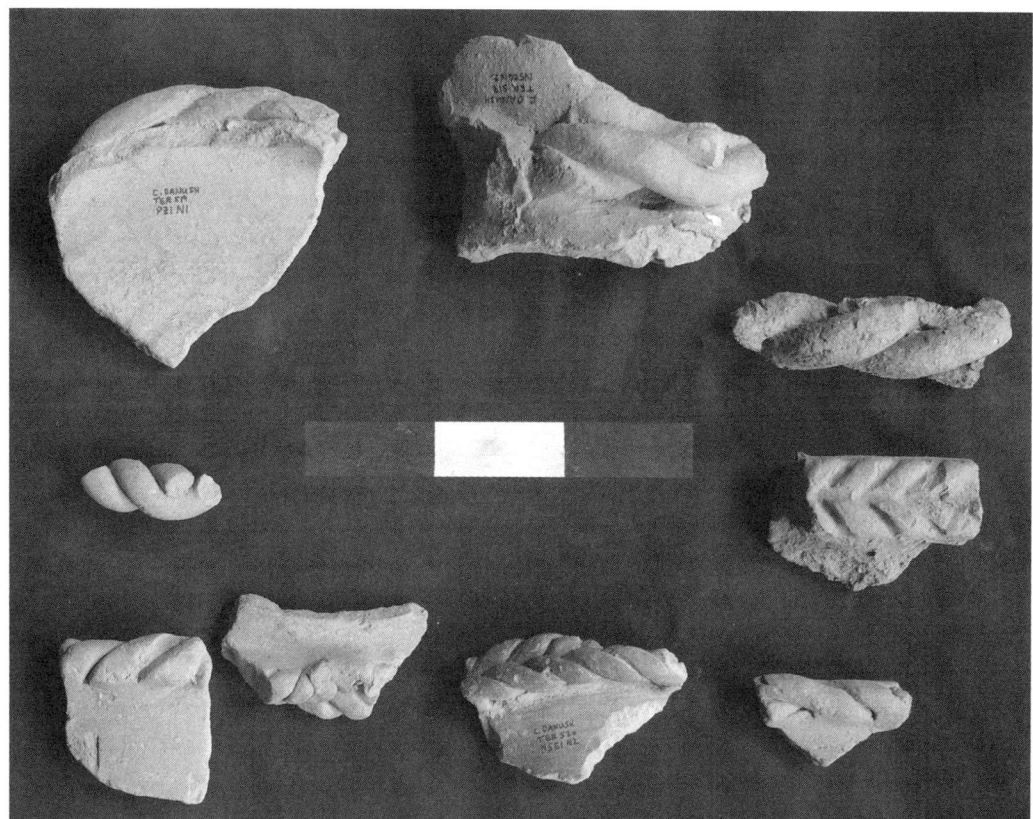

Figure B45. Fragments of cylindrical braziers with cord appliqué decoration (*top*) and hemispherical braziers with spine appliqué decoration (*bottom*).

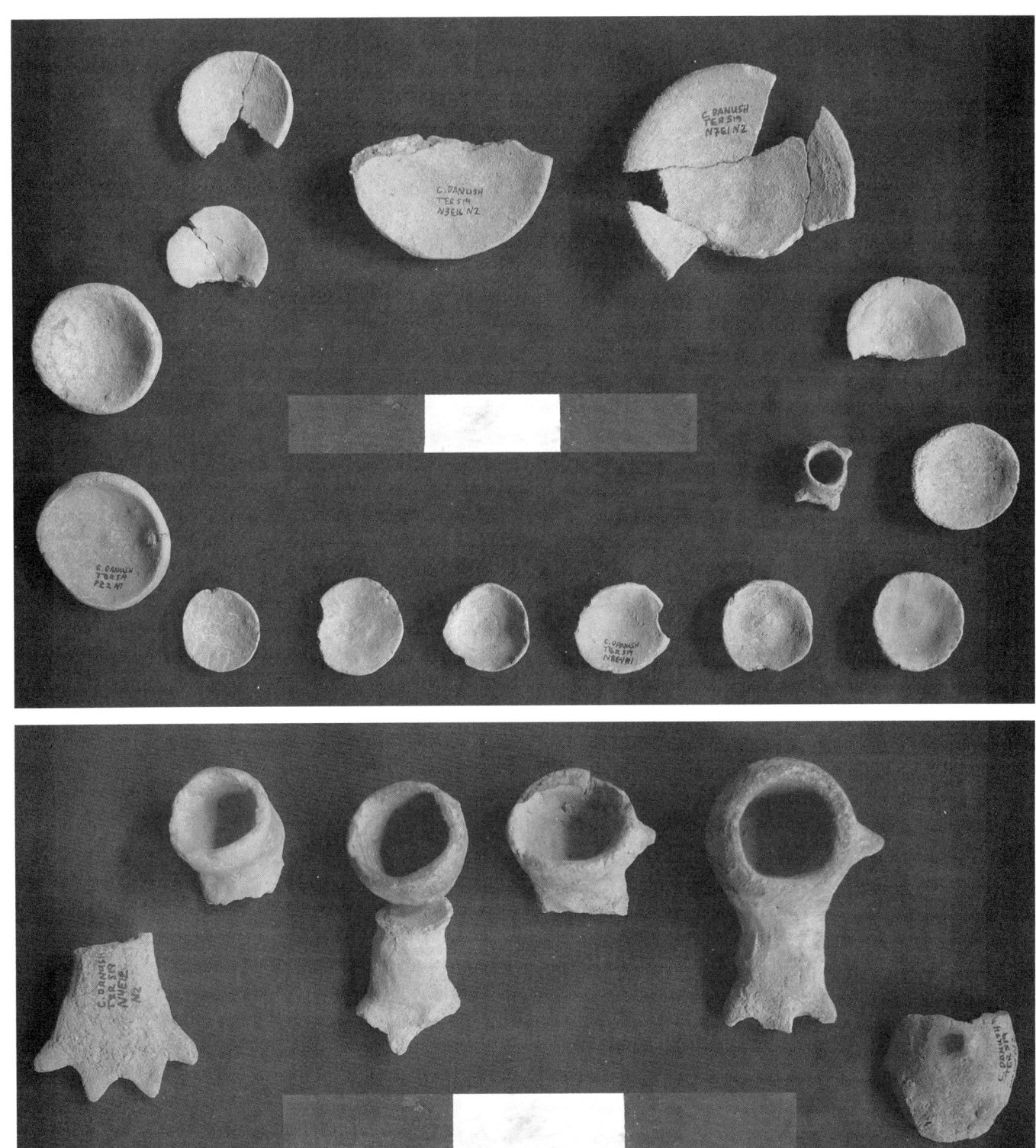

Figure B46. Miniature vessels. *top*, plates; *bottom*, claw cups.

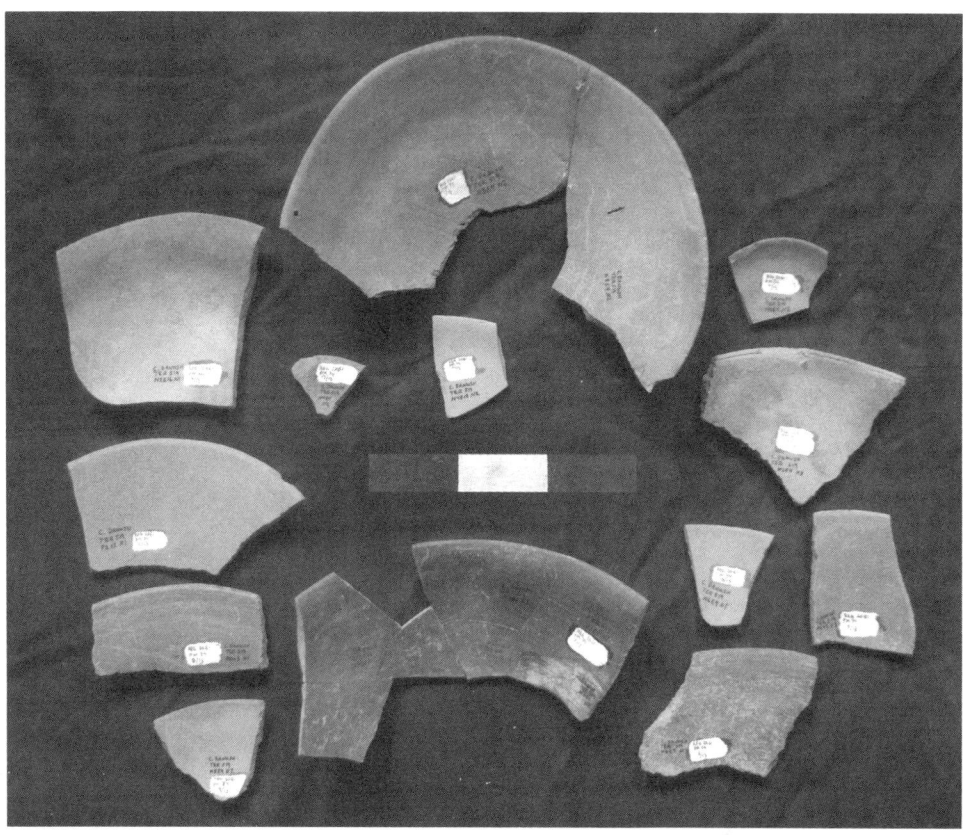

Figure B47. Fragments of shallow bowls or plates.

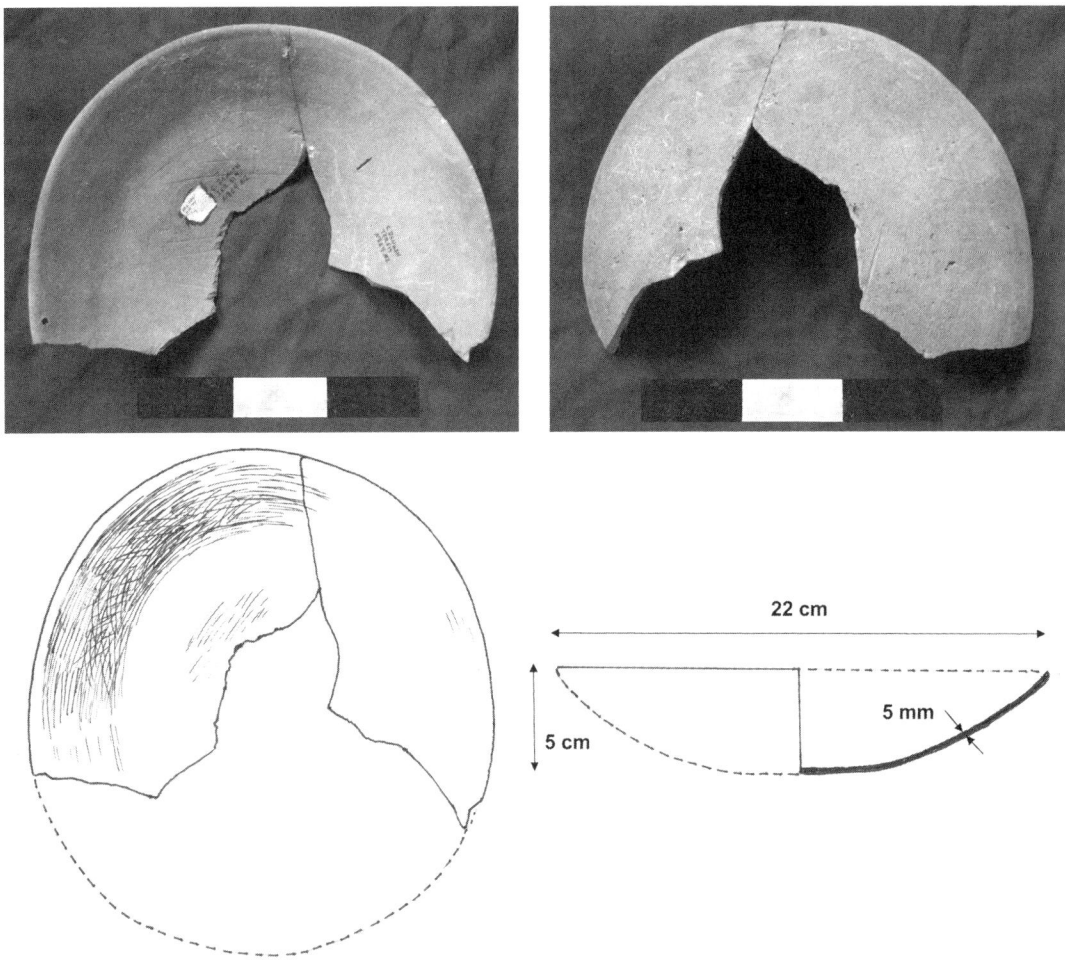

Figure B48. Fragments of shallow bowl or plate (drawing by Betty Cleeland).

Kiln Wasters

One hundred thirty-two items in the ceramic assemblage were classified as kiln wasters. Most appeared to be G35 bowl sherds with obvious bubbling or cracks (Fig. B50).

Stone Tools

Like the ceramic assemblage, stone tools were organized into categories based on form and construction material. Although there has not been a definitive valley-wide study of stone tools from the Late Classic and Early Postclassic periods, the tools from Cerro Danush and Dainzú-Macuilxóchitl match descriptions of other documented Valley of Oaxaca assemblages (e.g., Feinman, Nicholas, and Haines 2006; Haines, Feinman, and Nicholas 2004). In the case of chipped stone, source materials and chipping techniques do not seem to differ significantly from those reported for the Formative period (Parry 1987).

Ground Stone

The ground stone at Cerro Danush was made of a dense volcanic rock (probably ignimbrite) with colors varying between dark gray, gray-green, dark red, and whitish-yellow. While no source for this material has been found on Cerro Danush, Kowalewski et al. (1989) have located a possible source and manufacturing area within a few kilometers of the site. Because my sample of ground stone was so small in comparison to the chipped stone or ceramic collections, I conducted only qualitative analysis with the frequency count data set.

Most of the ground stone appeared to be fragments of tools that were broken during use and discarded. As with the ceramic assemblage, all of these materials were consistent with what one would expect for a domestic assemblage. The most abundant tools were related to domestic food processing activities; examples include manos (Fig. B51), metates (Fig. B52), tejolotes (Fig. B53), and molcajetes (Fig. B54). In addition to this, 6 axe or celt heads were

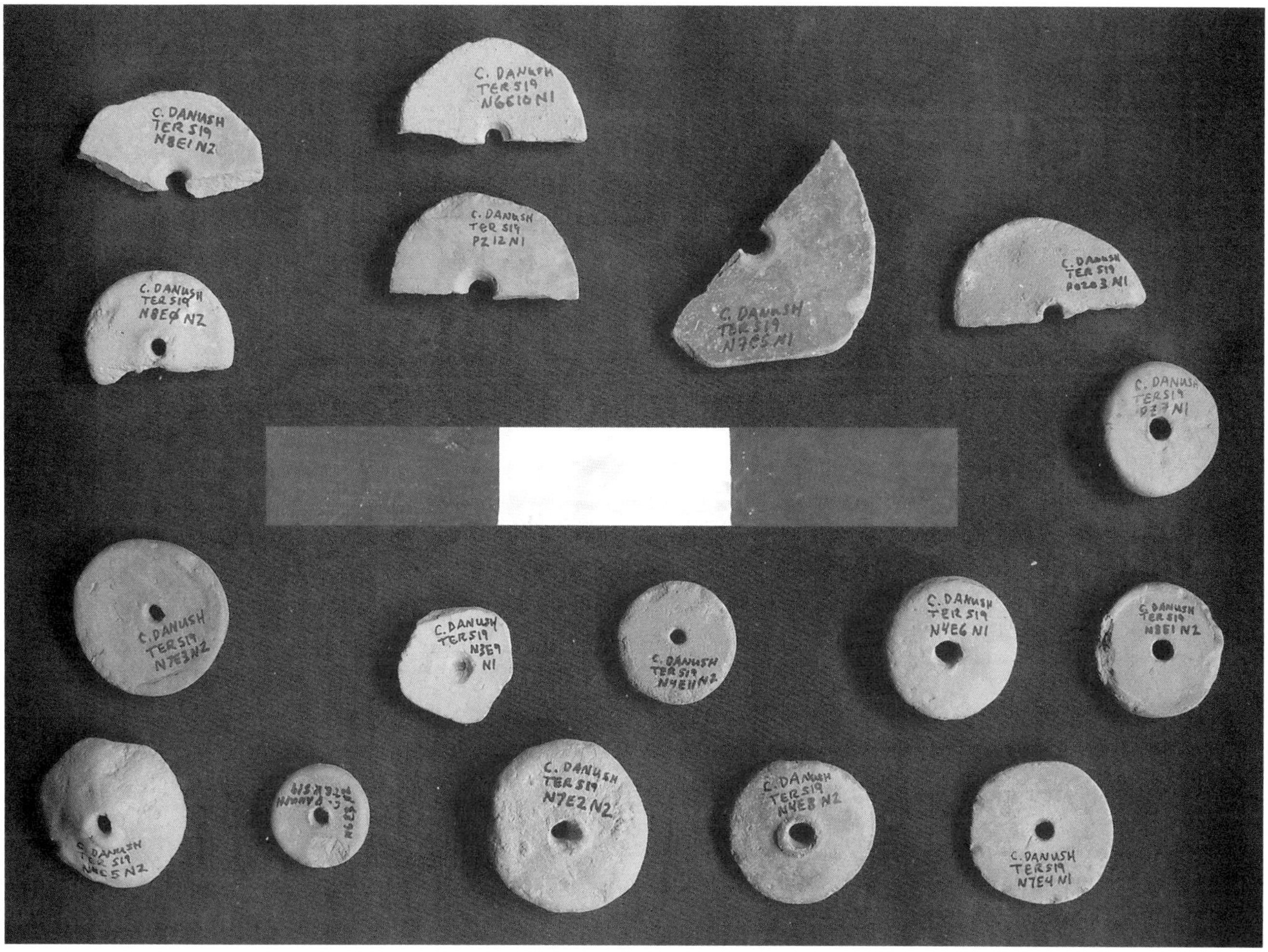

Appendix B 221

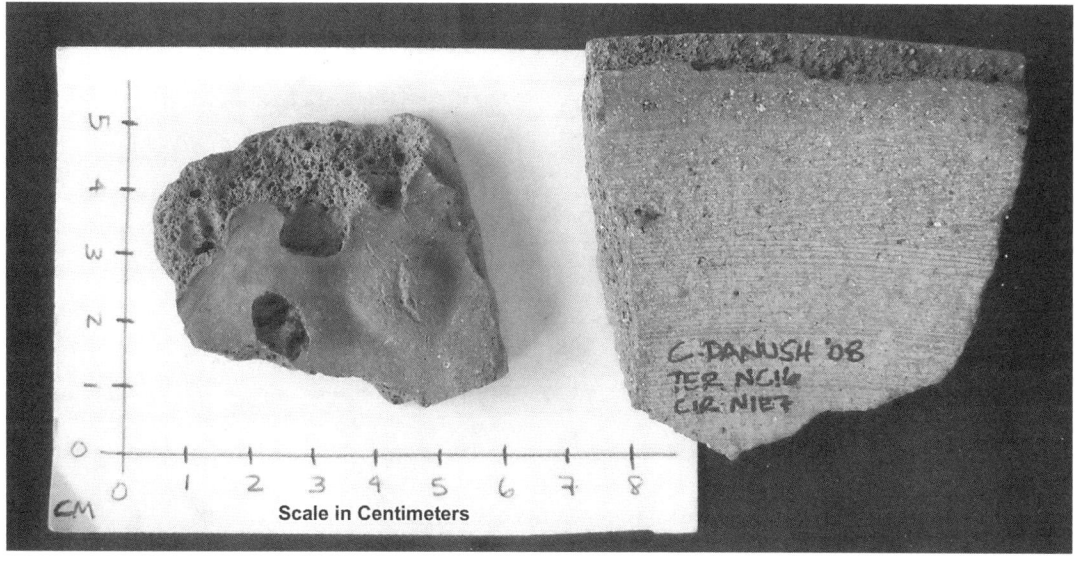

Figure B49. Perforated disks/spindle whorls.

Figure B50. Ceramic waster fragments.

Figure B51. Manos. *above*, two-handed manos; *left*, one-handed manos.

Figure B52. Metates.

Figure B53. Tejolotes.

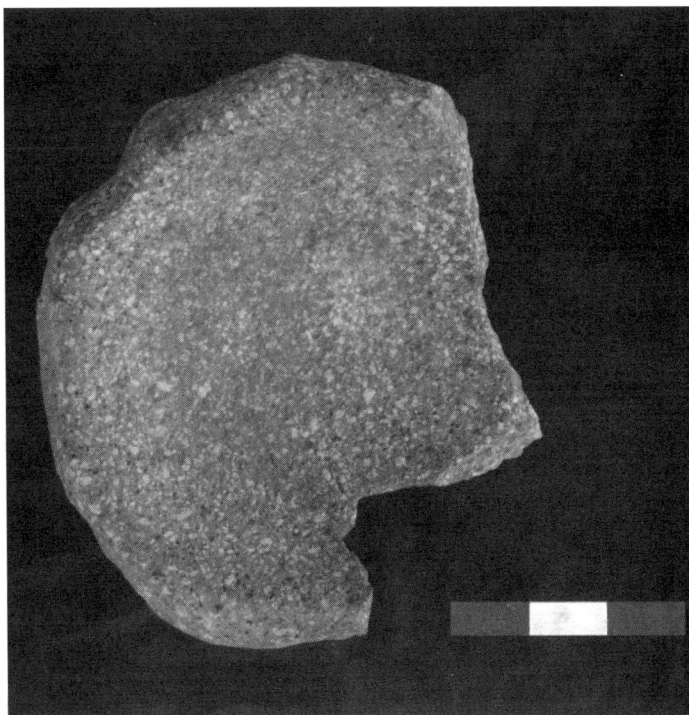

Figure B54. Molcajete.

recovered (Fig. B55). The 4 remaining ground stone items were fragments of flattened disks with holes in the center; I refer to these as ruedas (Fig. B56). Similar objects have been found in domestic contexts at Yagul (Bernal and Gamio 1974) and other sites, where they are sometimes interpreted as digging-stick weights.

Chipped Stone Tools

The raw materials for the chipped stone assemblage consisted of chert, obsidian, and silicified volcanic tuff. Chert was the most abundant, making up 936 items or 72.73% of the sample. Much of the chert was dark red, white, or a mosaic of the two, but other colors such as gray and black were present. There was also a significant amount of translucent quartzite in my sample. The variation in color and consistency found within the chert assemblage has been traced to individual sources in the Valley of Oaxaca (Whalen 1986; Haines, Feinman, and Nicholas 2004; Parry 1987). The second most abundant source material (181 pieces, or 14.06%) was a dark gray silicified volcanic tuff, which has been found at the Mitla Fortress and in arroyos in the Tlacolula-Mitla region (Whalen 1986).

Obsidian, no source of which is known in Oaxaca (Parry 1987:17), made up the remainder of the Cerro Danush sample (171 pieces, or 13.29%). It came in at least five colors—green, opaque black, cloudy gray, clear/translucent black, and clear with black striations. All these colors were present already in the Formative (Parry 1987:17–18), suggesting a long-term pattern of importing obsidian from sources in Hidalgo, the Basin of Mexico, Guanajuato, and even the Guatemala highlands.

I divided the chipped stone from Cerro Danush into 6 diagnostic categories: production debitage and debris, expedient flake tools, points, scrapers, spent cores, and prismatic obsidian blades.

Debitage

The bulk of the chipped stone—1063 pieces or 82.60% of my surface collection, and 684 pieces or 42.67% of my excavation assemblage—was classified as debitage (Fig. B57). The majority of the debitage consisted of chert (863 pieces from the surface, 552 from excavation) or silicified tuff (137 pieces from the surface, 58 from excavation). I also recovered 54 tiny flakes of obsidian from the surface and 74 from excavation. These are presumed to result from the use of obsidian, most of which arrived in the valley in the form of blades made elsewhere.

(*top, above*) Figure B55. Axes and celts.

Figure B56. Rueda.

Figure B57. Chert debitage.

Expedient Flake Tools

I classified 379 items as expedient flake tools. Some 321 of these came from the excavation of Terrace S19 (241 chert and 80 silicified tuff), and 58 were found on the surface (22 chert and 36 silicified tuff). These items all showed evidence of working, such as percussion bulbs and percussion rings, and displayed at least one edge sharpened through secondary flaking (Fig. B58). Similar items from El Palmillo have been identified as "expedient or informal tools" (Haines, Feinman, and Nicholas 2004:257). Silicified tuff was apparently deemed appropriate for expedient flake tools, but less appropriate for more formal tools; chert was more likely to be used for the latter.

Spent Cores

A total of 75 spent cores were found. There were 17 chert and 9 volcanic tuff examples from excavation, and 41 chert and 8 volcanic tuff examples from the surface collection. Most were conical or square pieces showing evidence of extensive flaking (Fig. B59).

Prismatic Obsidian Blades

Whole or fragmented obsidian blades made up 13% of the surface collection (107 pieces) and 33% of the excavation assemblage (531 pieces) (Fig. B60). All the remaining obsidian consisted of items derived from prismatic blades, or the debris left from reworking them. This suggests that obsidian was procured by the households on Cerro Danush either in the form of prismatic blades, or tools hafted with prismatic blade sections. The reworked items included a small point (Fig. B61), 3 E- and C-shaped eccentrics, which were probably nose ornaments (Fig. B62), and objects that appear to be slender perforators or awls (Fig. B63).

Figure B58. Expedient flake tools.

Figure B59. Spent cores.

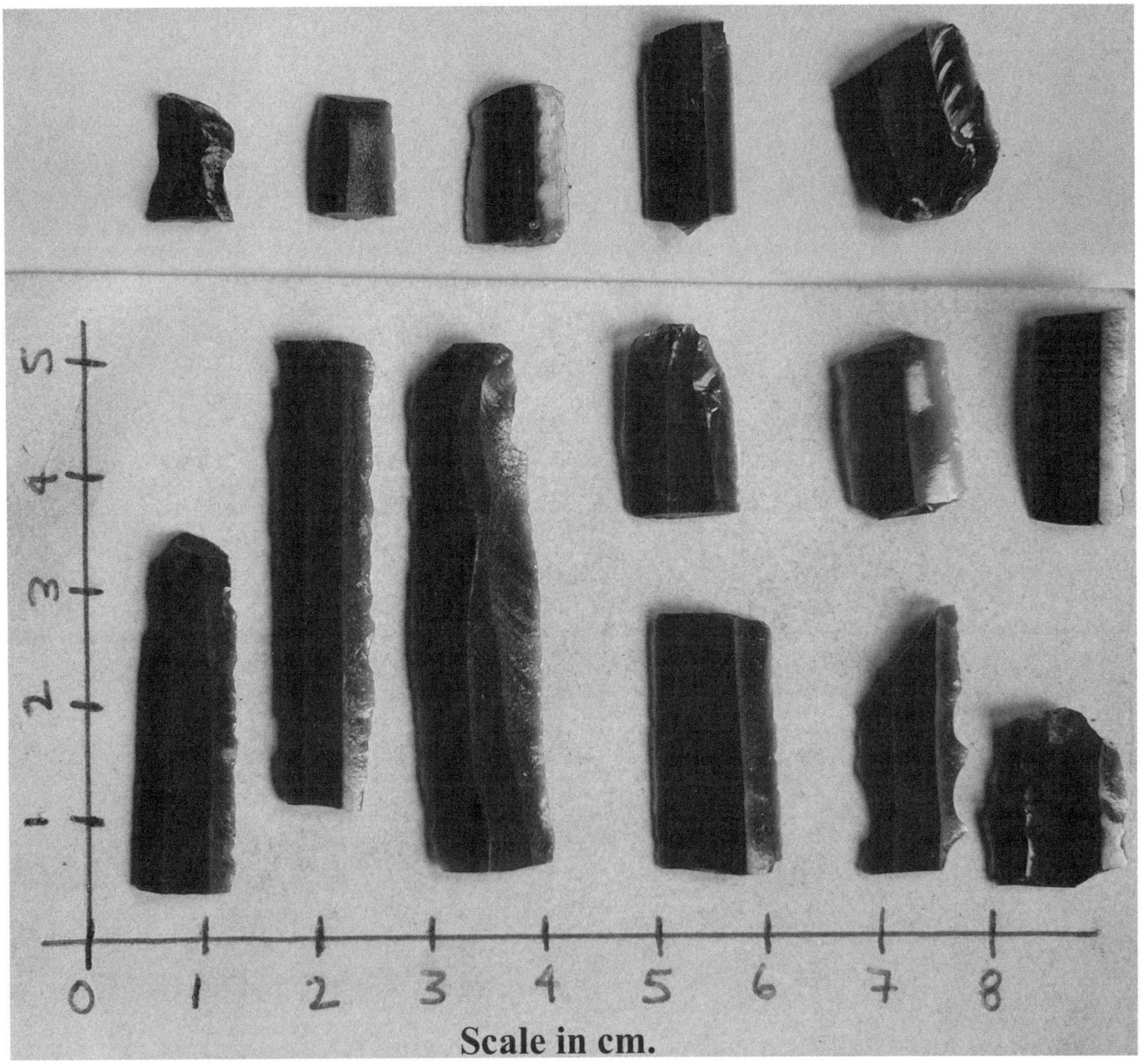

Figure B60. Prismatic blade fragments.

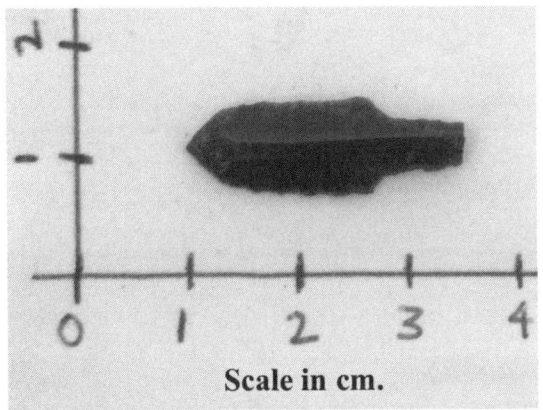

Figure B61. Small point derived from a prismatic blade.

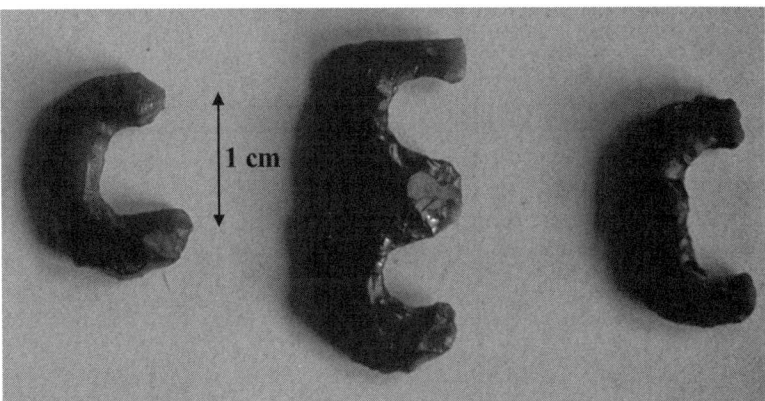

Figure B62. Obsidian eccentrics.

Chert Scrapers

These were dome-shaped scrapers with a steep working edge (Figs. B64, B65). I found 6 during surface collection, and another 4 during excavation. Haines, Feinman, and Nicholas (2004:259–60) found between 13 and 38 similar scrapers on five residential terraces at El Palmillo. They suggest that these scrapers were specialized tools for processing maguey fiber, and that households at El Palmillo were involved in producing cloth from this material. However, Williams and Heizer (1965) interpreted similar scrapers from Mitla as having been used to produce rope from maguey fiber. Whatever the case, the small number found at Cerro Danush does not suggest craft specialization.

Arrow Points

During surface survey at Cerro Danush I collected 5 points, 4 of chert, and 1 of obsidian (Fig. B61). The obsidian point was found on Terrace S18 and one of the chert points on Terrace S19, along with high concentrations of chert debitage and a couple of spent cores. The high concentration of chipped stone that I found on the surface there was one of the reasons that I chose to excavate Terraces S19 and S20. I was rewarded with abundant chipped stone during the excavation. Some 35 whole or broken points were recovered, some made from chert (Fig. B66), others from quartzite (Fig. B67), and some even from volcanic tuff (Fig. B68).

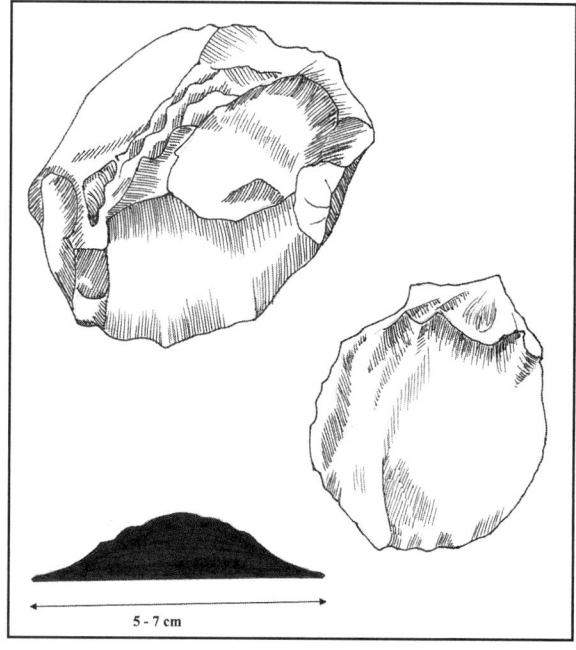

(*left*) Figure B63. Obsidian needles or awls derived from prismatic blades.

(*below left*) Figure B64. Chert raspadores.

(*below*) Figure B65. Illustration of raspador (drawing by Betty Cleeland).

Figure B66. Chert points.

Figure B67. Quartzite points.

Figure B68. Volcanic tuff points.

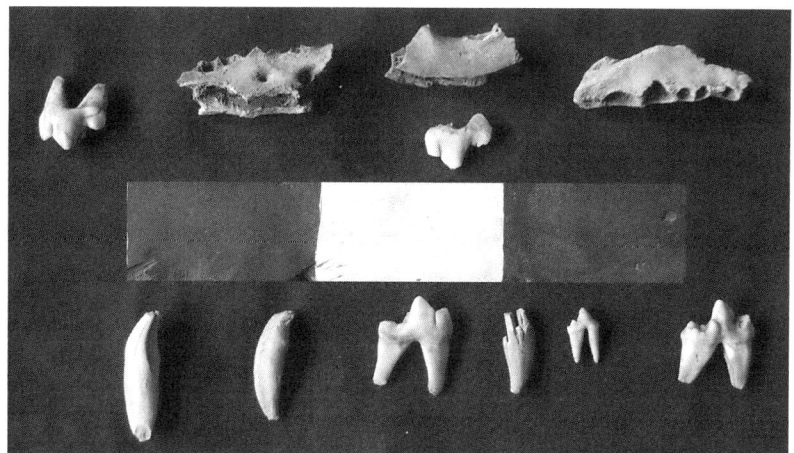

Figure B69. Fragments of dog mandibles and teeth.

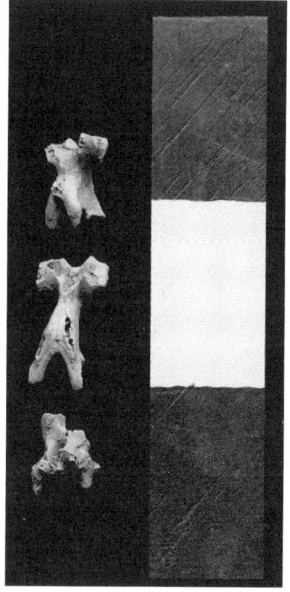

Figure B70. Fragments of turkey vertebrae.

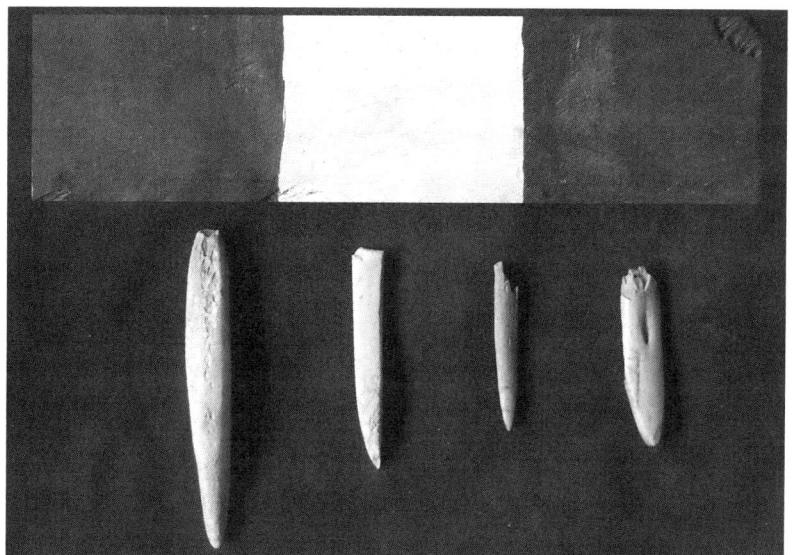

Figure B71. Bone needles or punches.

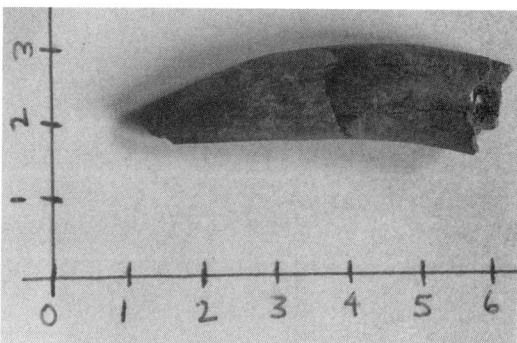

Figure B72. Charred and broken antler (possible billet).

Figure B73. Cal fragments.

Figure B74. Fragments of bajareque (daub).

Only a few of the points recovered were intact; many appear to have broken during production, or were discarded because they were poorly formed. The majority of the points we recovered were less than 5 cm long and just 1–3 cm wide, which suggests that they were probably arrow points. The quantities of debitage and spent cores, the high numbers of points, and the evidence that many were rejected for slight flaws all suggest that Terrace S19 was producing arrows or arrow points in excess of household needs.

Faunal Remains

During the excavation of Terrace S19, we recovered 373 fragments of animal bones. Most bones were so splintered or damaged that I was unable to say more than that they were not human. Of the diagnostic bones, the most notable were 22 pieces of mandibles and teeth from dogs (Fig. B69), and 5 fragments of turkey vertebrae (Fig. B70). In addition, we recovered 4 bone needles (Fig. B71) and what appears to be a broken and charred antler billet (Fig. B72).

Miscellaneous

Chalk (Cal)

During the excavation of Terrace S19, 70 fragments of lyme chalk blocks were recovered (Fig. B73). These may have been used for a variety of purposes: for example, to prepare lyme plaster for floors and walls, or for boiling dried corn kernels while preparing corn masa.

Bajareque (Daub)

Forty-eight fragments of bajareque (Fig. B74) were recovered during the excavation of Terrace S19, most of which were found alongside Structure A. The majority of these items were probably preserved because they were burned. These materials provide insight into the construction techniques for perishable structures that were probably built on top of the stone foundations that were excavated inside the house complex.

References Cited

Acosta, Jorge R., and Javier Romero
1992 *Exploraciones en Monte Negro, Oaxaca: 1937–1938, 1938–1939 y 1939–1940*. Instituto Nacional de Antropología e Historia, Mexico City.

Acuña, René
1984 [1580] *Relaciones geográficas del siglo XVI: Antequera*, tomo primero. Serie Antropológica, 54. Instituto de Investigaciones Antropológicas, Universidad Nacional Autónoma de México, Mexico City.

Adams, Robert McC.
1978 Strategies at maximization, stability, and resilience in Mesopotamian society, settlement, and agriculture. *Proceedings of the American Philosophical Society* 122(5):329–35.
1988 Contexts of civilizational collapse: A Mesopotamian view. In *The Collapse of Ancient States and Civilizations*, edited by Norman Yoffee and George L. Cowgill, pp. 20–43. University of Arizona Press, Tucson.

Allen, Mark
2008 Hillforts and cycling of Maori chiefdoms: Do good fences make good neighbors? In *Global Perspectives on the Collapse of Complex Systems*, edited by Jim A. Railey and Richard Martin Reycraft, pp. 65–82. Maxwell Museum of Anthropology, Anthropological Papers no. 8, Albuquerque, New Mexico.

Allison, Penelope M. (editor)
1999 *The Archaeology of Household Activities*. Routledge, New York.

Anderson, David G.
1994 *The Savannah River Chiefdoms: Political Change in the Late Prehistoric Southeast*. University of Alabama Press, Tuscaloosa.

Andrews, Anthony P., E. Wyllys Andrews V, and Fernando Robles Castellanos
2003 The northern Maya collapse and its aftermath. *Ancient Mesoamerica* 14(1):151–56.

Baird, Ellen T.
1989 Stars and war at Cacaxtla. In *Mesoamerica after the Decline of Teotihuacan A.D. 700–900*, edited by Richard A. Diehl and Janet C. Berlo, pp. 105–22. Dumbarton Oaks Research Library and Collection, Washington, D.C.

Balkansky, Andrew K.
1998 Origin and collapse of complex societies in Oaxaca (Mexico): Evaluating the era from 1965 to the present. *Journal of World Prehistory* 12(4):451–93.
2002 *The Sola Valley and the Monte Albán State: A Study of Zapotec Imperial Expansion*. Prehistory and Human Ecology of the Valley of Oaxaca, vol. 12, edited by Kent V. Flannery and Joyce Marcus. Memoirs, no. 36. Museum of Anthropology, University of Michigan, Ann Arbor.

2006 Surveys and Mesoamerican archaeology: The emerging macroregional paradigm. *Journal of Archaeological Research* 14(1):53–95.

Balkansky, Andrew K., and Michelle M. Crossier
2009 Multicrafting in preshispanic Oaxaca. In *Housework: Craft Production and Domestic Economy in Ancient Mesoamerica*, edited by Kenneth G. Hirth, pp. 58–74. Archaeological Papers of the American Anthropological Association, no. 19. Wiley Periodicals, Walden, Massachusetts.

Balkansky, Andrew K., Gary M. Feinman, and Linda M. Nicholas
1997 Pottery kilns of ancient Ejutla, Oaxaca, Mexico. *Journal of Field Archaeology* 24:139–60.

Barabas, Alicia M.
2003 Etnoterritorialidad sagrada en Oaxaca. In *Diálogos con el territorio: Simbolizaciones sobre el espacio en las culturas indígenas de México*, edited by Alicia M. Barabas, pp. 37–124. Instituto Nacional de Antropología e Historia, Mexico City.

Baudez, Claude-François
2011 Las batallas rituales en Mesoamérica: Parte 1. *Arqueología Mexicana* 112:20–29.

Berdan, Frances F.
1982 *The Aztecs of Central Mexico: An Imperial Society*. Harcourt Brace, New York.
1983 The reconstruction of ancient economies: Perspectives from archaeology and ethnohistory. In *Economic Anthropology: Topics and Theories*, edited by Sutti Ortiz, pp. 83–95. Monographs in Economic Anthropology, no. 1. Academic Press of America, Lanham, Maryland.

Berger, Martin
2011 The ballplayers of Dainzú? An alternative interpretation of the Dainzú iconography. *Mexicon* 33(2):46–51.

Bernal, Ignacio
1946 La Cerámica Preclásica de Monte Albán. Master's thesis, Escuela Nacional de Antropología e Historia, Mexico.
1965 Archaeological synthesis of Oaxaca. In *Archaeology of Southern Mesoamerica Part 2*, edited by Gordon R. Willey, pp. 788–813, *Handbook of Middle American Indians*, edited by Robert Wauchope. University of Texas Press, Austin.
1966 The Mixtecs in the archaeology of the Valley of Oaxaca. In *Ancient Oaxaca: Discoveries in Mexican Archaeology and History*, edited by John Paddock, pp. 345–66. Stanford University Press, California.
1967 Excavaciones en Dainzú. *Boletín del Instituto Nacional de Antropología e Historia* 27:7–13.
1968 The ball players of Dainzú. *Archaeology* 21(4):246–51.
1973 Stone reliefs in the Dainzu area. In *The Iconography of Middle American Sculpture*, pp. 13–23. Metropolitan Museum of Art, New York.

Bernal, Ignacio, and Lorenzo Gamio
1974 *Yagul, el palacio de los seis patios*. Serie Antropológica 16. Instituto de Investigaciones Antropológicas, Universidad Nacional Autónoma de México, Mexico City.

Bernal, Ignacio, and Arturo Oliveros
1988 *Exploraciones arqueológicas en Dainzú, Oaxaca*. Instituto Nacional de Antropología e Historia, Mexico City.

Bernal, Ignacio, and Andy Seuffert
1973 *Esculturas Asociadas del valle de Oaxaca*. Corpus Antiquitatum Americanensium no. VII. Instituto Nacional de Antropología e Historia, Mexico City.
1979 *The Ballplayers of Dainzú*. Akademische Druck-u. Verlagsanstalt, Graz, Austria.

Blanton, Richard E.
1978 *Monte Alban: Settlement Patterns at the Ancient Zapotec Capital*. Academic Press, New York.
1983 The urban decline of Monte Alban. In *The Cloud People: Divergent Evolution of the Zapotec and Mixtec Civilizations*, edited by Kent V. Flannery and Joyce Marcus, p. 186. Academic Press, New York.
1994 *Houses and Households: A Comparative Study*. Plenum Press, New York.

Blanton, Richard E., Gary M. Feinman, Stephen A. Kowalewski, and Linda M. Nicholas
1999 *Ancient Oaxaca*. Cambridge University Press, Cambridge.

Blanton, Richard E., and Stephen A. Kowalewski
1981 Monte Alban and after in the Valley of Oaxaca. In *Archaeology*, edited by Jeremy A. Sabloff, pp. 94–116, vol. 1, *Supplement to the Handbook of Middle American Indians*. University of Texas Press, Austin.

Blanton, Richard E., Gary M. Feinman, and Stephen A. Kowalewski
1984 Market system development in the prehispanic Valley of Oaxaca, Mexico. In *Trade and Exchange in Early Mesoamerica*, edited by Kenneth G. Hirth, pp. 157–78. University of New Mexico Press, Albuquerque.

Blanton, Richard E., Stephen A. Kowalewski, Gary M. Feinman, and Jill Appel
1982 *Monte Alban's Hinterland, Part I: The Prehistoric Settlement Patterns of the Central and Southern Parts of the Valley of Oaxaca, Mexico*. Prehistory and Human Ecology of the Valley of Oaxaca, vol. 7, edited by Kent V. Flannery and Richard E. Blanton. Memoirs, no. 15. Museum of Anthropology, University of Michigan, Ann Arbor.

Blanton, Richard E., Stephen A. Kowalewski, Gary M. Feinman, and Laura Finsten
1993 *Ancient Mesoamerica: A Comparison of Change in Three Regions*. Cambridge University Press, Cambridge.

Blomster, Jeffrey P. (editor)
2008 *After Monte Albán: Transformation and Negotiation in Oaxaca, Mexico*. University Press of Colorado, Boulder.

Boos, Frank H.
1966 *The Ceramic Sculptures of Ancient Oaxaca*. A. S. Barnes, South Brunswick, New Jersey.

Boone, Elizabeth H.
2000 *Stories in Red and Black: Pictorial Histories of the Aztecs and Mixtecs*. University of Texas Press, Austin.

Braswell, Geoffrey E. (editor)
2003 *The Maya and Teotihuacan: Reinterpreting Early Classic Interaction*. University of Texas Press, Austin.

Broda, Johanna
1991 The sacred landscape of the Aztec calendar festivals: Myth, nature, and society. In *Aztec Ceremonial Landscapes*, edited by David Carrasco, pp. 74–120. University Press of Colorado, Boulder.
1993 Astronomical knowledge, calendrics, and sacred geography in ancient Mesoamerica. In *Astronomies and Cultures*, edited by Clive L. N. Ruggles and Nicholas J. Saunders, pp. 253–95. University Press of Colorado, Boulder.
2001 La etnografía de la fiesta de Santa Cruz: Una perspectiva histórica. In *Cosmovisión, ritual e identidad de los pueblos indígenas de México*, edited by Johanna Broda and Félix Báez-Jorge, pp. 165–238. Instituto Nacional de Antropología e Historia, Mexico City.

Brumfiel, Elizabeth M.
1980 Specialization, market exchange, and the Aztec state: A view from Huexotla. *Current Anthropology* 21(4):459–78.

Canseco, Alonso de
1905 [1580] Relación de Tlacolula y Mitla hecha en los días 12 y 23 de agosto respectivamente. In *Papeles de Nueva España, Segunda Serie, Geografía y Estadística*, vol. 4, edited by Francisco del Paso y Troncoso, pp. 144–54. Est. Tipográfico "Sucesores de Rivadeneyra," Madrid.

Carmean, Kelly, Nicholas Dunning, and Jeff K. Kowalski
2004 High times in the hill country: A perspective from the Terminal Classic Puuc region. In *The Terminal Classic in the Maya Lowlands: Collapse, Transition, and Transformation*, edited by Arthur A. Demarest, Prudence M. Rice, and Don S. Rice, pp. 424–49. University Press of Colorado, Boulder.

Carpenter, Lacey, Gary M. Feinman, and Linda M. Nicholas
2012 Spindle whorls from El Palmillo: Economic implications. *Latin American Antiquity* 23(4):381–400.

Carrasco, Pedro
1971 Social organization of ancient Mexico. In *Archaeology of Northern Mesoamerica*, edited by G. F. Elkholm and I. Bernal, pp. 349–75, vol. 10, *Handbook of Middle American Indians*, edited by Robert Wauchope. University of Texas Press, Austin.
1978 La economía del México prehispánico. In *Economía política e ideología en el México prehispánico*, edited by Pedro Carrasco and Johanna Broda, pp. 15–76. Editorial Nueva Imagen, Mexico City.

Caso, Alfonso
1947 Calendario y escritura de las antiguas culturas de Monte Albán. In *Obras completes de Miguel Othón de Mendizábal*, vol. 1. Mexico.
2003a Las exploraciones en Mitla Temporada 1934–1935. In *Obras 2: El México Antiguo (Mixtecas y Zapotecas)*, edited by Rosa Campos de la Rosa, pp. 353–439. El Colegio Nacional, Mexico City.
2003b Las exploraciones en Monte Albán Temporada 1931–1932. In *Obras 2: El México Antiguo (Mixtecas y Zapotecas)*, edited by Rosa Campos de la Rosa, pp. 175–260. El Colegio Nacional, Mexico City.
2003c Las exploraciones en Monte Albán Temporada 1934–1935. In *Obras 2: El México Antiguo (Mixtecas y Zapotecas)*, edited by Rosa Campos de la Rosa, pp. 261–301. El Colegio Nacional, Mexico City.

Caso, Alfonso, and Ignacio Bernal
1952 *Urnas de Oaxaca*. Memorias, no. 2. Instituto Nacional de Antropología e Historia, Mexico City.
1965 Ceramics of Oaxaca. In *Archaeology of Southern Mesoamerica*, edited by Gordon R. Willey, pp. 871–95, vol. 3, pt. 2, *Handbook of Middle American Indians*, edited by Robert Wauchope. University of Texas Press, Austin.

Caso, Alfonso, Ignacio Bernal, and Jorge R. Acosta
1967 *La cerámica de Monte Albán*. Memorias, no. 13. Instituto Nacional de Antropología e Historia, Mexico City.

Casparis, Luca
2006 Early Classic Jalieza and the Monte Albán State: A Study of Political Fragmentation in the Valley of Oaxaca, Mexico. PhD dissertation, Science Department, University of Geneva, Switzerland.

Chang, K.-C.
1958 Study of the Neolithic social grouping: Examples from the New World. *American Anthropologist* 60(2):298–334.

Charlton, Cynthia O., Thomas H. Charlton, and Deborah Nichols
1993 Aztec household-based craft production: Archaeological evidence from the city-state of Otumba, Mexico. In *Pre-Hispanic Domestic Units in Western Mesoamerica*, edited by Robert S. Santley and Kenneth G. Hirth, pp. 147–72. CRC Press, Boca Raton, Florida.

Clark, John E.
1991 The beginnings of Mesoamerica: Apologia for the Soconusco Early Formative. In *The Formation of Complex Society in Southeastern Mesoamerica*, edited by William R. Fowler, pp. 13–26. CRC Press, Boca Raton, Florida.

Coe, Michael D., and Richard A. Diehl
1980 *In the Land of the Olmec*, vols. 1, 2. University of Texas Press, Austin.

Coe, Michael D., and Rex Koontz
2002 *Mexico: From the Olmecs to the Aztecs*, 5th ed. Thames and Hudson, London.

Costin, Cathy Lynne
1991 Craft specialization: Issues in defining, documenting, and explaining the organization of production. *Archaeological Method and Theory* 3:1–56.

Cowgill, George L.
1988 Onward and upward with collapse. In *The Collapse of Ancient States and Civilizations*, edited by Norman Yoffee and George L. Cowgill, pp. 244–76. University of Arizona Press, Tucson.
1997 State and society at Teotihuacan, Mexico. *Annual Review of Anthropology* 26:129–61.
2012 Concepts of collapse and regeneration in human history. In *The Oxford Handbook of Mesoamerican Archaeology*, edited by Deborah L. Nichols and Christopher A. Pool, pp. 301–8. Oxford University Press, Oxford.

Culbert, T. Patrick
1988 The collapse of Classic Maya civilization. In *The Collapse of Ancient States and Civilizations*, edited by Norman Yoffee and George L. Cowgill, pp. 69–101. University of Arizona Press, Tucson.

Culbert, T. Patrick (editor)
1973 *The Classic Maya Collapse*. University of New Mexico Press, Albuquerque.

de Córdova, Fray Juan
1987 *Vocabulario en Lengua Zapoteca*. Instituto Nacional de Antropología e Historia. Edicion Toledo, Mexico City. First published 1817.

Delcourt, Paul A., and Hazel R. Delcourt
2004 *Prehistoric Native Americans and Ecological Change*. Cambridge University Press, New York.

Demarest, Arthur A.
1992 Ideology in ancient Maya cultural evolution: The dynamics of galactic polities. In *Ideology and Pre-Columbian Civilizations*, edited by Geoffrey W. Conrad and Arthur A. Demarest, pp. 135–58. School of American Research Press, Santa Fe, New Mexico.
2004 *Ancient Maya: The Rise and Fall of a Rainforest Civilization*. Case Studies in Early Societies 3. Cambridge University Press, Cambridge.

Demarest, Arthur A., Prudence M. Rice, and Don S. Rice
2004 The Terminal Classic in the Maya Lowlands: Assessing collapses, terminations, and transformations. In *The Terminal Classic in the Maya Lowlands: Collapse, Transition, and Transformation*, edited by Arthur A. Demarest, Prudence M. Rice, and Don S. Rice, pp. 545–72. University Press of Colorado, Boulder.

Demarest, Arthur A., Prudence M. Rice, and Don S. Rice (editors)
2004 *The Terminal Classic in the Maya Lowlands: Collapse, Transition, and Transformation*. University Press of Colorado, Boulder.

Diamond, Jared
2005 *Collapse: How Societies Choose to Fail and Succeed*. Penguin Group, New York.

Diehl, Richard A.
1983 *Tula: The Toltec Capital of Ancient Mexico*. Thames and Hudson, London.

Diehl, Richard A., and Janet C. Berlo (editors)
1989 *Mesoamerica after the Decline of Teotihuacan A.D. 700–900*. Dumbarton Oaks Research Library and Collection, Washington, D.C.

Drennan, Robert D.
1976a *Fábrica San José and Middle Formative Society in the Valley of Oaxaca*. Prehistory and Human Ecology of the Valley of Oaxaca, vol. 4, edited by Kent V. Flannery. Memoirs, no. 8. Museum of Anthropology, University of Michigan, Ann Arbor.
1976b Religion and social evolution in Formative Mesoamerica. In *The Early Mesoamerican Village*, edited by Kent V. Flannery, pp. 345–68. Academic Press, New York.
1983 Radiocarbon dates for the Oaxaca region. In *The Cloud People: Divergent Evolution of Zapotec and Mixtec Civilizations*, edited by Kent V. Flannery and Joyce Marcus, pp. 363–70. Academic Press, New York.
1988 Household location and compact versus dispersed settlement in pre-Hispanic Mesoamerica. In *Household and Community in the Mesoamerican Past*, edited by Richard R. Wilk and Wendy Ashmore, pp. 273–94. University of New Mexico Press, Albuquerque.

Drews, Robert
1993 *The End of the Bronze Age: Changes in Warfare and the Catastrophe ca. 1200 B.C.* Princeton University Press, Princeton.

Durán, Diego
1971 *Book of the Gods and Rites and the Ancient Calendar*, translated and edited by Fernando Horcasitas and Doris Heyden. Civilizations of the American Indian, 102. University of Oklahoma Press, Norman.

Eisenstadt, Shmuel N.
1988 Beyond collapse. In *The Collapse of Ancient States and Civilizations*, edited by Norman Yoffee and George L. Cowgill, pp. 236–43. University of Arizona Press, Tucson.
1993 *The Political Systems of Empires*. Transaction Publishers, New Brunswick, New Jersey. First published 1963 by Free Press of Glencoe.

Elam, J. Michael
1989 Defensible and fortified sites. In *Monte Albán's Hinterland Part II: Pre-Hispanic Settlement Patterns in Tlacolula, Etla, and Ocotlan, the Valley of Oaxaca, Mexico*, edited by Stephen A. Kowalewski, Gary M. Feinman, Laura Finsten, Richard E. Blanton, and Linda M. Nicholas, pp. 385–407. Memoirs, no. 23. Museum of Anthropology, University of Michigan, Ann Arbor.

Elson, Christina M.
2007 *Excavations at Cerro Tilcajete: A Monte Albán II Administrative Center in the Valley of Oaxaca*. Prehistory and Human Ecology of the Valley of Oaxaca, vol. 14, edited by Kent V. Flannery and Joyce Marcus. Memoirs, no. 42. Museum of Anthropology, University of Michigan, Ann Arbor.
2011 Jalieza: Su transición de un centro secundario a un cacicazgo en la época Clásica Tardía. In *Monte Albán en la encrucijada regional y disciplinaria: Memoria de la Quinta Mesa Redonda de Monte Albán*, edited by Nelly M. Robles García and Angel Iván Rivera Guzmán, pp. 345–74. Instituto Nacional de Antropología e Historia, Mexico City.

Fargher, Lane F.
2004 A Diachronic Analysis of the Valley of Oaxaca Economy from the Classic through the Postclassic. PhD dissertation, Department of Anthropology, University of Wisconsin, Madison.

Faulseit, Ronald K.
2008 Cerro Danush: An Exploration of the Late Classic Transition in the Tlacolula Valley, Oaxaca. Report to the Foundation for the Advancement of Mesoamerican Studies.
2011 Community Resilience after State Collapse: The Archaeology of Late Classic/Early Postclassic Residential Terraces on Cerro Danush, Oaxaca, Mexico. PhD dissertation, Department of Anthropology, Tulane University, New Orleans, Louisiana.

2012a State collapse and household resilience in the Oaxaca Valley of Mexico. *Latin American Antiquity* 23(4):401–25.
2012b Late Classic to Early Postclassic community ritual at Dainzú-Macuilxóchitl, Oaxaca, Mexico. *Mexicon* 34(6):148–56.

Feinman, Gary M.
1999 Rethinking our assumptions: Economic specialization at the household scale in ancient Ejutla, Oaxaca, Mexico. In *Pottery and People: A Dynamic Interaction*, edited by James M. Skibo and Gary M. Feinman, pp. 81–98. University of Utah Press, Salt Lake City.
2007 The last quarter century of archaeological research in the central valleys of Oaxaca. *Mexicon* 29:3–15.

Feinman, Gary M., Sherman Banker, Reid F. Cooper, Glen B. Cook, and Linda M. Nicholas
1989 A technological perspective on changes in the ancient Oaxacan grayware ceramic tradition: Preliminary results. *Journal of Field Archaeology* 16:331–44.

Feinman, Gary M., and Linda M. Nicholas
1990 At the margins of the Monte Albán state: Settlement patterns in the Ejutla Valley, Oaxaca, Mexico. *Latin American Antiquity* 1:216–46.
1992 Pre-Hispanic interregional interaction in southern Mexico: The Valley of Oaxaca and the Ejutla Valley. In *Resources, Power, and Interregional Interaction*, edited by Edward M. Schortman and Patricia A. Urban, pp. 75–116. Plenum Press, New York.
1993 Shell-ornament production in Ejutla: Implications for highland-coastal interaction in ancient Oaxaca. *Ancient Mesoamerica* 4:103–19.
2000 High-intensity household-scale production in ancient Mesoamerica: A perspective from Ejutla, Oaxaca. In *Cultural Evolution: Contemporary Viewpoints*, edited by Gary M. Feinman and Linda Manzanilla, pp. 119–42. Kluwer Academic/Plenum Publishers, New York.
2004a *Hilltop Terrace Sites of Oaxaca, Mexico: Intensive Surface Survey at Guirún, El Palmillo, and the Mitla Fortress*. Fieldiana, Anthropology, n.s. 37. Field Museum of Natural History, Chicago.
2004b El Palmillo: Una perspectiva doméstica del period clásico en el valle de Oaxaca. *Cuadernos del Sur* 10(20):7–29.
2005 More than alluvial land and water: The late pre-Hispanic emergence of eastern Tlacolula, Oaxaca, Mexico. In *Settlement, Subsistence, and Social Complexity: Essays Honoring the Legacy of Jeffrey R. Parsons*, edited by Richard E. Blanton, pp. 229–59. Cotsen Institute of Archaeology, University of California, Los Angeles.
2007a Household production and the regional economy in ancient Oaxaca: Classic period perspectives from hilltop El Palmillo and valley-floor Ejutla. In *Pottery Economics in Mesoamerica*, edited by Christopher A. Pool and George J. Bey III, pp. 184–211. University of Arizona Press, Tucson.
2007b Craft production in Classic period Oaxaca: Implications for Monte Albán's political economy. In *Craft Production in Complex Societies: Multicraft and Producer Perspectives*, edited by Izumi Shimada, pp. 97–119. University of Utah Press, Salt Lake City.
2007c The socioeconomic organization of the Classic period Zapotec state: A bottom up perspective from El Palmillo. In *The Political Economy of Ancient Mesoamerica: Transformations during the Formative and Classic Periods*, edited by Vernon L. Scarborough and John E. Clark, pp. 135–47. University of New Mexico Press, Albuquerque

2009 Las bases socioeconómicas de la civilización zapoteca del periodo clásico: Una perspectiva desde El Palmillo. In *Bases de la complejidad social en Oaxaca: Memoria de la Cuarta Mesa Redonda de Monte Albán*, edited by Nelly M. Robles García, pp. 153–78. Instituto Nacional de Antropología e Historia, Mexico City.
2010 A multiscalar perspective on market exchange in the Classic-period Valley of Oaxaca. In *Archaeological Approaches to Market Exchange in Ancient Societies*, edited by Christopher P. Garraty and Barbara L. Stark, pp. 85–98. University Press of Colorado, Boulder.
2011 Monte Albán: Una perspectiva desde los límites del Valle de Oaxaca. In *Monte Albán en la encrucijada regional y disciplinaria: Memoria de la Quinta Mesa Redonda de Monte Albán*, edited by Nelly M. Robles García and Angel Iván Rivera Guzmán, pp. 241–84. Instituto Nacional de Antropología e Historia, Mexico City.
2012 Compact versus dispersed settlement in pre-Hispanic Mesoamerica: The role of neighborhood organization and collective action. In *The Neighborhood as a Social and Spatial Unit in Mesoamerican Cities*, edited by M. Charlotte Arnauld, Linda R. Manzanilla, and Michael E. Smith, pp. 132–58. University of Arizona Press, Tucson.

Feinman, Gary M., Linda M. Nicholas, and Helen R. Haines
2002 Houses on a hill: Classic period life at El Palmillo, Oaxaca, Mexico. *Latin American Antiquity* 13(3):251–77.
2006 Socioeconomic inequality and the consumption of chipped stone at El Palmillo, Oaxaca, Mexico. *Latin American Antiquity* 17(2):151–75.

Feinman, Gary M., Linda M. Nicholas, and Edward F. Maher
2008 Domestic offerings at El Palmillo: Implications for community organization. *Ancient Mesoamerica* 19:175–94.

Fernández Dávila, Enrique, and Susana Gómez Serafín
1993 Un conjunto habitacional del Formativo Terminal en Dainzú, Valle de Tlacolula, Oaxaca. *Cuadernos del Sur* año 2(5):5–29.

Finley, Moses I.
1973 *The Ancient Economy*. University of California Press, Berkeley.

Finsten, Laura
1983 The Classic-Postclassic Transition in the Valley of Oaxaca, Mexico: A Regional Analysis of the Process of Political Decentralization in a Prehistoric Complex Society. PhD dissertation, Department of Anthropology, Purdue University, West Lafayette, Indiana.
1995 *Jalieza, Oaxaca: Activity Specialization at a Hilltop Center*. Vanderbilt University Publications in Anthropology 48. Vanderbilt University Press, Nashville, Tennessee.

Fish, Suzanne K., and Stephen A. Kowalewski (editors)
1990 *The Archaeology of Regions: A Case for Full-Coverage Survey*. Smithsonian Institution Press, Washington, D.C.

Flannery, Kent V.
1972 The cultural evolution of civilizations. *Annual Review of Ecology and Systematics* 3:399–426.
1976 Research strategy and Formative Mesoamerica. In *The Early Mesoamerican Village*, edited by Kent V. Flannery, pp. 1–12. Academic Press, New York.
1999 Process and agency in early state formation. *Cambridge Archaeological Journal* 9(1):3–21.

Flannery, Kent V. (editor)
1976 *The Early Mesoamerican Village*. Academic Press, New York.
1986 *Guilá Naquitz: Archaic Foraging and Early Agriculture in Oaxaca, Mexico*. Academic Press, New York.

Flannery, Kent V., and Joyce Marcus
1994 Early Formative Pottery of the Valley of Oaxaca. Prehistory and Human Ecology of the Valley of Oaxaca, vol. 10, edited by Kent V. Flannery and Joyce Marcus. Memoirs, no. 27. Museum of Anthropology, University of Michigan, Ann Arbor.
2005 *Excavations at San José Mogote 1: The Household Archaeology*. Prehistory and Human Ecology of the Valley of Oaxaca, vol. 13, edited by Kent V. Flannery and Joyce Marcus. Memoirs, no. 40. Museum of Anthropology, University of Michigan, Ann Arbor.

Flannery, Kent V., and Joyce Marcus (editors)
1983 *The Cloud People: Divergent Evolution of the Zapotec and Mixtec Civilizations*. Academic Press, New York.

Flannery, Kent V., and Marcus C. Winter
1976 Analyzing household activities. In *The Early Mesoamerican Village*, edited by Kent V. Flannery, pp. 34–44. Academic Press, New York.

Franco Brizuela, María L.
1993 *La tumba zapoteca de Huijazoo en Oaxaca*. Cavallari Impresores y Editores, S.A. de C.V., Mexico City.

Garraty, Christopher P.
2010 Investigating market exchange in ancient societies: A theoretical review. In *Archaeological Approaches to Market Exchange in Ancient Societies*, edited by Christopher P. Garraty and Barbara L. Stark, pp. 3–32. University Press of Colorado, Boulder.

Gill, Richardson B.
2000 *The Great Maya Droughts: Water, Life, and Death*. University of New Mexico Press, Albuquerque.

Gill, Richardson B., Paul A. Mayeski, Johan Nyberg, Gerald H. Haug, and Larry C. Peterson
2007 Drought and the Maya collapse. *Ancient Mesoamerica* 18:283–302.

Gonlin, Nancy, and Jon C. Lohse (editors)
2007 *Commoner Ritual and Ideology in Ancient Mesoamerica*. University Press of Colorado, Boulder.

González Licón, Ernesto
2003 Social Inequality at Monte Albán Oaxaca: Household Analysis from the Terminal Formative to Early Classic. PhD dissertation, Department of Anthropology, University of Pittsburgh, Pennsylvania.
2009 Ritual and social stratification at Monte Albán, Oaxaca: Strategies from a household perspective. In *Domestic Life in Prehispanic Capitals: A Study of Specialization, Hierarchy, and Ethnicity*, edited by Linda Manzanilla and Claude Chapdelaine, pp. 7–20. Memoirs, no. 46. Museum of Anthropology, University of Michigan, Ann Arbor.

Gunderson, Lance H., and C. S. Holling (editors)
2002 *Panarchy: Understanding Transformations in Human and Natural Systems*. Island Press, Washington, D.C.

Haines, Helen R., Gary M. Feinman, and Linda M. Nicholas
2004 Household economic specialization and social differentiation: The stone tool assemblage at El Palmillo, Oaxaca. *Ancient Mesoamerica* 15(2):251–66.

Haug, Gerald H., Detlef Günther, Larry C. Peterson, Daniel M. Sigman, and Konrad A. Hughen
2003 Climate and the collapse of Maya civilization. *Science* 299:1731–35.

Healan, Dan M.
1972 *Surface Delineation of Functional Areas at a Mississippian Ceremonial Center*. Missouri Archaeological Society, Columbia, Missouri.
1989 *Tula of the Toltecs: Excavations and Survey*. University of Iowa Press, Iowa City.
1993 Urbanism at Tula from the perspective of residential archaeology. In *Pre-Hispanic Domestic Units in Western Mesoamerica: Studies of Household, Compound, and Residence*, edited by Robert S. Santley and Kenneth G. Hirth, pp. 105–20. CRC Press, Boca Raton, Florida.

Hegmon, Michelle, Margaret C. Nelson, and Susan M. Ruth
1998 Abandonment and reorganization in the Mimbres region of the American Southwest. *American Anthropologist* n.s. 100(1):148–62.

Hendon, Julia A.
2010 *Houses on a Landscape: Memory and Everyday Life in Mesoamerica*. Duke University Press, Durham, North Carolina.

Hernández, Pedro
1984 *Anecdotas narradas por el Señor Pedro Hernández*. Instituto Lingüístico de Verano (Summer Institute of Linguistics), Mexico City.

Hester, Thomas R., and Robert F. Heizer
1972 Problems in the functional interpretation of artifacts: Scraper planes from Mitla and Yagul, Oaxaca. *Contributions of the University of California Archaeological Research Facility* 14:107–23.

Hirth, Kenneth G.
1989 Militarism and social organization at Xochicalco, Morelos. In *Mesoamerica after the Decline of Teotihuacan A.D. 700–900*, edited by Richard A. Diehl and Janet C. Berlo, pp. 69–81. Dumbarton Oaks Research Library and Collection, Washington, D.C.
1998 The distributional approach: A new way to identify marketplace exchange in the archaeological record. *Current Anthropology* 39(4):451–76.
2000a *Archaeological Research at Xochicalco*, vol. 1, *Ancient Urbanism at Xochicalco: The Evolution and Organization of a Pre-Hispanic Society*. University of Utah Press, Salt Lake City.
2000b *Archaeological Research at Xochicalco*, vol. 2, *The Xochicalco Mapping Project*. University of Utah Press, Salt Lake City.

2009a Craft production, household diversification, and domestic economy in prehispanic Mesoamerica. In *Housework: Craft Production and Domestic Economy in Ancient Mesoamerica*, edited by Kenneth Hirth, pp. 2–32. Archaeological Papers of the American Anthropological Association, no. 19. Wiley Periodicals, Walden, Massachusetts.

2009b Household, workshop, guild, and barrio: The organization of obsidian craft production in a prehispanic urban center. In *Domestic Life in Prehispanic Capitals: A Study of Specialization, Hierarchy, and Ethnicity*, edited by Linda Manzanilla and Claude Chapdelaine, pp. 43–66. Memoirs, no. 46. Museum of Anthropology, University of Michigan, Ann Arbor.

Hirth, Kenneth G. (editor)
2009 *Housework: Craft Production and Domestic Economy in Ancient Mesoamerica*. Archaeological Papers of the American Anthropological Association, no. 19. Wiley Periodicals, Walden, Massachusetts.

Hodell, David A., Jason H. Curtis, and Mark Brenner
1995 Possible role of climate in the collapse of Classic Maya civilization. *Nature* 375:391–94.

Holling, C. S., and Lance H. Gunderson
2002 Resilience and adaptive cycles. In *Panarchy: Understanding Transformations in Human and Natural Systems*, edited by Lance H. Gunderson and C. S. Holling, pp. 25–62. Island Press, Washington, D.C.

Holling, C. S., Lance H. Gunderson, and Gary D. Peterson
2002 Sustainability and panarchies. In *Panarchy: Understanding Transformations in Human and Natural Systems*, edited by Lance H. Gunderson and C. S. Holling, pp. 63–102. Island Press, Washington, D.C.

Instituto Nacional de Estadística y Geografía (INEGI)
1999 *Tlalixtac de Cabrera*, E14D48, UTM, Datum ITRF92, Ellipsoid GRS80. Mexico City.

Inomata, Takeshi
2003 War, destruction, and abandonment: The fall of the Classic Maya center of Aguateca, Guatemala. In *The Archaeology of Settlement Abandonment in Middle America*, edited by Takeshi Inomata and Ronald W. Webb, pp. 43–60. University of Utah Press, Salt Lake City.

Inomata, Takeshi, and Ronald W. Webb (editors)
2003 *The Archaeology of Settlement Abandonment in Middle America*. Foundations of Archaeological Inquiry. University of Utah Press, Salt Lake City.

Joyce, Arthur A.
2000 The founding of Monte Alban: Sacred propositions and social practice. In *Agency in Archaeology*, edited by Marcia-Anne Dobres and John E. Robb, pp. 71–91. Routledge, New York.
2004 Sacred space and social relations in the Valley of Oaxaca. In *Mesoamerican Archaeology*, edited by Rosemary A. Joyce and Julia A. Hendon, pp. 192–216. Blackwell Publishers, Oxford.
2010 *Mixtecs, Zapotecs, and Chatinos: Ancient Peoples of Southern Mexico*. John Wiley and Sons, West Sussex.

Joyce, Arthur A., Laura Arnaud Bustamante, and Marc N. Levine
2001 Commoner power: A case study from the Classic period collapse on the Oaxaca coast. *Journal of Archaeological Method and Theory* 8(4):343–85.

Kirkby, Anne V. T.
1973 *The Use of Land and Water Resources in the Past and Present Valley of Oaxaca, Mexico*. Prehistory and Human Ecology of the Valley of Oaxaca, vol. 1, edited by Kent V. Flannery. Memoirs, no. 5. Museum of Anthropology, University of Michigan, Ann Arbor.

Kowalewski, Stephen A.
1970 "Tlaloc" in the Valley of Oaxaca. *Boletín de Estudios Oaxaqueños* 31:2–8.

Kowalewski, Stephen A., Gary M. Feinman, Laura Finsten, Richard E. Blanton, and Linda M. Nicholas
1989 *Monte Albán's Hinterland, Part II: Pre-Hispanic Settlement Patterns in Tlacolula, Etla, and Ocotlan, the Valley of Oaxaca, Mexico*. Memoirs, no. 23. Museum of Anthropology, University of Michigan, Ann Arbor.

Kowalewski, Stephen A., Arthur D. Murphy, and Ignacio F. Cabrera
1984 Yu?, Be?e, and Casa: 3500 years of continuity in residential construction. *Ekistics* 51:354–59.

Kowalewski, Stephen A., Charles S. Spencer, and Elsa M. Redmond
1978 Appendix II: Description of ceramic categories. In *Monte Albán: Settlement at the Ancient Zapotec Capital*, edited by Richard E. Blanton, pp. 167–93. Academic Press, New York.

LaMotta, Vincent M., and Michael B. Schiffer
1999 Formation processes of house floor assemblages. In *The Archaeology of Household Activities*, edited by Penelope M. Allison, pp. 19–29. Routledge, New York.
2001 Behavioral archaeology: Toward a new synthesis. In *Archaeological Theory Today*, edited by Ian Hodder, pp. 14–64. Blackwell Publishing Company, Malden, Massachusetts.

Lapham, Heather A., Gary M. Feinman, and Linda M. Nicholas
2013 Animal economies in prehispanic southern Mexico. In *The Archaeology of Mesoamerican Animals*, edited by Christopher M. Götz and Kitty F. Emery, pp. 153–91. Lockwood Press, Atlanta.

Lind, Michael
1991–1992 Unos problemas con la cronología de Monte Albán y una nueva serie de nombres para las fases. *Notas Mesoamericanas* 13:177–92.
2008 The Classic to Postclassic at Lambityeco. In *After Monte Albán: Transformation and Negotiation in Oaxaca, Mexico*, edited by Jeffrey P. Blomster, pp. 171–92. University Press of Colorado, Boulder.
2009 Unidades domésticas de Lambityeco durante la fase Xoo. In *Bases de la complejidad social en Oaxaca: Memoria de la Cuarta Mesa Redonda de Monte Albán*, edited by Nelly M. Robles García, pp. 107–22. Instituto Nacional de Antropología e Historia, Mexico City.

Lind, Michael, and Javier Urcid
1983 The lords of Lambityeco and their nearest neighbors. *Notas Mesoamericanas* 9:78–111.
2010 *The Lords of Lambityeco: Political Evolution in the Valley of Oaxaca during the Xoo Phase*. University Press of Colorado, Boulder.

MacNeish, Richard S., Antoinette Nelken-Terner, and Irmgard W. Johnson
1967 *The Prehistory of the Tehuacan Valley*, vol. 2, *Nonceramic Artifacts*. University of Texas Press, Austin.

Manning, Sturt W., and Linda Hulin
2005 Maritime commerce and geographies of mobility in the Late Bronze Age of the eastern Mediterranean: Problematizations. In *The Archaeology of Mediterranean Prehistory*, edited by Emma Blake and A. Bernard Knapp, pp. 270–302. Blackwell Publishing, Malden, Massachusetts.

Manzanilla, Linda
2003 The abandonment of Teotihuacan. In *The Archaeology of Settlement Abandonment in Middle America*, edited by Takeshi Inomata and Ronald W. Webb, pp. 91–102. University of Utah Press, Salt Lake City.

Marcus, Joyce
1974 The iconography of power among the Classic Maya. *World Archaeology* 6:83–94.
1976 The iconography of militarism at Monte Albán and neighboring sites in the Valley of Oaxaca. In *The Origins of Religious Art and Iconography in Pre-Classic Mesoamerica*, edited by Henry B. Nicholson, pp. 123–39. Latin American Center, University of California, Los Angeles.
1980 Zapotec writing. *Scientific American* 242:50–64.
1983a The first appearance of Zapotec writing and calendrics. In *The Cloud People: Divergent Evolution of the Zapotec and Mixtec Civilizations*, edited by Joyce Marcus and Kent V. Flannery, pp. 91–96. Academic Press, New York.
1983b Changing patterns of stone monuments after the fall of Monte Albán, A.D. 600–900. In *The Cloud People: Divergent Evolution of the Zapotec and Mixtec Civilizations*, edited by Kent V. Flannery and Joyce Marcus, pp. 191–97. Academic Press, New York.
1983c Monte Albán II in the Macuilxochitl area. In *The Cloud People: Divergent Evolution of the Zapotec and Mixtec Civilizations*, edited by Kent V. Flannery and Joyce Marcus, pp. 113–15. Academic Press, New York.
1983d Rethinking the Zapotec urn. In *The Cloud People: Divergent Evolution of the Zapotec and Mixtec Civilizations*, edited by Kent V. Flannery and Joyce Marcus, pp. 144–48. Academic Press, New York.
1983e The reconstructed chronology of the later Zapotec rulers, A.D. 1415–1563. In *The Cloud People: Divergent Evolution of the Zapotec and Mixtec Civilizations*, edited by Kent V. Flannery and Joyce Marcus, pp. 301–8. Academic Press, New York.
1983f Zapotec religion. In *The Cloud People: Divergent Evolution of the Zapotec and Mixtec Civilizations*, edited by Kent V. Flannery and Joyce Marcus, pp. 345–51. Academic Press, New York.
1983g Teotihuacán visitors on Monte Albán monuments and murals. In *The Cloud People: Divergent Evolution of the Zapotec and Mixtec Civilizations*, edited by Kent V. Flannery and Joyce Marcus, pp. 175–81. Academic Press, New York.
1989 From centralized systems to city-states: Possible models for the Epiclassic. In *Mesoamerica after the Decline of Teotihuacan A.D. 700–900*, edited by Richard A. Diehl and Janet C. Berlo, pp. 201–8. Dumbarton Oaks Research Library and Collection, Washington, D.C.
1992a Dynamic cycles of Mesoamerican states. *National Geographic Research and Exploration* 8:392–411.
1992b *Mesoamerican Writing Systems: Propaganda, Myth, and History in Four Ancient Civilizations*. Princeton University Press, Princeton, New Jersey.
1993 Ancient Maya political organization. In *Lowland Maya Civilization in the Eighth Century A.D.: A Symposium at Dumbarton Oaks, 7th and 8th October 1989*, edited by Jeremy A. Sabloff and John S. Henderson, pp. 111–83. Dumbarton Oaks Research Library and Collection, Washington, D.C.
1995 Where is Lowland Maya archaeology headed? *Journal of Archaeological Research* 3:3–53.
1998a The peaks and valleys of ancient states: An extension of the dynamic model. In *Archaic States*, edited by Gary M. Feinman and Joyce Marcus, pp. 59–94. School of American Research Press, Santa Fe, New Mexico.
1998b *Women's Ritual in Formative Oaxaca: Figurine-making, Divination, Death and the Ancestors*. Prehistory and Human Ecology of the Valley of Oaxaca, vol. 11, edited by Kent V. Flannery and Joyce Marcus. Memoirs, no. 33. Museum of Anthropology, University of Michigan, Ann Arbor.
2001 La zona maya en el clásico terminal. In *Historia antigua de México, Volumen II: El Horizonte Clásico*, edited by Linda Manzanilla and Leonardo López Luján, pp. 301–46. Instituto Nacional de Antropología e Historia, Mexico City.
2012 Maya political cycling and the story of the Kaan polity. In *The Ancient Maya of Mexico: Reinterpreting the Past of the Northern Maya Lowlands*, edited by Geoffrey Braswell, pp. 88–114. Equinox Publishing, London.
n.d. [ca. 1980] *Zapotec Monuments*. Manuscript in possession of author.

Marcus, Joyce (editor)
1990 *Debating Oaxaca Archaeology*. Anthropological Papers, no. 84. Museum of Anthropology, University of Michigan, Ann Arbor.

Marcus, Joyce, and Kent V. Flannery
1983 The Postclassic Balkanization of Oaxaca: An introduction to the Late Postclassic. In *The Cloud People: Divergent Evolution of the Zapotec and Mixtec Civilizations*, edited by Kent V. Flannery and Joyce Marcus, pp. 217–26. Academic Press, New York.
1990 Science and science fiction in Postclassic Oaxaca: Or "Yes, Virginia, there is a Monte Alban IV." In *Debating Oaxaca Archaeology*, edited by Joyce Marcus, pp. 191–205. Anthropological Papers, no. 84. Museum of Anthropology, University of Michigan, Ann Arbor.
1996 *Zapotec Civilization: How Urban Society Evolved in Mexico's Oaxaca Valley*. Thames and Hudson, New York.

Markens, Robert J.
2004 Ceramic Chronology in the Valley of Oaxaca, Mexico during the Late Classic and Postclassic Periods and the Organization of Ceramic Production. PhD dissertation, Department of Anthropology, Brandeis University, Waltham, Massachusetts.
2008 Advances in defining the Classic-Postclassic portion of the Valley of Oaxaca ceramic chronology: Occurrence and phyletic seriation. In *After Monte Albán: Transformation and Negotiation in Oaxaca, Mexico*, edited by Jeffrey P. Blomster, pp. 49–94. University Press of Colorado, Boulder.

2011 La transición del clásico al posclásico en el valle de Oaxaca: Hacia las causas y consecuencias de una crisis política. In *Monte Albán en la encrucijada regional y disciplinaria: Memoria de la Quinta Mesa Redonda de Monte Albán*, edited by Nelly M. Robles García and Angel Iván Rivera Guzmán, pp. 489–530. Instituto Nacional de Antropología e Historia, Mexico City.

Markens, Robert, Marcus Winter, and Cira Martínez López
2008 Ethohistory, oral history, and archaeology at Macuilxóchitl: Perspectives on the Postclassic period (800–1521 CE) in the Valley of Oaxaca. In *After Monte Albán: Transformation and Negotiation in Oaxaca, Mexico*, edited by Jeffrey P. Blomster, pp. 193–215. University Press of Colorado, Boulder.
2010 Appendix I: Calibrated radiocarbon dates for the Late Classic and Postclassic periods in the Valley of Oaxaca, Mexico. In *The Lords of Lambityeco: Political Evolution in the Valley of Oaxaca during the Xoo Phase*, by Michael Lind and Javier Urcid, pp. 345–64. University Press of Colorado, Boulder.

Martínez López, Cira
1994 La cerámica de estilo teotihuacano en Monte Albán. In *Monte Alban: Estudios Recientes*, edited by Marcus Winter, pp. 25–54. Proyecto Especial Monte Albán 1992–1994. Centro INAH Oaxaca, Oaxaca, Mexico.

Martínez López, Cira, Robert Markens, Marcus Winter, and Michael D. Lind
2000 *Cerámica de la fase Xoo (Monte Albán IIIb–IV) del Valle de Oaxaca*. Proyecto Especial Monte Albán 1992–1994. Centro INAH Oaxaca, Oaxaca, Mexico.

Martínez López, Cira, and Marcus Winter
1994 *Figurillas y silbatos de cerámica de Monte Albán*. Proyecto Especial Monte Albán 1992–1994. Centro INAH Oaxaca, Oaxaca, Mexico.

Mastache de Escobar, Alba Guadalupe, and Robert H. Cobean
1989 The Coyotlatelco culture and the origins of the Toltec state. In *Mesoamerica after the Decline of Teotihuacan A.D. 700–900*, edited by Richard A. Diehl and Janet C. Berlo, pp. 49–67. Dumbarton Oaks Research Library and Collection, Washington, D.C.

Mastache de Escobar, Alba Guadalupe, Robert H. Cobean, and Dan M. Healan
2002 *Ancient Tollan: Tula and the Toltec Heartland*. University Press of Colorado, Boulder.

McAnany, Patricia A., and Tomás Gallareta Negrón
2010 Bellicose rulers and climatological peril? In *Questioning Collapse: Human Resilience, Ecological Vulnerability, and the Aftermath of Empire*, edited by Patricia A. McAnany and Norman Yoffee, pp. 142–75. Cambridge University Press, Cambridge.

McAnany, Patricia A., and Norman Yoffee
2010 Why we question collapse and study human resilience, ecological vulnerability, and the aftermath of empire. In *Questioning Collapse: Human Resilience, Ecological Vulnerability, and the Aftermath of Empire*, edited by Patricia A. McAnany and Norman Yoffee, pp. 1–20. Cambridge University Press, Cambridge.

Michelet, Dominique
1995 La zona occidental en el posclásico. In *Historia Antigua de México. Volumen III: El Horizonte Posclásico*, edited by Linda Manzanilla and Leonardo López Luján, pp. 161–98. Instituto Nacional de Antropología e Historia, Mexico City.

Millon, René
1973 *Urbanization at Teotihuacán, Mexico*. University of Texas Press, Austin.
1988 The last years of Teotihuacan dominance. In *The Collapse of Ancient States and Civilizations*, edited by Norman Yoffee and George L. Cowgill, pp. 102–64. University of Arizona Press, Tucson.

Minc, Leah
2006 Monitoring regional market systems in prehistory: Models, methods, and metrics. *Journal of Anthropological Archaeology* 25:82–116.

Nelson, Ben A.
2003 A place of continued importance: The abandonment of Epiclassic La Quemada. In *The Archaeology of Settlement Abandonment in Middle America*, edited by Takeshi Inomata and Ronald W. Webb, pp. 77–90. University of Utah Press, Salt Lake City.

Nelson, Ben A., J. Andrew Darling, and David A. Kice
1992 Mortuary patterns and social order at La Quemada, Zacatecas. *Latin American Antiquity* 3(4):298–315.

Nelson, Margaret C., Michelle Hegmon, Stephanie Kulow, and Karen Gust Schollmeye
2006 Archaeological and ecological perspectives on reorganization: A case study from the Mimbres region of the U.S. Southwest. *American Antiquity* 71(3):403–32.

Netting, Robert M., Richard R. Wilk, and E. J. Arnould (editors)
1984 *Households: Comparative and Historical Studies of the Domestic Group*. University of California Press, Los Angeles.

Ochoa Salas, Lorenzo
1979 *Historia prehispánica de la Huaxteca*. Instituto de Investigaciones Antropológicas, Universidad Nacional Autónoma de México, Mexico City.
1995 La zona del golfo en el Posclásico. In *Historia Antigua de México. Volumen III: El Horizonte Posclásico*, edited by Linda Manzanilla and Leonardo López Luján, pp. 13–56. Instituto Nacional de Antropología e Historia, Mexico City.

Oliveros, Arturo
1997 Dainzú-Macuilxóchitl. *Arqueología Mexicana* 5(26):4–29.

Orr, Heather S.
1997 Power Games in the Late Formative Valley of Oaxaca: The Ballplayer Carvings at Dainzú. PhD dissertation, Department of Art History, University of Texas, Austin.
2001 Procession rituals and shrine sites: The politics of sacred space in the Late Formative Valley of Oaxaca. In *Landscapes and Power in Ancient Mesoamerica*, edited by Rex Koontz, K. Reese-Taylor, and A. Headrick, pp. 55–79. Westview Press, Boulder, Colorado.
2003 Stone balls and masked men: Ballgame as combat ritual, Dainzú, Oaxaca. *Ancient America* 5:73–103.

Oudijk, Michel R.
2000 *Historiography of the Benizaa: The Postclassic and Early Colonial Periods (1000–1600 AD)*. Research School of Asian, African, and Amerindian Studies (CNWS), vol. 84. University of Leiden, the Netherlands.
2001 La genealogía de Macuilxóchitl y la historia del Valle de Oaxaca. In *Procesos de cambio y conceptualización del tiempo: Memoria de la Primera Mesa Redonda de Monte Albán*, edited by Nelly M. Robles García, pp. 217–32. Instituto Nacional de Antropología e Historia, Mexico City.
2002 The Zapotec city state. In *A Comparative Study of 30 City-State Cultures*, edited by M. M. Hansen, pp. 73–90. Royal Danish Academy of Sciences and Letters, Copenhagen.
2008 The Postclassic period in the Valley of Oaxaca. In *After Monte Albán: Transformation and Negotiation in Oaxaca, Mexico*, edited by Jeffrey P. Blomster, pp. 95–118. University Press of Colorado, Boulder.

Paddock, John
1983a Some thoughts on the decline of Monte Albán. In *The Cloud People: Divergent Evolution of the Zapotec and Mixtec Civilizations*, edited by Kent V. Flannery and Joyce Marcus, pp. 186–88. Academic Press, New York.
1983b Lambityeco. In *The Cloud People: Divergent Evolution of the Zapotec and Mixtec Civilizations*, edited by Kent V. Flannery and Joyce Marcus, pp. 197–203. Academic Press, New York.
1983c Comments on the lienzos of Huilotepec and Guevea. In *The Cloud People: Divergent Evolution of the Zapotec and Mixtec Civilizations*, edited by Kent V. Flannery and Joyce Marcus, pp. 308–13. Academic Press, New York.

Paddock, John (editor)
1966 *Ancient Oaxaca: Discoveries in Mexican Archeology and History*. Stanford University Press, Stanford, California.

Paddock, John, Joseph R. Mogor, and Michael D. Lind
1968 Lambityeco Tomb 2: A preliminary report. *Boletín de Estudios Oaxaqueños* 25:2–24.

Parry, William J.
1987 *Chipped Stone Tools in Formative Oaxaca, Mexico: Their Procurement, Production, and Use*. Prehistory and Human Ecology of the Valley of Oaxaca, vol. 8, edited by Kent V. Flannery and Richard E. Blanton. Memoirs, no. 20. Museum of Anthropology, University of Michigan, Ann Arbor.

Parsons, Elsie Clews
1936 *Mitla, Town of Souls, and Other Zapoteco-Speaking Pueblos of Oaxaca, Mexico*. University of Chicago Press, Chicago.

Parsons, Mary H.
1972 Spindle whorls from the Teotihuacán Valley, Mexico. In *Miscellaneous Studies in Mexican Prehistory*, by Michael W. Spence, Jeffrey R. Parsons, and Mary H. Parsons, pp. 45–79. Anthropological Papers, no. 45. Museum of Anthropology, University of Michigan, Ann Arbor.

Payne, William O.
1970 A potter's analysis of the pottery from Lambityeco Tomb 2. *Boletín de Estudios Oaxaqueños* 29:1–8.

Peterson, David A.
1976 Ancient Commerce. PhD dissertation, Department of Anthropology, State University of New York, Binghamton.

Plunket, Patricia (editor)
2002 *Domestic Ritual in Ancient Mesoamerica*. Cotsen Institute of Archaeology, University of California, Los Angeles.

Polanyi, Karl, Conrad M. Arensberg, and Harry W. Pearson (editors)
1957 *Trade and Market in Early Empires*. Free Press, Glencoe, Illinois.

Railey, Jim A., and Richard Martin Reycraft
2008 Introduction. In *Global Perspectives on the Collapse of Complex Systems*, edited by Jim A. Railey and Richard Martin Reycraft, pp. 1–17. Anthropological Papers no. 8. Maxwell Museum of Anthropology, Albuquerque, New Mexico.

Rappaport, Roy
1978 Maladaptation in social systems. In *The Evolution of Social Systems*, edited by Jonathan Friedman and Michael J. Rowlands, pp. 49–71. University of Pittsburgh Press, Pittsburgh.

Rathje, William L.
1973 Classic Maya development and denouement: A research design. In *The Classic Maya Collapse*, edited by T. Patrick Culbert, pp. 405–54. University of New Mexico Press, Albuquerque.

Rattray, Evelyn C.
1993 *The Oaxaca Barrio at Teotihuacan*. Monografías mesoamericanas, no. 1. Instituto de Estudios Avanzados, Universidad de las Américas, Puebla, Mexico.

Redman, Charles
2005 Resilience theory in archaeology. *American Anthropologist* 107:70–77.

Redman, Charles, and Anne P. Kinzig
2003 Resilience of past landscapes: Resilience theory, society, and the longue dureé. *Conservation Ecology* 7:10–14.

Redman, Charles, Margaret Nelson, and Anne P. Kinzig
2009 The resilience of socioecological landscapes: Lessons from the Hohokam. In *The Archaeology of Environmental Change: Socionatural Legacies of Degradation and Resilience*, edited by Christopher T. Fisher, J. Brett Hill, and Gary M. Feinman, pp. 15–39. University of Arizona Press, Tucson.

Redmond, Elsa M.
1983 *A Fuego y Sangre: Early Zapotec Imperialism in the Cuicatlán Cañada, Oaxaca*. Studies in Latin American Ethnohistory and Archaeology, vol. 1, edited by Joyce Marcus. Memoirs, no. 16. Museum of Anthropology, University of Michigan, Ann Arbor.

Redmond, Elsa M., and Charles S. Spencer
2006 From raiding to conquest: Warfare strategies and early state development in Oaxaca, Mexico. In *The Archaeology of Warfare: Prehistories of Raiding and Conquest*, edited by Elizabeth N. Arkush and Mark W. Allen, pp. 336–93. University Press of Florida, Gainesville.

2008 Rituals of sanctification and the development of standardized temples in Oaxaca, Mexico. *Cambridge Archaeological Journal* 18(2):239–66.

Renfrew, Colin
1978 Trajectory discontinuity and morphogenesis: The implications of catastrophe theory for archaeology. *American Antiquity* 43:203–22.
1984 *Approaches to Social Archaeology*. Harvard University Press, Cambridge, Massachusetts.

Robles García, Nelly M.
1994 *Las canteras de Mitla, Oaxaca: Tecnología para la arquitectura monumental*. Publications in Anthropology, no. 47. Vanderbilt University, Nashville.

Robles García, Nelly M., and Agustín E. Andrade Cuautle
2011 El Proyecto Arqueológico del Conjunto Monumental de Atzompa. In *Monte Albán en la encrucijada regional y disciplinaria: Memoria de la Quinta Mesa Redonda de Monte Albán*, edited by Nelly M. Robles García and Angel Iván Rivera Guzmán, pp. 285–314. Instituto Nacional de Antropología e Historia, Mexico City.

Sánchez Santiago, Gonzalo A.
2005 *Los Artefactos Sonoros del Oaxaca Prehispánico*. Secretaría de Cultura del Estado de Oaxaca, Oaxaca City, Mexico.

Sanders, William, Jeffrey R. Parsons, and Robert S. Santley
1979 *The Basin of Mexico: Ecological Processes in the Evolution of a Civilization*. Academic Press, New York.

Sanders, William T., and Barbara J. Price
1968 *Mesoamerica: The Evolution of a Civilization*. Random House, New York.

Santley, Robert S., and Kenneth G. Hirth (editors)
1993 *Pre-Hispanic Domestic Units in Western Mesoamerica: Studies of the Household, Compound, and Residence*. CRC Press, Boca Raton, Florida.

Scarborough, Vernon L., and David R. Wilcox (editors)
1991 *The Mesoamerican Ballgame*. University of Arizona Press, Tucson.

Schiffer, Michael B.
1975 Archaeology as behavioral science. *American Anthropologist* 77(4):836–48.
2000 *Social Theory in Archaeology*. University of Utah Press, Salt Lake City.

Schwartz, Glenn M.
2006 From collapse to regeneration. In *After Collapse: The Regeneration of Complex Societies*, edited by Glenn M. Schwartz and John J. Nichols, pp. 3–17. University of Arizona Press, Tucson.

Schwartz, Glenn M., and John J. Nichols (editors)
2006 *After Collapse: The Regeneration of Complex Societies*. University of Arizona Press, Tucson.

Scott, Sue
1993 *Teotihuacan Mazapan Figurines and the Xipe Totec Statue*. Publications in Anthropology, no. 44. Vanderbilt University, Nashville.

Sellen, Adam T.
2002 Storm-god impersonators from ancient Oaxaca. *Ancient Mesoamerica* 13:3–19.

Sharer, Robert J.
2006 *The Ancient Maya*. Stanford University Press, Stanford, California.

Shennan, Stephen
1997 *Quantifying Archaeology*. University of Iowa Press, Iowa City.

Shimada, Izumi
2007 Introduction. In *Craft Production in Complex Societies: Multicraft and Producer Perspectives*, edited by Izumi Shimada, pp. 1–21. University of Utah Press, Salt Lake City.

Simon, Herbert A.
1965 The architecture of complexity. In *General Systems: Yearbook of the Society for General Systems Research*, edited by Ludwig von Bertalanffy and Anatol Rapoport, pp. 63–76. Society for General Systems Research, Ann Arbor, Michigan.

Smith, C. Earle, Jr.
1978 *The Vegetational History of the Oaxaca Valley*. Prehistory and Human Ecology of the Valley of Oaxaca, vol. 5, pt. 1, edited by Kent V. Flannery and Richard E. Blanton. Memoirs, no. 10. Museum of Anthropology, University of Michigan, Ann Arbor.

Smith, Michael E.
2003 *The Aztecs*. Blackwell Publishing, Malden, Massachusetts.

Smith, Michael E., and Juliana Novic
2012 Introduction: Neighborhoods and districts in ancient Mesoamerica. In *The Neighborhood as a Social Unit in Mesoamerican Cities*, edited by M. Charlotte Arnauld, Linda R. Manzanilla, and Michael E. Smith, pp. 1–26. University of Arizona Press, Tucson.

Spencer, Charles S.
1982 *The Cuicatlán Cañada and Monte Albán: A Study of Primary State Formation*. Academic Press, New York.

Spencer, Charles S., and Elsa M. Redmond
1997 *Archaeology of the Cañada de Cuicatlán, Oaxaca*. Anthropological Papers of the American Museum of Natural History 80. American Museum of Natural History, New York.
2001 Multilevel selection and political evolution in the Valley of Oaxaca, 500–100 B.C. *Journal of Anthropological Archaeology* 20:195–229.
2004 A Late Monte Albán I phase (300–100 B.C.) palace in the Valley of Oaxaca. *Latin American Antiquity* 15(4):441–55.
2005 Institutional development in Late Formative Oaxaca: The view from San Martín Tilcajete. In *New Perspectives on Formative Mesoamerican Cultures*, edited by Terry G. Powis, pp. 171–82. Archaeopress, Oxford, England.
2006 Resistance strategies and early state formation in Oaxaca, Mexico. In *Intermediate Elites in Pre-Columbian States and*

Empires, edited by Christina Elson and R. Alan Covey, pp. 21–43. University of Arizona Press, Tucson.

Spencer, Charles S., Elsa M. Redmond, and Christina M. Elson
2008 Ceramic microtypology and the territorial expansion of the early Monte Albán state in Oaxaca, Mexico. *Journal of Field Archaeology* 33(3):321–41.

Stark, Miriam T.
2006 From Funan to Angkor: Collapse and regeneration in ancient Cambodia. In *After Collapse: The Regeneration of Complex Societies*, edited by Glenn M. Schwartz and John J. Nichols, pp. 144–67. University of Arizona Press, Tucson.

Stark, Barbara L., and Christopher Garraty
2010 Detecting marketplace exchange in archaeology: A methodological review. In *Archaeological Approaches to Market Exchange in Ancient Societies*, edited by Christopher P. Garraty and Barbara L. Stark, pp. 33–60. University Press of Colorado, Boulder.

Strayer, Robert W.
1998 *Why Did the Soviet Union Collapse? Understanding Historical Change*. M. E. Sharpe, Armonk, New York.

Stuart, David E.
2000 *Anasazi America: Seventeen Centuries on the Road from Center Place*. University of New Mexico Press, Albuquerque.

Suhler, Charles, Traci Ardren, David Freidel, and Dave Johnstone
2004 The rise and fall of Terminal Classic Yaxuna, Yucatán, Mexico. In *The Terminal Classic in the Maya Lowlands: Collapse, Transition, and Transformation*, edited by Arthur A. Demarest, Prudence M. Rice, and Don S. Rice, pp. 450–84. University Press of Colorado, Boulder.

Sutro, Livingston D., and Theodore E. Downing
1988 A step toward a grammar of space: Domestic space use in Zapotec villages. In *Household and Community in the Mesoamerican Past*, edited by Richard R. Wilk and Wendy Ashmore, pp. 29–50. University of New Mexico Press, Albuquerque.

Tainter, Joseph A.
1988 *The Collapse of Complex Societies*. New Studies in Archaeology. Cambridge University Press, Cambridge.

Taube, Karl, and Marc Zender
2009 Ritual boxing in ancient Mesoamerica. In *Blood and Beauty: Organized Violence in the Art and Archaeology of Mesoamerica and Central America*, edited by Heather S. Orr and Rex Koontz, pp. 161–220. Cotsen Institute of Archaeology, University of California, Los Angeles.

Taylor, William B.
1972 *Landlord and Peasant in Colonial Oaxaca*. Stanford University Press, Stanford, California.

Thompson, Victor D., and John A. Turck
2009 Adaptive cycles of coastal hunter-gatherers. *American Antiquity* 74(2):255–78.

Urcid, Javier
2001 *Zapotec Hieroglyphic Writing*. Dumbarton Oaks Research Library and Collection, Washington, D.C.
2008 El arte de pintar las tumbas: Sociedad e ideología zapotecas (400–800 d.C.). In *La pintura mural prehispánica en México. Vol. III: Oaxaca*, edited by Beatriz de la Fuente, pp. 513–627. Universidad Nacional Autónoma de México, Mexico City.
n.d. *Otra narrativa de jugadores de pelota en Dainzú*. Manuscript on file in the Library of the Welte Institute for Oaxacan Studies, Oaxaca, Mexico.

Webb, Ronald W., and Kenneth G. Hirth
2003 Xochicalco Morelos: The abandonment of households at an Epiclassic urban center. In *The Archaeology of Settlement Abandonment in Middle America*, edited by Takeshi Inomata and Ronald W. Webb, pp. 29–42. University of Utah Press, Salt Lake City.

Webster, David L.
2002 *The Fall of the Ancient Maya: Solving the Mystery of the Maya Collapse*. Thames and Hudson, London.

Whalen, Michael E.
1981 *Excavations at Santo Domingo Tomaltepec: Evolution of a Formative Community in the Valley of Oaxaca, Mexico*. Prehistory and Human Ecology of the Valley of Oaxaca, vol. 6, edited by Kent V. Flannery and Richard E. Blanton. Memoirs, no. 12. Museum of Anthropology, University of Michigan, Ann Arbor.
1986 Sources of the Guilá Naquitz chipped stone. In *Guilá Naquitz*, edited by Kent V. Flannery, pp. 141–46. Academic Press, Orlando.
1988 House and household in Formative Oaxaca. In *Household and Community in the Mesoamerican Past*, edited by Richard R. Wilk and Wendy Ashmore, pp. 249–72. University of New Mexico Press, Albuquerque.

Whitecotton, Joseph W.
1977 *The Zapotecs: Princes, Priests and Peasants*. University of Oklahoma Press, Norman.
1983 The genealogy of Macuilxochitl: A 16th century Zapotec pictorial from the Valley of Oaxaca. *Notas Mesoamericanas* 9:58–75.
1990 *Zapotec Elite Ethnohistory: Pictorial Genealogies from Eastern Oaxaca*. Publications in Anthropology, no. 39. Vanderbilt University, Nashville.
2003 Las genealogías del Valle de Oaxaca, Epoca Colonial. In *Escritura Zapoteca: 2,500 Años de Historia*, edited by María de los Angeles Romero Frizzi, pp. 305–40. Instituto Nacional de Antropología e Historia, Mexico City.

Wilk, Richard R., and Wendy Ashmore (editors)
1988 *Household and Community in the Mesoamerican Past*. University of New Mexico Press, Albuquerque.

Wilk, Richard R., and William L. Rathje
1982 Household archaeology. *American Behavioral Scientist* 25(6):617–39.

Willey, Gordon R.
1982 Foreword. *American Behavioral Scientist* 25(6):613–16.

Williams, Howel, and Robert F. Heizer
1965   Geological notes on the ruins of Mitla and other Oaxacan sites, Mexico. *Contributions of the University of California Archaeological Research Facility* 1:41–54.

Winter, Marcus
1974   Residential patterns at Monte Albán, Oaxaca, Mexico. *Science* 186:981–87.
1986   Templo-patio-adoratorio: Un conjunto arquitectónico no-residencial en el Oaxaca prehispánico. *Cuadernos de Arquitectura Mesoamerica* 7:51–59.
1989a From Classic to Post-Classic in pre-Hispanic Oaxaca. In *Mesoamerica after the Decline of Teotihuacan A.D. 700–900*, edited by Richard A. Diehl and Janet C. Berlo, pp. 123–30. Dumbarton Oaks Research Library and Collection, Washington, D.C.
1989b *Oaxaca, the Archaeological Record*. Minutiae Mexicana, Mexico City.
2001   Palacios, templos y 1300 años de vida urbana en Monte Albán. In *Reconstruyendo la ciudad maya: El urbanismo en las sociedades antiguas*, edited by Andrés Ciudad Ruiz, María Josefa Iglesias Ponce de León, and María del Carmen Martínez Martínez, pp. 277–301. Publicaciones de la Sociedad Española de Estudios Mayas, vol. 6. Madrid.
2002   Monte Albán: Mortuary practices as domestic ritual and their relation to community religion. In *Domestic Ritual in Ancient Mesoamerica*, edited by Patricia Plunket, pp. 67–82. Cotsen Institute of Archaeology, University of California, Los Angeles.
2003   Monte Albán and Late Classic site abandonment in highland Oaxaca. In *The Archaeology of Settlement Abandonment in Middle America*, edited by Takeshi Inomata and Ronald W. Webb, pp. 103–19. University of Utah Press, Salt Lake City.
2007   *Cerro de Las Minas: Arqueología de la Mixteca Baja*. Arqueología Oaxaqueña 1. Centro INAH Oaxaca, Oaxaca City, Mexico.

Winter, Marcus, Robert Markens, Cira Martínez L., and Alicia T. Herrera Muzgo
2007   Shrines, offerings, and Postclassic continuity in Zapotec religion. In *Commoner Ritual and Ideology in Ancient Mesoamerica*, edited by Nancy Gonlin and Jon C. Lohse, pp. 185–212. University Press of Colorado, Boulder.

Winter, Marcus, and William O. Payne
1976   Hornos para cerámica hallados en Monte Albán. *Boletín del Instituto Nacional de Antropología e Historia* 16:37–40.

Yoffee, Norman
1988a Orienting collapse. In *The Collapse of Ancient States and Civilizations*, edited by Norman Yoffee and George L. Cowgill, pp. 1–19. University of Arizona Press, Tucson.
1988b The collapse of ancient Mesopotamian states and civilization. In *The Collapse of Ancient States and Civilizations*, edited by Norman Yoffee and George L. Cowgill, pp. 44–68. University of Arizona Press, Tucson.
2010   Collapse in ancient Mesopotamia: What happened, what didn't? In *Questioning Collapse: Human Resilience, Ecological Vulnerability, and the Aftermath of Empire*, edited by Patricia A. McAnany and Norman Yoffee, pp. 176–206. Cambridge University Press, Cambridge.

Plate 1

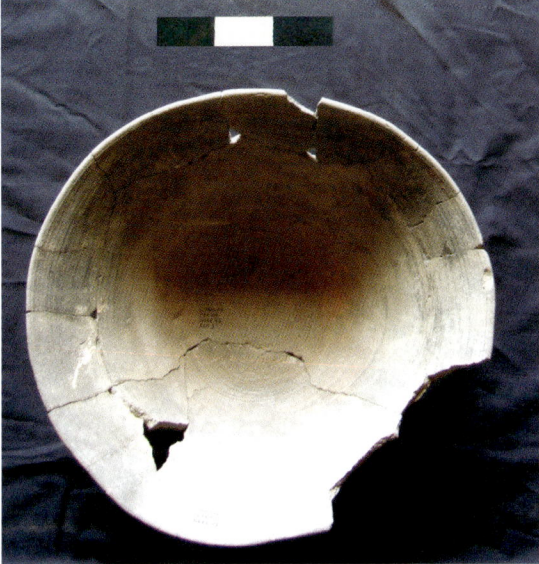

G35-type conical bowl, Burial 3.

(top left)
Layer 3, east side of Terrace S19.

(middle left)
Fire Pit 1, Layer 3, test unit 8
(prior to excavation).

(bottom left)
Fire Pit 1, Layer 3, test unit 8
(after excavation).

Plate 2

(above left, above rt) Cajete/patojo pair number 1.

(far left, left) Small G35-type conical bowl, cajete/patojo pair number 1.

(far left, left) Brown paste patojo, cajete/patojo pair number 1.

Plate 3

Postclassic-type conical bowl, cajete/patojo pair number 2 (scale has 5-cm sections).

Postclassic patojo, cajete/patojo pair number 2.

Cajete/patojo pair number 3.   Postclassic-style conical bowl, cajete/patojo pair number 3.

Plate 4

Postclassic-style patojo, cajete/patojo pair number 3.

Cajete/patojo pair number 6 (scale has 5-cm sections).

Plate 5

Postclassic brown paste conical bowl, cajete/patojo pair number 6 (scale has 5-cm sections).

Brown paste patojo, cajete/patojo pair number 6 (scale has 5-cm sections).

Plate 6

Large gray paste G35 conical bowl, test unit 3 (scale has 5-cm sections).

Gray ware conical bowl with corncob impression (scale has 5-cm sections).

Plate 7

Map of Macuilxóchitl and its jurisdiction, from the *Relación Geográfica de Macuilxóchitl*, 1580. © Real Academia de la Historia, Madrid, C-028-007 (9-4663/19).

Plate 8

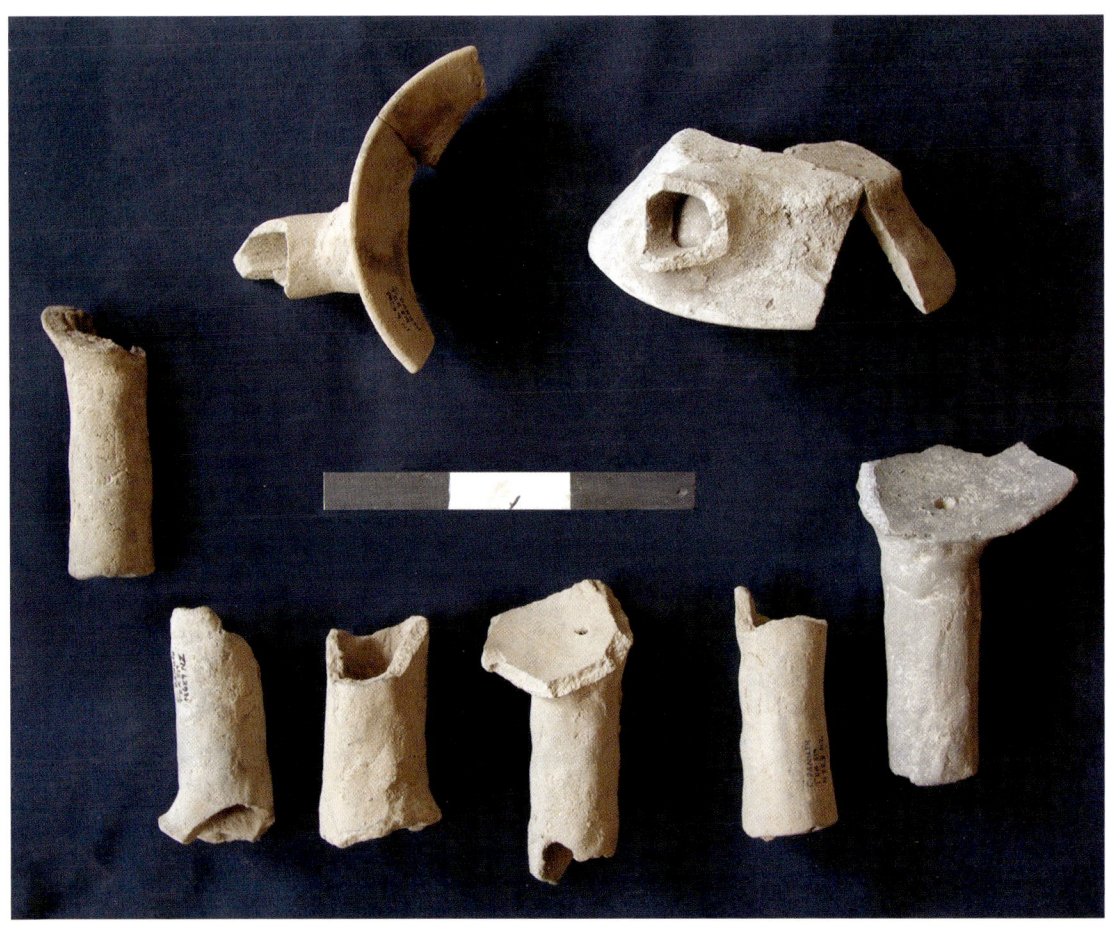

Fragments of hollow-handled sahumadores.

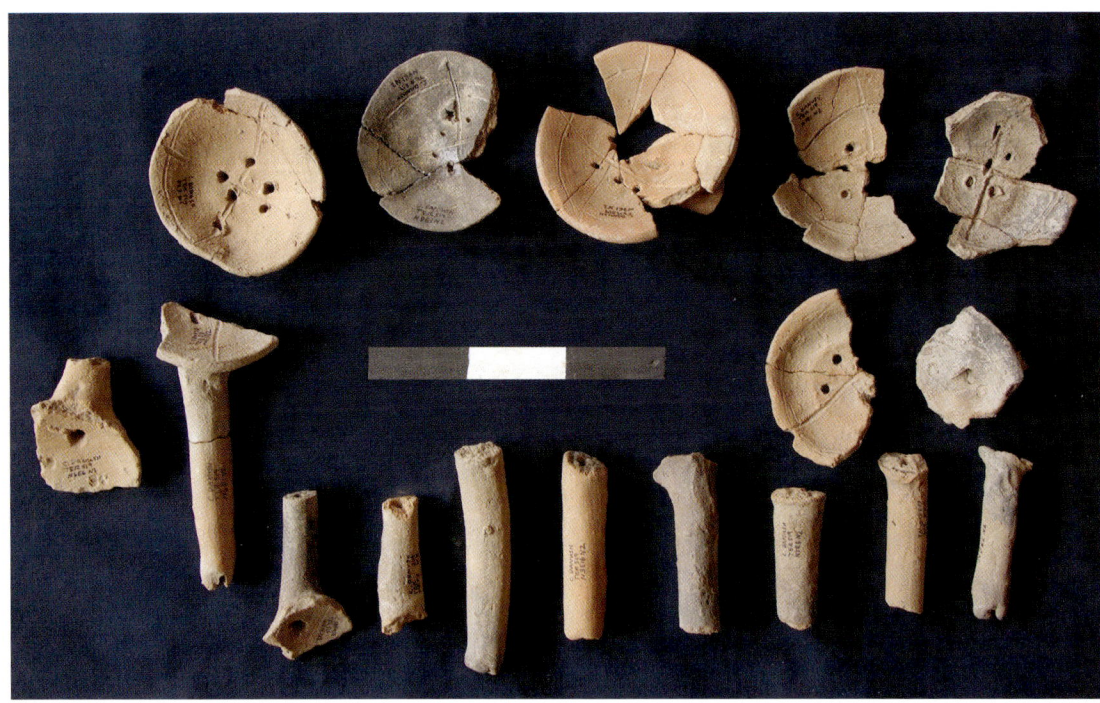

Fragments of solid-handled sahumadores.